reader

is

integrative
STUDIES

OTTERBEIN
COLLEGE

Third Printing

Custom Publishing

Boston   Burr Ridge, IL   Dubuque, IA   Madison, WI   New York
San Francisco   St. Louis   Bangkok   Bogotá   Caracas   Kuala Lumpur
Lisbon   London   Madrid   Mexico City   Milan   Montreal   New Delhi
Santiago   Seoul   Singapore   Sydney   Taipei   Toronto

Integrative Studies Reader

Third Printing

1 2 3 4 5 6 7 8 9 0   QSR   QSR   0 9 8 7 6 5 4

ISBN 0-256-80337-4

Editor: Tammy Immell
Production Editor: Carrie Braun
Printer/Binder: Quebecor World

ACKNOWLEDGMENTS

Page 24:   From Anchor Press/Doubleday, The Novelist as teacher, copyright © 1975 by Chinua Achebe. Reprinted with permission of the Publisher.

Page 72:   From Science & Spirit Resources, Trasition or Torture, Copyright © 2001 by Lucia Carruthers. Reprinted with permission of the publisher.

Page 295:   From Social Policy Corporation, The Uses of Poverty: The Poor Pay All, Copyright © 1971 by Herbert J. Gans. Reprinted with permission of the publisher.

Page 366   From Penguin Books Ltd., The Grand Inquisitor, Copyright © 1993 by Fyodor Dostoyevsky. Reprinted with permission of the publisher.

Page 418:   From Doubleday, At the Start: Genesis Made New, Copyright © 1992 by Mary Phil Korsak. Reprinted with permission of the author.

Page 477:   From Christian Century Foundation, Homosexuality and the Bible, Copyright © 1979 b6 Walter Wink. Reprinted with permission of the publisher.

Page 490:   From Harper & Row, Symbols of Faith, Copyright © 1957 by Paul Tillich. Reprinted with permission of the publisher.

Page 498:   From Augsburg Fortress, Loving Your Enemies, Copyright © 1981 by Martin Luther King Jr. Reprinted with permission.

Page 506:   From Augsburg Fortress, On Being a Good Neighbor, Copyright © 1981 by Martin Luther King Jr. Reprinted by arrangement with the Estate of Martin Luther King Jr., c/o Writers House as agent for the proprietor. Copyright Martin Luther King 2963, copyright renewed 1991 Corretta Scott King.

Page 616:   From Wadsworth Publishing, Defining the Issue: An Overview, Copyright © 1988 by Marcia Eaton. Reprinted with permission of the author.

Page 629:   From The New American Library of World Literature, Mathematical Creation in Brewster Ghiselin, © 1952 by Henri Poincare. Reprinted with permission of the publisher.

Page 663:   From Science & Spriit Resources, Spirit in the Sky, Copyright © 2001 by Rex Graham. Reprinted with permission of the publisher.

Page 833:   Paradigms Lot, Copyright © 1997 by Joanne Stichweh. Reprinted with permission of the artist.

Page 835:   Sanctuary, Copyright © 1996 by Nicholas Hill Reprinted with permission of the artist.

TABLE OF CONTENTS

PREFACE

Integrative Studies—The Otterbein Core Curriculum in the Liberal Arts and Sciences.

Dear Student,

It is safe to say that practically every institution of higher education in the United States has a **core curriculum** separate from the departmental majors and minors, and that the mission of the core courses is to complete your general education in the humanities, natural and social sciences, and fine arts. On some campuses, students must take a minimum number of required introductory courses in a variety of departments. At Otterbein College, however, we have established an Integrative Studies Department and intentionally developed specific, coordinated courses to accomplish the mission of the core curriculum. We believe the Otterbein College Integrative Studies Program is unique and innovative and of especially high quality, and that it is a leading program on the American college scene.

An Honored Program

Our program of Integrative Studies is the product of outstanding creative inspiration and hard work at the time of its development and implementation more than thirty years ago. It is also the product of the intense evaluation, revision, and development that has occurred since then and that continues to take place year by year. We are proud of our program, not least because it has been honored by the Ohio Board of Regents and by the Association of American Colleges for its quality and innovation. Our surveys of alumni tell us that the liberal education of our graduates is valued in the workplace. Alumni also tell us that the longer they have been away from the campus and the further they have moved on in their lives, the more they appreciate the skills, knowledge, and values gained in the I.S. courses. Integrative Studies truly is educaton for living.

The Central Theme: "HUMAN NATURE"

Our courses in integrative studies all deal with aspects of the question, **"What does it mean to be a human being?"** Each course you take in the program is like a different lens through which you see this subject. Sometimes the focus is sharp because the discipline is inherently people-centered, *psychology*, for example. Other courses look at the question from a different angle, and the focus is wider. But sharp or diffuse, narrow or wide, **Human Nature** is addressed in each course.

Structure of the Department

The Integrative Studies Program is administered by the chairperson in cooperation with department chairs all across the campus. That is because I.S. instructors are also members of a "home department" and thus model in their own lives a concurrent commitment to both liberal learning and depth of knowledge in a major discipline. The I.S. Advisory Committee meets bi-weekly. It is made up of 1) faculty representatives from among the I.S. instructors, 2) elected members from each curricular Division on campus, and 3) student volunteer members. If you have concerns about the I.S. Program and/or want to participate in its continuing work and programs, speak to a faculty or student member of the I.S. Advisory Committee. Better still, become a student member yourself and take part in this truly central aspect of the college life around you.

Our Goals

A group of common goals that the faculty support and work toward is the "glue" that binds the program together and gives it direction and purpose. These goals are listed in every I.S. course syllabus, in the college catalog, and a bit further ahead in this introductory section of the **Reader.** To paraphrase these five goals, I would say that as a result of your Integrative Studies courses, you will learn to

- Think, write, and speak more clearly, creatively, and accurately
- Gain unified understanding from many fields that helps you grow intellectually throughout your life
- Integrate the knowledge you have gained from a variety of disciplines into wisdom that allows you to deal with complex contemporary problems
- Understand human beings and the many facets of our existence more fully
- Know your own values and spirituality and appropriately respect those of others

Revisit the Reader

It is our hope that at least some of the material in this **Reader** will appear in more than one of your courses, and that you will approach ideas in it from several viewpoints. So if you are an entering student reading these words for the first time, "Welcome to the Otterbein learning community!" And if you are an upperclass woman or man returning to these words in a book of dog-eared pages, maybe with a coffee-stain here and there, "Welcome back!" In either case, I leave you with these words of John Henry Cardinal Newman from *The Idea of a University:*

> all knowledge forms one whole, because its subject-matter is one; for the universe in its length and breadth is so intimately knit together that we cannot separate off portion from portion, operation from operation.

Lyle Barkhymer, Chairperson
Department of Integrative Studies
BFAC-109
Office phone: 823-1210
Lbarkhymer@otterbein.edu

Otterbein's Integrative Studies Program: A Brief History

Alison H. Prindle, IS Chairperson, 1984–94

The Integrative Studies program began at Otterbein in 1968-69, at a time of significant change for the college. Majors were reorganized, the calendar moved from semesters to the quarter system, and distribution requirements were replaced by a core of 50 hours of general education courses, to be taken over four years by all students. To emphasize their centrality in the college curriculum, these courses were called the Common Courses, and were specifically designed for the core under the theme, "The Nature of Man." Dr. Harold Hancock, in his history of the college, said, "Future historians will look upon this transformation as a landmark in the academic life of the college."

In the years since, the original curricular design has been modified, new courses have been added, new focal points for study have emerged, a few course requirements have moved from the lower to the upper division, and some requirements have been added. In 1976 the program's theme became "Human Nature" and in 1980 the program's title became Integrative Studies. But the fundamental, original structure has proven sound and enduring.

Major disciplinary ways of knowing have been included from the beginning, in courses designed for all students: the natural sciences, the arts, the social sciences, and the humanities all developed Integrative Studies courses. At the program's center were a sequence of skills based courses in composition, under the thematic headings of The Individual and Society, The Dialogue of Men and Women, and The Dilemma of Existence. Among recent adjustments in the program, noteworthy in the area of new emphases was the emergence of a Non-Western cultures requirement (1991), now retitled the Global Studies requirement.

The change from Common Courses to Integrative Studies underlined the program's goal of making connections across disciplinary lines; we seek to integrate that breadth of knowledge earned by students in a liberal arts college. But the original title, Common Courses, also identifies a continuing and fundamental goal. The creators intended these courses to be the basis for cross-disciplinary conversations in the college as a whole: both students and faculty step out of their areas of specialization to engage in discussions of meaning and values, discussions that connect us all to the educated conversations of American culture. Our differences, questions, and knowledge can be integrated only "through dialogue," as the planners of this liberal arts core stated in 1967. To encourage these cross-disciplinary conversations, Integrative Studies annually sponsors an I.S. Festival of interdisciplinary programming, and its faculty and students participate in the college's required Common Book reading and events for freshmen.

Integrative Studies emphasizes that learning is a shared responsibility, that the disciplines are at the heart of knowledge but that each discipline has its limits, that the educated person needs the flexibility of mind to negotiate and integrate different ways of knowing, and that the final goal of such a liberal arts core is for students to become independent, life-long learners, able to participate in the important conversations of their time.

Why Should I Take IS Courses?

Beth Rigel Daugherty, IS Chairperson, 1994–2000

No one likes to hear "Because we say so," though that's what's implied by making these courses requirements, isn't it? Well, why do we say so? What makes the Integrative Studies courses so important that Otterbein thinks everyone receiving its degree should take ten of them? Why should you take them? Here's why.

They provide breadth. Your major provides depth. Once you declare a major, you decide to specialize in a discipline or field, and you work hard to develop more and more specialized knowledge within that field. The IS courses do the opposite. They provide you with general knowledge across a wide spectrum of fields. Your major keeps you from becoming dangerously superficial, whereas Integrative Studies courses keep you from becoming dangerously narrow. Your major provides a home, a place where everything feels right, the tools feel comfortable, and you feel confident, whereas IS courses send you out into the forest, where everything seems strange, the tools feel awkward, and you feel confused. Your major asks you to get below the surface, to dig; IS asks you to explore many surfaces, to skate.

They enlarge your sense of the world. As the core of liberal arts courses all students take, the IS courses open your mind to other viewpoints, other approaches to knowledge, other cultures. Integrative Studies reminds you that the world and learning and you are bigger than your specialty or your career. IS courses remind you that other people have totally different ways of thinking about the world. It's amazing to discover that some people actually like chemistry or music or philosophy or sociology. It's a little scary but also liberating to discover that not everyone sees things the way you do. That discovery affects everything, from one-on-one to global relationships.

They allow you to join the conversation of educated persons. It's funny how it happens. You struggle in the IS courses to learn names and concepts and ways of thinking are foreign to you; everything you read is difficult, and it seems as though you're looking up every other word and going back to your notes constantly to check: "Now who is that? And what did she believe?" But you keep at it, and suddenly, there comes day when you're reading a complex article and you come across a reference to Plato and you get it! Or there's an allusion to DNA, and you understand it. Or someone mentions Jane Addams' Hull House and you know what it is. Or someone uses the term Renaissance art, and you remember (vaguely perhaps, but you remember) what that is. You no longer feel dumb or excluded. You no longer have to look everything up because your general knowledge base is bigger. You're in a different place. The IS courses have done their work.

They remind you that all knowledge is connected. To make the world easier to study, schools divide knowledge up into subjects. But to some extent, those divisions are arbitrary. Leon Botstein, the president of Bard College, puts it this way: "The truth is that life is not divisible into majors. Neither is work or, believe it or not, learning or scholarship" (199). A discovery in physics affects literature, for example (see Thomas Pynchon's *Gravity's Rainbow*), or physicists use a metaphor to describe a scientific concept. The structure of the IS Program asks you to keep asking, "How is what I'm learning in this class related to what I learned in my other IS classes? To what I'm learning in my major?" Keep asking, and you'll have an epiphany, one of those moments when a light bulb comes on and illuminates everything in a blinding flash of insight: Oh! Biochemistry and religion have histories; history has been influenced by science and religion; modern art, music, theatre, dance, and literature are all after the same things; geography and psychology and biology all affect politics, which affects policy, which affects the way we live! It's all related.

They are practical. Yes, they are the most useful courses you'll take at Otterbein. Think about it: what do employers want? Well, first they want basic skills such as reading, speaking, researching, writing, and technology, along with the ability to increase them. Doesn't every single IS course ask you to use all these skills in one way or another? Second, they want people skills such as cooperation, listening, understanding, cultural sensitivity, and leadership, along with the ability to develop them. Don't all those group activities and projects in IS courses help you practice those skills? Finally, they want visionary skills such as critical thinking, creativity, awareness of the larger picture, and thinking outside the box, along with the knowledge of how to learn and the ability to adapt to change. Aren't you learning how to learn every time an IS course asks you to confront new or strange material? Isn't that why you may say "I have to work harder in my IS course than in my major"? Aren't you learning how to adapt to change every time you take an IS course outside your major's subject matter? Paradoxically, when you're most frustrated at having to learn something that seems impractical, you're actually gaining your most practical skill. According to Leon Botstein, "Learning for its own sake is the best preparation for functioning competitively and creatively" (196). Otterbein alumni agree, reporting that, contrary to what they thought while they were in school, it's their IS courses, not their majors, that they use every day on the job. In a very real way, then, IS courses prepare you for the world of work.

They provide a shared experience. Integrative Studies gives everyone at Otterbein something to talk about; you can all relate to each other through the experience of taking one course or another, even if it's only through complaint! So IS provides you with the camaraderie of a culture, a shared conversation, a sense of community. Even though Otterbein is a small college, not everyone lives on campus, which sometimes makes it hard to feel connected—IS helps. In addition, when you declare a major, you're choosing a cohort without knowing it, a group of people you'll continue to see and work with in class after class. Integrative Studies classes give you the chance to meet new people, to see and work with people outside your cohort, to keep in touch with the larger campus community. So think of these requirements as a social opportunity! In fact, alumni have identified the IS courses as the places where they saw and heard diversity in action, where they got practice in working with difference, where they confronted the variety of opinions and beliefs on campus and in the world, where they met people they would never have met otherwise.

They're personal. IS courses hit you where you live—they challenge you to think again about ideas and beliefs and values you thought you had settled. IS courses can be unsettling, even threatening, because they ask questions you would rather avoid. But they can also be deeply rewarding because they let you explore what you think and why. IS courses ask you, over and over again, to think about how your learning relates to your life: how does the subject matter in this course relate to you, to your background, to the people you know, to the person you want to be? That's what's neat about them. While the courses in your major provide you with disciplinary or professional training, IS courses give you the space and time to ponder, rethink, and strengthen personal values. Isn't that what college is about? Asking and trying to answer the big questions in IS courses—who am I? what are my talents? where do I fit? what are my responsibilities within a diverse society and complex world? what has gone before me and what will come after me? what is the purpose of life? what will I do if (or when)...?— prepares you for living your life, for participating in society as a family member and as a citizen of your community, nation, and world.

So there you have it. The seven most important reasons to take IS courses. You see, we know IS courses will give you breadth, enlarge your world, invite you to the table, bring fragments of your knowledge together, serve you well in your career, help you meet people, and provide opportunities for personal growth. How could we possibly withhold such riches from you? As one of the Otterbein Admission Counselors says, "You don't *have* to take IS courses; you *get* to take IS courses."

Work Cited

Botstein, Leon. *Jefferson's Children: Education and the Promise of American Culture*. New York: Doubleday, 1997.

Unique Features of the I.S. Program

- Carefully designed courses specific to the program
- Unifying theme of human nature
- Five coherent goals (see p. xiii)
- Courses spread across all four years
- Developmental structure: increasing complexity from lower to upper level courses

INTEGRATIVE STUDIES

Barkhymer (chairperson), and members of other departments.

The Integrative Studies Program explores the complexities of **human nature** throughout students' years of study at Otterbein. In doing so, the program builds self-knowledge as well as knowledge of the diversity of cultures, traditions, and points of view in the world. At each level in the program, the frame within which individuals see themselves widens and becomes both more complex and more inclusive. As a result, students going through the Integrative Studies Program gain a broad, general knowledge of the world in which they live. The Program, because of its multidisciplinary nature, may enrich students' graduate study or careers. It also provides Otterbein graduates with the basis for lifelong learning, which in turn may help them adjust to change and complexity, learn new fields, and shift careers. Most important, however, the Integrative Studies Program prepares graduates to become informed citizens in a democracy and to live their lives in family, community, country, and world.

To encourage the achievement of these outcomes, the Integrative Studies Program aims to:

1. teach students to communicate clearly, think critically, analyze. creatively, and view issues from several different points of view;
2. give students the breadth of knowledge and the understanding of a variety of disciplines that will allow them to be lifelong learners;
3. teach students to make connections across disciplines, helping them meet the complexity of contemporary life with interdisciplinary knowledge;
4. focus students on understanding human beings, their natures, their histories, and their place in the cosmos;
5. make students aware of moral and spiritual issues, including knowledge of their own beliefs and tolerance for those of others.

To reach the above **goals,** students take a core of 50 quarter hours, met through 10 requirements, from the list of Integrative Studies courses below. At some points in the program, all students take the same required course; at other points, students choose from among several options. Courses in the program explore the theme of **human nature** from a variety of disciplinary perspectives, ask students to think critically and to use oral and written communication skills, and encourage students to integrate classroom learning with learning from experience, discussion, performances, lectures, films, and/or service work. The requirements are designed to be taken in a sequence: freshmen take three courses at the 100 level, sophomores take two courses at the 200 level, and juniors generally take three courses and seniors two courses at the 300 and 400 level. **Students must take the freshman and sophomore level requirements before enrolling in the junior and senior level requirements.** Each requirement builds on the one before it, and as students move through the sequence of ten courses they are encouraged to make connections between and among their Integrative Studies courses, to connect their Integrative Studies courses to their majors courses, and to see the interconnectedness of all knowledge.

Thus, students and advisers must plan schedules carefully, working to coordinate the developmental sequences of both Integrative Studies and the major. Some flexibility is added through the Integrative Studies Policy on Substitutions described in this section.

Freshman Requirements

Choose one (writing)
- ❏ INST 100   Freshman Seminar
- ❏ INST 105   Growing Up in America
- ❏ INST 110   Composition and Literature: The Individual and Society

Choose one (social sciences)
- ❏ INST 130   Psychology and Human Nature
- ❏ INST 160   World Geography and Human Society
- ❏ INST 170   Inequality in Contemporary American Society
- ❏ INST 180   Encountering Cultural Systems

Required (social sciences)
- ❏ INST 150   Issues in Western Experience

Sophomore Requirements

Choose one (religion and philosophy)
- ❏ INST 250   Philosophy and Human Nature
- ❏ INST 260   Human Nature in the Christian Tradition

Required (writing)
- ❏ INST 270   Composition and Literature: Relationships and Dialogues

Students must take freshman and sophomore level requirements before enrolling in junior and senior level requirements.

Junior and Senior Requirements

Required (writing)
- ❏ INST 300   Composition and Literature: The Dilemma of Existence

Choose one (fine arts)
- ❏ INST 310   Art Forms: Images and Ideas
- ❏ INST 320   Music and Human Nature
- ❏ INST 330   Theatre and Human Nature

Choose two (natural sciences)
- ❏ INST 340   Chemistry Affects Our Lives
- ❏ INST 350   Biological Science: Being in Nature
- ❏ INST 360   Energy, Science, and Society
- ❏ INST 400   Earth Science and Humankind
- ❏ INST 410   Our Place in the Universe

Choose one (global thought)

- ❏ INST 380   Human Nature in World Religions and Philosophies
- ❏ INST 381   Aspects of World Music
- ❏ INST 382   African Cultures and Colonialism
- ❏ INST 383   Modern Indian Culture and Literatures
- ❏ INST 384   Approaching Japan Through Its Arts

Policy on Waivers

One INST course may be waived for participation in an approved off-campus study program (not an internship) for a quarter or a semester, and two INST courses may be waived for full-academic-year participation. In addition to any waived courses, courses in approved off-campus study programs may be used as substitutes for INST courses according to the Policy on Substitutions below. Please see the INST Department Chairperson for approval. Regardless of the number of quarters spent in off-campus study, only one of the composition and literature courses may be waived and only one of the two required natural sciences may be waived.

Policy on Substitutions

The substitution of the alternate courses shown below for specific Intergrative Studies requirements is permitted under the following conditions:

1. No more than three substitutions are permitted.

2. While up to three substitutions are permitted, only one of them may be used to fulfill both an INST requirement and a requirement in the student's major or minor. In other words, only one substitute course may be double-counted.

3. Only one substitution may be made in composition and literature (INST 270/300) and only one substitution may be made in the natural sciences (INST 340/350/360/400/410).

4. Substitute courses to be taken in an off-campus study program must be approved by the chairperson of the Integrative Studies Department.

5. To register for a substitution, select the section with the #sign (example: RELG 100-#1).

INST Course/Approved Alternate

INST 130   PSYC 100
INST 150   HIST 200, HIST 210 or HIST 220
INST 170   SOCL 160
INST 180   Philadelphia Center, SOCL 160 or SOCL 190
INST 250   PHIL 100, PHIL 200, PHIL 210, or PHIL 220
INST 260   PHIL 260, RELG 140, RELG 150, RELG 210, RELG 220, RELG 230,
           RELG 300 or RELG 310
INST 270   ENGL 230, ENGL 231, ENGL 232, or ENGL 233
INST 300   ENGL 350

INST 310   *ART 220, *ART 230 or *ART 240 **(see note below)**
INST 320   **MUSC 335 or **MUSC 338 **(see note below)**
INST 330   ***THR 251 **(see note below)**
INST 340   CHEM 220
INST 350   ENST 101
INST 360   PHYS 210
INST 380   RELG 100, RELG 270, RELG 290, RELG 340, RELG 350 or RELG 360
INST 400   ESC 201, ESC 202 or ESC 205

Integrative Studies Courses (INST)

Information about experimental courses, when offered, will be available at the Office of the Registrar late in the Spring Quarter preceding the academic year in which the Courses are scheduled. Such courses are numbered 191, 291, 391 or 491.

FRESHMAN REQUIREMENTS
Writing - Choose one; 5 hrs

Each option meets the freshman writing requirement and aims to develop skills needed in an academic community: to see an issue from more than one viewpoint, to support conclusions with evidence from texts, and to write expository prose. Composition includes personal responses and thesis papers. ***Honors students must register for an Honors Section of INST 100, 105, or 110.***

INST 100 FRESHMAN SEMINAR   5 hrs

Each seminar uses the approach of one or more disciplines to explore a different topic related to the theme of human nature. Topics in the past have included Food for Thought, Twenty-First Century Sounds, Death and Dying, Consumerism in America and Art, and the Arts Alive and Well.

INST 105 GROWING UP IN AMERICA   5 hrs

This course examines major movements in the United States from the Great Depression to the present to understand how the historical and social developments of the twentieth century have shaped the lives of our grandparents, parents, and selves. Readings are drawn from history, literature, sociology, and other disciplines. Films, lectures, music, and art supplement the readings.

INST 110 COMPOSITION AND LITERATURE:
THE INDIVIDUAL AND SOCIETY   5 hrs

This course uses literature to examine social issues, especially how individuals relate to the communities to which they belong. Readings include poetry, fiction, essays, and drama.

---

*Art majors must take INST 320, INST 330 or their substitutes — not ART 220/230/240
**Music majors must take INST 310, INST 330 or an INST Arts substitute — not MUSC 335/338.
***Theatre majors must take INST 310, INST 320 or their substitutes — not THR 251.

INST 150 ISSUES IN THE WESTERN EXPERIENCE   5 hrs

A study of how the past shapes the issues confronting individuals and societies today. Explores ideas and institutions of past and present Western societies in the context of cultural traditions and values, political systems, economic conditions, and social structures. Students learn to explore the interactions between past, present, and future as they examine major themes such as justice and freedom, faith and reason, war and nationalism.

Social Sciences - Choose one; 5 hrs

The social sciences requirement explores the methods and theories of psychology, sociology, anthropology, and political science to study human beings. Each option teaches students how to ask (and sometimes answer) important questions about human nature, encourages students to value the diversity of human beings and societies in the world, uses an historical approach, and emphasizes how the social sciences apply to individuals and society.

INST 130 PSYCHOLOGY AND HUMAN NATURE   5 hrs

A study of the human being from a range of psychological perspectives. Acquaints students with the philosophies, theories, methods, and major findings of psychology and encourages students to explore the relationships between psychology and other disciplines. Small-group discussions allow for elaboration of classroom material. *Required for teacher licensure and Nursing majors.*

INST 160 WORLD GEOGRAPHY AND HUMAN SOCIETY   5 hrs

A study of the relationship between *where* people live and the *way* they live. Topics, drawn from historical, economic, cultural, medical, and political geography, include the geography of economic development, world population patterns, changing natural environments, and the geography of politics. Students learn to use maps as tools for comprehending the world.

INST 170 INEQUALITY IN CONTEMPORARY AMERICAN SOCIETY   5 hrs

A study of the influence identity, power, and change have on everyday life in contemporary America, with emphasis on social hierarchies based on race, class and gender. Students observe their social environment through the use of tools, concepts, and perspectives of sociology. Focuses on how social inequalities affect people, how individuals cope with social inequality, and how they attempt to improve their place in society.

INST 180 ENCOUNTERING CULTURAL SYSTEMS   5 hrs

A study of human beings within cultures and the tools for studying cultures other than our own, both Western and non-Western. Provides students with a perspective from which to understand both their own and other cultures and a basis for examining crucial human concerns. Brings together political science and economics in the context of sociology and cultural anthropology.

SOPHOMORE REQUIREMENTS
Religion/Philosophy - Choose one; 5 hrs

This requirement focuses on human nature from the perspectives of the Christian faith and of several western philosophical traditions. Each option aims to acquaint students with the Hellenistic, Hebrew, and Christian heritages of western culture, to encourage students to be historically informed, to promote self-understanding in relation to one's own tradition and culture, and to sharpen skills in reading for comprehension, critical thinking, and oral and written communication.

INST 250 PHILOSOPHY AND HUMAN NATURE   5 hrs

An examination of the philosophical problems arising from the attempt to understand human nature, such as: free will and the possibility of determinism; the nature of the self and survival after death; the nature of justice; the nature and foundations of morality; the nature of the good life; and the implications of the existence of (and of various conceptions of) God. Course requirements include a writing component.

INST 260 HUMAN NATURE IN THE CHRISTIAN TRADITION   5 hrs

An examination of the human condition from the perspectives of the Christian tradition, including the Hellenistic and Hebraic backgrounds of the Pauline-Augustinian doctrinal mainstream and interpretations growing from that theological mainstream. Uses the perspective of biblical theology to study themes such as creation and human origin, image of God, sin, the problem of evil and suffering, freedom of the will, salvation, community, sexuality, death and immortality. Course requirements include a writing component.

Writing - Required; 5 hrs
INST 270 COMPOSITION AND LITERATURE: RELATIONSHIPS
AND DIALOGUES   5 hrs

The intermediate course in the writing sequence; stylistically and thematically complex readings present views of relationships, love and romance, marriage and partnerships in literary and other texts from classical times to the present, including works from a variety of cultures. Composition builds on the expository skills developed in freshman courses and emphasizes analysis and comparison/contrast. *Prereq: credit for INST 100 or 105 or 110. Honors students must register for an Honors section.*

INST 290 ECONOMICS AND SOCIETY   5 hrs

The course examines the fundamental principles of both micro- and macro-economics in the context of their effects on individuals and societies. Topics covered include: scarcity and opportunity cost, demand and supply, elasticity, market structures and market failures, national income determination, inflation, unemployment, fiscal and monetary policies, and international economics. The course uses the principles of economics to explore human and social themes such as poverty, income distribution, economic discrimination, crime, education, and environmental degradation. Open only to Continuing Studies students pursuing one of the B.A. degrees in Liberal Studies. Does not fulfill any I.S. requirement for other students.

JUNIOR AND SENIOR REQUIREMENTS

Please Note: Students must take the freshman and sophomore level requirements before enrolling in the junior and senior level requirements.

Writing - Required; 5 hrs

INST 300 COMPOSITION AND LITERATURE: THE DILEMMA OF EXISTENCE   **5 hrs**

The culminating course in the writing sequence; longer and more advanced readings respond to the great concerns of human existence: good and evil, justice and injustice, community and alienation, life and death. Traditional authors such as Sophocles and Shakespeare are central to the course, but contemporary and non-Western writers are also included. Composition builds on skills developed in the freshman and sophomore courses and emphasizes synthesis. **Prereq: credit for INST 270 and 90 quarter hours.**

Fine Arts - Choose one; 5 hrs

This requirement aims to present students with the nonverbal means which human beings have used to express their needs, desires, perceptions, and values. Each option explores the nature of a particular art form, its historical role in society, its connections to the other arts, and its insights about human nature. Special attention is also paid to the nature of artistic creativity.

INST 310 ART FORMS: IMAGES AND IDEAS   **5 hrs**

An examination of how the processes and products of the visual arts embody human nature. Students will consider the nature of artistic creativity and the role of the artist in society, view significant visual art objects, and learn about artistic production through the perspective of history. Although the course emphasizes the development of Western art, students will also view works reflecting the rich heritage of art throughout the world. **Art majors must register for INST 320, INST 330, or an INST 320 or 330 approved substitute.**

INST 320 MUSIC AND HUMAN NATURE   **5 hrs**

An introduction to the Western European concert music tradition from the listener's viewpoint, emphasizing music's relation to the human being and society. Students learn the vocabulary for discussing the basic elements of music, practice listening skills, and use an historical approach to become familiar with principal stylistic eras. Course requires attendance at music events outside the classroom. **Music majors must register for INST 310, INST 330, or an INST Fine Arts approved substitute.**

INST 330 THEATRE AND HUMAN NATURE   **5 hrs**

An introduction to the process of creating theatre. Students study dramatic literature, history, criticism, and the process of production to learn how to make critical judgments about current plays, films, and television shows. Course requires attendance at theatre events outside the classroom. **Theatre and musical theatre majors must register for INST 310 or INST 320 or an INST 310 or 320 approved substitute.**

Sciences – Choose two;   10 hrs

This requirement focuses on developing an understanding of human nature from a scientific perspective and on promoting scientific literacy. Scientific literacy consists of: a familiarity with the scientific method; an understanding of science as a way of knowing the world; an appreciation of the breadth of scientific inquiry; an awareness of how science affects contemporary life; the exploration of connections between the sciences and other disciplines and the ability to think critically and quantitatively. Each option seeks to discourage anti-science attitudes, to decrease science anxiety, and to promote stewardship of the Earth.

INST 340 CHEMISTRY AFFECTS OUR LIVES   5 hrs

Studies of the benefits and risks of chemical processes. Focuses on the society/science interface from perspectives of the economy, physical health, ethics, and culture. Discussion groups allow for elaboration of classroom material.

INST 350 BIOLOGICAL SCIENCE: BEING IN NATURE   5 hrs

A presentation and discussion of some economic, health, ethical and cultural concerns from the viewpoint of life science. Uses the study of the biological human, the place of humans in the ecosystem, and the effect of changing environments (e.g. rural to urban) on human beings to explore the theme of being in nature. Students must complete several laboratory and field experiments.

INST 360 ENERGY, SCIENCE AND SOCIETY   5 hrs

A study of the role of energy in our lives. Discussion of the physics of energy precedes a look at its uses, consequences for humanity, and the impact on resulting energy and environmental policies. Course requirements include a writing component.

INST 400 EARTH SCIENCE AND HUMANKIND   5 hrs

A study of the impact of earth science upon human life, and of human life upon the physical Earth, including volcanoes, earthquakes, water and energy resources, pollution, deforestation, and global change such as global warming. Students use essays, debates, and discussion groups to practice written and oral communication skills.

INST 410 OUR PLACE IN THE UNIVERSE   5 hrs

A study of the evolving human understanding of the universe and our place in it through the study of astronomy. Places the explorations of modern astronomy in the historical context. Students participate in several observational and experimental activities. Course requirements include a writing component.

Global Thought - Choose one; 5 hrs

This requirement focuses on human nature from a variety of perspectives and a variety of disciplines. The focus is on areas outside the U.S. and on cultures and traditions that are beyond the Western experience. Each option aims to broaden students' awareness of, and appreciation for, the many ways human beings understand themselves and the purpose of life, to encourage students to make connections across disciplines, and to continue to shape their own beliefs and values in light of other cultural points of view.

INST 380 HUMAN NATURE IN WORLD RELIGIONS AND PHILOSOPHIES 5 hrs

An examination of human nature from the viewpoint of several Asian religions and philosophies. Designed as a complementary sequel to INST 250 or INST 260, the course deals with basic questions about the purpose and meaning of life and the nature of the Ultimate or God. Topics include views of reality, definitions of human nature, the nature of right and wrong, the causes of evil and suffering, paths of salvation, and the interdependence of religion and culture. Course requirements include a writing component.

INST 381 ASPECTS OF WORLD MUSIC 5 hrs

A view of human nature through the lens of the world's music. Connections between music and society in cultures chosen from the following-Native America, Africa, Black America, Eastern Europe, the Indian Subcontinent, Japan, Indonesia, and South America-will be studied outside the context of the Western European concert music tradition. Students develop a vocabulary for describing each culture's music and a set of approaches for studying music in a sociocultural context. Course requirements include a written project and attendance at music events outside the classroom.

INST 382 AFRICAN CULTURES AND COLONIALISM 5 hrs

A study of African cultures, with emphasis on selected geographic areas and ethnic groups. Focuses on cultural encounters, their effects, and the relationship of culture to human nature by examining precolonial African civilization, the world view of colonizers, the impact of Western colonialism on Africa, and the African recovery of independence. Exploration of several perspectives is encouraged through the use of several disciplines (chosen from among history, literature, religion, political science, sociology, economics, and the arts). Course requirements include a writing component and a final project that requires synthesis.

INST 383 MODERN INDIAN CULTURE AND LITERATURES 5 hrs

This course uses literature as a major, though not the sole means, to introduce students to modern India after its independence in 1947. The course is interdisciplinary in approach. Literary readings are put in context by using two other focal points, India's religions such as Hinduism, Islam and Buddhism, and its experience of colonization by the British to understand its varied and complex present-day culture but also to compare it to their own. It seeks to show students how such a comparative exploration can help one gain a deeper understanding of one's own culture and individuality as well as better understand human nature.

INST 384 APPROACHING JAPAN THROUGH ITS ARTS 5 hrs

This team-taught course begins with the premise that Japan is a nation whose post-modern, high-tech exterior clothes a deeply traditional civilization, divergent in some ways from Euro-

American experience and values. Students will approach Japan by encountering the visual arts, music, literature, cinema, language, and athletic traditions. They will seek an understanding of common themes, motives, and forms that indicate Japanese perceptions of the world and of human nature. Course requirements include a final written project and attendance at events outside the class meeting time.

Internship - Optional

INST 490 INTERNSHIP   **1-15 hrs**

Internship associated with the Integrative Studies festival designed by the intern and the festival chairperson through a learning contract process. ***Registration must be approved by the chairperson of the Integrative Studies Department***

Chapter 1
SCHOOL AND COLLEGE

Andrew P. Mills (1968–   ) is an associate professor of philosophy at Otterbein College, where he teaches a wide array of philosophy courses. He received his B. A. from the University of Michigan, and his M.A. and Ph.D. in philosophy from The University of North Carolina at Chapel Hill. He is the author of scholarly articles in the philosophy of language and in philosophical logic.

What's So Good About A College Education?

Andrew P. Mills

Why is it good to go to college? What is so valuable about a college educa-   1
tion? College is expensive, and you wouldn't spend all that money on something that wasn't valuable. Moreover, college requires a great deal of work,
and it requires that you spend time reading and writing and studying and
going to class and taking tests—time that you could spend doing other
things—and you wouldn't spend your time on all those college-related tasks
unless you thought you were getting something valuable for all your effort.
You are in college, and so you think that getting a college education is a
good thing—that it is valuable in some way or other—but what sort of value
does it have? It's worthwhile to spend some time thinking about the answer
to this question, for it will affect the way you spend your time at college, and
it will affect the sort of education that you get there. If you don't know why
college is valuable, you're very likely wasting your time and money and
effort during your college years.

Most people give what I will call the simple "Can Opener Answer" to   2
this question. I think there are two serious problems with that answer, and
that is what I want to convince you of. Once we see what is wrong with the
simple Can Opener Answer, we can talk about some of the differences
between high school and college, and the right way to approach your college education.

The Can Opener Answer

Why is it good to have a can opener? People pay money for can openers, and   3
people spend time with can openers, so they must think that can openers
are valuable in some way or other, but how are they valuable? The answer
here is easy: can openers are valuable because they allow you to open cans.
There's tasty stuff inside of cans, and you can't get at the tasty stuff unless
the can is open, and you can't open the can unless you've got a can opener.
If you could open cans by snapping your fingers, then you wouldn't need a
can opener. Can openers are tools: they are valuable, but only as tools or
instruments are valuable. That is, they are valuable because of what you can
get with them. Once we acquire the ability to open cans by snapping our
fingers, or once they stop hiding the tasty stuff inside of cans, then can
openers will be useless. They will cease to have the sort of value they now
have. [1]

So what's the Can Opener Answer to the question about the value of   4
college? It's this: a college education is valuable because of what you can do
with it. In particular, it's valuable because you can trade it for a job. Crudely
put, you can take your diploma, show it to an employer, and then you'll get
a job. Of course the job interview process is not that easy, but in rough outline that's how many people (maybe even you!) think about the value of a
college education. I hope you can see the analogy with the can opener case.
The job is the analogue of the tasty stuff in the can. If you could get a job
without a college education, then, it would seem, it's silly and wasteful and
foolish to spend all that time and money and effort at college. Just as it
would be silly to spend money on a can opener if you could open the can by
snapping your fingers.

People who ask the question, "So, what are you going to do with an   5
English major?", or "How much money do Sociology majors make?" are
thinking in can opener terms. They think that the only thing valuable
about a college education is what sort of job (and how high-paying a job)
you can get with that college education. And they also think that people
who major in Classics or Philosophy or Women's Studies won't get very
good jobs. So, they think, since you're spending all that time and money
and effort on college, you should get yourself the sort of education that is
useful for getting a good job. So, they might say, you should major in

Nursing or Education or Business or Journalism or Computer Science because those are the sort of majors that you can trade for good jobs.

Now I think there is something right about the Can Opener Answer, but there are two serious problems with it.   6

The First Problem with the Can Opener Answer

What the Can Opener Answer has right is that a college education is use-   7
ful for getting a job. After all, college graduates, in general, have better, higher paying, more interesting, potentially more fulfilling jobs than those without college degrees. But that is not the only thing a college education is useful for. A college education—in particular, a broad-based, multidisciplinary, liberal arts education—is useful for so much more. The problem with the simple Can Opener Answer is that it misses this "so much more" when it focuses merely on the job-getting features of a college degree. Here are just some of the other things that college educated people are able to do.

- College can equip us for our leisure time just as much, if not more   8
  so, than it can equip us for our working lives. College-educated people are able to appreciate and enjoy literature, art, music, essays, movies, and other products of the culture. Or, to put it better, the sort of appreciation and enjoyment that they have is deeper because of their education: those with a liberal arts education see things in movies and music and literature that those without the education don't. And, as a consequence, their experience is richer.

- We live in a democracy, the success of which requires that each of   9
  us participates actively and intelligently in the democratic institutions. Such participation includes not simply voting, but critically examining the candidates' positions, speaking out as an advocate for policy change, perhaps even serving in a leadership role on a governmental body. Moreover, it requires being critical of the institutions themselves, and seeing what needs changing and why. The appreciation of history, the ability to formulate a persuasive argument, an analytic skill with budgets and statistics and polling data—these are all skills you get as a college-educated person and

they are skills necessary for successful participation as a citizen in a democracy.

- The developments in technology and the advances in science   10 (especially medical science) are an ever-present, and ever-more-important part of our lives. The growing presence of medications in the treatment of psychological maladies, the possibilities opened up by the study and manipulation of DNA, and the prospects for artificial intelligence (just to name a few) are developments that require an intelligent response. Which of the many possibilities opened up to us by science should be pursued? How reliable is DNA testing? Should we treat depression with a drug or with traditional therapy? College graduates are well-positioned to answer these questions because they know some science, and can distinguish quackery from good scientific practice. Moreover, they are accustomed to asking questions about value[2] and these are the sorts of questions which very much need to be asked about technological developments.

- This last point applies not simply to the advances in science and   11 technology, but to the information that comes to us via the media. We need to be able to distinguish the foolish fad from the important trend; we need to be able to determine which news outlets are reliable and which are overly biased; we need to be able to figure out where to turn for information and how to navigate between the twin vices of gullibility (believing everything you read in the newspaper, or see on the internet, or hear from a TV anchor) and skepticism (believing nothing that anybody else tells you). Because during your education college you will spend a significant amount of time doing research and evaluating sources, you will be, once you finish college, perfectly situated to be intelligent consumers of information.

- Finally, a college education equips people with the tools for self-   12 examination that renders them able to make informed and intelligent choices about the direction of their own lives. College may equip you for a career, but you have to decide which career to pursue, and how to balance the competing demands of work and family. At what point do you leave the comfort of a safe but boring job for the excitement of a new but less secure job? How important a role should your religious or political beliefs play in the life you lead? Should you work for (or buy the products of) a company that exploits child laborers? Should you buy your groceries from a large national chain or from the local, but perhaps more expensive, market? At what point should you put a moral principle ahead of economic interest? These are decisions that we all must make; if we don't, someone else will make them for us. And by providing the experience and guidance at thinking through these sorts of questions (and other, much more difficult ones) a college education will turn you into a reflective, morally mature person.

The point I'm making can be put this way. A college education isn't   13
valuable like a can opener is valuable. It's valuable like a Swiss army knife is valuable. Or like a computer is valuable. People who focus simply on the job-getting feature of a college education are like people who think that the belt-punch is the only useful feature of a Swiss army knife.

I would go even further and argue that the benefits of a college educa-   14
tion that I just listed are actually more valuable than the fact that you can get a good job with a college diploma. First, it is becoming increasingly unlikely you will spend the 40 years following college in one career, let alone in one job. To devote your college years to preparing for life as a lab assistant will turn out to be a waste when you leave the biomedical industry for a job in book publishing. But the features I listed above will be of use no matter what job you have. Secondly, and I think more importantly, the job you have is but one element in what I would hope is a complex and multi-layered life. Living your life involves so much more than working at a job. It involves being a citizen, a spouse, a friend, a parent, a decision-maker, and someone who has leisure time to fill, and a college education contributes toward improving these aspects of your life.

The Second Problem with the Can Opener Answer.

That's the first problem with the simple Can Opener Answer: it mistakes   15
something that has many uses for something that performs merely one task.

But even when we do focus on the way in which a college education translates into a job, I think many people fail fully to grasp precisely why employers value employees who are college-educated. And this failure is the second problem with the simple Can Opener Answer.

The reason that college degrees translate into high-end salaries and   16
good jobs has, I would argue, more to do with the skills one acquires in college than with the discipline-specific knowledge of the individual courses.
No one is going to give you a better job because of your knowledge of
Shakespeare or Plato or the Napoleonic Wars. But students who are successful in their English, Philosophy, and History classes are independent and
creative thinkers who can write and speak clearly, who can juggle many
responsibilities, who can conduct research, and who can take steps to educate themselves. And employers will be falling all over themselves to hire
people with these skills. Consequently, it doesn't matter so much what your
major is as much as it does that you acquire these more general skills. So
select a major you find interesting, which will challenge you, which will
make you smarter, and don't worry exclusively about "what you can do"
with a degree in, say, religious studies.

Even when it comes to the more vocationally-related majors like nurs-   17
ing or business or education or biology, it is sure to be the case that the
knowledge you will need in your job will far outstrip what you will learn in
your college classes. This is not a failing of the college classes, it is just a fact
that specific industries and jobs require highly specific knowledge. It is also
a fact that what you need to know to be an accountant or a teacher or a
nurse or a biologist will change in response to advances in those fields.
(Think, for example, about how much more today's middle school teachers
need to know about computers compared to their predecessors 30 years
ago.) One of the goals of a college education is to give you the general
knowledge into which you can fit the more specific knowledge required by
your particular job. And, more importantly, a college education will give
you the ability to teach yourself, so that when you need a new job skill,
you'll be prepared.

When you get a job, the employer very likely will train you to do what-   18
ever it is that needs to be done. Large corporations have entire human
resources departments and internal "universities" the sole purpose of which
is to train the new employees to perform the necessary tasks. The Widget
Corporation will understand if you can't come in on the first day of the job

and start making the widgets; their trainers will show you how to do that. But what they won't show you is how to write clearly, how to organize your time, how to give a presentation to the Board of Directors, how to ask questions, and how to make decisions. What an employer wants above all is an employee who can think, and that is what they expect from people with a college education. Once you understand that it is these more generally intellectual skills which employers desire, you'll realize that they can be acquired in just about any major.

The second problem, then, with the simple Can Opener Answer is   19 that it fails to recognize that it is the general skills and not simply the domain-specific content knowledge which turns college graduates into desirable employees. I think I can put the point this way. A college education does not, as most people believe, prepare you do to something. Rather, it prepares you to do anything. [3]

How To Get The Most Out of College

Now that we understand the value of a college education, we can think   20 about what you should do in college, and how you can make the most of your college years. Given that college is valuable not simply because it gets you a job, but because it prepares you to be a complete person, and given that what you want from college in the way of job-related skills are general intellectual abilities more than particular, task-specific knowledge, what should you do? I don't have all the answers, but here are some about which I'm fairly confident.

1. Write as much as you can. Then write some more. The written word   21 is the medium of academic communication. Academics talk to one another through books and published articles. Students talk to their professors through exams and term papers. If you cannot write well, you will not succeed in college, it's as simple as that. I once spoke to a group of college juniors, and I asked them what they wish they knew about college when they were entering freshmen. One of them[4] said that he wished he had known how much writing he would have to do, and to how high a standard his writing would be held. So now you know: writing is crucially important.

And since writing is a skill like juggling or playing the guitar, the only   22 way to get better at it is to practice. Write at every opportunity. Keep a class journal. Take notes when you read (and don't simply underline or highlight your books. This is next to worthless.). Write drafts of your assigned papers. Demand feedback on your writing from your professors. The more you write, the better a writer you will become. And, you will find, the better a thinker you will become, because more than anything else, writing is just thinking out loud on paper. Write for yourself, to clarify your own thinking, not simply because you have a paper due at the end of the term. Because writing is the medium of academic communication, you need to treat it that way—as a form of communication. Don't think of your papers as something that you turn in for a grade, but as an opportunity to talk to your professors and to tell them what you have been thinking about. I hardly need say that if you are a talented writer, you will succeed in the workplace. You won't have to write essays on Jane Austen or the Protestant Reformation once you leave college, but you will have to write memos and reports and presentations and speeches, and honing this skill in college will serve you well once you leave.

2. Talk. And not just about your weekend plans or about the details of   23
your friends' love lives. Talk about ideas that fascinate you. Talk about politics and religion and racism and abortion and all the other issues that are important but which are not usually talked about in "polite society". It is through talking about these issues that you may very well come to turn confusion into clarity. Many of these questions can only be solved when a number of minds come together at once, and gathering in a group and talking is the best way to bring minds together. How will you know if there is a flaw in your position if you don't show it to someone else? Moreover, you can use your talking about these issues as practice for the talking that you will have to do with your spouse, your children, your co-workers, your boss, and the members of your town council. Speaking to others in private and to groups in public is one of those life and job skills that I mentioned above, and if you can treat college as an opportunity for honing that skill, you will be ready to talk in these other sorts of situations. Finally, as you will soon learn, talking about ideas is valuable for its own sake. The late-night conversations at coffee houses or in dorm rooms about the meaning of life and the way to fix the world are just plain fun. Do it as often as you can.

3. Take responsibility for your education. Here's the part where college   24
distinguishes itself from high school. High school students are there because

they have to be. College students are in college because they want to be. (And make sure you really want to be in college before you go. It is a sizeable investment of time and money, and if there's something else you'd rather be doing, you should take some time and re-assess your situation. Taking a year off to figure out what you want, and entering college with a clear plan in mind can make all the difference in the world.) You are paying dearly for your college education, so you should go out and get it. Don't wait for someone else to hand it to you; it won't come. Taking responsibility for your own education manifests itself in small ways, and in larger ways. On the small side it means going to the dictionary when you run across a word you don't know. It also means asking your professor to read a draft of your essay, or raising your hand in class to ask for a difficult point to be repeated. But taking responsibility for your education means more than this. It means seeking out challenging courses and inspiring professors, for only if you push yourself by taking hard courses will you improve your academic and intellectual skills. It means having the courage to change your major if you find your current one uninteresting. It means engaging your friends in the dormitories and coffee shops about what you are learning in the classroom. It means speaking up and agitating for change if things aren't going the way you want. If you sit passively through your classes, skipping the readings, and taking only the easy courses, you will fail to gain the very education to which you are committing so much time and money.

It might help to think of college as a sort of health club—a health club   25
for the mind.[5] There are all sorts of machines in the health club: these are your professors, your classes, and the many extra-curricular activity opportunities. The machines at this intellectual health club can improve your mind in the way that the weights and stair-climbers at your gym can improve your body. But, just as at the gym, the machines are useless if you don't use them. Merely buying a health club membership won't turn flab into muscle; you have to lift weights and do sit-ups. And merely enrolling in college won't turn an uneducated person into an educated one. Doing the reading, talking in class, visiting your professors in office hours, pursuing research topics outside of class—this is the sort of "machine using" behavior that will turn the gray matter inside your head into a well-toned mental muscle.

4. <u>Do something completely different</u>. I see so many students who take 26 the same menu of courses they took in high school: history, English, math, science, and a foreign language. All of those are important classes, but a quick glance at any college's course catalog will show that there are dozens if not hundreds of comparatively exotic courses. Religious studies, communication, anthropology, economics, psychology, film theory—the list goes on. Take a course that is completely different from anything you have taken before. <u>Explore the unknown</u>. Not only might the strange and exotic be something you like (and have a talent for!), but the challenge of these new courses will push you to develop the intellectual skills I have been talking about. This injunction to do something completely different shouldn't stop at the course catalog, however. Find the person on campus most different from you and take them out to coffee. Try out for a play, join the debate team, write for the newspaper, join a campus service organization. Try your hand at some of those activities that you would never have done in high school. Of course you will meet new people, but the primary reason for engaging in these pursuits is to discover something about yourself. Maybe you would enjoy the theatre or find that you have a talent for organizing fund-drives (and can translate that into a career!). It is foolish to commit yourself to a life-plan before you have discovered what you like and what talents you have. And after you get a "real job" and "settle down" you will find precious little time for these extra curricular pursuits.

5. <u>Become curious</u>. The late Canadian novelist Robertson Davies has 27 hit upon the essence of college. "<u>Energy and curiosity are the lifeblood of universities</u>," Davies had one of his characters say. "<u>The desire to find out, to uncover, to dig deeper, to puzzle out obscurities, is the spirit of the university and it is a channeling of that unresting curiosity that holds mankind together</u>."[6] Since this 'unresting curiosity' is the essence of any college, succeeding during the next four years requires that you tap into this energy, and that you become an unrestingly curious person yourself. Feed your curiosity by taking courses that interest you, rather than the courses which might look good on a law school application. Find those issues and problems that interest you and pursue them doggedly. Become curious about everything— about medieval history, about the structure of the cell, about what your roommates are learning in their classes, about the research interests of your professors—and you will find not only that you are getting better grades, but

that you are becoming a smarter, more intellectually independent person. And that is, at the end, the goal of a college education.[7]

Notes

1. Of course in such a situation can openers may have value as antiques, or as objects of art. And that is a real sort of value, but it is not (at least not standardly) why we think can openers are valuable now.
2. Like this very essay: it's an examination of the value of a college education.
3. I learned of this way of putting the point from Ami Berger, though I don't think she was the originator of this thought.
4. His name is Caleb Bell.
5. For this health club analogy I am indebted to Craig Froehle.
6. This is from Davies' novel, *The Rebel Angels.*
7. An earlier, abbreviated, version of this essay was published under the title "College is more than job training" in *The Blade* (Toledo, Ohio) on September 30, 2000. For helpful conversation on this essay, I would like to thank Lori Aronson, Ami Berger, Brad Cohen, Craig Froehle, Glenna Jackson, Kristine LaLonde, Brian Lindeman, Mary MacLeod, Lisa Pollak, Charles Salter, and the audiences at Otterbein College to whom I have presented the main ideas contained above. I would like to dedicate this essay to Jack Meiland, who ignited my thinking on the question of why a college education is valuable. His little book, *College Thinking,* is as valuable a guide to college as I can think of.

Caroline Bird (1915–) a researcher, journalist, public-relations specialist, professor, and writer, attended Vassar College and received a B.A. from the University of Toledo (1938) before earning an M.A. from the University of Wisconsin–Madison in 1939. Her career has included posts at *Newsweek*, *Fortune*, and Russell Sage College, as well as freelance writing. She is a member of the Society for Magazine Writers, the American Sociological Association, Women in Communications, Women's Equity Action League, and the National Organization for Women. The American Library Association named *The Invisible Scar: The Great Depression and What It Did to American Life* one of the best books of 1966.

As a feminist scholar, Bird has documented job discrimination against women. Some of her books include *Born Female: The High Cost of Keeping Women Down* (1968; rev. 1970); *Everything a Woman Needs to Know to Get Paid What She's Worth* (1973; rev. 1981); *The Case Against College*, in which "Where College Fails Us" appears (1975); *Enterprising Women: Their Contribution to the American Economy, 1776–1976* (1976); *What Women Want* (1978); *The Two-Paycheck Marriage: How Women at Work Are Changing Life in America* (1979); and *The Good Years: Your Life in the Twenty-First Century* (1983).

Where College Fails Us

Caroline Bird

The case *for* college has been accepted without question for more than a gener-   1
ation. All high school graduates ought to go, says Conventional Wisdom and statistical evidence, because college will help them earn more money, become "better" people, and learn to be more responsible citizens than those who don't go.

But college has never been able to work its magic for everyone. And now   2
that close to half our high school graduates are attending, those who don't fit the
pattern are becoming more numerous, and more obvious. College graduates are
selling shoes and driving taxis; college students sabotage each other's experiments and forge letters of recommendation in the intense competition for admission to graduate school. Others find no stimulation in their studies, and drop
out—often encouraged by college administrators.

Some observers say the fault is with the young people themselves—they   3
are spoiled, stoned, overindulged, and expecting too much. But that's mass character assassination, and doesn't explain all campus unhappiness. Others blame
the state of the world, and they are partly right. We've been told that young
people have to go to college because our economy can't absorb an army of

"Where College Fails Us" From *The Case Against College* by Caroline Bird.

untrained 18-year-olds. But disillusioned graduates are learning that it can no longer absorb an army of trained 22-year-olds, either.

Some adventuresome educators and campus watchers have openly   4
begun to suggest that college may not be the best, the proper, the only place for every young person after the completion of high school. We may have been looking at all those surveys and statistics upside down, it seems, and through the rosy glow of our own remembered college experiences. Perhaps college doesn't make people intelligent, ambitious, happy, liberal, or quick to learn new things—maybe it's just the other way around, and intelligent, ambitious, happy, liberal, and quick-learning people are merely the ones who have been attracted to college in the first place. And perhaps all those successful college graduates would have been successful whether they had gone to college or not. This is heresy to those of us who have been brought up to believe that if a little schooling is good, more has to be much better. But contrary evidence is beginning to mount up.

The unhappiness and discontent of young people is nothing new, and   5
problems of adolescence are always painfully intense. But while traveling around the country, speaking at colleges, and interviewing students at all kinds of schools—large and small, public and private—I was overwhelmed by the prevailing sadness. It was as visible on campuses in California as in Nebraska and Massachusetts. Too many young people are in college reluctantly, because everyone told them they ought to go, and there didn't seem to be anything better to do. Their elders sell them college because it's good for them. Some never learn to like it, and talk about their time in school as if it were a sentence to be served.

Students tell us the same thing college counselors tell us—they go   6
because of pressure from parents and teachers, and stay because it seems to be an alternative to a far worse fate. It's "better" than the Army or a dead-end job, and it has to be pretty bad before it's any worse than staying at home.

College graduates say that they don't want to work "just" for the   7
money: They want work that matters. They want to help people and save the world. But the numbers are stacked against them. Not only are there not enough jobs in the world-saving fields, but in the current slowdown it has become evident that there never were, and probably never will be, enough jobs requiring higher education to go around.[1]

Students who tell their advisers they want to help people, for example, are   8
often directed to psychology. This year the Department of Labor estimates that
there will be 4300 new jobs for psychologists, while colleges will award 58,430
bachelor's degrees in psychology.[2]

Sociology has become a favorite major on socially conscious campuses, but   9
graduates find that social reform is hardly a paying occupation. Male sociologists
from the University of Wisconsin reported as gainfully employed a year after
graduation included a legal assistant, sports editor, truck unloader, Peace Corps
worker, publications director, and a stockboy—but no sociologist per se. The
highest paid worked for the post office.

Publishing, writing, and journalism are presumably the vocational goal of a   10
large proportion of the 104,000 majors in communications and letters expected
to graduate in 1975.[3] The outlook for them is grim. All of the daily newspapers
in the country combined are expected to hire a total of 2600 reporters this year.
Radio and television stations may hire a total of 500 announcers, most of them
in local radio stations.[4] Nonpublishing organizations will need 1100 technical
writers, and public-relations activities another 4400.[5] Even if new graduates
could get all these jobs (they can't, of course), over 90,000 of them will have to
find something less glamorous to do.

Other fields most popular with college graduates are also pathetically small.   11
Only 1900 foresters a year will be needed during this decade, although schools of
forestry are expected to continue graduating twice that many.[6] Some will get
subprofessional jobs as forestry aides. Schools of architecture are expected to turn
out twice as many as will be needed,[7] and while all sorts of people want to design
things, the Department of Labor forecasts that there will be jobs for only 400 new
industrial designers[8] a year. As for anthropologists, only 400 will be needed every
year in the 1970s[9] to take care of all the college courses, public-health research,
community surveys, museums, and all the archaeological digs on every continent. (For these jobs graduate work in anthropology is required.)

Many popular occupations may seem to be growing fast without necessarily   12
offering employment to very many. "Recreation work" is always cited as an
expanding field, but it will need relatively few workers who require more special
training than life guards. "Urban planning" has exploded in the media, so the
U.S. Department of Labor doubled its estimate of the number of jobs to be filled
every year in the 1970s—to a big, fat 800.[10] A mere 200 oceanographers[11] a year
will be able to do all the exploring of "inner space"—and all that exciting under-

water diving you see demonstrated on television—for the entire decade of the 1970s.

Whatever college graduates *want* to do, most of them are going to wind up   13
doing what *there* is to do. During the next few years, according to the Labor Department, the biggest demand will be for stenographers and secretaries, followed by retail-trade salesworkers, hospital attendants, bookkeepers, building custodians, registered nurses, foremen, kindergarten and elementary-school teachers, receptionists, cooks, cosmetologists, private-household workers, manufacturing inspectors, and industrial machinery repairmen.[12] These are the jobs which will eventually absorb the surplus archaeologists, urban planners, oceanographers, sociologists, editors, and college professors.

Vocationalism is the new look on campus because of the discouraging job   14
market faced by the generalists. Students have been opting for medicine and law in droves. If all those who check "doctor" as their career goal succeed in getting their MDs, we'll immediately have ten times the target ratio of doctors for the population of the United States. Law schools are already graduating twice as many new lawyers every year as the Department of Labor thinks we will need, and the oversupply grows annually.[13]

Specialists often find themselves at the mercy of shifts in demand, and the   15
narrower the vocational training, the more risky the long-term prospects. Engineers are the classic example of the "Yo-Yo" effect in supply and demand. Today's shortage is apt to produce a big crop of engineering graduates after the need has crested, and teachers face the same squeeze.

Worse than that, when the specialists turn up for work, they often find that   16
they have learned a lot of things in classrooms that they will never use, that they will have to learn a lot of things on the job that they were never taught, and that most of what they have learned is less likely to "come in handy later" than to fade from memory. One disillusioned architecture student, who had already designed and built houses, said, "It's the degree you need, not everything you learn getting it."

A diploma saves the employer the cost of screening candidates and gives   17
him a predictable product: He can assume that those who have survived the four-year ordeal have learned how to manage themselves. They have learned how to budget their time, meet deadlines, set priorities, cope with impersonal authority, follow instructions, and stick with a task that may be tiresome without direct supervision.

The employer is also betting that it will be cheaper and easier to train the college graduate because he has demonstrated his ability to learn. But if the diploma serves only to identify those who are talented in the art of schoolwork, it becomes, in the words of Harvard's Christopher Jencks, "a hell of an expensive aptitude test." It is unfair to the candidates because they themselves must bear the cost of the screening— the cost of college. Candidates without the funds, the academic temperament, or the patience for the four year obstacle race are ruled out, no matter how well they may perform on the job. But if "everyone" has a diploma, employers will have to find another way to choose employees, and it will become an empty credential.   18

(Screening by diploma may in fact already be illegal. The 1971 ruling of the Supreme Court in *Griggs* v. *Duke Power Co.* contended that an employer cannot demand a qualification which systematically excludes an entire class of applicants, unless that qualification reliably predicts success on the job. The requiring of a high school diploma was outlawed in the *Griggs* case, and this could extend to a college diploma.)   19

The bill for four years at an Ivy League college is currently climbing toward $25,000; at a state university, a degree will cost the student and his family about $10,000 (with taxpayers making up the difference).[14]   20

Not many families can afford these sums, and when they look for financial aid, they discover that someone else will decide how much they will actually have to pay. The College Scholarship Service, which establishes a family's degree of need for most colleges, is guided by noble principles: uniformity of sacrifice, need rather than merit. But families vary in their willingness to "sacrifice" as much as the bureaucracy of the CSS thinks they ought to. This is particularly true of middle-income parents, whose children account for the bulk of the country's college students. Some have begun to rebel against this attempt to enforce the same values and priorities on all. "In some families, a college education competes with a second car, a color television, or a trip to Europe—and it's possible that college may lose," one financial-aid officer recently told me.   21

Quite so. College is worth more to some middle-income families than to others. It is chilling to consider the undercurrent of resentment that families who "give up everything" must feel toward their college-age children, or the burden of guilt children must bear every time they goof off or receive less than top grades in their courses.   22

The decline in return for a college degree within the last generation has been substantial. In the 1950s, a Princeton student could pay his expenses   23 for the school year—eating club and all—on less than $3,000. When he graduated, he entered a job market which provided a comfortable margin over the earnings of his agemates who had not been to college. To be precise, a freshman entering Princeton in 1956, the earliest year for which the Census has attempted to project lifetime earnings, could expect to realize a12.5 percent return on his investment. A freshman entering in 1972, with the cost nearing $6,000 annually, could expect to realize only 9.3 percent, less than might be available in the money market. This calculation was made with the help of a banker and his computer, comparing college as an investment in future earnings with other investments available in the booming money market of 1974, and concluded that in strictly financial terms, college is not always the best investment a young person can make.

I postulated a young man (the figures are different with a young woman, but   24
the principle is the same) whose rich uncle would give him, in cash, the total cost of four years at Princeton—$34,181.[15] (The total includes what the young man would earn if he went to work instead of to college right after high school.) If he did not spend the money on Princeton, but put it in the savings bank at 7.5 percent interest compounded daily, he would have, at retirement age 64, more than five times as much as the $199,000 extra he could expect to earn between 22 and 60 as a college man rather than a mere high school graduate. And with all that money accumulating in the bank, he could invest in something with a higher return than a diploma. At age 28, when his nest egg had reached $73,113, he could buy a liquor store, which would return him well over 20 percent on his investment, as long as he was willing to mind the store. He might get a bit fidgety sitting there, but he'd have to be dim-witted to lose money on a liquor store, and right now we're talking only about dollars.

If the young man went to a public college rather than Princeton, the invest   25
ment would be lower, and the payoff higher, of course, because other people— the tax-payers—put up part of the capital for him. But the difference in return between an investment in public and private colleges is minimized because the biggest part of the investment in either case is the money a student might earn if he went to work, not to college—in economic terms, his "foregone income." That he bears himself.

Rates of return and dollar signs on education are a fascinating brain teaser,   26
and, obviously, there is a certain unreality to the game. But the same unreality extends to the traditional calculations that have always been used to convince taxpayers that college is a worthwhile investment.

The ultimate defense of college has always been that while it may not teach   27
you anything vocationally useful, it will somehow make you a better person, able
to do anything better, and those who make it through the process are initiated
into the "fellowship of educated men and women." In a study intended to probe
what graduates seven years out of college thought their colleges should have
done for them, the Carnegie Commission found that most alumni expected the
"development of my abilities to think and express myself." But if such respected
educational psychologists as Bruner and Piaget are right, specific learning skills
have to be acquired very early in life, perhaps even before formal schooling
begins.

So, when pressed, liberal-arts defenders speak instead about something more   28
encompassing, and more elusive. "College changed me inside," one graduate told
us fervently. The authors of a Carnegie Commission report, who obviously struggled for a definition, concluded that one of the common threads in the perceptions of a liberal education is that it provides "an integrated view of the world
which can serve as an inner guide." More simply, alumni say that college should
have "helped me to formulate the values and goals of my life."

In theory, a student is taught to develop these values and goals himself, but   29
in practice, it doesn't work quite that way. All but the wayward and the saintly
take their sense of the good, the true, and the beautiful from the people around
them. When we speak of students acquiring "values" in college, we often mean
that they will acquire the values—and sometimes that means only the tastes—
of their professors. The values of professors may be "higher" than many students
will encounter elsewhere, but they may not be relevant to situations in which
students find themselves in college and later.

Of all the forms in which ideas are disseminated, the college professor lec-   30
turing a class is the slowest and most expensive. You don't have to go to college
to read the great books or learn about the great ideas of Western Man. Today you
can find them everywhere—in paperbacks, in the public libraries, in museums,
in public lectures, in adult-education courses, in abridged, summarized, or adapted form in magazines, films, and television. The problem is no longer one of
access to broadening ideas; the problem is the other way around: how to choose
among the many courses of action proposed to us, how to edit the stimulations
that pour into our eyes and ears every waking hour. A college experience that
piles option on option and stimulation on stimulation merely adds to the contemporary nightmare.

What students and graduates say that they did learn on campus comes under   31
the heading of personal, rather than intellectual, development. Again and again
I was told that the real value of college is learning to get along with others, to
practice social skills, to "sort out my head," and these have nothing to do with
curriculum.

For whatever impact the academic experience used to have on college stu-   32
dents, the sheer size of many undergraduate classes in the 1970s dilutes faculty-
student dialogue, and, more often than not, they are taught by teachers who were
hired when colleges were faced with a shortage of qualified instructors, during
their years of expansion and when the big rise in academic pay attracted the
mediocre and the less than dedicated.

On the social side, colleges are withdrawing from responsibility for feeding,   33
housing, policing, and protecting students at a time when the environment of
college may be the most important service it could render. College officials are
reluctant to "intervene" in the personal lives of the students. They no longer
expect to take over from parents, but often insist that students—who have, most
often, never lived away from home before—take full adult responsibility for their
plans, achievements, and behavior.

Most college students do not live in the plush, comfortable country-clublike   34
surroundings their parents envisage, or, in some cases, remember. Open dorms,
particularly when they are coeducational, are noisy, usually overcrowded, and
often messy. Some students desert the institutional "zoos" (their own word for
dorms) and move into run-down, overpriced apartments. Bulletin boards in student centers are littered with notices of apartments to share and the drift of conversation suggests that a lot of money is dissipated in scrounging for food and
shelter.

Taxpayers now provide more than half of the astronomical sums that are   35
spent on higher education. But less than half of today's high school graduates go
on, raising a new question of equity: Is it fair to make all the taxpayers pay for the
minority who actually go to college? We decided long ago that it is fair for childless adults to pay school taxes because everyone, parents and non-parents alike,
profits by a literate population. Does the same reasoning hold true for state-sup-
ported higher education? There is no conclusive evidence on either side.

Young people cannot be expected to go to college for the general good of   36
mankind. They may be more altruistic than their elders, but no great numbers
are going to spend four years at hard intellectual labor, let alone tens of thousands
of family dollars, for "the advancement of human capability in society at large,"

one of the many purposes invoked by the Carnegie Commission report. Nor do any considerable number of them want to go to college to beat the Russians to Jupiter, improve the national defense, increase the Gross National Product, lower the crime rate, improve automobile safety, or create a market for the arts— all of which have been suggested at one time or other as benefits taxpayers get for supporting higher education.

One sociologist said that you don't have to have a reason for going to col- 37
lege because it's an institution. His definition of an institution is something everyone subscribes to without question. The burden of proof is not on why you should go to college, but why anyone thinks there might be a reason for not going. The implication—and some educators express it quite frankly—is that an 18-year-old high school graduate is still too young and confused to know what he wants to do, let alone what is good for him.

Mother knows best, in other words. 38

It had always been comfortable for students to believe that authorities, like 39
Mother, or outside specialists, like educators, could determine what was best for them. However, specialists and authorities no longer enjoy the credibility former generations accorded them. Patients talk back to doctors and are not struck suddenly dead. Clients question the lawyer's bills and sometimes get them reduced. It is no longer self-evident that all adolescents must study a fixed curriculum that was constructed at a time when all educated men could agree on precisely what it was that made them educated.

The same with college. If high school graduates don't want to continue 40
their education, or don't want to continue it right away, they may perceive more clearly than their elders that college is not for them.

College is an ideal place for those young adults who love learning for its 41
own sake, who would rather read than eat, and who like nothing better than writing research papers. But they are a minority, even at the prestigious colleges, which recruit and attract the intellectually oriented.

The rest of our high school graduates need to look at college more closely 42
and critically, to examine it as a consumer product, and decide if the cost in dollars, in time, in continued dependency, and in future returns, is worth the very large investment each student—and his family—must make.

Questions for Discussion

1. According to Bird, what are the faults of a college education? What is the "contrary evidence" (paragraph 4) against college education?

2. Do you agree with Bird's speculation in paragraph 4 that "maybe...intelligent, ambitious, happy, liberal, and quick-learning people are merely the ones who have been attracted to college in the first place"?
3. What is vocationalism? Would you rather be a generalist or a specialist? Why?
4. This article was written in 1975. Do you think anything has changed since then? Is Bird's article still relevant?
5. Is college becoming something that only the wealthy can afford? What are the consequences of viewing college as an investment?
6. Why might Bird have focused on the financial aspects of college? What aspects has she ignored, and why might she have done so?
7. How does Bird's use of statistics and footnotes establish her authority? What statistics can be questioned?

Questions for Reflection and Writing

1. What have been your experiences of college? Why are you in college? Do you think college is worth the time, effort, and expense?
2. Basing your comments on Bird's, suggest alternative methods of education besides college. Extend your essay by focusing on just one alternative and providing details, examples, and hypothetical cases.
3. What is the purpose of education? Is it to train a person for a career, to give that person job skills? Take your stance with Bird to argue that a college education should enhance a student's chances for a good job. Or take your stance against Bird to argue that job skills should not be the main goal of education; name what you think is the main goal of education. In either case, find current equivalents of the statistics Bird cites, such as the cost of tuition, student expenses, and projected salaries for various professions.

Notes

1. [Editors' Note: Ms. Bird's article appeared in 1975.] According to the Department of Labor Bureau of Statistics, 20.8 million college graduates will enter the work force from 1982 to 1995; the bureau predicts only 16.9 million job openings in traditional jobs for college graduates during that period. In 1982 figures: approximately 2076 new jobs for psychologists; 41,031 bachelor's degrees in psychology granted.
2. In 1982 figures: approximately 2076 new jobs for psychologists; 41031 bachelor's degrees inpsychology granted.
3. In 1982 figures: 74,915 graduates in communications and letters.
4. The Department of Labor Bureau of Statistics no longer calculates total yearly job openings in each field. Instead, it projects only the number of new jobs created in afield over a 13-year period. (New job openings account for only 10–20 percent of all job openings, with the other

80–90 percent resulting from workers vacating already established positions.) All figures quoted in the footnotes represent an estimated annual average based on this projection. For the period 1982–1995, the bureau projects 1153 new jobs in reporting and 1153 new jobs in radio and television announcing each year.

5. Statistics for technical writers and public relations personnel are not available.

6. Projected figures for the 1980s indicate there will be a need for an average of 1400 new foresters each year, while schools of forestry are expected to grant an average of 3000 bachelor's degrees each year.

7. In 1982, 9728 students graduated with BAs in architecture, while there were an estimated 2615 new job openings in the field that year.

8. Current projections indicate 500 new job openings for industrial designers each year in the 1980s.

9. In the 1980s, approximately 350 anthropologists will be needed every year.

10. This figure remains the same in the 1980s.

11. Only 150 in the 1980s.

12. This year, according to the Labor Department, the fastest-growing professions, in terms of new jobs created, are: building custodians, cashiers, secretaries, general office clerks, retail sales workers, registered nurses, waiters and waitresses, kindergarten and elementary school teachers, truck drivers, nursing aides and orderlies, technical sales representatives, automobile mechanics, supervisors of blue collar workers, kitchen helpers, guards and doorkeepers, fast food preparers, and service personnel, store managers, and electric and electronic technicians.

13. These figures are similar for the 1980s.

14. According to the National Center for Educational Statistics, the cost of four years at an Ivy League school is now approaching $50,000; the average cost of four years at a public institution is approximately $13,000.

15. Students in the class of 1985 will pay $48,352 for four years at Princeton.

The Novelist as Teacher

Chinua Achebe

Writing of the kind I do is relatively new in my part of the world and it is   1
too soon to try and describe in detail the complex of relationships between
us and our readers. However, I think I can safely deal with one aspect of
these relationships which is rarely mentioned. Because of our largely
European education our writers may be pardoned if they begin by thinking
that the relationship between European writers and their audience will
automatically reproduce itself in Africa. We have learnt from Europe that a
writer or an artist lives on the fringe of society—wearing a beard and a peculiar dress and generally behaving in a strange, unpredictable way. He is in
revolt against society, which in turn looks on him with suspicion if not hostility. The last thing society would dream of doing is to put him in charge of
anything.

All that is well known, which is why some of us seem too eager for our soci-   2
ety to treat us with the same hostility or even behave as though it already does.
But I am not interested now in what writers expect of society; that is generally
contained in their books, or should be. What is not so well documented is what
society expects of its writers.

I am assuming, of course, that our writer and his society live in the same   3
place. I realize that a lot has been made of the allegation that African writers
have to write for European and American readers because African readers where
they exist at all are only interested in reading textbooks. I don't know if African
writers always have a foreign audience in mind. What I do know is that they
don't have to. At least I know that I don't have to. Last year the pattern of sales
of *Things Fall Apart* in the cheap paperback edition was as follows: about 800
copies in Britain; 20,000 in Nigeria; and about 2,500 in all other places. The
same pattern was true also of *No Longer at Ease*.

Most of my readers are young. They are either in school or college or have   4
only recently left. And many of them look to me as a kind of teacher. Only the
other day I received this letter from Northern Nigeria:

Dear C. Achebe,   5

I do not usually write to authors, no matter how interesting their work is, but I feel I must tell you how much I enjoyed your editions of *Things Fall Apart* and *No Longer at Ease*. I look forward to reading your new edition *Arrow of God*. Your novels serve as advice to us young. I trust that you will continue to produce as many of this type of books. With friendly greetings and best wishes.

Yours sincerely,
BUBA YERO MAFINDI

It is quite clear what this particular reader expects of me. Nor is there much   6
doubt about another reader in Ghana who wrote me a rather pathetic letter to say that I had neglected to include questions and answers at the end of *Things Fall Apart* and could I make these available to him to ensure his success at next year's school certificate examination. This is what I would call in Nigerian pidgin "a how-for-do" reader and I hope there are not very many like him. But also in Ghana I met a young woman teacher who immediately took me to task for not making the hero of my *No Longer at Ease* marry the girl he is in love with. I made the kind of vague noises I usually make whenever a wise critic comes along to tell me I should have written a different book to the one I wrote. But my woman teacher was not going to be shaken off so easily. She was in deadly earnest. Did I know, she said, that there were many women in the kind of situation I had described and that I could have served them well if I had shown that it was possible to find one man with enough guts to go against custom?

I don't agree, of course. But this young woman spoke with so much feeling   7
that I couldn't help being a little uneasy at the accusation (for it was indeed a serious accusation) that I had squandered a rare opportunity for education on a whimsical and frivolous exercise. It is important to say at this point that no self-respecting writer will take dictation from his audience. He must remain free to disagree with his society and go into rebellion against it if need be. But I am for choosing my cause very carefully. Why should I start waging war as a Nigerian newspaper editor was doing the other day on the "soulless efficiency" of Europe's industrial and technological civilization when the very thing my society needs may well be a little technical efficiency?

My thinking on the peculiar needs of different societies was sharpened   8
when not long ago I heard an English pop song which I think was entitled "I

Ain't Gonna Wash for a Week." At first I wondered why it should occur to any-   9
one to take such a vow when there were so many much more worthwhile resolutions to make. But later it dawned on me that this singer belonged to the same
culture which in an earlier age of self-satisfaction had blasphemed and said that
cleanliness was next to godliness. So I saw him in a new light—as a kind of
divine administrator of vengeance. I make bold to say, however, that his particular offices would not be required in my society because we did not commit the
sin of turning hygiene into a god.

Needless to say, we do have our own sins and blasphemies recorded against   10
our name. If I were God I would regard as the very worst our acceptance—for
whatever reason—of racial inferiority. It is too late in the day to get worked up
about it or to blame others, much as they may deserve such blame and condemnation. What we need to do is to look back and try and find out where we went
wrong, where the rain began to beat us.

Let me give one or two examples of the result of the disaster brought upon   11
the African psyche in the period of subjection to alien races. I remember the
shock felt by Christians of my father's generation in my village in the early 40s
when for the first time the local girls' school performed Nigerian dances at the
anniversary of the coming of the gospel. Hitherto they had always put on something Christian and civilized which I believe was called the Maypole dance. In
those days—when I was growing up—I also remember that it was only the poor
benighted heathen who had any use for our local handicraft, e.g., our pottery.
Christians and the well-to-do (and they were usually the same people) displayed
their tins and other metalware. We never carried water pots to the stream. I had
a small cylindrical biscuit-tin suitable to my years while the older members of our
household carried four-gallon kerosene tins.

Today, things have changed a lot, but it would be foolish to pretend that   12
we have fully recovered from the traumatic effects of our first confrontation with
Europe. Three or four weeks ago my wife, who teaches English in a boys' school,
asked a pupil why he wrote about winter when he meant the harmattan. He said
the other boys would call him a bushman if he did such a thing! Now, you would-
n't have thought, would you, that there was something shameful in your
weather? But apparently we do. How can this great blasphemy be purged? I think
it is part of my business as a writer to teach that boy that there is nothing dis-
graceful about the African weather, that the palm tree is a fit subject for poetry.

Here then is an adequate revolution for me to espouse—to help my socie-   13
ty regain belief in itself and put away the complexes of the years of denigration
and self-abasement. And it is essentially a question of education, in the best sense

of that word. Here, I think, my aims and the deepest aspirations of my society meet. For no thinking African can escape the pain of the wound in our soul. You have all heard of the "African personality"; of African democracy, of the African way of socialism, of negritude, and so on. They are all props we have fashioned at different times to help us get on our feet again Once we are up we shan't need any of them anymore. But for the moment it is in the nature of things that we may need to counter racism with what Jean-Paul Sartre has called an anti-racist racism, to announce not just that we are as good as the next man but that we are much better.

The writer cannot expect to be excused from the task of re-education and regeneration that must be done. In fact, he should march right in front. For he is, after all—as Ezekiel Mphahlele says in his *African Image*—the sensitive point of his community. The Ghanaian professor of philosophy, William Abraham, puts it this way:

> Just as African scientists undertake to solve some of the scientific problems of Africa, African historians go into the history of Africa, African political scientists concern themselves with the politics of Africa; why should African literary creators be exempted from the services that they themselves recognize as genuine?

I for one would not wish to be excused. I would be quite satisfied if my novels (especially the ones I set in the past) did no more than teach my readers that their past—with all its imperfections—was not one long night of savagery from which the first Europeans acting on God's behalf delivered them. Perhaps what I write is applied art as distinct from pure. But who cares? Art is important, but so is education of the kind I have in mind. And I don't see that the two need be mutually exclusive. In a recent anthology a Hausa folk tale, having recounted the usual fabulous incidents, ends with these words:

> They all came and they lived happily together. He had several sons and daughters who grew up and helped in raising the standard of education of the country.

As I said elsewhere, if you consider this ending a naive anticlimax then you cannot know very much about Africa.

Leeds University, 1965

Maya Angelou (1928-   ) is a poet, an author, a performer, a stage and screen producer, a director, and a singer. She was born Marguerite Angelou in April 4, 1928, in St. Louis, Missouri. Angelou attended public schools in Arkansas and California before going on to study music and drama as well as studying dance with Martha Graham. Her wide-ranging career includes stints at the *Arab Observer* in Cairo, the University of Ghana, the *African Review* in Ghana, the University of California at Los Angeles, the University of Kansas, Wake Forest University, Wichita State University, California State University at Sacremento, the Southern Christian Leadership Conference, the American Revolution Bicentennial Council, and the national Commission on the Observance of International Women's Year. She has also served as a television host and an interviewer. Author of autobiographical nonfiction, poetry, plays, and children's literature, Angelou has won numerous honorary degrees and awards, including a Grammy for Best Spoken Word or Non-Traditional Album in 1994 for a recording of "On the Pulse of the Morning," a long poem penned for and delivered at President Bill Clinton's 1993 inauguration. Angelou is known equally well as a memoirist whose autobiographical books depict a painful past with warmth and wisdom, and as a poet whose short lyric poems utilize jazz rhythms to celebrate both the survival of the demeaning nature of the experience of blacks and women's process of self-creation. Her many books include the autobiographical works *I Know Why the Caged Bird Sings* (1970), *Gather Together in My Name* (1974), *Heart of a Woman* (1981), and *All God's Children Need Traveling Shoes* (1986). Her poetry volumes include *Just Give Me a Cool Drink of Water "Fore I Diiie* (1971), *Oh Pray My Wings Are Gonna Fit Me Well* (1975), *And Still I Rise* (1978), *Singin' and Swingin' and Gettin' Merry Like Christmas* (1976), and *Poems: Maya Angelou* (4 vols., 1986). Angelou speaks French, Spanish, Italian, Arabic, and Fanti.

Graduation Day

Maya Angelou

The children in Stamps trembled visibly with anticipation. Some adults were   1
excited too, but to be certain the whole young population had come down with
graduation epidemic. Large classes were graduating from both the grammar
school and the high school. Even those who were years removed from their own
day of glorious release were anxious to help with preparations as a kind of dry run.
The junior students who were moving into the vacating classes' chairs were tra-
dition-bound to show their talents for leadership and management. They strut-
ted through the school and around the campus exerting pressure on the lower

grades. Their authority was so new that occasionally if they pressed a little too hard it had to be overlooked. After all, next term was coming, and it never hurt a sixth grader to have a play sister in the eighth grade, or a tenth-year student to be able to call a twelfth grader Bubba. So all was endured in a spirit of shared understanding. But the graduating classes themselves were the nobility. Like travelers with exotic destinations on their minds, the graduates were remarkably forgetful. They came to school without their books, or tablets or even pencils. Volunteers fell over themselves to secure replacements for the missing equipment. When accepted, the willing workers might or might not be thanked, and it was of no importance to the pregraduation rites. Even teachers were respectful of the now quiet and aging seniors, and tended to speak to them, if not as equals, as beings only slightly lower than themselves. After tests were returned and grades given, the student body, which acted like an extended family, knew who did well, who excelled, and what piteous ones had failed.

Unlike the white high school, Lafayette County Training School distinguished itself by having neither lawn, nor hedges, nor tennis court, nor climbing ivy. Its two buildings (main classrooms, the grade school and home economics) were set on a dirt hill with no fence to limit either its boundaries or those of bordering farms. There was a large expanse to the left of the school which was used alternately as a baseball diamond or basketball court. Rusty hoops on swaying poles represented the permanent recreational equipment, although bats and balls could be borrowed from the P.E. teacher if the borrower was qualified and if the diamond wasn't occupied.

Over this rocky area relieved by a few shady persimmon trees the graduating class walked. The girls often held hands and no longer bothered to speak to the lower students. There was a sadness about them, as if this old world was not their home and they were bound for higher ground. The boys, on the other hand, had become more friendly, more outgoing. A decided change from the closed attitude they projected while studying for finals. Now they seemed not ready to give up the old school, the familiar paths and classrooms. Only a small percentage would be continuing on to college—one of the South's A & M (agricultural and mechanical) schools, which trained Negro youths to be carpenters, farmers, handymen, masons, maids, cooks and baby nurses. Their future rode heavily on their shoulders, and blinded them to the collective joy that had pervaded the lives of the boys and girls in the grammar school graduating class.

Parents who could afford it had ordered new shoes and ready-made clothes for themselves from Sears and Roebuck or Montgomery Ward. They also engaged the best seamstresses to make the floating graduating dresses and to cut down second-hand pants which would be pressed to a military slickness for the important event.

Oh, it was important, all right. White folks would attend the ceremony, and two or three would speak of God and home, and the Southern way of life, and Mrs. Parsons, the principal's wife, would play the graduation march while the lower-grade graduates paraded down the aisles and took their seats below the platform. The high school seniors would wait in empty classrooms to make their dramatic entrance.   5

In the Store I was the person of the moment. The birthday girl. The center. Bailey had graduated the year before, although to do so he had had to forfeit all pleasures to make up for his time lost in Baton Rouge.   6

My class was wearing butter-yellow piqué dresses, and Momma launched out on mine. She smocked the yoke into tiny crisscrossing puckers, then shirred the rest of the bodice. Her dark fingers ducked in and out of the lemony cloth as she embroidered raised daisies around the hem. Before she considered herself finished she had added a crocheted cuff on the puff sleeves, and a pointy crocheted collar.   7

I was going to be lovely. A walking model of all the various styles of fine hand sewing and it didn't worry me that I was only twelve years old and merely graduating from the eighth grade. Besides, many teachers in Arkansas Negro schools had only that diploma and were licensed to impart wisdom.   8

The days had become longer and more noticeable. The faded beige of former times had been replaced with strong and sure colors. I began to see my classmates' clothes, their skin tones, and the dust that waved off pussy willows. Clouds that lazed across the sky were objects of great concern to me. Their shiftier shapes might have held a message that in my new happiness and with a little bit of time I'd soon decipher. During that period I looked at the arch of heaven so religiously my neck kept a steady ache. I had taken to smiling more often, and my jaws hurt from the unaccustomed activity. Between the two physical sore spots, I suppose I could have been uncomfortable, but that was not the case. As a member of the winning team (the graduating class of 1940) I had outdistanced unpleasant sensations by miles. I was headed for the freedom of open fields.   9

Youth and social approval allied themselves with me and we trammeled memories of slights and insults. The wind of our swift passage remodeled my features. Lost tears were pounded to mud and then to dust. Years of withdrawal were brushed aside and left behind, as hanging ropes of parasitic moss.   10

My work alone had awarded me a top place and I was going to be one of 11
the first called in the graduating ceremonies. On the classroom blackboard, as
well as on the bulletin board in the auditorium, there were blue stars and white
stars and red stars. No absences, no tardinesses, and my academic work was
among the best of the year. I could say the preamble to the Constitution even
faster than Bailey. We timed ourselves often: "We the people of the United
States in order to form a more perfect union . . ." I had memorized the Presidents
of the United States from Washington to Roosevelt in chronological as well as
alphabetical order.

My hair pleased me too. Gradually the black mass had lengthened and 12
thickened, so that it kept at last to its braided pattern, and I didn't have to yank
my scalp off when I tried to comb it.

Louise and I had rehearsed the exercises until we tired out ourselves. Henry 13
Reed was class valedictorian. He was a small, very black boy with hooded eyes,
a long, broad nose and an oddly shaped head. I had admired him for years
because each term he and I vied for the best grades in our class. Most often he
bested me, but instead of being disappointed I was pleased that we shared top
places between us. Like many Southern Black children, he lived with his grandmother, who was as strict as Momma and as kind as she knew how to be. He was
courteous, respectful and soft spoken to elders, but on the playground he chose
to play the roughest games. I admired him. Anyone, I reckoned, sufficiently
afraid or sufficiently dull could be polite. But to be able to operate at a top level
with both adults and children was admirable.

His valedictory speech was entitled, "To Be or Not to Be." The rigid tenth- 14
grade teacher had helped him write it. He'd been working on the dramatic stresses for months.

The weeks until graduation were filled with heady activities. A group of 15
small children were to be presented in a play about buttercups and daisies and
bunny rabbits. They could be heard throughout the building practicing their
hops and their little songs that sounded like silver bells. The older girls (nongrad-
uates, of course) were assigned the task of making refreshments for the night's fes-
tivities. A tangy scent of ginger, cinnamon, nutmeg and chocolate wafted around
the home economics building as the budding cooks made samples for themselves
and their teachers.

In every corner of the workshop, axes and saws split fresh timber as the 16
woodshop boys made sets and stage scenery. Only the graduates were left out of

the general bustle. We were free to sit in the library at the back of the building or look in quite detachedly, naturally, on the measures being taken for our event.

Even the minister preached on graduation the Sunday before. His subject   17
was, "Let your light so shine that men will see your good works and praise your Father, Who is in Heaven." Although the sermon was purported to be addressed to us, he used the occasion to speak to backsliders, gamblers and general ne'er-do-wells. But since he had called our names at the beginning of the service we were mollified.

Among Negroes the tradition was to give presents to children going only   18
from one grade to another. How much more important this was when the person was graduating at the top of the class. Uncle Willie and Momma had sent away for a Mickey Mouse watch like Bailey's. Louise gave me four embroidered handkerchiefs. (I gave her crocheted doilies.) Mrs. Sneed, the minister's wife, made me an undershirt to wear for graduation, and nearly every customer gave me a nickel or maybe even a dime with the instruction "Keep on moving to higher ground," or some such encouragement.

Amazingly the great day finally dawned and I was out of bed before I knew   19
it. I threw open the back door to see it more clearly, but Momma said, "Sister, come away from that door and put your robe on."

I hoped the memory of that morning would never leave me. Sunlight was   20
itself young, and the day had none of the insistence maturity would bring it in a few hours. In my robe and barefoot in the backyard, under cover of going to see about my new beans, I gave myself up to the gentle warmth and thanked God that no matter what evil I had done in my life He had allowed me to live to see this day. Somewhere in my fatalism I had expected to die, accidentally, and never have the chance to walk up the stairs in the auditorium and gracefully receive my hard-earned diploma. Out of God's merciful bosom I had won reprieve.

Bailey came out in his robe and gave me a box wrapped in Christmas paper.   21
He said he had saved his money for months to pay for it. It felt like a box of chocolates, but I knew Bailey wouldn't save money to buy candy when we had all we could want under our noses.

He was as proud of the gift as I. It was a soft-leather-bound copy of a col-   22
lection of poems by Edgar Allan Poe, or, as Bailey and I called him, "Eap." I turned to "Annabel Lee" and we walked up and down the garden rows, the cool dirt between our toes, reciting the beautifully sad lines.

Momma made a Sunday breakfast although it was only Friday. After we fin-   23
ished the blessing, I opened my eyes to find the watch on my plate. It was a

dream of a day. Everything went smoothly and to my credit. I didn't have to be reminded or scolded for anything. Near evening I was too jittery to attend to chores, so Bailey volunteered to do all before his bath.

Days before, we had made a sign for the Store, and as we turned out the lights Momma hung the cardboard over the doorknob. It read clearly: CLOSED. GRADUATION.   24

My dress fitted perfectly and everyone said that I looked like a sunbeam in it. On the hill, going toward the school, Bailey walked behind with Uncle Willie, who muttered, "Go on, Ju." He wanted him to walk ahead with us because it embarrassed him to have to walk so slowly. Bailey said he'd let the ladies walk together, and the men would bring up the rear. We all laughed, nicely.   25

Little children dashed by out of the dark like fireflies. Their crepe-paper dresses and butterfly wings were not made for running and we heard more than one rip, dryly, and the regretful "uh uh" that followed.   26

The school blazed without gaiety. The windows seemed cold and unfriendly from the lower hill. A sense of ill-fated timing crept over me, and if Momma hadn't reached for my hand I would have drifted back to Bailey and Uncle Willie, and possibly beyond. She made a few slow jokes about my feet getting cold, and tugged me along to the now-strange building. *She knew something was wrong*   27

Around the front steps, assurance came back. There were my fellow "greats," the graduating class. Hair brushed back, legs oiled, new dresses and pressed pleats, fresh pocket handkerchiefs and little handbags, all homesewn. Oh, we were up to snuff, all right. I joined my comrades and didn't even see my family go in to find seats in the crowded auditorium.   28

The school band struck up a march and all classes filed in as had been rehearsed. We stood in front of our seats, as assigned, and on a signal from the choir director, we sat. No sooner had this been accomplished than the band started to play the national anthem. We rose again and sang the song, after which we recited the pledge of allegiance. We remained standing for a brief minute before the choir director and the principal signaled to us, rather desperately I thought, to take our seats. The command was so unusual that our carefully rehearsed and smooth-running machine was thrown off. For a full minute we fumbled for our chairs and bumped into each other awkwardly. Habits change or solidify under pressure, so in our state of nervous tension we had been ready to follow our usual assembly pattern: the American national anthem, then the pledge of allegiance, then the song every Black person I knew called the Negro   29

National Anthem. All done in the same key, with the same passion and most often standing on the same foot.

Finding my seat at last, I was overcome with a presentiment of worse things   30
to come. Something unrehearsed, unplanned, was going to happen, and we were going to be made to look bad. I distinctly remember being explicit in the choice of pronoun. It was "we," the graduating class, the unit, that concerned me then.

The principal welcomed "parents and friends" and asked the Baptist min-   31
ister to lead us in prayer. His invocation was brief and punchy, and for a second I thought we were getting on the high road to right action. When the principal came back to the dais, however, his voice had changed. Sounds always affected me profoundly and the principal's voice was one of my favorites. During assem-bly it melted and lowed weakly into the audience. It had not been in my plan to listen to him, but my curiosity was piqued and I straightened up to give him my attention.

He was talking about Booker T. Washington, our "late great leader," who   32
said we can be as close as the finger on the hand, etc.. . . Then he said a few vague things about friendship and the friendship of kindly people to those less fortunate than themselves. With that his voice nearly faded, thin, away. Like a river dimin-ishing to a stream and then to a trickle. But he cleared his throat and said, "Our speaker tonight, who is also our friend, came from Texarkana to deliver the com-mencement address, but due to the irregularity of the train schedule, he's going to, as they say, 'speak and run.'" He said that we understood and wanted the man to know that we were most grateful for the time he was able to give us and then something about how we were willing always to adjust to another's program, and without more ado—"I give you Mr. Edward Donleavy."

Not one but two white men came through the door off-stage. The shorter   33
one walked to the speaker's platform, and the tall one moved to the center seat and sat down. But that was our principal's seat, and already occupied. The dis-lodged gentleman bounced around for a long breath or two before the Baptist minister gave him his chair, then with more dignity than the situation deserved, the minister walked off the stage.

Donleavy looked at the audience once (on reflection, I'm sure that he   34
wanted only to reassure himself that we were really there), adjusted his glasses and began to read from a sheaf of papers.

He was glad "to be here and to see the work going on just as it was in the   35
other schools."

At the first "Amen" from the audience, I willed the offender to immediate   36
death by choking on the word. But Amens and Yes, sir's began to fall around the
room like rain through a ragged umbrella.

He told us of the wonderful changes we children in Stamps had in store.   37
The Central School (naturally, the white school was Central) had already been
granted improvements that would be in use in the fall. A well-known artist was
coming from Little Rock to teach art to them. They were going to have the
newest microscopes and chemistry equipment for their laboratory. Mr. Donleavy
didn't leave us long in the dark over who made these improvements available to
Central High. Nor were we to be ignored in the general betterment scheme he
had in mind.

He said that he had pointed out to people at a very high level that one of   38
the first-line football tacklers at Arkansas Agricultural and Mechanical College
had graduated from good old Lafayette County Training School. Here fewer
Amens were heard. Those few that did break through lay dully in the air with
the heaviness of habit.

He went on to praise us. He went on to say how he had bragged that "one   39
of the best basketball players at Fisk sank his first ball right here at Lafayette
County Training School."

The white kids were going to have a chance to become Galileos and   40
Madame Curies and Edisons and Gauguins, and our boys (the girls weren't even
in on it) would try to be Jesse Owenses and Joe Louises.

Owens and the Brown Bomber were great heroes in our world, but what   41
school official in the white-goddom of Little Rock had the right to decide that
those two men must be our only heroes? Who decided that for Henry Reed to
become a scientist he had to work like George Washington Carver, as a boot-
black, to buy a lousy microscope? Bailey was obviously always going to be too
small to be an athlete, so which concrete angel glued to what country seat had
decided that if my brother wanted to become a lawyer he had to first pay penance
for his skin by picking cotton and hoeing corn and studying correspondence
books at night for twenty years?

The man's dead words fell like bricks around the auditorium and too many   42
settled in my belly. Constrained by hard-learned manners I couldn't look behind
me, but to my left and right the proud graduating class of 1940 had dropped their
heads. Every girl in my row had found something new to do with her handkerchief. Some folded the tiny squares into love knots, some into triangles, but most
were wadding them, then pressing them flat on their yellow laps.

On the dais, the ancient tragedy was being replayed. Professor Parsons sat,   43
a sculptor's reject, rigid. His large, heavy body seemed devoid of will or willingness, and his eyes said he was no longer with us. The other teachers examined
the flag (which was draped stage right) or their notes, or the windows which
opened on our now-famous playing diamond.

Graduation, the hush-hush magic time of frills and gifts and congratula-   44
tions and diplomas, was finished for me before my name was called. The accomplishment was nothing. The meticulous maps, drawn in three colors of ink,
learning and spelling decasyllabic words, memorizing the whole of The Rape of
Lucrece—it was for nothing. Donleavy had exposed us.

We were maids and farmers, handymen and washerwomen, and anything   45
higher that we aspired to was farcical and presumptuous.

Then I wished that Gabriel Prosser and Nat Turner had killed all white-   46
folks in their beds and that Abraham Lincoln had been assassinated before the
signing of the Emancipation Proclamation, and that Harriet Tubman had been
killed by that blow on her head and Christopher Columbus had drowned in the
Santa Maria.

It was awful to be a Negro and have no control over my life. It was brutal   47
to be young and already trained to sit quietly and listen to charges brought
against my color with no chance of defense. We should all be dead. I thought I
should like to see us all dead, one on top of the other. A pyramid of flesh with
the white folks on the bottom, as the broad base, then the Indians with their silly
tomahawks and teepees and wigwams and treaties, the Negroes with their mops
and recipes and cotton sacks and spirituals sticking out of their mouths. The
Dutch children should all stumble in their wooden shoes and break their necks.
The French should choke to death on the Louisiana Purchase (1803) while silkworms ate all the Chinese with their stupid pig-tails. As a species, we were an
abomination. All of us.

Donleavy was running for election, and assured our parents that if he won   48
we could count on having the only colored paved playing field in that part of
Arkansas. Also—he never looked up to acknowledge the grunts of acceptance—
also, we were bound to get some new equipment for the home economics building and the workshop.

He finished, and since there was no need to give any more than the most   49
perfunctory thank-you's, he nodded to the men on the stage, and the tall white
man who was never introduced joined him at the door. They left with the atti-

tude that now they were off to something really important. (The graduation ceremonies at Lafayette County Training School had been a mere preliminary.)

The ugliness they left was palpable. An uninvited guest who wouldn't   50
leave. The choir was summoned and sang a modern arrangement of "Onward,
Christian Soldiers," with new words pertaining to graduates seeking their place
in the world. But it didn't work. Elouise, the daughter of the Baptist minister,
recited "Invictus," and I could have cried at the impertinence of "I am the master of my fate, I am the captain of my soul."

My name had lost its ring of familiarity and I had to be nudged to go and   51
receive my diploma. All my preparations had fled. I neither marched up to the
stage like a conquering Amazon, nor did I look in the audience for Bailey's nod
of approval. Marguerite Johnson. I heard the name again, my honors were read,
there were noises in the audience of appreciation, and I took my place on the
stage as rehearsed.

I thought about colors I hated: ecru, puce, lavender, beige and black.   52

There was shuffling and rustling around me, then Henry Reed was giving   53
his valedictory address, "To Be or Not to Be." Hadn't he heard the white-folks?
We couldn't be, so the question was a waste of time. Henry's voice came out clear
and strong. I feared to look at him. Hadn't he got the message? There was no
"nobler in the mind" for Negroes because the world didn't think we had minds,
and they let us know it. "Outrageous fortune"? Now, that was a joke. When the
ceremony was over I had to tell Henry Reed some things. That is, if I still cared.
Not "rub," Henry, "erase." "Ah, there's the erase." Us.

Henry had been a good student in elocution. His voice rose on tides of   54
promise and fell on waves of warnings. The English teacher had helped him to
create a sermon winging through Hamlet's soliloquy. To be a man, a doer, a
builder, a leader, or to be a tool, an unfunny joke, a crusher of funky toadstools.
I marveled that Henry could go through with the speech as if we had a choice.

I had been listening and silently rebutting each sentence with my eyes   55
closed; then there was a hush, which in an audience warns that something
unplanned is happening. I looked up and saw Henry Reed, the conservative, the
proper, the A student, turn his back to the audience and turn to us (the proud
graduating class of 1940) and sing, nearly speaking,

"Lift ev'ry voice and sing
Till earth and heaven ring
Ring with the harmonies of Liberty..."

It was the poem written by James Weldon Johnson. It was the music composed by J. Rosamond Johnson. It was the Negro National Anthem. Out of habit we were singing it.

Our mothers and fathers stood in the dark hall and joined the hymn of   56
encouragement. A kindergarten teacher led the small children onto the stage and the buttercups and daisies and bunny rabbits marked time and tried to follow:

"Stony the road we trod
Bitter the chastening rod
Felt in the days when hope, unborn, had died.
Yet with a steady beat
Have not our weary feet
Come to the place for which our fathers sighed?"

Each child I knew had learned that song with his ABC's and along with   57
"Jesus Loves Me This I Know." But I personally had never heard it before. Never heard the words, despite the thousands of times I had sung them. Never thought they had anything to do with me.

On the other hand, the words of Patrick Henry had made such an impres-   58
sion on me that I had been able to stretch myself tall and trembling and say, "I know not what course others may take, but as for me, give me liberty or give me death."

And now I heard, really for the first time: 59
"We have come over a way that with tears
has been watered,
We have come, treading our path through
the blood of the slaughtered."

While echoes of the song shivered in the air, Henry Reed bowed his head,   60
said "Thank you," and returned to his place in the line. The tears that slipped down many faces were not wiped away in shame.

We were then on top again. As always, again. We survived. The depths had   61
been icy and dark, but now a bright sun spoke to our souls. I was no longer simply a member of the proud graduating class of 1940; I was a proud member of the wonderful, beautiful Negro race.

Oh, Black known and unknown poets, how often have your auctioned   62
pains sustained us? Who will compute the lonely nights made less lonely by your
songs, or the empty pots made less tragic by your tales?

If we were a people much given to revealing secrets, we might raise mon-   63
uments and sacrifice to the memories of our poets, but slavery cured us of that
weakness. It may be enough, however, to have it said that we survive in exact
relationship to the dedication of our poets (include preachers, musicians and
blues singers).

Questions for Discussion

1. Why is graduation day so important to the children of Stamps? Does it have
   the same importance for the adults? Why might the college-bound students
   be "blinded . . . to the collective joy" (paragraph 3)?

2. What is the hierarchy of the grades? Why does the young Angelou see the
   graduating class as the "nobility" (paragraph 1), the junior class as the new
   authority, and the younger children as anxious to please the older children?
   What roles do the senior and junior students play for the younger students?

3. How did the Lafayette County Training School differ from the white high
   shools? Why?

4. What does Angelou admire in her competitor, Henry Reed? To what extent
   does she have the same characteristics?

5. What was misguided about Don Leavy's speech? Why was saying that
   Layfayette County Training School graduates had become good college athletes the wrong thing to say? Why are a playing field, and economics building, and a workshop not the right beneficiaries of funding? What attitude
   does the speech reflect?

6. What did Angelou learn at the graduation ceremony? What does it mean
   to choose? Why did Angelou, as an eighth grader, feel she did not have a
   choice?

7. How would you describe the emotional power of this excerpt from
   Angelou's memoir? What creates this power? What emotions did the author
   evoke in you as you read?

Questions for Reflection and Writing

1.   What is the function of gift giving? Why was Bailey's gift to Angelou particularly meaningful to her? After what happened during the graduation ceremony, do you think Angelou might have had different feelings about the gift? Write briefly about these questions.

2.   Write a narrative essay about an important event in your community's life, an event that has communal as well as personal importance. For example, "The Time I Won an Athletic Prize" would probably have only personal importance, but "Homecoming" would have both communal and personal importance. Include in your essay an explanation of why the event is so significant.

3.   Read some of Angelou's poems and compare them to her prose. What themes recur throughout her work? Report on what you discover.

Frederick Douglass (1817–1895) was born a slave near Easton, Maryland. Overcoming tremendous odds, Douglass first secretly taught himself to read and write, and then escaped slavery, settling in the free state of Massachusetts. He became a prominent abolitionist, women's rights leader, and public speaker. Douglass was also an advisor to Abraham Lincoln and publisher of the newspaper *The North Star*. His books include the autobiographies *My Bondage and My Freedom* (1855) and *The Life and Times of Frederick Douglass* (1882). "How I Learned to Read and Write," one of the most eloquent pleas for universal literacy ever written, is taken from Douglass's autobiography *Narrative of the Life of Frederick Douglass, an American Slave* (1845).

How I Learned to Read and Write

Frederick Douglass

Very soon after I went to live with Mr. and Mrs. Auld, she very kindly commenced to teach me the A, B, C. After I had learned this, she assisted me in learning to spell words of three or four letters. Just at this point of my progress, Mr. Auld found out what was going on, and at once forbade Mrs. Auld to instruct me further, telling her, among other things, that it was unlawful, as well as unsafe, to teach a slave to read. To use his own words, further, he said, "If you give a nigger an inch, he will take an ell. A nigger should know nothing but to obey his master—to do as he is told to do. Learning would spoil the best nigger in the world. Now," said he, "if you teach that nigger (speaking of myself) how to read, there would be no keeping him. It would forever unfit him to be a slave. He would at once become unmanageable, and of no value to his master. As to himself, it could do him no good, but a great deal of harm. It would make him discontented and unhappy." These words sank deep into my heart, stirred up sentiments within that lay slumbering, and called into existence an entirely new train of thought. It was a new and special revelation, explaining dark and mysterious things, with which my youthful understanding had struggled, but struggled in vain. I now understood what had been to me a most perplexing difficulty—to wit, the white man's power to enslave the black man. It was a grand achievement, and I prized it highly. From that moment, I understood the pathway from slavery to freedom. It was just what I wanted, and I got it at a time when I the

1

least expected it. Whilst I was saddened by the thought of losing the aid of my kind mistress, I was gladdened by the invaluable instruction which, by the merest accident, I had gained from my master. Though conscious of the difficulty of learning without a teacher, I set out with high hope, and a fixed purpose, at whatever cost of trouble, to learn how to read. The very decided manner with which he spoke, and strove to impress his wife with the evil consequences of giving me instruction, served to convince me that he was deeply sensible of the truths he was uttering. It gave me the best assurance that I might rely with the utmost confidence on the results which, he said, would flow from teaching me to read. What he most dreaded, that I most desired. What he most loved, that I most hated. That which to him was a great evil, to be carefully shunned, was to me a great good, to be diligently sought; and the argument which he so warmly urged, against my learning to read, only served to inspire me with a desire and determination to learn. In learning to read, I owe almost as much to the bitter opposition of my master, as to the kindly aid of my mistress. I acknowledge the benefit of both....

I lived in Master Hugh's family about seven years. During this time, I succeeded in learning to read and write. In accomplishing this, I was compelled to resort to various stratagems. I had no regular teacher. My mistress, who had kindly commenced to instruct me, had, in compliance with the advice and direction of her husband, not only ceased to instruct, but had set her face against my being instructed by any one else. It is due, however, to my mistress to say of her, that she did not adopt this course of treatment immediately. She at first lacked the depravity indispensable to shutting me up in mental darkness. It was at least necessary for her to have some training in the exercise of irresponsible power, to make her equal to the task of treating me as though I were a brute.

My mistress was, as I have said, a kind and tender-hearted woman; and in the simplicity of her soul she commenced, when I first went to live with her, to treat me as she supposed one human being ought to treat another. In entering upon the duties of a slaveholder, she did not seem to perceive that I sustained to her the relation of a mere chattel, and that for her to treat me as a human being was not only wrong, but dangerously so. Slavery proved as injurious to her as it did to me. When I went there, she was a pious, warm, and tender-hearted woman. There was no sorrow or suffering for which she had not a tear. She had bread for the hungry, clothes for the naked, and comfort for every mourner that came within her reach. Slavery soon proved its ability to divest her of these heavenly qualities. Under its influence, the tender heart became stone, and the lamb like disposition gave way to one of tiger-like fierceness. The first step in her downward course was in her ceasing to instruct me. She now commenced to practise her husband's precepts. She finally became even more violent in her opposition than her husband himself. She was not satisfied with simply doing as well as he had commanded; she seemed anxious to do better. Nothing seemed to make her more angry than to see me with a newspaper. She seemed to think that here lay the danger. I have had her rush at me with a face made all up of fury, and snatch from me a newspaper, in a manner that fully revealed her apprehension. She was an apt woman; and a little experience soon demonstrated, to her satisfaction, that education and slavery were incompatible with each other.

From this time I was most narrowly watched. If I was in a separate room   4
any considerable length of time, I was sure to be suspected of having a book, and was at once called to give an account of myself. All this, however, was too late. The first step had been taken. Mistress, in teaching me the alphabet, had given me the inch, and no precaution could prevent me from taking the *ell*.

The plan which I adopted, and the one by which I was most successful, was   5
that of making friends of all the little white boys whom I met in the street. As many of these as I could, I converted into teachers. With their kindly aid, obtained at different times and in different places, I finally succeeded in learning to read. When I was sent on errands, I always took my book with me, and by doing one part of my errand quickly, I found time to get a lesson before my return. I used also to carry bread with me, enough of which was always in the house, and to which I was always welcome; for I was much better off in this regard than many of the poor white children in our neighborhood. This bread I used to bestow upon the hungry little urchins, who, in return, would give me that more valuable bread of knowledge. I am strongly tempted to give the names of two or three of those little boys, as a testimonial of the gratitude and affection I bear them; but prudence forbids;—not that it would injure me, but it might embarrass them; for it is almost an unpardonable offence to teach slaves to read in this Christian country. It is enough to say of the dear little fellows, that they lived in Philpot Street, very near Durgin and Bailey's shipyard. I used to talk this matter of slavery over with them. I would sometimes say to them, I wished I could be as free as they would be when they got to be men. "You will be free as soon as you are twenty-one, but I am a slave for life! Have not I as good a right to be free as you have?" These words used to trouble them; they would express for me the liveliest sympathy, and console me with the hope that something would occur by which I might be free.

I was now about twelve years old, and the thought of being a slave for life   6
began to bear heavily upon my heart. Just about this time, I got hold of a book
entitled "The Columbian Orator." Every opportunity I got, I used to read this
book. Among much of other interesting matter, I found in it a dialogue between
a master and his slave. The slave was represented as having run away from his
master three times. The dialogue represented the conversation which took place
between them, when the slave was retaken the third time. In this dialogue, the
whole argument in behalf of slavery was brought forward by the master, all of
which was disposed of by the slave. The slave was made to say some very smart
as well as impressive things in reply to his master—things which had the desired
though unexpected effect; for the conversation resulted in the voluntary emancipation of the slave on the part of the master.

In the same book, I met with one of Sheridan's mighty speeches on and in   7
behalf of Catholic emancipation. These were choice documents to me. I read
them over and over again with unabated interest. They gave tongue to interesting thoughts of my own soul, which had frequently flashed through my mind,
and died away for want of utterance. The moral which I gained from the dialogue
was the power of truth over the conscience of even a slaveholder. What I got
from Sheridan was a bold denunciation of slavery, and a powerful vindication of
human rights. The reading of these documents enabled me to utter my thoughts,
and to meet the arguments brought forward to sustain slavery; but while they
relieved me of one difficulty, they brought on another even more painful than
the one of which I was relieved. The more I read, the more I was led to abhor
and detest my enslavers. I could regard them in no other light than a band of successful robbers, who had left their homes, and gone to Africa, and stolen us from
our homes, and in a strange land reduced us to slavery. I loathed them as being
the meanest as well as the most wicked of men. As I read and contemplated the
subject, behold! that very discontentment which Master Hugh had predicted
would follow my learning to read had already come, to torment and sting my soul
to unutterable anguish. As I writhed under it, I would at times feel that learning
to read had been a curse rather than a blessing. It had given me a view of my
wretched condition, without the remedy. It opened my eyes to the horrible pit,
but to no ladder upon which to get out. In moments of agony, I envied my fellow-slaves for their stupidity. I have often wished myself a beast. I preferred the
condition of the meanest reptile to my own. Any thing, no matter what, to get
rid of thinking! It was this everlasting thinking of my condition that tormented
me. There was no getting rid of it. It was pressed upon me by every object with-

in sight or hearing, animate or inanimate. The silver trump of freedom had roused my soul to eternal wakefulness. Freedom now appeared, to disappear no more forever. It was heard in every sound, and seen in every thing. It was ever present to torment me with a sense of my wretched condition. I saw nothing without seeing it, I heard nothing without hearing it, and felt nothing without feeling it. It looked from every star, it smiled in every calm, breathed in every wind, and moved in every storm.

I often found myself regretting my own existence, and wishing myself dead;   8
and but for the hope of being free, I have no doubt but that I should have killed myself, or done something for which I should have been killed. While in this state of mind, I was eager to hear any one speak of slavery. I was a ready listener. Every little while, I could hear something about the abolitionists. It was some time before I found what the word meant. It was always used in such connections as to make it an interesting word to me. If a slave ran away and succeeded in get-ting clear, or if a slave killed his master, set fire to a barn, or did any thing very wrong in the mind of a slaveholder, it was spoken of as the fruit of abolition. Hearing the word in this connection very often, I set about learning what it meant. The dictionary afforded me little or no help. I found it was "the act of abolishing"; but then I did not know what was to be abolished. Here I was per-plexed. I did not dare to ask any one about its meaning, for I was satisfied that it was something they wanted me to know very little about. After a patient wait-ing, I got one of our city papers, containing an account of the number of peti-tions from the north, praying for the abolition of slavery in the District of Columbia, and of the slave trade between the States. From this time I understood the words abolition and abolitionist, and always drew near when that word was spoken, expecting to hear something of importance to myself and fellow-slaves. The light broke in upon me by degrees. I went one day down on the wharf of Mr. Waters; and seeing two Irishmen unloading a scow of stone, I went, unasked, and helped them. When we had finished, one of them came to me and asked, "Are ye a slave for life?" I told him that I was. The good Irishman seemed to be deeply affected by the statement. He said to the other that it was a pity so fine a little fellow as myself should be a slave for life. He said it was a shame to hold me. They both advised me to run away to the north; that I should find friends there, and that I should be free. I pretended not to be interested in what they said, and treat-ed them as if I did not understand them; for I feared they might be treacherous. White men have been known to encourage slaves to escape, and then, to get the reward, catch them and return them to their masters. I was afraid that these

seemingly good men might use me so; but I nevertheless remembered their advice, and from that time I resolved to run away. I looked forward to a time at which it would be safe for me to escape. I was too young to think of doing so immediately; besides, I wished to learn how to write, as I might have occasion to write my own pass. I consoled myself with the hope that I should one day find a good chance. Meanwhile, I would learn to write.

The idea as to how I might learn to write was suggested to me by being in   9
Durgin and Bailey's shipyard, and frequently seeing the ship carpenters, after hewing, and getting a piece of timber ready for use, write on the timber the name of that part of the ship for which it was intended. When a piece of timber was intended for the larboard side, it would be marked thus—"L." When a piece was for the starboard side, it would be marked thus—"S." A piece for the larboard side forward, would be marked thus—"L. F." When a piece was for starboard side forward, it would be marked thus— "S. F." For larboard aft, it would be marked thus—"L. A." For starboard aft, it would be marked thus—"S. A." I soon learned the names of these letters, and for what they were intended when placed upon a piece of timber in the shipyard. I immediately commenced copying them, and in a short time was able to make the four letters named. After that, when I met with any boy who I knew could write, I would tell him I could write as well as he. The next word would be, "I don't believe you. Let me see you try it." I would then make the letters which I had been so fortunate as to learn, and ask him to beat that. In this way I got a good many lessons in writing, which it is quite possible I should never have gotten in any other way. During this time, my copy-book was the board fence, brick wall, and pavement; my pen and ink was a lump of chalk. With these, I learned mainly how to write. I then commenced and continued copying the Italics in Webster's Spelling Book, until I could make them all without looking on the book. By this time, my little Master Thomas had gone to school, and learned how to write, and had written over a number of copy-books. These had been brought home, and shown to some of our near neighbors, and then laid aside. My mistress used to go to class meeting at the Wilk Street meetinghouse every Monday afternoon, and leave me to take care of the house. When left thus, I used to spend this time writing in the spaces left in Master Thomas's copy-book, copying what he had written. I continued to do this until I could write a hand very similar to that of Master Thomas. Thus, after a long, tedious effort for years, I finally succeeded in learning how to write.

Questions for Discussion

1. Why does Mr. Auld tell Mrs. Auld that she can't continue her lessons with Douglass?

2. What effect does Mr. Auld's prohibition have on Mrs. Auld? Why? What effect does it have on Douglass?

3. What is "The Columbian Orator"?

4. Describe Douglass's changing understanding of the word abolition.

5. What relationship does Douglass see between writing and freedom?

Questions for Reflection and Writing

1. This piece was written more than 150 years ago. What effect do you think this historical distance has on your understanding of the essay? What other factors might make your reading of the text different from that of one of Douglass's contemporaries?

2. Consider Douglass's efforts to learn. Now think about the history of your own education. How are his story and yours different? Are there also similarities?

3. Do some research on Douglass's later life. As a starting point, you might want to research something in the essay that left you scratching your head. (Consider, for example, your response to Question for Reflection and Writing #1.) If you're interested in doing some research online, you might simply type "Frederick Douglass" into a search engine like Google.com. Alternatively, you could look into some of Douglass's later writings available online at Project Gutenberg (www.gutenberg.net/). How essential do you think reading and writing was to what Douglass became, and what he eventually achieved?

Joan Didion (1934–   ) earned a B.A. from the University of California—Berkeley in 1956. Her first writing job was as a copywriter for *Vogue*, where she later became an associate feature editor. Didion has also been a regular columnist for *The Saturday Evening Post* and a contributing editor for *The National Review*. Her major works include the novels *Play It as It Lays* (1971), *A Book of Common Prayer* (1977), and *Democracy* (1984), and the nonfiction books *Salvador* (1983) and *Miami* (1987). Her essays have been collected as *Slouching Towards Bethlehem* (1968), *The White Album* (1979), and *After Henry* (1992), later republished as *Sentimental Journeys*.

On Keeping a Notebook

Joan Didion

"'That woman Estelle,'" the note reads, "'is partly the reason why George Sharp   1
and I are separated today.' *Dirty crêpe-de-Chine wrapper, hotel bar, Wilmington RR, 9:45 a.m. August Monday morning.*"

Since the note is in my notebook, it presumably has some meaning to me.   2
I study it for a long while. At first I have only the most general notion of what I was doing on an August Monday morning in the bar of the hotel across from the Pennsylvania Railroad station in Wilmington, Delaware (waiting for a train? missing one? 1960? 1961? why Wilmington?), but I do remember being there. The woman in the dirty crêpe-de-Chine wrapper had come down from her room for a beer, and the bartender had heard before the reason why George Sharp and she were separated today. "Sure," he said, and went on mopping the floor. "You told me." At the other end of the bar is a girl. She is talking, pointedly, not to the man beside her but to a cat lying in the triangle of sunlight cast through the open door. She is wearing a plaid silk dress from Peck & Peck, and the hem is coming down.

Here is what it is: the girl has been on the Eastern Shore, and now she is   3
going back to the city, leaving the man beside her, and all she can see ahead are the viscous summer sidewalks and the 3 A.M. long-distance calls that will make her lie awake and then sleep drugged through all the steaming mornings left in August (1960? 1961?). Because she must go directly from the train to lunch in New York, she wishes that she had a safety pin for the hem of the plaid silk dress,

and she also wishes that she could forget about the hem and the lunch and stay in the cool bar that smells of disinfectant and malt and make friends with the woman in the crêpe-de-Chine wrapper. She is afflicted by a little self-pity, and she wants to compare Estelles. That is what that was all about.

Why did I write it down? In order to remember, of course, but exactly what   4
was it I wanted to remember? How much of it actually happened? Did any of it? Why do I keep a notebook at all? It is easy to deceive oneself on all those scores. The impulse to write things down is a peculiarly compulsive one, inexplicable to those who do not share it, useful only accidentally, only secondarily, in the way that any compulsion tries to justify itself. I suppose that it begins or does not begin in the cradle. Although I have felt compelled to write things down since I was five years old, I doubt that my daughter ever will, for she is a singularly blessed and accepting child, delighted with life exactly as life presents itself to her, unafraid to go to sleep and unafraid to wake up. Keepers of private notebooks are a different breed altogether, lonely and resistant rearrangers of things, anxious malcontents, children afflicted apparently at birth with some presentiment of loss.

My first notebook was a Big Five tablet, given to me by my mother with   5
the sensible suggestion that I stop whining and learn to amuse myself by writing down my thoughts. She returned the tablet to me a few years ago; the first entry is an account of a woman who believed herself to be freezing to death in the Arctic night, only to find, when day broke, that she had stumbled onto the Sahara Desert, where she would die of the heat before lunch. I have no idea what turn of a five-year-old's mind could have prompted so insistently "ironic" and exotic a story, but it does reveal a certain predilection for the extreme which has dogged me into adult life; perhaps if I were analytically inclined I would find it a truer story than any I might have told about Donald Johnson's birthday party or the day my cousin Brenda put Kitty Litter in the aquarium.

So the point of my keeping a notebook has never been, nor is it now, to   6
have an accurate factual record of what I have been doing or thinking. That would be a different impulse entirely, an instinct for reality which I sometimes envy but do not possess. At no point have I ever been able successfully to keep a diary; my approach to daily life ranges from the grossly negligent to the merely absent, and on those few occasions when I have tried dutifully to record a day's events, boredom has so overcome me that the results are mysterious at best. What is this business about "shopping, typing piece, dinner with E, depressed"?

Shopping for what? Typing what piece? Who is E? Was this "E" depressed, or was I depressed? Who cares?

In fact I have abandoned altogether that kind of pointless entry; instead I   7
tell what some would call lies. "That's simply not true," the members of my family frequently tell me when they come up against my memory of a shared event. "The party was not for you, the spider was not a black widow, it wasn't that way at all." Very likely they are right, for not only have I always had trouble distinguishing between what happened and what merely might have happened, but I remain unconvinced that the distinction, for my purposes, matters. The cracked crab that I recall having for lunch the day my father came home from Detroit in 1945 must certainly be embroidery, worked into the day's pattern to lend verisimilitude; I was ten years old and would not now remember the cracked crab. The day's events did not turn on cracked crab. And yet it is precisely that fictitious crab that makes me see the afternoon all over again, a home movie run all too often, the father bearing gifts, the child weeping, an exercise in family love and guilt. Or that is what it was to me. Similarly, perhaps it never did snow that August in Vermont; perhaps there never were flurries in the night wind, and maybe no one else felt the ground hardening and summer already dead even as we pretended to bask in it, but that was how it felt to me, and it might as well have snowed, could have snowed, did snow.

How it felt to me: that is getting closer to the truth about a notebook. I   8
sometimes delude myself about why I keep a notebook, imagine that some thrifty virtue derives from preserving everything observed. See enough and write it down, I tell myself, and then some morning when the world seems drained of wonder, some day when I am only going through the motions of doing what I am supposed to do, which is write—on that bankrupt morning I will simply open my notebook and there it will all be, a forgotten account with accumulated interest, paid passage back to the world out there: dialogue overheard in hotels and elevators and at the hat-check counter in Pavillon (one middle-aged man shows his hat-check to another and says, "That's my old football number"); impressions of Bettina Aptheker and Benjamin Sonnenberg and Teddy ("Mr. Acapulco") Stauffer; careful aperçus about tennis bums and failed fashion models and Greek shipping heiresses, one of whom taught me a significant lesson (a lesson I could have learned from F. Scott Fitzgerald, but perhaps we all must meet the very rich for ourselves) by asking, when I arrived to interview her in her orchid-filled sitting room on the second day of a paralyzing New York blizzard, whether it was snowing outside.

I imagine, in other words, that the notebook is about other people. But of 9 course it is not. I have no real business with what one stranger said to another at the hat-check counter in Pavillon; in fact I suspect that the line "That's my old football number" touched not my own imagination at all, but merely some memory of something once read, probably "The Eighty-Yard Run." Nor is my concern with a woman in a dirty crêpe-de-Chine wrapper in a Wilmington bar. My stake is always, of course, in the unmentioned girl in the plaid silk dress. Remember what it was to be me: that is always the point.

It is a difficult point to admit. We are brought up in the ethic that others, 10 any others, all others, are by definition more interesting than ourselves; taught to be diffident, just this side of self-effacing. ("You're the least important person in the room and don't forget it," Jessica Mitford's governess would hiss in her ear on the advent of any social occasion; I copied that into my notebook because it is only recently that I have been able to enter a room without hearing some such phrase in my inner ear.) Only the very young and the very old may recount their dreams at breakfast, dwell upon self, interrupt with memories of beach picnics and favorite Liberty lawn dresses and the rainbow trout in a creek near Colorado Springs. The rest of us are expected, rightly, to affect absorption in other people's favorite dresses, other people's trout.

And so we do. But our notebooks give us away, for however dutifully we 11 record what we see around us, the common denominator of all we see is always, transparently, shamelessly, the implacable "I." We are not talking here about the kind of notebook that is patently for public consumption, a structural conceit for binding together a series of graceful pensées; we are talking about something private, about bits of the mind's string too short to use, an indiscriminate and erratic assemblage with meaning only for its maker.

And sometimes even the maker has difficulty with the meaning. There 12 does not seem to be, for example, any point in my knowing for the rest of my life that, during 1964, 720 tons of soot fell on every square mile of New York City, yet there it is in my notebook, labeled "FACT." Nor do I really need to remember that Ambrose Bierce liked to spell Leland Stanford's name "£eland $tanford" or that "smart women almost always wear black in Cuba," a fashion hint without much potential for practical application. And does not the relevance of these notes seem marginal at best?:

In the basement museum of the Inyo County Courthouse in Independence, California, sign pinned to a mandarin coat: "This MAN-

DARIN COAT was often worn by Mrs. Minnie
S. Brooks when giving lectures on her TEAPOT COLLECTION."

Redhead getting out of car in front of Beverly Wilshire Hotel, chin-
chilla stole, Vuitton bags with tags reading:

MRS. LOU
FOX HOTEL SAHARA
VEGAS

Well, perhaps not entirely marginal. As a matter of fact, Mrs. Minnie S.   13
Brooks and her mandarin coat pull me back into my own childhood, for
although I never knew Mrs. Brooks and did not visit Inyo County until I was
thirty, I grew up in just such a world, in houses cluttered with Indian relics and
bits of gold ore and ambergris and the souvenirs my Aunt Mercy Farnsworth
brought back from the Orient. It is a long way from that world to Mrs. Lou Fox's
world, where we all live now, and is it not just as well to remember that? Might
not Mrs. Minnie S. Brooks help me to remember what I am? Might not Mrs. Lou
Fox help me to remember what I am not?

But sometimes the point is harder to discern. What exactly did I have in   14
mind when I noted down that it cost the father of someone I know $650 a
month to light the place on the Hudson in which he lived before the Crash?
What use was I planning to make of this line by Jimmy Hoffa: "I may have my
faults, but being wrong ain't one of them"? And although I think it interesting
to know where the girls who travel with the Syndicate have their hair done
when they find themselves on the West Coast, will I ever make suitable use of
it? Might I not be better off just passing it on to John O'Hara? What is a recipe
for sauerkraut doing in my notebook? What kind of magpie keeps this notebook?
"He was born the night the Titanic went down." That seems a nice enough line, and
I even recall who said it, but is it not really a better line in life than it could ever
be in fiction?

But of course that is exactly it: not that I should ever use the line, but that   15
I should remember the woman who said it and the afternoon I heard it. We were
on her terrace by the sea, and we were finishing the wine left from lunch, trying
to get what sun there was, a California winter sun. The woman whose husband
was born the night the Titanic went down wanted to rent her house, wanted to
go back to her children in Paris. I remember wishing that I could afford the
house, which cost $1,000 a month. "Someday you will," she said lazily. "Someday

it all comes." There in the sun on her terrace it seemed easy to believe in some-day, but later I had a low-grade afternoon hangover and ran over a black snake on the way to the supermarket and was flooded with inexplicable fear when I heard the checkout clerk explaining to the man ahead of me why she was final-ly divorcing her husband. "He left me no choice," she said over and over as she punched the register. "He has a little seven-month-old baby by her, he left me no choice." I would like to believe that my dread then was for the human con-dition, but of course it was for me, because I wanted a baby and did not then have one and because I wanted to own the house that cost $1,000 a month to rent and because I had a hangover.

It all comes back. Perhaps it is difficult to see the value in having one's self back in that kind of mood, but I do see it; I think we are well advised to keep on nodding terms with the people we used to be, whether we find them attractive company or not. Otherwise they turn up unannounced and surprise us, come hammering on the mind's door at 4 A.M. of a bad night and demand to know who deserted them, who betrayed them, who is going to make amends. We for-get all too soon the things we thought we could never forget. We forget the loves and the betrayals alike, forget what we whispered and what we screamed, forget who we were. I have already lost touch with a couple of people I used to be; one of them, a seventeen-year-old, presents little threat, although it would be of some interest to me to know again what it feels like to sit on a river levee drinking vodka-and-orange-juice and listening to Les Paul and Mary Ford and their echoes sing "How High the Moon" on the car radio. (You see I still have the scenes, but I no longer perceive myself among those present, no longer could even improvise the dialogue.) The other one, a twenty-three-year-old, bothers me more. She was always a good deal of trouble, and I suspect she will reappear when I least want to see her, skirts too long, shy to the point of aggravation, always the injured party, full of recriminations and little hurts and stories I do not want to hear again, at once saddening me and angering me with her vulnerabil-ity and ignorance, an apparition all the more insistent for being so long banished.

It is a good idea, then, to keep in touch, and I suppose that keeping in touch is what notebooks are all about. And we are all on our own when it comes to keeping those lines open to ourselves: your notebook will never help me, nor mine you. "So what's new in the whiskey business?" What could that possibly mean to you? To me it means a blonde in a Pucci bathing suit sitting with a cou-ple of fat men by the pool at the Beverly Hills Hotel. Another man approaches, and they all regard one another in silence for a while. "So what's new in the whiskey business?" one of the fat men finally says by way of welcome, and the blonde stands up, arches one foot and dips it in the pool, looking all the while at the cabaña where Baby Pignatari is talking on the telephone. That is all there is to that, except that several years later I saw the blonde coming out of Saks Fifth Avenue in New York with her California complexion and a voluminous mink coat. In the harsh wind that day she looked old and irrevocably tired to me, and even the skins in the mink coat were not worked the way they were doing them that year, not the way she would have wanted them done, and there is the point of the story. For a while after that I did not like to look in the mirror, and my eyes would skim the newspapers and pick out only the deaths, the cancer victims, the premature coronaries, the suicides, and I stopped riding the Lexington Avenue IRT because I noticed for the first time that all the strangers I had seen for years—the man with the seeing-eye dog, the spinster who read the classified pages every day, the fat girl who always got off with me at Grand Central—looked older than they once had.

It all comes back. Even that recipe for sauerkraut: even that brings it back. 18
I was on Fire Island when I first made that sauerkraut, and it was raining, and we drank a lot of bourbon and ate the sauerkraut and went to bed at ten, and I listened to the rain and the Atlantic and felt safe. I made the sauerkraut again last night and it did not make me feel any safer, but that is, as they say, another story.

Questions for Discussion

1. What intrigues you about the opening notes? What possible stories about the woman spring to mind?

2. What is the point of keeping a notebook, besides recording events? What is a notebook really about?

3. Why is accuracy not important in keeping a notebook? In fact, what benefits does being inaccurate provide the writer?

4. What makes a writer a writer? Didion implies that it is a compulsion to write things down. Do you agree?

5. If notebooks are mainly about the note taker, is writing an essay about keeping a notebook mainly about the essayist? If so, why might Didion feel compelled to write about herself to this extent?

6. How does Didion work things out about herself by rereading her old notebooks? What happens when you read through your old notebooks, diaries, or journals?

7.   Why might Didion have referred to herself in paragraph 3 as "the girl" and "she" instead of using the first person "I"?

Questions for Reflection and Writing

1.   Over the next week or several days, jot down bits and pieces of overheard conversations, things you notice during the day, anything that strikes you. Begin to keep a notebook of details.

2.   Flesh out your notebook into an essay on the process of keeping the notebook, on topics written about in your notebook, or on several of the entries, tying the disparate entries together in a creative way. Your essay could be serious or humorous.

3.   Read what other writers say about keeping notebooks or about their writing processes. How do writers do what they do? How do they collect the material for their stories, essays, poetry, articles, and books?

Henry Louis Gates, Jr. (1950–), a prominent and controversial African American literary scholar, was born on September 16 in Keyser, West Virginia. Gates began studying at a community college but went on to Yale, graduating summa cum laude in 1973; he subsequently earned M.A. and Ph.D. degrees from Clare College. Gates familiarized himself with African culture during a 15-country African tour as a Carnegie Foundation fellow and Phelps fellow (1970–1971). He studied with the well-known African writer Wole Soyinka at Cambridge University. Gates was awarded a "genius grant" by the MacArthur Foundation in 1981. He taught at Yale University and Cornell University before winning an endowed chair at Duke University.

Gates describes his literary criticism as nonextremist and eclectic, contending that our literary canon needs to be enlarged according to a view of the interrelationship between black and white cultures in America that avoids what he calls "ethnic absolutism." Gates has worked as a general anesthetist, researcher, journalist, and educator. He has a long list of memberships, awards, and honors. In 1984 Gates edited *Black Literature and Literary Theory*, a collection of essays that connect contemporary literary theory with black literature. *Loose Canons: Notes on the Culture Wars* (1992) counters arguments by both the left, which demands that literary canons reflect demographics, and the right, which takes a protectionist view of the traditional canon. Gates has written or edited a long list of critical books.

Whose Canon Is It, Anyway?

Henry Louis Gates, Jr.

William Bennett and Allan Bloom, the dynamic duo of the new cultural right, have become the easy targets of the cultural left, which I am defining here loosely and generously as that uneasy, shifting set of alliances formed by feminist critics, critics of so-called minority culture and Marxist and post structuralist critics generally—in short, the rainbow coalition of contemporary critical theory. These two men (one a former United States Secretary of Education and now President Bush's "drug czar," the other a professor at the University of Chicago and author of *The Closing of the American Mind*) symbolize the nostalgic return to what I think of as the "antebellum esthetic position," when men were men and men were white, when scholar-critics were white men and when women and people of color were voiceless, faceless servants and laborers, pouring tea and filling brandy snifters in the boardrooms of old boys' clubs. Inevitably, these two men have come to play the roles that George Wallace and Orville Faubus played for the civil rights movement, or that Richard Nixon and Henry Kissinger played during Vietnam—the "feel good" targets who, despite internal differences and contradictions, the cultural left loves to hate.

And how tempting it is to juxtapose their "civilizing mission" to the racial   2 violence that has swept through our campuses since 1986–at traditionally liberal Northern institutions such as the University of Massachusetts at Amherst, Mount Holyoke College, Smith College, the University of Chicago, Columbia, the University of Pennsylvania, and at Southern institutions such as the University of Alabama, the University of Texas and the Citadel. Add to this the fact that affirmative action programs on campus have become window dressing operations, necessary "evils" maintained to preserve the fiction of racial fairness and openness but deprived of the power to enforce their stated principles. When unemployment among black youth is 40 percent, when 44 percent of black Americans can't read the front page of a newspaper, when less than two percent of the faculty on campuses is black, and when only 40 percent of black students in higher education are men, well, you look for targets close at hand.

And yet there's a real danger of localizing our grievances; of the easy per-   3 sonification, assigning celebrated faces to the forces of reaction and so giving too much credit to a few men who are really symptomatic of a larger political current. (In a similar vein, our rhetoric sometimes depicts the high canonical as the reading matter of the power elite. You have to imagine James Baker curling up with the *Pisan Cantos*, Dan Quayle leafing through *The Princess Casamassima*.) Maybe our eagerness to do so reflects a certain vanity that academic cultural critics are prone to. We make dire predictions, and when they come true, we think we've changed the world.

It's a tendency that puts me in mind of my father's favorite story about   4 Father Divine, that historic con man of the cloth. In the 1930s, he was put on trial and convicted for using the mails to defraud. At sentencing, Father Divine stood up and told the judge: I'm warning you, you send me to jail, something terrible is going to happen to you. Father Divine, of course, was sent to prison, and a week later, by sheer coincidence, the judge had a heart attack and died. When the warden and the guards found out about it in the middle of the night, they raced to Father Divine's cell and woke him up. Father Divine, they said, your judge just dropped dead of a heart attack. Without missing a beat, Father Divine lifted his head and told them: "I *hated* to do it."

As writers, teachers or intellectuals, most of us would like to claim greater   5
efficacy for our labors than we're entitled to. These days, literary criticism likes
to think of itself as "war by other means." But it should start to wonder: have its
victories come too easily? The recent turn toward politics and history in literary
studies has turned the analysis of texts into a marionette theater of the political,
to which we bring all the passions of our real-world commitments. And that's
why it is sometimes necessary to remind ourselves of the distance from the classroom to the streets. Academic critics write essays, "readings" of literature, where
the bad guys (you know, racism or patriarchy) lose, where the forces of oppression are subverted by the boundless powers of irony and allegory that no prison
can contain, and we glow with hard-won triumph. We pay homage to the mar-
ginalized and demonized, and it feels almost as if we've righted an actual injustice. (Academic battles are so fierce—the received wisdom has it—because so
little is truly at stake.) I always think of the folk tale about the fellow who killed
seven with one blow: flies, not giants.

Ours was the generation that took over buildings in the late 1960s and   6
demanded the creation of black and women's studies programs and now, like the
return of the repressed, has come back to challenge the traditional curriculum.
And some of us are even attempting to redefine the canon by editing anthologies. Yet it sometimes seems that blacks are doing better in the college curriculum than they are in the streets or even on the campuses.

This is not a defeatist moan, just an acknowledgment that the relation   7
between our critical postures and the social struggles they reflect is far from transparent. That doesn't mean there's no relation, of course, only that it's a highly
mediated one. In all events, I do think we should be clear about when we've
swatted a fly and when we've toppled a giant. Still, you can't expect people who
spend their lives teaching literature to be dispassionate about the texts they
teach; no one went into literature out of an interest in literature-in-general.

I suppose the literary canon is, in no very grand sense, the commonplace   8
book of our shared culture, the archive of those texts and titles we wish to
remember. And how else did those of us who teach literature fall in love with our
subject than through our very own commonplace books, in which we inscribed
secretly, as we might in a private diary, those passages of books that names for us
what we had deeply felt, but could not say?

I kept mine from the age of 12, turning to it to repeat those marvelous   9
words that named me in some private way. From H. H. Munro to Dickens and
Austen, to Hugo and de Maupassant, each resonant sentence would find its way

into my book. (There's no point in avoiding the narcissism here: We are always transfixed by those passages that seem to read us.) Finding James Baldwin and writing him down at an Episcopal church camp in 1965—I was fifteen, and the Watts riots were raging—probably determined the direction of my intellectual life more than anything else I could name. I wrote and rewrote verbatim his elegantly framed paragraphs, full of sentences that were somehow both Henry Jamesian and King Jamesian, garbed as they were in the figures and cadences of the spirituals. Of course, we forget the private pleasures that brought us to the subject in the first place once we adopt the alienating strategies of formal analysis; our professional vanity is to insist that the study of literature be both beauty and truth, style and politics and everything in between.

In the swaddling clothes of our academic complacencies, then, few of us are 10 prepared when we bump against something hard, and sooner or later, we do. One of the first talks I ever gave was to a packed audience at a college honors seminar, and it was one of those mistakes you don't make twice. Fresh out of graduate school, immersed in the arcane technicalities of contemporary literary theory. I was going to deliver a crunchy structuralist analysis of a slave narrative by Frederick Douglass, tracing the intricate play of its "binary oppositions." Everything was neatly schematized, formalized, analyzed; this was my Sunday-best structuralism: crisp white shirt and shiny black shoes. And it wasn't playing. If you've seen an audience glaze over, this was double glazing. Bravely, I finished my talk and, of course, asked for questions. "Yeah, brother," said a young man in the very back of the room, breaking the silence that ensued, "all we want to know is, was Booker T. Washington an Uncle Tom or not?"

The funny thing is, this happens to be an interesting question, a lot more 11 interesting than my talk was. It raised all the big issues about the politics of style, about what it means to speak for another, about how you were to distinguish between canny subversion and simple co-optation—who was manipulating whom? And while I didn't exactly appreciate it at the time, the exchange did draw my attention, a little rudely perhaps, to the yawning chasm between our critical discourse and the traditions they discourse upon.

Obviously, some of what I'm saying is by way of *mea cupla*, because I'm 12 speaking here as a participant in a moment of canon formation in a so-called marginal tradition. As it happens, W. W. Norton, the "canonical" anthology publisher, will be publishing *The Norton Anthology of Afro-American Literature*. The editing of this anthology has been a great dream of mine for a long time, and it represents, in the most concrete way, the project of black canon formation. But my pursuit of this project has required me to negotiate a position between those on the cultural right who claim that black literature can have no canon, no masterpieces, and those on the cultural left who wonder why anyone wants to establish the existence of a canon, any canon, in the first place.

We face the outraged reactions of those custodians of Western culture who   13
protest that the canon, that transparent decanter of Western values, may become—breathe the word—*politicized.* That people can maintain a straight face while they protest the irruption of politics into something that has always been political—well, it says something about how remarkably successful official literary histories have been in presenting themselves as natural objects, untainted by wordly interests.

I agree with those conservatives who have raised the alarm about our stu-   14
dents' ignorance of history. But part of the history we need to teach has to be the history of the very idea of the "canon," which involves the history both of literary pedagogy and the very institution of the school. One function of literary history is then to conceal all connections between institutionalized interests and the literature we remember. Pay no attention to the men behind the curtain, booms the Great Oz of literary history.

Cynthia Ozick once chastised feminists by warning that strategies become   15
institutions. But isn't that really another way of warning that their strategies, Heaven forfend, may *succeed?*

Here we approach the scruples of those on the cultural left who worry   16
about, well, the price of success. "Who's co-opting whom?" might be their slogan. To them, the very idea of the canon is hierarchical, patriarchal and otherwise politically suspect. They'd like us to disavow it altogether.

But history and its institutions are not just something we study, they're also   17
something we live, and live through. And how effective and how durable our inventions in contemporary cultural politics will be depends upon our ability to mobilize the institutions that buttress and reproduce that culture. We could seclude ourselves from the real world and keep our hands clean, free from the taint of history. But that is to pay obeisance to the status quo, to the entrenched arsenal of sexual and racial authority, to say that things shouldn't change, become something other and, let's hope, better.

Indeed, this is one case where we've got to borrow a leaf from the right,   18
which is exemplarily aware of the role of education in the reproduction of values. We must engage in this sort of canon reformation precisely because Mr. Bennett is correct: the teaching of literature is the teaching of values, not inher-

ently, no, but contingently, yes; it is—it has become—the teaching of an esthetic and political order, in which no person of color, no woman, was ever able to discover the reflection or representation of his or her cultural image or voice. The return of "the" canon, the high canon of Western masterpieces, represents the return of an order in which my people were the subjugated, the voiceless, the invisible, the unpresented and the unrepresentable.

Let me be specific. Those of us working in my own tradition confront the   19 hegemony of the Western tradition, generally, and of the larger American tradition, more locally, as we theorize about our tradition and engage in canon formation. Long after white American literature has been anthologized and canonized, and recanonized, our efforts to define a black American canon are often decried as racist, separatist, nationalist, or "essentialist." Attempts to derive theories about our literary tradition from the black tradition—a tradition, I might add, that must include black vernacular forms as well as written literary forms—are often greeted by our colleagues in traditional literature departments as a misguided desire to secede from a union that only recently, and with considerable kicking and screaming, has been forged. What is wrong with you people? our friends ask us in genuine passion and concern; after all, aren't we all just citizens of literature here?

Well, yes and no. Every black American text must confess to a complex   20 ancestry, one high and low (that is, literary and vernacular) but also one white and black. There can be no doubt that white texts inform and influence black texts (and vice versa), so that a thoroughly integrated canon of American literature is not only politically sound, it is intellectually sound as well. But the attempts of black scholars to define a black American canon, and to derive indigenous theories of interpretation from within this canon, are not meant to refute the soundness of these gestures of integration. Rather, it is a question of perspective, a question of emphasis. Just as we can and must cite a black text within the larger American tradition, we can and must cite it within its own tradition, a tradition not defined by a pseudoscience of racial biology, or a mystically shared essence called blackness, but by the repetition and revision of shared themes, topoi and tropes, the call and response of voices, their music and cacophony.

And this is our special legacy: what in 1849 Frederick Douglass called the   21 "live, calm, grave, clear, pointed, warm, sweet, melodious and powerful human voice." The presence of the past in the African-American tradition comes to us most powerfully as voice, a voice that is never quite our own—or *only* our own—

however much we want it to be. One of my earliest childhood memories tells this story clearly.

I remember my first public performance, which I gave at the age of four in   22 the all-black Methodist church that my mother attended, and that her mother had attended for fifty years. It was a religious program, at which each of the children of the Sunday school was to deliver a "piece"—as the people in our church referred to a religious recitation. Mine was the couplet "Jesus was a boy like me,/ And like Him I want to be." Not much of a recitation, but then I was only four. So, after weeks of practice in elocution, hair pressed and greased down, shirt starched and pants pressed, I was ready to give my piece. I remember skipping along to the church with all of the other kids, driving everyone crazy, repeating that couplet over and over. "Jesus was a boy like me, / And like Him I want to be."

Finally we made it to the church, and it was packed—bulging and glisten-   23 ing with black people, eager to hear pieces, despite the fact that they had heard all of the pieces already, year after year, like bits and fragments of a repeated master text. Because I was the youngest child on the program, I was the first to go. Miss Sarah Russell (whom we called Sister Holy Ghost—behind her back, of course) started the program with a prayer, then asked if little Skippy Gates would step forward. I did so.

And then the worst happened: I completely forgot the words of my piece.   24 Standing there, pressed and starched, just as clean as I could be, in front of just about everybody in our part of town, I could not for the life of me remember one word of that piece.

After standing there I don't know how long, struck dumb and captivated   25 by all of those staring eyes, I heard a voice from near the back of the church proclaim, "Jesus was a boy like me, / And like Him I want to be."

And my mother, having arisen to find my voice, smoothed her dress and   26 sat down again. The congregation's applause lasted as long as its laughter as I crawled back to my seat.

What this moment crystallizes for me is how much of my scholarly and crit-   27 ical work has been an attempt to learn how to speak in the strong, compelling cadences of my mother's voice. As the black feminist scholar Hortense Spillers has recently insisted, in moving words that first occasioned this very recollection, it is "the heritage of the mother that the African-American male must regain as an aspect of his own personhood—the power of 'yes' to the 'female' within.

To reform core curriculums, to account for the comparable eloquence of   28
the African, the Asian and the Middle Eastern traditions, is to begin to prepare
our students for their roles as citizens of a world culture, educated through a truly
human notion of "the humanities," rather than—as Mr. Bennett and Mr. Bloom
would have it—as guardians at the last frontier outpost of white male Western
culture, the keepers of the masterpieces. And for us as scholar-critics, learning to
speak in the voice of the black mother is perhaps the ultimate challenge of producing a discourse of the Other.

Questions for Discussion

1. What is meant by a "canon"?
2. What is the main social problem that Gates describes here? What does he
    see as the root cause of the problem? Does he suggest any solutions?
3. What does Gates find at fault with the "cultural right"? What does he find
    at fault with the "cultural left"? Why does he find fault with either?
4. How does what Gates is saying about the difficulties of teaching also apply
    to the difficulties of being a student?
5. What does Gates say or imply about how literature, especially the literature
    outside the traditional white male canon, be taught?
6. How does literary history relate to the political history usually taught in his-
    tory departments? What is literary history, and why is it important?
7. What are Gates' politics? How do you know? What about his style and word
    choice reveals his bias?

Questions for Reflection and Writing

1. Find a few sentences in this essay that puzzle you. Write an informal
    response, paraphrasing the sentences and speculating on what they mean.
2. Find one passage (as little as a sentence or as long as a paragraph) in this
    essay that delights or annoys you. Write a response, summarizing Gates
    objectively, then evaluating his essay.
3. What works are in the traditional literary canon? How is this canon chang-
    ing and why? What works should be in the canon? Find possible answers to
    these questions by reading critical articles, by comparing tables of contents
    from literature anthologies, and by interviewing literature teachers at your
    school.

Chapter 2
FAMILY ROLES AND GENDER ROLES

Margaret Atwood (1939–   ) studied at the University of Toronto (B.A. 1961),
Radcliffe College (M.A. 1962), and did graduate work at Harvard University (1962–63,
1965–67). She began her career as a lecturer at the University of British Columbia in
Vancouver and at Williams University in Montreal, and was an editor at House of Anansi
Press. Since 1972, she has been a writer-in-residence at the University of Toronto (1972-73),
the University of Alabama, Tuscaloosa (1985), New York University (1986), and Macquarie
University, Australia (1987). She is a member of PEN, the Royal Society of Canada, and the
American Academy of Arts and Sciences, and has received numerous awards and honorary
degrees for her work. She is a prolific writer; her work includes novels, poetry, short stories, nonfiction, and radio and television plays. A few of her best-known books are the novels *The Edible
Women* (1969), *Surfacing* (1972), *The Handmaid's Tale* (1985), and *Cat's Eye* (1988), and the
short story collections *Dancing Girls and Other Stories* (1977) and *Bluebeard's Egg and Other
Stories* (1983). Atwood's fictional works often blend fiction, history, science fiction, the goth-
ic, and realism; her nonfiction works tend to be acerbic political pieces with a decidedly feminist stance. Atwood is one of the few Canadian authors to enjoy a widespread popularity in the
United States; in Canada she has achieved celebrity status.

The Female Body

Margaret Atwood

> . . . entirely devoted to the subject of "The Female Body." Knowing how
> well you have written on this topic . . . this capacious topic . . .
> —letter from *Michigan Quarterly Review*

1.

I agree, it's a hot topic. But only one? Look around, there's a wide range. Take my   1
own, for instance.

I get up in the morning. My topic feels like hell. I sprinkle it with water,   2
brush parts of it, rub it with towels, powder it, add lubricant. I dump in the fuel
and away goes my topic, my topical topic, my controversial topic, my capacious
topic, my limping topic, my nearsighted topic, my topic with back problems, my
badly behaved topic, my vulgar topic, my outrageous topic, my aging topic, my
topic that is out of the question and anyway still can't spell, in its oversized coat
and worn winter boots, scuttling along the sidewalk as if it were flesh and blood,

hunting for what's out there, an avocado, an alderman, an adjective, hungry as ever.

2.

The basic Female Body comes with the following accessories: garter belt, panti-   3
girdle, crinoline, camisole, bustle, brassiere, stomacher, chemise, virgin zone, spike heels, nose ring, veil, kid gloves, fishnet stockings, fichu, bandeau, Merry Widow, weepers, chokers, barrettes, bangles, beads, lorgnette, feather boa, basic black, compact, Lycra stretch one-piece with modesty panel, designer peignoir, flannel nightie, lace teddy, bed, head.

3.

The Female Body is made of transparent plastic and lights up when you plug it   4
in. You press a button to illuminate the different systems. The circulatory system is red, for the heart and arteries, purple for the veins; the respiratory system is blue; the lymphatic system is yellow; the digestive system is green, with liver and kidneys in aqua. The nerves are done in orange and the brain is pink. The skeleton, as you might expect, is white.

The reproductive system is optional, and can be removed. It comes with or   5
without a miniature embryo. Parental judgment can thereby be exercised. We do not wish to frighten or offend.

4.

He said, I won't have one of those things in the house. It gives a young girl a false   6
notion of beauty, not to mention anatomy. If a real woman was built like that she'd fall on her face.

She said, If we don't let her have one like all the other girls she'll feel sin-   7
gled out. It'll become an issue. She'll long for one and she'll long to turn into one. Repression breeds sublimation. You know that.

He said, It's not just the pointy plastic tits, it's the wardrobes. The   8
wardrobes and that stupid male doll, what's his name, the one with the underwear glued on.

She said, Better to get it over with when she's young. He said, All right, but   9
don't let me see it.

She came whizzing down the stairs, thrown like a dart. She was stark   10
naked. Her hair had been chopped off, her head was turned back to front, she was missing some toes and she'd been tattooed all over her body with purple ink

in a scrollwork design. She hit the potted azalea, trembled there for a moment like a botched angel, and fell.

He said, I guess we're safe.   11

5.

The Female Body has many uses. It's been used as a door knocker, a bottle open-   12
er, as a clock with a ticking belly, as something to hold up lampshades, as a nut-
cracker, just squeeze the brass legs together and out comes your nut. It bears
torches, lifts victorious wreaths, grows copper wings and raises aloft a ring of neon
stars; whole buildings rest on its marble heads.

It sells cars, beer, shaving lotion, cigarettes, hard liquor; it sells diet plans   13
and diamonds, and desire in tiny crystal bottles. Is this the face that launched a
thousand products? You bet it is, but don't get any funny big ideas, honey, that
smile is a dime a dozen.

It does not merely sell, it is sold. Money flows into this country or that   14
country, flies in, practically crawls in, suitful after suitful, lured by all those hair-
less preteen legs. Listen, you want to reduce the national debt, don't you? Aren't
you patriotic? That's the spirit. That's my girl.

She's a natural resource, a renewable one luckily, because those things wear   15
out so quickly. They don't make 'em like they used to. Shoddy goods.

6.

One and one equals another one. Pleasure in the female is not a requirement.   16
Pair-bonding is stronger in geese. We're not talking about love, we're talking
about biology. That's how we all got here, daughter.

Snails do it differently. They're hermaphrodites, and work in threes.   17

7.

Each Female Body contains a female brain. Handy. Makes things work. Stick   18
pins in it and you get amazing results. Old popular songs. Short circuits. Bad
dreams.

Anyway: each of these brains has two halves. They're joined together by a   19
thick cord; neural pathways flow from one to the other, sparkles of electric information washing to and from. Like light on waves. Like a conversation. How does
a woman know? She listens. She listens in.

The male brain, now, that's a different matter. Only a thin connection.   20
Space over here, time over there, music and arithmetic in their own sealed com-

partments. The right brain doesn't know what the left brain is doing. Good for aiming though, for hitting the target when you pull the trigger. What's the target? Who's the target? Who cares? What matters is hitting it. That's the male brain for you. Objective.

This is why men are so sad, why they feel so cut off, why they think of 21 themselves as orphans cast adrift, footloose and stringless in the deep void. What void? she asks. What are you talking about? The void of the universe, he says, and she says Oh and looks out the window and tries to get a handle on it, but it's no use, there's too much going on, too many rustlings in the leaves, too many voices, so she says, Would you like a cheese sandwich, a piece of cake, a cup of tea? And he grinds his teeth because she doesn't understand, and wanders off, not just alone but Alone, lost in the dark, lost in the skull, searching for the other half, the twin who could complete him.

Then it comes to him: he's lost the Female Body! Look, it shines in the 22 gloom, far ahead, a vision of wholeness, ripeness, like a giant melon, like an apple, like a metaphor for "breast" in a bad sex novel; it shines like a balloon, like a foggy noon, a watery moon, shimmering in its egg of light.

Catch it. Put it in a pumpkin, in a high tower, in a compound, in a cham- 23 ber, in a house, in a room. Quick, stick a leash on it, a lock, a chain, some pain, settle it down, so it can never get away from you again.

Questions for Discussion

1. What is the type of female body that is being described in each of the seven numbered sections? What point does Atwood make about each type of female body? What point does she make about the female body in general?
2. What is the central issue of each of the sections?
3. What is the body "hunting for" in the first section?
4. What comparisons does Atwood make between female and male bodies? What does Atwood think about men?
5. Why might Atwood have chosen the accessories that she lists in the second section?
6. Atwood writes some of her passages as lists, such as the list of descriptive phrases in the first section, and the list of accessories in the second section. What tone do these lists establish? What purpose do the lists serve?
7. How would you characterize the humor in this essay? What kind of humor is it? How does Atwood want you to respond to the humor? What is serious about her humor?

Questions for Reflection and Writing

1. Using Atwood's format and style, write a satire about another controversial topic, such as managed health care, higher education, political correctness, multiculturalism, alternative lifestyles, or freedom of speech.

2. Compare the style of this essay to another piece in your anthology that uses unusual formatting, style, or point of view. What techniques do both pieces use? In your opinion, how effective are the techniques?

3. Reread Atwood's essay, looking for the points she makes or implies about how false images of the female body have been created. Using outside sources about advertising, cinema, fashion dolls, and so forth, write an essay in which you explain how false images have been or can be created.

Mary and Martha

Luke 10:38-42

Now as they went along, he came to this village where a woman named Martha welcomed him into her home. And she had a sister named Mary, who sat at the Lord's feet and listened to his words. But Martha kept getting distracted because she was doing all the serving. So she went up <to Jesus> and said, "Lord, doesn't it matter to you that my sister has left me with all the serving? Tell her to give me a hand."

"But the Lord answered her, "Martha, Martha, you are worried and upset about a lot of things. But only one thing is necessary. Mary has made the better choice, and it is something she will never lose."

Tradition or Torture?

Human rights activists and healthcare providers strive to abolish female circumcision.

Lucia Carruthers

In the battle to end female circumcision activists face a fierce and resilient adversary: 1
tradition. In Africa, where an estimated 60 to 90 million women are circumcised,
female genital mutilation is a revered custom and a part of the peoples' identity.

"It's deeply connected with sacredness, religion, social status, and perceptions of 2
sexuality," says Dr. Oyeronke Olajubu, a visiting scholar and lecturer on Women's
Studies in Religion at Harvard University and a professor at the University of Llorin
in Nigeria.

Opponents insist that despite its long-standing role in African culture, female cir- 3
cumcision is a flagrant human rights violation that results in devastating physical and
mental consequences. One point everyone can agree on: The decision to end this
ancient practice must come from the people.

A Brutal Legacy

The type of circumcision and age at which girls undergo the procedure vary among 4
regions, says Hanny Lightfoot-Klein, a leading author and researcher on female genital mutilation. This practice is found primarily in Africa, in some Middle Eastern
countries, and in immigrant populations virtually all over the world.

Most African women undergo a clitoridectomy, the removal of all or part of the 5
clitoris. About 15 percent of women experience the most severe form of circumcision, which is called infibulation. In this procedure, the clitoris and labia minora are
removed and the labia majora stitched together with thread or thorns, leaving a
matchstick-size hole for urine and menstrual blood to escape. The girls are then
bound from ankles to hips while they heal.

Lightfoot-Klein says circumcision is often performed under unsanitary conditions 6
with primitive, dull instruments and no antibiotics. Medical repercussions are grave.
Common complications include hemorrhage, shock, urine retention, HIV, chronic
pain, infection in the urinary and reproductive tracts, bladder and urethra stones,
damming of menstrual blood, and infertility. In Sudan, where Lightfoot-Klein conducted most of her research, she estimates a 10 to 30 percent fatality rate.

The discomfort and health risks don't end, even for those who experience few   7
complications. For intercourse and childbirth, the infibulation must be cut, torn, or
stretched and the woman again sutured. Frequent recircumcision can lead to excessive scar tissue buildup, disease, and life-long pain.

Anecdotal evidence suggests this practice also leaves deep mental scars.   8
Circumcised women report feelings of anxiety, betrayal, lack of confidence, worth-
lessness, and depression. For African girls and their mothers, the prospect of being
unmarried is worse than being mutilated.

"In Sudan, men would not under any circumstances consider marrying an uncir-   9
cumcised or unclean girl," Lightfoot-Klein says. "Since marriage and childbearing
are virtually the only options for most African women, this leaves them little choice
but to submit to the practice."

A Nation's Identity

Despite the custom's apparent brutality, Olajubu says circumcision is an inherent part   10
of the tribal system.

"African men and women perceive circumcision as a requirement to become an   11
adult, and most of the time, they don't need an explanation for it," she says. "It's simply part of their life experience."

Many proponents believe circumcision offers social, moral, and health benefits.   12
Some use this rite to impart tribal law and teachings about women's role in society.
In his book Facing Mt. Kenya, Jomo Kenyatta, the late president of Kenya, explains
that the Gikuyu use the rite of passage from childhood to adulthood to record events
of national importance.

"The history and legends of the people are explained and remembered according   13
to the names given to various age-groups at the time of the initiation ceremony," he
says. The Gikuyu have been able to record the time when the European introduced
syphilis. Those initiated at the time when this disease first emerged are called gatego,
[meaning] syphilis."

Other common reasons for circumcision: to ensure women don't indulge in ille-   14
gitimate sex and to enhance the husband's sexual pleasure. Some people, including
the Sudanese, believe the clitoris will grow and hang between a woman's legs if not
circumcised. This so-called male part is considered dangerous if it touches an emerging baby or a man's penis. In most societies that practice female genital mutilation,
circumcision marks a girl's purification and transformation into womanhood.

A Faith Debate

In Egypt, 97 percent of women still endure circumcision despite urging from the   15
Sheikh of al-Azhar, the highest religious authority in the country, to ban the practice. Most communities that practice female genital mutilation today follow animist
religions; however, Amnesty International reports circumcision practices among
small numbers of Christian, Jewish, and Islamic women.

Female circumcision often is erroneously tied to Islam, Lightfoot-Klein says,   16
despite the fact that 80 percent of Muslims don't practice the custom. The small percentage who cite religion as the reason say the mandate comes directly from sayings
attributed to Mohammed, even though the Qur'an never mentions the procedure.

Most opponents deny any religious connection and insist it is a regional practice.   17

The minority Ethiopian Jewish population and some Christian converts still   18
practice female genital mutilation, as well. Christian missionaries have had little success stopping this tradition, and in some cases have overlooked it to gain converts.

A Campaign of Understanding

Female genital mutilation is a human rights issue that has captured world attention, says   19
Jane Connors, Chief of the Women's Rights Unit of the United Nations Division for the
Advancement of Women.

The UN's efforts to abolish this practice combine policymaking and education. During   20
the 1990s, nine African countries adopted legislation to criminalize this circumcision,
Connors says. Nevertheless, the practice thrives.

"Legislation sets a standard that not everyone will follow," she says. "It provides an   21
important framework, but laws alone won't stop this practice."

So what will? Most efforts focus on education, with the hope of spawning a grass-roots   22
movement to abolish female genital mutilation. Like the anti-foot-binding societies in
China, anti-circumcision societies have squelched the practice among some people in
Senegal, Lightfoot-Klein says.

"Now that they understand the monstrous health problems associated with FGM,   23
whole villages have decided that they won't circumcise their daughters, and they won't let
their sons marry a circumcised woman," she says. "This spreads to other communities, and
soon there are six or eight other villages from which they can draw men and women to
marry."

Change is slowgoing, in part because of what Olajubu sees as a class problem.   24

"This movement is coming from the elites and academicians—people who don't   25
always take into consideration that this is part of the people's identity," she says. "We
shouldn't condemn them but seek to understand and appreciate why they do this and then
modify what's harmful about the custom. Only then can meaningful conversation take
place."

Simone de Beauvoir (1908–1986), a teacher, editor, essayist, short story writer, and novelist, was born in Paris and earned a degree in Philosophy from the Sorbonne in 1929. In 1943 de Beauvoir founded the left-wing review *Les Temps Modernes* with Jean-Paul Sartre. Among her enduring works are the groundbreaking *The Second Sex* (1952), a feminist classic, and *The Coming of Age* (1973), a philosophical look at the aging process. Her novel *The Blood of Others* (1948) was made into a movie in 1984, directed by Claude Chabrol and starring Jodie Foster. "The Making of a Woman," in which she examines how society and culture determine gender roles, is an excerpt from *The Second Sex.*

The Making of a Woman

Simone de Beauvoir

The passivity that is the essential characteristic of the "feminine" woman is a 1
trait that develops in her from the earliest years. But it is wrong to assert that a
biological datum is concerned; it is in fact a destiny imposed upon her by her
teachers and by society. The great advantage enjoyed by the boy is that his mode
of existence in relation to others leads him to assert his subjective freedom. His
apprenticeship for life consists in free movement toward the outside world; he
contends in hardihood and independence with other boys, he scorns girls.
Climbing trees, fighting with his companions, facing them in rough games, he
feels his body as a means for dominating nature and as a weapon for fighting; he
takes pride in his muscles as in his sex; in games, sports, fights, challenges, trials
of strength, he finds a balanced exercise of his powers; at the same time he
absorbs the severe lessons of violence; he learns from an early age to take blows,
to scorn pain, to keep back the tears. He undertakes, he invents, he dares.
Certainly he tests himself also as if he were another; he challenges his own manhood, and many problems result in relation to adults and to other children. But
what is very important is that there is no fundamental opposition between his
concern for that objective figure which is his, and his will to self-realization in
concrete projects. It is by *doing* that he creates his existence, both in one and the
same action.

    In woman, on the contrary, there is from the beginning a conflict between 2
her autonomous existence and her objective self, her "being-the-other"; she is

taught that to please she must try to please, she must make herself object; she should therefore renounce her autonomy. She is treated like a live doll and is refused liberty. Thus a vicious circle is formed; for the less she exercises her freedom to understand, to grasp and discover the world about her, the less resources will she find within herself, the less will she dare to affirm herself as subject. If she were encouraged in it, she could display the same lively exuberance, the same curiosity, the same initiative, the same hardihood, as a boy. This does happen occasionally, when the girl is given a boyish bringing up; in this case she is spared many of the problems.[1] It is noteworthy that this is the kind of education a father prefers to give his daughter; and women brought up under male guidance very largely escape the defects of femininity. But custom is opposed to treating girls like boys. I have known of little village girls of three or four being compelled by their fathers to wear trousers.[2] All the other children teased them: "Are they girls or boys?"—and they proposed to settle the matter by examination. The victims begged to wear dresses. Unless the little girl leads an unusually solitary existence, a boyish way of life, though approved by her parents, will shock her entourage, her friends, her teachers. There will always be aunts, grandmothers, cousins around to counteract the father's influence. Normally he is given a secondary role with respect to his daughters' training. One of the curses that weigh heavily upon women—as Michelet has justly pointed out—is to be left in women's hands during childhood. The boy, too, is brought up at first by his mother, but she respects his maleness and he escapes very soon,[3] whereas she fully intends to fit her daugh-ter into the feminine world.

We shall see later how complex the relations of mother to daughter are: the daughter is for the mother at once her double and another person, the mother is at once overweeningly affectionate and hostile toward her daughter; she saddles her child with her own destiny: a way of proudly laying claim to her own femininity and also a way of revenging herself for it. The same process is to be found in pederasts, gamblers, drug addicts, in all who at once take pride in belonging to a certain confraternity and feel humiliated by the association: they endeavor with eager proselytism to gain new adherents. So, when a child comes under their care, women apply themselves to changing her into a woman like themselves, manifesting a zeal in which arrogance and resentment are mingled; and even a generous mother, who sincerely seeks her child's welfare, will as a rule think that it is wiser to make a "true woman" of her, since society will more readily accept her if this is done. She is therefore given little girls for playmates, she is entrusted to female teachers, she lives among the older women as in the days of the Greek gynaeceum, books and games are chosen for her which initiate her into her destined sphere, the treasures of feminine wisdom are poured into her ears, feminine virtues are urged upon her, she is taught cooking, sewing, housekeeping, along with care of her person, charm, and modesty; she is dressed in inconvenient and frilly clothes of which she has to be careful, her hair is done up in fancy style, she is given rules of deportment: "Stand up straight, don't walk like a duck"; to develop grace she must repress her spontaneous movements; she is told not to act like a would-be boy, she is forbidden violent exercises, she is not allowed to fight. In brief, she is pressed to become, like her elders, a servant and an idol. Today, thanks to the conquests of feminism, it is becoming more and more normal to encourage the young girl to get an education, to devote herself to sports; but lack of success in these fields is more readily pardoned in her than in a boy; and success is made harder by the demands made upon her for another kind of accomplishment: at any rate she must be also a woman, she must not lose her femininity.

When very young the girl child resigns herself to all this without too much trouble. The child moves on the play and dream level, playing at being, playing at doing; to do and to be are not clearly distinguished when one is concerned only with imaginary accomplishments. The little girl can compensate for the present superiority of the boys by the promises that are inherent in her womanly destiny and that she already fulfills in play. Because she knows as yet only her childhood universe, her mother at first seems to her to be endowed with more authority than her father; she imagines the world to be a kind of matriarchate; she imitates her mother and identifies herself with her; frequently she even reverses their respective roles: "When I am big and you are little . . ." she likes to say to her mother. The doll is not only her double; it is also her child. These two functions do not exclude each other, inasmuch as the real child is also an alter ego for the mother. When she scolds, punishes, and then consoles her doll, she is at once vindicating herself as against her mother and assuming, herself, the dignity of a mother: she combines in herself the two elements of the mother-daughter pair. She confides in her doll, she brings it up, exercises upon it her sovereign authority, sometimes even tears off its arms, beats it, tortures it. Which is to say she experiences subjective affirmation and identification through the doll. The child plays with her mother at being father and mother of the doll, making a couple that excludes the man. Here again there is no "maternal instinct," innate and mysterious. The little girl ascertains that the care of children falls upon the mother, she is so taught; stories heard, books read, all her little experiences confirm the

4

idea. She is encouraged to feel the enchantment of these future riches, she is given dolls so that these values may henceforth have a tangible aspect. Her "vocation" is powerfully impressed upon her. . . .

In addition to this hope which playing with dolls makes concrete, family   5
life provides the little girl with other possibilities for self-expression. A large part of the housework is within the capability of a very young child; the boy is commonly excused, but his sister is allowed, even asked, to sweep, dust, peel vegetables, wash the baby, watch the soup kettle. In particular, the eldest sister is often concerned in this way with motherly tasks; whether for convenience or because of hostility and sadism, the mother thus rids herself of many of her functions; the girl is in this manner made to fit precociously into the universe of serious affairs; her sense of importance will help her in assuming her femininity. But she is deprived of happy freedom, the carefree aspect of childhood; having become precociously a woman, she learns all too soon the limitations this estate imposes upon a human being; she reaches adolescence as an adult, which gives her history a special character. A child overburdened with work may well become prematurely a slave, doomed to a joyless existence. But if no more than an effort suited to her powers is asked of her, she is proud to feel herself as capable as a grown-up and she enjoys sharing responsibility with adults. This equal sharing is possible because it is not a far cry from child to housekeeper. A man expert in his trade is separated from the stage of childhood by his years of apprenticeship. Thus the little boy finds his father's activities quite mysterious, and the man he is to become is hardly sketched out in him at all. On the contrary, the mother's activities are quite accessible to the girl; "she is already a little woman," as her parents say; and it is sometimes held that she is more precocious than the boy. In truth, if she is nearer to the adult stage it is because this stage in most women remains traditionally more or less infantile. The fact is that the girl is conscious of her precocity, that she takes pride in playing the little mother toward the younger children; she is glad to become important, she talks sensibly, she gives orders, she assumes airs of superiority over her brothers of infantile rank, she converses on a footing of equality with her mother.

In spite of all these compensations, she does not accept without regret the   6
fate assigned to her; as she grows, she envies the boys their vigor. Parents and grandparents may poorly conceal the fact that they would have preferred male offspring to female; or they may show more affection for the brother than the sister. Investigations make it clear that the majority of parents would rather have sons than daughters. Boys are spoken to with greater seriousness and esteem, they

are granted more rights; they themselves treat girls scornfully; they play by themselves, not admitting girls to their group, they offer insults: for one thing, calling girls "prissy" or the like and thus recalling the little girls' secret humiliation. In France, in mixed schools, the boys' caste deliberately oppresses and persecutes the girls' caste.

If the girls want to struggle with the boys and fight for their rights, they are   7
reprimanded. They are doubly envious of the activities peculiar to the boys: first, because they have a spontaneous desire to display their power over the world, and, second, because they are in protest against the inferior status to which they are condemned. For one thing, they suffer under the rule forbidding them to climb trees and ladders or on roofs. Adler remarks that the notions of high and low have great importance, the idea of elevation in space implying a spiritual superiority, as may be seen in various heroic myths; to attain a summit, a peak, is to stand out beyond the common world of fact as sovereign subject (ego); among boys, climbing is frequently a basis for challenge. The little girl, to whom such exploits are forbidden and who, seated at the foot of a tree or cliff, sees the triumphant boys high above her, must feel she is, body and soul, their inferior. And it is the same if she is left behind in a race or jumping match, if she is thrown down in a scuffle or simply kept on the side lines.

As she becomes more mature, her universe enlarges, and masculine superi-   8
ority is perceived still more clearly. Very often identification with the mother no longer seems to be a satisfying solution; if the little girl at first accepts her feminine vocation, it is not because she intends to abdicate; it is, on the contrary, in order to rule; she wants to be a matron because the matrons' group seems privileged; but when her company, her studies, her games, her reading, take her out of the maternal circle, she sees that it is not the women but the men who control the world. It is this revelation—much more than the discovery of the penis—that irresistibly alters her conception of herself.

The relative rank, the hierarchy, of the sexes is first brought to her atten-   9
tion in family life; little by little she realizes that if the father's authority is not that which is most often felt in daily affairs, it is actually supreme; it only takes on more dignity from not being degraded to daily use; and even if it is in fact the mother who rules as mistress of the household, she is commonly clever enough to see to it that the father's wishes come first; in important matters the mother demands, rewards, and punishes in his name and through his authority. The life of the father has a mysterious prestige: the hours he spends at home, the room where he works, the objects he has around him, his pursuits, his hobbies, have a

sacred character. He supports the family, and he is the responsible head of the family. As a rule his work takes him outside, and so it is through him that the family communicates with the rest of the world: he incarnates that immense, difficult, and marvelous world of adventure; he personifies transcendence, he is God.[4] This is what the child feels physically in the powerful arms that lift her up, in the strength of his frame against which she nestles. Through him the mother is dethroned as once was Isis by Ra, and the Earth by the Sun.

But here the child's situation is profoundly altered: she was to become one   10
day a woman like her all-powerful mother—she will never be the sovereign father; the bond attaching her to her mother was an active emulation—from her father she can but passively await an expression of approval. The boy thinks of his father's superiority with a feeling of rivalry; but the girl has to accept it with impotent admiration. I have already pointed out that what Freud calls the Electra complex is not, as he supposes, a sexual desire; it is a full abdication of the subject, consenting to become object in submission and adoration. If her father shows affection for his daughter, she feels that her existence is magnificently justified; she is endowed with all the merits that others have to acquire with difficulty; she is fulfilled and deified. All her life she may longingly seek that lost state of plenitude and peace. If the father's love is withheld, she may ever after feel herself guilty and condemned; or she may look elsewhere for a valuation of herself and become indifferent to her father or even hostile. Moreover, it is not alone the father who holds the keys to the world: men in general share normally in the prestige of manhood; there is no occasion for regarding them as "father substitutes." It is directly, as men, that grandfathers, older brothers, uncles, playmates' fathers, family friends, teachers, priests, doctors, fascinate the little girl. The emotional concern shown by adult women toward Man would of itself suffice to perch him on a pedestal.[5]

Everything helps to confirm this hierarchy in the eyes of the little girl. The   11
historical and literary culture to which she belongs, the songs and legends with which she is lulled to sleep, are one long exaltation of man. It was men who built up Greece, the Roman Empire, France, and all other nations, who have explored the world and invented the tools for its exploitation, who have governed it, who have filled it with sculptures, paintings, works of literature. Children's books, mythology, stories, tales, all reflect the myths born of the pride and the desires of men; thus it is that through the eyes of men the little girl discovers the world and reads therein her destiny.

The superiority of the male is, indeed, overwhelming: Perseus, Hercules, 12 David, Achilles, Lancelot, the old French warriors Du Guesclin and Bayard, Napoleon—so many men for one Joan of Arc; and behind her one descries the great male figure of the archangel Michael! Nothing could be more tiresome than the biographies of famous women: they are but pallid figures compared with great men; and most of them bask in the glory of some masculine hero. Eve was not created for her own sake but as a companion for Adam, and she was made from his rib. There are few women in the Bible of really high renown: Ruth did no more than find herself a husband. Esther obtained favor for the Jews by kneeling before Ahasuerus, but she was only a docile tool in the hands of Mordecai; Judith was more audacious, but she was subservient to the priests, and her exploit, of dubious aftertaste, is by no means to be compared with the clean, brilliant triumph of young David. The goddesses of pagan mythology are frivolous or capricious, and they all tremble before Jupiter. While Prometheus magnificently steals fire from the sun, Pandora opens her box of evils upon the world.

There are in legend and story, to be sure, witches and hags who wield fear- 13 ful powers. Among others, the figure of the Mother on the Winds in Andersen's Garden of Paradise recalls the primitive Great Goddess: her four gigantic sons obey her in fear and trembling, she beats them and shuts them up in sacks when they misbehave. But these are not attractive personages. More pleasing are the fairies, sirens, and undines, and these are outside male domination; but their existence is dubious, hardly individualized; they intervene in human affairs but have no destiny of their own: from the day when Andersen's little siren becomes a woman, she knows the yoke of love, and suffering becomes her lot. . . .

Endnotes

1. At least during early childhood. Under present social conditions, the conflicts of adolescence, on the contrary, may well be exaggerated.
2. Quite in accordance with current American fashion!–Tr.
3. There are of course many exceptions; but we cannot undertake here to study the part played by the mother in the boy's development.
4. "His generous presence inspired great love and extreme fear in me," says Mme de Noailles in speaking of her father. "At first he astounded me. The first man astounds a little girl. I felt strongly that everything depended upon him."
5. It is noteworthy that the worship of the father is to be met with especially in the eldest of the children, and indeed a man is more interested in his first

paternity than in later ones; he often consoles his daughter, as he consoles his son, when their mother is monopolized by newcomers, and she is likely to become ardently attached to him. On the contrary, a younger sister never can have her father all to herself, without sharing him; she is commonly jealous at once of him and of her elder sister; she attaches herself to that same elder sister whom the father's favor invests with high prestige, or she turns to her mother, or she revolts against the family and looks for help outside. In many families the youngest daughter gains a privileged position in some other way. Many things, of course, can motivate special preferences in the father. But almost all the cases I know of confirm this observation on the different attitudes of the older and younger sisters.

Questions for Discussion

1. Why does the author put quotation marks around the word "feminine" in the first paragraph?
2. The author makes use of many examples to bolster her claims. Do these provide effective support for her claims? Explain why or why not.
3. How does the figure of the doll function as a symbol in this essay?
4. According to de Beauvoir, what role does upbringing have in promoting gender difference?
5. How does the author describe girls' shifting views of the hierarchy of the family as they grow up? Explain with details from the reading.

Questions for Reflection and Writing

1. How would you describe your relationship with your mother? How does your own gender relate to this relationship? Can you relate this relationship to your reading of de Beauvoir's piece?
2. Since this piece was written in 1953, major changes have occurred in family structure in the United States. Identify some of these changes. Do these changes affect the way we read this essay today? Is the essay as relevant now as it was when it was written?
3. Do you think gender is culturally shaped or biologically determined? Take a position on this notoriously thorny issue and respond to de Beauvoir's piece. Personal experience may be used as partial support, but be sure to look outside your own history for evidence. Online, try searching on +"biology" +"destiny" +"feminism" (or a similar combination of terms).

Charlotte Perkins Gilman (1860–1935), a feminist, a suffragist, and a writer, also wrote under the name Charlotte Perkins Stetson. Her writing took a wide variety of forms: novels, nonfiction, science fiction, and poetry. Similarly, she herself took a variety of roles: teacher, commercial artist, editor, lecturer, and social activist. Gilman edited periodicals in California in the 1890s, cofounded the Women's Peace Party, and wrote and published the periodical *Forerunner* almost single-handedly between the years 1909 and 1916.

Abandoned by her father as an infant, Gilman later received lists from her father of books he considered important. Gilman's mother withheld affection from her in the belief that she could prevent her daughter from needing love. Therefore, Gilman spent considerable time with relatives such as Harriet Beecher Stowe, the abolitionist author of *Uncle Tom's Cabin*.

Gilman became involved in California's Women's Congresses in the mid-1890s and toured the United States and England advocating reform of women's rights and labor. Some of her many works include *In This Our World* (poems, 1893); *Women and Economics* (1898); *Concerning Children* (1900); *The Home: Its Work and Influence* (1903); *Human Work* (1904); *The Punishment That Educates* (1907); and *His Religion and Hers: A Study of the Faith of Our Fathers and the Work of Our Mothers* (1923). Her novels include *Moving the Mountain* (1911), *Herland* (1915), and *With Her in Ourland* (1916). Gilman also penned utopian novels celebrating the inspirational, communal nature of motherhood. Gilman is best known today for her autobiographical novella *The Yellow Wallpaper* (1892). She divorced her first husband in 1894 after suffering postpartum depression, she married George Gilman in 1900 and apparently enjoyed this marriage until terminal cancer drove her to suicide in 1935.

The Yellow Wallpaper

Charlotte Perkins Gilman

It is very seldom that mere ordinary people like John and myself secure ancestral halls for the summer.   1

A colonial mansion, a hereditary estate, I would say a haunted house and reach the height of romantic felicity—but that would be asking too much of fate!   2

Still I will proudly declare that there is something queer about it.   3

Else, why should it be let so cheaply? And why have stood so long untenanted?   4

John laughs at me, of course, but one expects that.   5

John is practical in the extreme. He has no patience with faith, an intense horror of superstition, and he scoffs openly at any talk of things not to be felt and seen and put down in figures.   6

John is a physician, and *perhaps*—(I would not say it to a living soul, of   7
course, but this is dead paper and a great relief to my mind)—*perhaps* that is one
reason I do not get well faster.

You see, he does not believe I am sick! And what can one do?   8

If a physician of high standing, and one's own husband, assures friends and   9
relatives that there is really nothing the matter with one but temporary nervous
depression—a slight hysterical tendency—what is one to do?

My brother is also a physician, and also of high standing, and he says the   10
same thing.

So I take phosphates or phosphites—whichever it is—and tonics, and air   11
and exercise, and journeys, and am absolutely forbidden to "work" until I am well
again.

Personally, I disagree with their ideas.   12

Personally, I believe that congenial work, with excitement and change,   13
would do me good.

But what is one to do?   14

I did write for a while in spite of them; but it *does* exhaust me a good deal—   15
having to be so sly about it, or else meet with heavy opposition.

I sometimes fancy that in my condition, if I had less opposition and more   16
society and stimulus—but John says the very worst thing I can do is to think
about my condition, and I confess it always makes me feel bad.

So I will let it alone and talk about the house.   17

The most beautiful place! It is quite alone, standing well back from the   18
road, quite three miles from the village. It makes me think of English places that
you read about, for there are hedges and walls and gates that lock, and lots of separate little houses for the gardeners and people.

There is a *delicious* garden! I never saw such a garden—large and shady, full   19
of box-bordered paths, and lined with long grape-covered arbors with seats under
them.

There were greenhouses, but they are all broken now.   20

There was some legal trouble, I believe, something about the heirs and co-   21
heirs; anyhow, the place has been empty for years.

That spoils my ghostliness, I am afraid, but I don't care—there is something   22
strange about the house—I can feel it.

I even said so to John one moonlight evening, but he said what I felt was   23
a draught, and shut the window.

I get unreasonably angry with John sometimes. I'm sure I never used to be   24
so sensitive. I think it is due to this nervous condition.

But John says if I feel so I shall neglect proper self-control; so I take pains   25
to control myself—before him, at least, and that makes me very tired.

I don't like our room a bit. I wanted one downstairs that opened onto the   26
piazza and had roses all over the window, and such pretty old-fashioned chintz
hangings! But John would not hear of it.

He said there was only one window and not room for two beds, and no near   27
room for him if he took another.

He is very careful and loving, and hardly lets me stir without special direc-   28
tion.

I have a schedule prescription for each hour in the day; he takes all care   29
from me, and so I feel basely ungrateful not to value it more.

He said he came here solely on my account, that I was to have perfect rest   30
and all the air I could get. "Your exercise depends on your strength, my dear," said
he, "and your food somewhat on your appetite; but air you can absorb all the
time." So we took the nursery at the top of the house.

It is a big, airy room, the whole floor nearly, with windows that look all   31
ways, and air and sunshine galore. It was nursery first, and then playroom and
gymnasium, I should judge, for the windows are barred for little children, and
there are rings and things in the walls.

The paint and paper look as if a boys' school had used it. It is stripped off—   32
the paper—in great patches all around the head of my bed, about as far as I can
reach, and in a great place on the other side of the room low down. I never saw
a worse paper in my life. One of those sprawling, flamboyant patterns committing every artistic sin.

It is dull enough to confuse the eye in following, pronounced enough con-   33
stantly to irritate and provoke study, and when you follow the lame uncertain
curves for a little distance they suddenly commit suicide—plunge off at outrageous angles, destroy themselves in unheard-of contradictions.

The color is repellent, almost revolting: a smouldering unclean yellow,   34
strangely faded by the slow-turning sunlight. It is a dull yet lurid orange in some
places, a sickly sulphur tint in others.

No wonder the children hated it! I should hate it myself if I had to live in   35
this room long.

There comes John, and I must put this away—he hates to have me write   36
a word.

We have been here two weeks, and I haven't felt like writing before, since   37
that first day.

I am sitting by the window now, up in this atrocious nursery, and there is   38
nothing to hinder my writing as much as I please, save lack of strength.

John is away all day, and even some nights when his cases are serious.   39

I am glad my case is not serious!   40

But these nervous troubles are dreadfully depressing.   41

John does not know how much I really suffer. He knows there is no reason   42
to suffer, and that satisfies him.

Of course it is only nervousness. It does weigh on me so not to do my duty   43
in any way!

I meant to be such a help to John, such a real rest and comfort, and here I   44
am a comparative burden already!

Nobody would believe what an effort it is to do what little I am able—to   45
dress and entertain, and order things.

It is fortunate Mary is so good with the baby. Such a dear baby!   46

And yet I *cannot* be with him, it makes me so nervous.   47

I suppose John never was nervous in his life. He laughs at me so about this   48
wallpaper!

At first he meant to repaper the room, but afterward he said that I was let-   49
ting it get the better of me, and that nothing was worse for a nervous patient than
to give way to such fancies.

He said that after the wallpaper was changed it would be the heavy bed-   50
stead, and then the barred windows, and then that gate at the head of the stairs,
and so on.

"You know the place is doing you good," he said, "and really, dear, I don't   51
care to renovate the house just for a three months' rental."

"Then do let us go downstairs," I said. "There are such pretty rooms there."   52

Then he took me in his arms and called me a blessed little goose, and said   53
he would go down cellar, if I wished, and have it whitewashed into the bargain.

But he is right enough about the beds and windows and things.   54

It is as airy and comfortable a room as anyone need wish, and, of course, I   55
would not be so silly as to make him uncomfortable just for a whim.

I'm really getting quite fond of the big room, all but that horrid paper.   56

Out of one window I can see the garden—those mysterious deep-shaded   57
arbors, the riotous old-fashioned flowers, and bushes and gnarly trees.

Out of another I get a lovely view of the bay and a little private wharf   58
belonging to the estate. There is a beautiful shaded lane that runs down there
from the house. I always fancy I see people walking in these numerous paths and
arbors, but John has cautioned me not to give way to fancy in the least. He says
that with my imaginative power and habit of story-making, a nervous weakness
like mine is sure to lead to all manner of excited fancies, and that I ought to use
my will and good sense to check the tendency. So I try.

I think sometimes that if I were only well enough to write a little it would   59
relieve the press of ideas and rest me.

But I find I get pretty tired when I try.   60

It is so discouraging not to have any advice and companionship about my   61
work. When I get really well, John says we will ask Cousin Henry and Julia down
for a long visit; but he says he would as soon put fireworks in my pillow-case as
to let me have those stimulating people about now.

I wish I could get well faster.   62

But I must not think about that. This paper looks to me as if it *knew* what   63
a vicious influence it had!

There is a recurrent spot where the pattern lolls like a broken neck and two   64
bulbous eyes stare at you upside down.

I get positively angry with the impertinence of it and the everlastingness.   65
Up and down and sideways they crawl, and those absurd unblinking eyes are
everywhere. There is one place where two breadths didn't match, and the eyes
go all up and down the line, one a little higher than the other.

I never saw so much expression in an inanimate thing before, and we all   66
know how much expression they have! I used to lie awake as a child and get
more entertainment and terror out of blank walls and plain furniture than most
children could find in a toy-store.

I remember what a kindly wink the knobs of our big old bureau used to   67
have, and there was one chair that always seemed like a strong friend.

I used to feel that if any of the other things looked too fierce I could always   68
hop into that chair and be safe.

The furniture in this room is no worse than inharmonious, however, for we   69
had to bring it all from downstairs. I suppose when this was used as a playroom
they had to take the nursery things out, and no wonder! I never saw such ravages as the children have made here.

The wallpaper, as I said before, is torn off in spots, and it sticketh closer   70
than a brother—they must have had perseverance as well as hatred.

Then the floor is scratched and gouged and splintered, the plaster itself is   71
dug out here and there, and this great heavy bed, which is all we found in the
room, looks as if it had been through the wars.

But I don't mind it a bit—only the paper.   72

There comes John's sister. Such a dear girl as she is, and so careful of me! I   73
must not let her find me writing.

She is a perfect and enthusiastic housekeeper, and hopes for no better pro-   74
fession. I verily believe she thinks it is the writing which made me sick!

But I can write when she is out, and see her a long way off from these win-   75
dows.

There is one that commands the road, a lovely shaded winding road, and   76
one that just looks off over the country. A lovely country, too, full of great elms
and velvet meadows.

This wallpaper has a kind of sub-pattern in a different shade, a particularly   77
irritating one, for you can only see it in certain lights, and not clearly then.

But in the places where it isn't faded and where the sun is just so—I can   78
see a strange, provoking, formless sort of figure that seems to skulk about behind
that silly and conspicuous front design.

There's sister on the stairs!   79

Well, the Fourth of July is over! The people are all gone, and I am tired out.   80
John thought it might do me good to see a little company, so we just had Mother
and Nellie and the children down for a week.

Of course I didn't do a thing. Jennie sees to everything now.   81

But it tired me all the same.   82

John says if I don't pick up faster he shall send me to Weir Mitchell in the   83
fall.

But I don't want to go there at all. I had a friend who was in his hands once,   84
and she says he is just like John and my brother, only more so!

Besides, it is such an undertaking to go so far.   85

I don't feel as if it was worthwhile to turn my hand over for anything, and   86
I'm getting dreadfully fretful and querulous.

I cry at nothing, and cry most of the time.   87

Of course I don't when John is here, or anybody else, but when I am alone.   88

And I am alone a good deal just now. John is kept in town very often by   89
serious cases, and Jennie is good and lets me alone when I want her to.

So I walk a little in the garden or down that lovely lane, sit on the porch 90
under the roses, and lie down up here a good deal.

I'm getting really fond of the room in spite of the wallpaper. Perhaps 91
because of the wallpaper.

It dwells in my mind so! 92

I lie here on this great immovable bed—it is nailed down, I believe—and 93
follow that pattern about by the hour. It is as good as gymnastics, I assure you. I
start, we'll say, at the bottom, down in the corner over there where it has not
been touched, and I determine for the thousandth time that I *will* follow that
pointless pattern to some sort of a conclusion.

I know a little of the principle of design, and I know this thing was not 94
arranged on any laws of radiation, or alternation, or repetition, or symmetry, or
anything else that I ever heard of.

It is repeated, of course, by the breadths, but not otherwise. 95

Looked at in one way, each breadth stands alone; the bloated curves and 96
flourishes—a kind of "debased Romanesque" with delirium tremens go waddling
up and down in isolated columns of fatuity.

But, on the other hand, they connect diagonally, and the sprawling out- 97
lines run off in great slanting waves of optic horror, like a lot of wallowing sea-
weeds in full chase.

The whole thing goes horizontally, too, at least it seems so, and I exhaust 98
myself trying to distinguish the order of its going in that direction.

They have used a horizontal breadth for a frieze, and that adds wonderful- 99
ly to the confusion.

There is one end of the room where it is almost intact, and there, when the 100
crosslights fade and the low sun shines directly upon it, I can almost fancy radiation after all—the interminable grotesque seems to form around a common
center and rush off in headlong plunges of equal distraction.

It makes me tired to follow it. I will take a nap, I guess. 101

I don't know why I should write this. 102

I don't want to. 103

I don't feel able. 104

And I know John would think it absurd. But I must say what I feel and 105
think in some way—it is such a relief!

But the effort is getting to be greater than the relief. 106

Half the time now I am awfully lazy, and lie down ever so much. John says   107
I mustn't lose my strength, and has me take cod liver oil and lots of tonics and
things, to say nothing of ale and wine and rare meat.

Dear John! He loves me very dearly, and hates to have me sick. I tried to   108
have a real earnest reasonable talk with him the other day, and tell him how I
wish he would let me go and make a visit to Cousin Henry and Julia.

But he said I wasn't able to go, nor able to stand it after I got there; and I   109
did not make out a very good case for myself, for I was crying before I had finished.

It is getting to be a great effort for me to think straight. Just this nervous   110
weakness, I suppose.

And dear John gathered me up in his arms, and just carried me upstairs and   111
laid me on the bed, and sat by me and read to me till it tired my head.

He said I was his darling and his comfort and all he had, and that I must   112
take care of myself for his sake, and keep well.

He says no one but myself can help me out of it, that I must use my will   113
and self-control and not let any silly fancies run away with me.

There's one comfort—the baby is well and happy, and does not have to   114
occupy this nursery with the horrid wallpaper.

If we had not used it, that blessed child would have! What a fortunate   115
escape! Why, I wouldn't have a child of mine, an impressionable little thing, live
in such a room for worlds.

I never thought of it before, but it is lucky that John kept me here after all;   116
I can stand it so much easier than a baby, you see.

Of course I never mention it to them any more—I am too wise—but I keep   117
watch for it all the same.

There are things in that wallpaper that nobody knows about but me, or   118
ever will.

Behind that outside pattern the dim shapes get clearer every day.   119

It is always the same shape, only very numerous.   120

And it is like a woman stooping down and creeping about behind that pat-   121
tern. I don't like it a bit. I wonder—I begin to think—I wish John would take me
away from here!

It is so hard to talk with John about my case, because he is so wise, and   122
because he loves me so.

But I tried it last night.   123

It was moonlight. The moon shines in all around just as the sun does.   124

I hate to see it sometimes, it creeps so slowly, and always comes in by one 125 window or another.

John was asleep and I hated to waken him, so I kept still and watched the 126 moonlight on that undulating wallpaper till I felt creepy.

The faint figure behind seemed to shake the pattern, just as if she wanted 127 to get out.

I got up softly and went to feel and see if the paper did move, and when I 128 came back John was awake.

"What is it, little girl?" he said. "Don't go walking about like that—you'll 129 get cold."

I thought it was a good time to talk, so I told him that I really was not gain- 130 ing here, and that I wished he would take me away.

"Why, darling!" said he. "Our lease will be up in three weeks, and I can't 132 see how to leave before."

"The repairs are not done at home, and I cannot possibly leave town just 132 now. Of course, if you were in any danger, I could and would, but you really are better, dear, whether you can see it or not. I am a doctor, dear, and I know. You are gaining flesh and color, your appetite is better, I feel really much easier about you."

"I don't weigh a bit more," said I, "nor as much; and my appetite may be 133 better in the evening when you are here but it is worse in the morning when you are away!"

"Bless her little heart!" said he with a big hug. "She shall be as sick as she 134 pleases! But now let's improve the shining hours by going to sleep, and talk about it in the morning!"

"And you won't go away?" I asked gloomily. 135

"Why, how can I, dear? It is only three weeks more and then we will take 136 a nice little trip of a few days while Jennie is getting the house ready. Really, dear, you are better!"

"Better in body perhaps—" I began, and stopped short, for he sat up straight 137 and looked at me with such a stern, reproachful look that I could not say anoth- er word.

"My darling," said he, "I beg of you, for my sake and for our child's sake, as 138 well as for your own, that you will never for one instant let that idea enter your mind! There is nothing so dangerous, so fascinating, to a temperament like yours. It is a false and foolish fancy. Can you not trust me as a physician when I tell you so?"

So of course I said no more on that score, and we went to sleep before long. 139
He thought I was asleep first, but I wasn't, and lay there for hours trying to decide whether that front pattern and the back pattern really did move together or separately.

On a pattern like this, by daylight, there is a lack of sequence, a defiance of 140
law, that is a constant irritant to a normal mind but the pattern is torturing.

The color is hideous enough, and unreliable enough, and infuriating 141
enough, but the pattern is torturing.

You think you have mastered it, but just as you get well under way in fol- 142
lowing, it turns a back-somersault and there you are. It slaps you in the face, knocks you down, and tramples upon you. It is like a bad dream.

The outside pattern is a florid arabesque, reminding one of a fungus. If you 143
can imagine a toadstool in joints, an interminable string of toadstools, budding and sprouting in endless convolutions—why, that is something like it.

That is, sometimes! 144

There is one marked peculiarity about this paper, a thing nobody seems to 145
notice but myself, and that is that it changes as the light changes.

When the sun shoots in through the east window—I always watch for that 146
first long, straight ray—it changes so quickly that I never can quite believe it.

That is why I watch it always. 147

By moonlight—the moon shines in all night when there is a moon—I 148
wouldn't know it was the same paper.

At night in any kind of light, in twilight, candlelight, lamplight, and worst 149
of all by moonlight, it becomes bars! The outside pattern, I mean, and the woman behind it is as plain as can be.

I didn't realize for a long time what the thing was that showed behind, that 150
dim sub-pattern, but now I am quite sure it is a woman.

By daylight she is subdued, quiet. I fancy it is the pattern that keeps her so 151
still. It is so puzzling. It keeps me quiet by the hour.

I lie down ever so much now. John says it is good for me, and to sleep all I 152
can.

Indeed he started the habit by making me lie down for an hour after each 153
meal.

It is a very bad habit, I am convinced, for you see, I don't sleep. 154
And that cultivates deceit, for I don't tell them I'm awake—oh, no! 155
The fact is I am getting a little afraid of John. 156
He seems very queer sometimes, and even Jennie has an inexplicable look. 157

It strikes me occasionally, just as a scientific hypothesis, that perhaps it is 158 the paper!

I have watched John when he did not know I was looking, and come into 159 the room suddenly on the most innocent excuses, and I've caught him several times *looking at the paper!* And Jennie too. I caught Jennie with her hand on it once.

She didn't know I was in the room, and when I asked her in a quiet, a very 160 quiet voice, with the most restrained manner possible, what she was doing with the paper, she turned around as if she had been caught stealing, and looked quite angry—asked me why I should frighten her so!

Then she said that the paper stained everything it touched, that she had 161 found yellow smooches on all my clothes and John's and she wished we would be more careful!

Did not that sound innocent? But I know she was studying that pattern, 162 and I am determined that nobody shall find it out but myself!

Life is very much more exciting now than it used to be. You see, I have 163 something more to expect, to look forward to, to watch. I really do eat better, and am more quiet than I was.

John is so pleased to see me improve! He laughed a little the other day, and 164 said I seemed to be flourishing in spite of my wallpaper.

I turned it off with a laugh. I had no intention of telling him it was *because* 165 of the wallpaper—he would make fun of me. He might even want to take me away.

I don't want to leave now until I have found it out. There is a week more, 166 and I think that will be enough.

I'm feeling so much better! 167

I don't sleep much at night, for it is so interesting to watch developments; 168 but I sleep a good deal during the daytime.

In the daytime it is tiresome and perplexing. 169

There are always new shoots on the fungus, and new shades of yellow all 170 over it. I cannot keep count of them, though I have tried conscientiously.

It is the strangest yellow, that wallpaper! It makes me think of all the yel- 171 low things I ever saw—not beautiful ones like buttercups, but old, foul, bad yellow things.

But there is something else about that paper—the smell! I noticed it the 172 moment we came into the room, but with so much air and sun it was not bad.

Now we have had a week of fog and rain, and whether the windows are open or not, the smell is here.

It creeps all over the house.   173

I find it hovering in the dining-room, skulking in the parlor, hiding in the   174
hall, lying in wait for me on the stairs.

It gets into my hair.   175

Even when I go to ride, if I turn my head suddenly and surprise it—there   176
is that smell!

Such a peculiar odor, too! I have spent hours in trying to analyze it, to find   177
what it smelled like.

It is not bad—at first—and very gentle, but quite the subtlest, most endur-   178
ing odor I ever met.

In this damp weather it is awful. I wake up in the night and find it hang-   179
ing over me.

It used to disturb me at first. I thought seriously of burning the house—to   180
reach the smell.

But now I am used to it. The only thing I can think of that it is like is the   181
color of the paper! A yellow smell.

There is a very funny mark on this wall, low down, near the mopboard. A   182
streak that runs around the room. It goes behind every piece of furniture, except
the bed, a long, straight, even *smooch*, as if it had been rubbed over and over.

I wonder how it was done and who did it, and what they did it for. Round   183
and round and round—round and round and round—it makes me dizzy!

I really have discovered something at last.   184

Through watching so much at night, when it changes so, I have finally   185
found out.

The front pattern *does* move—and no wonder! The woman behind shakes   186
it!

Sometimes I think there are a great many women behind, and sometimes   187
only one, and she crawls around fast, and her crawling shakes it all over.

Then in the very bright spots she keeps still, and in the very shady spots   188
she just takes hold of the bars and shakes them hard.

And she is all the time trying to climb through. But nobody could climb   189
through that pattern—it strangles so; I think that is why it has so many heads.

They get through and then the pattern strangles them off and turns them   190
upside down, and makes their eyes white!

If those heads were covered or taken off it would not be half so bad.   191

I think that woman gets out in the daytime! 192

And I'll tell you why—privately—I've seen her! 193

I can see her out of every one of my windows! 194

It is the same woman, I know, for she is always creeping, and most women 195 do not creep by daylight.

I see her in that long shaded lane, creeping up and down. I see her in those 196 dark grape arbors, creeping all around the garden.

I see her on that long road under the trees, creeping along, and when a car- 197 riage comes she hides under the blackberry vines.

I don't blame her a bit. It must be very humiliating to be caught creeping 198 by daylight!

I always lock the door when I creep by daylight. I can't do it at night, for I 199 know John would suspect something at once.

And John is so queer now that I don't want to irritate him. I wish he would 200 take another room! Besides, I don't want anybody to get that woman out at night but myself.

I often wonder if I could see her out of all the windows at once. 201

But, turn as fast as I can, I can only see out of one at one time. 202

And though I always see her, she *may* be able to creep faster than I can 203 turn! I have watched her sometimes away off in the open country, creeping as fast as a cloud shadow in a wind.

If only that top pattern could be gotten off from the under one! I mean to 204 try it, little by little.

I have found out another funny thing, but I shan't tell it this time! It does 205 not do to trust people too much.

There are only two more days to get this paper off, and I believe John is 206 beginning to notice. I don't like the look in his eyes.

And I heard him ask Jennie a lot of professional questions about me. She 207 had a very good report to give.

She said I slept a good deal in the daytime. 208

John knows I don't sleep very well at night, for all I'm so quiet! 209

He asked me all sorts of questions, too, and pretended to be very loving and 210 kind.

As if I couldn't see through him! 211

Still, I don't wonder he acts so, sleeping under this paper for three months. 212 It only interests me, but I feel sure John and Jennie are affected by it.

Hurrah! This is the last day, but it is enough. John is to stay in town over 214
night, and won't be out until this evening.

Jennie wanted to sleep with me—the sly thing; but I told her I should 215
undoubtedly rest better for a night all alone.

That was clever, for really I wasn't alone a bit! As soon as it was moonlight 216
and that poor thing began to crawl and shake the pattern, I got up and ran to
help her.

I pulled and she shook. I shook and she pulled, and before morning we had 217
peeled off yards of that paper.

A strip about as high as my head and half around the room.   218

And then when the sun came and that awful pattern began to laugh at me, 219
I declared I would finish it today!

We go away tomorrow, and they are moving all my furniture down again 220
to leave things as they were before.

Jennie looked at the wall in amazement, but I told her merrily that I did it 221
out of pure spite at the vicious thing.

She laughed and said she wouldn't mind doing it herself, but I must not get 222
tired.

How she betrayed herself that time!   223

But I am here, and no person touches this paper but Me—not *alive!*   224

She tried to get me out of the room—it was too patent! But I said it was so 225
quiet and empty and clean now that I believed I would lie down again and sleep
all I could, and not to wake me even for dinner—I would call when I woke.

So now she is gone, and the servants are gone, and the things are gone, and 226
there is nothing left but that great bedstead nailed down, with the canvas mat-
tress we found on it.

We shall sleep downstairs tonight, and take the boat home tomorrow.   227

I quite enjoy the room, now it is bare again.   228

How those children did tear about here!   229

This bedstead is fairly gnawed!   230

But I must get to work.   231

I have locked the door and thrown the key down into the front path.   232

I don't want to go out, and I don't want to have anybody come in, till John 233
comes.

I want to astonish him.   234

I've got a rope up here that even Jennie did not find. If that woman does 235
get out, and tries to get away, I can tie her!

But I forgot I could not reach far without anything to stand on!   236

This bed will *not* move!   237

I tried to lift and push it until I was lame, and then I got so angry I bit off   238
a little piece at one corner—but it hurt my teeth.

Then I peeled off all the paper I could reach standing on the floor. It sticks   239
horribly and the pattern just enjoys it! All those strangled heads and bulbous eyes
and waddling fungus growths just shriek with derision.

I am getting angry enough to do something desperate. To jump out of the   240
window would be admirable exercise, but the bars are too strong to even try.

Besides I wouldn't do it. Of course not. I know well enough that a step like   241
that is improper and might be misconstrued.

I don't like to *look* out of the windows even—there are so many of those   242
creeping women, and they creep so fast.

I wonder if they all come out of that wallpaper as I did?   243

But I am securely fastened now by my well-hidden rope—you don't get *me*   244
out in the road there!

I suppose I shall have to get back behind the pattern when it comes night,   245
and that is hard!

It is so pleasant to be out in this great room and creep around as I please!   246

I don't want to go outside. I won't even if Jennie asks me to.   247

For outside you have to creep on the ground, and everything is green   248
instead of yellow.

But here I can creep smoothly on the floor, and my shoulder just fits in that   249
long smooch around the wall, so I cannot lose my way.

Why, there's John at the door!   250

It is no use, young man, you can't open it!   251

How he does call and pound!   252

Now he's crying to Jennie for an axe.   253

It would be a shame to break down that beautiful door!   254

"John, dear!" said I in the gentlest voice. "The key is down by the front   255
steps, under a plantain leaf!"

That silenced him for a few moments.   256

Then he said, very quietly indeed, "Open the door, my darling!"   257

"I can't," said I. "The key is down by the front door under a plantain leaf!"   258
And then I said it again, several times, very gently and slowly, and said it so often
that he had to go and see, and he got it of course, and came in. He stopped short
by the door.

"What is the matter?" he cried. "For God's sake, what are you doing!"   259

I kept on creeping just the same, but I looked at him over my shoulder.   260

"I've got out at last," said I, "in spite of you and Jane. And I've pulled off   261
most of the paper, so you can't put me back!"

Now why should that man have fainted? But he did, and right across my   262
path by the wall, so that I had to creep over him every time!

Question for Discussion

1. What does the yellow wallpaper represent—to the narrator, to other characters, to readers?

2. How would you characterize the relationship between the narrator and her husband? What does the story say about women's experiences?

3. What criticisms of the medical profession does the story make?

4. Is the narrator insane or not? What passages in the story indicate this to you?

5. What senses are used in this story? Why might Gilman have made the narrator so sensitive to physical sensation?

6. Why does the narrator tell her story in short sentences? What is the general effect of so many short sentences and paragraphs? What image is created of the narrator by the sentence style?

7. What objects besides the wallpaper does Gilman personify? How do these things have a life of their own? How do they "interact" with the human characters?

Questions for Reflection and Writing

1. What might John's story be? Write the tale from the point of view of John or another character.

2. Interpret this story. What is Gilman telling us?

3. Compare this story to another story or essay on the topic of marriage, insanity, or women's experiences. How does each author construct a tale about the topic? How do themes, settings, and characters interact?

Patricia Hill Collins (1948–   ) was born in Philadelphia and earned a Ph.D. from Brandeis University in 1984. She has taught sociology and African American studies at the University of Cincinnati since 1987. She often writes about gender, race, and class, and her books include *Race, Class, and Gender: An Anthology* (1992) (which she compiled with Margaret L. Andersen), and *Fighting Words: Black Women and the Search for Justice* (1998). Here, Collins analyzes previous studies of black motherhood and comes up with some very different conclusions. "Black Women and Motherhood" is an excerpt from *Black Feminist Thought: Knowledge, Consciousness, and the Politics of Empowerment* (1990).

Black Women and Motherhood

Patricia Hill Collins

Just yesterday I stood for a few minutes at the top of the stairs leading to a white doctor's office in a white neighborhood. I watched one Black woman after another trudge to the corner, where she then waited to catch the bus home. These were Black women still cleaning somebody else's house or Black women still caring for somebody else's sick or elderly, before they came back to the frequently thankless chores of their own loneliness, their own families. And I felt angry and I felt ashamed. And I felt, once again, the kindling heat of my hope that we, the daughters of these Black women, will honor their sacrifice by giving them thanks. We will undertake, with pride, every transcendent dream of freedom made possible by the humility of their love.

June Jordan 1985, 105

June Jordan's words poignantly express the need for Black feminists to honor our   1
mothers' sacrifice by developing an Afrocentric feminist analysis of Black motherhood. Until recently analyses of Black motherhood have largely been the province of men, both white and Black, and male assumptions about Black women as mothers have prevailed. Black mothers have been accused of failing to discipline their children, of emasculating their sons, of defeminizing their daughters, and of retarding their children's academic achievement (Wade-Gayles 1980). Citing high rates of divorce, female-headed households, and out-of-wedlock births, white male scholars and their representatives claim that African-American mothers wield unnatural power in allegedly deteriorating

"Black Women and Motherhood" in *Black Feminist Thought* by Patricia Hill Collins. Reprinted by permission of HarperCollins Publishers—UK.

family structures (Moynihan 1965; Zinn 1989). The African-American mothers observed by Jordan vanish from these accounts.

White feminist work on motherhood has failed to produce an effective cri-   2
tique of elite white male analyses of Black motherhood. Grounded in a white, middle-class women's standpoint, white feminist analyses have been profoundly affected by the limitations that this angle of vision has on race (Chodorow 1974, 1978; Chodorow and Contratto 1982). While white feminists have effectively confronted white male analyses of their own experiences as mothers, they rarely challenge controlling images such as the mammy, the matriarch, and the welfare mother and therefore fail to include Black mothers "still cleaning somebody else's house or . . . caring for somebody else's sick or elderly." As a result, white feminist theories have had limited utility for African-American women (Joseph 1984).

In African-American communities the view has been quite different. As   3
Barbara Christian contends, the "concept of motherhood is of central impor-tance in the philosophy of both African and Afro-American peoples" (1985, 213). But in spite of its centrality, Black male scholars in particular typically glo-rify Black motherhood by refusing to acknowledge the issues faced by Black mothers who "came back to the frequently thankless chores of their own loneli-ness, their own families." By claiming that Black women are richly endowed with devotion, self-sacrifice, and unconditional love—the attributes associated with archetypal motherhood—Black men inadvertently foster a different controlling image for Black women, that of the "super-strong Black mother" (Stapes 1973; Dance 1979). In many African-American communities so much sanctification surrounds Black motherhood that "the idea that mothers should live lives of sac-rifice has come to be seen as the norm" (Christian 1985, 234).

Far too many Black men who praise their own mothers feel less account-   4
able to the mothers of their own children. They allow their wives and girlfriends to support the growing numbers of African-American children living in poverty (Frazier 1948; Burnham 1985; U.S. Department of Commerce 1986, 1989). Despite the alarming deterioration of economic and social supports for Black mothers, large numbers of young men encourage their unmarried teenaged girl-friends to give birth to children whose futures are at risk (Ladner 1972; Ladner and Gourdine 1984; Simms 1988). Even when they are aware of the poverty and struggles these women face, many Black men cannot get beyond the powerful controlling image of the super-strong Black mother in order to see the very real

costs of mothering to African-American women. Michele Wallace describes the tenacity of this controlling image:

> I remember once I was watching a news show with a black male friend of mine who had a Ph.D. in psychology and was the director of an out-patient clinic. We were looking at some footage of a black woman. . . . She was in bed wrapped in blankets, her numerous small, poorly clothed children huddled around her. Her apartment looked rat-infested, cramped, and dirty. She had not, she said, had heat and hot water for days. My friend, a solid member of the middle class now but surely no stranger to poverty in his childhood, felt obliged to comment . . . "That's a strong sister," as he bowed his head in reverence. (1978, 108–9)

The absence of a fully articulated Afrocentric feminist standpoint on motherhood is striking but not particularly surprising. While Black women have produced insightful critiques of both white male and white feminist analyses of motherhood (King 1973; Davis 1981; Gilkes 1983a; Hooks 1981), we have paid far less attention to Black male views. This silence partly reflects the self-imposed restrictions that accompany African-Americans' efforts to present a united front to the dominant group. Part of Black women's reluctance to challenge Black men's ideas in particular stems from the vehement attacks sustained by those Black feminist scholars, such as Michele Wallace, Alice Walker, and Ntozake Shange, who have been perceived as critical of Black men (see, for example, Stapes 1979). But much of our silence emanates from an unwillingness to criticize Black men's well-intentioned efforts to defend and protect Black womanhood. Glorifying the strong Black mother represents Black men's attempts to replace negative white male interpretations with positive Black male ones. But no matter how sincere, externally defined definitions of Black womanhood— even those offered by sympathetic African-American men— are bound to come with their own set of problems.

In the case of Black motherhood, the problems have been a stifling of dialogue among African-American women and the perpetuation of troublesome, controlling images, both negative and positive. As Renita Weems observes: "We have simply sat and nodded while others talked about the magnificent women who bore and raised them and who, along with God, made a way out of no way. . . . We paid to hear them lecture about the invincible strength and genius of the

Black mother, knowing full well that the image can be as bogus as the one of the happy slave" (1984, 27).

African-American women need an Afrocentric feminist analysis of moth-   7
erhood that debunks the image of "happy slave," whether the white-male-creat-
ed "matriarch" or the Black-male-perpetuated "superstrong Black mother." Some
of the classic sociological and ethnographic work on African-American families
gives a comprehensive sense of how Black women mother (Herskovits 1941;
Young 1970; Ladner 1972; Stack 1974; Aschenbrenner 1975; Dougherty 1978;
Dill 1980). This emphasis on Black women's actions has recently been enriched
by an outpouring of research on Black women's ideas by Black women scholars
(McCray 1980; Joseph 1981, 1984; Rollins 1985; D. White 1985; Sage 1984,
1987). When coupled with the explorations of Black women's consciousness
extant in Black women's autobiographies, fiction, and Black feminist literary
criticism (Walker 1983; Washington 1984; Christian 1985), these sources offer
the rich conceptual terrain of a Black women's standpoint from which an
Afrocentric feminist analysis of African-American motherhood can emerge.

Exploring A Black Women's Standpoint on Mothering

The institution of Black motherhood consists of a series of constantly renegoti-   8
ated relationships that African-American women experience with one another,
with Black children, with the larger African-American community, and with
self. These relationships occur in specific locations such as the individual households that make up African-American extended family networks, as well as in
Black community institutions (Martin and Martin 1978; Sudarkasa 1981b).
Moreover, just as Black women's work and family experiences varied during the
transition from slavery to the post–World War II political economy, how Black
women define, value, and shape Black motherhood as an institution shows comparable diversity.

Black motherhood as an institution is both dynamic and dialectical. An   9
ongoing tension exists between efforts to mold the institution of Black motherhood to benefit systems of race, gender, and class oppression and efforts by
African-American women to define and value our own experiences with motherhood. The controlling images of the mammy, the matriarch, and the welfare
mother and the practices they justify are designed to oppress. In contrast, motherhood can serve as a site where Black women express and learn the power of
self-definition, the importance of valuing and respecting ourselves, the necessity
of self-reliance and independence, and a belief in Black women's empowerment.

This tension leads to a continuum of responses. Some women view motherhood as a truly burdensome condition that stifles their creativity, exploits their labor, and makes them partners in their own oppression. Others see motherhood as providing a base for self-actualization, status in the Black community, and a catalyst for social activism. These alleged contradictions can exist side by side in African-American communities and families and even within individual women.

Embedded in these changing relationships are five enduring themes that   10 characterize a Black women's standpoint on Black motherhood. For any given historical moment, the particular form that Black women's relationships with one another, children, community, and self actually take depends on how this dialectical relationship between the severity of oppression facing African-American women and our actions in resisting that oppression is expressed.

Bloodmothers, Othermothers, and Women-Centered Networks
In African-American communities, fluid and changing boundaries often distin-   11 guish biological mothers from other women who care for children. Biological mothers, or bloodmothers, are expected to care for their children. But African and African-American communities have also recognized that vesting one person with full responsibility for mothering a child may not be wise or possible. As a result, othermothers—women who assist bloodmothers by sharing mothering responsibilities—traditionally have been central to the institution of Black motherhood (Troester 1984).

The centrality of women in African-American extended families reflects   12 both a continuation of West African cultural values and functional adaptations to race and gender oppression (Tanner 1974; Stack 1974; Aschenbrenner 1975; Martin and Martin 1978; Sudarkasa 1981b; Reagon 1987). This centrality is not characterized by the absence of husbands and fathers. Men may be physically present and/or have well-defined and culturally significant roles in the extended family and the kin unit may be woman-centered. Bebe Moore Campbell's (1989) parents separated when she was small. Even though she spent the school year in the North Philadelphia household maintained by her grandmother and mother, Campbell's father assumed an important role in her life. "My father took care of me," Campbell remembers. "Our separation didn't stunt me or condemn me to a lesser humanity. His absence never made me a fatherless child. I'm not fatherless now" (p. 271). In woman-centered kin units such as Campbell's—whether a mother-child household unit, a married couple household, or a larger unit extending over several households—the centrality of mothers is not predicated on male powerlessness (Tanner 1974, 133).

Organized, resilient, women-centered networks of bloodmothers and oth-   13
ermothers are key in understanding this centrality. Grandmothers, sisters, aunts, or cousins act as othermothers by taking on child-care responsibilities for one another's children. When needed, temporary child-care arrangements can turn into long-term care of informal adoption (Stack 1974; Gutman 1976). Despite strong cultural norms encouraging women to become biological mothers, women who choose not to do so often receive recognition and status from oth-ermother relationships that they establish with Black children.

In African-American communities these women-centered networks of   14
community-based child care often extend beyond the boundaries of biologically related individuals and include "fictive kin" (Stack 1974). Civil rights activist Ella Baker describes how informal adoption by othermothers functioned in the rural southern community of her childhood:

> My aunt who had thirteen children of her own raised three more. She had
> become a midwife, and a child was born who was covered with sores.
> Nobody was particularly wanting the child, so she took the child and raised
> him . . . and another mother decided she didn't want to be bothered with
> two children. So my aunt took one and raised him . . . they were part of the
> family. (Cantarow 1980, 59)

Even when relationships are not between kin or fictive kin, African-   15
American community norms traditionally were such that neighbors cared for one anothers' children. Sara Brooks, a southern domestic worker, describes the importance that the community-based child care a neighbor offered her daugh-ter had for her: "She kept Vivian and she didn't charge me nothin either. You see, people used to look after each other, but now its not that way. I reckon its because we all was poor, and I guess they put theirself in the place of the person that they was helpin" (Simonsen 1986, 181). Brooks's experiences demonstrate how the African-American cultural value placed on cooperative child care tra-ditionally found institutional support in the adverse conditions under which so many Black women mothered.

Othermothers are key not only in supporting children but also in helping   16
bloodmothers who, for whatever reason, lack the preparation or desire for moth-erhood. In confronting racial oppression, maintaining community-based child

care and respecting othermothers who assume child-care responsibilities serve a critical function in African-American communities. Children orphaned by sale or death of their parents under slavery, children conceived through rape, children of young mothers, children born into extreme poverty or to alcoholic or drug-addicted mothers, or children who for other reasons cannot remain with their bloodmothers have all been supported by othermothers, who, like Ella Baker's aunt, take in additional children even when they have enough of their own.

Young women are often carefully groomed at an early age to become other- 17
mothers. As a ten-year-old, civil rights activist Ella Baker learned to be an othermother by caring for the children of a widowed neighbor: "Mama would say, 'You must take the clothes to Mr. Powell's house, and give so-and-so a bath.' The children were running wild. . . . The kids . . . would take off across the field. We'd chase them down, and bring them back, and put 'em in the tub, and wash 'em off, and change clothes, and carry the dirty ones home, and wash them. Those kind of things were routine" (Cantarow 1980, 59).

Many Black men also value community-based child care but exercise these 18
values to a lesser extent. Young Black men are taught how to care for children (Young 1970; Lewis 1975). During slavery, for example, Black children under age ten experienced little division of labor. They were dressed alike and performed similar tasks. If the activities of work and play are any dictation of the degree of gender role differentiation that existed among slave children, "then young girls probably grew up minimizing the difference between the sexes while learning far more about the differences between the races" (D. White 1985, 94). Differences among Black men and women in attitudes toward children may have more to do with male labor force patterns. As Ella Baker observes, "my father took care of people too, but . . . my father had to work" (Cantarow 1980, 60).

Historically, community-based child care and the relationships among 19
bloodmothers and othermothers in women-centered networks have taken diverse institutional forms. In some polygynous West African societies, the children of the same father but different mothers referred to one another as brothers and sisters. While a strong bond existed between the biological mother and her child—one so strong that, among the Ashanti for example, "to show disrespect towards one's mother is tantamount to sacrilege" (Fortes 1950, 263)—children could be disciplined by any of their other "mothers." Cross-culturally, the high status given to othermothers and the cooperative nature of child-care arrangements among bloodmothers and othermothers in Caribbean and other Black

societies gives credence to the importance that people of African descent place on mothering (Clarke 1966; Shimkin et al. 1978; Sudarkasa 1981a, 1981b).

Although the political economy of slavery brought profound changes to   20 enslaved Africans, cultural values concerning the importance of motherhood and the value of cooperative approaches to child care continued. While older women served as nurses and midwives, their most common occupation was caring for the children of parents who worked (D. White 1985). Informal adoption of orphaned children reinforced the importance of social motherhood in African-American communities (Gutman 1976).

The relationship between bloodmothers and othermothers survived the   21 transition from a slave economy to postemancipation southern rural agriculture. Children in southern rural communities were not solely the responsibility of their biological mothers. Aunts, grandmothers, and others who had time to supervise children served as othermothers (Young 1970; Dougherty 1978). The significant status women enjoyed in family networks and in African-American communities continued to be linked to their bloodmother and othermother activities.

The entire community structure of bloodmothers and othermothers is   22 under assault in many inner-city neighborhoods, where the very fabric of African-American community life is being eroded by illegal drugs. But even in the most troubled communities, remnants of the othermother tradition endure. Bebe Moore Campbell's 1950s North Philadelphia neighborhood underwent some startling changes when crack cocaine flooded the streets in the 1980s. Increases in birth defects, child abuse, and parental neglect left many children without care. But some residents, such as Miss Nee, continue the othermother tradition. After raising her younger brothers and sisters and five children of her own, Miss Nee cares for three additional children whose families fell apart. Moreover, on any given night Miss Nee's house may be filled by up to a dozen children because she has a reputation for never turning away a needy child ("Children of the Underclass" 1989).

Traditionally, community-based child care certainly has been functional for   23 African-American communities and for Black women. Black feminist theorist Bell Hooks suggests that the relationships among bloodmothers and othermothers may have greater theoretical importance than currently recognized:

This form of parenting is revolutionary in this society because it takes place in opposition to the ideas that parents, especially mothers, should be the only childrearers. . . . This kind of shared responsibility for child care can happen in small community settings where people know and trust one another. It cannot happen in those settings if parents regard children as their "property," their possession. (1984, 144)

The resiliency of women-centered family networks illustrates how tradi-   24
tional cultural values—namely, the African origins of community-based child care—can help people cope with and resist oppression. By continuing commu- nity-based child care, African-American women challenge one fundamental assumption underlying the capitalist system itself: that children are "private property" and can be disposed of as such. Notions of property, child care, and gender differences in parenting styles are embedded in the institutional arrange- ments of any given political economy. Under the property model stemming from capitalist patriarchal families, parents may not literally assert that their children are pieces of property, but their parenting may reflect assumptions analogous to those they make in connection with property (Smith 1983). For example, the exclusive parental "right" to discipline children as parents see fit, even if disci- pline borders on abuse, parallels the widespread assumption that property own- ers may dispose of their property without consulting members of the larger com- munity. By seeing the larger community as responsible for children and by giv- ing othermothers and other nonparents "rights" in child rearing, African- Americans challenge prevailing property relations. It is in this sense that tradi- tional bloodmother/othermother relationships in women-centered networks are "revolutionary."

Motherhood as a Symbol of Power
Motherhood—whether bloodmother, othermother, or community othermoth-   25
er—can be invoked by African-American women as a symbol of power. Much of Black women's status in African-American communities stems not only from actions as mothers in Black family networks but from contributions as commu- nity othermothers.

Black women's involvement in fostering African-American community   26
development forms the basis for community-based power. This is the type of power many African-Americans have in mind when they describe the "strong Black women" they see around them in traditional African-American commu- nities. Community othermothers work on behalf of the Black community by expressing ethics of caring and personal accountability which embrace concep-

tions of transformative power and mutuality (Kuykendall 1983). Such power is transformative in that Black women's relationships with children and other vulnerable community members is not intended to dominate or control. Rather, its purpose is to bring people along, to—in the words of late-nineteenth-century Black feminists—"uplift the race" so that vulnerable members of the community will be able to attain the self-reliance and independence essential for resistance.

When older African-American women invoke their power as community   27 othermothers, the results can be quite striking. Karen Fields recounts a telling incident:

> One night . . . as Grandmother sat crocheting alone at about two in the morning, a young man walked into the living room carrying the portable TV from upstairs. She said, "Who are you looking for this time of night?" As Grandmother [described] the incident to me over the phone, I could hear a tone of voice that I know well. It said, "Nice boys don't do that." So I imagine the burglar heard his own mother or grandmother at that moment. He joined in the familial game just created: "Well, he told me that I could borrow it." "Who told you?" "John." "Um um, no John lives here. You got the wrong house." (Fields and Fields 1983, xvi)

After this dialogue, the teenager turned around, went back upstairs, and returned the television.

In local African-American communities, community othermothers   28 become identified as powerful figures through furthering the community's well-being. Sociologist Charles Johnson (1934/1979) describes the behavior of an elderly Black woman at a church service in rural 1930s Alabama. Even though she was not on the program, the woman stood up to speak. The master of ceremonies rang for her to sit down, but she refused to do so claiming, "I am the mother of this church, and I will say what I please" (p. 172). The master of ceremonies offered the following explanation to the congregation as to why he let the woman continue: "Brothers, I know you all honor Sister Moore. Course our time is short but she has acted as a mother to me. . . . Any time old folks get up I give way to them" (p. 173).

The View From the Inside: The Personal Meaning of Mothering

Within African-American communities, women's innovative and practical ap-   29
proaches to mothering under oppressive conditions often bring power and recognition. But this situation should not obscure the costs of motherhood to many
Black women. Black motherhood is fundamentally a contradictory institution.
African-American communities value motherhood, but Black mothers' ability
to cope with race, class, and gender oppression should not be confused with transcending those conditions. Black motherhood can be rewarding, but it can also
extract high personal costs. The range of Black women's reactions to motherhood reflect motherhood's contradictory nature.

Certain dimensions of Black motherhood are clearly problematic. Coping   30
with unwanted pregnancies and being unable to care for one's children is oppressive. Sara Brooks remembers, "I had babies one after another because I never
knew how to avoid havin babies and I didn't ask nobody, so I didn't know nothin. . . . After I separated from my husband, I still didn't know nothin, so there
come Vivian" (Simonsen 1986, 174). Brooks became pregnant again even
though she was unmarried and had three children from a previous marriage
whom she could not support. Brooks describes the strain placed on Black women
who must mother under oppressive conditions: "I hated it. . . . I didn't want no
other baby. I couldn't hardly take care of myself, and I had other kids I'da loved
to have taken care of, and I couldn't do that" (p. 177). Like Brooks, many Black
women have children they really do not want. When combined with Black community values claiming that good Black women always want their children,
ignorance about reproductive issues leaves many Black women with unplanned
pregnancies and the long-term responsibilities of parenting.

Ann Moody's mother also did not celebrate her repeated pregnancies.   31
Moody remembers her mother's feelings when her mother started "getting fat"
and her boyfriend stopped coming by: "Again Mama started crying every night.
. . . When I heard Mama crying at night, I felt so bad. She wouldn't cry until we
were all in bed and she thought we were sleeping. Every night I would lie awake
for hours listening to her sobbing quietly in her pillow. The bigger she got the
more she cried, and I did too" (Moody 1968, 46). To her children, Moody's
mother may have appeared to be the stereotypical strong Black mother, but Ann
Moody was able to see the cost her mother paid for living with this controlling
image.

Dealing with an unwanted pregnancy can have tragic consequences. All   32
Sara Brooks could think about was "doing away with this baby." She self-med-

icated herself and almost died. But she was luckier than her mother. As Brooks recalls, "my momma, she got pregnant too close behind me—it was an unwanted pregnancy—and so she taken turpentine and she taken too much, I guess, and she died. She bled to death and died" (Simonsen 1986, 160). She was not alone. Prior to the 1973 Roe v. Wade U.S. Supreme Court decision that a woman's right to personal privacy gave her the right to decide whether or not to have an abortion, large numbers of women who died from illegal abortions were Black. In New York, for example, during the several years preceding the decriminalization of abortions, 80 percent of the deaths from illegal abortions involved Black and Puerto Rican women (Davis 1981).

Strong pronatalist values in African-American communities may stem in part from traditional Black values that vest adult status on women who become biological mothers. For many, becoming a biological mother is often seen as a significant first step toward womanhood. Annie Amiker, an elderly Black woman, describes the situation in the rural Mississippi of her childhood. When asked if there were many girls with out-of-wedlock children, she replied, "there was some but not many—not many because when you run upon a girl who had a child the other girls wouldn't have nothing to do with her . . . she was counted as a grown person so she wasn't counted among the young people" (Parker 1979, 268). Joyce Ladner describes how this link between adult status and motherhood operates in low-income, urban communities: "If there was one common standard for becoming a woman that was accepted by the majority of the people in the community, it was the time when girls gave birth to their first child. This line of demarcation was extremely clear and separated the *girls* from the *women*" (1972, 212).   33

In spite of the high personal costs, Ann Moody's mother, Sara Brooks, and an overwhelming majority of unmarried Black adolescent mothers choose to keep their children (Simms 1988). Those women who give up their children can also pay high personal costs. In Alice Walker's *Meridian*, the fact that mothers cannot attend her prestigious, Black women's college forces Meridian to choose between keeping her child and going to college. After relinquishing her child, Meridian suffers physiological and psychological illness. Although she knows that her son is better cared for by others, she feels "condemned, consigned to penitence for life," for she has committed the ultimate sin against Black motherhood. Knowing that she had parted with her baby when her enslaved maternal ancestors had done anything and everything to keep their children was almost too much for Meridian to bear (Christian 1985).   34

The pain of knowing what lies ahead for Black children while feeling pow- 35
erless to protect them is another problematic dimension of Black mothering.
Michele Wallace remembers, "I can understand why my mother felt desperate.
No one else thought it would be particularly horrible if I got pregnant or got married before I had grown up, if I never completed college. I was a black girl" (1978,
98). Nineteen-year-old Harriet Jacobs, a slave mother, articulates the feelings of
Black mothers who must raise their children in dangerous and impoverished
environments: "When they told me my new-born babe was a girl, my heart was
heavier than it had ever been before. Slavery is terrible for men; but it is far more
terrible for women" (1860/1987, 46). In a 1904 letter, a Black mother in the
South wrote to a national magazine:

> I dread to see my children grow. I know not their fate. Where the white girl
> has one temptation, mine will have many. Where the white boy has every
> opportunity and protection, mine will have few opportunities and no pro-
> tection. It does not matter how good or wise my children may be, they are
> colored. When I have said that, all is said. Everything is forgiven in the
> South but color. (Lerner 1972, 158)

Protecting Black children remains a primary concern of African-American 36
mothers because Black children are at risk. Nearly 40 percent of all Black mothers receive no prenatal care in the first trimester of pregnancy. One in every eight
Black infants has a low birth weight, a factor contributing to an infant mortality rate among Black babies that remains twice that for white infants. During the
first year of life Black babies die from fires and burns at a rate 4.5 times greater
than that of white infants. The number of cases of pediatric AIDS has doubled
between 1986 and 1989, and more than 75 percent of children with AIDS are
Black or Hispanic, more than half of them the offspring of intravenous drug users
("Children of the Underclass" 1989, 27). An anonymous mother expresses her
concern for Black children:

> I turn my eyes on the little children, and keep on praying that one of them
> will grow up at the right second, when the school teachers have time to say
> hello and give him the lessons he needs, and when they get rid of the build-
> ing here and let us have a place you can breathe in and not get bitten all
> the time, and when the men can find work—because *they* can't have chil-

dren, and so they have to drink or get on drugs to find some happy moments, and some hope about things. (Lerner 1972, 315)

To this mother, even though her children are her hope, the conditions under which she must mother are intolerable.

Black mothers also pay the cost of giving up their own dreams of achieving   37
full creative ability. Because many spend so much time feeding the physical needs of their children, as Alice Walker queries, "when . . . did my overworked mother have time to know or care about feeding the creative spirit?" (1983, 239). Much of that creativity goes into dimensions of Black culture that are relatively protected from the incursions of the dominant group. Many Black women blues singers, poets, and artists manage to incorporate their art into their daily responsibilities as bloodmothers and othermothers. But for far too many African-American women who are weighed down by the incessant responsibilities of mothering others, that creative spark never finds full expression.

Harriet Jacobs's autobiography gives a clear example of one mother's denial   38
of her own self-actualization and illustrates the costs paid by Black mothers who assume the heavy responsibilities inherent in their bloodmother and othermother relationships. Jacobs desperately wanted to escape slavery but explains how having children created a particular dilemma:

> I could have made my escape alone; but it was more for my helpless children than for myself that I longed for freedom. Though the boon would have been precious to me, above all price, I would not have taken it at the expense of leaving them in slavery. Every trial I endured, every sacrifice I made for their sakes, drew them closer to my heart, and gave me fresh courage. (1860/1987, 59)

Black mothers like those of Ann Moody and June Jordan and women like Harriet Jacobs and Sara Brooks are examples of women who gave up their freedom for the sake of their children. Community othermothers like Mamie Fields and Miss Nee pay a similar cost, not for the sakes of their own biological children but for the Black community's children.

Despite the obstacles and costs, motherhood remains a symbol of hope for   39
many of even the poorest Black women. One anonymous mother describes how she feels about her children:

> To me, having a baby inside me is the only time I'm really alive. I know I
> can make something, do something, no matter what color my skin is, and
> what names people call me. . . . You can see the little one grow and get larg-
> er and start doing things, and you feel there must be some hope, some
> chance that things will get better; because there it is, right before you, a
> real, live, growing baby. . . . The baby is a good sign, or at least he's some
> sign. If we didn't have that, what would be the difference from death?
> (Lerner 1972, 314)

Given the harshness of this mother's environment, her children offer hope. They
are all she has.

Mothering is an empowering experience for many African-American   40
women. Gwendolyn Brooks (1953) explores this issue of reproductive power in
her novel *Maud Martha*. Maud Martha is virtually silent until she gives birth to
her daughter, when "pregnancy and the birth of a child connect Maud to some
power in herself, some power to speak, to be heard, to articulate feelings"
(Washington 1987, 395). Her child serves as a catalyst for her movement into
self-definition, self-valuation, and eventual empowerment. Marita Golden
describes a similar experience that illustrates how the special relationship
between mother and child can foster a changed definition of self and an accompanying empowerment:

> Now I belonged to me. No parents or husband claiming me. . . . There was
> only my child who consumed and replenished me . . . my son's love was
> unconditional and, as such, gave me more freedom than any love I had
> known. . . . I at last accepted mama as my name. Realized that it did not
> melt down any other designations. Discovered that it expanded them—
> and me. (1983, 240–241)

This special relationship that Black mothers have with their children can also
foster a creativity, a mothering of the mind and soul, for all involved. It is this gift
that Alice Walker alludes to when she notes, "and so our mothers and grandmothers have, more often than not anonymously, handed on the creative spark,
the seed of the flower they themselves never hoped to see" (1983, 240).

But what cannot be overlooked in work emphasizing mothers' influences   41
on their children is how Black children affirm their mothers and how important
that affirmation can be in a society that denigrates Blackness and womanhood.

In her essay "One Child of One's Own," Alice Walker offers a vision of what African-American mother-child relationships can be:

> It is not my child who tells me: I have no femaleness white women must affirm. Not my child who says: I have no rights black men must respect. It is not my child who has purged my face from history and herstory, and left mystory just that, a mystery; my child loves my face and would have it on every page, if she could, as I have loved my own parents' faces above all others. . . . We are together, my child and I. Mother and child, yes, but *sisters* really, against whatever denies us all that we are. (Walker 1979b, 75)

References

Aschenbrenner, Joyce. 1975. *Lifelines, Black Families in Chicago.* Prospect Heights, IL: Waveland Press.

Brooks, Gwendolyn. 1953. *Maud Martha.* Boston: Atlantic Press.

Brown, Elsa Barkley. 1989. "African-American Women's Quilting: A Framework for Conceptualizing and Teaching African-American Women's History." *Signs* 14(4): 921–29.

Burnham, Linda. 1985. "Has Poverty Been Feminized in Black America?" *Black Scholar* 16(2): 14–24.

Campbell, Bebe Moore. 1989. *Sweet Summer: Growing Up with and without My Dad.* New York: Putnam.

Cantarow, Ellen. 1980. *Moving the Mountain: Women Working for Social Change.* Old Westbury, NY: Feminist Press.

"Children of the Underclass." 1989. *Newsweek,* September 11, 16–27.

Chodorow, Nancy. 1974. "Family Structure and Feminine Personality." In *Women, Culture, and Society,* edited by Michelle Zimbalist Rosaldo and Louise Lamphere, 43–66. Stanford: Stanford University Press.

Chodorow, Nancy. 1978. *The Reproduction of Mothering.* Berkeley: University of California Press.

Chodorow, Nancy, and Susan Contratto. 1982. "The Fantasy of the Perfect Mother." In *Rethinking the Family: Some Feminist Questions,* edited by Barrie Thorne and Marilyn Yalom, 54–75. New York: Longman.

Christian, Barbara. 1985. *Black Feminist Criticism, Perspectives on Black Women Writers.* New York: Pergamon.

Clarke, Edith. 1966. *My Mother Who Fathered Me.* 2d ed. London: Allen and Unwin.

Coleman, Willi. 1987. "Closets and Keepsakes." *Sage: A Scholarly Journal on Black Women* 4(2): 34–35.

Dance, Daryl. 1979. "Black Eve or Madonna? A Study of the Antithetical View of the Mother in Black American Literature." In *Sturdy Black Bridges: Visions of Black Women in Literature*, edited by Roseann Bell, Bettye Parker, and Beverly Guy-Sheftall, 123–132. Garden City, NY: Anchor.

Davis, Angela Y. 1981. *Women, Race and Class*. New York: Random House.

Dill, Bonnie Thornton. 1980. " 'The Means to Put My Children Through': Child-Rearing Goals and Strategies among Black Female Domestic Servants." In *The Black Woman*, edited by La Frances Rodgers-Rose, 107–123. Beverly Hills, CA: Sage.

Dougherty, Molly C. 1978. *Becoming a Woman in Rural Black Culture*. New York: Holt, Rinehart and Winston.

Fields, Mamie Garvin, and Karen Fields. 1983. *Lemon Swamp and Other Places: A Carolina Memoir*. New York: Free Press.

Fortes, Meyer. 1950. "Kinship and Marriage among the Ashanti." In *African Systems of Kinship and Marriage*, edited by A. R. Radcliffe-Brown and Daryll Forde, 252–284. New York: Oxford University Press.

Frazier, E. Franklin. 1948. *The Negro Family in the United States*. New York: Dryden Press.

Giddings, Paula. 1984. *When and Where I Enter . . . The Impact of Black Women on Race and Sex in America*. New York: William Morrow.

Gilkes, Cheryl Townsend. 1980. " 'Holding Back the Ocean with a Broom': Black Women and Community Work." In *The Black Woman*, edited by La Frances Rodgers-Rose, 217–32. Beverly Hills, CA: Sage.

Gilkes, Cheryl Townsend. 1982. "Successful Rebellious Professionals: The Black Women's Professional Identity and Community Commitment." *Psychology of Women Quarterly* 6(3): 289–311.

Gilkes, Cheryl Townsend. 1983a. "From Slavery to Social Welfare: Racism and the Control of Black Women." In *Class, Race, and Sex: The Dynamics of Control*, edited by Amy Swerdlow and Hanna Lessinger, 288–300. Boston: G. K. Hall.

Gilkes, Cheryl Townsend. 1983b. "Going Up for the Oppressed: The Career Mobility of Black Women Community 'Workers." *Journal of Social Issues* 39(3): 115–39.

Golden, Marita. 1983. *Migrations of the Heart*. New York: Ballantine.

Gutman, Herbert. 1976. *The Black Family in Slavery and Freedom, 1750–1925.* New York: Random House.

Herskovits, Melville J. [1941] 1958. *The Myth of the Negro Past.* Boston: Beacon.

hooks, bell. 1981. *Ain't I a Woman: Black Women and Feminism.* Boston: South End Press.

hooks, bell. 1984. *From Margin to Center.* Boston: South End Press.

hooks, bell. 1989. *Talking Back: Thinking Feminist, Thinking Black.* Boston: South End Press.

Jacobs, Harriet. [1860] 1987. "The Perils of a Slave Woman's Life." In *Invented Lives: Narratives of Black Women 1860–1960,* edited by Mary Helen Washington, 16–67. Garden City, NY: Anchor.

Johnson, Charles S. [1934] 1979. *Shadow of the Plantation.* Chicago: University of Chicago Press.

Jordan, June. 1985. *On Call.* Boston: South End Press.

Joseph, Gloria. 1981. "Black Mothers and Daughters: Their Roles and Functions in American Society." In *Common Differences,* edited by Gloria Joseph and Jill Lewis, 75–126. Garden City, NY: Anchor.

Joseph, Gloria. 1984. "Black Mothers and Daughters: Traditional and New Perspectives." *Sage: A Scholarly Journal on Black Women* 1(2): 17–21.

King, Mae. 1973. "The Politics of Sexual Sereotypes." *Black Scholar* 4(6–7): 12–23.

Kuykendall, Eleanor H. 1983. "Toward an Ethic of Nurturance: Luce Irigaray on Mothering and Power." In *Motherhood: Essays in Feminist Theory,* edited by Joyce Treblicot, 263–274. Totowa, NJ: Rowman & Allanheld.

Ladner, Joyce. 1972. *Tomorrow's Tomorrow.* Garden City, NY: Doubleday.

Ladner, Joyce, and Ruby Morton Gourdine. 1984. "Intergenerational Teenage Motherhood: Some Preliminary Findings." *Sage: A Scholarly Journal on Black Women* 1(2): 22–24.

Lerner, Gerda, ed. 1972. *Black Women in White America: A Documentary History.* New York: Vintage.

Lewis, Diane K. 1975. "The Black Family: Socialization and Sex Roles." *Phylon* 36(3): 221–237.

Marshall, Paule. 1959. *Brown Girl, Brownstones.* New York: Avon.

Martin, Elmer, and Joanne Mitchell Martin. 1978. *The Black Extended Family.* Chicago: University of Chicago Press.

McCray, Carrie Allen. 1980. "The Black Woman and Family Roles." In *The Black Woman*, edited by La Frances Rodgers-Rose, 67–78. Beverly Hills, CA: Sage.

Moody, Ann. 1968. *Coming of Age in Mississippi*. New York: Dell.

Morrison, Tony. 1974. *Sula*. New York: Random House.

Moynihan, Daniel Patrick. 1965. *The Negro Family: The Case of National Action*. Washington, DC: GPO.

Parker, Bettye J. 1979. "Mississippi Mothers: Roots." In *Sturdy Black Bridges*, edited by Rosann Bell, Bettye Parker, and Beverly Guy-Sheftall, 263–281. Garden City, NY: Anchor.

Reagon, Bernice Johnson. 1983. "Coalition Politics: Turning the Century." In *Home Girls—A Black Feminist Anthology*, edited by Barbara Smith, 356–68. New York: Kitchen Table Press.

Reagon, Bernice Johnson. 1978. "African Diaspora Women: The Making of Cultural Workers." In *Women in Africa and the African Diaspora*, edited by Rosalyn Terborg-Penn, Sharon Harley, and Andrea Benton Rushing, 167–180. Washington, DC: Howard University Press.

Rollins, Judith. 1985. *Between Women, Domestics and Their Employers*. Philadelphia: Temple University Press.

Sage: A Scholarly Journal on Black Women. 1984. "Mothers and Daughters I." Special Issue, 1(2).

Sage: A Scholarly Journal on Black Women. 1987. "Mothers and Daughters II." Special Issue, 4(2).

Shimkin, Demitri B., Edith M. Shimkin, and Dennis A. Frate, eds. 1978. *The Extended Family in Black Societies*. Chicago: Aldine.

Simms, Margaret C. 1988. *The Choices that Young Black Women Make: Education, Employment, and Family Formation*. Working Paper No. 190, Wellesley, MA: Center for Research on Women, Wellesley College.

Simonsen, Thordis, ed. 1986. *You May Plow Here: The Narrative of Sara Brooks*. New York: Touchstone.

Smith, Janet Farrell. 1983. "Parenting as Property." In *Mothering: Essays in Feminist Theory*, edited by Joyce Trebilcot, 199–212. Totawa, NJ: Rowman & Allanheld.

Stack, Carol D. 1974. *All Our Kin: Strategies for Survival in a Black Community*. New York: Harper & Row.

Stapes, Robert. 1973. *The Black Woman in America*. Chicago: Nelson-Hall.

Stapes, Robert. 1979. "The Myth of Black Macho: A Response to Angry Black Feminists." *Black Scholar* 10(6): 24–33.

Sudarkasa, Niara. 1981a. "Female Employment and Family Organizations in West Africa." In *The Black Woman Cross-Culturally*, edited by Filomina Chioma Steady, 49–64. Cambridge, MA: Schenkman.

Sudarkasa, Niara. 1981b. "Interpreting the African Heritage in Afro-American Family Organization." In *Black Families*, edited by Harriette Pipes McAdoo, 37–53. Beverly Hills, CA: Sage.

Tanner, Nancy. 1974. "Matrifocality in Indonesia and Africa and among Black Americans." In *Woman, Culture, and Society*, edited by Michelle Z. Rosaldo and Louise Lamphere, 129–156. Stanford: Stanford University Press.

Troester, Rosalie Riegle. 1984. "Turbulence and Tenderness: Mothers, Daughters, and 'Othermothers' in Paule Marshall's *Brown Girl, Bornwstones*." *Sage: A Scholarly Journal on Black Women* 1(2): 13–16.

U.S. Department of Commerce, Bureau of the Census. 1986. *Money Income and Poverty Status of Families and Persons in the United States: 1985*. Series P-60, No. 154. Washington, DC: GPO.

U.S. Department of Commerce, Bureau of the Census. 1989. *Money Income of Households, Families, and Persons in the United States: 1987*. Series P-60, No. 162. Washington, DC: GPO.

WadeGayles, Gloria. 1980. "She Who Is Black and Mother: In Sociology and Fiction, 1940–1970." In *The Black Woman*, edited by La Frances Rodgers-Rose, 89–106. Beverly Hills, CA: Sage.

WadeGayles, Gloria. 1984. "The Truths of Our Mothers' Lives: Mother-Daughter Relationships in Black Women's Fiction." *Sage: A Scholarly Journal on Black Women* 1(2): 8–12.

Walker, Alice. 1976. *Meridian*. New York: Pocket Books.

Walker, Alice. 1979 "One Child of One's Own: A Meaningful Digression Within the Work(s)." *Ms.* 8(2), August: 47–50, 72–75.

Walker, Alice. 1983. *In Search of Our Mothers' Gardens*. New York: Harcourt Brace Jovanovich.

Wallace, Michele. 1978. *Black Macho and the Myth of the Superwoman*. New York: Dial Press.

Washington, Mary Helen. 1984. "I Sign My Mother's Name: Alice Walker, Dorothy West and Paule Marshall." In *Mothering the Mind: Twelve Studies of Writers and Their Silent Partners*, edited by Ruth Perry and Matine Watson Broronley, 143–163. New York: Holmes and Meier.

Washington, Mary Helen, ed. 1987. *Invented Lives: Narratives of Black Women 1860–1960.* Garden City, NY: Anchor.

Weems, Renita. 1984. " 'Hush. Mama's Gotta Go Bye Bye': A Personal Narrative." *Sage: A Scholarly Journal on Black Women* 1(2): 25–28.

West, Cheryl, 1987. "Lesbian Daughter." *Sage: A Scholarly Journal on Black Women* 4(2): 42–44.

White, Deborah Gray. 1985. *Ar'n't I a Woman? Female Slaves in the Plantation South.* New York: W. W. Norton.

Young, Virginia Heyer. 1970. "Family and Childhood in a Southern Negro Community." *American Anthropologist* 72(32): 269–288.

Zinn, Maxine Baca. 1989. "Family, Race, and Poverty in the Eighties." *Signs* 14(4): 856–74.

Questions for Discussion

1. How does the quoted paragraph that opens this selection function? What effect does it have on the reader?

2. What does the author see as the problem with most analyses of black motherhood that were done prior to the writing of this piece? Does her piece effectively address this problem?

3. What are "othermothers"? Why does the author coin a word to describe the concept?

4. What does the author mean when she refers to black motherhood as an "institution"? Does her use of the term make sense to you?

5. Collins has broken up this piece and given titles to the sections. Why do you think she did this? How can you characterize the titles? What would the piece lose without them?

Questions for Reflection and Writing

1. Describe your relationship with your mother. Is Collins's discussion of motherhood relevant to it in any way? Why or why not?

2. Discuss motherhood as a symbol of power. Use specific references from the text in your discussion. Does Collins's analysis make sense to you? Endorse/amplify/correct it, as necessary, using examples from your own experience and from other texts with which you are familiar.

3. The author states that white males studying black mothers have been quite critical of them, whereas these same mothers hold a place of high esteem within black communities. What do you think accounts for these differing

views? Specifically, do you think it has to do with race, gender, or both? If you'd like to go online to research this question further, you might start at The Gender Issues Research Center (www.gendercenter.org), where a site search on "African American" currently calls up several interesting studies on related topics.

Anthony Brandt (1936–   ) was born in Cranford, New Jersey, on November 21, 1936. He received a B.A. degree from Princeton University in 1958 and an M.A. degree from Columbia University in 1961. Brandt characterizes his main interest as "uncovering . . . unquestioned assumptions, the characteristic fears, obsessions, and desires" of Americans. His published works include *Reality Police: The Experience of Insanity in America* (1975), as well as articles and poems that he has also contributed to journals.

Rite of Passage

Anthony Brandt

Some things that happen to us can't be borne, with the paradoxical result that we carry them on our backs the rest of our lives. I have been half obsessed for almost thirty years with the death of my grandmother. I should say with her dying: with the long and terrible changes that came at the worst time for a boy of twelve and thirteen, going through his own difficult changes. It felt like and perhaps was the equivalent of a puberty rite: dark, frightening, aboriginal, an obscure emotional exchange between old and young. It has become part of my character.

I grew up in New Jersey in a suburban town where my brother still lives and practices law. One might best describe it as quiet, protected, and green; it was no preparation for death. Tall, graceful elm trees lined both sides of the street where we lived. My father's brother-in-law, a contractor, built our house; we moved into it a year after I was born. My grandmother and grandfather (my mother's parents; they were the only grandparents who mattered) lived up the street "on the hill"; it wasn't much of a hill, the terrain in that part of New Jersey being what it is, but we could ride our sleds down the street after it snowed, and that was hilly enough.

Our family lived, or seemed to a young boy to live, in very stable, very ordinary patterns. My father commuted to New York every day, taking the Jersey Central Railroad, riding in cars that had windows you could open, getting off the train in Jersey City and taking a ferry to Manhattan. He held the same job in the same company for more than thirty years. The son of Swedish immigrants, he

1

2

3

was a funny man who could wiggle his ears without raising his eyebrows and made up the most dreadful puns. When he wasn't being funny he was quiet, the newspaper his shield and companion, or the *Saturday Evening Post*, which he brought home without fail every Wednesday evening, or *Life*, which he brought home Fridays. It was hard to break through the quiet and the humor, and after he died my mother said, as much puzzled as disturbed, that she hardly knew him at all.

She, the backbone of the family, was fierce, stern, the kind of person who   4
can cow you with a glance. My brother and I, and my cousins, were all a little in awe of her. The ruling passion in her life was to protect her family; she lived in a set of concentric circles, sons and husband the closest, then nieces, nephews, brothers, parents, then more distant relatives, and outside that a few friends, very few. No one and nothing else existed for her; she had no interest in politics, art, history, or even the price of eggs. "Fierce" is the best word for her, or single-minded. In those days (I was born in 1936) polio was every parent's bugbear; she, to keep my brother and me away from places where the disease was supposed to be communicated, particularly swimming pools, took us every summer for the entire summer to the Jersey shore, first to her parents' cottage, later to a little cottage she and my father bought. She did that even though it meant being separated from my father for nearly three months, having nobody to talk to, having to handle my brother and me on her own. She hated it, she told us years later, but she did it: fiercely. Or there's the story of one of my cousins who got pregnant when she was sixteen or seventeen; my mother took her into our house, managed somehow to hide her condition from the neighbors, then, after the birth, arranged privately to have the child adopted by a family the doctor recommended, all this being done without consulting the proper authorities, and for the rest of her life never told a single person how she made these arrangements or where she had placed the child. She was a genuine primitive, like some tough old peasant woman. Yet her name was Grace, her nickname Bunny; if you saw through the fierceness, you understood that it was a version of love.

Her mother, my grandmother, seemed anything but fierce. One of our   5
weekly routines was Sunday dinner at their house on the hill, some five or six houses from ours. When I was very young, before World War II, the house had a mansard roof, a barn in the back, lots of yard space, lots of rooms inside, and a cherry tree. I thought it was a palace. Actually it was rather small, and became smaller when my grandmother insisted on tearing down the mansard roof and replacing it with a conventional peaked roof: the house lost three attic rooms in

the process. Sunday dinner was invariably roast beef or chicken or leg of lamb with mashed potatoes and vegetables, standard American fare but cooked by my grandparents' Polish maid, Josephine, not by my grandmother. Josephine made wonderful pies in an old cast iron coal stove and used to let me tie her with string to the kitchen sink. My grandfather was a gentle man who smoked a pipe, had a bristly reddish moustache, and always seemed to wind up paying everybody else's debts in the family: my mother worshipped him. There were usually lots of uncles at these meals, and they were a playful bunch. I have a very early memory of two of them tossing me back and forth between them, and another of the youngest, whose name was Don, carrying me on his shoulders into the surf. I also remember my grandmother presiding at these meals. She was gray-haired and benign.

Later they sold that house. My benign grandmother, I've been told since,   6
was in fact a restless, unsatisfied woman: changing the roof line, moving from house to house, were her ways of expressing that dissatisfaction. In the next house, I think it was, my grandfather died; my grandmother moved again, then again, and then to a house down the street, at the bottom of the hill this time, and there I got to know her better. I was 9 or 10 years old. She let me throw a tennis ball against the side of the house for hours at a time; the noise must have been terribly aggravating. She cooked lunch for me and used to make pancakes the size of dinner plates, and corn fritters. She also made me a whole set of yarn figures a few inches long, rolling yarn around her hand, taking the roll and tying off arms, legs, and a head, then sewing a face onto the head with black thread. I played with these and an odd assortment of hand-me-down toy soldiers for long afternoons, setting up wars, football games, contests of all kinds, and designating particular yarn figures as customary heroes. Together we played a spelling game: I'd be on the floor playing with the yarn figures, she'd be writing a letter and ask me how to spell "appreciate" (it was always that word), and I'd spell it for her while she pretended to be impressed with my spelling ability and I pretended that she hadn't asked me to spell that same word a dozen times before. I was good, too, at helping her find her glasses.

One scene at this house stands out. My uncle Bob came home from the war   7
and the whole family, his young wife, other uncles, my mother and father and brother and I, gathered at the house to meet him, and he came in wearing his captain's uniform and looking to me, I swear it, like a handsome young god. In fact he was an ordinary man who spent the rest of his life selling insurance. He had been in New Guinea, a ground officer in the Air Corps, and the story I remember is of the native who came into his tent one day and took a great deal

of interest in the scissors my uncle was using. The native asked in pidgin English what my uncle would require for the scissors in trade, and he jokingly said, well, how about a tentful of bananas. Sure enough, several days later two or three hundred natives came out of the jungle, huge bunches of bananas on their shoulders, and filled my uncle's tent.

Things went on this way for I don't know how long, maybe two years,   8 maybe three. I don't want to describe it as idyllic. Youth has its problems. But this old woman who could never find her glasses was wonderful to me, a grandmother in the true likeness of one, and I couldn't understand the changes when they came. She moved again, against all advice, this time to a big, bare apartment on the other side of town. She was gradually becoming irritable and difficult, not much fun to be around. There were no more spelling games; she stopped writing letters. Because she moved I saw her less often, and her home could no longer be a haven for me. She neglected it, too; it grew dirtier and dirtier, until my mother eventually had to do her cleaning for her.

Then she began to see things that weren't there. A branch in the back yard   9 became a woman, I remember, who apparently wasn't fully clothed, and a man was doing something to her, something unspeakable. She developed diabetes and my mother learned to give her insulin shots, but she wouldn't stop eating candy, the worst thing for her, and the diabetes got worse. Her face began to change, to slacken, to lose its shape and character. I didn't understand these things; arteriosclerosis, hardening of the arteries, whatever the explanation, it was only words. What I noticed was that her white hair was getting thinner and harder to control, that she herself seemed to be shrinking even as I grew, that when she looked at me I wasn't sure it was me she was seeing anymore.

After a few months of this, we brought her to live with us. My mother was   10 determined to take care of her, and certain family pressures were brought to bear too. That private man my father didn't like the idea at all, but he said nothing, which was his way. And she was put in my brother's bedroom over the garage, my brother moving in with me. It was a small house, six rooms and a basement, much too small for what we had to face.

What we had to face was a rapid deterioration into senile dementia and the   11 rise from beneath the surface of this smiling, kindly, white-haired old lady of something truly ugly. Whenever she was awake she called for attention, calling, calling a hundred times a day. Restless as always, she picked the bedclothes off, tore holes in sheets and pillows, took off her nightclothes and sat naked talking to herself. She hallucinated more and more frequently, addressing her dead husband, a dead brother, scolding, shouting at their apparitions. She became incontinent and smeared feces on herself, the furniture, the walls. And always calling—"Bunny, where are you? Bunny, I want you!"—scolding, demanding; she could seldom remember what she wanted when my mother came. It became an important event when she fell asleep; to make sure she stayed asleep the radio was kept off, the four of us tiptoed around the house, and when I went out to close the garage door, directly under the window (it was an overhead door and had to be pulled down), I did it so slowly and carefully, half an inch at a time, that it sometimes took me a full fifteen minutes to get it down.

That my mother endured this for six months is a testimony to her strength   12
and determination, but it was really beyond her and almost destroyed her health. My grandmother didn't often sleep through the night; she would wake up, yell, cry, a creature of disorder, a living memento mori, and my mother would have to tend to her. The house began to smell in spite of all my mother's efforts to keep my grandmother's room clean. My father, his peace gone, brooded in his chair behind his newspaper. My brother and I fought for Lebensraum, each of us trying to grow up in his own way. People avoided us. My uncles were living elsewhere—Miami, Cleveland, Delaware. My grandmother's two surviving sisters, who lived about ten blocks away, never came to see her. Everybody seemed to sense that something obscene was happening, and stayed away. Terrified, I stayed away, too. I heard my grandmother constantly, but in the six months she lived with us I think I went into her room only once. That was as my mother wished it. She was a nightmare, naked and filthy without warning.

After six months, at my father's insistence, after a night nurse had been   13
hired and left, after my mother had reached her limits and beyond, my parents started looking for a nursing home, any place they could put her. It became a family scandal; the two sisters were outraged that my mother would consider putting her own mother in a home, there were telephone calls back and forth between them and my uncles, but of course the sisters had never come to see her themselves, and my mother never forgave them. One of my uncles finally came from Cleveland, saw what was happening, and that day they put my grandmother in a car and drove her off to the nearest state mental hospital. They brought her back the same day; desperate as they were, they couldn't leave her in hell. At last, when it had come time to go to the shore, they found a nursing home in the middle of the Pine Barrens, miles from anywhere, and kept her there for awhile. That, too, proving unsatisfactory, they put her in a small nursing home in western New Jersey, about two hours away by car. We made the drive every Sunday

for the next six months, until my grandmother finally died. I always waited in the car while my mother visited her. At the funeral I refused to go into the room for one last look at the body. I was afraid of her still. The whole thing had been a subtle act of violence, a violation of the sensibilities, made all the worse by the fact that I knew it wasn't really her fault, that she was a victim of biology, of life itself. Hard knowledge for a boy just turned 14. She became the color of all my expectations.

Life is savage, then, and even character is insecure. Call no man happy until he be dead, said the Greek lawgiver Solon. But what would a wise man say to this? In that same town in New Jersey, that town I have long since abandoned as too flat and too good to be true, my mother, 30 years older now, weighing in at 92 pounds, incontinent, her white hair wild about her head sits strapped into a chair in another nursing home talking incoherently to her fellow patients and working her hands at the figures she thinks she sees moving around on the floor. It's enough to make stones weep to see this fierce, strong woman, who paid her dues, surely, ten time over, reduced to this.   14

Yet she is cheerful. This son comes to see her and she quite literally babbles with delight, introduces him (as her father, her husband—the connections are burnt out) to the aides, tells him endless stories that don't make any sense at all, and shines, shines with a clear light that must be her soul. Care and bitterness vanish in her presence. Helpless, the victim of numerous tiny strokes—"shower strokes," the doctors call them—that are gradually destroying her brain, she has somehow achieved a radiant serenity that accepts everything that happens and incorporates and transforms it.   15

Is there a lesson in this? Is some pattern larger than life working itself out; is this some kind of poetic justice on display, a mother balancing a grandmother, gods demonstrating reasons beyond our comprehension? It was a bitter thing to put her into that place, reeking of disinfectant, full of senile, dying old people, and I used to hate to visit her there, but as she has deteriorated she has also by sheer force of example managed to change my attitude. If she can be reconciled to all this, why can't I? It doesn't last very long, but after I've seen her, talked to her for half an hour, helped feed her, stroked her hair, I walk away amazed, as if I had been witness to a miracle.   16

Questions for Discussion

1. How is the relationship between Brandt's mother and grandmother analogous to the relationship between Brandt and his mother?

2. How does Brandt's relationship with his mother differ from the relationship she had with her mother?

3. What is the role of pretense in Brandt's family? When do family members pretend, and why? What form does the pretense take?

4. What questions are you left with at the end of the essay? What else do you wish Brandt had told you about his mother?

5. What details about his family did Brandt seem to leave out of his narrative? What kinds of things would he have had to leave out in order to focus on his mother as the central figure?

6. How does the introductory paragraph set the scene for the essay? What phrases did you find most striking?

7. Where does Brandt shift from narrative to general commentary? How effective is this shift? Why is such a shift necessary in writing memoirs?

Questions for Reflection and Writing

1. What do you remember of your own grandparent or another elderly person of importance to your family?

2. List the important details in this narrative essay, details that Brandt obviously wants to stand out, to represent his mother, grandmother, and other family members. Choose a few of the details and explain how they function in the essay. In other words, what does each detail say implicitly about the person, so that Brandt does not need to say it explicitly?

3. Write a personal narrative about one of these people, using a few key details and events to depict that person clearly for readers.

Kate Chopin (1850–1904), the daughter of a well-to-do businessman, was educated at the Academy of the Sacred Heart in St. Louis, Missouri. She was fluent in French and German and well versed in music, reading, and writing. In 1870 she married Oscar Chopin and moved to his home state of Louisiana, living first in New Orleans and later on their plantation in Cloutierville, north of the city, where her husband was a prosperous cotton factor. In 1882 Oscar died of fever; at first, Chopin ran the plantation herself, but in 1884 she moved with her six children back to St. Louis where she began teaching herself biology and anthropology. She also began writing fiction, publishing her first two stories in 1889. Over the course of her life she wrote nearly 100 stories and sketches, most of which are set in Louisiana. The stories were published in two collections, *Banyon Folk* (1894) and *A Night in Acadie* (1897). Though her stories were published in national as well as regional magazines, she was never considered more than a regional writer, and since she had no correspondence with other writers, she had no real influence upon them. As a result, she was never studied or read much after her early death in 1904. The critical reaction to her (now) best-known novel, *The Awakening,* may have added to that lack of academic interest. When *The Awakening* was published in 1899, critics condemned the book for being immoral and not a fit subject for women to write about or read. Libraries banned it, and the book got such bad press that Chopin wrote only five stories after its publication. Though interest in Chopin languished for decades, in the late 1950s scholars began to reappraise her. In 1963, the scholar Per Seyersted wrote a biography of her that convinced others of Chopin's place in literary history.

The Story of an Hour

Kate Chopin

Knowing that Mrs. Mallard was afflicted with a heart trouble, great care was   1
taken to break to her as gently as possible the news of her husband's death.

It was her sister Josephine who told her, in broken sentences, veiled hints   2
that revealed in half concealing. Her husband's friend Richards was there, too,
near her. It was he who had been in the newspaper office when intelligence of
the railroad disaster was received, with Brently Mallard's name leading the list of
"killed." He had only taken the time to assure himself of its truth by a second
telegram, and had hastened to forestall any less careful, less tender friend in bearing the sad message.

She did not hear the story as many women have heard the same, with a   3
paralyzed inability to accept its significance. She wept at once, with sudden, wild

abandonment, in her sister's arms. When the storm of grief had spent itself she went away to her room alone. She would have no one follow her.

There stood, facing the open window, a comfortable, roomy armchair. Into   4 this she sank, pressed down by a physical exhaustion that haunted her body and seemed to reach into her soul.

She could see in the open square before her house the tops of trees that   5 were all aquiver with the new spring life. The delicious breath of rain was in the air. In the street below a peddler was crying his wares. The notes of a distant song which some one was singing reached her faintly, and countless sparrows were twittering in the eaves.

There were patches of blue sky showing here and there through the clouds   6 that had met and piled above the other in the west facing her window.

She sat with her head thrown back upon the cushion of the chair, quite   7 motionless, except when a sob came up into her throat and shook her, as a child who has cried itself to sleep continues to sob in its dreams.

She was young, with a fair, calm face, whose lines bespoke repression and   8 even a certain strength. But now there was a dull stare in her eyes, whose gaze was fixed away off yonder on one of those patches of blue sky. It was not a glance of reflection, but rather indicated a suspension of intelligent thought.

There was something coming to her and she was waiting for it, fearfully.   9 What was it? She did not know; it was too subtle and elusive to name. But she felt it, creeping out of the sky, reaching toward her through the sounds, the scents, the color that filled the air.

Now her bosom rose and fell tumultuously. She was beginning to recognize   10 this thing that was approaching to possess her, and she was striving to beat it back with her will—as powerless as her two white slender hands would have been.

When she abandoned herself a little whispered word escaped her slightly   11 parted lips. She said it over and over under her breath: "Free, free, free!" The vacant stare and the look of terror that had followed it went from her eyes. They stayed keen and bright. Her pulses beat fast, and the coursing blood warmed and relaxed every inch of her body.

She did not stop to ask if it were or were not a monstrous joy that held her.   12 A clear and exalted perception enabled her to dismiss the suggestion as trivial.

She knew that she would weep again when she saw the kind, tender hands   13 folded in death; the face that had never looked save with love upon her, fixed and gray and dead. But she saw beyond that bitter moment a long procession of years to come that would belong to her absolutely. And she opened and spread her arms out to them in welcome.

There would be no one to live for her during those coming years; she would   14
live for herself. There would be no powerful will bending her in that blind persistence with which men and women believe they have a right to impose a private will upon a fellow-creature. A kind intention or a cruel intention made the act seem no less a crime as she looked upon it in that brief moment of illumination.

And yet she had loved him—sometimes. Often she had not. What did it   15
matter! What could love, the unsolved mystery, count for in the face of this possession of self-assertion which she suddenly recognized as the strongest impulse of her being!

"Free! Body and soul free!" she kept whispering.   16

Josephine was kneeling before the closed door with her lips to the keyhole,   17
imploring for admission. "Louise, open the door! I beg; open the door—you will make yourself ill. What are you doing, Louise? For heaven's sake open the door."

"Go away. I am not making myself ill." No; she was drinking in a very elixir   18
of life through that open window.

Her fancy was running riot along those days ahead of her. Spring days, and   19
summer days, and all sorts of days that would be her own. She breathed a quick prayer that life might be long. It was only yesterday she had thought with a shudder that life might be long.

She arose at length and opened the door to her sister's importunities. There   20
was a feverish triumph in her eyes, and she carried herself unwittingly like a goddess of Victory. She clasped her sister's waist, and together they descended the stairs. Richards stood waiting for them at the bottom.

Some one was opening the front door with a latchkey. It was Brently   21
Mallard who entered, a little travel-stained, composedly carrying his grip-sack and umbrella. He had been far from the scene of accident, and did not even know there had been one. He stood amazed at Josephine's piercing cry; at Richards' quick motion to screen him from the view of his wife.

But Richards was too late.   22

When the doctors came they said she had died of heart disease—of joy that   23
kills.

Questions for Discussion

1. What goes through Louise Mallard's mind as she sits in her room alone, adjusting to the news of her husband's death? What is the process of her thinking?

2. What was the "subtle and elusive" (paragraph 9) thing that comes to Louise as she gazes out the window?

3. What are Louise's feelings toward her husband? What are her feelings toward marriage and men in general?

4. What is the "joy that kills" (paragraph 23)? Why is this phrase ironic?

5. Why is the time of year (early spring) and the setting (Louise Mallard's room with a window) important to the story? What do the room, window, and spring symbolize?

6. Why is it important that readers see into Louise Mallard's thoughts? How might the story have been told without this knowledge of what she was thinking?

7. In what ways would this story be different if it were told from the point of view of one of the male characters?

Questions for Reflection and Writing

1. Write a story with a sudden, ironic twist at the end. What techniques did you use to show readers what your main character was thinking and to create irony?

2. Look up "irony," "cosmic irony," and "dramatic irony" in a dictionary of literary terms. Discuss Chopin's use of irony in this story.

3. Compare "The Story of an Hour" with another of Chopin's stories, such as "The Storm" or "A Pair of Silk Stockings," or if you have time to read it, her novel, *The Awakening*. What themes are present in both or all of the stories? What character types are common?

Ellen Goodman (1941–   ) received her bachelor's degree from Radcliffe College in 1963 and attended Harvard University on a Nieman Fellowship in 1973 and 1974. Goodman began her journalistic career with *Newsweek* (1963–1965), then moved to the *Detroit Free Press* (1965–1967), and since 1967 has been writing for the *Boston Globe*. Her syndicated column, "At Large," appears in more than two hundred newspapers across the country. She has won several awards for her commentary, including a Pulitzer Prize for commentary in 1980. She has also been a commentator on the television show *Spectrum* (CBS) and is a weekly guest commentator on the *Today* show (NBC). Many of her columns have been collected in *Close to Home* (1979), *At Large* (1981), and *Value Judgments* (1993).

The Tapestry of Friendships

Ellen Goodman

It was, in many ways, a slight movie. Nothing actually happened. There was no   1
big-budget chase scene, no bloody shootout. The story ended without any cosmic conclusions.

Yet she found Claudia Weill's film *Girlfriends* gentle and affecting. Slowly,   2
it panned across the tapestry of friendship—showing its fragility, its resiliency, its
role as the connecting tissue between the lives of two young women.

When it was over, she thought about the movies she'd seen this year—   3
Julia, *The Turning Point* and now *Girlfriends*. It seemed that the peculiar eye, the
social lens of the cinema, had drastically shifted its focus. Suddenly the Male
Buddy movies had been replaced by the Female Friendship flicks.

This wasn't just another binge of trendiness, but a kind of *cinéma vérité*. For   4
once the movies were reflecting a shift, not just from men to women but from
one definition of friendship to another.

Across millions of miles of celluloid, the ideal of friendship had always been   5
male—a world of sidekicks and "pardner," of Butch Cassidys and Sundance kids.
There had been something almost atavistic about these visions of attachments—
as if producers culled their plots from some pop anthropology book on male
bonding. Movies portrayed the idea that only men, those direct descendants of
hunters and Hemingways, inherited a primal capacity for friendship. In contrast,
they portrayed women picking on each other, the way they once picked berries.

Well, that duality must have been mortally wounded in some shootout at   6
the You're OK, I'm OK Corral. Now, on the screen, they were at least aware of
the subtle distinction between men and women as buddies and friends.

About 150 years ago, Coleridge had written, "A woman's friendship bor-   7
ders more closely on love than man's. Men affect each other in the reflection of
noble or friendly acts, whilst women ask fewer proofs and more signs and expressions of attachment."

Well, she thought, on the whole, men had buddies, while women had   8
friends. Buddies bonded, but friends loved. Buddies faced adversity together, but
friends faced each other. There was something palpably different in the way they
spent their time. Buddies seemed to "do" things together; friends simply "were"
together.

Buddies came linked, like accessories, to one activity or another. People   9
have golf buddies and business buddies, college buddies and club buddies. Men
often keep their buddies in these categories, while women keep a special category for friends.

A man once told her that men weren't real buddies until they'd been   10
"through the wars" together—corporate or athletic or military. They had to soldier together, he said. Women, on the other hand, didn't count themselves as
friends until they'd shared three loathsome confidences.

Buddies hang tough together; friends hang onto each other.   11

It probably had something to do with pride. You don't show off to a friend;   12
you show need. Buddies try to keep the worst from each other; friends confess it.

A friend of hers once telephoned her lover, just to find out if he were home.   13
She hung up without a hello when he picked up the phone. Later, wretched with
embarrassment, the friend moaned, "Can you believe me? A 35-year-old lawyer,
making a chicken call?" Together they laughed and made it better.

Buddies seek approval. But friends seek acceptance.   14

She knew so many men who had been trained in restraint, afraid of each   15
other's judgment or awkward with each other's affection. She wasn't sure which.
Like buddies in the movies, they would die for each other, but never hug each
other.

She'd read *Babbitt* recently, that extraordinary catalogue of male griev-   16
ances. The only relationship that gave meaning to the claustrophobic life of
George Babbitt had been with Paul Riesling. But not once in the tragedy of their
lives had one been able to say to the other: You make a difference.

Even now men shocked her at times with their description of friendship. 17
Does this one have a best friend? "Why, of course, we see each other every
February." Does that one call his most intimate pal long distance? "Why, certainly, whenever there's a real reason." Do those two old chums ever have dinner
together? "You mean alone? Without our wives?"

Yet, things were changing. The ideal of intimacy wasn't this parallel play- 18
mate, this teammate, this trenchmate. Not even in Hollywood. In the double
standard of friendship, for once the female version was becoming accepted as the
general ideal.

After all, a buddy is a fine life-companion. But one's friends, as Santayana 19
once wrote, "are that part of the race with which one can be human."

Questions for Discussion

1. What is a Male Buddy film? What is a Female Friendship film? Why are two
    terms needed?
2. How are the Female Friendship films changing the definition of friendship?
3. How have older films portrayed women and relationships between women?
    Why is this a problem?
4. Does Goodman favor one or the other, a buddy or a friend? Does she need
    to be unbiased?
5. How is this essay a "woman's essay"?
6. Who is the ideal reader for this essay? Do you think Goodman would prefer
    men or women as the main readers? Or does she write to both sexes equal-
    ly? What in her essay shows who her readers are?
7. Who is "she"? Why might Goodman have chosen to use just a pronoun to
    create a perspective?

Questions for Reflection and Writing

1. Goodman uses short sentences with a repeated structure when she compares
    and contrasts buddies and friends. Try this technique in your own writing,
    comparing two closely related terms, such as pet and companion animal,
    teacher and mentor, or business partner and marriage partner.
2. Write your definition of friendship, using examples from your own life or
    from literature and film.
3. See a Male Buddy or a Female Friendship film and write either a film review
    (use reviews in newspapers as models) or a commentary about how friend-
    ship is portrayed in the film.

Phyllis Rose (1942–   ), feminist essayist, literary historian, and biographer of Virginia Woolf and Josephine Baker, was born on October 26 in New York City. She was graduated with a B.A. from Radcliffe College in 1964, from Yale University with an M.A. in 1965, and from Harvard University with a Ph.D. in 1970. Rose won a National Book Award nomination for her first book, *Woman of Letters: A Life of Virginia Woolf* (1978), which emphasizes Woolf's writing, her struggles with mental illness, and sexuality. Some of her other writings include *Writing of Women: Essays in a Renaissance* (1985) and *Never Say Goodbye: Essays* (1991). She has also edited *The Norton Book of Women's Lives* (1993). Rose is a former columnist for the *New York Times* as well as a book reviewer and a contributor to periodicals.

Mothers and Fathers

Phyllis Rose

My mother always said: "The daughters come back to you eventually. When the   1
sons go they're gone." She has other favorite sayings—"A father's not a mother,"
"The beginning is the half of all things," and "De gustibus non disputandum est,"
which she translated as "That's what makes horse races"—all of which have
become increasingly meaningful to me with time. Recently I told her that she
was right in a fight we had twenty-seven years go about which language I should
study in high school. This came up because I had just had the same discussion
with my son and took the side my mother took (French). She laughed when I
told her that she was right twenty-seven years ago. There have been more and
more nice moments like that with my mother as we both grow older.

She is 75, ash blond, blue-eyed, a beauty. When my father died three years   2
ago she suddenly developed glaucoma and lost a lot of her vision. She says she
literally "cried her eyes out." She can read only very slowly, with the help of a
video enhancer supplied by the Lighthouse for the Blind. Nevertheless, her lipstick is always perfect. She doesn't use a mirror. She raises her hand to her lips
and applies it. When I praise her for this, she says, "By now I should know where
my mouth is."

She doesn't walk alone at night and during the day rarely gets beyond the   3
area she can reach on foot, between 50th and 60th Streets, First Avenue and
Fifth. She loves to transgress those boundaries, so when I come in from

Connecticut I usually pick her up in my car and drive her to distant parts of Manhattan: the Lower East Side, the Seaport, TriBeCa, SoHo, the Village. One of our favorite things to do together is to have Sunday brunch at a restaurant on West Broadway near Houston Street. We go there especially for the pecan pancakes and the scrambled eggs with salmon and dill.

One day this winter we went there for Sunday brunch. It was a particular- 4 ly cold day and I was suffering from a pulled muscle in my neck. I walked with one shoulder higher than the other. My mother walked slowly and with a slight stoop. But as soon as we entered the door, the restaurant buoyed us up. We were patrons, to be pampered. We had a reservation. We could share in the general atmosphere of youth, energy, chic, competence, success. The waiters were stylishly dressed with an accent of the 1940s. This was SoHo.

One young man, wearing a plaid shirt and pinch-pleated trousers, showed 5 us to a table in a bright front section overlooking the sidewalk. This was excellent for my mother, who often finds restaurants too dark and carries a spelunker's light to read menus by. But we didn't need a menu; we ordered pecan pancakes and scrambled eggs with salmon and dill. When they arrived we split them and I began with the eggs. "Eat the pancakes first," my mother said. I didn't ask why. She's my mother. She has to tell me how to do things.

Three beautiful women dressed in black who were eating lunch at a table 6 nearby finished eating, cleared their table, and moved it aside. From the corner they took a cello, a violin, and a flute, removed their covers and positioned themselves to play. They started with Schubert and went on to a medley of Strauss waltzes. My spirits soared. I looked at my mother to see if she was listening to the music. She was. I could see she was as ravished by it as I was, and for the same reason. Without exchanging a word both of us moved simultaneously thirty years backward in our minds and to another place.

"Palm Beach," I said. 7

My mother nodded. "Hoops, crinolines, strapless dresses with net skirts, 8 white fox stoles. Each of us took three suitcases. Those days are gone forever."

In the 1950s my father, in his proud and powerful middle age, took my 9 mother, my brother, my sister, and me to Palm Beach for two weeks every winter until just after New Year's Day. We stayed at a hotel called the Whitehall; its core was originally the mansion of Henry F. Flagler, the railroad man and Florida pioneer. The lobby had floors of inlaid marble and variegated marble pillars.

The Whitehall dining room was a gigantic sunken area that, family legend 10 said, was Mr. Flagler's indoor swimming pool. Whether it was or not didn't matter then, doesn't now. It was a magical place. The families as they came in for dinner and took their usual places were brilliantly dressed; fathers in the light-colored raw silk jackets appropriate for the South; mothers in strapless dresses with wide skirts supported by hoops and crinolines; children, after a day on the beach and the tennis courts, scraped, peeling, but burnished for dinner. Nothing was casual. The hotel hairdresser was heavily booked. Elaborate sets and comb-outs several times a week were not unusual. Jewelry was not left in the vault at home. The room sparkled. There was general splendor, the result of all that effort and the discipline of dressing for dinner. And at the center of the room a quintet in black formal clothes played music throughout the four-course meal. Every night, usually during the clear consommé, they played a medley of Strauss waltzes.

My mother and I are tied together because we share the same memories. 11 My brother and sister share them, too. We are a family because the Whitehall, a certain dude ranch in the Great Smokies, the layout of our house on Central Avenue and other recondite geographies exist in our minds and no others. We move in the same mental spaces. In some of our dreams we wander the same streets, trying to get back to the same house. One form of loneliness is to have a memory and no one to share it with. If, in twenty years, I want to reminisce about Sunday brunch in a certain SoHo restaurant I may have nobody to reminisce with. That will be lonely.

Often I feel I do not do enough for my mother. When I read King Lear I 12 realize that I'd be flattering myself to identify with Cordelia. I have the awful suspicion that I am much more like Regan or Goneril—from Lear's point of view monsters of ingratitude; from their own just two women taking their turn at the top, enjoying their middle-aged supremacy. When these guilty thoughts afflict me a folk tale comes to mind.

There once was a bird with three young to carry across a river. She put the 13 first on her back and, halfway across, asked, "Will you care for me in my old age as I have cared for you?" "Yes, Mama," said the first bird, and the mother dumped him in the river, calling him a liar. Second bird, same result. "Will you care for me in my old age as I have cared for you?" "Yes." "Liar." But the third bird, asked if he would care for his mother in her old age as she had cared for him, answered: "I can't promise that. I can only promise to care for my own children as you have cared for me."

It's a truthful response and it satisfied the mother bird, a philosophic spirit 14 if ever there was one. But when I imagine my son saying the same thing to me—

"I can only promise to care for my own children as you have cared for me"—I don't seem to find much comfort in it.

Questions for Discussion

1. What is the actual translation of "De gustibus non disputandum est" in Paragraph 1? Why is Rose's mother's "translation" still an apt one?
2. What does Rose consider significant about her relationship with her mother?
3. Why might Rose not feel any comfort in imagining her son saying he would care for his children as she has cared for him?
4. Why is King Lear (Paragraph 12) a surprising but apt comparison to illustrate Rose's relationship with her mother?
5. Where does a touch of sadness show up in this memoir? What emotion does the sadness balance?
6. What is the role of Rose's father in the memoir? Why does Rose seem more attached to her mother than to her father?
7. Does Rose come across as overly sentimental? If so, how so? In other words, what makes her prose not only sentimental, but overly so? If not, how does Rose manage to keep her prose from becoming over sentimental?

Questions for Reflection and Writing

1. Write an essay in which you reflect on the statement, "One form of loneliness is to have a memory and no one to share it with" (Paragraph 11). What is meant in general by this statement? How does it connect to your life?
2. Write an essay about your mother or father. Your essay is a memoir, but it should also make a point about your parents that is meaningful to readers outside of your family.
3. Find a folk tale or a short story on the subject of motherhood or fatherhood. Respond to it, explaining how motherhood or fatherhood is presented.

Chapter 3
HISTORY AND CULTURE

Sarvepalli Radhakrishnan was born in 1888 in Tiruttani, India. He received his initial education at Christian missionary schools. Exposed to Christian criticisms of Hinduism, he resolved to understand his native Hinduism more deeply. He pursued graduate studies at Madras Christian College, where he wrote a thesis on the ethics of Hindu Ved-anta philosophy and received his degree in 1909. Radhakrishnan then began a career as a philosopher, teaching at Presidency College in Madras (1909–1917), Mysore University (1918–1921), and Calcutta University (1921–1931). From 1931 to 1936 he was vice chancellor of Andhra University in Waltair. In 1936 Radhakrishnan was knighted by King George V of England and was appointed Spalding Professor of Eastern Religions and Ethics at Oxford University. In 1946, after serving as an administrator at Benares Hindu University and the University of Delhi, he embarked on a career in politics by heading the Indian delegation to the United Nations Educational, Scientific, and Cultural Organization (UNESCO). Three years later he was appointed ambassador to the Soviet Union. He became vice president of India in 1952 and president ten years later. In 1967, after completing his five-year term as president, Radhakrishnan retired from politics. He died in Madras in 1975.

Radhakrishnan's major works are *Indian Philosophy* (two volumes; 1923, 1927), *An Idealist View of Life* (1932), *Eastern Religions and Western Thought* (1939), *The Bhagavadgītā* (translation and commentary; 1948), and *The Principal Upaniṣads* (translation and commentary; 1953).

Our reading is taken from Chapter 7 of *An Idealist View of Life*, "Human Personality and Its Destiny." In this section of the chapter, entitled "Karma and Freedom," Radhakrishnan argues that the Hindu doctrine of karma is compatible with human freedom. According to the doctrine of karma (a Sanskrit word that means, literally, "action," "deed"), our actions create a force that affects our destiny. In the physical world every event is the effect of past causes and affects the future; similarly, in the moral world everything we think or say or do "enters into the living chain of causes which makes us what we are." Hindus believe in rebirth and hold that the law of karma operates from one life to the next: Our status in the present life is the result of how we acted during our previous life, and what we do in this life affects our status in the next one.

Radhakrishnan argues that karma is compatible with freedom because, although karma links us to our past, we have the creative power to shape our self. Freedom means self-determination, and we can determine how we will act within the context of karma and the limitations it puts on our range of options. Radhakrishnan compares life to a game of bridge: We are dealt a hand (our present status is due to karma), but we can play the hand as we wish (we have free choice). Radhakrishnan concludes by observing that belief in karma makes us more compassionate toward the less fortunate. We should not feel superior to those who are faring badly because we share the human frailty that, through karma, led to their misfortune.

From Sarvepalli Radhakrishnan, *An Idealist View of Life*, 2nd ed., George Allen & Unwin, 1937.

An Idealist View of Life

Sarvepalli Radhakrishnan

Human Personality and Its Destiny

Karma and Freedom The two pervasive features of all nature, connection with   1
the past and creation of the future, are present in the human level. The connection with the past at the human stage is denoted by the word "karma" in the
Hindu systems. The human individual is a self-conscious, ef-ficient portion of
universal nature with his own uniqueness. His history stretching back to an
indefinite period of time binds him with the physical and vital conditions of the
world. Human life is an organic whole where each successive phase grows out of
what has gone before. We are what we are on account of our affinity with the
past. Human growth is an ordered one and its orderedness is indicated by saying
that it is governed by the law of karma.

Karma, literally, means "action," "deed." All acts produce their effects,   2
which are recorded both in the organism and the environment. Their physical
effects may be short-lived, but their moral effects (samskara) are worked into the
character of the self. Every single thought, word and deed enters into the living
chain of causes which makes us what we are. Our life is not at the mercy of blind
chance or capricious fate. The conception is not peculiar to the Oriental creeds.
The Christian scriptures refer to it. "Be not deceived; God is not mocked: for
whatsoever a man soweth, that shall he also reap."[1] Jesus is reported to have said
on the Mount, "Judge not that ye be not judged, for with what judgment ye
judge, ye shall be judged, and with what measure ye mete, it shall be measured
to you again."[2]

Karma is not so much a principle of retribution as one of continuity. Good   3
produces good, evil evil. Love increases our power of love, hatred our power of
hatred. It emphasises the great importance of right action. Man is continuously
shaping his own self. The law of karma is not to be confused with either a hedonistic or a juridical theory of rewards and punishments. The reward for virtue is
not a life of pleasure nor is the punishment for sin pain. Pleasure and pain may
govern the animal nature of man but not his human. Love, which is a joy in
itself, suffers; hatred too often means a perverse kind of satisfaction. Good and
evil are not to be confused with material well-being and physical suffering.

All things in the world are at once causes and effects. They embody the   4
energy of the past and exert energy on the future. Karma or connection with the
past is not inconsistent with creative freedom. On the other hand, it is implied

by it. The law that links us with the past also asserts that it can be subjugated by our free action. Though the past may present obstacles, they must all yield to the creative power in man in proportion to its sincerity and insistence. The law of karma says that each individual will get the return according to the energy he puts forth. The universe will respond to and implement the demands of the self. Nature will reply to the insistent call of spirit. "As is his desire, such is his purpose; as is his purpose, such is the action he performs; what action he performs, that he procures for himself."[3] "Verily I say unto you that whoever shall say to this mountain, 'Be lifted up and cast into the sea,' and shall not doubt in his heart but believe fully that what he says shall be, it shall be done for him."[4] When Jesus said, "Destroy this temple and I will raise it again in three days,"[5] he is asserting the truth that the spirit within us is mightier than the world of things. There is nothing we cannot achieve if we want it enough. Subjection to spirit is the law of universal nature. The principle of karma has thus two aspects, a retrospective and a prospective, continuity with the past and creative freedom of the self.

The urge in nature which seeks not only to maintain itself at a particular   5
level but to advance to a higher becomes conscious in man, who deliberately seeks after rules of life and principles of progress. "My father worketh hitherto, and I work."[6] Human beings are the first among nature's children who can say "I" and consciously collaborate with the "father," the power that controls and directs nature, in the fashioning of the world. They can substitute rational direction for the slow, dark, blundering growth of the subhuman world. We cannot deny the free action of human beings however much their origin may be veiled in darkness. The self has conative tendencies, impulses to change by its efforts the given conditions, inner and outer, and shape them to its own purpose.

The problem of human freedom is confused somewhat by the distinction   6
between the self and the will. The will is only the self in its active side and freedom of the will really means the freedom of the self. It is determination by the self.

It is argued that self-determination is not really freedom. It makes little dif-   7
ference whether the self is moved from without or from within. A spinning top moved from within by a spring is as mechanical a top as one whipped into motion from without. The self may well be an animated automaton. A drunkard who takes to his glass habitually does so in obedience to an element in his nature. The habit has become a part of his self. If we analyse the contents of the self, many of them are traceable to the influence of the environment and the inheritance from the past. If the individual's view and character are the product of a long evolution, his actions which are the outcome of these cannot be free. The feeling of freedom may be an illusion of the self which lives in each moment of

the present, ignoring the determining past. In answer to these difficulties, it may be said that the self represents a form of relatedness or organisation, closer and more intimate than that which is found in animal, plant or atom. Self-de-termination means not determination by any fragment of the self's nature but by the whole of it. Unless the individual employs his whole nature, searches the different possibilities and selects one which commends itself to his whole self, the act is not really free.

Sheer necessity is not to be found in any aspect of nature; complete freedom is divine and possible only when the self becomes coextensive with the whole. Human freedom is a matter of degree. We are most free when our whole self is active and not merely a fragment of it. We generally act according to our conventional or habitual self and sometimes we sink to the level of our subnormal self.

Freedom is not caprice, nor is karma necessity. Human choice is not unmotivated or uncaused. If our acts were irrelevant to our past, then there would be no moral responsibility or scope for improvement. Undetermined beginnings, upstart events are impossible either in the physical or the human world. Free acts cannot negate continuity. They arise within the order of nature. Freedom is not caprice, since we carry our past with us. The character, at any given point, is the condensation of our previous history. What we have been enters into the "me" which is now active and choosing. The range of one's natural freedom of action is limited. No man has the universal field of possibilities for himself. The varied possibilities of our nature do not all get a chance, and the cosmic has its influence in permitting the development of certain possibilities and closing down others. Again, freedom is dogged by automatism. When we make up our mind to do a thing, our mind is different from what it was before. When a possibility becomes an actuality, it assumes the character of necessity. The past can never be cancelled, though it may be utilised. Mere defiance of the given may mean disaster, though we can make a new life spring up from the past. Only the possible is the sphere of freedom. We have a good deal of present constraint and previous necessity in human life. But necessity is not to be mistaken for destiny, which we can neither defy nor delude. Though the self is not free from the bonds of determination, it can subjugate the past to a certain extent and turn it into a new course. Choice is the assertion of freedom over necessity, by which it converts necessity to its own use and thus frees itself from it. "The human agent is free."[7] He is not the plaything of fate or driftwood on the tide of uncontrolled events. He can actively mould the future instead of passively suffering the past. The past may become either an opportunity or an obstacle. Everything depends on what we make of it and not what it makes of us. Life is not bound to move in a specific direction. Life is a growth and a growth is undetermined in a measure. Though the future is the sequel of the past, we cannot say what it will be. If there is no indetermination, then human consciousness is an unnecessary luxury.

Our demand for freedom must reckon with a universe that is marked by   10 order and regularity. Life is like a game of bridge. The cards in the game are given to us. We do not select them. They are traced to past karma but we are free to make any call as we think fit and lead any suit. Only we are limited by the rules of the game. We are more free when we start the game than later on when the game has developed and our choices become restricted. But till the very end there is always a choice. A good player will see possibilities which a bad one does not. The more skilled a player, the more alternatives does he perceive. A good hand may be cut to pieces by unskilful play and the bad play need not be attributed to the frowns of fortune. Even though we may not like the way in which the cards are shuffled, we like the game and we want to play. Sometimes wind and tide may prove too strong for us and even the most noble may come down. The great souls find profound peace in the consciousness that the stately order of the world, now lovely and luminous, now dark and terrible, in which man finds his duty and destiny, cannot be subdued to known aims. It seems to have a purpose of its own of which we are ignorant. Misfortune is not fate but providence.

The law of karma does not support the doctrine of predestination. There   11 are some who believe that only the predestination of certain souls to destruction is consistent with divine sovereignty. God has a perfect right to deal with his creatures even as a potter does with his clay. St. Paul speaks of "vessels of wrath fitted to destruction."[8] Life eternal is a gracious gift of God. Such a view of divine sovereignty is unethical. God's love is manifested in and through law.

In our relations with human failures, belief in karma inclines us to take a   12 sympathetic attitude and develop reverence before the mystery of misfortune. The more understanding we are, the less do we pride ourselves on our superiority. Faith in karma induces in us the mood of true justice or charity, which is the essence of spirituality. We realise how infinitely helpless and frail human beings are. When we look at the warped lives of the poor, we see how much the law of karma is true. If they are lazy and criminal, let us ask what chance they had of choosing to be different. They are more unfortunate than wicked. Again, failures are due not so much to "sin" as to errors which lead us to our doom. In Greek tragedy, man is held individually less responsible and circumstances or the decisions of Moira[9] more so. The tale of Oedipus Rex tells us how he could not avoid his fate to kill his father and marry his mother, in spite of his best efforts. The parting of Hector and Andromache in Homer is another illustration. In Shakespeare again, we see the artist leading on his characters to their destined ends by what seems a very natural development of their foibles, criminal folly in Lear or personal ambition in Macbeth. The artist shows us these souls in pain. Hamlet's reason is puzzled, his will confounded. He looks at life and at death and wonders which is worse. Goaded by personal ambition, Macbeth makes a mess of it all. Othello kills his wife and kills himself because a jealous villain shows him a handkerchief. When these noble souls crash battling with adverse forces, we feel with them and for them; for it might happen to any of us. We are not free from the weaknesses that broke them, whatever we call them, stupidity, disorder, vacillation or, if you please, insane ambition and self-seeking. Today the evil stars of the Greek tragedians are replaced by the almighty laws of economics. Thousands of young men the world over are breaking their heads in vain against the iron walls of society like trapped birds in cages. We see in them the essence of all tragedy, something noble breaking down, something sublime falling with a crash. We can only bow our heads in the presence of those broken beneath the burden of their destiny. The capacity of the human soul for suffering and isolation is immense. Take the poor creatures whom the world passes by as the lowly and the lost. If only we had known what they passed through, we would have been glad of their company. It is utterly wrong to think that misfortune comes only to those who deserve it. The world is a whole and we are members one of another, and we must suffer one for another. In Christianity, it needed a divine soul to reveal how much grace there is in suffering. To bear pain, to endure suffering, is the quality of the strong in spirit. It adds to the spiritual resources of humanity.

Notes

1. Galatians 6:7 [S.R.]
2. Matthew 7:1–2 [D.C.A., ed.]
3. Bṛihadāraṇyaka Upaniṣad, Part 4, Chapter 4, verse 5 [S.R.]
4. Mark 11:23 [D.C.A.]
5. John 2:19 [D.C.A.]
6. John 5:17 [S.R.] a..a.
7. Pāṇini, Aṣṭādhyāyi, Book I, Chapter 4, Section 54. [S.R.] Pāṇini was an Indian grammarian and philosopher who flourished about 400 B.C.E. [D.C.A.]
8. Romans 9:22 [D.C.A.]
9. Moira: in Greek mythology, the goddess of Fate; usually spoken of in the plural (Moirai), as three goddesses [D.C.A.]

N. Scott Momaday (1934–   ), who was half Kiowan and part Cherokee, was born in Lawton, Oklahoma, and grew up on Navajo, Apache, and Pueblo reservations in northern New Mexico. A distinguished writer and a professor of English at the University of Arizona, Momaday is also an accomplished painter, photographer, and tribal dancer. His prose, poetry, illustrations, and photographs celebrate the culture of Native Americans and their reverence for the land. Momaday is best known for *The Way to Rainy Mountain* (1969), a book that grew from an autobiographical essay, "The Journey of Tai-me," published two years earlier. But his works are many and varied. In 1968, he won the Pulitzer Prize for *House Made of Dawn*, a novel. He has written two volumes of poetry: *Angle of Geese and Other Poems* (1973) and *The Gourd Dancer* (1976). A second autobiographical work, *The Names: A Memoir*, appeared in 1977. In 1982, he coauthored a pictorial history entitled *American Indian Photographic Images, 1868–1931.*

FROM The Way to Rainy Mountain

N. Scott Momaday

A single knoll rises out of the plain in Oklahoma, north and west of the Wichita   1
range. For my people, the Kiowas, it is an old landmark, and they gave it the name Rainy Mountain. The hardest weather in the world is there. Winter brings blizzards, hot tornadic winds arise in the spring, and in summer the prairie is an anvil's edge. The grass turns brittle and brown, and it cracks beneath your feet. There are green belts along the rivers and creeks, linear groves of hickory and pecan, willow and witch hazel. At a distance in July or August the steaming foliage seems almost to writhe in fire. Great green and yellow grasshoppers are everywhere in the tall grass, popping up like corn to sting the flesh, and tortoises crawl about on the red earth, going nowhere in the plenty of time. Loneliness is an aspect of the land. All things in the plain are isolate; there is no confusion of objects in the eye, but one hill or one tree or one man. To look upon that landscape in the early morning, with the sun at your back, is to lose the sense of proportion. Your imagination comes to life, and this, you think, is where Creation was begun.

I returned to Rainy Mountain in July. My grandmother had died in the   2
spring, and I wanted to be at her grave. She had lived to be very old and at last
infirm. Her only living daughter was with her when she died, and I was told that
in death her face was that of a child.

I like to think of her as a child. When she was born, the Kiowas were liv-   3
ing the last great moment of their history. For more than a hundred years they
had controlled the open range from the Smoky Hill River to the Red, from the
headwaters of the Canadian to the fork of the Arkansas and Cimarron. In
alliance with the Comanches, they had ruled the whole of the Southern Plains.
War was their sacred business, and they were the finest horsemen the world has
ever known. But warfare for the Kiowas was preeminently a matter of disposition
rather than of survival, and they never understood the grim, unrelenting
advance of the U.S. Cavalry. When at last, divided and ill provisioned, they were
driven onto the Staked Plains in the cold of autumn, they fell into panic. In Palo
Duro Canyon they abandoned their crucial stores to pillage and had nothing
then but their lives. In order to save themselves, they surrendered to the soldiers
at Fort Sill and were imprisoned in the old stone corral that now stands as a military museum. My grandmother was spared the humiliation of those high gray
walls by eight or ten years, but she must have known from birth the affliction of
defeat, the dark brooding of old warriors.

Her name was Aho, and she belonged to the last culture to evolve in North   4
America. Her forebears came down from the high country in western Montana
nearly three centuries ago. They were a mountain people, a mysterious tribe of
hunters whose language has never been classified in any major group. In the late
seventeenth century they began a long migration to the south and east. It was a
journey toward the dawn, and it led to a golden age. Along the way the Kiowas
were befriended by the Crows, who gave them the culture and religion of the
Plains. They acquired horses, and their ancient nomadic spirit was suddenly free
of the ground. They acquired Tai-me, the sacred sun-dance doll, from that
moment the object and symbol of their wor-ship, and so shared in the divinity
of the sun. Not least, they acquired the sense of destiny, therefore courage and
pride. When they entered upon the Southern Plains they had been transformed.
No longer were they slaves to the simple necessity of survival; they were a lordly and dangerous society of fighters and thieves, hunters and priests of the sun.
According to their origin myth, they entered the world through a hollow log.
From one point of view, their migration was the fruit of an old prophecy, for
indeed they emerged from a sunless world.

Though my grandmother lived out her long life in the shadow of Rainy   5
Mountain, the immense landscape of the continental interior lay like memory
in her blood. She could tell of the Crows, whom she had never seen, and of the
Black Hills, where she had never been. I wanted to see in reality what she had
seen more perfectly in the mind's eye, and drove fifteen hundred miles to begin
my pilgrimage.

A dark mist lay over the Black Hills, and the land was like iron. At the top   6
of a ridge I caught sight of Devil's Tower upthrust against the gray sky as if in the
birth of time the core of the earth had broken through its crust and the motion
of the world was begun. There are things in nature that engender an awful quiet
in the heart of man; Devil's Tower is one of them. Two centuries ago, because of
their need to explain it, the Kiowas made a legend at the base of the rock. My
grandmother said:

"Eight children were there at play, seven sisters and their brother. Suddenly   7
the boy was struck dumb; he trembled and began to run upon his hands and feet.
His fingers became claws, and his body was covered with fur. There was a bear
where the boy had been. The sisters were terrified; they ran, and the bear after
them. They came to the stump of a great tree, and the tree spoke to them. It bade
them climb upon it, and as they did so, it began to rise into the air. The bear
came to kill them, but they were just beyond its reach. It reared against the tree
and scored the bark all around with its claws. The seven sisters were borne into
the sky, and they became the stars of the Big Dipper." From that moment, and
so long as the legend lives, the Kiowas have kinsmen in the night sky. Whatever
they were in the mountains, they could be no more. However tenuous their well-
being, however much they had suffered and would suffer again, they had found
a way out of the wilderness.

My grandmother had a reverence for the sun, a holy regard that now is all   8
but gone out of mankind. There was a wariness in her, and an ancient awe. She
was a Christian in her later years, but she had come a long way about, and she
never forgot her birthright. As a child she had been to the sun dances; she had
taken part in that annual rite, and by it she had learned the restoration of her
people in the presence of Tai-me. She was about seven when the last Kiowa sun
dance was held in 1887 on the Washita River above Rainy Mountain Creek.
The buffalo were gone. In order to consummate the ancient sacrifice—to impale
the head of a buffalo bull upon the Tai-me tree—a delegation of old men journeyed into Texas, there to beg and barter for an animal from the Goodnight
herd. She was ten when the Kiowas came together for the last time as a living

sun-dance culture. They could find no buffalo; they had to hang an old hide from the sacred tree. Before the dance could begin, a company of soldiers rode out from Fort Sill under orders to disperse the tribe. Forbidden without cause the essential act of their faith, having seen the wild herds slaughtered and left to rot upon the ground, the Kiowas backed away forever from the tree. That was July 20, 1890, at the great bend of the Washita. My grandmother was there. Without bitterness, and for as long as she lived, she bore a vision of deicide.

Now that I can have her only in memory, I see my grandmother in the several postures that were peculiar to her: standing at the wood stove on a winter morning and turning meat in a great iron skillet; sitting at the south window, bent above her beadwork, and afterwards, when her vision failed, looking down for a long time into the fold of her hands; going out upon a cane, very slowly as she did when the weight of age came upon her; praying. I remember her most often at prayer. She made long, rambling prayers out of suffering and hope, having seen many things. I was never sure that I had the right to hear, so exclusive were they of all mere custom and company. The last time I saw her she prayed standing by the side of her bed at night, naked to the waist, the light of a kerosene lamp moving upon her dark skin. Her long black hair, always drawn and braided in the day, lay upon her shoulders and against her breasts like a shawl. I do not speak Kiowa, and I never understood her prayers, but there was something inherently sad in the sound, some merest hesitation upon the syllables of sorrow. She began in a high and descending pitch, exhausting her breath to silence; then again and again—and always the same intensity of effort, of something that is, and is not, like urgency in the human voice. Transported so in the dancing light among the shadows of her room, she seemed beyond the reach of time. But that was illusion; I think I knew then that I should not see her again.   9

Houses are like sentinels in the plain, old keepers of the weather watch. There, in a very little while, wood takes on the appearance of great age. All colors wear soon away in the wind and rain, and then the wood is burned gray and the grain appears and the nails turn red with rust. The window panes are black and opaque; you imagine there is nothing within, and indeed there are many ghosts, bones given up to the land. They stand here and there against the sky, and you approach them for a longer time than you expect. They belong in the distance; it is their domain.   10

Once there was a lot of sound in my grandmother's house, a lot of coming and going, feasting and talk. The summers there were full of excitement and reunion. The Kiowas are a summer people; they abide the cold and keep to   11 themselves, but when the season turns and the land becomes warm and vital they cannot hold still; an old love of going returns upon them. The aged visitors who came to my grandmother's house when I was a child were made of lean and leather, and they bore themselves upright. They wore great black hats and bright ample shirts that shook in the wind. They rubbed fat upon their hair and wound their braids with strips of colored cloth. Some of them painted their faces and carried the scars of old and cherished enmities. They were an old council of war-lords, come to remind and be reminded of who they were. Their wives and daughters served them well. The women might indulge themselves; gossip was at once the mark and compensation of their servitude. They made loud and elaborate talk among themselves, full of jest and gesture, fright and false alarm. They went abroad in fringed and flowered shawls, bright beadwork and German silver. They were at home in the kitchen, and they prepared meals that were banquets.

There were frequent prayer meetings, and nocturnal feasts. When I was a   12
child I played with my cousins outside, where the lamplight fell upon the ground and the singing of the old people rose up around us and carried away into the darkness. There were a lot of good things to eat, a lot of laughter and surprise. And afterwards, when the quiet returned, I lay down with my grandmother and could hear the frogs away by the river and feel the motion of the air.

Now there is a funereal silence in the rooms, the endless wake of some final   13
word. The walls have closed in upon my grandmother's house. When I returned to it in mourning, I saw for the first time in my life how small it was. It was late at night, and there was a white moon, nearly full. I sat for a long time on the stone steps by the kitchen door. From there I could see out across the land; I could see the long row of trees by the creek, the low light upon the rolling plains, and the stars of the Big Dipper. Once I looked at the moon and caught sight of a strange thing. A cricket had perched upon the handrail, only a few inches away. My line of vision was such that the creature filled the moon like a fossil. It had gone there, I thought, to live and die, for there, of all places, was its small definition made whole and eternal. A warm wind rose up and purled like the longing within me.

The next morning, I awoke at dawn and went out on the dirt road to Rainy   14
Mountain. It was already hot, and the grasshoppers began to fill the air. Still, it was early in the morning, and birds sang out of the shadows. The long yellow grass on the mountain shone in the bright light, and a scissortail hied above the land. There, where it ought to be, at the end of a long and legendary way, was

my grandmother's grave. She had at last succeeded to that holy ground. Here and there on the dark stones were ancestral names. Looking back once, I saw the mountain and came away.

Questions for Discussion

1. Why does Momaday return to Rainy Mountain? What are his stated reasons? What might be other reasons, unstated?
2. What does Momaday remember about his grandmother and where she lived that is different from the reality? What does this say about memory?
3. How does Momaday's memory betray him when he returns to his grandmother's house?
4. Why might Momaday have written so much about his memories of his grandmother and childhood, yet written only a short line about his grandmother's grave, the supposed goal of his journey?
5. What is the effect of the many metaphors and similes? What do they add to the atmosphere of the piece?
6. What does Rainy Mountain symbolize to the Kiowas and to Momaday's grandmother? What does it symbolize to Momaday?
7. How is the "way" of the title used metaphorically?

Questions for Reflection and Writing

1. Describe the most memorable images you have of a person you once knew well. Why did those images gel in your memory?
2. What are some of the rituals of childhood that Momaday recalls? What makes them rituals? Define "ritual" and show where they appear in Momaday's essay. Compare them to childhood rituals that you practiced.
3. Research the life of one of your grandparents or other ancestors. What was happening when that person was a child and young adult? As an alternative, research and report on the history and culture of the Kiowas or another Plains nation.

Langston Hughes (1902–1967) was born in Joplin, Missouri, and raised in Lawrence, Kansas, and Cleveland, Ohio. Hughes evolved into one of the most original, versatile, and prolific authors of African-American literature. He wrote poetry, drama, fiction, essays, autobiography, songs, opera libretti, children's books, and a history of the NAACP. In all, he produced more than sixty books: perhaps best known are the early verse collection *The Weary Blues* (1926); *Mulatto* (1935), a play; and his two volumes of autobiography, *The Big Sea* (1940), from which "Salvation" is taken, and *I Wonder As I Wander* (1954). Hughes was a dominant voice in twentieth-century American literature and the century's most influential African-American poet, serving as a model for poets like Gwendolyn Brooks and playwrights like Lorraine Hansberry. "I explain and illuminate the Negro condition in America. This applies to 90 percent of my work," declared Hughes.

Salvation

Langston Hughes

I was saved from sin when I was going on thirteen. But not really saved It happened like this. There was a big revival at my Auntie Reed's church. Every night for weeks there had been much preaching, singing, praying, and shouting, and some very hardened sinners had been brought to Christ, and the membership of the church had grown by leaps and bounds. Thenjust before the revival ended, they held a special meeting for children, "to bring the young lambs to the fold." My aunt spoke of it for days ahead. That night I was escorted to the front row and placed on the mourners' bench with all the other young sinners, who had not yet been brought to Jesus.   1

My aunt told me that when you were saved you saw a light, and something happened to you inside! And Jesus came into your life! And God was with you from then on! She said you could see and hear and feel Jesus in your soul. I believed her. I had heard a great many old people say the same thing and it seemed to me they ought to know. So I sat there calmly in the hot. crowded church, waiting for Jesus to come to me.   2

The preacher preached a wonderful rythmical sermon, all moans and shouts and lonely cries and dire pictures of hell, and then he sang a song about the ninety and nine safe in the fold, but one little lamb was left out in the   3 cold. Then he said: "Won't you come? Won't you come to Jeses? Young lambs, won't you come?" And he held out his arms to all us young sinners there on the mourners' bench. And the little girls cried. And some of them jumped up and went to Jesus right away. But most of us just sat there.

A great many old people came and knelt around us and prayed, old women with jet-black faces and braided hair, old men with work-gnarled hands. And the church sang a song about the lower lights are burning, some poor sinners to be saved. And the whole building rocked with prayer and song.   4

Still I kept waiting to *see* Jesus.   5

Finally all the young people had gone to the altar and were saved, but one boy and me. He was a rounder's son named Westley. Westley and I were surrounded by sisters and deacons praying. It was very hot in the church, and getting late now. Finally Westley said to me in a whisper: "God damn! I'm tired o' sitting here. Let's get up and be saved." So he got up and was saved.   6

Then I was left all alone on the mourners' bench. My aunt came and knelt at my knees and cried, while prayers and song swirled all around me in the little church. The whole congregation prayed for me alone, in a mighty wail of moans and voices. And I kept waiting serenely for Jesus, waiting, waiting—but he didn't come. I wanted to see him, but nothing happened to me. Nothing! I wanted something to happen to me, but nothing happened.   7

I heard the songs and the minister saying: "Why don't you come? My dear child, why don't you come to Jesus? Jesus is waiting for you. He want you. Why don't you come? Sister Reed, what is this child's name?"   8

"Langston," my aunt sobbed.   9

"Langston, why don't you come? Why don't you come and be saved? Oh, Lamb of God! Why don't you come?"   10

Now it was really getting late. I began to be ashamed of myself, holding every thing up so long. I began to wonder what God thought about Westley, who certainly hadn't seen Jesus either, but who was now sitting proudly on the platform, swinging his knickerbockered legs and grinning down at me, surrounded by deacons and old women on their knees praying. God had not struck Westley dead for taking his name in vain or for lying in the temple. So I decided that maybe to save further trouble, I'd better lie, too, and say that Jesus had come, and get up and be saved.   11

So I got up.   12

Suddenly the whole room broke into a sea of shouting, as they saw me rise.   13
Waves of rejoicing swept the place. Women leaped in the air. My aunt threw her
arms around me. The minister took me by the hand and led me to the platform.

When things quieted down, in a hushed silence, punctuated by a few   14
ecstatic "Amens," all the new young lambs were blessed in the name of God.
Then joyous singing filled the room.

That night, for the last time in my life but one—for I was a big boy twelve   15
years old—I cried. I cried, in bed alone, and couldn't stop. I buried my head
under the quilts, but my aunt heard me. She woke up and told my uncle I was
crying because the Holy Ghost had come into my life, and because I had seen
Jesus. But I was really crying because I couldn't bear to tell her that I had lied,
that I had deceived everybody in the church, that I hadn't seen Jesus, and that
now I didn't believe there was a Jesus any more, since he didn't come to help me.

Questions for Discussion

1. What's the effect of Hughes's opening sentence: "I was saved from sin when
   I was going on thirteen." How is this effect moderated by the second sentence?
2. What's the effect of the repeated exclamation points in the first three sentences of the second paragraph?
3. What is a "rounder" (paragraph 6)? Do some research to find out if you don't
   know. Do you think that Hughes expected his audience to be familiar with
   the term?
4. What finally convinces the boy to stand up?
5. Do you think the rest of the congregation believed that the boy had seen
   Jesus? On what do you base your conclusion?

Questions for Reflection and Writing

1. How does the boy explain the fact that he didn't "see" Jesus? Do you accept
   his explanation?
2. Why do you think Hughes recounts this event? Do we have access to the
   mature writer's reflections on his experience, or only of the boy's experience
   of the events? Use textual evidence to support your answer.
3. How much do you know about the tradition of revivals? Do a little
   research—online, you might try "African-American Religion in the
   Nineteenth Century" (www.nhc. rtp.nc.us:8080/tserve/nineteen/nkeyin-
   fo/nafrican.htm), from the National Humanities Center. Write an essay in
   which you put Hughes's account into this broader perspective, explaining
   how your research expanded your understanding of the story, and vice versa.

Maxine Hong Kingston, author of two prize-winning nonfiction books, has also published numerous poems, stories and articles. Her autobiography, *The Woman Warrior: Memories of a Girlhood among Ghosts* (1976), won the National Book Critics Circle award for nonfiction. This excerpt from that autobiography reveals some of the cultural obstacles she encountered as a female child in a Chinese family, as well as her troubled responses to those difficulties.

Prereading: Questions

1. Have you ever been expected to behave in a certain way because you were a girl or a boy? How did you feel about this situation?
2. What fairy tales or stories do you remember from your childhood? What did you like about them?
3. Have you ever rebelled against a parent or some other authority? What was the result?

Helpful Definitions

talking-story (1)—telling a story
alighted (1)—came to rest
emigrant (8)—a person who leaves his or her homeland
grievances (15)—complaints
Berkeley (20)—The University of California at Berkeley
gloat (24)—brag, boast

The Woman Warrior

Maxine Hong Kingston

When we Chinese girls listened to the adults talking-story, we learned that we   1
failed if we grew up to be but wives or slaves. We could be heroines, swordswomen. Even if she had to rage across all China, a swordswoman got even with anybody who hurt her family. Perhaps women were once so dangerous that they had to have their feet bound. It was a woman who invented white crane

boxing only two hundred years ago. She was already an expert pole fighter, daughter of a teacher trained at the Shao-lin temple, where there lived an order of fighting monks. She was combing her hair one morning when a white crane alighted outside her window. She teased it with her pole, which it pushed aside with a soft brush of its wing. Amazed, she dashed outside and tried to knock the crane off its perch. It snapped her pole in two. Recognizing the presence of great power, she asked the spirit of the white crane if it would teach her to fight. It answered with a cry that white crane boxers imitate today. Later the bird returned as an old man, and he guided her boxing for many years. Thus she gave the world a new martial art.

This was one of the tamer, more modern stories, mere introduction. My   2
mother told others that followed swordswomen through woods and palaces for years. Night after night my mother would talk-story until we fell asleep. I couldn't tell where the stories left off and the dreams began, her voice the voice of the heroines in my sleep. And on Sundays, from noon to midnight, we went to the movies at the Confucius Church. We saw swordswomen jump over houses from a standstill; they didn't even need a running start.

At last I saw that I too had been in the presence of great power, my moth-   3
er talking-story. After I grew up, I heard the chant of Fa Mu Lan, the girl who took her father's place in battle. Instantly I remembered that as a child I had followed my mother about the house, the two of us singing about how Fa Mu Lan fought gloriously and returned alive from war to settle in the village. I had forgotten this chant that was once mine, given me by my mother, who may not have known its power to remind. She said I would grow up a wife and a slave, but she taught me the song of the warrior woman, Fa Mu Lan. I would have to grow up a warrior woman. . . .

My American life has been such a disappointment.   4

"I got straight A's, Mama."   5

"Let me tell you a true story about a girl who saved her village."   6

I could not figure out what was my village. And it was important that I do   7
something big and fine, or else my parents would sell me when we made our way back to China. In China there were solutions for what to do with little girls who ate up food and threw tantrums. You can't eat straight A's.

When one of my parents or the emigrant villagers said, "Feeding girls is   8
feeding cowbirds," I would thrash on the floor and scream so hard I couldn't talk. I couldn't stop.

"What's the matter with her?"   9

"I don't know. Bad, I guess. You know how girls are. 'There's no profit in   10
raising girls. Better to raise geese than girls.'"

"I would hit her if she were mine. But then there's no use wasting all that   11
discipline on a girl. 'When you raise girls, you're raising children for strangers.'"

"Stop that crying!" my mother would yell. 'I'm going to hit you if you don't   12
stop. Bad girl! Stop!" I'm going to remember never to hit or to scold my children
for crying, I thought, because then they will only cry more.

"I'm not a bad girl," I would scream. "I'm not a bad girl. I'm not a bad girl."   13
I might as well have said, "I'm not a girl."

"When you were little, all you had to say was 'I'm not a bad girl,' and you   14
could make yourself cry," my mother says, talking-story about my childhood.

I minded that the emigrant villagers shook their heads at my sister and me.   15
"One girl—and another girl," they said, and made our parents ashamed to take
us out together. The good part about my brothers being born was that people
stopped saying, "All girls," but I learned new grievances. "Did you roll an egg on
my face like that when I was born?" "Did you have a full-month party for me?"
"Did you turn on all the lights?" "Did you send my picture to Grandmother?"
"Why not? Because I'm a girl? Is that why not?" "Why didn't you teach me
English?" "You like having me beaten up at school, don't you?"

"She is very mean, isn't she?" the emigrant villagers would say.   16

"Come, children. Hurry. Hurry. Who wants to go out with Great-Uncle?"   17
On Saturday mornings my great-uncle, the ex-river pirate, did the shopping.
"Get your coats, whoever's coming."

"I'm coming. I'm coming. Wait for me."   18

When he heard girls' voices, he turned to us and roared, "No girls!" and left   19
my sisters and me hanging our coats back up, not looking at one aother. The boys
came back with candy and new toys. When they walked through Chinatown,
the people must have said, "A boy—and another boy— and another boy!" At
my great-uncle's funeral I secretly tested out feeling glad that he was dead—the
six-foot bearish masculinity of him.

I went away to college—Berkeley in the sixties—and I studied, and I   20
marched to change the world, but I did not turn into a boy. I would have liked
to bring myself back as a boy for my parents to welcome with chickens and pigs.
That was for my brother, who returned alive from Vietnam.

If I went to Vietnam, I would not come back; females desert families. It was   21
said, "There is an outward tendency in females," which meant that I was getting
straight A's for the good of my future husband's family, not my own. I did not plan

ever to have a husband. I would show my mother and father and the nosey emigrant villagers that girls have no outward tendency. I stopped getting straight A's.

And all the time I was having to turn myself American-feminine, or no   22
dates.

There is a Chinese word for the female I—which is "slave." Break the   23
women with their own tongues!

I refused to cook. When I had to wash dishes, I would crack one or two.   24
"Bad girl," my mother yelled, and sometimes that made me gloat rather than cry.
Isn't a bad girl almost a boy?

"What do you want to be when you grow up, little girl?"   25

"A lumberjack in Oregon."   26

Even now, unless I'm happy, I burn the food when I cook. I do not feed peo-   27
ple. I let dirty dishes rot. I eat at other people's tables but won't invite them to
mine, where the dishes are rotting.

If I could not eat, perhaps I could make myself a warrior like the   28
swordswoman who drives me. I will—I must—rise and plow the fields as soon as
the baby comes out.

Questions on Content

1. How does Kingston feel about the stories of women warriors her mother told her?

2. How does Kingston make it clear that girl children were less valued than boy children?

3. Why does Kingston's family not appreciate her good grades? Why did Kingston stop getting A's?

4. As a child, how did Kingston react to the cultural values reflected in the reading selection? As an adult, how does she react?

5. What is the "outward tendency" (paragraph 21) in females?

Questions on Technique

1. In her opening paragraph, Kingston suggests that women were once so dangerous that their feet were bound. She is referring to a now-illegal practice of binding girls' feet in linen to prevent them from growing. This was considered a mark of breeding and beauty; it also crippled the girls. Why does Kingston mention this practice?

2. Kingston often uses dialogue (conversation). Cite two or three examples of dialogue that you like. What does the dialogue contribute?

3.   What do you think of Kingston's last paragraph? What does her reference to plowing the fields "as soon as the baby comes out" mean? Does that reference provide a suitable closing for the selection? Explain.

For Further Consideration

1.   Why do you think Kingston's mother tells her the stories of the women warriors?
2.   Why do you think that Kingston says her American life is "a disappointment" (paragraph 4)?
3.   What do you think Kingston means when she says, "Break the women with their own tongues" (paragraph 23)?
4.   Does American culture value boys more than girls? Cite examples to support your view.

Journal Entry

In a paragraph or two, write a description of the kind of person you think Kingston is. You can consider some or all of these questions: What kind of woman is she? What does she value? What is her view of men? Of women? Of Chinese culture? Of American culture?

Collaborative Activity

In groups of three or four, discuss several well-known fairy tales or sto-ries told to American children. What values do these stories reveal? What roles do men and women play in them?

Writing Topics

1.   Kingston feels that her straight-A grades were not enough to please her family. Tell about a time when you achieved something that did not satisfy someone else's expectations. As an alternative, tell about a time when you did meet someone's expectations.
2.   Create a story or fairy tale of your own for American children, one that demonstrates the value of women (or men) in American culture.
3.   Write an essay about a time or times when you were treated differently because of your gender. Be sure to include how you were affected and how you responded. (Cause-and-Effect Analysis)
4.   Many of us have rebelled, as Kingston says she did, against our parents' authority or values. Write about a time when you rebelled. Explain why you

rebelled, as well as the consequences of your behavior. (Cause-and-Effect Analysis)

5. Explain how you have been affected by some fact of your family life: for example, being the oldest or youngest, your parents' divorce, moving to new towns often, living in an older house, or being an only child. (Cause-and-Effect Analysis)

Oliver Goldsmith (1728—1774) was born in Ireland and attended Trinity College. After wandering around Europe for a few years, he turned his hand to literature and ultimately became one of Britain's enduring literary voices. Goldsmith wrote novels, plays, poems, and essays. His best known works include the poem *The Deserted Village* (1770), the play *She Stoops to Conquer* (1773), and the novel *The Vicar of Wakefield* (1766). "National Prejudices," from the *Citizen of the World* (1762), examines the interplay between national and global loyalties.

National Prejudices

Oliver Goldsmith

As I am one of that sauntering tribe of mortals, who spend the greatest part of 1 their time in taverns, coffee houses, and other places of public resort, I have thereby an opportunity of observing an infinite variety of characters, which, to a person of a contemplative turn, is a much higher entertainment than a view of all the curiosities of art or nature. In one of these, my late rambles, I accidentally fell into the company of half a dozen gentlemen, who were engaged in a warm dispute about some political affair; the decision of which, as they were equally divided in their sentiments, they thought proper to refer to me, which naturally drew me in for a share of the conversation.

Amongst a multiplicity of other topics, we took occasion to talk of the dif- 2 ferent characters of the several nations of Europe; when one of the gentlemen, cocking his hat, and assuming such an air of importance as if he had possessed all the merit of the English nation in his own person, declared that the Dutch were a parcel of avaricious wretches; the French a set of flattering sycophants; that the Germans were drunken sots, and beastly gluttons; and the Spaniards proud, haughty, and surly tyrants; but that in bravery, generosity, clemency, and in every other virtue, the English excelled all the rest of the world.

This very learned and judicious remark was received with a general smile 3 of approbation by all the company—all, I mean, but your humble servant; who, endeavoring to keep my gravity as well as I could, and reclining my head upon my arm, continued for some time in a posture of affected thoughtfulness, as if I had been musing on something else, and did not seem to attend to the subject of conversation; hoping by these means to avoid the disagreeable necessity of explaining myself, and thereby depriving the gentleman of his imaginary happiness.

But my pseudo-patriot had no mind to let me escape so easily. Not satisfied   4
that his opinion should pass without contradiction, he was determined to have
it ratified by the suffrage of every one in the company; for which purpose addressing himself to me with an air of inexpressible confidence, he asked me if I was
not of the same way of thinking. As I am never forward in giving my opinion,
especially when I have reason to believe that it will not be agreeable; so, when I
am obliged to give it, I always hold it for a maxim to speak my real sentiments. I
therefore told him that, for my own part, I should not have ventured to talk in
such a peremptory strain, unless I had made the tour of Europe, and examined
the manners of these several nations with great care and accuracy: that, perhaps,
a more impartial judge would not scruple to affirm that the Dutch were more frugal and industrious, the French more temperate and polite, the Germans more
hardy and patient of labour and fatigue, and the Spaniards more staid and sedate,
than the English; who, though undoubtedly brave and generous, were at the
same time rash, headstrong, and impetuous; too apt to be elated with prosperity,
and to despond in adversity.

I could easily perceive that all the company began to regard me with a jeal-   5
ous eye before I had finished my answer, which I had no sooner done, than the
patriotic gentleman observed, with a contemptuous sneer, that he was greatly
surprised how some people could have the conscience to live in a country which
they did not love, and to enjoy the protection of a government, to which in their
hearts they were inveterate enemies. Finding that by this modest declaration of
my sentiments I had forfeited the good opinion of my companions, and given
them occasion to call my political principles in question, and well knowing that
it was in vain to argue with men who were so very full of themselves, I threw
down my reckoning and retired to my own lodgings, reflecting on the absurd and
ridiculous nature of national prejudice and prepossession.

Among all the famous sayings of antiquity, there is none that does greater   6
honour to the author, or affords greater pleasure to the reader (at least if he be a
person of a generous and benevolent heart), than that of the philosopher, who,
being asked what "countryman he was," replied, that he was, "a citizen of the
world."—How few are there to be found in modern times who can say the same,
or whose conduct is consistent with such a profession!—We are now become so
much Englishmen, Frenchmen, Dutchmen, Spaniards, or Germans, that we are
no longer citizens of the world; so much the natives of one particular spot, or

members of one petty society, that we no longer consider ourselves as the general inhabitants of the globe, or members of that grand society which comprehends the whole human kind.

Did these prejudices prevail only among the meanest and lowest of the   7
people, perhaps they might be excused, as they have few, if any, opportunities of correcting them by reading, travelling, or conversing with foreigners; but the misfortune is, that they infect the minds, and influence the conduct, even of our gentlemen; of those, I mean, who have every title to this appellation but an exemption from prejudice, which however, in my opinion, ought to be regarded as the characteristical mark of a gentleman; for let a man's birth be ever so high, his station ever so exalted, or his fortune ever so large, yet if he is not free from national and other prejudices, I should make bold to tell him, that he had a low and vulgar mind, and had no just claim to the character of a gentleman. And in fact, you will always find that those are most apt to boast of national merit, who have little or no merit of their own to depend on; than which, to be sure, nothing is more natural: the slender vine twists around the sturdy oak, for no other reason in the work but because it has not strength sufficient to support itself.

Should it be alleged in defense of national prejudice, that it is the natural   8
and necessary growth of love to our country, and that therefore the former cannot be destroyed without hurting the latter, I answer, that this is a gross fallacy and delusion. That it is the growth of love to our country, I will allow; but that it is the natural and necessary growth of it, I absolutely deny. Superstition and enthusiasm too are the growth of religion; but who ever took it in his head to affirm that they are the necessary growth of this noble priciple? They are, if you will, the bastard sprouts of this heavenly plant, but not its natural and genuine branches, and may safely enough be loped off, this goodly tree can never flourish in perfect health and vigour.

It is not very possible that I may love my own country, without hating the   9
natives of other countries? that I may exert the most heroic bravery, the most undaunted resolution, in defending its laws and liberty, without despising all the rest of the world as cowards and poltroons? Most certainly it is; and if it were not, I must own, I should prefer the title of the ancient philosopher, viz. a citizen of the world, to that of an Englishman, a Frenchman, a European, or to any other appellation whatever.

Questions for Discussion

1. Where does the author say he spends the most time meeting people? Does this surprise you?

2. Describe the conversation that's central to this essay. What do you think its setting looked like?

3. What is the thesis of this piece? Can you write one sentence that expresses it?

4. Goldsmith calls one of conversationalists a "pseudo-patriot." Why? Do you agree?

5. Which is a better title for this piece: "National Prejudices" or "A Citizen of the World"? Explain.

Questions for Reflection and Writing

1. Recall a time you had a discussion with someone about the country in which you were born. What was the nature of the conversation? Did it resemble the conversation featured in this essay? Compare and contrast the two, and in so doing, say something about the different worlds in which they took place.

2. Did you find this essay funny? If so, characterize the humor. If not, why not? Was any of it offensive?

3. Does Goldsmith believe that you can live in a country that you do not love? What about the "patriotic gentleman" from question 4 above? Considering their implicit reasoning, make up your own mind on this question, and argue logically for your position. You might want to do some research along the way on the history and meaning of patriotism; online, start at the Museum of Patriotism (www. museumofpatriotism.org/).

Etty Hillesum (1914–1943) is remembered for her World War II diaries. She was born in Middleburg, Netherlands, in 1914 and died in the Nazi concentration camp in Auschwitz, Poland, on November 30, 1943, at age twenty-nine. Hillesum portrays her last three years in *An Interrupted Life: The Diaries of Etty Hillesum, 1941–1943*. She delivered eight handwritten volumes of these diaries to her friend Maria Tuinzing, who passed them on to writer Klaas Smelik. Smelik's son subsequently obtained a publisher for the diaries in 1980. Hillesum's diaries offer a glimpse into her spiritual struggle in the midst of wartime persecution.

Letter from a Nazi Concentration Camp

Etty Hillesum

24 August 1943

There was a moment when I felt in all seriousness that, after this night, it would be a sin ever to laugh again. But then I reminded myself that some of those who had gone away had been laughing, even if only a handful of them this time . . . There will be some who will laugh now and then in Poland, too, though not many from this transport, I think.   1

When I think of the faces of that squad of armed, green-uniformed guards—my God, those faces! I looked at them, each in turn, from behind the safety of a window, and I have never been so frightened of anything in my life as I was of those faces. I sank to my knees with the words that preside over human life: And God made man after His likeness. That passage spent a difficult morning with me.   2

I have told you often enough that no words and images are adequate to describe nights like these. But still I must try to convey something of it to you. One always has the feeling here of being the ears and eyes of a piece of Jewish history, but there is also the need sometimes to be a still, small voice. We must keep one another in touch with everything that happens in the various outposts of this world, each one contributing his own little piece of stone to the great mosaic that will take shape once the war is over.   3

After a night in the hospital barracks, I took an early morning walk past   4
the punishment barracks, and prisoners were being moved out. The deportees,
mainly men, stood with their packs behind the barbed wire. So many of them
looked tough and ready for anything. An old acquaintance—I didn't recognise
him straightaway, a shaven head often changes people completely—called out to
me with a smile, 'If they don't manage to do me in, I'll be back.'

But the babies, those tiny piercing screams of the babies, dragged from their   5
cots in the middle of the night . . . I have to put it all down quickly, in a muddle
because if I leave it until later I probably won't be able to go on believing that it
really happened. It is like a vision, and drifts further and further away. The babies
were easily the worst.

And then there was that paralysed young girl, who didn't want to take her   6
dinner plate along and found it so hard to die. Or the terrified young boy: he had
thought he was safe, that was his mistake, and when he realised he was going to
have to go anyway, he panicked and ran off. His fellow Jews had to hunt him
down—if they didn't find him, scores of others would be put on the transport in
his place. He was caught soon enough, hiding in a tent, but 'notwithstanding' . . .
'notwithstanding,' all those others had to go on transport anyway, as a deterrent,
they said. And so, many good friends were dragged away by that boy. Fifty victims for one moment of insanity. Or rather: he didn't drag them away—our commandant did, someone of whom it is sometimes said that he is a gentleman. Even
so, will the boy be able to live with himself, once it dawns on him exactly what
he's been the cause of ? And how will all the other Jews on board the train react
to him? That boy is going to have a very hard time. The episode might have been
overlooked, perhaps, if there hadn't been so much unnerving activity over our
heads that night. The commandant must have been affected by that too.
'*Donnerwetter*, some flying tonight!' I heard a guard say as he looked up at the
stars.

People still harbour such childish hopes that the transport won't get   7
through. Many of us were able from here to watch the bombardment of a nearby town, probably Emden. So why shouldn't it be possible for the railway line to
be hit too, and for the train be stopped from leaving? It's never been known to
happen yet, but people keep hoping it will with each new transport and with
never-flagging hope . . .

The evening before that night, I walked through the camp. People were   8
grouped together between the barracks, under a grey, cloudy sky. 'Look, that's just
how people behave after a disaster, standing about on street corners discussing

what's happened,' my companion said to me. 'But that's what makes it so impossible to understand,' I burst out. 'This time, it's before the disaster!'

Whenever misfortune strikes, people have a natural instinct to lend a helping hand and to save what can be saved. Tonight I shall be 'helping' to dress babies and to calm mothers and that is all I can hope to do. I could almost curse myself for that. For we all know that we are yielding up our sick and defenceless brothers and sisters to hunger, heat, cold, exposure and destruction, and yet we dress them and escort them to the bare cattle trucks—and if they can't walk we carry them on stretchers. What is going on, what mysteries are these, in what sort of fatal mechanism have we become enmeshed? The answer cannot simply be that we are all cowards. We're not that bad. We stand before a much deeper question . . . 9

In the afternoon I did a round of the hospital barracks one more time, going from bed to bed. Which beds would be empty the next day? The transport lists are never published until the very last moment, but some of us know well in advance that our names will be down. A young girl called me. She was sitting bolt upright in her bed, eyes wide open. This girl has thin wrists and a peaky little face. She is partly paralysed, and has just been learning to walk again, between two nurses, one step at a time. 'Have you heard? I have to go.' We look at each other for a long moment. It is as if her face has disappeared, she is all eyes. Then she says in a level, grey little voice, 'Such a pity, isn't it? That everything you have learned in life goes for nothing.' And, 'How hard it is to die.' Suddenly the unnatural rigidity of her expression gives way and she sobs, 'Oh, and the worst of it all is having to leave Holland!' And, 'Oh, why wasn't I allowed to die before . . .' Later, during the night, I saw her again, for the last time. 10

There was a little woman in the wash-house, a basket of dripping clothes on her arm. She grabbed hold of me. She looked deranged. A flood of words poured over me. 'That isn't right, how can that be right, I've got to go and I won't even be able to get my washing dry by tomorrow. And my child is sick, he's feverish, can't you fix things so that I don't have to go? And I don't have enough things for the child, the rompers they sent me are too small, I need the bigger size, oh, it's enough to drive you mad. And you're not even allowed to take a blanket along, we're going to freeze to death, you didn't think of that, did you? There's a cousin of mine here, he came here the same time I did, but he doesn't have to go, he's got the right papers. Couldn't you help me to get some, too? Just say I don't have to go, do you think they'll leave the children with their moth- 11 ers, that's right, you come back again tonight, you'll help me then, won't you, what do you think, would my cousin's papers . . . ?'

If I were to say that I was in hell that night, what would I really be telling   12
you? I caught myself saying it aloud in the night, aloud to myself and quite sober-
ly, 'So that's what hell is like.' You really can't tell who is going and who isn't this
time. Almost everyone is up, the sick help each other to get dressed. There are
some who have no clothes at all, whose luggage has been lost or hasn't arrived
yet. Ladies from the 'Welfare' walk about doling out clothes, which may fit or
not, it doesn't matter so long as you've covered yourself with something. Some
old women look a ridiculous sight. Small bottles of milk are being prepared to
take along with the babies, whose pitiful screams punctuate all the frantic activity in the barracks. A young mother says to me almost apologetically, 'My baby
doesn't usually cry, it's almost as if he can tell what's happening.' She picks up the
child, a lovely baby about eight months old, from a makeshift crib and smiles at
it, 'If you don't behave yourself, mummy won't take you along with her!' She tells
me about some friends, 'When those men in green came to fetch them in
Amsterdam, their children cried terribly. Then their father said, "If you don't
behave yourselves, you won't be allowed to go in that green car, this green gentleman won't take you." And that helped—the children calmed down.' She
winks at me bravely, a trim, dark little woman with a lively, olive-skinned face,
dressed in long grey trousers and a green woolen sweater, 'I may be smiling, but
I feel pretty awful.' The little woman with the wet washing is on the point of hys-
terics. 'Can't you hide my child for me? Go on, please, won't you hide him, he's
got a high fever, how can I possibly take him along?' She points to a little bundle of misery with blonde curls and a burning, bright-red little face. The child
tosses about in his rough wooden cot. The nurse wants the mother to put on an
extra woolen sweater, tries to pull it over her dress. She refuses, 'I'm not going to
take anything along, what use would it be . . . my child.' And she sobs, 'They take
the sick children away and you never get them back.'

Then a woman comes up to her, a stout working-class woman with a kind-   13
ly snubnosed face, draws the desperate mother down with her on to the edge of
one of the iron bunk beds and talks to her almost crooningly, 'There now, you're
just an ordinary Jew, aren't you, so you'll just have to go, won't you . . . ?'

A few beds further along I suddenly catch sight of the ash-grey, freckled   14
face of a colleague. She is squatting beside the bed of a dying woman who has
swallowed some poison and who happens to be her mother . . .

'God Almighty, what are you doing to us?' The words just escape me. Over 15
there is that affectionate little woman from Rotterdam. She is in her ninth
month. Two nurses try to get her dressed. She just stands there, her swollen body
leaning against her child's cot. Drops of sweat run down her face. She stares into
the distance, a distance into which I cannot follow her, and says in a toneless,
worn-out voice, 'Two months ago I volunteered to go with my husband to
Poland. And then I wasn't allowed to, because I always have such difficult con-
finements. And now I do have to go . . . just because someone tried to run away
tonight.' The wailing of the babies grows louder still, filling every nook and cran-
ny of the barracks, now bathed in ghostly light. It is almost too much to bear. A
name occurs to me: Herod.

On the stretcher, on the way to the train, her labour pains begin, and we 16
are allowed to carry the woman to hospital instead of to the goods train, which,
this night, seems a rare act of humanity . . .

I pass the bed of the paralysed girl. The others have helped to dress her. I 17
never saw such great big eyes in such a little face. 'I can't take it all in,' she whispers to me. A few steps away stands my little hunchbacked Russian woman, I
told you about her before. She stands there as if spun in a web of sorrow. The
paralysed girl is a friend of hers. Later she said sadly to me, 'She doesn't even have
a plate, I wanted to give her mine but she wouldn't take it, she said, "I'll be dead
in ten days' time anyway, and then those horrible Germans will get it ."'

She stands there in front of me, a green silk kimono wrapped round her 18
small, misshapen figure. She has the very wise, bright eyes of a child. She looks
at me for a long time in silence, searchingly, and then says, 'I would like, oh, I
really would like, to be able to swim away in my tears.' And, 'I long so desperately for my dear mother.' (Her mother died a few months ago from cancer, in the
washroom near the WC. At least she was left alone there for a moment, left to
die in peace.) She asks me with her strange accent in the voice of a child that
begs for forgiveness, 'Surely God will be able to understand my doubts in a world
like this, won't He?' Then she turns away from me, in an almost loving gesture
of infinite sadness, and throughout the night I see the misshapen, green, silk-clad
figure moving between the beds, doing small services for those about to depart.
She herself doesn't have to go, not this time anyway . . .

I'm sitting here squeezing tomato juice for the babies. A young woman sits 19
beside me. She appears ready and eager to leave, and is beautifully turned out. It
is something like a cry of liberation when she exclaims, arms flung wide, 'I'm
embarking on a wonderful journey, I might find my husband.' A woman oppo-

site cuts her short bitterly, 'I'm going as well, but I certainly don't think it's wonderful.' I remembered admitting the young woman beside me. She has only been here for a few days and she came from the punishment block. She seems so level-headed and independent, with a touch of defiance about her mouth. She has been ready to leave since the afternoon, dressed in a long pair of trousers and a woollen jumper and cardigan. Next to her on the floor stands a heavy rucksack and a blanket roll. She is trying to force down a few sandwiches. They are mouldy. 'I'll probably get quite a lot of mouldy bread to eat,' she laughs. 'In prison I didn't eat anything at all for days.' A bit of her history in her own words: 'My time wasn't far off when they threw me into prison. And the taunts and the insults! I made the mistake of saying that I couldn't stand, so they made me stand for hours, but I managed it without making a sound.' She looks defiant.' My husband was in the prison as well. I won't tell you what they did to him! But my God, he was tough! They sent him through last month. I was in my third day of labour and couldn't go with him. But how brave he was!' She is almost radiant.

'Perhaps I shall find him again.' She laughs defiantly. 'They may drag us   20 through the dirt, but we'll come through all right in the end!' She looks at the crying babies all round and says, 'I'll have good work to do on the train, I still have lots of milk.'

'What, you here as well?' I suddenly call out in dismay. A woman turns and   21 comes up between the tumbled beds of the poor wailing babies, her hands groping round her for support. She is dressed in a long, black old-fashioned dress. She has a noble brow and white, wavy hair piled up high. Her husband died here a few weeks ago. She is well over eighty, but looks less than sixty. I always admired her for the aristocratic way in which she reclined on her shabby bunk. She answers in a hoarse voice, 'Yes, I'm here as well, they wouldn't let me share my husband's grave.'

'Ah, there she goes again!' It is the tough little ghetto woman who is racked   22 with hunger the whole time because she never gets any parcels. She has seven children here. She trips pluckily and busily about on her little short legs.' All I know is I've got seven children and they need a proper mother, you can be sure of that!'

With nimble gestures she is busy stuffing a jute bag full of her belongings.   23 'I'm not leaving anything behind, my husband was sent through here a year ago and my two oldest boys have been through as well.' She beams, 'My children are real treasures!' She bustles about, she packs, she's busy, she has a kind word for everyone who goes by. A plain, dumpy ghetto woman with greasy black hair and little short legs. She has a shabby, short-sleeved dress on, which I can imagine her wearing when she used to stand behind the washtub, back in Jodenbreestraat. And now she is off to Poland in the same old dress, a three days' journey with seven children. 'That's right, seven children, and they need a proper mother, believe me!'

You can tell that the young woman over there is used to luxury and that   24 she must have been very beautiful. She is a recent arrival. She had gone into hiding to save her baby. Now she is here, through treachery, like so many others. Her husband is in the punishment barracks. She looks quite pitiful now. Her bleached hair has black roots with a greenish tinge. She has put on many different sets of underwear and other clothing all on top of one another—you can't carry everything by hand, after all, particularly if you have a little child to carry as well. Now she looks lumpy and ridiculous. Her face is blotchy. She stares at everyone with a veiled, tentative gaze, like some defenceless and abandoned young animal.

What will this young woman, already in a state of collapse, look like after   25 three days in an overcrowded goods wagon with men, women, children and babies all thrown together, bags and baggage, a bucket in the middle their only convenience?

Presumably they will be sent on to another transit camp, and then on again   26 from there.

We are being hunted to death right through Europe . . .   27

I wander in a daze through other barracks. I walk past scenes that loom up   28 before my eyes in crystal-clear detail, and at the same time seem like blurred age-old visions. I see a dying old man being carried away, reciting the Sh'ma to himself . . .

Slowly but surely six o'clock in the morning has arrived. The train is due   29 to depart at eleven, and they are starting to load it with people and luggage. Paths to the train have been staked out by men of the Ordedienst, the Camp Service Corps. Anyone not involved with the transport has to keep to barracks. I slip into one just across from the siding .'There's always been a splendid view from here . . .' I hear a cynical voice say. The camp has been cut in two halves since yesterday by the train: a depressing series of bare, unpainted goods wagons in the front, and a proper carriage for the guards at the back. Some of the wagons have paper mattresses on the floor. These are for the sick. There is more and more movement now along the asphalt path beside the train.

Men from the 'Flying Column' in brown overalls are bringing the luggage   30 up on wheelbarrows. Among them I spot two of the commandant's court jesters:

the first is a comedian and a song-writer. Some time ago his name was down, irrevocably, for transport, but for several nights in a row he sang his lungs out for a delighted audience, including the commandant and his retinue. He sang 'Ich kann es nicht verstehen, dass die Rosen blühen' ('I know not why the roses bloom') and other topical songs. The commandant, a great lover of art, thought it all quite splendid. The singer got his 'exemption'. He was even allocated a house where he now lives behind redchecked curtains with his peroxide-blonde wife, who spends all her days at a mangle in the boiling hot laundry. Now here he is, dressed in khaki overalls, pushing a wheelbarrow piled high with the luggage of his fellow Jews. He looks like death warmed up. And over there is another court jester: the commandant's favourite pianist. Legend has it that he is so accomplished that he can play Beethoven's Ninth as a jazz number, which is certainly saying something . . .

Suddenly there are a lot of green-uniformed men swarming over the 31 asphalt. I can't imagine where they have sprung from. Knapsacks and guns over their shoulders. I study their faces. I try to look at them without prejudice.

I can see a father, ready to depart, blessing his wife and child and being 32 himself blessed in turn by an old rabbi with a snow-white beard and the profile of a fiery prophet. I can see . . . ah, I can't begin to describe it all . . .

On earlier transports, some of the guards were simple, kindly types with 33 puzzled expressions, who walked about the camp smoking their pipes and speaking in some incomprehensible dialect, and one would have found their company not too objectionable on the journey. Now I am transfixed with terror. Oafish, jeering faces, in which one seeks in vain for even the slightest trace of human warmth. At what fronts did they learn their business? In what punishment camps were they trained? For after all this is a punishment, isn't it? A few young women are already sitting in a goods wagon. They hold their babies on their laps, their legs dangling outside— they are determined to enjoy the fresh air as long as possible. Sick people are carried past on stretchers. After all, it is meant as a punishment. I almost find myself laughing, the disparity between the guards and the guarded is too absurd. My companion at the window shudders. Months ago he was brought here from Amersfoort, in bits and pieces. 'Oh, yes, that's what those fellows were like,' he says. 'That's what they looked like.'

A couple of young children stand with their noses pressed to the window- 34 pane. I listen in to their earnest conversation, 'Why do those nasty, horrid men wear green, why don't they wear black? Bad people wear black, don't they?' 'Look over there, that man is really sick!' A shock of grey hair above a rumpled blanket on a stretcher. 'Look, there's another sick one . . .'

And, pointing at the green uniforms, 'Look at them, now they're laughing!'   35
'Look, look, one of them's already drunk!'

More and more people are filling up the spaces in the goods wagons. A tall,   36
lonely figure paces the asphalt, a briefcase under his arm. He is the head of the
so-called *Antragstelle*, the camp 'appeals department'. He strives right up to the
last moment to get people out of the commandant's clutches. Horse-trading here
always continues until the train has actually pulled out. It's even been known for
him to manage to free people from the moving train. The man with the briefcase
has the brow of a scholar, and tired, very tired shoulders. A bent, little old
woman, with a black, oldfashioned hat on her grey, wispy hair, bars his way, gesticulating and brandishing a bundle of papers under his nose. He listens to her
for a while, then shakes his head and turns away, his shoulders sagging just a little bit more. This time it won't be possible to get many people off the train in the
nick of time. The commandant is annoyed. A young Jew has had the effrontery
to run away. One can't really call it a serious attempt to escape—he absconded
from the hospital in a moment of panic, a thin jacket over his blue pyjamas, and
in a clumsy, childish way took refuge in a tent where he was picked up quickly
enough after a search of the camp. But if you are a Jew you may not run away,
may not allow yourself to be stricken with panic. The commandant is remorseless. As a reprisal, and without warning, scores of others are being sent on the
transport with the boy, including quite a few who had thought they were firmly
at anchor here. This system happens to believe in collective punishment. And
all those planes overhead couldn't have helped to improve the commandant's
mood, though that is a subject on which he prefers to keep his own counsel.

The goods wagons are now what you might call full. But that's what you   37
think. God Almighty, does all this lot have to get in as well? A large new group
has turned up. The children are still standing with their noses glued to the window-pane, they don't miss a thing . . . 'Look over there, a lot of people are getting
off, it must be too hot in the train.' Suddenly one of them calls out. 'Look, the
commandant!'

He appears at the end of the asphalt path, like a famous star making his   38
entrance during agrand finale. This near-legendary figure is said to be quite
charming and so well-disposed towards the Jews. For the commandant of a camp
for Jews he has some strange ideas. Recently he decided that we needed more
variety in our diet, and we were promptly served marrowfat peas—just once—

instead of cabbage. He could also be said to be our artistic patron here, and is a regular at all our cabaret nights. On one occasion he came three times in succession to see the same performance and roared with laughter at the same old jokes each time. Under his auspices, a male choir has been formed that sang 'Bei mir bist du schön' on his personal orders. It sounded very moving here on the heath, it must be said. Now and then he even invites some of the artistes to his house and talks and drinks with them into the early hours. One night not so long ago he escorted an actress back home, and when he took his leave of her he offered her his hand, just imagine, his hand! They also say that he specially loves children. Children must be looked after. In the hospital they even get a tomato each day. And yet many of them seem to die all the same . . . I could go on quite a bit longer about 'our' commandant. Perhaps he sees himself as a prince dispensing largesse to his many humble subjects. God knows how he sees himself. A voice behind me says, 'Once upon a time we had a commandant who used to kick people off to Poland. This one sees them off with a smile.'

He now walks along the train with military precision, a relatively young   39
man who has 'arrived' early in his career, if one may call it that. He is absolute master over the life and death of Dutch and German Jews here on this remote heath in Drenthe Province. A year ago he probably had not the slightest idea that it so much as existed. I didn't know about it myself, to tell the truth. He walks along the train, his grey, immaculately brushed hair just showing beneath his flat, light-green cap. That grey hair, which makes such a romantic contrast with his fairly young face, sends many of the silly young girls here into raptures, although they dare not, of course, express their feelings openly. On this cruel morning his face is almost iron-grey. It is a face that I am quite unable to read. Sometimes it seems to me to be like along thin scar in which grimness mingles with joylessness and hypocrisy. And there is something else about him, halfway between a dapper hairdresser's assistant and a stage-door Johnny. But the grimness and the rigidly forced bearing predominate. With military step he walks along the goods wagons, bulging now with people. He is inspecting his troops: the sick, infants in arms, young mothers and shaven-headed men. A few more ailing people are being brought up on stretchers, he makes an impatient gesture, they're taking too long about it. Behind him walks his Jewish secretary, smartly dressed in fawn riding breeches and brown sports jacket. He has the sporty demeanour yet vacuous expression of the English whisky drinker. Suddenly they are joined by a handsome brown gun-dog, where from heaven knows. With studied gestures the fawn secretary plays with it, like something from a picture in an

English society paper. The green squad stare at him goggle-eyed. They probably think—though think is a big word—that some of the Jews here look quite different from what their propaganda sheets have led them to believe. A few Jewish big-shots from the camp now also walk along the train. 'Trying to air their "importance",' mutters someone behind me. 'Transport Boulevard,' I say. 'Could one ever hope to convey to the outside world what has happened here today?' I ask my companion. The outside world probably thinks of us as a grey, uniform, suffering mass of Jews, and knows nothing of the gulfs and abysses and subtle differences that exist between us. They could never hope to understand.

The commandant has now been joined by the *Oberdienstleiter*, the head of   40
the Camp Service Corps. The Oberdienstleiter is a German Jew of massive build, and the commandant looks slight and insignificant by his side. Black topboots, black cap, black army coat with yellow star. He has a cruel mouth and a powerful neck. A few years ago he was still a digger in the outworkers' corps. When the story of his meteoric rise is written up later, it will be an important historical account of the mentality of our age. The light-green commandant with his military bearing, the fawn, impassive secretary, the black bully-boy figure of the Oberdienstleiter, parade past the train. People fall back around them, but all eyes are on them.

My God, are the doors really being shut now? Yes, they are. Shut on the   41
herded, densely packed, mass of people inside. Through small openings at the top we can see heads and hands, hands that will wave to us later when the train leaves. The commandant takes a bicycle and rides once again along the entire length of the train. Then he makes a brief gesture, like royalty in an operetta. A little orderly comes flying up and deferentially relieves him of the bicycle. The train gives a piercing whistle, and 1020 Jews leave Holland.

This time the quota was really quite small, all considered: a mere thousand   42
Jews, the extra twenty being reserves, for it is always possible, indeed quite certain this time, that a few will die or be crushed to death on the way. So many sick people and not a single nurse . . .

The tide of helpers gradually recedes; people go back to their sleeping quarters.   43
So many exhausted, pale and suffering faces. One more piece of our camp has been amputated. Next week yet another piece will follow. This is what has been happening now for over a year, week in, week out. We are left with just a few thousand. A hundred thousand Dutch members of our race are toiling away under an unknown sky or lie rotting in some unknown soil. We know nothing of their fate. It is only a short while, perhaps, before we find out, each one of us

in his own time, for we are all marked down to share that fate, of that I have not a moment's doubt. But I must go now and lie down and sleep for a little while. I am a bit tired and dizzy. Then later I have to go to the laundry to track down the face cloth that got lost. But first I must sleep. As for the future, I am firmly resolved to return to you after my wanderings. In the meantime, my love once again, you dear people.

Questions for Discussion

1. According to Hillesum, who or what is to blame for the fate of the Dutch Jews?

2. Why did the Jews not only not try to escape but also help bring about their own and their neighbors' deaths?

3. What does this essay tell us about how people react as a group in times of mi fortune?

4. What is Hillesum's "job" at the staging camp? Why does she have this position?

5. Which of the people at the camp does Hillesum find fascinating, and why?

6. How would you describe Hillesum's persona as a narrator of events? How does she position herself as an observer?

7. How does knowing that the author of this letter was killed soon after writing it affect your reading of it?

Questions for Reflection and Writing

1. Which of the people in Hillesum's letter interest you the most. Why?

2. Why did people not do more to save themselves? What should they have done? Write in response to Hillesum's essay, but also consider what people should do if something like this were to happen again.

3. Find other personal narratives written about experiences during wars. Read one or two of them, or parts of several. What do the narratives teach you about war, humanity, and human behavior? What do they teach you about writing as a way of dealing with overwhelming events?

John Hersey (1914–1993), novelist, writer, educator, and professor, was born on June 17 in Tientsin, China. He received a B.A. from Yale University in 1936 and attended Clare College, Cambridge. A resident of Connecticut, Hersey enjoyed a long and varied career, including serving as personal secretary and driver to Sinclair Lewis and working as a World War II correspondent, a writer, and an educator.

His extensive list of memberships, awards, and honors included memberships in the National Institute of Arts and Letters, the American Academy of Arts and Letters, the American Academy of Arts and Sciences, and PEN. He was awarded the Pulitzer Prize in 1945 for *A Bell for Adano* and received several honorary degrees. Hersey considered fiction the best literary vehicle for truth. His writing was primarily concerned with conveying historical and political truths, and Hersey maintained that literature was moral in nature. *Hiroshima* was first published in the *New Yorker* on August 31, 1946 (1946; 1948); his other nonfiction work includes editing *The Writer's Craft* (1974) and authoring *Aspects of the Presidency: Truman and Ford in Office* (1980). His novels include *A Bell for Adano* (1944), *The Wall* (1950), *The War Lover* (1959), and *The Call: An American Missionary in China* (1985).

A Noiseless Flash from Hiroshima

John Hersey

At exactly fifteen minutes past eight in the morning, on August 6, 1945, Japanese time, at the moment when the atomic bomb flashed above Hiroshima, Miss Toshiko Sasaki, a clerk in the personnel department of the East Asia Tin Works, had just sat down at her place in the plant office and was turning her head to speak to the girl at the next desk. At that same moment, Dr. Masakazu Fujii was settling down crosslegged to read the Osaka *Asahi* on the porch of his private hospital, overhanging one of the seven deltaic rivers which divide Hiroshima; Mrs. Hatsuyo Nakamura, a tailor's widow, stood by the window of her kitchen, watching a neighbor tearing down his house because it lay in the path of an air-raid-defense fire lane; Father Wilhelm Kleinsorge, a German priest of the Society of Jesus, reclined in his underwear on a cot on the top floor of his order's three-story mission house, reading a Jesuit magazine, *Stimmen der Zeit*; Dr. Terufumi Sasaki, a young member of the surgical staff of the city's large, modern Red Cross Hospital, walked along one of the hospital corridors with a blood specimen for a Wassermann test in his hand; and the Reverend Mr. Kiyoshi

1

Tanimoto, pastor of the Hiroshima Methodist Church, paused at the door of a rich man's house in Koi, the city's western suburb, and prepared to unload a handcart full of things he had evacuated from town in fear of the massive B-29 raid which everyone expected Hiroshima to suffer. A hundred thousand people were killed by the atomic bomb, and these six were among the survivors. They still wonder why they lived when so many others died. Each of them counts many small items of chance or volition—a step taken in time, a decision to go indoors, catching one streetcar instead of the next—that spared him. And now each knows that in the act of survival he lived a dozen lives and saw more death than he ever thought he would see. At the time, none of them knew anything.

The Reverend Mr. Tanimoto got up at five o'clock that morning. He was   2
alone in the parsonage, because for some time his wife had been commuting with their yearold baby to spend nights with a friend in Ushida, a suburb to the north. Of all the important cities of Japan, only two, Kyoto and Hiroshima, had not been visited in strength by *B-san*, or Mr. B, as the Japanese, with a mixture of respect and unhappy familiarity, called the B-29; and Mr. Tanimoto, like all his neighbors and friends, was almost sick with anxiety. He had heard uncomfortably detailed accounts of mass raids on Kure, Iwakuni, Tokuyama, and other nearby towns; he was sure Hiroshima's turn would come soon. He had slept badly the night before, because there had been several air-raid warnings. Hiroshima had been getting such warnings almost every night for weeks, for at that time the B-29s were using Lake Biwa, northeast of Hiroshima, as a rendezvous point, and no matter what city the Americans planned to hit, the Superfortresses streamed in over the coast near Hiroshima. The frequency of the warnings and the continued abstinence of Mr. B with respect to Hiroshima had made its citizens jittery; a rumor was going around that the Americans were saving something special for the city.

Mr. Tanimoto is a small man, quick to talk, laugh, and cry. He wears his   3
black hair parted in the middle and rather long; the prominence of the frontal bones just above his eyebrows and the smallness of his mustache, mouth, and chin give him a strange, old-young look, boyish and yet wise, weak and yet fiery. He moves nervously and fast, but with a restraint which suggests that he is a cautious, thoughtful man. He showed, indeed, just those qualities in the uneasy days before the bomb fell. Besides having his wife spend the nights in Ushida, Mr. Tanimoto had been carrying all the portable things from his church, in the close-packed residential district called Nagaragawa, to a house that belonged to a rayon manufacturer in Koi, two miles from the center of town. The rayon man,

a Mr. Matsui, had opened his then unoccupied estate to a large number of his friends and acquaintances, so that they might evacuate whatever they wished to a safe distance from the probable target area. Mr. Tanimoto had had no difficulty in moving chairs, hymnals, Bibles, altar gear, and church records by pushcart himself, but the organ console and an upright piano required some aid. A friend of his named Matsuo had, the day before, helped him get the piano out to Koi; in return, he had promised this day to assist Mr. Matsuo in hauling out a daughter's belongings. That is why he had risen so early.

Mr. Tanimoto cooked his own breakfast. He felt awfully tired. The effort of   4
moving the piano the day before, a sleepless night, weeks of worry and unbalanced diet, the cares of his parish—all combined to make him feel hardly adequate to the new day's work. There was another thing, too; Mr. Tanimoto had studied theology at Emory College, in Atlanta, Georgia; he had graduated in 1940; he spoke excellent English; he dressed in American clothes; he had corresponded with many American friends right up to the time the war began; and among a people obsessed with a fear of being spied upon—perhaps almost obsessed himself—he found himself growing increasingly uneasy. The police had questioned him several times, and just a few days before, he had heard that an influential acquaintance, a Mr. Tanaka, a retired officer of the Toyo Kisen Kaisha steamship line, an anti-Christian, a man famous in Hiroshima for his showy philanthropies and notorious for his personal tyrannies, had been telling people that Tanimoto should not be trusted. In compensation, to show himself publicly a good Japanese, Mr. Tanimoto had taken on the chairmanship of his local *tonarigumi*, or Neighborhood Association, and to his other duties and concerns this position had added the business of organizing air-raid defense for about twenty families.

Before six o'clock that morning, Mr. Tanimoto started for Mr. Matsuo's   5
house. There he found that their burden was to be a *tansu*, a large Japanese cabinet, full of clothing and household goods. The two men set out. The morning was perfectly clear and so warm that the day promised to be uncomfortable. A few minutes after they started, the air-raid siren went off—a minute-long blast that warned of approaching planes but indicated to the people of Hiroshima only a slight degree of danger, since it sounded every morning at this time, when an American weather plane came over. The two men pulled and pushed the handcart through the city streets. Hiroshima was a fan-shaped city, lying mostly on the six islands formed by the seven estuarial rivers that branch out from the Ota River; its main commercial and residential districts, covering about four square

miles in the center of the city, contained threequarters of its population, which had been reduced by several evacuation programs from a wartime peak of 380,000 to about 245,000. Factories and other residential districts, or suburbs, lay compactly around the edges of the city. To the south were the docks, an airport, and the island-studded Inland Sea. A rim of mountains runs around the other three sides of the delta. Mr. Tanimoto and Mr. Matsuo took their way through the shopping center, already full of people, and across two of the rivers to the sloping streets of Koi, and up them to the outskirts and foothills. As they started up a valley away from the tight-ranked houses, the all-clear sounded. (The Japanese radar operators, detecting only three planes, supposed that they comprised a reconnaissance.) Pushing the handcart up to the rayon man's house was tiring, and the men, after they had maneuvered their load into the driveway and to the front steps, paused to rest awhile. They stood with a wing of the house between them and the city. Like most homes in this part of Japan, the house consisted of a wooden frame and wooden walls supporting a heavy tile roof. Its front hall, packed with rolls of bedding and clothing, looked like a cool cave full of fat cushions. Opposite the house, to the right of the front door, there was a large, finicky rock garden. There was no sound of planes. The morning was still; the place was cool and pleasant.

Then a tremendous flash of light cut across the sky. Mr. Tanimoto has a dis-   6
tinct recollection that it travelled from east to west, from the city toward the hills. It seemed a sheet of sun. Both he and Mr. Matsuo reacted in terror—and both had time to react (for they were 3500 yards, or two miles, from the center of the explosion). Mr. Matsuo dashed up the front steps into the house and dived among the bedrolls and buried himself there. Mr. Tanimoto took four or five steps and threw himself between two big rocks in the garden. He bellied up very hard against one of them. As his face was against the stone, he did not see what happened. He felt a sudden pressure, and then splinters and pieces of board and fragments of tile fell on him. He heard no roar. (Almost no one in Hiroshima recalls hearing any noise of the bomb. But a fisherman in his sampan on the Inland Sea near Tsuzu, the man with whom Mr. Tanimoto's mother-in-law and sister-in-law were living, saw the flash and heard a tremendous explosion; he was nearly twenty miles from Hiroshima, but the thunder was greater than when the B-29s hit Iwakuni, only five miles away.)

When he dared, Mr. Tanimoto raised his head and saw that the rayon   7
man's house had collapsed. He thought a bomb had fallen directly on it. Such clouds of dust had risen that there was a sort of twilight around. In panic, not

thinking for the moment of Mr. Matsuo under the ruins, he dashed out into the street. He noticed as he ran that the concrete wall of the estate had fallen over—toward the house rather than away from it. In the street, the first thing he saw was a squad of soldiers who had been burrowing into the hillside opposite, making one of the thousands of dugouts in which the Japanese apparently intended to resist invasion, hill by hill, life for life; the soldiers were coming out of the hole, where they should have been safe, and blood was running from their heads, chests, and backs. They were silent and dazed.

    Under what seemed to be a local dust cloud, the day grew darker and darker.   8

    At nearly midnight, the night before the bomb was dropped, an announc-   9
er on the city's radio station said that about two hundred B-29s were approaching southern Honshu and advised the population of Hiroshima to evacuate to their designated "safe areas." Mrs. Hatsuyo Nakamura, the tailor's widow, who lived in the section called Noboricho and who had long had a habit of doing as she was told, got her three children—a ten-year-old boy, Toshio, an eight-year-old girl, Yaeko, and a five-year-old girl, Myeko—out of bed and dressed them and walked with them to the military area known as the East Parade Ground, on the northeast edge of the city. There she unrolled some mats and the children lay down on them. They slept until about two, when they were awakened by the roar of the planes going over Hiroshima.

    As soon as the planes had passed, Mrs. Nakamura started back with her   10
children. They reached home a little after two-thirty and she immediately turned on the radio, which, to her distress, was just then broadcasting a fresh warning. When she looked at the children and saw how tired they were, and when she thought of the number of trips they had made in past weeks, all to no purpose, to the East Parade Ground, she decided that in spite of the instructions on the radio, she simply could not face starting out all over again. She put the children in their bedrolls on the floor, lay down herself at three o'clock, and fell asleep at once, so soundly that when planes passed over later, she did not waken to their sound.

    The siren jarred her awake at about seven. She arose, dressed quickly, and   11
hurried to the house of Mr. Nakamoto, the head of her Neighborhood Association, and asked him what she should do. He said that she should remain at home unless an urgent warning—a series of intermittent blasts of the siren—was sounded. She returned home, lit the stove in the kitchen, set some rice to cook, and sat down to read the morning's Hiroshima *Chugoku*. To her relief, the all-clear sounded at eight o'clock. She heard the children stirring, so she went

and gave each of them a handful of peanuts and told them to stay on their bedrolls, because they were tired from the night's walk. She had hoped that they would go back to sleep, but the man in the house directly to the south began to make a terrible hullabaloo of hammering, wedging, ripping, and splitting. The prefectural government, convinced, as everyone in Hiroshima was, that the city would be attacked soon, had begun to press with threats and warnings for the completion of wide fire lanes, which, it was hoped, might act in conjunction with the rivers to localize any fires started by an incendiary raid: and the neighbor was reluctantly sacrificing his home to the city's safety. Just the day before, the prefecture had ordered all ablebodied girls from the secondary schools to spend a few days helping to clear these lanes, and they started work soon after the all-clear sounded.

Mrs. Nakamura went back to the kitchen, looked at the rice, and began watching the man next door. At first, she was annoyed with him for making so much noise, but then she was moved almost to tears by pity. Her emotion was specifically directed toward her neighbor, tearing down his home, board by board, at a time when there was so much unavoidable destruction, but undoubtedly she also felt a generalized, community pity, to say nothing of self-pity. She had not had an easy time. Her husband, Isawa, had gone into the Army just after Myeko was born, and she had heard nothing from or of him for a long time, until, on March 5, 1942, she received a sevenword telegram: "Isawa died an honorable death at Singapore." She learned later that he had died on February 15th, the day Singapore fell, and that he had been a corporal. Isawa had been a not particularly prosperous tailor, and his only capital was a Sankoku sewing machine. After his death, when his allotments stopped coming, Mrs. Nakamura got out the machine and began to take in piecework herself, and since then had supported the children, but poorly, by sewing.   12

As Mrs. Nakamura stood watching her neighbor, everything flashed whiter than any white she had ever seen. She did not notice what happened to the man next door; the reflex of a mother set her in motion toward her children. She had taken a single step (the house was 1350 yards, or three quarters of a mile, from the center of the explosion) when something picked her up and she seemed to fly into the next room over the raised sleeping platform, pursued by parts of her house.   13

Timbers fell around her as she landed, and a shower of tiles pommelled her; everything became dark, for she was buried. The debris did not cover her deeply. She rose up and freed herself. She heard a child cry, "Mother, help me!" and saw   14 her youngest—Myeko, the five-year-old—buried up to her breast and unable to move. As Mrs. Nakamura started frantically to claw her way toward the baby, she could see or hear nothing of her other children.

In the days right before the bombing, Dr. Masakazu Fujii, being prosperous, hedonistic, and at the time not too busy, had been allowing himself the luxury of sleeping until nine or nine-thirty, but fortunately he had to get up early the morning the bomb was dropped to see a house guest off on a train. He rose at six, and half an hour later walked with his friend to the station, not far away, across two of the rivers. He was back home by seven, just as the siren sounded its sustained warning. He ate breakfast and then, because the morning was already hot, undressed down to his underwear and went out on the porch to read the paper. This porch—in fact, the whole building—was curiously constructed. Dr. Fujii was the proprietor of a peculiarly Japanese institution: a private, single-doctor hospital. This building, perched beside and over the water of the Kyo River, and next to the bridge of the same name, contained thirty rooms for thirty patients and their kinfolk—for, according to Japanese custom, when a person falls sick and goes to a hospital, one or more members of his family go and live there with him, to cook for him, bathe, massage, and read to him, and to offer incessant familial sympathy, without which a Japanese patient would be miserable indeed. Dr. Fujii had no beds—only straw mats—for his patients. He did, however, have all sorts of modern equipment: an X-ray machine, diathermy apparatus, and a fine tiled laboratory. The structure rested two-thirds on the land, onethird on piles over the tidal waters of the Kyo. This overhang, the part of the building where Dr. Fujii lived, was queer-looking, but it was cool in summer and from the porch, which faced away from the center of the city, the prospect of the river, with pleasure boats drifting up and down it, was always refreshing. Dr. Fujii had occasionally had anxious moments when the Ota and its mouth branches rose to flood, but the piling was apparently firm enough and the house had always held.

Dr. Fujii had been relatively idle for about a month because in July, as the number of untouched cities in Japan dwindled and as Hiroshima seemed more and more inevitably a target, he began turning patients away, on the ground that in case of a fire raid he would not be able to evacuate them. Now he had only two patients left—a woman from Yano, injured in the shoulder, and a young man of twenty-five recovering from burns he had suffered when the steel factory near Hiroshima in which he worked had been hit. Dr. Fujii had six nurses to tend his patients. His wife and children were safe; his wife and one son were living out-

15

16

side Osaka, and another son and two daughters were in the country on Kyushu. A niece was living with him, and a maid and a man-servant. He had little to do and did not mind, for he had saved some money. At fifty, he was healthy, convivial, and calm, and he was pleased to pass the evenings drinking whiskey with friends, always sensibly and for the sake of conversation. Before the war, he had affected brands imported from Scotland and America; now he was perfectly satisfied with the best Japanese brand, Suntory.

Dr. Fujii sat down cross-legged in his underwear on the spotless matting of the porch, put on his glasses, and started reading the Osaka *Asahi*. He liked to read the Osaka news because his wife was there. He saw the flash. To him—faced away from the center and looking at his paper—it seemed a brilliant yellow. Startled, he began to rise to his feet. In that moment (he was 1550 yards from the center), the hospital leaned behind him rising and, with a terrible ripping noise, toppled into the river. The Doctor, still in the act of getting to his feet, was thrown forward and around and over; he was buffeted and gripped; he lost track of everything, because things were so speeded up; he felt the water. 17

Dr. Fujii hardly had time to think that he was dying before he realized that he was alive, squeezed tightly by two long timbers in a V across his chest, like a morsel suspended between two huge chopsticks—held upright, so that he could not move, with his head miraculously above water and his torso and legs in it. The remains of his hospital were all around him in a mad assortment of splintered lumber and materials for the relief of pain. His left shoulder hurt terribly. His glasses were gone. 18

Father Wilhelm Kleinsorge, of the Society of Jesus, was, on the morning of the explosion, in rather frail condition. The Japanese wartime diet had not sustained him, and he felt the strain of being a foreigner in an increasingly xenophobic Japan; even a German, since the defeat of the Fatherland, was unpopular. Father Kleinsorge had, at thirty-eight, the look of a boy growing too fast—thin in the face, with a prominent Adam's apple, a hollow chest, dangling hands, big feet. He walked clumsily, leaning forward a little. He was tired all the time. To make matters worse, he had suffered for two days, along with Father Cieslik, a fellow-priest, from a rather painful and urgent diarrhea, which they blamed on the beans and black ration bread they were obliged to eat. Two other priests then living in the mission compound, which was in the Nobori-cho section—Father Superior LaSalle and Father Schiffer—had happily escaped this affliction. 19

Father Kleinsorge woke up about six the morning the bomb was dropped, and half an hour later—he was a bit tardy because of his sickness—he began to 20 read Mass in the mission chapel, a small Japanese-style wooden building which was without pews, since its worshippers knelt on the usual Japanese matted floor, facing an altar graced with splendid silks, brass, silver, and heavy embroideries. This morning, a Monday, the only worshippers were Mr. Takemoto, a theological student living in the mission house; Mr. Fukai, the secretary of the diocese; Mrs. Murata, the mission's devoutly Christian housekeeper; and his fellow-priests. After Mass, while Father Kleinsorge was reading the Prayers of Thanksgiving, the siren sounded. He stopped the service and the missionaries retired across the compound to the bigger building. There, in his room on the ground floor, to the right of the front door, Father Kleinsorge changed into a military uniform which he had acquired when he was teaching at the Rokko Middle School in Kobe and which he wore during air-raid alerts.

After an alarm, Father Kleinsorge always went out and scanned the sky, 21 and in this instance, when he stepped outside, he was glad to see only the single weather plane that flew over Hiroshima each day about this time. Satisfied that nothing would happen, he went in and breakfasted with the other Fathers on substitute coffee and ration bread, which, under the circumstances, was especially repugnant to him. The Fathers sat and talked awhile, until, at eight, they heard the all-clear. They went then to various parts of the building. Father Schiffer retired to his room to do some writing. Father Cieslik sat in his room in a straight chair with a pillow over his stomach to ease his pain, and read. Father Superior LaSalle stood at the window of his room, thinking. Father Kleinsorge went up to a room on the third floor, took off all his clothes except his underwear, and stretched out on his right side on a cot and began reading his *Stimmen der Zeit*.

After the terrible flash—which, Father Kleinsorge later realized, reminded 22 him of something he had read as a boy about a large meteor colliding with the earth—he had time (since he was 1400 yards from the center) for one thought: A bomb has fallen directly on us. Then, for a few seconds or minutes, he went out of his mind.

Father Kleinsorge never knew how he got out of the house. The next 23 things he was conscious of were that he was wandering around in the mission's vegetable garden in his underwear, bleeding slightly from small cuts along his left flank; that all the buildings round about had fallen down except the Jesuits' mission house, which had long before been braced and doublebraced by a priest named Gropper, who was terrified of earthquakes; that the day had turned dark;

and that Muratasan, the housekeeper, was nearby, crying over and over, "*Shu Jesusu, awaremi tamai! Our Lord Jesus, have pity on us!*"

On the train on the way into Hiroshima from the country, where he lived   24 with his mother, Dr. Terufumi Sasaki, the Red Cross Hospital surgeon, thought over an unpleasant nightmare he had had the night before. His mother's home was in Mukaihara, thirty miles from the city, and it took him two hours by train and tram to reach the hospital. He had slept uneasily all night and had wakened an hour earlier than usual, and, feeling sluggish and slightly feverish, had debated whether to go to the hospital at all; his sense of duty finally forced him to go, and he had started out on the earlier train than he took most mornings. The dream had particularly frightened him because it was so closely associated, on the surface at least, with a disturbing actuality. He was only twenty-five years old and had just completed his training at the Eastern Medical University, in Tsingtao, China. He was something of an idealist and was much distressed by the inadequacy of medical facilities in the country town where his mother lived. Quite on his own, and without a permit, he had begun visiting a few sick people out there in the evenings, after his eight hours at the hospital and four hours commuting. He had recently learned that the penalty for practicing without a permit was severe; a fellow doctor whom he had asked about it had given him a serious scolding. Nevertheless, he had continued to practice. In his dream, he had been at the bedside of a country patient when the police and the doctor he had consulted burst into the room, seized him, dragged him outside, and beat him up cruelly. On the train, he just about decided to give up the work in Mukaihara, since he felt it would be impossible to get a permit, because the authorities would hold that it would conflict with his duties at the Red Cross Hospital.

At the terminus, he caught a streetcar at once. (He later calculated that if   25 he had taken his customary train that morning, and if he had had to wait a few minutes for the streetcar, as often happened, he would have been close to the center at the time of the explosion and would surely have perished.) He arrived at the hospital at seven-forty and reported to the chief surgeon. A few minutes later, he went to a room on the first floor and drew blood from the arm of a man in order to perform a Wassermann test. The laboratory containing the incubators for the test was on the third floor. With the blood specimen in his left hand, walking in a kind of distraction he had felt all morning, probably because of the dream and his restless night, he started along the main corridor on his way toward the stairs. He was one step beyond an open window when the light of the bomb was reflected, like a gigantic photographic flash, in the corridor. He ducked down on one knee and said to himself, as only a Japanese would, "Sasaki, *gambare!* Be brave!" Just then (the building was 1650 yards from the center), the blast ripped through the hospital. The glasses he was wearing flew off his face; the bottle of blood crashed against one wall; his Japanese slippers zipped out from under his feet—but otherwise, thanks to where he stood, he was untouched.

Dr. Sasaki shouted the name of the chief surgeon and rushed around to the man's office and found him terribly cut by glass. The hospital was in horrible confusion: heavy partitions and ceilings had fallen on patients, beds had overturned, windows had blown in and cut people, blood was spattered on the walls and floors, instruments were everywhere, many of the patients were running about screaming, many more lay dead. (A colleague working in the laboratory to which Dr. Sasaki had been walking was dead; Dr. Sasaki's patient, whom he had just left and who a few moments before had been dreadfully afraid of syphilis, was also dead.) Dr. Sasaki found himself the only doctor in the hospital who was unhurt.   26

Dr. Sasaki, who believed that the enemy had hit only the building he was in, got bandages and began to bind the wounds of those inside the hospital; while outside, all over Hiroshima, maimed and dying citizens turned their unsteady steps toward the Red Cross Hospital to begin an invasion that was to make Dr. Sasaki forget his private nightmare for a long, long time.   27

Miss Toshiko Sasaki, the East Asia Tin Works clerk, who is not related to Dr. Sasaki, got up at three o'clock in the morning on the day the bomb fell. There was extra housework to do. Her eleven-month-old brother, Akio, had come down the day before with a serious stomach upset; her mother had taken him to the Tamura Pediatric Hospital and was staying there with him. Miss Sasaki, who was about twenty, had to cook breakfast for her father, a brother, a sister, and herself, and—since the hospital, because of the war, was unable to provide food—to prepare a whole day's meals for her mother and the baby, in time for her father, who worked in a factory making rubber earplugs for artillery crews, to take the food by on his way to the plant. When she had finished and had cleaned and put away the cooking things, it was nearly seven. The family lived in Koi, and she had a forty-five-minute trip to the tin works, in the section of town called Kannonmachi. She was in charge of the personnel records in the factory. She left Koi at seven, and as soon as she reached the plant, she went with some of the other girls from the personnel department to the factory auditorium. A prominent local Navy man, a former employee, had committed suicide the day before by throwing himself under a train—a death considered honorable enough to warrant a memorial service, which was to be held at the tin works at   28

ten o'clock that morning. In the large hall, Miss Sasaki and the others made suitable preparations for the meeting. This work took about twenty minutes.

Miss Sasaki went back to her office and sat down at her desk. She was quite   29
far from the windows, which were off to her left, and behind her were a couple
of tall bookcases containing all the books of the factory library, which the personnel department had organized. She settled herself at her desk, put some things
in a drawer, and shifted papers. She thought that before she began to make
entries in her lists of new employees, discharges, and departures for the Army, she
would chat for a moment with the girl at her right. Just as she turned her head
away from the windows, the room was filled with a blinding light. She was paralyzed by fear, fixed still in her chair for a long moment (the plant was 1600 yards
from the center). Everything fell, and Miss Sasaki lost consciousness. The ceiling dropped suddenly and the wooden floor above collapsed in splinters and the
people up there came down and the roof above them gave way; but principally
and first of all, the bookcases right behind her swooped forward and the contents
threw her down, with her left leg horribly twisted and breaking underneath her.
There, in the tin factory, in the first moment of the atomic age, a human being
was crushed by books.

Questions for Discussion

1. How are the lives of the six people described in this essay similar, when they
   are considered together? How does each individual's life combine with the
   others to create a unified story?
2. What is Hersey's point? Why does he not come right out and state it directly?
3. Hersey does not make any explicit comments about the bombing of
   Hiroshima, but how do the six people implicitly comment?
4. Why might Hersey have chosen these six people and not others? What
   about these six helps Hersey make his point?
5. This article was first published in the *New Yorker* in 1946. What about the
   article shows that it was written for this particular magazine? Who typically reads the *New Yorker*, and what about this article would appeal to them?
6. What is the effect of the extremely personal details of these six people's
   lives? When you feel that you know the people, how does that change your
   mental image of the bombing of Hiroshima?
7. How does this article differ from most investigative articles you have read?

Questions for Reflection and Writing

1. What do these narratives teach you about history?
2. Interview one person you know who lived through a memorable (negative or positive) event. Try to get as much detail as possible. Write up the interview as a narrative essay that reveals a side to the historical event that one would not necessarily read in a history textbook.
3. Research the bombing of Hiroshima and Nagasaki, and write an informational essay on one aspect of the event.

James Robert Atlas (1949–   ) was born in Chicago on March 22, 1949. He was graduated summa cum laude from Harvard College in 1971 and conducted postgraduate study at New College, Oxford. A writer, a biographer, a critic, and an editor, Atlas has worked for *The New York Times Magazine*, *The Harvard Advocate*, *Time*, *The New York Times Book Review*, *The Atlantic Monthly*, and *Vanity Fair*. His well-known *The Book Wars: What It Takes to Be Educated in America* (1990) argues that our culture is producing an apathetic generation, a trend that he attributes to the lack of study of "great books" at universities. He has edited an anthology, *Ten American Poets* (1973), and has written biographies of Delmore Schwartz and Saul Bellow, as well as the autobiographical novel *The Great Pretender* (1986).

The Battle of the Books

James Atlas

The philosopher George Santayana was once asked which books young people   1
should read. It didn't matter, he replied, as long as they read the same ones. Generations of Eng. lit. majors in American colleges followed his advice. You started with the Bible, moved briskly through Beowulf and Chaucer, Shakespeare and Milton, the 18th-century novel, the Romantics, a few big American books like "The Scarlet Letter" and "Moby-Dick"—and so on, masterpiece by masterpiece, century by century, until you'd read (or browsed through) the corpus.

Occasional disputes broke out, reputations flourished and declined. T. S.   2
Eliot smuggled in the 17th-century metaphysical poets, Malcolm Cowley promoted Faulkner, there was a Henry James revival. For the most part, though, the canon was closed: You were either on the syllabus or off the syllabus.

It was in the academic journals that I first noticed the word canon.   3
Originally, it referred to those works that the church considered part of the Bible: now, apparently, it had a new meaning. PMLA, the journal of the Modern Language Association, proposed a future issue on "the idea of the literary canon in relation to concepts of judgment, taste and value." This spring, the Princeton

English department held a symposium on "Masterpieces: Canonizing the Literary."

Canon formation, canon revision, canonicity: the mysterious, often indeci-   4
pherable language of critical theory had yielded up a whole new terminology. What was this canon? The books that constituted the intellectual heritage of educated Americans, that had officially been defined as great. The kinds of books you read, say, in Columbia's famed lit. hum. course, virtually unchanged since 1937: Homer, Plato, Dante, Milton . . . The masterpieces of Western civilization. The Big Boys.

In the academic world, I kept hearing the canon was "a hot issue."   5
Everything these days has to do with the canon," one of my campus sources reported. Then, early this year, a flurry of articles appeared in the press. "From Western Lit to Westerns as Lit," joked The Wall Street Journal in a piece about some English professors down at Duke University who have been teaching "The Godfather"—book and movie—"E.T." and the novels of Louis L'Amour. An article in *The New York Times*, "U.S. Literature: Canon Under Siege," quoted a heretical brigade of academics who were fed up with hierarchies of literary value.

Why should Melville and Emerson dominate the syllabus? argued renegade   6
professors from Johns Hopkins and Northwestern, Queens College and Berkeley. What about Zora Neale Hurston, a hero of the Harlem Renaissance? What about Harriet Beecher Stowe? "It's no different from choosing between a hoagy and a pizza," explained Houston Baker, a professor of literature at the University of Pennsylvania. (Did he mean that all literature, like all junk food, was essentially the same?) "To hell with Shakespeare and Milton, Emerson and Faulkner!" retorted Jonathan Yardley in *The Washington Post*, setting a high standard for the debate. "Let's boogie!"

By the end of March, when Stanford University announced plans to revise   7
the series of Western culture courses it required of freshmen, eliminating the core list of classics and substituting works by "women, minorities, and persons of color," what began as an academic squabble had burgeoned into a full blown Great Books Debate. Comp. lit. and humanities professors, Afro-American specialists, historians, college administrators and government spokesmen entered the fray. All over the country, editorials appeared decrying the sorry developments at Stanford, where last year students on a march with Jesse Jackson had chanted, "Hey hey, ho ho, Western culture's got to go."

Days after the new course was unveiled, William J. Bennett, the Secretary   8
of Education, showed up in Palo Alto, Calif., to deplore the university's decision.

Speaking before an overflow crowd, Bennett expressed contempt for the faculty senate that had voted for the change.

"The West is the culture in which we live," Bennett asserted. "It has set the   9
moral, political, economic and social standards for the rest of the world." By giving in to a vocal band of student radicals, "a great university was brought low by the very forces which modern universities came into being to oppose: ignorance, irrationality and intimidation."

Bennett's polemic ignored the fine print. Instead of dealing with 15 "clas-   10
sic texts," students would read the Old and New Testaments as well as the works of five authors: Plato, St. Augustine, Machiavelli, Rousseau and Marx. The other works assigned would concentrate on "at least one non-European culture," with "substantial attention to issues of race, gender and class." No one was proposing to "junk Western culture," insisted Stanford's president, Donald Kennedy. The point was simply to reflect "the diversity of contemporary American culture and values."

Never mind. For Bennett, what happened at Stanford was another oppor-   11
tunity to rehearse one of his favorite themes: the decline of the West. In 1984, as chairman of the National Endowment for the Humanities, he published a report titled "To Reclaim a Legacy," which decried the influence of the 1960's on higher education in America, working in the obligatory reference to Matthew Arnold's famous definition of culture as the best that has been thought and said.

The trouble with this "Matthew Arnold view of literature and culture," as   12
Gerald Graff, a professor at Northwestern University and one of the more reasoned commentators on the debate, observes, is that there never was any consensus about the best that has been thought and said—or, for that matter, why the West should have a corner on the high culture market. The idea of literature as a fixed and immutable canon—the Great Books, the Five-Foot Shelf—is a historical illusion. "Canon-busting is nothing new," Graff says. "There have always been politics. Teaching Shakespeare instead of the classics was a radical innovation."

So why is this debate over the canon different from all other debates? The   13
fierce arguments about Socialist Realism that raged among American intellectuals in the 1930's and 40's were a lot more acrimonious. As for what's literature and what isn't, the critic Leslie Fiedler was anatomizing the cultural significance of Superman decades ago.

What's different is who's doing the debating. A new generation of scholars   14
has emerged, a generation whose sensibilities were shaped by intellectual trends that originated in the 60's: Marxism, feminism, deconstruction, a skepticism

about the primacy of the West. For these scholars, the effort to widen the canon is an effort to define themselves, to validate their own identities. In the 80's, literature is us.

On the shelves in Jane Tompkins's office at Duke are rows of 19th-century   15
novels; she is one of the few who read them now. Her book "Sensational Designs: The Cultural Work of American Fiction 1790 -1860" is a brilliant exhumation of what she considers lost masterpieces, the history of a different American literature from the one I read in college in the 1960's.

Writers like Charles Brockden Brown, Harriet Beecher Stowe and Susan   16
Warner still deserve an audience, Tompkins argues with considerable persuasiveness. If they're no longer read, it's because our values have changed. The way to read these books is from the vantage of the past. Only by reconstructing the culture in which they were written and the audience to whom they were addressed can we learn to appreciate their intrinsic worth and see them for what they are: "man-made, historically produced objects" whose reputations were created in their day by a powerful literary establishment. In other words, the Great Books aren't the only books.

Tompkins is one of the jewels in the crown of Duke's English department,   17
which in the last few years has assembled a faculty that can now claim to rival any in the country. Attracted by salaries that in some cases approach six figures and a university willing to let them teach pretty much whatever interests them, the new recruits compose a formidable team: Frank Lentricchia, the author of "After the New Criticism" and other works; Fredric Jameson, probably the foremost Marxist critic in the country; Barbara Herrnstein Smith, president of the Modern Language Association, and Tompkins's husband, Stanley Fish, chairman of the department. (Duke is known in academic circles as "the Fish tank.")

Canon revision is in full swing down at Duke, where students lounge on   18
the manicured quad of the imitation-Cotswold campus and the magnolias blossom in the spring. In the Duke catalogue, the English department lists, besides the usual offerings in Chaucer and Shakespeare, courses in American popular culture; advertising and society; television, technology and culture.

Lentricchia teaches a course titled "Paranoia, Politics and Other Pleasures"   19
that focuses on the works of Joan Didion, Don DeLillo and Michel Foucault. Tompkins, an avid reader of contemporary fiction—on a shelf in her office I spotted copies of "Princess Daisy" and "Valley of the Dolls"—is teaching all kinds of things, from a course on American literature and culture in the 1850's to one called "Home on the Range: The Western in American Culture."

Tompkins talks about her work with a rhetorical intensity that reminded   20
me of the fervent Students for a Democratic Society types I used to know in college. Like so many of those in the vanguard of the new canonical insurrection,
she is a child of the 60's and a dedicated feminist. In her book "Sensational
Designs," she recounts how she gradually became aware of herself as a woman
working in a "male-dominated scholarly tradition that controls both the canon
of American literature and the critical perspective that interprets the canon for
society." The writers offered up as classics didn't speak to Tompkins; they didn't
address her own experience.

"If you look at the names on Butler Library up at Columbia, they're all   21
white males," she notes one afternoon over lunch in the faculty dining hall. "We
wanted to talk about civil rights in the classroom, to prove that literature wasn't
a sacred icon above the heat and dust of conflict."

The English literature syllabus, Tompkins and her colleagues on other cam-   22
puses discovered, was a potential instrument of change: "This is where it all came
out in the wash." By the 1970's, Afro-American departments and women's studies majors had been installed on college campuses across the land. Books on gender, race, ethnicity poured from the university presses. Seminars were offered in
Native American literature, Hispanic literature, Asian-American literature. "It
wasn't only women we'd neglected," says Marjorie Garber, director of English
graduate studies at Harvard University. "It was the whole third world."

The ideology behind these challenges to the canon is as unambiguous as   23
the vanity plates on Frank Lentricchia's old Dodge: GO LEFT. Pick up any
recent academic journal and you'll find it packed with articles on "Maidens,
Maps and Mines: the Reinvention of Patriarchy in Colonial South Africa" or
"Dominance, Hegemony and the Modes of Minority Discourse." The critical
vocabulary of the 1980's bristles with militant neologisms: *Eurocentrism, phallo-
centrism, logophallocentrism*. (Why not *Europhallologocentrism?*)"This is not an
intellectual agenda, it is a political agenda," Secretary of Education Bennett
declared on the "MacNeil/Lehrer News-Hour" the night after his Stanford
speech.

Why should a revolutionary curricular struggle be happening at a time   24
when radical politics in America is virtually extinct? Walk into any classroom
and you'll find the answer. Enormous sociological changes have occurred in
American universities over the last 20 years; the ethnic profile of both students
and faculty has undergone a dramatic transformation.

There's a higher proportion of minorities in college than ever before. By   25
the end of this century, Hispanic, black and Asian-American undergraduates at

Stanford may well outnumber whites. Their professors, many of whom were on the barricades in the 60's, are now up for tenure.

"It's a demographic phenomenon," Jane Tompkins says. "There are   26
women, Jews, Italians teaching literature in universities. The people who are teaching now don't look the way professors used to look. Frank Lentricchia does- n't look like Cleanth Brooks."

I had never seen Cleanth Brooks, the eminent Yale professor emeritus, but   27
I could imagine him striding across campus in a conservative gray suit and neat bow tie—not at all the way Frank Lentricchia looks. The photograph on the book jacket of "Criticism and Social Change" shows a guy in a sports shirt, posed against a graffiti-scarred wall—"the Dirty Harry of contemporary critical theory," a reviewer in The Village Voice called him.

In person, Lentricchia is a lot less intimidating. I found him mild-man-   28
nered, easygoing, and surprisingly conventional in his approach to literature. Standing before his modern poetry class in a faded blue workshirt open at the neck, he made his way through "The Waste Land" just the way professors used to, line by line, pointing out the buried allusions to Ovid and Dante, Marvell and Verlaine.

His work is densely theoretical, yet there's nothing doctrinaire about it.   29
What comes through is a devotion to the classics that is more visceral than abstract. "I'm interested in social issues as they bear on literature, but what real- ly interests me is the mainline stuff, like Faulkner," he says after class, popping open a beer—no sherry—on the porch of his comfortable home in the nearby town of Hillsborough. "I'm too American to be a Marxist."

One afternoon I talk with Stanley Fish, the chairman of Duke's English   30
department, in his newly renovated office in the Allen Building. Fish has on slacks and a sports jacket, but he doesn't look any more like Cleanth Brooks— or my image of Cleanth Brooks—than Frank Lentricchia does. He's never been comfortable with the T. S. Eliot tradition, he says, though he's one of the lead- ing Milton scholars in America.

Now 50, Fish is maybe a decade older than the generation of radical schol-   31
ars who came of age in the 60's; but like many of them, he discovered his voca- tion largely on his own. "You come from a background where there were no books, the son and daughter of immigrants," he says. In such a world, Milton was a first name.

For American Jewish writers who grew up in the Depression, the art critic   32
Clement Greenberg once noted, literature offered "a means of flight from the restriction and squalor of the Brooklyns and Bronxes to the wide open world

which rewards the successful fugitive with space, importance and wealth." Making it in those days meant making it on others' terms: in this case, the terms established by tradition-minded English departments dominated by white, Anglo-Saxon Protestants, which even in the 1940's looked with skeptical distaste upon the Jewish assistant professors who were trying to storm the gates.

Diana Trilling has written movingly about the humiliation her celebrated   33
husband, Lionel, suffered at the beginning of his career, when he was briefly banished from Columbia by the English department on the grounds that he was "a Freudian, a Marxist and a Jew." There was nothing subversive about Trilling's ambition; for him, as for Jewish critics like Philip Rahv and Harry Levin, literature was an escape from ethnic identity, not an affirmation of it.

Fish and his radical colleagues are no less ambitious. They, too, aspire to   34
"space, importance and wealth," but on their own terms. Frank Lentricchia has a swimming pool in his backyard. In his work, though, he writes openly and with unashamed ardor, in the autobiographical fashion of the day, about his Italian-American origins, his grandfather in Utica, his working-class Dad.

"To become an intellectual from this kind of background means typically   35
to try to forget where you've come from," he writes in "Criticism and Social Change." It means becoming "a cosmopolitan gentleman of the world of letters, philosophy and art."

That's not Lentricchia's style. For the scholars of his generation, it's no   36
longer a matter of proving their claim on literature; that struggle has been won. What they're demanding now is a literature that reflects their experience, a literature of their own. "Assimilation is a betrayal," says Fish. "The whole idea of 'Americanness' has been thrown in question."

In a way, this was what the debate at Stanford was about. "If you think we   37
are talking about a handful of good books you are mistaken," Bill King, a senior and president of the university's Black Student Union, declared in an eloquent speech before the faculty senate. "We are discussing the foundations of education in America and the acceptance of Euro-America's place in the world as contributor, not creator." Why had he never been taught that Socrates, Herodotus, Pythagoras and Solon owed much of what they knew to African cultures in Egypt, or that "many of the words of Solomon" were borrowed from the black Pharaoh Amen-En- Eope? Where, in the great scheme of things, were *his* people to be found?

Yet "opening up the canon," as the effort to expand the curriculum is   38
called, isn't as radical as it seems. It's a populist, grassroots phenomenon, American to the core. What could be more democratic than the new "Columbia

Literary History of the United States," which incorporates Chippewa poems and Whitman's "Song of Myself," Mark Twain and Jay McInerney? There are chapters on Afro-American literature, Mexican-American literature, Asian-American literature, on immigrant writers of the 19th century and slave narratives of the Civil War.

"There isn't just one story of American literature," says Emory Elliott, chairman of Princeton's English department and the volume's general editor. "Things are wide open." 39

No group has been more assiduous in the effort to institutionalize new canonical discoveries than the feminists. Gynocriticism, the study of women's literature, is a flourishing academic field. Catalogues list English department courses in "Feminism, Modernism and Post-Modernism," "Shakespeare and Feminism," "Feminist Theory and the Humanities." Margaret Williams Ferguson of Columbia University teaches a course on "Renaissance Women of Letters"— Christine de Pisan, Mary Sidney, Aphra Behn. "This is just the tip of the iceberg," says Harvard's Marjorie Garber. "These aren't just oddities or curiosities, but major writers." 40

But the feminist enterprise is more than a matter of introducing works by women into the curriculum, or "mainstreaming." Men and women, it is now believed, have different responses to literature. What is needed, says Princeton's Elaine Showalter, one of the most articulate feminist critics around, is a "defamiliarization of masculinity," "a poetics of the Other"— a critical methodology that addresses gender and sexual difference. 41

On campus bulletin boards I saw notices for lectures on "Coming Unstrung: Women, Men, Narrative and Principles of Pleasure"; "Men's Reading, Women's Writing: Canon-Formation and the Case of the 18th-Century French Novel"; "Abulia: Crises of Male Desire in Freud, Thomas Mann and Musil." 42

Lit. crit. in the 80's is like child-raising in the 80's: Both sexes share the burden. Lentricchia's work on Wallace Stevens attempts to sort out the poet's attitude toward his own masculinity—to "feminize" his image. At Harvard, Marjorie Garber is at work on a book about "cross-dressing" that discusses Sherlock Holmes, Laurie Anderson, old movies. "There's a lot of work to be done on cross-dressing," she says. Her most recent book is "Shakespeare's Ghost Writers: Literature as Uncanny Causality." "I'll sell you a copy," she offers. "I have a whole box of them." I put down my $14 and read it on the shuttle back to New York. 43

Garber has written a shrewd, idiosyncratic book, full of curious lore and lively speculation about hidden sexual motifs in Shakespeare's plays. But isn't the focus somewhat narrow? "They're looking for things to write," says Garber's col- 44 league Walter Jackson Bate, the great biographer of Keats and Samuel Johnson. "You can't write the 40th book on the structure of 'Paradise Lost.'" Bate is convinced that the humanities are in "their worst state of crisis since the modern university was formed a century ago"—and that specialization is the cause. "The aim and tradition of literature is to give, if possible, the *whole* experience of life."

The idea that literature should reflect our unique identity is "the new academic shibboleth," Gertrude Himmelfarb, a historian and highly visible proponent of the traditional curriculum, objected last month on the Op-Ed page of *The New York Times*. "It used to be thought that ideas transcend race, gender and class, that there are such things as truth, reason, morality and artistic excellence, which can be understood and aspired to by everyone, of whatever race, gender or class." Now we have democracy in the syllabus, affirmative action in the classroom. "No one believes in greatness," Bate says mournfully. "That's gone."   45

All these "texts" that are being rediscovered, republished, "revalorized"—   46
the sermons and spinsters' diaries, the popular fiction of 1850: Are any of them neglected masterpieces? Jane Tompkins makes a persuasive case for the merits of Susan Warner's "The Wide, Wide World" (reissued last year in paperback by the Feminist Press), and it is a powerful book. The story of a young woman orphaned and exiled to bullying relatives in Scotland, Warner's novel portrays an experience of physical and spiritual renunciation that was obviously familiar to its 19th-century audience. The writing is energetic and vivid, and the humiliations endured by the heroine recall the trials of Lily Bart in Edith Wharton's "The House of Mirth" or Dreiser's "Sister Carrie."

Only how do you know whether a book is "good" or not? Who decides and   47
by what criteria? There are no universals, Tompkins insists: "It is the context— which eventually includes the work itself—that creates the value its readers 'discover' there." The critic is only part of the story.

What the Duke critics discovered was "the historicization of value," says   48
Stanley Fish. It's not that texts have no literal meaning, as the deconstructors who dominated literary studies in the 1970's believed; they have "an infinite plurality of meanings." The only way that we can hope to interpret a literary work is by knowing the vantage from which we perform the act of interpretation—in contemporary parlance, where we're coming from.

Barbara Herrnstein Smith, a power at Duke and a specialist in matters   49
canonical, has written the definitive text on value relativity. "Contingencies of Value," to be published this fall by Harvard University Press, is an exasperating book, especially in the first chapter, where Smith goes on about her life as a pro-

fessor, and claims to be so close to Shakespeare's sonnets that "there have been times when I believed that I had written them myself."

Still, for all her confessional posturing, her self-professed "monstrous" immodesty, Smith is on to something. What is taste? What do we experience when we contemplate a work of art? Like Fish, Smith is less interested in the status of a given work than in how that status is established. Who decides what's in and what's out? Those who possess "cultural power." What is art? Whatever the literary establishment says it is.   50

Smith's recent work is, among other things, a shrewd polemic against "highculture critics" intent upon "epistemic self-stabilization" (that is to say, maintaining the status quo). Just who are these critics? A tribe of "nonacculturated intellectuals," "post-modern cosmopolites," "exotic visitors and immigrants." In other words, professors.   51

The vanguard of this new professoriate has transformed the landscape of contemporary literature. Many of them are tenured; they publish books. So why do they cultivate an image of themselves as literary outlaws? Frank Lentricchia isn't the only heavy academic dude around. D. A. Miller, a professor of comparative literature at Berkeley, has adorned his latest book with a photograph that mimes Lentricchia's notorious pose on the back of "Criticism and Social Change"—biceps rippling, arms folded across his chest like Mr. Clean.   52

Lentricchia's new book is titled "Ariel and the Police." Miller's is "The Novel and the Police." Both are ostensibly works of literary criticism— Lentricchia is writing largely about William James and Michel Foucault; Miller, about the Victorian novel—but their real subject is the repressive nature of society, power and the containment of power, how our culture "polices" us.   53

"Where are the police in 'Barchester Towers' (1857)?" Miller asks in a chapter on Trollope. Where, indeed? They're "literally nowhere to be found . . ." But not so fast. Their very absence is significant. Miller claims proof that Victorian England was a repressed society. The novel, then, is a form of concealment as well as of disclosure. Its truths are latent, murky, undeclared. Miller's own aim as a critic is to "bring literature out of the classroom and into the closet."   54

What's going on here? Reading between the lines, one begins to get the message. The questioning of authority that's such a pervasive theme in criticism now is a theoretical version of the battles that were fought on campuses 20 years ago—with real police. "The new epistemology—structuralism, deconstruction— provided the interpretive framework for challenging the canon," says Tompkins. "It's out in the hinterlands now. It's everywhere."   55

How will the New Canonicity—to coin a term—affect the way literature   56
is taught in America? What will students in the next generation read? It would
be presumptuous to guess. But at least the debate has focused public attention on
books—not an easy thing to do.

"It's an issue that's made literary studies suddenly vital and exciting," says   57
Gerald Graff. The struggle over who belongs in the canon and what it means is
more than a literary matter, Tompkins asserts. "It is a struggle among contending
factions for the right to be represented in the picture America draws of itself."

Questions for Discussion

1. Why should all young people read the same books?
2. What is a canon? Why can creating a literary canon pose such a problem to
   students and teachers of literature? What problems might a literary canon
   pose for aspiring writers?
3. What is "critical theory" (paragraph 4)? What value does it have for education and for society as a whole?
4. Why should Melville and Emerson dominate a literature syllabus? Why
   should they not?
5. Who are on what sides of the debate? Why is the debate about the canon
   different now than in previous years?
6. Where does Atlas stand on this issue? What passages give away his opinions?
7. What is different about the "new generation of scholars" (paragraph 14)?
   How does Atlas portray them as different from their predecessors?

Questions for Reflection and Writing

1. Design your ideal reading list of "great books" that not just you but also other
   students should read. Explain why you put each book on the list.
2. What is "Western culture"? Write your own definition.
3. Collect syllabuses from the literature teachers at your school and compare
   their reading lists. Or interview your English teachers to find out their views
   about the canon issue. Report on your findings, and add your own comments about the issue.

Barbara Wertheim Tuchman (1912–   ), a best-selling narrative historian and twotime Pulitzer Prize-winner, was born on January 30 in New York City. She was graduated from Radcliffe College in 1933 with a B.A. degree. Her family was prominent in politics and banking, and her father was an owner of the *Nation* magazine. Nevertheless, it was an impressive achievement when Barbara Tuchman, who had no advanced degrees but did have three small children, became a published historian Tuchman researches information for her books and then visits pertinent historical sites.

She achieved success with her new third book, *The Zimmerman Telegram* (1958; new ed., 1966), which narrates the historical significance of the telegram from Germany to Mexico that promised land from the American Southwest to Mexico if that country would enter World War I in support of Germany. Tuchman followed *Zimmerman* with another book on World War I, *The Guns of August* (1963). In 1972 she published *Stilwell and the American Experience in China, 1911–45*, which became a Book-of-the-Month Club selection. *The Proud Tower: A Portrait of the World before the War, 1890–1914* (1966; another Book-of-the-Month Club selection) further explains how World War I created what Tuchman calls a "gulf between two epochs."

In *A Distant Mirror: The Calamitous Fourteenth Century* (1978), Tuchman draws comparisons between the fourteenth and the twentieth centuries: both have endured nearly continuous war, crises of faith, the rise of individualism, and political instability. In the fourteenth century, bubonic plague, known as the "Black Death," killed almost one-third of the population; Tuchman compares that devastation with the possible loss of life that would be precipitated by nuclear war. In *The March of Folly: From Troy to Vietnam* (1984), Tuchman develops the thesis that four major historical periods represent governmental folly: the Trojans' wooden horse, the corruption of the Renaissance papacy, English policy regarding the colonies in America, and American intervention in Vietnam.

"This is the End of the World": The Black Death

Barbara Tuchman

In October 1347, two months after the fall of Calais, Genoese trading ships put   1
into the harbor of Messina in Sicily with dead and dying men at the oars. The ships had come from the Black Sea port of Caffa (now Feodosiya) in the Crimea, where the Genoese maintained a trading post. The diseased sailors showed strange black swellings about the size of an egg or an apple in the armpits and groin. The swellings oozed blood and pus and were followed by spreading boils and black blotches on the skin from internal bleeding. The sick suffered severe

pain and died quickly within five days of the first symptoms. As the disease spread, other symptoms of continuous fever and spitting of blood appeared instead of the swellings or buboes. These victims coughed and sweated heavily and died even more quickly, within three days or less, sometimes in 24 hours. In both types everything that issued from the body—breath, sweat, blood from the buboes and lungs, bloody urine, and bloodblackened excrement—smelled foul. Depression and despair accompanied the physical symptoms, and before the end "death is seen seated on the face."

The disease was bubonic plague, present in two forms: one that infected   2 the bloodstream, causing the buboes and internal bleeding, and was spread by contact; and a second, more virulent pneumonic type that infected the lungs and was spread by respiratory infection. The presence of both at once causes the high mortality and speed of contagion. So lethal was the disease that cases were known of persons going to bed well and dying before they woke, of doctors catching the illness at a bedside and dying before the patient. So rapidly did it spread from one to another that to a French physician, Simon de Covino, it seemed as if one sick person "could infect the whole world." The malignity of the pestilence appeared more terrible because its victims knew no prevention and no remedy.

The physical suffering of the disease and its aspect of evil mystery were   3 expressed in a strange Welsh lament which saw "death coming into our midst like black smoke, a plague which cuts off the young, a rootless phantom which has no mercy for fair countenance. Woe is me of the shilling in the armpit! It is seething, terrible . . . a head that gives pain and causes a loud cry . . . a painful angry knob . . . Great is its seething like a burning cinder . . . a grievous thing of ashy color." Its eruption is ugly like the "seeds of black peas, broken fragments of brittle seacoal . . . the early ornaments of black death, cinders of the peelings of the cockle weed, a mixed multitude, a black plague like halfpence, like berries. . . ."

Rumors of a terrible plague supposedly arising in China and spreading   4 through Tartary (Central Asia) to India and Persia, Mesopotamia, Syria, Egypt, and all of Asia Minor had reached Europe in 1346. They told of a death toll so devastating that all of India was said to be depopulated, whole territories covered by dead bodies, other areas with no one left alive. As added up by Pope Clement VI at Avignon, the total of reported dead reached 23,840,000. In the absence of a concept of contagion, no serious alarm was felt in Europe until the trading ships brought their black burden of pestilence into Messina while other infected ships from the Levant carried it to Genoa and Venice.

By January 1348 it penetrated France via Marseille, and North Africa via   5
Tunis. Shipborne along coasts and navigable rivers, it spread westward from
Marseille through the ports of Languedoc to Spain and northward up the Rhône
to Avignon, where it arrived in March. It reached Narbonne, Montpellier,
Carcassonne, and Toulouse between February and May, and at the same time in
Italy spread to Rome and Florence and their hinterlands. Between June and
August it reached Bordeaux, Lyon, and Paris, spread to Burgundy and
Normandy, and crossed the Channel from Normandy into southern England.
From Italy during the same summer it crossed the Alps into Switzerland and
reached eastward to Hungary.

In a given area the plague accomplished its kill within four to six months   6
and then faded, except in the larger cities, where, rooting into the close quar-
tered population, it abated during the winter, only to reappear in spring and rage
for another six months.

In 1349 it resumed in Paris, spread to Picardy, Flanders, and the Low   7
Countries, and from England to Scotland and Ireland as well as to Norway,
where a ghost ship with a cargo of wool and a dead crew drifted offshore until it
ran aground near Bergen. From there the plague passed into Sweden, Denmark,
Prussia, Iceland, and as far as Greenland. Leaving a strange pocket of immunity
in Bohemia, and Russia unattacked until 1351, it had passed from most of Europe
by mid-1350. Although the mortality rate was erratic, ranging from one-fifth in
some places to nine-tenths or almost total elimination in others, the overall estimate of modern demographers has settled— for the area extending from India to
Iceland—around the same figure expressed in Froissart's casual words: "a third of
the world died." His estimate, the common one at the time, was not an inspired
guess but a borrowing of St. John's figure for mortality from plague in Revelation,
the favorite guide to human affairs of the Middle Ages.

A third of Europe would have meant about 20 million deaths. No one   8
knows in truth how many died. Contemporary reports were an awed impression,
not an accurate count. In crowded Avignon, it was said, 400 died daily; 7000
houses emptied by death were shut up; a single graveyard received 11,000 corpses
in six weeks; half the city's inhabitants reportedly died, including nine cardinals
or one third of the total, and seventy lesser prelates. Watching the endlessly passing death carts, chroniclers let normal exaggeration take wings and put the
Avignon death toll at 62,000 and even at 120,000, although the city's total population was probably less than 50,000.

When graveyards filled up, bodies at Avignon were thrown into the Rhône   9
until mass burial pits were dug for dumping the corpses. In London in such pits
corpses piled up in layers until they overflowed. Everywhere reports speak of the
sick dying too fast for the living to bury. Corpses were dragged out of homes and
left in front of doorways. Morning light revealed new piles of bodies. In Florence
the dead were gathered up by the Compagnia della Misericordia—founded in
1244 to care for the sick—whose members wore red robes and hoods masking
the face except for the eyes. When their efforts failed, the dead lay putrid in the
streets for days at a time. When no coffins were to be had, the bodies were laid
on boards, two or three at once, to be carried to graveyards or common pits.
Families dumped their own relatives into the pits, or buried them so hastily and
thinly "that dogs dragged them forth and devoured their bodies."

Amid accumulating death and fear of contagion, people died without last   10
rites and were buried without prayers, a prospect that terrified the last hours of
the stricken. A bishop in England gave permission to laymen to make confession
to each other as was done by the Apostles, "or if no man is present then even to
a woman," and if no priest could be found to administer extreme unction, "then
faith must suffice." Clement VI found it necessary to grant remissions of sin to
all who died of the plague because so many were unattended by priests. "And no
bells tolled," wrote a chronicler of Siena, "and nobody wept no matter what his
loss because almost everyone expected death. . . . And people said and believed,
'This is the end of the world.'"

In Paris, where the plague lasted through 1349, the reported death rate was   11
800 a day, in Pisa 500, in Vienna 500 to 600. The total dead in Paris numbered
50,000 or half the population. Florence, weakened by the famine of 1347, lost
three to fourfifths of its citizens, Venice two-thirds, Hamburg and Bremen,
though smaller in size, about the same proportion. Cities, as centers of transportation, were more likely to be affected than villages, although once a village
was infected, its death rate was equally high. At Givry, a prosperous village in
Burgundy of 1200 to 1500 people, the parish register records 615 deaths in the
space of fourteen weeks, compared to an average of thirty deaths a year in the
previous decade. In three villages of Cambridgeshire, manorial records show a
death rate of 47 percent, 57 percent, and in one case 70 percent. When the last
survivors, too few to carry on, moved away, a deserted village sank back into the
wilderness and disappeared from the map altogether leaving only a grass-covered
ghostly outline to show where mortals once had lived.

In enclosed places such as monasteries and prisons, the infection of one 12
person usually meant that of all, as happened in the Franciscan convents of
Carcassonne and Marseille, where every inmate without exception died. Of the
140 Dominicans at Montpellier only seven survived. Petrarch's brother
Gherardo, member of a Carthusian monastery, buried the prior and 34 fellow
monks one by one, sometimes three a day, until he was left alone with his dog
and fled to look for a place that would take him in. Watching every comrade die,
men in such places could not but wonder whether the strange peril that filled the
air had not been sent to exterminate the human race. In Kilkenny, Ireland,
Brother John Clyn of the Friars Minor, another monk left alone among dead
men, kept a record of what had happened lest "things which should be remembered perish with time and vanish from the memory of those who come after us."
Sensing "the whole world, as it were, placed within the grasp of the Evil One,"
and waiting for death to visit him too, he wrote, "I leave parchment to continue this work, if perchance any man survive and any of the race of Adam escape
this pestilence and carry on the work which I have begun." Brother John, as
noted by another hand, died of the pestilence, but he foiled oblivion.

The largest cities of Europe, with populations of about 100,000, were Paris 13
and Florence, Venice and Genoa. At the next level, with more than 50,000,
were Ghent and Bruges in Flanders, Milan, Bologna, Rome, Naples, Palermo,
and Cologne. London hovered below 50,000, the only city in England except
York with more than 10,000. At the level of 20,000 to 50,000 were Bordeaux,
Toulouse, Montpellier, Marseille, and Lyon in France, Barcelona, Seville, and
Toledo in Spain, Siena, Pisa, and other secondary cities in Italy, and the
Hanseatic trading cities of the Empire. The plague raged through them all,
killing anywhere from one-third to two-thirds of their inhabitants. Italy, with a
total population of 10 to 11 million, probably suffered the heaviest toll.
Following the Florentine bankruptcies, the crop failures and workers' riots of
1346-47, the revolt of Cola di Rienzi that plunged Rome into anarchy, the
plague came as the peak of successive calamities. As if the world were indeed in
the grasp of the Evil One, its first appearance on the European mainland in
January 1348 coincided with a fearsome earthquake that carved a path of wreckage from Naples up to Venice. Houses collapsed, church towers toppled, villages
were crushed, and the destruction reached as far as Germany and Greece.
Emotional response, dulled by horrors, underwent a kind of atrophy epitomized
by the chronicler who wrote, "And in these days was burying without sorrowe
and wedding without friendschippe."

In Siena, where more than half the inhabitants died of the plague, work   14
was abandoned on the great cathedral, planned to be the largest in the world,
and never resumed, owing to loss of workers and master masons and "the melancholy and grief" of the survivors. The cathedral's truncated transept still stands
in permanent witness to the sweep of death's scythe. Agnolo di Tura, a chronicler of Siena, recorded the fear of contagion that froze every other instinct.
"Father abandoned child, wife husband, one brother another," he wrote, "for this
plague seemed to strike through the breath and sight. And so they died. And no
one could be found to bury the dead for money or friendship. . . . And I, Agnolo
di Tura, called the Fat, buried my five children with my own hands, and so did
many others likewise."

There were many to echo his account of inhumanity and few to balance it,   15
for the plague was not the kind of calamity that inspired mutual help. Its loath-
someness and deadliness did not herd people together in mutual distress, but only
prompted their desire to escape each other. "Magistrates and notaries refused to
come and make the wills of the dying," reported a Franciscan friar of Piazza in
Sicily; what was worse, "even the priests did not come to hear their confessions."
A clerk of the Archbishop of Canterbury reported the same of English priests
who "turned away from the care of their benefices from fear of death." Cases of
parents deserting children and children their parents were reported across Europe
from Scotland to Russia. The calamity chilled the hearts of men, wrote
Boccaccio in his famous account of the plague in Florence that serves as introduction to the *Decameron.* "One man shunned another . . . kinsfolk held aloof,
brother was forsaken by brother, oftentimes husband by wife; nay, what is more,
and scarcely to be believed, fathers and mothers were found to abandon their
own children in their fate, untended, unvisited as if they had been strangers."
Exaggeration and literary pessimism were common in the 14th century, but the
Pope's physician, Guy de Chauliac, was a sober, careful observer who reported
the same phenomenon: "A father did not visit his son, nor the son his father.
Charity was dead."

Yet not entirely. In Paris, according to the chronicler Jean de Venette, the   16
nuns of the Hôtel Dieu or municipal hospital, "having no fear of death, tended
the sick with all sweetness and humility." New nuns repeatedly took the places
of those who died, until the majority "many times renewed by death now rest in
peace with Christ as we may piously believe."

When the plague entered northern France in July 1348, it settled first in   17
Normandy and, checked by winter, gave Picardy a deceptive interim until the

next summer. Either in the mourning or warning, black flags were flown from church towers of the worst-stricken villages of Normandy. "And in that time," wrote a monk of the abbey of Fourcarment, "the mortality was so great among the people of Normandy that those of Picardy mocked them." The same unneighborly reaction was reported of the Scots, separated by a winter's immunity from the English. Delighted to hear of the disease that was scourging the "southrons," they gathered forces for an invasion, "laughing at their enemies." Before they could move, the savage mortality fell upon them too, scattering some in death and the rest in panic to spread the infection as they fled.

In Picardy in the summer of 1349 the pestilence penetrated the castle of 18
Coucy to kill Enguerrand's mother, Catherine, and her new husband. Whether her 9-yearold son escaped by chance or was perhaps living elsewhere with one of his guardians is unrecorded. In nearby Amiens, tannery workers, responding quickly to losses in the labor force, combined to bargain for higher wages. In another place villagers were seen dancing to drums and trumpets, and on being asked the reason, answered that, seeing their neighbors die day by day while their village remained immune, they believed they could keep the plague from entering "by the jollity that is in us. That is why we dance." Further north in Tournai on the border of Flanders, Gilles li Muisis, Abbot of St. Martin's, kept one of the epidemic's most vivid accounts. The passing bells rang all day and all night, he recorded, because sextons were anxious to obtain their fees while they could. Filled with the sound of mourning, the city became oppressed by fear, so that the authorities forbade the tolling of bells and the wearing of black and restricted funeral services to two mourners. The silencing of funeral bells and of criers' announcements of deaths were ordained by most cities. Siena imposed a fine on the wearing of mourning clothes by all except widows.

Flight was the chief recourse of those who could afford it or arrange it. The 19
rich fled to their country places like Boccaccio's young patricians of Florence, who settled in a pastoral palace "removed on every side from the roads" with "wells of cool water and vaults of rare wines." The urban poor died in their burrows, "and only the stench of their bodies informed neighbors of their death." That the poor were more heavily afflicted than the rich was clearly remarked at the time, in the north as in the south. A Scottish chronicler, John of Fordun, stated flatly that the pest "attacked especially the meaner sort and common people—seldom the magnates." Simon de Covino of Montpellier made the same observation. He ascribed it to the misery and want and hard lives that made the poor more susceptible, which was half the truth. Close contact and lack of sani-

tation was the unrecognized other half. It was noticed too that the young died in greater proportion than the old; Simon de Covino compared the disappearance of youth to the withering of flowers in the fields.

In the countryside peasants dropped dead on the roads, in the fields, in   20 their houses. Survivors in growing helplessness fell into apathy, leaving ripe wheat uncut and livestock untended. Oxen and asses, sheep and goats, pigs and chickens ran wild and they too, according to local reports, succumbed to the pest. English sheep, bearers of the precious wool, died throughout the country. The chronicler Henry Knighton, canon of Leicester Abbey, reported 5000 dead in one field alone, "their bodies so corrupted by the plague that neither beast nor bird would touch them," and spreading an appalling stench. In the Austrian Alps wolves came down to prey upon sheep and then, "as if alarmed by some invisible warning, turned and fled back into the wilderness." In remote Dalmatia bolder wolves descended upon a plague-stricken city and attacked human survivors. For want of herdsmen, cattle strayed from place to place and died in hedgerows and ditches. Dogs and cats fell like the rest.

The dearth of labor held a fearful prospect because the 14th century lived   21 close to the annual harvest both for food and for next year's seed. "So few servants and laborers were left," wrote Knighton, "that no one knew where to turn for help." The sense of a vanishing future created a kind of dementia of despair. A Bavarian chronicler of Neuberg on the Danube recorded that "Men and women . . . wandered around as if mad" and let their cattle stray "because no one had any inclination to concern themselves about the future." Fields were uncultivated, spring seed unsown. Second growth with nature's awful energy crept back over cleared land, dikes crumbled, salt water reinvaded and soured the lowlands. With so few hands remaining to restore the work of centuries, people felt, in Walsingham's words, that "the world could never again regain its former prosperity."

Though the death rate was higher among the anonymous poor, the known   22 and the great died too. King Alfonso XI of Castile was the only reigning monarch killed by the pest, but his neighbor King Pedro of Aragon lost his wife, Queen Leonora, his daughter Marie, and a niece in the space of six months. John Cantacuzene, Emperor of Byzantium, lost his son. In France the lame Queen Jeanne and her daughter-in-law Bonne de Luxemburg, wife of the Dauphin, both died in 1349 in the same phase that took the life of Enguerrand's mother. Jeanne, Queen of Navarre, daughter of Louis X, was another victim. Edward III's second daughter, Joanna, who was on her way to marry Pedro, the heir of Castile, died in Bordeaux. Women appear to have been more vulnerable than men, perhaps because, being more housebound, they were more exposed to fleas. Boccaccio's mistress Fiammetta, illegitimate daughter of the King of Naples, died, as did Laura, the beloved—whether real or fictional—of Petrarch. Reaching out to us in the future, Petrarch cried, "Oh happy posterity who will not experience such abysmal woe and will look upon our testimony as a fable."

In Florence Giovanni Villani, the great historian of his time, died at 68 in the midst of an unfinished sentence: . . . *e dure questo pistolenza fino a* . . . (in the midst of this pestilence there came to an end . . .)." Siena's master painters, the brothers Ambrogio and Pietro Lorenzetti, whose names never appeared after 1348, presumably perished in the plague, as did Andrea Pisano, architect and sculptor of Florence. William of Ockham and the English mystic Richard Rolle of Hample both disappear from mention after 1349. Francisco Datini, merchant of Prato, lost both his parents and two siblings. Curious sweeps of mortality afflicted certain bodies of merchants in London. All eight wardens of the Company of Cutters, all six wardens of the Hatters, and four wardens of the Goldsmiths died before July 1350. Sir John Pulteney, master draper and four times Mayor of London, was a victim, likewise Sir John Montgomery, Governor of Calais.

Among the clergy and doctors the mortality was naturally high because of the nature of their professions. Out of 24 physicians in Venice, 20 were said to have lost their lives in the plague, although, according to another account, some were believed to have fled or to have shut themselves up in their houses. At Montpellier, site of the leading medieval medical school, the physician Simon de Covino reported that, despite the great number of doctors, "hardly one of them escaped." In Avignon, Guy de Chauliac confessed that he performed his medical visits only because he dared not stay away for fear of infamy, but "I was in continual fear." He claimed to have contracted the disease but to have cured himself by his own treatment; if so, he was one of the few who recovered.

Clerical mortality varied with rank. Although the one-third toll of cardinals reflects the same proportion as the whole, this was probably due to their concentration in Avignon. In England, in strange and almost sinister procession, the Archbishop of Canterbury, John Stratford, died in August 1348, his appointed successor died in May 1349, and the next appointee three months later, all three within a year. Despite such weird vagaries, prelates in general managed to sustain a higher survival rate than the lesser clergy. Among bishops the deaths have been estimated at about one in twenty. The loss of priests, even if many avoided their fearful duty of attending the dying, was about the same as among the population as a whole.

Government officials, whose loss contributed to the general chaos, found, on the whole, no special shelter. In Siena four of the nine members of the governing oligarchy died, in France one-third of the royal notaries, in Bristol 15 out of the 52 members of the Town Council or almost one-third. Tax-collecting obviously suffered, with the result that Philip VI was unable to collect more than a fraction of the subsidy granted him by the Estates in the winter of 1347–48.   26

Lawlessness and debauchery accompanied the plague as they had during the great plague of Athens of 430 b.c., when according to Thucydides, men grew bold in the indulgence of pleasure: "For seeing how the rich died in a moment and those who had nothing immediately inherited their property, they reflected that life and riches were alike transitory and they resolved to enjoy themselves while they could." Human behavior is timeless. When St. John had his vision of plague in Revelation, he knew from some experience or race memory that those who survived "repented not of the work of their hands. . . . Neither repented they of their murders, nor of their sorceries, nor of their fornication, nor of their thefts."   27

Ignorance of the cause augmented the sense of horror. Of the real carriers, rats and fleas, the 14th century had no suspicion, perhaps because they were so familiar. Fleas, though a common household nuisance, are not once mentioned in contemporary plague writings, and rats only incidentally, although folklore commonly associated them with pestilence. The legend of the Pied Piper arose from an outbreak of 1284. The actual plague bacillus, *Pasturella pestis*, remained undiscovered for another 500 years. Living alternatively in the stomach of the flea and the bloodstream of the rat who was the flea's host, the bacillus in its bubonic form was transferred to humans and animals by the bite of either rat or flea. It traveled by virtue of *Rattus rattus*, the small medieval black rat that lived on ships, as well as by the heavier brown or sewer rat. What precipitated the turn of the bacillus from innocuous to virulent form is unknown, but the occurrence is now believed to have taken place not in China but somewhere in central Asia and to have spread along the caravan routes. Chinese origin was a mistaken notion of the 14th century based on real but belated reports of huge death tolls in China from drought, famine, and pestilence which have since been traced to the 1330s, too soon to be responsible for the plague that appeared in India in 1346.   28

The phantom enemy had no name. Called the Black Death only in later   29
recurrences, it was known during the first epidemic simply as the Pestilence or
Great Mortality. Reports from the East, swollen by fearful imaginings, told of
strange tempests and "sheets of fire" mingled with huge hailstones that "slew
almost all," or a "vast rain of fire" that burned up men, beasts, stones, trees, villages, and cities. In another version, "foul blasts of wind" from the fires carried
the infection to Europe "and now as some suspect it cometh round the seacoast."
Accurate observation in this case could not make the mental jump to ships and
rats because no idea of animal- or insectborne contagion existed.

The earthquake was blamed for releasing sulfurous and foul fumes from the   30
earth's interior, or as evidence of a titanic struggle of planets and oceans causing
waters to rise and vaporize until fish died in masses and corrupted the air. All
these explanations had in common a factor of poisoned air, of miasmas and thick,
stinking mists traced to every kind of natural or imagined agency from stagnant
lakes to malign conjunction of the planets, from the hand of the Evil One to the
wrath of God. Medical thinking, trapped in the theory of astral influences,
stressed air as the communicator of disease, ignoring sanitation or visible carriers. The existence of two carriers confused the trail, the more so because the flea
could live and travel independently of the rat for as long as a month and, if
infected by the particularly virulent septicemic form of the bacillus, could infect
humans without reinfecting itself from the rat. The simultaneous presence of the
pneumonic form of the disease, which was indeed communicated through the
air, blurred the problem further.

The mystery of the contagion was "the most terrible of all the terrors," as   31
an anonymous Flemish cleric in Avignon wrote to a correspondent in Bruges.
Plagues had been known before, from the plague of Athens (believed to have
been typhus) to the prolonged epidemic of the 6th century a.d., to the recurrence
of sporadic outbreaks in the 12th and 13th centuries, but they had left no accumulated store of understanding. That the infection came from contact with the
sick or with their houses, clothes, or corpses was quickly observed but not com-
prehended. Gentile da Foligno, renowned physician of Perugia and doctor of
medicine at the universities of Bologna and Padua, came close to respiratory
infection when he surmised that poisonous material was "communicated by
means of air breathed out and in." Having no idea of microscopic carriers, he had
to assume that the air was corrupted by planetary influences. Planets, however,
could not explain the ongoing contagion. The agonized search for an answer
gave rise to such theories as transference by sight. People fell ill, wrote Guy de

Chauliac, not only by remaining with the sick but "even by looking at them." Three hundred years later Joshua Barnes, the 17th century biographer of Edward III, would write that the power of infection had entered into beams of light and "darted death from the eyes."

Doctors struggling with the evidence could not break away from the terms   32 of astrology, to which they believed all human physiology was subject. Medicine was the one aspect of medieval life, perhaps because of its links with the Arabs, not shaped by Christian doctrine. Clerics detested astrology, but could not dislodge its influence. Guy de Chauliac, physician to three popes in succession, practiced in obedience to the zodiac. While his *Cirurgia* was the major treatise on surgery of its time, while he understood the use of anesthesia made from the juice of opium, mandrake, or hemlock, he nevertheless prescribed bleeding and purgatives by the planets and divided chronic from acute diseases on the basis of one being under the rule of the sun and the other of the moon.

In October 1348 Philip VI asked the medical faculty of the University of   33 Paris for a report on the affliction that seemed to threaten human survival. With careful thesis, antithesis, and proofs, the doctors ascribed it to a triple conjunction of Saturn, Jupiter, and Mars in the 40th degree of Aquarius said to have occurred on March 20, 1345. They acknowledged, however, effects "whose cause is hidden from even the most highly trained intellects." The verdict of the masters of Paris became the official version. Borrowed, copied by scribes, carried abroad, translated from Latin into various vernaculars, it was everywhere accepted, even by the Arab physicians of Cordova and Granada, as the scientific if not the popular answer. Because of the terrible interest of the subject, the translations of the plague tracts stimulated use of national languages. In that one respect, life came from death.

Questions for Discussion

1. Why did Europeans feel no alarm on hearing rumors of a plague in Asia? How did their sense of being immune from the plague leave them unprepared for it?

2. What is the process by which the plague moved through Europe? Why did the plague behave as if on a cycle?

3. What is known with certainty about the plague? What is still uncertain? Why?

4. What made the Black Death particularly and psychologically terrifying?

5. What do the many statistics and quotes help Tuchman do?

6. What techniques does Tuchman use to make the subject matter even more interesting than it already naturally is? How does she enliven the historical events?

7. What does Tuchman do to clarify possible misconceptions that her readers may have about the Black Death?

Questions for Reflection and Writing

1. Before you read, list what you know or assume or remember hearing about the plague. After reading, make another list, of what you learned from Tuchman's essay.

2. What was the effect of the plague on the communities of Europe? How did it change the way people behaved, lived, and thought? Explain, with references to Tuchman.

3. Choose one country or, even better, city, or area within a country, in Europe or Asia. Find out how the Black Death affected that country, city, or area.

Chapter 4
GOVERNMENT, POLITICS, AND SOCIAL JUSTICE

Niccolò **Machiavelli** (1469–1527) was born in Florence and studied Roman law. He was a public servant, diplomat, historian, writer, and one of the most important political scientists of all time. Besides *The Discourses* (1531), from which "The Circle of Governments" is taken, *The Art of War* (1519–1520), and *The Prince* (1532), Machiavelli also wrote comedies and histories. While today *The Prince* is sometimes called "a handbook for dictators," Machiavelli strongly believed in a republican government. Machiavelli's entire body of work was put on the Roman Catholic Church's Index of Prohibited Books in 1559. In this essay, Machiavelli illustrates a pattern in governments' dissolution and re-formation.

The Circle of Governments

Niccolò Machiavelli

Having proposed to myself to treat of the kind of government established at   1
Rome, and of the events that led to its perfection, I must at the beginning
observe that some of the writers on politics distinguished three kinds of government, vis. the monarchical, the aristocratic, and the democratic; and maintain
that the legislators of a people must choose from these three the one that seems
to them most suitable. Other authors, wiser according to the opinion of many,
count six kinds of governments, three of which are very bad, and three good in
themselves, but so liable to be corrupted that they become absolutely bad. The
three good ones are those which we have just named; the three bad ones result
from the degradation of the other three, and each of them resembles its corresponding original, so that the transition from the one to the other is very easy.
Thus monarchy becomes tyranny; aristocracy degenerates into oligarchy; and
the popular government lapses readily into licentiousness. So that a legislator
who gives to a state which he founds either of these three forms of government,
constitutes it but for a brief time; for no precautions can prevent either one of
the three that are reputed good from degenerating into its opposite kind; so great
are in these the attractions and resemblances between the good and the evil.

Chance has given birth to these different kinds of governments amongst   2
men; for at the beginning of the world the inhabitants were few in number and
lived for a time dispersed, like beasts. As the human race increased, the necessity for uniting themselves for defence made itself felt; the better to attain this
object they chose the strongest and most courageous from amongst themselves

and placed him at their head promising to obey him. Thence they began to know the good and the honest, and to distinguish them from the bad and vicious; for seeing a man injure his benefactor aroused at once two sentiments in every heart, hatred against the ingrate and love for the benefactor. They blamed the first, and on the contrary honoured those the more who showed themselves grateful, for each felt that he in turn might be subject to a like wrong; and to prevent similar evils, they set to work to make laws, and to institute punishments for those who contravened them. Such was the origin of justice. This caused them, when they had afterwards to choose a prince, neither to look to the strongest nor bravest, but to the wisest and most just. But when they began to make sovereignty hereditary and non-elective, the children quickly degenerated from their fathers; and, so far from trying to equal their virtues, they considered that a prince had nothing else to do than to excel all the rest in luxury, indulgence, and every other variety of pleasure. The prince consequently soon drew upon himself the general hatred. An object of hatred, he naturally felt fear; fear in turn dictated to him precautions and wrongs, and thus tyranny quickly developed itself. Such were the beginning and causes of disorders, conspiracies, and plots against the sovereigns, set on foot, not by the feeble and timid, but by those citizens who, surpassing the others in grandeur of soul, in wealth, and in courage, could not submit to the outrages and excesses of their princes.

Under such powerful leaders the masses armed themselves against the tyrant, and after having rid themselves of him, submitted to these chiefs as their liberators. These, abhorring the very name of prince, constituted themselves a new government; and at first bearing in mind the past tyranny, they governed in strict accordance with the laws which they had established themselves; preferring public interests to their own, and to administer and protect with greatest care both public and private affairs. The children succeeded their fathers, and ignorant of the changes of fortune, having never experienced its reverses, and indisposed to remain content with this civil equality, they in turn gave themselves up to cupidity, ambition, libertinage, and violence, and soon caused the aristocratic government to degenerate into an oligarchic tyranny, regardless of all civil rights. They soon, however, experienced the same fate as the first tyrant; the people, disgusted with their government, placed themselves at the command of whoever was willing to attack them, and this disposition soon produced an avenger, who was sufficiently well seconded to destroy them. The memory of the prince and the wrongs committed by him being still fresh in their minds, and having overthrown the oligarchy, the people were not willing to return to the government of a prince. A popular government was therefore resolved upon, and it was so organized that the authority would not again fall into the hands of a prince or a small number of nobles. And as all governments are at first looked up to with some degree of reverence, the popular state also maintained itself for a time, but which was never of long duration, and lasted generally only about as long as the generation that had established it; for it soon ran into that kind of licence which inflicts injury upon public as well as private interests. Each individual only consulted his own passions, and a thousand acts of injustice were daily committed, so that, constrained by necessity, or directed by the counsels of some good man, or for the purpose of escaping from this anarchy, they returned anew to the government of a prince, and from this they generally lapsed again into anarchy, step-by-step, in the same manner and from the same causes as we have indicated.

Such is the circle which all republics are destined to run through. Seldom, 4 however, do they come back to the original form of government, which results from the fact that their duration is not sufficiently long to be able to undergo these repeated changes and preserve their existence. But it may well happen that a republic lacking strength and good counsel in its difficulties becomes subject after a while to some neighbouring state, that is better organized than itself; and if such is not the case, then they will be apt to revolve indefinitely in the circle of revolutions. I say, then, that all kinds of government are defective; those three which we have qualified as good because they are too short-lived, and the three bad ones because of their inherent viciousness. Thus sagacious legislators, knowing the vices of each of these systems of government by themselves, have chosen one that should partake of all of them, judging that to be the most stable and solid. In fact, when there is combined under the same constitution a prince, a nobility, and the power of the people, then these three powers will watch and keep each other reciprocally in check.

Questions for Discussion

1. According to the author, what is "the origin of justice"?
2. To what effect does Machiavelli use examples in this piece? What other means of support does he use?
3. According to Machiavelli, why were governments formed in the first place?
4. Briefly discuss the types of governments Machiavelli describes. Do they all seem familiar, or do you think some no longer exist?

5. Discuss Machiavelli's view of the circular nature of the rise and fall of government, using specific examples from your reading.

Questions for Reflection and Writing

1. This piece was written in the sixteenth century. How accurately does it describe governments of today? What has changed?

2. How does the author structure this essay? In what order are the different types of governments discussed? Why do you think Machiavelli chose this order? What would change with a change in the ordering?

3. Machiavelli's name has become synonymous today with a certain type of behavior performed very often but not always in the sphere of politics. What is this type of behavior? From your reading of this piece (and, if you care to delve further, of Machiavelli's *The Prince*), does the use of his name in this context seem fair? If you knew of the term beforehand, do you think it colored your reading of the piece?

Thomas Jefferson (1743–1826), one of the Founding Fathers and, later, president of the United States, was also a lawyer, congressman, statesman, ambassador, and inventor. He was educated first by Anglicans and later at the College of William and Mary. Admitted to the bar in 1767, Jefferson became familiar with Virginia by attending quarter sessions of county courts. When Virginia agreed to support Massachusetts against what became known as the Intolerable Acts, Jefferson penned *A Summary View of the Rights of British America* (1774); he subsequently became a delegate to the Continental Congress in Philadelphia. In 1776 Jefferson drafted the Declaration of Independence, which was amended somewhat both by committee and by Congress. He also coauthored a new legal code for Virginia and wrote a plan to phase out slavery, although he declined to present it to the House of Delegates.

In 1779 Jefferson became governor of Virginia and had to contend with both the move of the capital from Williamsburg to Richmond and the British invasion of Virginia. Depressed by the death of his wife in 1782, Jefferson nevertheless accepted reappointment to Congress, where he helped develop the American economic system and advocated local self-government. In 1785 Jefferson replaced Benjamin Franklin as minister to France, returning to the U.S. capital, New York, in 1789. He helped establish a District of Columbia, although the federal government moved temporarily to Philadelphia. In 1791 Jefferson organized the first opposition party with James Madison in order to oust Washington's secretary of the Treasury, Alexander Hamilton. Jefferson became vice president in 1797 after losing a close election to his friend John Adams.

Jefferson was elected president in 1798 in a close election which was sent to Congress. Eventually Jefferson had Aaron Burr, his vice president, arrested and tried for treason. During Jefferson's presidency the Twelfth Amendment to the Constitution was passed, clarifying presidential and vice presidential votes; the whiskey tax was repealed; and Jefferson sent ships to the Mediterranean to deter piracy. Jefferson doubled the size of the United States with the purchase of the Louisiana Territory from Napoleon, and he sent Lewis and Clark on their famous expedition up the Missouri and Columbia rivers to gather scientific and geographic information. Jefferson won reelection in 1804, but faced both external opposition from France, which wanted Florida, and internal opposition.

The Declaration of Independence

Thomas Jefferson

In CONGRESS, July 4, 1776.

The Unanimous Declaration of the thirteen united States of America.

When in the Course of human events, it becomes necessary for one peo-   1
ple to dissolve the political bands which have connected them with another, and
to assume among the powers of the earth, the separate and equal station to which

the Laws of Nature and of Nature's God entitle them, a decent respect to the opinions of mankind requires that they should declare the causes which impel them to the separation.—— We hold these truths to be self-evident, that all men are created equal, that they are endowed by their Creator with certain unalienable Rights, that among these are Life, Liberty and the pursuit of Happiness.—That to secure these rights, Governments are instituted among Men, deriving their just powers from the consent of the governed,—That whenever any Form of Government becomes destructive of these ends, it is the Right of the People to alter or to abolish it, and to institute new Government, laying its foundation on such principles and organizing its powers in such form, as to them shall seem most likely to effect their Safety and Happiness. Prudence, indeed, will dictate that Governments long established should not be changed for light and transient causes; and accordingly all experience hath shewn, that mankind are more disposed to suffer, while evils are sufferable, than to right themselves by abolishing the forms to which they are accustomed. But when a long train of abuses and usurpations, pursuing invariably the same Object, evinces a design to reduce them under absolute Despotism, it is their right, it is their duty, to throw off such Government, and to provide new Guards for their future security.—Such has been the patient sufferance of these Colonies; and such is now the necessity which constrains them to alter their former Systems of Government. The history of the present King of Great Britain is a history of repeated injuries and usurpations, all having in direct object the establishment of an absolute Tyranny over these States. To prove this, let Facts be submitted to a can did world.——He has refused his Assent to Laws, the most wholesome and necessary for the public good.——He has forbidden his Governors to pass Laws of immediate and pressing importance, unless suspended in their operation till his Assent should be obtained; and when so suspended, he has utterly neglected to attend to them.——He has refused to pass other Laws for the accommodation of large districts of people, unless those people would relinquish the right of Representation in the Legislature, a right inestimable to them and formidable to tyrants only.——He has called together legislative bodies at places unusual, uncomfortable, and distant from the depository of their public Records, for the sole purpose of fatiguing them into compliance with his measures.——He has dissolved Representative Houses repeatedly, for opposing with manly firmness his invasions on the rights of the people.——He has refused for a long time, after such dissolutions, to cause others to be elected; whereby the Legislative powers, incapable of Annihilation, have returned to the People at large for their exercise; the State remaining in the mean time exposed to all the dangers of invasion from without, and convulsions within.——He has endeavoured to prevent the population of these States; for that purpose obstructing the Laws for Naturalization of Foreigners; refusing to pass others to encourage their migrations hither, and raising the conditions of new Appropriations of Lands.——He has obstructed the Administration of Justice, by refusing his Assent to Laws for establishing Judiciary powers.——He has made Judges dependent on his Will alone, for the tenure of their offices, and the amount and payment of their salaries.——He has erected a multitude of New Offices, and sent hither swarms of Officers to harass our people, and eat out their substance.—— He has kept among us, in times of peace, Standing Armies without the Consent of our legislatures.——He has affected to render the Military independent of and superior to the Civil power.——He has combined with others to subject us to a jurisdiction foreign to our constitution, and unacknowledged by our laws; giving his Assent to their Acts of pretended Legislation:—For Quartering large bodies of armed troops among us:—For protecting them, by a mock Trial, from punishment for any Murders which they should commit on the Inhabitants of these States:—For cutting off our Trade with all parts of the world:—For imposing Taxes on us without our Consent:— For depriving us in many cases, of the benefits of Trial by Jury:—For transporting us beyond Seas to be tried for pretended offences:—For abolishing the free System of English Laws in a neighbouring Province, establishing therein an Arbitrary government, and enlarging its Boundaries so as to render it at once an example and fit instrument for introducing the same absolute rule into these Colonies:—For taking away our Charters, abolishing our most valuable Laws, and altering fundamentally the Forms of our Governments:—For suspending our own Legislatures, and declaring themselves invested with power to legislate for us in all cases whatsoever.—He has abdicated Government here, by declaring us out of his Protection and waging War against us:— He has plundered our seas, ravaged our Coasts, burnt our towns, and destroyed the lives of our people.—He is at this time transporting large Armies of foreign Mercenaries to compleat the works of death, desolation and tyranny, already begun with circumstances of Cruelty & perfidy scarcely paralleled in the most barbarous ages, and totally unworthy the Head of a civilized nation.—He has constrained our fellow Citizens taken Captive on the high Seas to bear Arms against their Country, to become the executioners of their friends and Brethren, or to fall themselves by their Hands.—He has excited domestic insurrections amongst us, and has endeavoured to bring on the inhabitants of our frontiers, the merciless

Indian Savages, whose known rule of warfare, is an undistinguished destruction of all ages, sexes and conditions. In every stage of these Oppressions We have Petitioned for Redress in the most humble terms: Our repeated Petitions have been answered only by repeated injury. A Prince, whose character is thus marked by every act which may define a Tyrant, is unfit to be the ruler of a free people. Nor have We been wanting in attentions to our British brethren. We have warned them from time to time of attempts by their legislature to extend an unwarrantable jurisdiction over us. We have reminded them of the circumstances of our emigration and settlement here. We have appealed to their native justice and magnanimity, and we have conjured them by the ties of our common kindred to disavow these usurpations, which, would inevitably interrupt our connections and correspondence. They too have been deaf to the voice of justice and of consanguinity. We must, therefore, acquiesce in the necessity, which denounces our Separation, and hold them, as we hold the rest of mankind, Enemies in War, in Peace Friends.

We, therefore, the Representatives of the United States of America, in General Congress Assembled, appealing to the Supreme Judge of the world for the rectitude of our intentions, do, in the Name and by Authority of the good People of these Colonies, solemnly publish and declare, That these United Colonies are, and of Right ought to be Free and Independent States; that they are Absolved from all Allegiance to the British Crown, and that all political connection between them and the State of Great Britain, is and ought to be totally dissolved; and that as Free and Independent States, they have full Power to levy War, conclude Peace, contract Alliances, establish Commerce, and to do all other Acts and Things which Independent States may of right do.—And for the support of this Declaration, with a firm reliance on the protection of divine Providence, we mutually pledge to each other our Lives, our Fortunes and our sacred Honor.

Questions for Discussion

1. What are "unalienable Rights" and why should they have priority in a country?
2. What did Jefferson and the Continental Congress expect to happen as a result of writing the Declaration of Independence? What does Jefferson include in the text that shows that they expected an angry response?

3. What is the structure of the Declaration of Independence? What do each of the two paragraphs do? Can the text be divided into smaller sections, with each section having a special purpose?

4. What strong language does Jefferson use? Do you think he is always justified in using such language? How does he justify it?

5. What are the stated reasons for declaring independence? Might there be any other reasons, that are left unsaid?

6. What is the claim and what are the points supporting that claim?

7. What concrete evidence does Jefferson provide to support his argument?

Questions for Reflection and Writing

1. Describe the typical (from your point of view) American opinion of monarchy. What does this opinion share with the ideas stated in the Declaration of Independence?

2. Analyze the rhetoric of the Declaration of Independence. What makes this a powerful document? Include in your analysis specific examples from the text of effective rhetoric, and explain why these examples are effective.

3. Research the writing of the Declaration of Independence. How many drafts did Jefferson write? What kind of help did he receive? How was the finished Declaration received by the Continental Congress? Why was Jefferson chosen to write it?

Martin Luther King, Jr. (1929–1968) had at first planned to become a doctor or a lawyer, but when he graduated from Morehouse College in Atlanta at the age of nineteen, he abandoned these ambitions and went into the seminary. After seminary, he went to Boston University, where he received his Ph.D. in 1955. He was ordained as a Baptist minister in his father's church, the Ebenezer Baptist Church in Atlanta, a church he copastored with his father from 1960 to 1968. He was also founder and director of the Southern Christian Leadership Conference from 1957 to 1968, and a member of the Montgomery Improvement Association, an activist group protesting racial segregation. Inspired by Mahatma Gandhi's principles of nonviolent protest, King led this group in several demonstrations. In May 1963, he was arrested and imprisoned in Birmingham for demonstrating against segregation in hotels and restaurants. It was while in jail that he wrote his famous "Letter from Birmingham Jail," a work that was published in 1963 and expanded and republished in 1968. It was also in 1963 that King made the speech entitled "I Have a Dream" to over 200,000 people at the March on Washington. King received numerous awards for his work for human rights, including the Nobel Prize for Peace in 1964. On April 4, 1968, while talking with other human rights activists on a motel balcony in Memphis, King was assassinated.

I Have a Dream

Martin Luther King, Jr.

Five score years ago, a great American, in whose symbolic shadow we stand, signed the Emancipation Proclamation. This momentous decree came as a great beacon light of hope to millions of Negro slaves who had been seared in the flames of withering injustice. It came as a joyous daybreak to end the long night of captivity.   1

But 100 years later, we must face the tragic fact that the Negro is still not free. One hundred years later, the life of the Negro is still sadly crippled by the manacles of segregation and the chains of discrimination. One hundred years later, the Negro lives on a lonely island of poverty in the midst of a vast ocean of material prosperity. One hundred years later, the Negro is still languished in the corners of American society and finds himself an exile in his own land. So we have come here today to dramatize an appalling condition.   2

In a sense we have come to our nation's capital to cash a check. When the architects of our republic wrote the magnificent words of the Constitution and   3 the Declaration of Independence, they were signing a promissory note to which every American was to fall heir. This note was a promise that all men would be guaranteed the unalienable rights of life, liberty, and the pursuit of happiness.

It is obvious today that America has defaulted on this promissory note inso- 4
far as her citizens of color are concerned. Instead of honoring this sacred obligation, America has given the Negro people a bad check; a check which has come
back marked "insufficient funds." But we refuse to believe that the bank of justice is bankrupt. We refuse to believe that there are insufficient funds in the great
vaults of opportunity of this nation. So we have come to cash this check—a
check that will give us upon demand the riches of freedom and the security of
justice. We have also come to this hallowed spot to remind America of the fierce
urgency of *now*. This is no time to engage in the luxury of cooling off or to take
the tranquilizing drug of gradualism. *Now* is the time to make real the promises
of Democracy. *Now* is the time to rise from the dark and desolate valley of segregation to the sunlit path of racial justice. *Now* is the time to open the doors of
opportunity to all of God's children. *Now* is the time to lift our nation from the
quicksands of racial injustice to the solid rock of brotherhood.

It would be fatal for the nation to overlook the urgency of the moment and 5
to underestimate the determination of the Negro. This sweltering summer of the
Negro's legitimate discontent will not pass until there is an invigorating autumn
of freedom and equality. Nineteen sixty-three is not an end, but a beginning.
Those who hope that the Negro needed to blow off steam and will now be content will have a rude awakening if the nation returns to business as usual. There
will be neither rest nor tranquility in America until the Negro is granted his citizenship rights. The whirlwinds of revolt will continue to shake the foundations
of our nation until the bright day of justice emerges.

But there is something that I must say to my people who stand on the warm 6
threshold which leads into the palace of justice. In the process of gaining our
rightful place we must not be guilty of wrongful deeds. Let us not seek to satisfy
our thirst for freedom by drinking from the cup of bitterness and hatred. We must
forever conduct our struggle on the high plane of dignity and discipline. We must
not allow our creative protest to degenerate into physical violence. Again and
again we must rise to the majestic heights of meeting physical force with soul
force. The marvelous new militancy which has engulfed the Negro community
must not lead us to a distrust of all white people, for many of our white brothers,
as evidenced by their presence here today, have come to realize that their destiny

is tied up with our destiny and their freedom is inextricably bound to our freedom. We cannot walk alone.

And as we walk, we must make the pledge that we shall march ahead. We   7
cannot turn back. There are those who are asking the devotees of civil rights, "When will you be satisfied?" We can never be satisfied as long as the Negro is the victim of the unspeakable horrors of police brutality. We can never be satisfied as long as our bodies, heavy with fatigue of travel, cannot gain lodging in the motels of the highways and the hotels of the cities. We cannot be satisfied as long as the Negro's basic mobility is from a smaller ghetto to a larger one. We can never be satisfied as long as a Negro in Mississippi cannot vote and a Negro in New York believes he has nothing for which to vote. No, no, we are not satisfied, and we will not be satisfied until justice rolls down like waters and righteousness like a mighty stream.

I am not unmindful that some of you have come here out of great trials and   8
tribulations. Some of you have come fresh from narrow jail cells. Some of you have come from areas where your quest for freedom left you battered by the storms of persecution and staggered by the winds of police brutality. You have been the veterans of creative suffering. Continue to work with the faith that unearned suffering is redemptive.

Go back to Mississippi, go back to Alabama, go back to South Carolina, go   9
back to Georgia, go back to Louisiana, go back to the slums and ghettos of our northern cities, knowing that somehow this situation can and will be changed. Let us not wallow in the valley of despair.

I say to you today, my friends, that in spite of the difficulties and frustrations   10
of the moment I still have a dream. It is a dream deeply rooted in the American dream.

I have a dream that one day this nation will rise up and live out the true   11
meaning of its creed: "We hold these truths to be self-evident; that all men are created equal."

I have a dream that one day on the red hills of Georgia the sons of former   12
slaves and the sons of former slaveowners will be able to sit down together at the table of brotherhood.

I have a dream that one day even the state of Mississippi, a desert state   13
sweltering with the heat of injustice and oppression, will be transformed into an oasis of freedom and justice.

I have a dream that my four little children will one day live in a nation   14
where they will not be judged by the color of their skin but by the content of
their character.

I have a dream today.   15

I have a dream that one day the state of Alabama, whose governor's lips are   16
presently dripping with the words of interposition and nullification, will be transformed into a situation where little black boys and black girls will be able to join
hands with little white boys and white girls and walk together as sisters and
brothers.

I have a dream today.   17

I have a dream that one day every valley shall be exalted, every hill and   18
mountain shall be made low, the rough places will be made plains, and the
crooked places will be made straight, and the glory of the Lord shall be revealed,
and all flesh shall see it together.

This is our hope. This is the faith with which I return to the South. With   19
this faith we will be able to hew out of the mountain of despair a stone of hope.
With this faith we will be able to transform the jangling discords of our nation
into a beautiful symphony of brotherhood. With this faith we will be able to
work together, to pray together, to struggle together, to go to jail together, to
stand up for freedom together, knowing that we will be free one day.

This will be the day when all of God's children will be able to sing with   20
new meaning

My country, 'tis of thee,   21
Sweet land of liberty,
     Of thee I sing.
Land where my fathers died,
Land of the pilgrims' pride,
From every mountainside
Let freedom ring.

And if America is to be a great nation this must become true. So let free-   22
dom ring from the prodigious hilltops of New Hampshire. Let freedom ring from
the mighty mountains of New York. Let freedom ring from the heightening
Alleghenies of Pennsylvania!

Let freedom ring from the snowcapped Rockies of Colorado!   23
Let freedom ring from the curvacious peaks of California!   24

But not only that; let freedom ring from Stone Mountain of Georgia.   25

Let freedom ring from Lookout Mountain of Tennessee!   26

Let freedom ring from every hill and molehill of Mississippi. From every   27
mountainside, let freedom ring.

When we let freedom ring, when we let it ring from every village and every   28
hamlet, from every state and every city, we will be able to speed up that day when
all of God's children, black men and white men, Jews and Gentiles, Protestants
and Catholics, will be able to join hands and sing in the words of the old Negro
spiritual, "Free at last! free at last! thank God almighty, we are free at last!"

Questions for Discussion

1. What is King urging his listeners to do? Why must he urge them to do this?
2. What effect does the repetition of "I have a dream" have on you as you read
   or hear this speech? Read passages aloud, paying attention to the effect of
   that phrase. How does the phrase help carry the speech forward?
3. How is the inset song, and especially the repetition of the song's last line,
   used to drive the message home? What is the message?
4. Why does King repeat and emphasize the word "now" in Paragraph 4?
5. What are the audience and the purpose of this speech?
6. Why is the use of metaphors, such as "bad check" and "promissory note" in
   Paragraph 4, an effective strategy for this audience and this purpose?
7. Why does King not mention Abraham Lincoln by name in the first paragraph?

Questions for Reflection and Writing

1. Identify and list the metaphors used in this speech. Which metaphor do you
   like most or do you find most interesting?
2. Do a rhetorical analysis of this speech. What strategies does King use? For
   what purpose? Identify and label the rhetorical techniques, providing examples from the text.
3. Read about the events surrounding this speech. What were the events leading up to the speech? What was the effect on the audience?

Martin Luther King, Jr. (1929–1968) had at first planned to become a doctor or a lawyer, but when he graduated from Morehouse College in Atlanta at the age of nineteen, he abandoned these ambitions and went into the seminary. After seminary, he went to Boston University, where he received his Ph.D. in 1955. He was ordained as a Baptist minister in his father's church, the Ebenezer Baptist Church in Atlanta, a church he copastored with his father from 1960 to 1968. He was also founder and director of the Southern Christian Leadership Conference from 1957 to 1968, and a member of the Montgomery Improvement Association, an activist group protesting racial segregation. Inspired by Mahatma Gandhi's principles of nonviolent protest, King led this group in several demonstrations. In May 1963, he was arrested and imprisoned in Birmingham for demonstrating against segregation in hotels and restaurants. It was while in jail that he wrote his famous "Letter from Birmingham Jail," a work that was published in 1963 and expanded and republished in 1968. It was also in 1963 that King made the speech entitled "I Have a Dream" to over 200,000 people at the March on Washington. King received numerous awards for his work for human rights, including the Nobel Prize for Peace in 1964. On April 4, 1968, while talking with other human rights activists on a motel balcony in Memphis, King was assassinated.

Letter From Birmingham Jail

Martin Luther King, Jr.

April 16, 1963
My Dear Fellow Clergymen:

While confined here in Birmingham city jail, I came across your recent state- 1
ment calling my present activities "unwise and untimely." Seldom do I pause to
answer criticism of my work and ideas. If I sought to answer all the criticisms that
cross my desk, my secretaries would have little time for anything other than such
correspondence in the course of the day, and I would have no time for constructive work. But since I feel that you are men of genuine good will and that your
criticisms are sincerely set forth, I want to try to answer your statement in what
I hope will be patient and reasonable terms.

I think I should indicate why I am here in Birmingham, since you have 2
been influenced by the view which argues against "outsiders coming in." I have
the honor of serving as president of the Southern Christian Leadership

Conference, an organization operating in every southern state, with headquarters in Atlanta, Georgia. We have some eighty-five affiliated organizations across the South, and one of them is the Alabama Christian Movement for Human Rights. Frequently we share staff, educational and financial resources with our affiliates. Several months ago the affiliate here in Birmingham asked us to be on call to engage in a nonviolent direct-action program if such were deemed necessary. We readily consented, and when the hour came we lived up to our promise. So I, along with several members of my staff, am here because I was invited here. I am here because I have organizational ties here.

But more basically, I am in Birmingham because injustice is here. Just as   3
the prophets of the eighth century b.c. left their villages and carried their "thus saith the Lord" far beyond the boundaries of their home towns, and just as the Apostle Paul left his village of Tarsus and carried the gospel of Jesus Christ to the far corners of the Greco-Roman world, so am I compelled to carry the gospel of freedom beyond my own home town. Like Paul, I must constantly respond to the Macedonian call for aid.

Moreover, I am cognizant of the interrelatedness of all communities and   4
states. I cannot sit idly by in Atlanta and not be concerned about what happens to Birmingham. Injustice anywhere is a threat to justice everywhere. We are caught in an inescapable network of mutuality, tied in a single garment of destiny. Whatever affects one directly, affects all indirectly. Never again can we afford to live with the narrow, provincial "outside agitator" idea. Anyone who lives inside the United States can never be considered an outsider anywhere within its bounds.

You deplore the demonstrations taking place in Birmingham. But your   5
statement, I am sorry to say, fails to express a similar concern for the conditions that brought about the demonstrations. I am sure that none of you would want to rest content with the superficial kind of social analysis that deals merely with effects and does not grapple with underlying causes. It is unfortunate that demonstrations are taking place in Birmingham, but it is even more unfortunate that the city's white power structure left the Negro community with no alternative.

In any nonviolent campaign there are four steps: collection of the facts to   6
determine whether injustices exist; negotiation; self-purification; and direct action. We have gone through all these steps in Birmingham. There can be no gain saying the fact that racial injustice engulfs this community. Birmingham is probably the most thoroughly segregated city in the United States. Its ugly record

of brutality is widely known. Negroes have experienced grossly unjust treatment in the courts. There have been more unsolved bombings of Negro homes and churches in Birmingham than in any other city in the nation. These are the hard brutal facts of the case. On the basis of these conditions, Negro leaders sought to negotiate with the city fathers. But the latter consistently refused to engage in good-faith negotiation.

Then, last September, came the opportunity to talk with leaders of   7
Birmingham economic community. In the course of negotiations, certain promises were made by the merchants—for example, to remove the stores' humiliating racial signs. On the basis of these promises, the Reverend Fred Shuttlesworth and the leaders of the Alabama Christian Movement for Human Rights agreed to a moratorium on all demonstrations. As the weeks and months went by, we realized that we were the victims of a broken promise. A few signs, briefly removed, returned; the others remained.

As in so many past experiences, our hopes had been blasted, and the shad-   8
ow of deep disappointment settled upon us. We had no alternative except to prepare for direct action, whereby we would present our very bodies as a means of laying our case before the conscience of the local and the national community. Mindful of the difficulties involved, we decided to undertake a process of self-purification. We began a series of workshops on nonviolence, and we repeatedly asked ourselves: "Are you able to accept blows without retaliating?" "Are you able to endure the ordeal of jail?" We decided to schedule our direct-action program for the Easter season, realizing that except for Christmas, this is the main shopping period of the year. Knowing that a strong economic-withdrawal program would be the by-product of direct action, we felt that this would be the best time to bring pressure to bear on the merchants for the needed change.

Then it occurred to us that Birmingham's mayoralty election was coming   9
up in March, and we speedily decided to postpone action until after election day. When we discovered that the Commissioner of Public Safety, Eugene "Bull" Connor, had piled up enough votes to be in the run-off, we decided again to postpone action until the day after the run-off so that the demonstrations could not be used to cloud the issues. Like many others, we waited to see Mr. Connor defeated, and to this end we endured postponement after postponement. Having aided in this community need, we felt that our direct-action program could be delayed no longer.

You may well ask: "Why direct action? Why sit-ins, marches and so forth?   10
Isn't negotiation a better path?" You are quite right in calling for negotiation.

Indeed, this is the very purpose of direct action. Nonviolent direct action seeks to create such a crisis and foster such a tension that a community which has constantly refused to negotiate is forced to confront the issue. It seeks so to dramatize the issue that it can no longer be ignored. My citing the creation of tension as part of the work of the nonviolent-resister may sound rather shocking. But I must confess that I am not afraid of the word "tension." I have earnestly opposed violent tension, but there is a type of constructive nonviolent tension which is necessary for growth. Just as Socrates felt that it was necessary to create a tension in the mind so that individuals could rise from the bondage of myths and half-truths to the unfettered realm of creative analysis and objective appraisal, so must we see the need for nonviolent gadflies to create the kind of tension in society that will help men rise from the dark depths of prejudice and racism to the majestic heights of understanding and brotherhood.

11   The purpose of our direct-action program is to create a situation so crisis-packed that it will inevitably open the door to negotiation. I therefore concur with you in your call for negotiation. Too long has our beloved Southland been bogged down in a tragic effort to live in monologue rather than dialogue.

12   One of the basic points in your statement is that the action that I and my associates have taken in Birmingham is untimely. Some have asked: "Why didn't you give the new city administration time to act?" The only answer that I can give to this query is that the new Birmingham administration must be prodded about as much as the outgoing one, before it will act. We are sadly mistaken if we feel that the election of Albert Boutwell as mayor will bring the millennium to Birmingham. While Mr. Boutwell is a much more gentle person than Mr. Connor, they are both segregationists, dedicated to maintenance of the status quo. I have hope that Mr. Boutwell will be reasonable enough to see the futility of massive resistance to desegregation. But he will not see this without pressure from devotees of civil rights. My friends, I must say to you that we have not made a single gain in civil rights without determined legal and nonviolent pressure. Lamentably, it is an historical fact that privileged groups seldom give up their privileges voluntarily. Individuals may see the moral light and voluntarily give up their unjust posture; but, as Reinhold Niebuhr has reminded us, groups tend to be more immoral than individuals.

13   We know through painful experience that freedom is never voluntarily given by the oppressor; it must be demanded by the oppressed. Frankly, I have yet to engage in a direct-action campaign that was "well timed" in the view of those who have not suffered unduly from the disease of segregation. For years

now I have heard the word "Wait!" It rings in the ear of every Negro with piercing familiarity. This "Wait" has almost always meant "Never." We must come to see, with one of our distinguished jurists, that "justice too long delayed is justice denied."

We have waited for more than 340 years for our constitutional and God   14 given rights. The nations of Asia and Africa are moving with jetlike speed toward gaining political independence, but we still creep at horse-and-buggy pace toward gaining a cup of coffee at a lunch counter. Perhaps it is easy for those who have never felt the stinging darts of segregation to say, "Wait." But when you have seen vicious mobs lynch your mothers and fathers at will and drown your sisters and brothers at whim; when you have seen hate-filled policemen curse, kick and even kill your black brothers and sisters; when you see the vast majority of your 20 million Negro brothers smothering in an airtight cage of poverty in the midst of an affluent society; when you suddenly find your tongue twisted and your speech stammering as you seek to explain to your 6-year-old daughter why she can't go to the public amusement park that has just been advertised on television, and see tears welling up in her eyes when she is told that Funtown is closed to colored children, and see ominous clouds of inferiority beginning to form in her little mental sky, and see her beginning to distort her personality by developing an unconscious bitterness toward white people; when you have to concoct an answer for a 5-year-old son who is asking: "Daddy, why do white people treat colored people so mean?"; when you take a cross-country drive and find it necessary to sleep night after night in the uncomfortable corners of your automobile because no motel will accept you; when you are humiliated day in and day out by nagging signs reading "white" and "colored"; when your first name becomes "nigger," your middle name becomes "boy" (however old you are) and your last name becomes "John," and your wife and mother are never given the respected title "Mrs."; when you are harried by day and haunted by night by the fact that you are a Negro, living constantly at tiptoe stance, never quite knowing what to expect next, and are plagued with inner fears and outer resentments; when you are forever fighting a degenerating sense of "nobodiness"—then you will understand why we find it difficult to wait. There comes a time when the cup of endurance runs over, and men are no longer willing to be plunged into the abyss of despair. I hope, sirs, you can understand our legitimate and unavoidable impatience.

You express a great deal of anxiety over our willingness to break laws. This   15 is certainly a legitimate concern. Since we so diligently urge people to obey the

Supreme Court's decision of 1954 outlawing segregation in the public schools, at first glance it may seem rather paradoxical for us consciously to break laws. One may well ask: "How can you advocate breaking some laws and obeying others?" The answer lies in the fact that there are two types of laws: just and unjust. I would be the first to advocate obeying just laws. One has not only a legal but a moral responsibility to obey just laws. Conversely, one has a moral responsibility to disobey unjust laws. I would agree with St. Augustine that "an unjust law is no law at all."

Now, what is the difference between the two? How does one determine   16 whether a law is just or unjust? A just law is a man-made code that squares with the moral law or the law of God. An unjust law is a code that is out of harmony with the moral law. To put it in the terms of St. Thomas Aquinas: An unjust law is a human law that is not rooted in eternal law and natural law. Any law that uplifts human personality is just. Any law that degrades human personality is unjust. All segregation statutes are unjust because segregation distorts the soul and damages the personality. It gives the segregator a false sense of superiority and the segregated a false sense of inferiority. Segregation, to use the terminology of the Jewish philosopher Martin Buber, substitutes an "I-it" relationship for an "I-thou" relationship and ends up relegating persons to the status of things. Hence segregation is not only politically, economically and sociologically unsound, it is morally wrong and sinful. Paul Tillich has said that sin is separation. Is not segregation an existential expression of man's tragic separation, his awful estrangement, his terrible sinfulness? Thus it is that I can urge men to obey the 1954 decision of the Supreme Court, for it is morally right; and I can urge them to disobey segregation ordinances, for they are morally wrong.

Let us consider a more concrete example of just and unjust laws. An unjust   17 law is a code that a numerical or power majority group compels a minority group to obey but does not make binding on itself. This is *difference* made legal. By the same token, a just law is a code that a majority compels a minority to follow and that it is willing to follow itself. This is *sameness* made legal.

Let me give another explanation. A law is unjust if it is inflicted on a   18 minority that, as a result of being denied the right to vote, had no part in enacting or devising the law. Who can say that the legislature of Alabama which set up that state's segregation laws was democratically elected? Throughout Alabama all sorts of devious methods are used to prevent Negroes from becoming registered voters, and there are some counties in which even though Negroes constitute a majority of the population, not a single Negro is registered. Can any law enacted under such circumstances be considered democratically structured?

Sometimes a law is just on its face and unjust in its application. For instance, I have been arrested on a charge of parading without a permit. Now, there is nothing wrong in having an ordinance which requires a permit for a parade. But such an ordinance becomes unjust when it is used to maintain segregation and to deny citizens the First-Amendment privilege of peaceful assembly and protest.   19

I hope you are able to see the distinction I am trying to point out. In no sense do I advocate evading or defying the law, as would the rabid segregationist. That would lead to anarchy. One who breaks an unjust law must do so openly, lovingly, and with a willingness to accept the penalty. I submit that an individual who breaks a law that conscience tells him is unjust, and who willingly accepts the penalty of imprisonment in order to arouse the conscience of the community over its injustice, is in reality expressing the highest respect for law.   20

Of course, there is nothing new about this kind of civil disobedience. It was evidenced sublimely in the refusal of Shadrach, Meshach and Abednego to obey the laws of Nebuchadnezzar, on the ground that a higher moral law was at stake. It was practiced superbly by the early Christians, who were willing to face hungry lions and the excruciating pain of chopping blocks rather than submit to certain unjust laws of the Roman Empire. To a degree, academic freedom is a reality today because Socrates practiced civil disobedience. In our own nation, the Boston Tea Party represented a massive act of civil disobedience.   21

We should never forget that everything Adolf Hitler did in Germany was "legal" and everything the Hungarian freedom fighters did in Hungary was "illegal." It was "illegal" to aid and comfort a Jew in Hitler's Germany. Even so, I am sure that, had I lived in Germany at the time, I would have aided and comforted my Jewish brothers. If today I lived in a Communist country where certain principles dear to the Christian faith are suppressed, I would openly advocate disobeying that country's anti-religious laws.   22

I must make two honest confessions to you, my Christian and Jewish brothers. First, I must confess that over the past few years I have been gravely disappointed with the white moderate. I have almost reached the regrettable conclusion that the Negro's great stumbling block in his stride toward freedom is not the White Citizen's Counciler or the Ku Klux Klanner, but the white moderate, who is more devoted to "order" than to justice; who prefers a negative peace which is the absence of tension to a positive peace which is the presence of jus-   23 tice; who constantly says: "I agree with you in the goal you seek, but I cannot agree with your methods of direct action"; who paternalistically believes he can set the timetable for another man's freedom; who lives by a mythical concept of time and who constantly advises the Negro to wait for a "more convenient season." Shallow understanding from people of good will is more frustrating than absolute misunderstanding from people of ill will. Lukewarm acceptance is much more bewildering than outright rejection.

I had hoped that the white moderate would understand that law and order   24 exist for the purpose of establishing justice and that when they fail in this purpose they become the dangerously structured dams that block the flow of social progress. I had hoped that the white moderate would understand that the present tension in the South is a necessary phase of the transition from an obnoxious negative peace, in which the Negro passively accepted his unjust plight, to a substantive and positive peace, in which all men will respect the dignity and worth of human personality. Actually, we who engage in nonviolent direct action are not the creators of tension. We merely bring to the surface the hidden tension that is already alive. We bring it out in the open, where it can be seen and dealt with. Like a boil that can never be cured so long as it is covered up but must be opened with all its ugliness to the natural medicines of air and light, injustice must be exposed, with all the tension its exposure creates, to the light of human conscience and the air of national opinion before it can be cured.

In your statement you assert that our actions, even though peaceful, must   25 be condemned because they precipitate violence. But is this a logical assertion? Isn't this like condemning a robbed man because his possession of money precipitated the evil act of robbery? Isn't this like condemning Jesus because his uniqueGod-consciousness and never-ceasing devotion toGod'swill precipitated the evil act of crucifixion? We must come to see that, as the federal courts have consistently affirmed, it is wrong to urge an individual to cease his efforts to gain his basic constitutional rights because the quest may precipitate violence. Society must protect the robbed and punish the robber.

I had also hoped that the white moderate would reject the myth concern-   26 ing time in relation to the struggle for freedom. I have just received a letter from a white brother in Texas. He writes: "All Christians know that the colored people will receive equal rights eventually, but it is possible that you are in too great a religious hurry. It has taken Christianity almost two thousand years to accomplish what it has. The teachings of Christ take time to come to earth." Such an attitude stems from a tragic misconception of time, from the strangely irrational notion that there is something in the very flow of time that will inevitably cure all ills. Actually, time itself is neutral; it can be used either destructively or constructively. More and more I feel that the people of ill will have used time much more effectively than have the people of good will. We will have to repent in this generation not merely for the hateful words and actions of the bad people but for the appalling silence of the good people. Human progress never rolls in on wheels of inevitability; it comes through the tireless efforts of men willing to be co-workers with God, and without this hard work, time itself becomes an ally of the forces of social stagnation. We must use time creatively, in the knowledge that the time is always ripe to do right. Now is the time to make real the promise of democracy and transform our pending national elegy into a creative psalm of brotherhood. Now is the time to lift our national policy from the quicksand of racial injustice to the solid rock of human dignity.

You speak of our activity in Birmingham as extreme. At first I was rather   27
disappointed that fellow clergymen would see my nonviolent efforts as those of an extremist. I began thinking about the fact that I stand in the middle of two opposing forces in the Negro community. One is a force of complacency, made up in part of Negroes who, as a result of long years of oppression, are so drained of selfrespect and a sense of "somebodiness" that they have adjusted to segregation; and in part of a few middle-class Negroes who, because of a degree of academic and economic security and because in some ways they profit by segregation, have become insensitive to the problems of the masses. The other force is one of bitterness and hatred, and it comes perilously close to advocating violence. It is expressed in the various black nationalist groups that are springing up across the nation, the largest and best-known being Elijah Muhammad's Muslim movement. Nourished by the Negro's frustration over the continued existence of racial discrimination, this movement is made up of people who have lost faith in America, who have absolutely repudiated Christianity, and who have concluded that the white man is an incorrigible "devil."

I have tried to stand between these two forces, saying that we need emu-   28
late neither the "do-nothingism" of the complacement nor the hatred and despair of the black nationalist. For there is the more excellent way of love and nonviolent protest. I am grateful to God that, through the influence of the Negro church, the way of nonviolence became an integral part of our struggle.

If this philosophy had not emerged, by now many streets of the South   29
would, I am convinced, be flowing with blood. And I am further convinced that if our white brothers dismiss as "rabble-rousers" and "outside agitators" those of

us who employ nonviolent direct action, and if they refuse to support our non-violent efforts, millions of Negroes will, out of frustration and despair, seek solace and security in blacknationalist ideologies—a development that would inevitably lead to a frightening racial nightmare.

Oppressed people cannot remain oppressed forever. The yearning for free- 30 dom eventually manifests itself, and that is what has happened to the American Negro. Something within has reminded him that it can be gained. Consciously or unconsciously, he has been caught up by the *Zeitgeist*, and with his black brothers of Africa and his brown and yellow brothers of Asia, South America and the Caribbean, the United States Negro is moving with a sense of great urgency toward the promised land of racial justice. If one recognizes this vital urge that has engulfed the Negro community, one should readily understand why public demonstrations are taking place. The Negro has many pent-up resentments and latent frustrations, and he must release them. So let him march; let him make prayer pilgrimages to the city hall; let him go on freedom rides—and try to understand why he must do so. If his repressed emotions are not released in nonviolent ways, they will seek expression through violence; this is not a threat but a fact of history. So I have not said to my people: "Get rid of your discontent." Rather, I have tried to say that this normal and healthy discontent can be channeled into the creative outlet of nonviolent direct action. And now this approach is being termed extremist.

But though I was initially disappointed at being categorized as an extrem- 31 ist, as I continued to think about the matter I gradually gained a measure of satisfaction from the label. Was not Jesus an extremist for love: "Love your enemies, bless them that curse you, do good to them that hate you, and pray for them which despitefully use you, and persecute you." Was not Amos an extremist for justice: "Let justice roll down like waters and righteousness like an ever-flowing stream." Was not Paul an extremist for the Christian gospel: "I bear in my body the marks of the Lord Jesus." Was not Martin Luther an extremist: "Here I stand; I cannot do otherwise, so help me God." And John Bunyan: "I will stay in jail to the end of my days before I make a butchery of my conscience." And Abraham Lincoln: "This nation cannot survive half slave and half free." And Thomas Jefferson: "We hold these truths to be selfevident, that all men are created equal. . . . " So the question is not whether we will be extremists, but what kind of extremists we will be. Will we be extremists for hate or for love? Will we be extremists for the preservation of injustice or for the extension of justice? In that dramatic scene on Calvary's hill three men were crucified. We must never forget that all three were crucified for the same crime—the crime of extremism. Two were extremists for immorality, and thus fell below their environment. The other, Jesus Christ, was an extremist for love, truth and goodness, and thereby rose above his environment. Perhaps the South, the nation and the world are in dire need of creative extremists.

I had hoped that the white moderate would see this need. Perhaps I was   32 too optimistic; perhaps I expected too much. I suppose I should have realized that few members of the oppressor race can understand the deep groans and passionate yearnings of the oppressed race, and still fewer have the vision to see that injustice must be rooted out by strong, persistent and determined action. I am thankful, however, that some of our white brothers in the South have grasped the meaning of this social revolution and committed themselves to it. They are still all too few in quantity, but they are big in quality. Some—such as Ralph McGill, Lillian Smith, Harry Golden, James McBride Dabbs, Ann Braden and Sarah Patton Boyle—have written about our struggle in eloquent and prophetic terms. Others have marched with us down nameless streets of the South. They have languished in filthy, roachinfested jails, suffering the abuse and brutality of policemen who view them as "dirty nigger-lovers." Unlike so many of their moderate brothers and sisters, they have recognized the urgency of the moment and sensed the need for powerful "action" antidotes to combat the disease of segregation.

Let me take note of my other major disappointment. I have been so great-   33 ly disappointed with the white church and its leadership. Of course, there are some notable exceptions. I am not unmindful of the fact that each of you has taken some significant stands on this issue. I commend you, Reverend Stallings, for your Christian stand on this past Sunday, in welcoming Negroes to your worship service on a nonsegregated basis. I commend the Catholic leaders of this state for integrating Spring Hill College several years ago.

But despite these notable exceptions, I must honestly reiterate that I have   34 been disappointed with the church. I do not say this as one of those negative critics who can always find something wrong with the church. I say this as a minister of the gospel, who loves the church; who was nurtured in its bosom; who has been sustained by its spiritual blessings and who will remain true to it as long as the cord of life shall slengthen.

When I was suddenly catapulted into the leadership of the bus protest in   35 Montgomery, Ala., a few years ago, I felt we would be supported by the white church. I felt that the white ministers, priests and rabbis of the South would be among our strongest allies. Instead, some have been outright opponents, refusing to understand the freedom movement and misrepresenting its leaders; all too many others have been more cautious than courageous and have remained silent behind the anesthetizing security of stained-glass windows.

In spite of my shattered dreams, I came to Birmingham with the hope that   36
the white religious leadership of this community would see the justice of our cause and, with deep moral concern, would serve as the channel through which our just grievances could reach the power structure. I had hoped that each of you would understand. But again I have been disappointed.

I have heard numerous southern religious leaders admonish their wor-   37
shipers to comply with a desegregation decision because it is the law, but I have longed to hear white ministers declare: "Follow this decree because integration is morally right and because the Negro is your brother." In the midst of blatant injustices inflicted upon the Negro, I have watched white churchmen stand on the sideline and mouth pious irrelevancies and sanctimonious trivialities. In the midst of a mighty struggle to rid our nation of racial and economic injustice, I have heard many ministers say: "Those are social issues, with which the gospel has no real concern." And I have watched many churches commit themselves to a completely other-worldly religion which makes a strange, un-Biblical distinction between body and soul, between the sacred and the secular.

I have traveled the length and breadth of Alabama, Mississippi and all the   38
other southern states. On sweltering summer days and crisp autumn mornings I have looked at the South's beautiful churches with their lofty spires pointing heavenward. I have beheld the impressive outlines of her massive religious-education buildings. Over and over I have found myself asking: "What kind of people worship here? Who is their God? Where were their voices when the lips of Governor Barnett dripped with words of interposition and nullification? Where were they when Governor Wallace gave a clarion call for defiance and hatred? Where were their voices of support when bruised and weary Negro men and women decided to rise from the dark dungeons of complacency to the bright hills of creative protest?"

Yes, these questions are still in my mind. In deep disappointment I have   39
wept over the laxity of the church. But be assured that my tears have been tears of love. There can be no deep disappointment where there is not deep love. Yes, I love the church. How could I do otherwise? I am in the rather unique position of being the son, the grandson and the great-grandson of preachers. Yes, I see the

church as the body of Christ. But, oh! How we have blemished and scarred that body through social neglect and through fear of being nonconformists.

There was a time when the church was very powerful—in the time when 40 the early Christians rejoiced at being deemed worthy to suffer for what they believed. In those days the church was not merely a thermometer that recorded the ideas and principles of popular opinion; it was a thermostat that transformed the mores of society. Whenever the early Christians entered a town, the people in power became disturbed and immediately sought to convict the Christians for being "disturbers of the peace" and "outside agitators." But the Christians pressed on, in the conviction that they were "a colony of heaven," called to obey God rather than man. Small in number, they were big in commitment. They were too God-intoxicated to be "astronomically intimidated." By their effort and example they brought an end to such ancient evils as infanticide and gladiatorial contests.

Things are different now. So often the contemporary church is a weak, 41 ineffectual voice with an uncertain sound. So often it is an archdefender of the status quo. Far from being disturbed by the presence of the church, the power structure of the average community is consoled by the church's silent—and often even vocal—sanction of things as they are.

But the judgment of God is upon the church as never before. If today's 42 church does not recapture the sacrificial spirit of the early church, it will lose its authenticity, forfeit the loyalty of millions, and be dismissed as an irrelevant social club with no meaning for the twentieth century. Every day I meet young people whose disappointment with the church has turned into outright disgust.

Perhaps I have once again been too optimistic. Is organized religion too 43 inextricably bound to the status quo to save our nation and the world? Perhaps I must turn my faith to the inner spiritual church, the church within the church, as the true *ekklesia* and the hope of the world. But again I am thankful to God that some noble souls from the ranks of organized religion have broken loose from the paralyzing chains of conformity and joined us as active partners in the struggle for freedom. They have left their secure congregations and walked the streets of Albany, Ga, with us. They have gone down the highways of the South on tortuous rides for freedom. Yes, they have gone to jail with us. Some have been dismissed from their churches, have lost the support of their bishops and fellow ministers. But they have acted in the faith that right defeated is stronger than evil triumphant. Their witness has been the spiritual salt that has preserved the true meaning of the gospel in these troubled times. They have carved a tunnel of hope through the dark mountain of disappointment.

I hope the church as a whole will meet the challenge of this decisive hour.   44
But even if the church does not come to the aid of justice, I have no despair
about the future. I have no fear about the outcome of our struggle in
Birmingham, even if our motives are at present misunderstood. We will reach
the goal of freedom in Birmingham and all over the nation, because the goal of
America is freedom. Abused and scorned though we may be, our destiny is tied
up with America's destiny. Before the pilgrims landed at Plymouth, we were here.
Before the pen of Jefferson etched the majestic words of the Declaration of
Independence across the pages of history, we were here. For more than two centuries our forebears labored in this country without wages; they made cotton
king; they built the homes of their masters while suffering gross injustice and
shameful humiliation—and yet out of a bottomless vitality they continued to
thrive and develop. If the inexpressible cruelties of slavery could not stop us, the
opposition we now face will surely fail. We will win our freedom because the
sacred heritage of our nation and the eternal will of God are embodied in our
echoing demands.

Before closing I feel impelled to mention one other point in your statement   45
that has troubled me profoundly. You warmly commended the Birmingham
police force for keeping "order" and "preventing violence." I doubt that you
would have so warmly commended the police force if you had seen its dogs sink-
ing their teeth into unarmed, nonviolent Negroes. I doubt that you would so
quickly commend the policemen if you were to observe their ugly and inhumane
treatment of Negroes here in the city jail; if you were to watch them push and
curse old Negro women and young Negro girls; if you were to see them slap and
kick old Negro men and young boys; if you were to observe them as they did on
two occasions, refuse to give us food because we wanted to sing our grace together. I cannot join you in your praise of the Birmingham police department.

It is true that the police have exercised a degree of discipline in handling   46
the demonstrators. In this sense they have conducted themselves rather "nonviolently" in public. But for what purpose? To preserve the evil system of segregation. Over the past few years I have consistently preached that nonviolence
demands that the means we use must be as pure as the ends we seek. I have tried
to make clear that it is wrong to use immoral means to attain moral ends. But
now I must affirm that it is just as wrong, or perhaps even more so, to use moral
means to preserve immoral ends. Perhaps Mr. Connor and his policemen have
been rather nonviolent in public, as was Chief Pritchett in Albany, Ga., but they
have used the moral means of nonviolence to maintain the immoral end of racial

injustice. As T. S. Eliot has said: "The last temptation is the greatest treason: To do the right deed for the wrong reason."

I wish you had commended the Negro sit-inners and demonstrators of 47 Birmingham for their sublime courage, their willingness to suffer and their amazing discipline in the midst of great provocation. One day the South will recognize its real heroes. They will be the James Merediths, with the noble sense of purpose that enables them to face jeering and hostile mobs, and with the agonizing loneliness that characterizes the life of the pioneer. They will be old, oppressed, battered Negro women, symbolized in a 72-year-old woman in Montgomery, Ala., who rose up with a sense of dignity and with her people decided not to ride segregated buses, and who responded with ungrammatical profundity to one who inquired about her weariness: "My feet is tired, but my soul is at rest." They will be the young high school and college students, the young ministers of the gospel and a host of their elders, courageously and nonviolently sitting in at lunch counters and willingly going to jail for conscience's sake. One day the South will know that when these disinherited children of God sat down at lunch counters, they were in reality standing up for what is best in the American dream and for the most sacred values in our Judaeo-Christian heritage, thereby bringing our nation back to those great wells of democracy which were dug deep by the founding fathers in their formulation of the Constitution and the Declaration of Independence.

Never before have I written so long a letter. I'm afraid it is much too long 48 to take your precious time. I can assure you that it would have been much shorter if I had been writing from a comfortable desk, but what else can one do when he is alone in a narrow jail cell, other than write long letters, think long thoughts and pray long prayers?

If I have said anything in this letter that overstates the truth and indicates 49 an unreasonable impatience, I beg you to forgive me. If I have said anything that understates the truth and indicates my having a patience that allows me to settle for anything less than brotherhood, I beg God to forgive me.

I hope this letter finds you strong in the faith. I also hope that circum- 50 stances will soon make it possible for me to meet each of you, not as an integrationist or a civil rights leader but as a fellow clergyman and a Christian brother. Let us all hope that the dark clouds of racial prejudice will soon pass away and the deep fog of misunderstanding will be lifted from our fear drenched communities, and in some not too distant tomorrow the radiant stars of love and brotherhood will shine over our great nation with all their scintillating beauty.

Questions for Discussion

1. Why does King feel compelled to write to his "Fellow Clergymen"?
2. What is King's criticism of his audience? What have they failed to do?
3. What does King hope his readers will do? Do you think they will do it? Why or why not?
4. What is the difference between a just and an unjust law? How does King make the distinction? What examples does he use to illustrate the distinction?
5. What emotional images does King evoke to sway his readers?
6. Where does King anticipate his readers' reactions and supply arguments to counter those reactions? How effective is he at this strategy? When have you tried this strategy, and how well did it work?
7. Where does King use the Bible to support his political activities? How are political and religious goals similar?

Questions for Reflection and Writing

1. Do you think that King's plan to use nonviolent resistance such as sit-ins and marches was the right one? In general, do you think that nonviolent resistance is the best course to take?
2. Write an essay about a recent protest or conflict that used—or should have used—nonviolent resistance. How was nonviolent resistance used, or how could it have been used?
3. Research the Civil Rights era and King's role in it. Choose just one event on which to focus, such as a particular civil action, speech, or legal case. Report on what you find.

Mary Wollstonecraft (1759–1797), feminist social reformer and novelist, was the second of seven children born in London to a hard-drinking weaver and farmer who abused his wife. Although she received little formal education, Mary Wollstonecraft studied casually throughout her life and defied social convention by seeking her own living as a single woman. She served as superintendent of a girls' school and then as a governess before embarking upon a career as a writer.

Wollstonecraft became associated with Joseph Johnson and the Radical Dissenters, a Protestant group that was dedicated to reason and supportive of female authorship. Johnson hired her as a reviewer for the *Analytical Review* and began publishing her educational stories and her first novel. Wollstonecraft wrote her first controversial piece in response to Edmund Burke's opposition to the French Revolution. Her "A Vindication of the Rights of Men" (1790) began a maelstrom of rebuttals to Burke's arguments. She followed it in 1792 with the discussion of gender inequality on which her reputation now rests, "A Vindication of the Rights of Woman" (1792). Wollstonecraft contended that deprecating views of women such as those held by Jean-Jacques Rousseau reflect how men wish to perceive women and not how women really are; she called upon women to reconsider their roles and to assert their rights. However, Wollstonecraft expressed skepticism about whether women could actually transcend societal expectations.

She wrote several other books in her short lifetime, including sentimental novels whose main characters became vehicles for her agenda of gender equality. Although her writing style has never been considered sophisticated, Wollstonecraft is today appreciated for her willingness to flout societal conventions and for her role in initiating the feminist movement. Her private life revealed less certainty than her writing, however. She embarked upon a series of affairs and had a child outside marriage. Later she did marry her old friend William Godwin while pregnant with his child. She died in childbirth on September 10, 1797, after giving birth to a daughter, Mary, who became Mary Wollstonecraft Shelley, author of *Frankenstein*.

A Vindication of the Rights of Woman

Mary Wollstonecraft

My own sex, I hope, will excuse me, if I treat them like rational creatures, instead   1
of flattering their *fascinating* graces, and viewing them as if they were in a state of perpetual childhood, unable to stand alone. I earnestly wish to point out in what true dignity and human happiness consists—I wish to persuade women to endeavor to acquire strength, both of mind and body, and to convince them that the soft phrases, susceptibility of heart, delicacy of sentiment, and refinement of

taste, are almost synonymous with epithets of weakness, and that those beings who are only the objects of pity and that kind of love, which has been termed its sister, will soon become objects of contempt.

Dismissing, then, those pretty feminine phrases, which the men condescendingly use to soften our slavish dependence, and despising that weak elegancy of mind, exquisite sensibility, and sweet docility of manners, supposed to be the sexual characteristics of the weaker vessel, I wish to show that elegance is inferior to virtue, that the first object of laudable ambition is to obtain a character as a human being, regardless of the distinction of sex; and that secondary views should be brought to this simple touchstone. 2

This is a rough sketch of my plan; and should I express my conviction with the energetic emotions that I feel whenever I think of the subject, the dictates of experience and reflection will be felt by some of my readers. Animated by this important object, I shall disdain to cull my phrases or polish my style; I aim at being useful, and sincerity will render me unaffected; for, wishing rather to persuade by the force of my arguments, than dazzle by the elegance of my language, I shall not waste my time in rounding periods, or in fabricating the turgid bombast of artificial feelings, which, coming from the head, never reach the heart. I shall be employed about things, not words! and, anxious to render my sex more respectable members of society, I shall try to avoid that flowery diction which has slided from essays into novels, and from novels into familiar letters and conversation. 3

These pretty superlatives, dropping glibly from the tongue, vitiate the taste, and create a kind of sickly delicacy that runs away from simple unadorned truth; and a deluge of false sentiments and overstretched feelings, stifling the natural emotions of the heart, render the domestic pleasures insipid, that ought to sweeten the exercise of those severe duties, which educate a rational and immortal being for a nobler field of action. 4

The education of women has, of late, been more attended to than formerly; yet they are still reckoned a frivolous sex, and ridiculed or pitied by the writers who endeavor by satire or instruction to improve them. It is acknowledged that they spend many of the first years of their lives in acquiring a smattering of accomplishments; meanwhile strength of body and mind are sacrificed to libertine notions of beauty, to the desire of establishing themselves—the only way women can rise in the world—by marriage. And this desire making mere animals of them, when they marry they act as such children may be expected to act— they dress; they paint, and nickname God's creatures. Surely these weak beings 5 are only fit for a seraglio!—Can they be expected to govern a family with judgment, or take care of the poor babes whom they bring into the world?

If then it can be fairly deduced from the present conduct of the sex, from the prevalent fondness for pleasure which takes place of ambition, and those nobler passions that open and enlarge the soul; that the instruction which women have hitherto received has only tended, with the constitution of civil society, to render them insignificant objects of desire—mere propagators of fools!—if it can be proved that in aiming to accomplish them, without cultivating their understandings, they are taken out of their sphere of duties, and made ridiculous and useless when the shortlived bloom of beauty is over,[1] I presume that *rational* men will excuse me for endeavoring to persuade them to become more masculine and respectable.

6

Indeed the word masculine is only a bugbear: there is little reason to fear that women will acquire too much courage or fortitude; for their apparent inferiority with respect to bodily strength, must render them, in some degree, dependent on men in the various relations of life; but why should it be increased by prejudices that give a sex to virtue, and confound simple truths with sensual reveries?

7

Women are, in fact, so much degraded by mistaken notions of female excellence, that I do not mean to add a paradox when I assert, that this artificial weakness produces a propensity to tyrannize, and gives birth to cunning, the natural opponent of strength, which leads them to play off those contemptible infantine airs that undermine esteem even whilst they excite desire. Let men become more chaste and modest, and if women do not grow wiser in the same ratio, it will be clear that they have weaker understandings. It seems scarcely necessary to say, that I now speak of the sex in general. Many individuals have more sense than their male relatives; and, as nothing preponderates where there is a constant struggle for an equilibrium, without it has naturally more gravity, some women govern their husbands without degrading themselves, because intellect will always govern.

8

Notes

1. A lively writer, I cannot recollect his name, asks what business women turned of forty have to do in the world?

Questions for Discussion

1.   How were women viewed by men in Wollstonecraft's time? To what extent have these views changed (or not changed)?

2.   In what ways should women become strong? How should they change? What are the weaknesses they should free themselves of?

3.   What blame for women's status does Wollstonecraft lay on society (laws, traditions), what on her male contemporaries, and what on women themselves?

4.   How are women "degraded" (Paragraph 8) by being considered excellent?

5.   What does "intellect will always govern" (Paragraph 8) mean?

6.   What feminine traits does Wollstonecraft condemn? With what does she contrast these traits?

7.   How would you describe Wollstonecraft's tone? One adjective could be "passionate"—what other adjectives would describe her tone in various places?

Questions for Reflection and Writing

1.   Write an essay defining masculinity or femininity, or both.

2.   What are the rights of women, as delineated by Wollstonecraft? Summarize her essay by listing the rights of women. Comment.

3.   When was this piece written? Who was Mary Wollstonecraft? How did her theories fit into and reflect her times? Find out and report to the class.

Sojourner Truth (1797–1883) was born a slave in Hurley, New York, under the name Isabella Baumfree. She became a free woman in 1827 when New York State abolished slavery, and changed her name to Sojourner Truth in 1843 to express her religious convictions. Although unable to read or write, Truth made a name for herself as an electrifying speaker. She toured the nation with black leaders like Frederick Douglass, speaking out for equality, both racial and sexual. Truth met with Abraham Lincoln in 1864, advising him about the problems the newly freed slaves faced. She gave her "Ain't I a Woman" speech in 1851 at the Women's Rights Convention in Akron, Ohio. This speech was faithfully recorded in the June 21, 1851, issue of the *Anti-Slavery Bugle*, edited by Marcus Robinson (with whom Truth worked). In 1863, Truth's speech was rewritten by Frances Dana Gage, the organizer of the 1851 Akron convention, and published in the April 23, 1863, issue of the New York *Independent*. Though well-meaning, Gage's version perpetuated inaccuracies about Truth and her speech, most notably in characterizing the northern-born Truth as speaking in Southern dialect. Robinson's text and Gage's version are both reproduced below.

Ain't I a Woman?

Sojourner Truth

MARCUS ROBINSON, FROM THE ANTI-SLAVERY BUGLE, JUNE 21, 1851

One of the most unique and interesting speeches of the convention was made by   1
Sojourner Truth, an emancipated slave. It is impossible to transfer it to paper, or convey any adequate idea of the effect it produced upon the audience. Those only can appreciate it who saw her powerful form, her whole-souled, earnest gesture, and listened to her strong and truthful tones. She came forward to the platform and addressing the President said with great simplicity: "May I say a few words?" Receiving an affirmative answer, she proceeded:

> I want to say a few words about this matter. I am a woman's rights. I have as much muscle as any man, and can do as much work as any man. I have plowed and reaped and husked and chopped and mowed, and can any man do more than that? I have heard much about the sexes being equal. I can carry as much as any man, and can eat as much too, if I can get it. I am as strong as any man that is now. As for intellect, all I can say is, if a woman have a pint, and a man a quart—why can't she have her little pint full? You need not be afraid to give us our rights for fear we will take too much—for we can't take more than our pint'll hold. The poor men seems to be all in confusion, and don't know what to do. Why children, if you have woman's rights, give it to her and you will feel better. You will have your own rights, and they

won't be so much trouble. I can't read, but I can hear. I have heard the bible and have learned that Eve caused man to sin. Well, if woman upset the world, do give her a chance to set it right side up again. The Lady has spoken about Jesus, how he never spurned woman from him, and she was right. When Lazarus died, Mary and Martha came to him with faith and love and besought him to raise their brother. And Jesus wept and Lazarus came forth. And how came Jesus into the world? Through God who created him and the woman who bore him. Man, where was your part? But the women are coming up blessed be God and a few of the men are coming up with them. But man is in a tight place, the poor slave is on him, woman is coming on him, he is surely between a hawk and a buzzard.

FRANCES DANA GAGE, FROM THE NEW YORK INDEPENDENT, APRIL 23, 1863

The leaders of the movement trembled upon seeing a tall, gaunt black woman   2
in a gray dress and white turban, surmounted with an uncouth sunbonnet, march deliberately into the church, walk with the air of a queen up the aisle, and take her seat upon the pulpit steps. A buzz of disapprobation was heard all over the house, and there fell on the listening ear, "An abolition affair!" "Woman's rights and niggers!" "I told you so!" "Go it, darkey!"

I chanced on that occasion to wear my first laurels in public life as presi-   3
dent of the meeting. At my request order was restored and the business of the Convention went on. Morning, afternoon, and evening exercises came and went. . . . Again and again, timorous and trembling ones came to me and said, with earnestness, "Don't let her speak, Mrs. Gage, it will ruin us. Every newspaper in the land will have our cause mixed up with abolition and niggers and we shall be utterly denounced." My only answer was, "We shall see when the time comes."

The second day the work waxed warm. Methodist, Baptist, Episcopal,   4
Presbyterian, and Universalist ministers came in to hear and discuss the resolutions presented. One claimed superior rights and privileges for man, on the grounds of "superior intellect"; another, because of the "manhood of Christ; if God had desired the equality of woman, He would have given some token of His will through the birth, life and death of the Saviour." Another gave us a theological view of the "sin of the first mother."

There were very few women in those days who dared to "speak in meeting"   5
and the august teachers of the people were seemingly getting the best of us, while the boys in the galleries, and the sneerers among the pews, were hugely enjoying the discomfiture, as they supposed of the "strong-minded." . . . When, slowly from her seat in the corner rose Sojourner Truth, who till now had scarcely lift-

ed her head. "Don't let her speak!" gasped half a dozen in my ear. She moved slowly and solemnly to the front, laid her old bonnet at her feet, and turned her great speaking eyes to me. There was a hissing sound of disapprobation above and below. I rose and announced "Sojourner Truth," and begged the audience to keep silence for a few moments.

The tumult subsided at once, and every eye was fixed on this almost   6
Amazon form, which stood nearly six feet high, head erect, and eyes piercing the upper air like one in a dream. At her first word there was a profound hush. She spoke in deep tones, which, though not loud, reached every ear in the house, and away through the throng at the doors and windows.

"Wall, chilern, whar dar is so much racket dar must be somethin' out o' kil-   7
ter. I tink dat 'twixt de nigger of de Souf and de womin at de Norf, all talkin' 'bout rights, de white men will be in a fix pretty soon. But what's all dis here talkin' 'bout?

"Dat man ober dar say dat womin needs to be helped into carriages, and   8
lifted ober ditches, and to hab de best place everywhar. Nobody eber halps me into carriages, or ober mudpuddles, or gibs me any best place!"

And raising herself to her full height, and her voice to a pitch like rolling   9
thunder, she asked, "And ar'n't I a woman? Look at me! Look at my arm! [And here she bared her right arm to the shoulder, showing her tremendous muscular power] " I have ploughed, and planted, and gathered into barns, and no man could head me! And ar'n't I a woman? I could work as much and eat as much as a man—when I could get it—and bear de lash as well! And ar'n't' I a woman? I have borne thirteen chilern, and seen 'em mos' all sold off the slavery, and when I cried out with my mother's grief, none but Jesus heard me! And ar'n't I a woman?

"Den dey talks 'bout dis ting in de head; what dis dey call it?" "Intellect,"   10
whispered someone near. "Dat's it, honey. What's dat got to do wid womin's rights or nigger's rights? If my cup won't hold but a pint, and yourn holds a quart, wouldn't ye be mean not to let me have my little half-measure full?" And she pointed her significant finger, and sent a keen glance at the minister who had made the argument. The cheering was long and loud.

"Den dat little man in black dar, he say women can't have as much rights   11
as men, 'cause Christ wan't a woman! Whar did your Christ come from?" Rolling thunder couldn't have stilled that crowd, as did those deep, wonderful tones, as she stood there with outstretched arms and eyes of fire. Raising her voice still louder, she repeated, "Whar did your Christ come from? From God and a

woman! Man had nothin' to do wid Him." Oh, what a rebuke that was to the little man.

Turning again to another objector, she took up the defense of Mother Eve, 12
I cannot follow her through it all. It was pointed and witty, and solemn; eliciting at almost every sentence deafening applause; and she ended by asserting, "If de fust woman God ever made was strong enough to turn de world upside down all alone, dese women togedder [and she glanced her eye over the platform] ought to be able to turn it back, and get it right side up again! And now dey is asking to do it, de men better let 'em." Long continued cheering greeted this. "Bleeged to ye for hearin' on me, and now ole Sojourner han't got nothin' more to say."

Amid roars of applause, she returned to her corner, leaving more than one 13
of us with streaming eyes, and hearts beating with gratitude. She had taken us up in her strong arms and carried us safely over the slough of difficulty, turning the whole tide in our favor. I have never in my life seen anything like the magical influence that subdued the mobbish spirit of the day, and turned the sneers and jeers of an excited crowd into notes of respect and admiration. Hundreds rushed up to shake hands with her, and congratulate the glorious old mother, and bid her God-speed on her mission of "testifyin' agin concerning the wickedness of this 'ere people."

Questions for Discussion

1. In Robinson's version, what is Truth's primary message?
2. When Truth says "I am a woman's rights," what does she mean?
3. What kinds of evidence does Truth use to convince her audience of her point?
4. What "men" does Truth refer to when she says, in Robinson's version, "the women are coming up blessed be God and a few of the men are coming up with them"?
5. Truth mentions slavery in the final sentence of Robinson's version of her speech. Why? Does this make her primary argument more or less effective, in your opinion?

Questions for Reflection and Writing

1. The speech as recorded by Robinson was delivered in 1851. Does the language feel unfamiliar? Does the argument? Why should we read Sojourner Truth today (if, in fact, you agree that we should)?

2. Take a good look at Gage's version of Truth's speech. Note in particular the "framing," or introductory and concluding text; the use of dialect; and the representation of Truth's argument, as well as the kinds of evidence she brings to bear in order to prove it. What has Gage changed from Robinson's version? Why do you think she changed them?

3. Would it matter if Truth had *not* actually composed the text most often re presented as authentic? In what way(s)? If you like, consider the cases (in some ways parallel) of Chief Seattle's Letter to President Pierce, Harriet Jacobs's *Incidents in the Life of a Slave Girl*, or Anne Frank's *Diary*. How much should questions of sole authorship/unacknowledged collaboration affect our reading of texts widely admired for their power?

Elizabeth Cady Stanton (1815–1902) was born in Johnstown, New York, and attended Emma Willard's Troy Female Seminary. She was a pioneering women's rights leader and a writer. Stanton was also the editor of the national feminist newspaper *Revolution*, a contemporary of Susan B. Anthony, and president of the National Women's Suffrage Association from 1869 to 1890. She and Anthony can reasonably be said to have started the women's movement in the United States. "Declaration of Sentiments and Resolutions" was delivered at the Seneca Falls Conference in 1848 and was first published in 1870 as the *Address of Mrs. Elizabeth Cady Stanton: Delivered at Seneca Falls & Rochester, N.Y., July 19th & August 2d, 1848.*

Declaration of Sentiments

Elizabeth Cady Stanton

When, in the course of human events, it becomes necessary for one portion of 1 the family of man to assume among the people of the earth a position different from that which they have hitherto occupied, but one to which the laws of nature and of nature's God entitle them, a decent respect to the opinions of mankind requires that they should declare the causes that impel them to such a course.

We hold these truths to be self-evident: that all men and women are cre- 2 ated equal; that they are endowed by their Creator with certain inalienable rights; that among these are life, liberty, and the pursuit of happiness; that to secure these rights governments are instituted, deriving their just powers from the consent of the governed. Whenever any form of government becomes destructive of these ends, it is the right of those who suffer from it to refuse allegiance to it, and to insist upon the institution of a new government, laying its foundation on such principles, and organizing its powers in such form, as to them shall seem most likely to effect their safety and happiness. Prudence indeed, will dictate that governments long established should not be changed for light and transient causes; and accordingly all experience hath shown that mankind are more disposed to suffer, while evils are sufferable, than to right themselves by abolishing the forms to which they were accustomed. But when a long train of abuses and usurpations, pursuing invariably the same object evinces a design to

From *A History of Woman Suffrage*, ed. Elizabeth Cady Stanton, Susan B. Anthony, and Matilda Joslyn Gage (1881).

reduce them under absolute despotism, it is their duty to throw off such government, and to provide new guards for their future security. Such has been the patient sufferance of the women under this government, and such is now the necessity which constrains them to demand the equal station to which they are entitled.

The history of mankind is a history of repeated injuries and usurpations on   3
the part of man toward woman, having in direct object the establishment of an absolute tyranny over her. To prove this, let facts be submitted to a candid world.

He has never permitted her to exercise her inalienable right to the elective   4
franchise.

He has compelled her to submit to laws, in the formation of which she had   5
no voice.

He has withheld from her rights which are given to the most ignorant and   6
degraded men—both natives and foreigners.

Having deprived her of this first right of a citizen, the elective franchise,   7
thereby leaving her without representation in the halls of legislation, he has oppressed her on all sides.

He has made her, if married, in the eye of the law, civilly dead.   8

He has taken from her all right in property, even to the wages she earns.   9

He has made her, morally, an irresponsible being, as she can commit many   10
crimes with impunity, provided they be done in the presence of her husband. In the covenant of marriage, she is compelled to promise obedience to her husband, he becoming, to all intents and purposes, her master—the law giving him power to deprive her of her liberty, and to administer chastisement.

He has so framed the laws of divorce, as to what shall be the proper caus-   11
es, and in case of separation, to whom the guardianship of the children shall be given, as to be wholly regardless of the happiness of women—the law, in all cases, going upon a false supposition of the supremacy of man, and giving all power into his hands.

After depriving her of all rights as a married woman, if single, and the   12
owner of property, he has taxed her to support a government which recognizes her only when her property can be made profitable to it.

He has monopolized nearly all the profitable employments, and from those   13
she is permitted to follow, she receives but a scanty remuneration. He closes against her all the avenues to wealth and distinction which he considers most honorable to himself. As a teacher of theology, medicine, or law, she is not known.

He has denied her the facilities for obtaining a thorough education, all colleges being closed against her. 14

He allows her in Church, as well as State, but a subordinate position, claiming Apostolic authority for her exclusion from the ministry, and, with some exceptions, from any public participation in the affairs of the Church. 15

He has created a false public sentiment by giving to the world a different code of morals for men and women, by which moral delinquencies which exclude women from society, are not only tolerated, but deemed of little account in man. 16

He has usurped the prerogative of Jehovah himself, claiming it as his right to assign for her a sphere of action, when that belongs to her conscience and to her God. 17

He has endeavored, in every way that he could, to destroy her confidence in her own powers, to lessen her self-respect, and to make her willing to lead a dependent and abject life. 18

Now, in view of this entire disfranchisement of one-half the people of this country, their social and religious degradation—in view of the unjust laws above mentioned, and because women do feel themselves aggrieved, oppressed, and fraudulently deprived of their most sacred rights, we insist that they have immediate admission to all the rights and privileges which belong to them as citizens of the United States. 19

In entering upon the great work before us, we anticipate no small amount of misconception, misrepresentation, and ridicule; but we shall use every instrumentality within our power to effect our object. We shall employ agents, circulate tracts, petition the State and National legislatures, and endeavor to enlist the pulpit and the press in our behalf. We hope this Convention will be followed by a series of Conventions embracing every part of the country. 20

Questions for Discussion

1. "When in the course of human events, it becomes necessary . . ." also starts what other declaration? Is the echo deliberate? What effect does it have?
2. The word "he" is repeated quite frequently in this piece. What is the effect of this repetition?
3. Describe the structure of this speech. How does the structure help convey the author's points?
4. What does Stanton mean when she says that men have made women morally irresponsible (paragraph 10)?

5.   How does Stanton feel about women's right to vote? How do you know?

Questions for Reflection and Writing

1.   Describe a time someone treated you unfairly solely due to your sex, race, ethnicity, or any other characteristic. Try to formulate your own "declaration" against such behavior.

2.   Is a declaration such as Stanton's still needed today? Explain.

3.   Stanton states in paragraph 3, "The history of mankind is a history of repeated injuries and usurpations on the part of man toward woman. . . ." Is this a reasonable view? Take Stanton's position or an opposing one and argue your point, stating your thesis clearly.

Andrew Sullivan (1963–   ) was born and raised in England and educated at Oxford and Harvard University, where he earned both a Master's degree in Public Administration and a Ph.D. in Political Science. He worked as editor of *The New Republic* from 1991 until 1996, garnering numerous awards for exellence, and has co tributed many articles to that magazine and to *The Wall Street Journal*, *The Washington Post*, *The Daily Telegraph*, *Esquire*, *The New York Times*, *The New York Review of Books*, and *The Sunday Times* of London. Sullivan went public with his homosexuality in the early 1990s, and he has since made the topic one of his areas of journalistic focus. Among the books he has written and edited are *Virtually Normal: An Argument about Homosexuality* (1995), *Same-Sex Marriage: Pro and Con* (1996), and *Love Undetectable: Notes on Friendship, Sex, and Survival* (1998). "This Is a Religious War" was published on October 7, 2001 in *The New York Times Magazine*.

This Is a Religious War

Andrew Sullivan

Perhaps the most admirable part of the response to the conflict that began on   1
September 11 has been a general reluctance to call it a religious war. Officials and commentators have rightly stressed that this is not a battle between the Muslim world and the West, that the murderers are not representative of Islam. President Bush went to the Islamic Center in Washington to reinforce the point. At prayer meetings across the United States and throughout the world, Muslim leaders have been included alongside Christians, Jews, and Buddhists.

    The only problem with this otherwise laudable effort is that it doesn't hold   2
up under inspection. The religious dimension of this conflict is central to its meaning. The words of Osama bin Laden are saturated with religious argument and theological language. Whatever else the Taliban regime is in Afghanistan, it is fanatically religious. Although some Muslim leaders have criticized the terrorists, and even Saudi Arabia's rulers have distanced themselves from the militants, other Muslims in the Middle East and elsewhere have not denounced these acts, have been conspicuously silent, or have indeed celebrated them. The terrorists' strain of Islam is clearly not shared by most Muslims and is deeply unrepresentative of Islam's glorious, civilized, and peaceful past. But it surely represents a part

of Islam—a radical, fundamentalist part—that simply cannot be ignored or denied.

In that sense, this surely is a religious war—but not of Islam versus   3
Christianity and Judaism. Rather, it is a war of fundamentalism against faiths of all kinds that are at peace with freedom and modernity. This war even has far gentler echoes in America's own religious conflicts between newer, more viru- lent strands of Christian fundamentalism and mainstream Protestantism and Catholicism. These conflicts have ancient roots, but they seem to be gaining new force as modernity spreads and deepens. They are our new wars of religion— and their victims are in all likelihood going to mount with each passing year.

Osama bin Laden himself couldn't be clearer about the religious underpin-   4
nings of his campaign of terror. In 1998, he told his followers, "The call to wage war against America was made because America has spearheaded the crusade against the Islamic nation, sending tens of thousands of its troops to the land of the two holy mosques over and above its meddling in its affairs and its politics and its support of the oppressive, corrupt and tyrannical regime that is in con- trol." Notice the use of the word "crusade," an explicitly religious term, and one that simply ignores the fact that the last few major American interventions abroad—in Kuwait, Somalia, and the Balkans—were all conducted in defense of Muslims.

Notice also that as bin Laden understands it, the "crusade" America is   5
alleged to be leading is not against Arabs but against the Islamic nation, which spans many ethnicities. This nation knows no nation-states as they actually exist in the region—which is why this form of Islamic fundamentalism is also so wor- rying to the rulers of many Middle Eastern states. Notice also that bin Laden's beef is with American troops defiling the land of Saudi Arabia—"the land of the two holy mosques," in Mecca and Medina. In 1998, he also told followers that his terrorism was "of the commendable kind, for it is directed at the tyrants and the aggressors and the enemies of Allah." He has a litany of grievances against Israel as well, but his concerns are not primarily territorial or procedural. "Our religion is under attack," he said baldly. The attackers are Christians and Jews. When asked to sum up his message to the people of the West, bin Laden could- n't have been clearer: "Our call is the call of Islam that was revealed to Muhammad. It is a call to all mankind. We have been entrusted with good cause to follow in the footsteps of the messenger and to communicate his message to all nations."

This is a religious war against "unbelief and unbelievers," in bin Laden's 6
words. Are these cynical words designed merely to use Islam for nefarious ends?
We cannot know the precise motives of bin Laden, but we can know that he
would not use these words if he did not think they had salience among the people he wishes to inspire and provoke. This form of Islam is not restricted to bin
Laden alone.

Its roots lie in an extreme and violent strain in Islam that emerged in the 7
eighteenth century in opposition to what was seen by some Muslims as Ottoman
decadence but has gained greater strength in the twentieth. For the past two
decades, this form of Islamic fundamentalism has racked the Middle East. It has
targeted almost every regime in the region and, as it failed to make progress, has
extended its hostility into the West. From the assassination of Anwar Sadat to
the fatwa against Salman Rushdie to the decade-long campaign of bin Laden to
the destruction of ancient Buddhist statues and the hideous persecution of
women and homosexuals by the Taliban to the World Trade Center massacre,
there is a single line. That line is a fundamentalist, religious one. And it is an
Islamic one.

Most interpreters of the Koran find no arguments in it for the murder of 8
innocents. But it would be naive to ignore in Islam a deep thread of intolerance
toward unbelievers, especially if those unbelievers are believed to be a threat to
the Islamic world. There are many passages in the Koran urging mercy toward
others, tolerance, respect for life, and so on. But there are also passages as violent
as this: "And when the sacred months are passed, kill those who join other gods
with God wherever ye shall find them; and seize them, besiege them, and lay
wait for them with every kind of ambush." And this: "Believers! Wage war
against such of the infidels as are your neighbors, and let them find you rigorous."
Bernard Lewis, the great scholar of Islam, writes of the dissonance within Islam:
"There is something in the religious culture of Islam which inspired, in even the
humblest peasant or peddler, a dignity and a courtesy toward others never
exceeded and rarely equaled in other civilizations. And yet, in moments of
upheaval and disruption, when the deeper passions are stirred, this dignity and
courtesy toward others can give way to an explosive mixture of rage and hatred
which impels even the government of an ancient and civilized country— even
the spokesman of a great spiritual and ethical religion—to espouse kidnapping
and assassination, and try to find, in the life of their prophet, approval and indeed
precedent for such actions." Since Muhammad was, unlike many other religious

leaders, not simply a sage or a prophet but a ruler in his own right, this exploitation of his politics is not as great a stretch as some would argue.

This use of religion for extreme repression, and even terror, is not, of course,   9
restricted to Islam. For most of its history, Christianity has had a worse record.
From the Crusades to the Inquisition to the bloody religious wars of the sixteenth
and seventeenth centuries, Europe saw far more blood spilled for religion's sake
than the Muslim world did. And given how expressly nonviolent the teachings
of the Gospels are, the perversion of Christianity in this respect was arguably
greater than bin Laden's selective use of Islam. But it is there nonetheless. It
seems almost as if there is something inherent in religious monotheism that lends
itself to this kind of terrorist temptation. And our bland attempts to ignore this—
to speak of this violence as if it did not have religious roots—is some kind of
denial. We don't want to denigrate religion as such, and so we deny that religion
is at the heart of this. But we would understand this conflict better, perhaps, if
we first acknowledged that religion is responsible in some way, and then figured
out how and why.

The first mistake is surely to condescend to fundamentalism. We may dis-   10
agree with it, but it has attracted millions of adherents for centuries, and for a
good reason. It elevates and comforts. It provides a sense of meaning and direction to those lost in a disorienting world. The blind recourse to texts embraced
as literal truth, the injunction to follow the commandments of God before anything else, the subjugation of reason and judgment and even conscience to the
dictates of dogma: these can be exhilarating and transformative. They have led
human beings to perform extraordinary acts of both good and evil. And they
have an internal logic to them. If you believe that there is an eternal afterlife and
that endless indescribable torture awaits those who disobey God's law, then it
requires no huge stretch of imagination to make sure that you not only conform
to each diktat but that you also encourage and, if necessary, coerce others to do
the same. The logic behind this is impeccable. Sin begets sin. The sin of others
can corrupt you as well. The only solution is to construct a world in which such
sin is outlawed and punished and constantly purged—by force if necessary. It is
not crazy to act this way if you believe these things strongly enough. In some
ways, it's crazier to believe these things and not act this way.

In a world of absolute truth, in matters graver than life and death, there is   11
no room for dissent and no room for theological doubt. Hence the reliance on
literal interpretations of texts—because interpretation can lead to error, and
error can lead to damnation. Hence also the ancient Catholic insistence on

absolute church authority. Without infallibility, there can be no guarantee of truth. Without such a guarantee, confusion can lead to hell.

Dostoyevsky's Grand Inquisitor makes the case perhaps as well as anyone.   12
In the story told by Ivan Karamazov in *The Brothers Karamazov*, Jesus returns to earth during the Spanish Inquisition. On a day when hundreds have been burned at the stake for heresy, Jesus performs miracles. Alarmed, the Inquisitor arrests Jesus and imprisons him with the intent of burning him at the stake as well. What follows is a conversation between the Inquisitor and Jesus. Except it isn't a conversation because Jesus says nothing. It is really a dialogue between two modes of religion, an exploration of the tension between the extraordinary, transcendent claims of religion and human beings, inability to live up to them, or even fully believe them.

According to the Inquisitor, Jesus' crime was revealing that salvation was   13
possible but still allowing humans the freedom to refuse it. And this, to the Inquisitor, was a form of cruelty. When the truth involves the most important things imaginable— the meaning of life, the fate of one's eternal soul, the difference between good and evil—it is not enough to premise it on the capacity of human choice. That is too great a burden. Choice leads to unbelief or distraction or negligence or despair. What human beings really need is the certainty of truth, and they need to see it reflected in everything around them—in the cultures in which they live, enveloping them in a seamless fabric of faith that helps them resist the terror of choice and the abyss of unbelief. This need is what the Inquisitor calls the "fundamental secret of human nature." He explains: "These pitiful creatures are concerned not only to find what one or the other can worship, but to find something that all would believe in and worship; what is essential is that all may be together in it. This craving for community of worship is the chief misery of every man individually and of all humanity since the beginning of time."

This is the voice of fundamentalism. Faith cannot exist alone in a single   14
person. Indeed, faith needs others for it to survive—and the more complete the culture of faith, the wider it is, and the more total its infiltration of the world the better. It is hard for us to wrap our minds around this today, but it is quite clear from the accounts of the Inquisition and, indeed, of the religious wars that continued to rage in Europe for nearly three centuries, that many of the fanatics who burned human beings at the stake were acting out of what they genuinely thought were the best interests of the victims. With the power of the state, they used fire, as opposed to simple execution, because it was thought to be spiritual-

ly cleansing. A few minutes of hideous torture on earth were deemed a small price to pay for helping such souls avoid eternal torture in the afterlife. Moreover, the example of such government-sponsored executions helped create a culture in which certain truths were reinforced and in which it was easier for more weak people to find faith. The burden of this duty to uphold the faith lay on the men required to torture, persecute, and murder the unfaithful. And many of them believed, as no doubt some Islamic fundamentalists believe, that they were acting out of mercy and godliness.

This is the authentic voice of the Taliban. It also finds itself replicated in   15
secular form. What, after all, were the totalitarian societies of Nazi Germany or Soviet Russia if not an exact replica of this kind of fusion of politics and ultimate meaning? Under Lenin's and Stalin's rules, the imminence of salvation through revolutionary consciousness was in perpetual danger of being undermined by those too weak to have faith—the bourgeois or the kulaks or the intellectuals. So they had to be liquidated or purged. Similarly, it is easy for us to dismiss the Nazis as evil, as they surely were. It is harder for us to understand that in some twisted fashion, they truly believed that they were creating a new dawn for humanity, a place where all the doubts that freedom brings could be dispelled in a rapture of racial purity and destiny. Hence the destruction of all dissidents and the Jews—carried out by fire as the Inquisitors had before, an act of purification different merely in its scale, efficiency, and Godlessness.

Perhaps the most important thing for us to realize today is that the defeat   16
of each of these fundamentalisms required a long and arduous effort. The conflict with Islamic fundamentalism is likely to take as long. For unlike Europe's religious wars, which taught Christians the futility of fighting to the death over something beyond human understanding and so immune to any definitive resolution, there has been no such educative conflict in the Muslim world. Only Iran and Afghanistan have experienced the full horror of revolutionary fundamentalism, and only Iran has so far seen reason to moderate to some extent. From everything we see, the lessons Europe learned in its bloody history have yet to be absorbed within the Muslim world. There, as in sixteenth-century Europe, the promise of purity and salvation seems far more enticing than the mundane allure of mere peace. That means that we are not at the end of this conflict but in its very early stages.

America is not a neophyte in this struggle. The United States has seen several waves of religious fervor since its founding. But American evangelicalism has   17
always kept its distance from governmental power. The Christian separation

between what is God's and what is Caesar's—drawn from the Gospels—helped restrain the fundamentalist temptation. The last few decades have proved an exception, however. As modernity advanced, and the certitudes of fundamentalist faith seemed mocked by an increasingly liberal society, evangelicals mobilized and entered politics. Their faith sharpened, their zeal intensified, the temptation to fuse political and religious authority beckoned more insistently.

Mercifully, violence has not been a significant feature of this trend but it has not been absent. The murders of abortion providers show what such zeal can lead to. And indeed, if people truly believe that abortion is the same as mass murder, then you can see the awful logic of the terrorism it has spawned. This is the same logic as bin Laden's. If faith is that strong, and it dictates a choice between action or eternal damnation, then violence can easily be justified. In retrospect, we should be amazed not that violence has occurred—but that it hasn't occurred more often.   18

The critical link between Western and Middle Eastern fundamentalism is surely the pace of social change. If you take your beliefs from books written more than a thousand years ago, and you believe in these texts literally, then the appearance of the modern world must truly terrify. If you believe that women should be consigned to polygamous, concealed servitude, then Manhattan must appear like Gomorrah. If you believe that homosexuality is a crime punishable by death, as both fundamentalist Islam and the Bible dictate, then a world of same-sex marriage is surely Sodom. It is not a big step to argue that such centers of evil should be destroyed or undermined, as bin Laden does, or to believe that their destruction is somehow a consequence of their sin, as Jerry Falwell argued. Look again at Falwell's now infamous words in the wake of September 11: "I really believe that the pagans, and the abortionists, and the feminists, and the gays and lesbians who are actively trying to make that an alternative lifestyle, the A.C.L.U., People for the American Way—all of them who have tried to secularize America—I point the finger in their face and say, 'You helped this happen.'   19

And why wouldn't he believe that? He has subsequently apologized for the insensitivity of the remark but not for its theological underpinning. He cannot repudiate the theology—because it is the essence of what he believes in and must believe in for his faith to remain alive.   20

The other critical aspect of this kind of faith is insecurity. American fundamentalists know they are losing the culture war. They are terrified of failure and of the Godless world they believe is about to engulf or crush them. They speak and think defensively. They talk about renewal, but in their private dis-   21

course they expect damnation for an America that has lost sight of the fundamentalist notion of God.

Similarly, Muslims know that the era of Islam's imperial triumph has long   22
since gone. For many centuries, the civilization of Islam was the center of the
world. It eclipsed Europe in the Dark Ages, fostered great learning and expanded territorially well into Europe and Asia. But it has all been downhill from there.
From the collapse of the Ottoman Empire onward, it has been on the losing side
of history. The response to this has been an intermittent flirtation with
Westernization but far more emphatically a reaffirmation of the most irredentist
and extreme forms of the culture under threat. Hence the odd phenomenon of
Islamic extremism beginning in earnest only in the last 200 years.

With Islam, this has worse implications than for other cultures that have   23
had rises and falls. For Islam's religious tolerance has always been premised on its
own power. It was tolerant when it controlled the territory and called the shots.
When it lost territory and saw itself eclipsed by the West in power and civilization, tolerance evaporated. To cite Lewis again on Islam: "What is truly evil and
unacceptable is the domination of infidels over true believers. For true believers
to rule misbelievers is proper and natural, since this provides for the maintenance
of the holy law and gives the misbelievers both the opportunity and the incentive to embrace the true faith. But for misbelievers to rule over true believers is
blasphemous and unnatural, since it leads to the corruption of religion and
morality in society and to the flouting or even the abrogation of God's law."

Thus the horror at the establishment of the State of Israel, an infidel coun-   24
try in Muslim lands, a bitter reminder of the eclipse of Islam in the modern
world. Thus also the revulsion at American bases in Saudi Arabia. While colonialism of different degrees is merely political oppression for some cultures, for
Islam it was far worse. It was blasphemy that had to be avenged and countered.

I cannot help thinking of this defensiveness when I read stories of the sui-   25
cide bombers sitting poolside in Florida or racking up a $48 vodka tab in an
American restaurant. We tend to think that this assimilation into the West
might bring Islamic fundamentalists around somewhat, temper their zeal. But in
fact, the opposite is the case. The temptation of American and Western culture—indeed, the very allure of such culture—may well require a repression all
the more brutal if it is to be overcome. The transmission of American culture
into the heart of what bin Laden calls the Islamic nation requires only two
responses—capitulation to unbelief or a radical strike against it. There is little
room in the fundamentalist psyche for a moderate accommodation. The very

psychological dynamics that lead repressed homosexuals to be viciously homo-phobic or that entice sexually tempted preachers to inveigh against immorality are the very dynamics that lead vodka-drinking fundamentalists to steer planes into buildings. It is not designed to achieve anything, construct anything, argue anything. It is a violent acting out of internal conflict.

And America is the perfect arena for such acting out. For the question of   26 religious fundamentalism was not only familiar to the founding fathers. In many ways, it was the central question that led to America's existence. The first American immigrants, after all, were refugees from the religious wars that engulfed England and that intensified under England's Taliban, Oliver Cromwell. One central influence on the founders' political thought was John Locke, the English liberal who wrote the now famous "Letter on Toleration." In it, Locke argued that true salvation could not be a result of coercion, that faith had to be freely chosen to be genuine and that any other interpretation was counter to the Gospels. Following Locke, the founders established as a central element of the new American order a stark separation of church and state, ensur-ing that no single religion could use political means to enforce its own orthodox-ies.

We cite this as a platitude today without absorbing or even realizing its rad-   27 ical nature in human history—and the deep human predicament it was designed to solve. It was an attempt to answer the eternal human question of how to pur-sue the goal of religious salvation for ourselves and others and yet also maintain civil peace. What the founders and Locke were saying was that the ultimate claims of religion should simply not be allowed to interfere with political and religious freedom. They did this to preserve peace above all—but also to preserve true religion itself.

The security against an American Taliban is therefore relatively simple: it's   28 the Constitution. And the surprising consequence of this separation is not that it led to a collapse of religious faith in America—as weak human beings found themselves unable to believe without social and political reinforcement, but that it led to one of the most vibrantly religious civil societies on earth. No other country has achieved this. And it is this achievement that the Taliban and bin Laden have now decided to challenge. It is a living, tangible rebuke to every-thing they believe in.

That is why this coming conflict is indeed as momentous and as grave as   29 the last major conflicts, against Nazism and Communism, and why it is not hyperbole to see it in these epic terms. What is at stake is yet another battle against a religion that is succumbing to the temptation Jesus refused in the desert—to rule by force. The difference is that this conflict is against a more formidable enemy than Nazism or Communism. The secular totalitarianisms of the twentieth century were, in President Bush's memorable words, "discarded lies." They were fundamentalisms built on the very weak intellectual conceits of a master race and a Communist revolution.

But Islamic fundamentalism is based on a glorious civilization and a great   30
faith. It can harness and coopt and corrupt true and good believers if it has a propitious and toxic enough environment. It has a more powerful logic than either Stalin's or Hitler's Godless ideology, and it can serve as a focal point for all the other societies in the world, whose resentment of Western success and civilization comes more easily than the arduous task of accommodation to modernity. We have to somehow defeat this without defeating or even opposing a great religion that is nonetheless extremely inexperienced in the toleration of other ascendant and more powerful faiths. It is hard to underestimate the extreme delicacy and difficulty of this task.

In this sense, the symbol of this conflict should not be Old Glory, howev-   31
er stirring it is. What is really at issue here is the simple but immensely difficult principle of the separation of politics and religion. We are fighting not for our country as such or for our flag. We are fighting for the universal principles of our Constitution—and the possibility of free religious faith it guarantees. We are fighting for religion against one of the deepest strains in religion there is. And not only our lives but our souls are at stake.

Questions for Discussion

1. Why does Sullivan call the "general refusal" to call the war on terrorism a *religious* war "the most admirable part of the response to the conflict that began on September 11?"

2. Why does Sullivan insist that it *is* a religious war? How does he define his terms?

3. According to Sullivan, what "form of Islam" does Bin Laden represent? What is its history?

4. How does Sullivan support his perception of a "dissonance within Islam?" Does he see a similar dissonance within Christianity? What, if anything, is the difference?

5. How does Sullivan explain the enduring popularity of religious fundamentalism(s)?

Questions for Reflection and Writing

1. Describe the "single line" Sullivan draws between the assassination of Anwar Sadat and the destruction of the World Trade Center. What argument underlies his drawing of the line in this way? Could it be drawn differently? How?

2. In his essay, Sullivan explicitly links the practices of the Taliban with those of the Spanish Inquisition and the Nazis. With what evidence does he support his position? Do you find it credible? Write an essay in which you either explain and then expand upon his position, or point out its limitations.

3. Do you agree with Sullivan that we are actually "fighting for religion" in combatting terrorism? Outline Sullivan's reasoning in support of this claim, and then write an essay in which you either defend his position or take up a contrary one.

Paul M. Harrison (1923–   ), a sociologist, educator, and Christian ethicist, was born on May 7, in Philadelphia. He earned a B.A. from Pennsylvania State University in 1949, a B.D. from Colgate-Rochester Divinity School in 1952, and a Ph.D. from Yale University in 1958. Harrison has taught at Princeton University and Pennsylvania State University. He served in the U.S. Army Air Forces during World War II, ascending to second lieutenant. His memberships include the American Sociological Association, the Society for Scientific Study of Religion, and American Society of Christian Ethics Professors. Some of his writings include *Authority and Power in the Free Church Tradition* (1959; 3d ed., 1971); and contributions to *Religion as Dramatic Experience: A Study in Myth Symbolism and Dramatic Enactment through Role Play and the Religious Situation* (1969). Harrison has also contributed to professional periodicals.

The Westernization of the World

Paul Harrison

> The bourgeoisie has, through its exploitation of the world market, given a cosmo-politan character to production and consumption in every country.
>
> —Karl Marx

In Singapore, Peking opera still lives, in the back streets. On Boat Quay, where   1
great barges moor to unload rice from Thailand, raw rubber from Malaysia, or timber from Sumatra, I watched a troupe of traveling actors throw up a canvas-and-wood booth stage, paint on their white faces and lozenge eyes, and don their resplendent vermilion, ultramarine, and gold robes. Then, to raptured audiences of bent old women and little children with perfect circle faces, they enacted tales of feudal princes and magic birds and wars and tragic love affairs, sweeping their sleeves and singing in strange metallic voices.

The performance had been paid for by a local cultural society as part of a   2
religious festival. A purple cloth temple had been erected on the quayside, painted papiermâché sculptures were burning down like giant joss sticks, and middle-aged men were sharing out gifts to be distributed among members' families: red buckets, roast ducks, candies, and moon cakes. The son of the organizer, a fashionable young man in Italian shirt and gold-rimmed glasses, was looking on with

amused benevolence. I asked him why old people and children were watching the show.

"Young people don't like these operas," he said. "They are too old fashioned. We would prefer to see a high-quality Western variety show, something like that." 3

He spoke for a whole generation. Go to almost any village in the Third World and you will find youths who scorn traditional dress and sport denims and T-shirts. Go into any bank and the tellers will be dressed as would their European counterparts; at night the manager will climb into his car and go home to watch TV in a home that would not stick out on a European or North American estate. Every capital city in the world is getting to look like every other; it is Marshall McLuhan's global village, but the style is exclusively Western. And not just in consumer fashions: the mimicry extends to architecture, industrial technology, approaches to health care, education, and housing. 4

To the ethnocentric Westerner or the Westernized local, that may seem the most natural thing in the world. That is modern life, they might think. That is the way it will all be one day. That is what development and economic growth are all about. 5

Yet the dispassionate observer can only be puzzled by this growing world uniformity. Surely one should expect more diversity, more indigenous styles and models of development. Why is almost everyone following virtually the same European road? The Third World's obsession with the Western way of life has perverted development and is rapidly destroying good and bad in traditional cultures, flinging the baby out with the bathwater. It is the most totally pervasive example of what historians call cultural diffusion in the history of mankind. 6

Its origins, of course, lie in the colonial experience. European rule was something quite different from the general run of conquests. Previous invaders more often than not settled down in their new territories, interbred, and assimilated a good deal of local culture. Not so the Europeans. Some, like the Iberians or the Dutch, were not averse to cohabitation with native women; unlike the British, they seemed free of purely racial prejudice. But all the Europeans suffered from the same cultural arrogance. Perhaps it is the peculiar self-righteousness of Pauline Christianity that accounts for this trait. Whatever the cause, never a doubt entered their minds that native cultures could be in any way, materially, morally, or spiritually, superior to their own, and that the supposedly benighted inhabitants of the darker continents needed enlightening. 7

And so there grew up, alongside political and economic imperialism, that   8
more insidious form of control—cultural imperialism. It conquered not just the
bodies, but the souls of its victims, turning them into willing accomplices.

Cultural imperialism began its conquest of the Third World with the   9
indoctrination of an elite of local collaborators. The missionary schools sought
to produce converts to Christianity who would go out and proselytize among
their own people, helping to eradicate traditional culture. Later the government
schools aimed to turn out a class of junior bureaucrats and lower military officers
who would help to exploit and repress their own people. The British were subtle
about this, since they wanted the natives, even the Anglicized among them, to
keep their distance. The French, and the Portuguese in Africa, explicitly aimed
at the "assimilation" of gifted natives, by which was meant their metamorphosis
into model Frenchmen and Lusitanians, distinguishable only by the tint of their
skin.

The second channel of transmission was more indirect and voluntary. It   10
worked by what sociologists call reference-group behavior, found when someone
copies the habits and lifestyle of a social group he wishes to belong to, or to be
classed with, and abandons those of his own group. This happened in the West
when the new rich of early commerce and industry aped the nobility they secretly aspired to join. Not surprisingly the social climbers in the colonies started to
mimic their conquerors. The returned slaves who carried the first wave of
Westernization in West Africa wore black woolen suits and starched collars in
the heat of the dry season. The new officer corps of India were molded into what
the Indian writer Nirad Chaudhuri has called "imitation, polo-playing English
subalterns," complete with waxed mustaches and peacock chests. The elite of
Indians, adding their own caste-consciousness to the class-consciousness of their
rulers, became more British than the British (and still are).

There was another psychological motive for adopting Western ways, deriv-   11
ing from the arrogance and haughtiness of the colonialists. As the Martiniquan
political philosopher, Frantz Fanon, remarked, colonial rule was an experience in
racial humiliation. Practically every leader of the newly independent state could
recall some experience such as being turned out of a club or manhandled on the
street by whites, often of low status. The local elite were made to feel ashamed
of their color and of their culture. "I began to suffer from not being a white man,"
Fanon wrote, "to the degree that the white man imposes discrimination on me,
makes me a colonized native, robs me of all worth, all individuality. . . . Then I
will quite simply try to make myself white: that is, I will compel the white man

to acknowledge that I am human." To this complex Fanon attributes the colonized natives' constant preoccupation with attracting the attention of the white man, becoming powerful like the white man, proving at all costs that blacks too can be civilized. Given the racism and culturism of the whites, this could only be done by succeeding in their terms, and by adopting their ways.

This desire to prove equality surely helps to explain why Ghana's Nkrumah   12
built the huge stadium and triumphal arch of Black Star Square in Accra. Why the tiny native village of Ivory Coast president Houphouët-Boigny has been graced with a four-lane motorway starting and ending nowhere, a fivestar hotel and ultramodern conference center. Why Sukarno transformed Indonesia's capital, Jakarta, into an exercise in gigantism, scarred with sixlane highways and neofascist monuments in the most hideous taste. The aim was not only to show the old imperialists, but to impress other Third World leaders in the only way everyone would recognize: the Western way.

The influence of Western lifestyles spread even to those few nations who   13
escaped the colonial yoke. By the end of the nineteenth century, the elites of the entire non-Western world were taking Europe as their reference group. The progress of the virus can be followed visibly in a room of Topkapi, the Ottoman palace in Istanbul, where a sequence of showcases display the costumes worn by each successive sultan. They begin with kaftans and turbans. Slowly elements of Western military uniform creep in, until the last sultans are decked out in brocade, epaulettes, and cocked hats.

The root of the problem with nations that were never colonized, like   14
Turkey, China, and Japan, was probably their consciousness of Western military superiority. The beating of these three powerful nations at the hands of the West was a humiliating, traumatic experience. For China and Japan, the encounter with the advanced military technology of the industrialized nations was as terrifying as an invasion of extraterrestrials. Europe's earlier discovery of the rest of the world had delivered a mild culture shock to her ethnocentric attitudes. The Orient's contact with Europe shook nations to the foundations, calling into question the roots of their civilizations and all the assumptions and institutions on which their lives were based.

In all three nations groups of Young Turks grew up, believing that their   15
countries could successfully take on the West only if they adopted Western culture, institutions, and even clothing, for all these ingredients were somehow involved in the production of Western technology. As early as the 1840s, Chinese intellectuals were beginning to modify the ancient view that China was

in all respects the greatest civilization in the world. The administrator Wei Yüan urged his countrymen to "learn the superior technology of the barbarians in order to control them." But the required changes could not be confined to the technical realm. Effectiveness in technology is the outcome of an entire social system. "Since we were knocked out by cannon balls," wrote M. Chiang, "naturally we became interested in them, thinking that by learning to make them we could strike back. From studying cannon balls we came to mechanical inventions which in turn lead to political reforms, which lead us again to the political philosophies of the West." The republican revolution of 1911 attempted to modernize China, but her subjection to the West continued until another Young Turk, Mao Tse-tung, applied that alternative brand of Westernization: communism, though in a unique adaptation.

The Japanese were forced to open their border to Western goods in 1853,   16
after a couple of centuries of total isolation. They had to rethink fast in order to survive. From 1867, the Meiji rulers Westernized Japan with astonishing speed, adopting Western science, technology, and even manners: short haircuts became the rule, ballroom dancing caught on, and *moningku* with *haikara* (morning coats and high collars) were worn. The transformation was so successful that by the 1970s the Japanese were trouncing the West at its own game. But they had won their economic independence at the cost of losing their cultural autonomy.

Turkey, defeated in the First World War, her immense empire in fragments,   17
set about transforming herself under that compulsive and ruthless Westernizer, Kemal Atatürk. The Arabic script was abolished and replaced with the Roman alphabet. Kemal's strange exploits as a hatter will probably stand as the symbol of Westernization carried to absurd lengths. His biographer, Lord Kinross, relates that while traveling in the West as a young man, the future president had smarted under Western insults and condescension about the Turkish national hat, the fez. Later, he made the wearing of the fez a criminal offense. "The people of the Turkish republic," he said in a speech launching the new policy, "must prove that they are civilized and advanced persons in their outward respect also. . . . A civilized, international dress is worthy and appropriate for our nation and we will wear it. Boots or shoes on our feet, trousers on our legs, shirt and tie, jacket and waistcoat—and, of course, to complete these, a cover with a brim on our heads. I want to make this clear. This head covering is called a hat.

Questions for Discussion

1. What countries are included under the terms "the West" and "the Third World"?

2. What is cultural imperialism? Why is it "insidious" (Paragraph 8)? How is it different than colonialism?

3. What is Harrison's opinion of the West's influence in the Third World?

4. How does the opening scene lead to the rest of the essay?

5. How would you describe Harrison's tone? What language creates this tone?

6. In this cause-and-effect essay, what causes what?

7. How does Harrison's background explain his stance on his subject?

Questions for Reflection and Writing

1. After a first reading, brainstorm a list of questions you have about the essay, or create a running list of questions as you read. Respond to one of your own questions or use the questions to contribute to class discussion.

2. How did the term "Third World" come about? Research the origins of this term and how the term is used to develop government policy. Look into one Third World country's history and relationship with the West.

3. Trace one country's colonization of another country. Relate what you find to what Harrison says.

Chapter 5
WORK, BUSINESS, AND ECONOMICS

Karl Marx was born in 1818 in Trier, Prussia. He began studying law at the University of Bonn at the age of seventeen, but he soon transferred to the University of Berlin, where he became interested in philosophy. In 1841 he received his doctorate in philosophy from the University of Jena. Unable to get a teaching position because of his association with the politically radical Young Hegelians, Marx in 1842 became editor of the *Rhenish Gazette*, a liberal newspaper in the Rhineland. When the paper was closed down by the Prussian government the following year, Marx moved to Paris to take a job as coeditor of a new socialist publication, the *German-French Annals*. There he met Friedrich Engels, a German socialist and fellow Young Hegelian who was to become his lifelong friend and collaborator. The *Annals* was soon shut down by the authorities, and Marx was expelled from Paris in 1844. He moved to Brussels, Belgium, where he worked to promote communism. In 1849 he settled in London, where he studied capitalism and helped to found the International Workingmen's Association (later known as the First International). Marx died in London in 1883.

Marx's works include *Economic and Philosophic Manuscripts of 1844* (unfinished essays, first published in 1932), *The German Ideology* (coauthored with Engels; written in 1845, first published in full in 1932), *Manifesto of the Communist Party* (coauthored with Engels; 1848), *A Contribution to the Critique of Political Economy* (1859), and *Capital* (vol. 1, 1867; vols. 2 and 3 [unfinished], edited and published by Engels, 1885 and 1894).

Our readings are excerpts from two of the essays in the *Economic and Philosophic Manuscripts of 1844*. In "Estranged Labor," Marx explains how capitalism (the system of "political economy" described by Adam Smith and others, based on private ownership of the means of production) causes alienation (estrangement). Under capitalism, workers do not labor as a way to express themselves and to contribute to the human community; they work only to get enough money to survive. Workers put part of themselves into their products, but the capitalist owners take the products away, making the products alien (foreign, strange) to the workers. Marx shows how this alienation from the product of labor leads to alienation in the act of production, alienation from the human species, and alienation of human beings from one another.

In "The Meaning of Human Requirements," Marx explains how capitalists create artificial human needs in order to sell products and thus profit from their fellow human beings. True human needs, meanwhile, go unfulfilled. Marx criticizes capitalism for placing value on what a person *has* rather than on what he or she *is*.

Economic and Philosophic Manuscripts of 1844

Karl Marx

Estranged Labor

We have proceeded from the premises of political economy. We have accepted   1
its language and its laws. We presupposed private property,[1] the separation of
labor, capital and land, and of wages, profit of capital and rent of land—likewise

Karl Marx, excerpts from *Economics and Philosophic Manuscripts of 1844*, edited by Dirk J. Struik. Translated by Martin Mulligan. Pages 106 (part), 107 (part), 108–115, 116 (part), 118 (part), 147 (part), 148 (part), 149 (part), 150 (part), 151 (part), 152 (part), 154 (part), 155 (part), 240 (part). Copyright © 1964. Used by permission of International Publishers Co.

division of labor, competition, the concept of exchangevalue, etc. On the basis of political economy itself, in its own words, we have shown that the worker sinks to the level of a commodity and becomes indeed the most wretched of commodities; that the wretchedness of the worker is in inverse proportion to the power and magnitude of his production; that the necessary result of competition is the accumulation of capital in a few hands, and thus the restoration of monopoly in a more terrible form; and that finally the distinction between capitalist and land rentier,[2] like that between the tiller of the soil and the factory worker, disappears and that the whole of society must fall apart into the two classes—the property *owners* and the propertyless *workers*. . . .

The worker becomes all the poorer the more wealth he produces, the more 2 his production increases in power and size. The worker becomes an ever cheaper commodity the more commodities he creates. With the *increasing value* of the world of things proceeds in direct proportion the *devaluation* of the world of men. Labor produces not only commodities: it produces itself and the worker as a *commodity*—and this in the same general proportion in which it produces commodities.

This fact expresses merely that the object which labor produces—labor's 3 product—confronts it as *something alien*, as a *power independent* of the producer. The product of labor is labor which has been embodied in an object, which has become material: it is the *objectification*[3] of labor. Labor's realization is its objectification. In the sphere of political economy this realization of labor appears as *loss of realization*[4] for the workers; objectification as *loss of the object* and *bondage to it*; appropriation as *estrangement*, as *alienation*.

So much does labor's realization appear as loss of realization that the work- 4 er loses realization to the point of starving to death. So much does objectification appear as loss of the object that the worker is robbed of the objects most necessary not only for his life but for his work. Indeed, labor itself becomes an object which he can obtain only with the greatest effort and with the most irregular interruptions. So much does the appropriation of the object appear as estrangement that the more objects the worker produces, the less he can possess and the more he falls under the sway of his product, capital.

All these consequences result from the fact that the worker is related to the 5 *product of his labor* as to an *alien* object. For on this premise it is clear that the more the worker spends himself, the more powerful becomes the alien world of objects which he creates over and against himself, the poorer he himself—his inner world—becomes, the less belongs to him as his own. It is the same in religion. The more man puts into God, the less he retains in himself. The worker puts his life into the object; but now his life no longer belongs to him but to the object. Hence, the greater this activity, the greater is the worker's lack of objects. Whatever the product of his labor is, he is not. Therefore the greater this product, the less is he himself. The *alienation* of the worker in his product means not only that his labor becomes an object, an *external* existence, but that it exists *outside him,* independently, as something alien to him, and that it becomes a power on its own confronting him. It means that the life which he has conferred on the object confronts him as something hostile and alien.

Let us now look more closely at the *objectification,* at the production of the worker; and in it at the *estrangement,* the *loss* of the object, of his product.   6

The worker can create nothing without *nature,* without the *sensuous*[5] *external world.* It is the material on which his labor is realized, in which it is active, from which and by means of which it produces.   7

But just as nature provides labor with the *means of life* in the sense that labor cannot *live* without objects on which to operate, on the other hand, it also provides the *means of life* in the more restricted sense, that is, the means for the physical subsistence of the *worker* himself.   8

Thus the more the worker by his labor *appropriates* the external world, hence sensuous nature, the more he deprives himself of *means of life* in a double manner: first, in that the sensuous external world more and more ceases to be an object belonging to his labor—to be his labor's *means of life;* and secondly, in that it more and more ceases to be *means of life* in the immediate sense, means for the physical subsistence of the worker.   9

In both respects, therefore, the worker becomes a slave of his object, first, in that he receives an *object of labor,* that is, in that he receives *work;* and secondly, in that he receives *means of subsistence.* Therefore, it enables him to exist, first as a *worker,* and second as a *physical subject.* The height of this bondage is that it is only as a *worker* that he continues to maintain himself as a *physical subject,* and that it is only as a *physical subject* that he is a *worker.*   10

(The laws of political economy express the estrangement of the worker in his object thus: the more the worker produces, the less he has to consume; the more values he creates, the more valueless, the more unworthy he becomes; the better formed his product, the more deformed becomes the worker; the more civilized his object, the more barbarous becomes the worker; the more powerful labor becomes, the more powerless becomes the worker; the more ingenious   11 labor becomes, the less ingenious becomes the worker and the more he becomes nature's bondsman.)

Political economy conceals the estrangement inherent in the nature of labor by not   12
considering the direct relationship between the worker (labor) and production. It is true that labor produces for the rich wonderful things—but for the worker it produces privation. It produces palaces—but for the worker, hovels. It produces beauty—but for the worker, deformity. It replaces labor by machines, but it throws a section of the workers back to a barbarous type of labor, and it turns the other workers into machines. It produces intelligence—but for the worker stupidity, cretinism.

The direct relationship of labor to its products is the relationship of the worker to   13
the objects of his production. The relationship of the man of means to the objects of production and to production itself is only a *consequence* of this first relationship—and confirms it. We shall consider this other aspect later.

When we ask, then, what is the essential relationship of labor we are ask-   14
ing about the relationship of the *worker* to production.

Till now we have been considering the estrangement, the alienation of the   15
worker only in one of its aspects, that is, the worker's *relationship to the products of his labor*. But the estrangement is manifested not only in the result but in the *act of production*, within the *producing activity*, itself. How could the worker come to face the product of his activity as a stranger, were it not that in the very act of production he was estranging himself from himself? The product is after all but the summary of the activity, of production. If then the product of labor is alienation, production itself must be active alienation, the alienation of activity, the activity of alienation. In the estrangement of the object of labor is merely summarized the estrangement, the alienation, in the activity of labor itself.

What, then, constitutes the alienation of labor?   16

First, the fact that labor is *external* to the worker—that is, it does not belong   17
to his essential being; that in his work, therefore, he does not affirm himself but denies himself, does not feel content but unhappy, does not develop freely his physical and mental energy but mortifies his body and ruins his mind. The worker therefore only feels himself outside his work, and in his work feels outside himself. He is at home when he is not working, and when he is working he is not at home. His labor is therefore not voluntary, but coerced; it is *forced labor*. It is therefore not the satisfaction of a need; it is merely a *means* to satisfy needs external to it. Its alien character emerges clearly in the fact that as soon as no physical or other compulsion exists, labor is shunned like the plague. External labor,

labor in which man alienates himself, is a labor of self-sacrifice, of mortification. Lastly, the external character of labor for the worker appears in the fact that it is not his own, but someone else's, that it does not belong to him, that in it he belongs, not to himself, but to another. Just as in religion the spontaneous activity of the human imagination, of the human brain and the human heart, operates independently of the individual—that is, operates on him as an alien, divine or diabolical activity—so is the worker's activity not his spontaneous activity. It belongs to another; it is the loss of his self.

As a result, therefore, man (the worker) only feels himself freely active in   18 his animal functions—eating, drinking, procreating, or at most in his dwelling and in dressing-up, etc.; and in his human functions he no longer feels himself to be anything but an animal. What is animal becomes human and what is human becomes animal.

Certainly eating, drinking, procreating, etc., are also genuinely human   19 functions. But abstractly taken, separated from the sphere of all other human activity and turned into sole and ultimate ends, they are animal functions.

We have considered the act of estranging practical human activity, labor,   20 in two of its aspects. (1) The relation of the worker to the *product of labor* as an alien object exercising power over him. This relation is at the same time the relation to the sensuous external world, to the objects of nature, as an alien world inimically opposed to him. (2) The relation of labor to the *act of production* within the *labor* process. This relation is the relation of the worker to his own activity as an alien activity not belonging to him; it is activity as suffering, strength as weakness, begetting as emasculating, the worker's *own* physical and mental energy, his personal life—indeed, what is life but activity?—as an activity which is turned against him, independent of him and not belonging to him. Here we have *self-estrangement*, as previously we had the estrangement of the *thing*.

We have still a third aspect of *estranged labor* to deduce from the two   21 already considered.

Man is a species being,[6] not only because in practice and in theory he   22 adopts the species as his object (his own as well as those of other things), but— and this is only another way of expressing it—also because he treats himself as the actual, living species; because he treats himself as a *universal* and therefore a free being.

The life of the species, both in man and in animals, consists physically in   23 the fact that man (like the animal) lives on inorganic nature; and the more universal man is compared with an animal, the more universal is the sphere of inorganic nature on which he lives. Just as plants, animals, stones, air, light, etc., constitute theoretically a part of human consciousness, partly as objects of natural science, partly as objects of art—his spiritual inorganic nature, spiritual nourishment which he must first prepare to make palatable and digestible—so also in the realm of practice they constitute a part of human life and human activity. Physically man lives only on these products of nature, whether they appear in the form of food, heating, clothes, a dwelling, etc. The universality of man appears in practice precisely in the universality which makes all nature his *inorganic* body—both inasmuch as nature is (1) his direct means of life and (2) the material, the object, and the instrument of his life activity. Nature is man's *inorganic body*—nature, that is, in so far as it is not itself the human body. Man *lives* on nature—means that nature is his *body*, with which he must remain in continuous interchange if he is not to die. That man's physical and spiritual life is linked to nature means simply that nature is linked to itself, for man is a part of nature.

In estranging from man (1) nature and (2) himself, his own active func-   24
tions, his life activity, estranged labor estranges the *species* from man. It changes for him the *life of the species* into a means of individual life. First it estranges the life of the species, and individual life, and secondly it makes individual life in its abstract form the purpose of the life of the species, likewise in its abstract and estranged form.

Indeed, labor, *life activity, productive life* itself, appears in the first place mere-   25
ly as a *means* of satisfying a need—the need to maintain physical existence. Yet the productive life is the life of the species. It is life-engendering life. The whole character of a species—its species character—is contained in the character of its life activity; and free, conscious activity is man's species character. Life itself appears only as a *means to life*.

The animal is immediately one with its life activity. It does not distinguish   26
itself from it. It is *its life activity*. Man makes his life activity itself the object of his will and of his consciousness. He has conscious life activity. It is not a determination with which he directly merges. Conscious life activity distinguishes man immediately from animal life activity. It is just because of this that he is a species being. Or rather, it is only because he is a species being that he is a conscious being—that is, that his own life is an object for him. Only because of that is his activity free activity. Estranged labor reverses this relationship, so that it is just because man is a conscious being that he makes his life activity, his *essential* being, a mere means to his *existence*.

In creating a *world of objects* by his practical activity, in *his work upon* inor-   27
ganic nature, man proves himself a conscious species being, that is, as a being
that treats the species as its own essential being, or that treats itself as a species
being. Admittedly animals also produce. They build themselves nests, dwellings,
like the bees, beavers, ants, etc. But an animal only produces what it immediately needs for itself or its young. It produces one-sidedly, while man produces universally. It produces only under the dominion of immediate physical need, while
man produces even when he is free from physical need and only truly produces
in freedom therefrom. An animal produces only itself, while man reproduces the
whole of nature. An animal's product belongs immediately to its physical body,
while man freely confronts his product. An animal forms things in accordance
with the standard and the need of the species to which it belongs, while man
knows how to produce in accordance with the standard of every species, and
knows how to apply everywhere the inherent standard to the object. Man therefore also forms things in accordance with the laws of beauty.

It is just in his work upon the objective world, therefore, that man first real-   28
ly proves himself to be a *species being.* This production is his active species life.
Through and because of this production, nature appears as *his* work and his reality. The object of labor is, therefore, the *objectification of man's species life:* for he
duplicates himself not only, as in consciousness, intellectually, but also actively,
in reality, and therefore he contemplates himself in a world that he has created.
In tearing away from man the object of his production, therefore, estranged labor
tears from him his *species life,* his real objectivity as a member of the species, and
transforms his advantage over animals into the disadvantage that his inorganic
body, nature, is taken away from him.

Similarly, in degrading spontaneous, free, activity, to a means, estranged   29
labor makes man's species life a means to his physical existence.

The consciousness which man has of his species is thus transformed by   30
estrangement in such a way that species life becomes for him a means.

Estranged labor turns thus: 31

(3) *Man's species being,* both nature and his spiritual species property, into   32
a being *alien* to him, into a *means* to his *individual existence.* It estranges from man
his own body, as well as external nature and his spiritual essence, his *human*
being.

(4) An immediate consequence of the fact that man is estranged from the   33
product of his labor, from his life activity, from his species being is the *estrangement of man from man.* When man confronts himself, he confronts the *other* man.

What applies to a man's relation to his work, to the product of his labor and to himself, also holds of a man's relation to the other man, and to the other man's labor and object of labor.

In fact, the proposition that man's species nature is estranged from him   34 means that one man is estranged from the other, as each of them is from man's essential nature.

The estrangement of man, and in fact every relationship in which man   35 stands to himself, is first realized and expressed in the relationship in which a man stands to other men.

Hence within the relationship of estranged labor each man views the other   36 in accordance with the standard and the relationship in which he finds himself as a worker.

We took our departure from a fact of political economy—the estrangement   37 of the worker and his production. We have formulated this fact in conceptual terms as *estranged, alienated* labor. We have analyzed this concept—hence analyzing merely a fact of political economy.

Let us now see, further, how the concept of estranged, alienated labor must   38 express and present itself in real life.

If the product of labor is alien to me, if it confronts me as an alien power,   39 to whom, then, does it belong?

If my own activity does not belong to me, if it is an alien, a coerced activ-   40 ity, to whom, then, does it belong?

To a being *other* than myself.   41

Who is this being?   42

The *gods?* To be sure, in the earliest times the principal production (for   43 example, the building of temples, etc., in Egypt, India and Mexico) appears to be in the service of the gods, and the product belongs to the gods. However, the gods on their own were never the lords of labor. No more was *nature.* And what a contradiction it would be if, the more man subjugated nature by his labor and the more the miracles of the gods were rendered superfluous by the miracles of industry, the more man were to renounce the joy of production and the enjoyment of the product in favor of these powers.

The *alien* being, to whom labor and the product of labor belongs, in whose   44 service labor is done and for whose benefit the product of labor is provided, can only be *man* himself.

If the product of labor does not belong to the worker, if it confronts him as   45 an alien power, then this can only be because it belongs to some *man other than the worker.* If the worker's activity is a torment to him, to another it must be *delight* and his life's joy. Not the gods, not nature, but only man himself can be this alien power over man.

We must bear in mind the previous proposition that man's relation to him-   46
self only becomes for him *objective* and *actual* through his relation to the other man. Thus, if the product of his labor, his labor *objectified*, is for him an *alien*, hostile, powerful object independent of him, then his position towards it is such that someone else is master of this object, someone who is alien, hostile, powerful, and independent of him. If his own activity is to him related as an unfree activity, then he is related to it as an activity performed in the service, under the dominion, the coercion, and the yoke of another man.

Every self-estrangement of man, from himself and from nature, appears in   47
the relation in which he places himself and nature to men other than and differentiated from himself. For this reason religious selfestrangement necessarily appears in the relationship of the layman to the priest, or again to a mediator, etc., since we are here dealing with the intellectual world. In the real practical world self-estrangement can only become manifest through the real practical relationship to other men. The medium through which estrangement takes place is itself *practical*. Thus through estranged labor man not only creates his relationship to the object and to the act of production as to men that are alien and hostile to him; he also creates the relationship in which other men stand to his production and to his product, and the relationship in which he stands to these other men. Just as he creates his own production as the loss of his reality, as his punishment; his own product as a loss, as a product not belonging to him; so he creates the domination of the person who does not produce, over production and over the product. Just as he estranges his own activity from himself, so he confers to the stranger an activity which is not his own. . . .

The emancipation of society from private property, etc., from servitude, is   48
expressed in the *political* form of the *emancipation of the workers*; not that *their* emancipation alone is at stake, but because the emancipation of the workers contains universal human emancipation—and it contains this, because the whole of human servitude is involved in the relation of the worker to production, and every relation of servitude is but a modification and consequence of this relation. . . .

The Meaning of Human Requirements

. . . Under private property . . . every person speculates on creating a *new* need in   49
another, so as to drive him to a fresh sacrifice, to place him in a new dependence
and to seduce him into a new mode of *gratification* and therefore economic ruin.
Each tries to establish over the other an *alien power,* so as thereby to find satisfaction of his own selfish need. The increase in the quantity of objects is accompanied by an extension of the realm of the alien powers to which man is subjected, and every new product represents a new *possibility* of mutual swindling and
mutual plundering. Man becomes ever poorer as man, his need for *money*
becomes ever greater if he wants to overpower hostile being. The power of his
money declines so to say in inverse proportion to the increase in the volume of
production: that is, his neediness grows as the *power* of money increases.

The need for money is therefore the true need produced by the modern   50
economic system, and it is the only need which the latter produces. The *quantity* of money becomes to an ever greater degree its sole *effective* quality. Just as it
reduces everything to its abstract form, so it reduces itself in the course of its own
movement to *quantitative* entity. *Excess* and *intemperance* come to be its true
norm. Subjectively, this is partly manifested in that the extension of products
and needs falls into *contriving* and ever-*calculating* subservience to inhuman,
unnatural and *imaginary* appetites. Private property does not know how to
change crude need into *human* need. Its *idealism* is *fantasy, caprice* and *whim;* and
no eunuch flatters his despot more basely or uses more despicable means to stimulate his dulled capacity for pleasure in order to sneak a favor for himself than
does the industrial eunuch (the producer) in order to sneak for himself a few pennies—in order to charm the golden birds out of the pockets of his dearly beloved
neighbors in Christ. He puts himself at the service of the other's most depraved
fancies, plays the pimp between him and his need, excites in him morbid
appetites, lies in wait for each of his weaknesses—all so that he can then demand
the cash for this service of love. (Every product is a bait with which to seduce
away the other's very being, his money; every real and possible need is a weakness which will lead the fly to the gluepot. General exploitation of communal
human nature, just as every imperfection in man, is a bond with heaven—an
avenue giving the priest access to his heart; every need is an opportunity to
approach one's neighbor under the guise of the utmost amiability and to say to
him: Dear friend, I give you what you need, but you know the *conditio sine qua
non;*[7] you know the ink in which you have to sign yourself over to me; in providing for your pleasure, I fleece you.). . .

To [the political economist] every *luxury* of the worker seems to be repre-   51
hensible, and everything that goes beyond the most abstract need—be it in the
realm of passive enjoyment, or a manifestation of activity—seems to him a luxury. Political economy, this science of *wealth*, is therefore simultaneously the science of renunciation, of want, of *saving*—and it actually reaches the point where
it *spares* man the *need* of either fresh air or physical exercise. This science of marvelous industry is simultaneously the science of *asceticism*, and its true ideal is the
ascetic but *extortionate* miser and the *ascetic* but *productive* slave. Its moral ideal is
the *worker* who takes part of his wages to the savings bank, and it has even found
ready-made an abject *art* in which to embody this pet idea: they have presented
it, bathed in sentimentality, on the stage. Thus political economy—despite its
worldly and wanton appearance—is a true moral science, the most moral of all
the sciences. Self-renunciation, the renunciation of life and of all human needs,
is its principal thesis. The less you eat, drink and buy books; the less you go to the
theater, the dance hall, the public house; the less you think, love, theorize, sing,
paint, fence, etc., the more you *save*—the *greater* becomes your treasure which
neither moths nor rust will devour[8]—your *capital*. The less you *are*, the less you
express your own life, the greater is your *alienated* life, the more you *have*, the
greater is the store of your estranged being. Everything which the political econ-
omist takes from you in life and in humanity, he replaces for you in *money* and
in *wealth*; and all the things which you cannot do, your money can do. It can eat
and drink, go to the dance hall and the theater; it can travel, it can appropriate
art, learning, the treasures of the past, political power—all this it *can* appropriate
for you—it can buy all this for you: it is the true *endowment*. Yet being all this, it
is *inclined* to do nothing but create itself, buy itself; for everything else is after all
its servant. And when I have the master I have the servant and do not need his
servant. All passions and all activity must therefore be submerged in *greed*. The
worker may only have enough for him to want to live, and may only want to live
in order to have that. . . .

And you must not only stint the immediate gratification of your senses, as   52
by stinting yourself on food, etc.; you must also spare yourself all sharing of general interest, all sympathy, all trust, etc. If you want to be economical, if you do
not want to be ruined by illusions.

You must make everything that is yours *saleable*, that is, useful. If I ask the   53
political economist: Do I obey economic laws if I extract money by offering my
body for sale, by surrendering it to another's lust? (The factory workers in France
call the prostitution of their wives and daughters the nth working hour, which is

literally correct.) Or am I not acting in keeping with political economy if I sell my friend to the Moroccans? (And the direct sale of men in the form of a trade in conscripts, etc., takes place in all civilized countries.) Then the political econ-omist replies to me: You do not transgress my laws; but see what Cousin Ethics and Cousin Religion have to say about it. My *political economic* ethics and reli-gion have nothing to reproach you with, but—but whom am I now to believe, political economy or ethics? The ethics of political economy is *acquisition*, work, thrift, sobriety—but political economy promises to satisfy my needs. The politi-cal economy of ethics is the opulence of a good conscience, of virtue, etc.; but how can I live virtuously if I do not live? And how can I have a good conscience if I am not conscious of anything? It stems from the very nature of estrangement that each sphere applies to me a different and opposite yardstick— ethics one and political economy another. . . .

In order to abolish the *idea* of private property, the *idea* of communism is completely sufficient. It takes *actual* communist action to abolish actual private property. History will come to it; and this movement, which in *theory* we already know to be a self-transcending movement, will constitute *in actual fact* a very severe and protracted process. But we must regard it as a real advance to have gained beforehand a consciousness of the limited character as well as of the goal of this historical movement—and a consciousness which reaches out beyond it.

When communist *artisans* associate with one another, theory, propaganda, etc., is their first end. But at the same time, as a result of this association, they acquire a new need—the need for society—and what appears as a means becomes an end. In this practical process the most splendid results are to be observed whenever French socialist workers are seen together. Such things as smoking, drinking, eating, etc., are no longer means of contact or means that bring together. Company, association, and conversation, which again has socie-ty as its end, are enough for them; the brotherhood of man is no mere phrase with them, but a fact of life, and the nobility of man shines upon us from their work-hardened bodies.

Notes

1. *private property:* private ownership of the means of producing goods [D.C.A., ed.]
2. *land rentier:* a person who receives income from land [D.C.A.]
3. *objectification:* the process of becoming an object [D.J.S., ed.]

4. *loss of realization (Entwirklichung)*: the loss of reality; diminishment [D.C.A.]

5. *sensuous:* able to be sensed [D.C.A.]

6. *species being:* a being that is conscious of itself not only as an individual but as a member of a particular species. In being conscious of its own species, a species being is also conscious of other species. A species being is also conscious of the distinction between itself and its activity and can freely pursue its own ends. Only human beings are species beings. [D.C.A.]

7. *condition sine qua non:* an indispensable condition (literally, in Latin, "a condition without which not") [D.C.A.]

8. See Matthew 6:19–20. [D.C.A.]

Pulitzer Prize winner Ellen Goodman has written a syndicated column for the *Boston Globe*, where she is an associate editor, since 1972. Her experience as a journalist includes reporting for *Newsweek* and serving as a commentator for the *Today Show*. Among her books are *Turning Point*, *Close to Home* (both published in 1979), *At Large* (1981) and *Value Judgments* (1993). In "Being a Secretary Can Be Hazardous to Your Health," Goodman uses her trademark humor to unmask a very real problem.

Prereading: Questions

1. Have you ever held a job that you found stressful? What was the job? What created the stress?
2. Do you know people whose work has affected their health? In what ways?

Helpful Definitions

token (1)—symbol, sign

cardiogram (1)—curve traced by a cardiograph, which traces heart movements and disorders

syndrome (2)—group of symptoms or pattern of behavior

cardiovascular (3)—involving the heart and blood vessels

prestigious (4)—impressive, distinguished

epidemiologist (4)—specialist dealing with diseases in populations

irony (9)—use of words that express a different meaning from what they appear to mean

sundry (9)—various, assorted

automatons (12)—people or machines who act in a repetitive manner

intrinsically (13)—by nature

Being a Secretary Can Be Hazardous to Your Health

Ellen Goodman

They used to say it with flowers or celebrate it with a somewhat liquid lunch. 1
National Secretaries Week was always good for at least a token of appreciation.

But the way the figures add up now, the best thing a boss can do for a secretary this week is cough up for her cardiogram.

"Stress and the Secretary" has become the hottest new syndrome on the heart circuit.   2

It seems that it isn't those Daring Young Women in their Dress-for-Success Suits who are following men down the cardiovascular trail to ruin. Nor is it the female professionals who are winning their equal place in intensive care units.   3

It is powerlessness and not power that corrupts women's hearts. And clerical workers are the number one victims.   4

In the prestigious Framingham study, Dr. Suzanne Haynes, an epidemiologist with the National Heart, Lung and Blood Institute, found that working women as a whole have no higher rate of heart disease than housewives. But women employed in clerical and sales occupations do. Their coronary disease rates are twice that of other women.   5

"This is not something to ignore," says Dr. Haynes, "since such a high percent of women work at clerical jobs." In fact, 35 percent of all working women, or 18 million of us, hold these jobs.   6

When Dr. Haynes looked into their private lives, she found the women at greatest risk—with a one in five chance of heart disease—were clerical workers with blue-collar husbands, and three or more children. When she then looked at their work lives, she discovered that the ones who actually developed heart disease were those with nonsupportive bosses who hadn't changed jobs very often and who had trouble letting their anger out.   7

In short, being frustrated, dead-ended, without a feeling of control over your life is bad for your health.   8

The irony in all the various and sundry heart statistics is that we now have a weird portrait of the Cardiovascular Fun Couple of the Office: The Type A Boss and his secretary. The male heart disease stereotype is, after all, the Type A aggressive man who always needs to be in control, who lives with a great sense of time urgency . . . and is likely to be a white-collar boss.   9

"The Type A man is trying to be in control. But given the way most businesses are organized there are, in fact, few ways for them to be in control of their jobs," says Dr. Haynes. The only thing the Type A boss can be in control of is his secretary who in turn feels . . . well you get the picture. He's not only getting heart disease, he's giving it.   10

As if all this weren't enough to send you out for the annual three martini 11
lunch, clerical workers are increasingly working for a new Type A boss: the computer.

These days fewer women are sitting in front of bosses with notepads and 12
more are sitting in front of Visual Display Terminals. Word processors, data
processors, microprocessors . . . these are the demanding, time-conscious, new
automatons of automation.

There is nothing intrinsically evil about computers. I am writing this on a 13
VDT and if you try to take it away from me, I will break your arm. But as
Working Women, the national association of office workers, puts it in their
release this week, automation is increasingly producing clerical jobs that are deskilled, down-graded, dead-ended and dissatisfying.

As Karen Nussbaum of the Cleveland office described it, the office of the 14
future may well be the factory of the past. Work on computers is often reduced
to simple, repetitive, monotonous tasks. Workers are often expected to produce
more for no more pay, and there are also reports of a disturbing trend to process-
ing speed-ups and piece-rate pay, and a feeling among clerical workers that their
jobs are computer controlled.

"It's not the machine, but the way it's used by employers," says Working 15
Women's research director, Judith Gregory. Too often, automation's most important product is stress.

Groups, like Working Women, are trying to get clerical workers to organ- 16
ize in what they call "a race against time" so that computers will become their
tools instead of their supervisors.

But in the meantime, if you are 1) a female clerical worker, 2) with a blue- 17
collar husband, 3) with three or more children, 4) in a dead-end job, 5) without
any way to express anger, 6) with a Type A boss, 7) or a Type A computer controlling your work day . . . *you better start jogging.*

Questions On Content

1. In your own words, write out Goodman's main idea (thesis). Where does the
   author state her thesis most clearly?
2. Who does Goodman expect to be the victims of heart disease? Who are
   actually the victims? What causes heart disease in these people?
3. What is a Type A boss? Why does Goodman think that such a boss would
   be damaging to a secretary's health?
4. What is Goodman's opinion of working at a computer?

Questions on Technique

1. Goodman uses humor in her title and introductory paragraph, despite the seriousness of her topic. Why do you think she does this?
2. In what other paragraphs does Goodman use humor?
3. Goodman cites authorities and statistics in her essay. What does this material contribute?
4. What approach does the author take to her concluding paragraph? Does that paragraph bring the essay to a satisfying close? Explain why or why not.

For Further Consideration

1. Are you surprised by the information in the essay? Explain why or why not.
2. Paragraph 9 describes the Type A person in negative terms. What advantages might there be to having a Type A personality?
3. What other jobs have so much powerlessness associated with them that they might cause heart disease?
4. What do you think Karen Nussbaum means when she says in paragraph 14 that "the office of the future may well be the factory of the past"?

Journal Entry

Secretarial work is not the only work that can cause stress. Write a journal entry with the title "Being a _____ Can be Hazardous to Your Health" (you fill in the blank). Explain why the position is stressful.

Collaborative Activity

With some classmates, list the causes of stress among college students. Then list ways to combat the stress.

Writing Topics

1. Tell about a stressful situation you have experienced while working. Explain the nature of the stress and how you dealt with it.
2. Describe a Type A person you know—perhaps a friend, a boss, an instructor, or a relative. Give the person's characteristics and examples of behavior that illustrate those characteristics.
3. Tell about the best or worst job you have had, being sure to explain what you liked or did not like about it.
4. Goodman explains that feeling frustrated and powerless can cause stress. Tell about a time when you felt frustrated and powerless, being sure to explain how you responded to the situation.
5. Tell about the stress in your life, being sure to explain the causes of that stress and how it affects you. (*Cause-and-Effect Analysis*)

The Persistence of Social Inequality
The Uses of Poverty: The Poor Pay All

Herbert J. Gans

Some 20 years ago Robert K. Merton applied the notion of functional analysis to   1
explain the continuing though maligned existence of the urban political machine: if
it continued to exist, perhaps it fulfilled latent—unintended or unrecognized—positive functions. Clearly it did. Merton pointed out how the political machine provided central authority to get things done when a decentralized local government could
not act, humanized the services of the impersonal bureaucracy for fearful citizens,
offered concrete help (rather than abstract law or justice) to the poor, and otherwise
performed services needed or demanded by many people but considered unconventional or even illegal by formal public agencies.

Today, poverty is more maligned than the political machine ever was; yet it,   2
too, is a persistent social phenomenon. Consequently, there may be some merit in
applying functional analysis to poverty, in asking whether it also has positive functions that explain its persistence.

Merton defined functions as "those observed consequences [of a phenomenon]   3
which make for the adaptation or adjustment of a given [social] system." I shall use a
slightly different definition; instead of identifying functions for an entire social system, I shall identify them for the interest groups, socioeconomic classes, and other
population aggregates with shared values that "inhabit" a social system. I suspect that
in a modern heterogeneous society, few phenomena are functional or dysfunctional
for the society as a whole, and that most result in benefits to some groups and costs
to others. Nor are any phenomena indispensable; in most instances, one can suggest
what Merton calls "functional alternatives" or equivalents for them, i.e., other social
patterns or policies that achieve the same positive functions but avoid the dysfunc-
tion. (I shall henceforth abbreviate positive functions as functions and negative func-
tions as dysfunctions. I shall also describe functions and dysfunctions, in the planner's
terminology, as benefits and costs.)

Associating poverty with positive functions seems at first glance unimaginable.   4
Of course, the slumlord and the loan shark are commonly known to profit from the

existence of poverty, but they are viewed as evil men, so their activities are classified among the dysfunctions of poverty. However, what is less often recognized, at least by the conventional wisdom, is that poverty also makes possible the existence or expansion of respectable professions and occupations; for example, penology, criminology, social work, and public health. More recently, the poor have provided jobs for professional and paraprofessional "poverty warriors," and for journalists and social scientists, this author included, who have supplied the information demanded by the revival of public interest in poverty.

Clearly, then, poverty and the poor may well satisfy a number of positive func-   5
tions for many nonpoor groups in American society. I shall describe 13 such functions—economic, social, and political—that seem to me most significant.

The Functions of Poverty

First, the existence of poverty ensures that society's "dirty work" will be done. Every   6
society has such work: physically dirty or dangerous, temporary, dead-end and underpaid, undignified, and menial jobs. Society can fill these jobs by paying higher wages than for "clean" work, or it can force people who have no other choice to do the dirty work—and at low wages. In America, poverty functions to provide a low-wage labor pool that is willing—or, rather, unable to be un-willing—to perform dirty work at low cost. Indeed, this function of the poor is so important that in some Southern states, welfare payments have been cut off during the summer months when the poor are needed to work in the fields. Moreover, much of the debate about the Negative Income Tax and the Family Assistance Plan has concerned their impact on the work incentive, by which is actually meant the incentive of the poor to do the needed dirty work if the wages therefrom are no larger than the income grant. Many economic activities that involve dirty work depend on the poor for their existence: restaurants, hospitals, parts of the garment industry, and "truck farming," among others, could not persist in their present form without the poor.

Second, because the poor are required to work at low wages, they subsidize a   7
variety of economic activities that benefit the affluent. For example, domestics subsidize the upper middle and upper classes, making life easier for their employers and freeing affluent women for a variety of professional, cultural, civic, and partying activities. Similarly, because the poor pay a higher proportion of their income in property and sales taxes, among others, they subsidize many state and local governmental services that benefit more affluent groups. In addition, the poor support innovation in medical practice as patients in teaching and research hospitals and as guinea pigs in medical experiments.

Third, poverty creates jobs for a number of occupations and professions that   8
serve or "service" the poor, or protect the rest of society from them. As already noted,
penology would be minuscule without the poor, as would the police. Other activities
and groups that flourish because of the existence of poverty are the numbers game,
the sale of heroin and cheap wines and liquors, pentecostal ministers, faith healers,
prostitutes, pawn shops, and the peacetime army, which recruits its enlisted men
mainly from among the poor.

Fourth, the poor buy goods others do not want and thus prolong the econom-   9
ic usefulness of such goods—day-old bread, fruit and vegetables that would otherwise
have to be thrown out, secondhand clothes, and deteriorating automobiles and buildings. They also provide incomes for doctors, lawyers, teachers, and others who are
too old, poorly trained, or incompetent to attract more affluent clients.

In addition to economic functions, the poor perform a number of social functions.   10

Fifth, the poor can be identified and punished as alleged or real deviants in   11
order to uphold the legitimacy of conventional norms. To justify the desirability of
hard work, thrift, honesty, and monogamy, for example, the defenders of these norms
must be able to find people who can be accused of being lazy, spendthrift, dishonest,
and promiscuous. Although there is some evidence that the poor are about as moral
and law-abiding as anyone else, they are more likely than middle-class transgressors
to be caught and punished when they participate in deviant acts. Moreover, they
lack the political and cultural power to correct the stereotypes that other people hold
of them and thus continue to be thought of as lazy, spendthrift, etc., by those who
need living proof that moral deviance does not pay.

Sixth, and conversely, the poor offer vicarious participation to the rest of the   12
population in the uninhibited sexual, alcoholic, and narcotic behavior in which they
are alleged to participate and which, being freed from the constraints of affluence,
they are often thought to enjoy more than the middle classes. Thus many people,
some social scientists included, believe that the poor not only are more given to
uninhibited behavior (which may be true, although it is often motivated by despair
more than by lack of inhibition) but derive more pleasure from it than affluent people (which research by Lee Rainwater, Walter Miller, and others shows to be patently untrue). However, whether the poor actually have more sex and enjoy it more is
irrelevant; so long as middle-class people believe this to be true, they can participate
in it vicariously when instances are reported in factual or fictional form.

Seventh, the poor also serve a direct cultural function when culture created by   13
or for them is adopted by the more affluent. The rich often collect artifacts from
extinct folk cultures of poor people; and almost all Americans listen to the blues,

Negro spirituals, and country music, which originated among the Southern poor. Recently they have enjoyed the rock styles that were born, like the Beatles, in the slums; and in the last year, poetry written by ghetto children has become popular in literary circles. The poor also serve as culture heroes, particularly, of course, to the left; but the hobo, the cowboy, the hipster, and the mythical prostitute with a heart of gold have performed this function for a variety of groups.

Eighth, poverty helps to guarantee the status of those who are not poor. In   14 every hierarchical society someone has to be at the bottom; but in American society, in which social mobility is an important goal for many and people need to know where they stand, the poor function as a reliable and relatively permanent measuring rod for status comparisons. This is particularly true for the working class, whose politics is influenced by the need to maintain status distinctions between themselves and the poor, much as the aristocracy must find ways of distinguishing itself from the *nouveaux riches*.

Ninth, the poor also aid the upward mobility of groups just above them in the   15 class hierarchy. Thus a goodly number of Americans have entered the middle class through the profits earned from the provision of goods and services in the slums, including illegal or nonrespectable ones that upper-class and upper-middle-class businessmen shun because of their low prestige. As a result, members of almost every immigrant group have financed their upward mobility by providing slum housing, entertainment, gambling, narcotics, etc., to later arrivals—most recently to blacks and Puerto Ricans.

Tenth, the poor help to keep the aristocracy busy, thus justifying its continued   16 existence. "Society" uses the poor as clients of settlements houses and beneficiaries of charity affairs; indeed, the aristocracy must have the poor to demonstrate its superiority over other elites who devote themselves to earning money.

Eleventh, the poor, being powerless, can be made to absorb the costs of change   17 and growth in American society. During the nineteenth century, they did the backbreaking work that built the cities; today, they are pushed out of their neighborhoods to make room for "progress." Urban renewal projects to hold middle-class taxpayers in the city and expressways to enable suburbanites to commute downtown have typically been located in poor neighborhoods, since no other group will allow itself to be displaced. For the same reason, universities, hospitals, and civic centers also expand into land occupied by the poor. The major costs of the industrialization of agriculture have been borne by the poor, who are pushed off the land without recompense; and they have paid a large share of the human cost of the growth of American power overseas, for they have provided many of the foot soldiers for Vietnam and other wars.

Twelfth, the poor facilitate and stabilize the American political process.   18 Because they vote and participate in politics less than other groups, the political system is often free to ignore them.   Moreover, since they can rarely support Republicans, they often provide the Democrats with a captive constituency that has no other place to go. As a result, the Democrats can count on their votes, and be more responsive to voters—for example, the white working class—who might otherwise switch to the Republicans.

Thirteenth, the role of the poor in upholding conventional norms (see the fifth   19 point, above) also has a significant political function. An economy based on the ideology of laissez-faire requires a deprived population that is allegedly unwilling to work or that can be considered inferior because it must accept charity or welfare in order to survive. Not only does the alleged moral deviancy of the poor reduce the moral pressures on the present political economy to eliminate poverty but socialist alternatives can be made to look quite unattractive if those who will benefit most from them can be described as lazy, spendthrift, dishonest, and promiscuous.

The Alternatives

I have described 13 of the more important functions poverty and the poor satisfy in   20 American society, enough to support the functionalist thesis that poverty, like any other social phenomenon, survives in part because it is useful to society or some of its parts. This analysis is not intended to suggest that because it is often functional, poverty should exist, or that it must exist. For one thing, poverty has many more dysfunctions than functions; for another, it is possible to suggest functional alternatives.

For example, society's dirty work could be done without poverty, either by   21 automation or by paying "dirty workers" decent wages. Nor is it necessary for the poor to subsidize the many activities they support through their low-wage jobs. This would, however, drive up the costs of these activities, which would result in higher prices to their customers and clients. Similarly, many of the professionals who flourish because of the poor could be given other roles. Social workers could provide counseling to the affluent, as they prefer to do anyway; and the police could devote themselves to traffic and organized crime. Other roles would have to be found for badly trained or incompetent professionals now relegated to serving the poor, and someone else would have to pay their salaries. Fewer penologists would be employable, however. And pentecostal religion could probably not survive without the poor, nor would parts of the second- and third-hand-goods market. And in many cities, "used" housing that no one else wants would then have to be torn down at public expense.

Alternatives for the cultural functions of the poor could be found more easily   22 and cheaply. Indeed, entertainers, hippies, and adolescents are already serving as the deviants needed to uphold traditional morality and as devotees of orgies to "staff" the fantasies of vicarious participation.

The status functions of the poor are another matter. In a hierarchical society,   23 some people must be defined as inferior to everyone else with respect to a variety of attributes, but they need not be poor in the absolute sense. One could conceive of a society in which the "lower class," though last in the pecking order, received 75 percent of the median income, rather than 15-40 percent, as is now the case. Needless to say, this would require considerable income redistribution.

The contribution the poor make to the upward mobility of the groups that pro-   24 vide them with goods and services could also be maintained without the poor's having such low incomes. However, it is true that if the poor were more affluent, they would have access to enough capital to take over the provider role, thus competing with, and perhaps rejecting, the "outsiders." (Indeed, owing in part to anti-poverty programs, this is already happening in a number of ghettos, where white storeowners are being replaced by blacks.) Similarly, if the poor were more affluent, they would make less willing clients for upper-class philanthropy, although some would still use settlement houses to achieve upward mobility, as they do now. Thus "Society" could continue to run its philanthropic activities.

The political functions of the poor would be more difficult to replace. With   25 increased affluence the poor would probably obtain more political power and be more active politically. With higher incomes and more political power, the poor would be likely to resist paying the costs of growth and change. Of course, it is possible to imagine urban renewal and highway projects that properly reimbursed the displaced people, but such projects would then become considerably more expensive, and many might never be built. This, in turn, would reduce the comfort and convenience of those who now benefit from urban renewal and expressways. Finally, hippies could serve also as more deviants to justify the existing political economy—as they already do. Presumably, however, if poverty were eliminated there would be fewer attacks on that economy.

In sum, then, many of the functions served by the poor could be replaced if   26 poverty were eliminated, but almost always at higher costs to others, particularly more affluent others. Consequently, a functional analysis must conclude that poverty persists not only because it fulfills a number of positive functions but also because many of the functional alternatives to poverty would be quite dysfunctional for the affluent members of society. A functional analysis thus ultimately arrives at much the same conclusions as radical sociology, except that radical thinkers treat as manifest what I describe as latent: that social phenomena that are functional for affluent or powerful groups and dysfunctional for poor or powerless ones persist; that when the elimination of such phenomena through functional alternatives would generate dysfunctions for the affluent or powerful, they will continue to persist; and that phenomena like poverty can be eliminated only when they become dysfunctional for the affluent or powerful, or when the powerless can obtain enough power to change society.

Jonathan Swift (1667–1745) was born in Dublin, Ireland; studied at Trinity College, Dublin; and took an M.A. at Oxford. He stayed for a while in England, where he was secretary to the diplomat Sir William Temple. Ordained an Anglican priest in 1695, he was eventually made Dean of St. Patrick's Cathedral in Dublin in 1714. Before 1714, he spent his time in both England and Ireland, but after the death of Queen Anne in 1714 (and after the fall of the Tory government that same year), Swift traveled only twice more to England. In Ireland he wrote many essays defending the Irish against English oppression. "A Modest Proposal" is one of a series of satirical essays that exposed English cruelties. Of course, his position as Dean forced Swift to publish his works anonymously, but he is now hailed for his satires, the most famous of which are *A Tale of a Tub* (1704), a vicious satire on government abuses in education and religion, and *Gulliver's Travels* (1726).

A Modest Proposal

For Preventing the Children of Poor People in Ireland from Being a Burden to Their Parents or Country, and for Making Them Beneficial to the Public

Jonathan Swift

It is a melancholy object to those who walk through this great town or travel in   1
the country, when they see the streets, the roads, and cabin doors crowded with beggars of the female sex, followed by three, four, or six children, all in rags and importuning every passenger for an alms. These mothers, instead of being able to work for their honest livelihood, are forced to employ all their time in strolling to beg sustenance for their helpless infants, who, as they grow up, either turn thieves for want of work, or leave their dear native country to fight for the Pretender in Spain, or sell themselves to the Barbadoes.

I think it is agreed by all parties that this prodigious number of children in   2
the arms, or on the backs, or at the heels of their mothers, and frequently of their fathers, is in the present deplorable state of the kingdom a very great additional grievance; and therefore whoever could find out a fair, cheap, and easy method of making these children sound and useful members of the commonwealth would deserve so well of the public as to have his statue set up for a preserver of the nation.

But my intention is very far from being confined to provide only for the   3
children of professed beggars; it is of a much greater extent, and shall take in the
whole number of infants at a certain age who are born of parents in effect as little able to support them as those who demand our charity in the streets.

As to my own part, having turned my thoughts for many years upon this   4
important subject, and maturely weighed the several schemes of other projectors,
I have always found them grossly mistaken in their computation. It is true a child
just dropped from its dam may be supported by her milk for a solar year with little other nourishment, at most not above the value of two shillings, which the
mother may certainly get, or the value in scraps, by her lawful occupation of begging; and it is exactly at one year old that I propose to provide for them in such
a manner as instead of being a charge upon their parents or the parish, or wanting food and raiment for the rest of their lives, they shall, on the contrary, contribute to the feeding and partly to the clothing of many thousands.

There is likewise another great advantage in my scheme, that it will pre-   5
vent those voluntary abortions, and that horrid practice of women murdering
their bastard children, alas! too frequent among us, sacrificing the poor innocent
babes, I doubt, more to avoid the expense than the shame, which would move
tears and pity in the most savage and inhuman breast. The number of souls in
this kingdom being usually reckoned one million and a half, of these I calculate
there may be about two hundred thousand couples whose wives are breeders;
from which number I subtract thirty thousand couples who are able to maintain
their own children, although I apprehend there cannot be so many, under the
present distress of the kingdom; but this being granted, there will remain an hundred and seventy thousand breeders. I again subtract fifty thousand for those
women who miscarry, or whose children die by accident or disease within the
year. There only remain an hundred and twenty thousand children of poor parents annually born. The question therefore is, how this number shall be reared
and provided for, which, as I have already said, under the present situation of
affairs is utterly impossible by all the methods hitherto proposed. For we can neither employ them in handicraft or agriculture; we neither build houses (I mean
in the country) nor cultivate land: they can very seldom pick up a livelihood by
stealing till they arrive at six years old, except where they are of towardly parts;
although I confess they learn the rudiments much earlier, during which time they
can, however, be properly looked upon only as probationers, as I have been
informed by a principal gentleman in the county of Cavan, who protested to me

that he never knew above one or two instances under the age of six, even in a part of the kingdom so renowned for the quickest proficiency in that art.

I am assured by our merchants that a boy or girl before twelve years old is   7
no salable commodity; and even when they come to this age they will not yield above three pounds or three pounds and half-a-crown at most on the Exchange; which cannot turn to account either to the parents or the kingdom, the charge of nutriment and rags having been at least four times that value.

I shall now therefore humbly propose my own thoughts, which I hope will   8
not be liable to the least objection.

I have been assured by a very knowing American of my acquaintance in   9
London that a young healthy child well nursed is at a year old a most delicious, nourishing, and wholesome food, whether stewed, roasted, baked, or boiled; and I make no doubt that it will equally serve in a fricassee or a ragout.

I do therefore humbly offer it to public consideration that of the hundred   10
and twenty thousand children already computed, twenty thousand may be reserved for breed, whereof only one-fourth part to be males, which is more than we allow to sheep, black cattle or swine; and my reason is that these children are seldom the fruits of marriage, a circumstance not much regarded by our savages; therefore one male will be sufficient to serve four females. That the remaining hundred thousand may at a year old be offered in sale to the persons of quality and fortune through the kingdom, always advising the mother to let them suck plentifully in the last month, so as to render them plump and fat for a good table. A child will make two dishes at an entertainment for friends; and when the family dines alone, the fore or hind quarter will make a reasonable dish, and seasoned with a little pepper or salt will be very good boiled on the fourth day, especially in winter.

I have reckoned upon a medium that a child just born will weigh twelve   11
pounds, and in a solar year if tolerably nursed increaseth to twenty-eight pounds.

I grant this food will be somewhat dear, and therefore very proper for land-   12
lords, who, as they have already devoured most of the parents, seem to have the best title to the children.

Infants' flesh will be in season throughout the year, but more plentiful in   13
March, and a little before and after; for we are told by a grave author, an eminent French physician, that fish being a prolific diet, there are more children born in Roman Catholic countries about nine months after Lent than at any other season; therefore reckoning a year after Lent, the markets will be more glutted than usual, because the number of popish infants is at least three to one in this king-

dom; and therefore it will have one other collateral advantage, by lessening the number of Papists among us.

I have already computed the charge of nursing a beggar's child (in which   14 list I reckon all cottagers, laborers, and four-fifths of the farmers) to be about two shillings per annum, rags included; and I believe no gentleman would repine to give ten shillings for the carcass of a good fat child, which, as I have said, will make four dishes of excellent nutritive meat, when he hath only some particular friend or his own family to dine with him. Thus the squire will learn to be a good landlord, and grow popular among his tenants; the mother will have eight shillings net profit, and be fit for work till she produces another child.

Those who are more thrifty (as I must confess the times require) may flay   15 the carcass; the skin of which artificially dressed will make admirable gloves for ladies, and summer boots for fine gentlemen.

As to our city of Dublin, shambles may be appointed for this purpose in the   16 most convenient parts of it, and butchers we may be assured will not be wanting; although I rather recommend buying the children alive, and dressing them hot from the knife, as we do roasting pigs.

A very worthy person, a true lover of his country, and whose virtues I high-   17 ly esteem, was lately pleased, in discoursing on this matter, to offer a refinement upon my scheme. He said that many gentlemen of this kingdom, having of late destroyed their deer, he conceived that the want of venison might be well sup- plied by the bodies of young lads and maidens, not exceeding fourteen years of age nor under twelve, so great a number of both sexes in every country being now ready to starve for want of work and service: and these to be disposed of by their parents, if alive, or otherwise by their nearest relations. But with due deference to so excellent a friend and so deserving a patriot, I cannot be altogether in his sentiments. For as to the males, my American acquaintance assured me from fre- quent experience that their flesh was generally tough and lean, like that of our schoolboys, by continual exercise, and their taste disagreeable; and to fatten them would not answer the charge. Then as to the females, it would, I think, with humble submission, be a loss to the public, because they soon would become breeders themselves: and besides, it is not improbable that some scrupu- lous people might be apt to censure such a practice (although indeed very unjust- ly) as a little bordering upon cruelty; which, I confess, hath always been with me the strongest objection against any project, how well soever intended.

But in order to justify my friend, he confessed that this expedient was put   18 into his head by the famous Psalmanazar, a native of the island Formosa, who came from thence to London above twenty years ago, and in conversation told my friend that in his country when any young person happened to be put to death, the executioner sold the carcass to persons of quality as a prime dainty, and that in his time the body of a plump girl of fifteen, who was crucified for an attempt to poison the emperor, was sold to his Imperial Majesty's prime minister of state, and other great mandarins of the court, in joints from the gibbet, at four hundred crowns. Neither indeed can I deny that if the same use were made of several plump young girls in this town, who, without one single groat to their fortunes, cannot stir abroad without a chair, and appear at the playhouse and assemblies in foreign fineries, which they never will pay for, the kingdom would not be the worse.

Some persons of a desponding spirit are in great concern about that vast   19
number of poor people, who are aged, diseased, or maimed, and I have been desired to employ my thoughts what course may be taken to ease the nation of so grievous an encumbrance. But I am not in the least pain upon that matter, because it is very well known that they are every day dying and rotting, by cold and famine, and filth and vermin, as fast as can be reasonably expected. And as to the younger laborers, they are now in almost as hopeful a condition. They cannot get work, and consequently pine away for want of nourishment, to a degree that if at any time they are accidentally hired to common labor, they have not strength to perform it; and thus the country and themselves are happily delivered from the evils to come.

I have too long digressed, and therefore shall return to my subject. I think   20
the advantages by the proposal which I have made are obvious and many, as well as of the highest importance.

For first, as I have already observed, it would greatly lessen the number of   21
Papists, with whom we are yearly overrun, being the principal breeders of the nation as well as our most dangerous enemies; and who stay at home on purpose with a design to deliver the kingdom to the Pretender, hoping to take their advantage by the absence of so many good Protestants, who have chosen rather to leave their country than stay at home and pay tithes against their conscience to an Episcopal curate.

Secondly, the poorer tenants will have something valuable of their own,   22
which by law may be made liable to distress, and help to pay their landlord's rent; their corn and cattle being already seized, and money a thing unknown.

Thirdly, whereas the maintenance of an hundred thousand children, from   23
two years old and upwards, cannot be computed at less than ten shillings apiece

per annum, the nation's stock will be thereby increased fifty thousand pounds per annum, besides the profit of a new dish introduced to the tables of all gentlemen of fortune in the kingdom who have any refinement in taste. And the money will circulate among ourselves, the goods being entirely of our own growth and manufacture.

Fourthly, the constant breeders, besides the gain of eight shillings sterling per annum by the sale of their children, will be rid of the charge of maintaining them after the first year. 24

Fifthly, this food would likewise bring great custom to taverns, where the vintners will certainly be so prudent as to procure the best receipts for dressing it to perfection, and consequently have their houses frequented by all the fine gentlemen, who justly value themselves upon their knowledge in good eating; and a skillful cook, who understands how to oblige his guests, will contrive to make it as expensive as they please. 25

Sixthly, this would be a great inducement to marriage, which all wise nations have either encouraged by rewards or enforced by laws and penalties. It would increase the care and tenderness of mothers toward their children, when they were sure of a settlement for life to the poor babes, provided in some sort by the public, to their annual profit instead of expense. We should see an honest emulation among the married women, which of them could bring the fattest child to the market. Men would become as fond of their wives during the time of their pregnancy as they are now of their mares in foal, their cows in calf, or sows when they are ready to farrow; nor offer to beat or kick them (as is too frequent a practice) for fear of miscarriage. 26

Many other advantages might be enumerated. For instance, the addition of some thousand carcasses in our exportation of barreled beef, the propagation of swine's flesh, and improvement in the art of making good bacon, so much wanted among us by the great destruction of pigs, too frequent at our tables, and are no way comparable in taste or magnificence to a well-grown, fat yearling child, which roasted whole will make a considerable figure at a lord mayor's feast, or any other public entertainment. But this and many others I omit, being studious of brevity. 27

Supposing that one thousand families in this city would be constant customers for infants' flesh, besides others who might have it at merry meetings, particularly weddings and christenings, I compute that Dublin would take off annually about twenty thousand carcasses, and the rest of the kingdom (where probably they will be sold somewhat cheaper) the remaining eighty thousand. 28

I can think of no one objection that will possibly be raised against this pro-   29
posal, unless it should be urged that the number of people will be thereby much
lessened in the kingdom. This I freely own, and it was indeed one principal
design in offering it to the world. I desire the reader will observe that I calculate
my remedy for this one individual kingdom of Ireland, and for no other than ever
was, is, or, I think, ever can be upon earth. Therefore let no man talk to me of
other expedients: of taxing our absentees at five shillings a pound; of using neither clothes nor household furniture except what is of our own growth and manufacture; of utterly rejecting the materials and instruments that promote foreign
luxury; of cursing the expensiveness of pride, vanity, idleness, and gaming in our
women; of introducing a vein of parsimony, prudence, and temperance; of learning to love our country, in the want of which we differ even from Laplanders and
the inhabitants of Topinamboo; of quitting our animosities and factions, nor act
any longer like the Jews, who were murdering one another at the very moment
their city was taken; of being a little cautious not to sell our country and consciences for nothing; of teaching landlords to have at least one degree of mercy
toward their tenants; lastly, of putting a spirit of honesty, industry, and skill into
our shopkeepers, who, if a resolution could now be taken to buy only our native
goods, would immediately unite to cheat and exact upon us in the price, the
measure, and the goodness, nor could ever yet be brought to make one fair proposal of just dealing, though often and earnestly invited to it.

Therefore I repeat, let no man talk to me of these and the like expedients,   30
till he has at least some glimpse of hope that there will be ever some hearty and
sincere attempt to put them in practice.

But as to myself, having been wearied out for many years with offering vain,   31
idle, visionary thoughts, and at length utterly despairing of success, I fortunately
fell upon this proposal, which, as it is wholly new, so it has something solid and
real, of no expense and little trouble, full in our own power, and whereby we can
incur no danger in disobliging England. For this kind of commodity will not bear
exportation, the flesh being of too tender a consistence to admit a long continuance in salt, although perhaps I could name a country which would be glad to
eat up our whole nation without it.

After all, I am not so violently bent upon my own opinion as to reject any   32
offer proposed by wise men, which shall be found equally innocent, cheap, easy,
and effectual. But before something of that kind shall be advanced in contradiction to my scheme, and offering a better, I desire the author or authors will be
pleased maturely to consider two points. First, as things now stand, how they will

be able to find food and raiment for an hundred thousand useless mouths and backs. And secondly, there being a round million of creatures in human figure throughout this kingdom, whose whole subsistence put into a common stock would leave them in debt two millions of pounds sterling, adding those who are beggars by profession to the bulk of farmers, cottagers, and laborers, with their wives and children, who are beggars in effect; I desire those politicians who dislike my overture, and may perhaps be so bold as to attempt an answer, that they will first ask the parents of these mortals whether they would not at this day think it a great happiness to have been sold for food at a year old in the manner I prescribe, and thereby have avoided such a perpetual scene of misfortunes as they have since gone through by the oppression of landlords, the impossibility of paying rent without money or trade, the want of common sustenance, with neither house nor clothes to cover them from the inclemencies of the weather, and the most inevitable prospect of entailing the like or greater miseries upon their breed for ever.

I profess, in the sincerity of my heart, that I have not the least personal   33 interest in endeavoring to promote this necessary work, having no other motive than the public good of my country, by advancing our trade, providing for infants, relieving the poor, and giving some pleasure to the rich. I have no children by which I can propose to get a single penny; the youngest being nine years old, and my wife past child-bearing.

Questions for Discussion

1. Exactly what is Swift proposing? How serious is he?
2. What is the relationship between the poor and the wealthy as depicted in this essay?
3. Who is the speaker in "A Modest Proposal"? In other words, what persona does Swift create to be his "frontman," the imaginary person who is doing the actual proposing in this piece? How is this persona different from Swift himself?
4. Where is Swift being particularly ironic?
5. When you first read the "proposal," where in the piece did you figure out that Swift was not entirely serious? Why do you think Swift would not want you to see his essay as a satire right away?
6. Near the end of the piece Swift does present some realistic solutions. How realistic are these solutions?

7. Why would a writer use such a seemingly absurd approach to write about such a serious problem?

Questions for Reflection and Writing

1. Write your own "Modest Proposal," describing an extreme solution to a current problem in order to satirize the ineffectuality of dealing with the problem.
2. Look up the term "satire" in a dictionary of literary terms. Then analyze Swift's essay, pointing out how it is a satire.
3. Read more about the conditions in Ireland during the time that Swift is writing (1714). To what events is Swift responding? Extend the project by finding out whether Swift's writing had any impact on events.

Benjamin Franklin (1706–1790), natural philosopher, printer, journalist, postmaster, scientist, inventor, pamphleteer, satirist, and diplomat, was one of the Founding Fathers of the United States. Born in Boston to Puritan immigrants, Franklin was apprenticed to his brother James, a printer. He taught himself to write by outlining and paraphrasing essays from the *Spectator*. He wrote anonymously at first so his writing would not be rejected, and taught himself a reading knowledge of German, French, Spanish, Italian, and Latin before launching *Poor Richard's Almanac* in 1732. Franklin retired from printing in 1748 but continued to write for *Poor Richard's Almanac* until 1757.

While Franklin's long and multifaceted career included a few failures—such as a Germanlanguage newspaper, the first bilingual newspaper, and a magazine—he made significant strides in natural philosophy, politics, and literature. His *Proposal for Promoting Useful Knowledge* became the founding document of the American Philosophical Society in 1743. He theorized that lightning was electrical, writing *Experiments and Observations on Electricity* in 1751 and conducting his famous kite experiment in 1752.

He fought in King George's War (1740–1748), after which time he turned to civic duties, accepting appointment as postmaster general of North America in 1753 and publishing more tracts and pamphlets on his political views. Franklin spent a total of 25 years in London and Paris, beginning in 1757. He remained involved in politics as speaker of the Pennsylvania Assembly (1764) and was a prolific writer of letters to editors and humorous essays. His *Autobiography* emphasized the values of industry and frugality as keys to success and moral growth. Three weeks before his death, Franklin composed his brilliant satire "On the Slave-Trade." Though he did own slaves at one time, Franklin had been active in abolitionist publishing since the 1720s. Franklin's style is notable for its logic, simple diction, common sense, direct appeal to the reader, and didactic quality. "The Way to Wealth" is the reprint title of the final copy of *Poor Richard's Almanac*.

The Way to Wealth

Benjamin Franklin

Courteous Reader,

I have heard, that nothing gives an author so great pleasure as to find his works   1
respectfully quoted by others. Judge, then, how much I must have been gratified
by an incident I am going to relate to you. I stopped my horse lately, where a
great number of people were collected at an auction of merchants' goods. The
hour of the sale not being come, they were conversing on the badness of the

times; and one of the company called to a plain, clean, old man, with white locks, "Pray, Father Abraham, what think you of the times? Will not these heavy taxes quite ruin the country? How shall we ever be able to pay them? What would you advise us to?" Father Abraham stood up, and replied, "If you would have my advice, I will give it you in short; for *A word to the wise is enough*, as Poor Richard says." They joined in desiring him to speak his mind, and gathering round him, he proceeded as follows.

"Friends," said he, "the taxes are indeed very heavy, and, if those laid on by   2 the government were the only ones we had to pay, we might more easily discharge them; but we have many others, and much more grievous to some of us. We are taxed twice as much by our idleness, three times as much by our pride, and four times as much by our folly; and from these taxes the commissioners cannot ease or deliver us, by allowing an abatement. However, let us hearken to good advice, and something may be done for us; *God helps them that help themselves*, as Poor Richard says.

"I. It would be thought a hard government, that should tax its people one-   3 tenth part of their time, to be employed in its service; but idleness taxes many of us much more; sloth, by bringing on diseases, absolutely shortens life. *Sloth, like rust, consumes faster than labor wears; while the used key is always bright*, as Poor Richard says. *But dost thou love life, then do not squander time, for that is the stuff life is made of*, as Poor Richard says. How much more than is necessary do we spend in sleep, forgetting, that *The sleeping fox catches no poultry*, and that *There will be sleeping enough in the grave*, as Poor Richard says.

"*If time be of all things the most precious, wasting time must be*, as Poor Richard   4 says, *the greatest prodigality*; since, as he elsewhere tells us, *Lost time is never found again; and what we call time enough, always proves little enough*. Let us then up and be doing, and doing to the purpose; so by diligence shall we do more with less perplexity. *Sloth makes all things difficult, but industry all easy*; and *He that riseth late must trot all day, and shall scarce overtake his business at night*; while *Laziness travels so slowly, that Poverty soon overtakes him*. *Drive thy business, let not that drive thee*; and *Early to bed, and early to rise, makes a man healthy, wealthy, and wise*, as Poor Richard says.

"So what signifies wishing and hoping for better times? We may make these   5 times better, if we bestir ourselves. *Industry need not wish, and he that lives upon hopes will die fasting. There are no gains without pains; then help, hands, for I have no lands*; or, if I have, they are smartly taxed. *He that hath a trade hath an estate; and he that hath a calling, hath an office of profit and honor*, as Poor Richard says; but then the trade must be worked at, and the calling followed, or neither the estate nor the office will enable us to pay our taxes. If we are industrious, we shall never starve; for, *At the working man's house hunger looks in, but dares not enter.* Nor will the bailiff or the constable enter, for *Industry pays debts, while despair increaseth them.* What though you have found no treasure, nor has any rich relation left you a legacy, *Diligence is the mother of good luck, and God gives all things to industry.* Then *plough deep while sluggards sleep, and you shall have corn to sell and to keep.* Work while it is called to-day, for you know not how much you may be hindered to-morrow. *One to-day is worth two to-morrows,* as Poor Richard says; and further, *Never leave that till to-morrow, which you can do to-day.* If you were a servant, would you not be ashamed that a good master should catch you idle? Are you then your own master? Be ashamed to catch yourself idle, when there is so much to be done for yourself, your family, your country, and your king. Handle your tools without mittens; remember, that *The cat in gloves catches no mice,* as Poor Richard says. It is true there is much to be done, and perhaps you are weak-handed; but stick to it steadily, and you will see great effects; for *Constant dropping wears away stones;* and *By diligence and patience the mouse ate in two the cable;* and *Little strokes fell great oaks.*

"Methinks I hear some of you say, 'Must a man afford himself no leisure?' I   6
will tell thee, my friend, what Poor Richard says, *Employ thy time well, if thou meanest to gain leisure; and, since thou art not sure of a minute, throw not away an hour.* Leisure is time for doing something useful; this leisure the diligent man will obtain, but the lazy man never; for *A life of leisure and a life of laziness are two things. Many, without labor, would live by their wits only, but they break for want of stock;* whereas industry gives comfort, and plenty, and respect. *Fly pleasures, and they will follow you. The diligent spinner has a large shift; and now I have a sheep and a cow, everybody bids me good morrow.*

"II. But with our industry we must likewise be steady, settled, and careful,   7
and oversee our own affairs with our own eyes, and not trust too much to others; for, as Poor Richard says,

I never saw an oft-removed tree,   8
Nor yet an oft-removed family,
That throve so well as those that settled be.

And again, *Three removes are as bad as a fire*; and again, *Keep thy shop, and*   9
thy shop will keep thee; and again, *If you would have your business done, go; if not,*
send. And again,

> He that by the plough would thrive,   10
> Himself must either hold or drive.

And again, *The eye of a master will do more work than both his hands*; and again,   11
Want of care does us more damage than want of knowledge; and again, *Not to over-*
see workmen, is to leave them your purse open. Trusting too much to others' care is
the ruin of many; for *In the affairs of this world men are saved, not by faith, but by*
the want of it; but a man's own care is profitable; for, *If you would have a faithful*
servant, and one that you like, serve yourself. A little neglect may breed great mischief;
for *want of a nail the shoe was lost; for want of a shoe the horse was lost; and for want*
of a horse the rider was lost, being overtaken and slain by the enemy; all for want of a
little care about a horse-shoe nail.

"III. So much for industry, my friends, and attention to one's own business;   12
but to these we must add frugality, if we would make our industry more certainly successful. A man may, if he knows not how to save as he gets, keep his nose
all his life to the grindstone, and die not worth a groat at last. *A fat kitchen makes*
a lean will; and

> Many estates are spent in the getting,   13
> Since women for tea forsook spinning and knitting,
> And men for punch forsook hewing and splitting.

If you would be wealthy, think of saving as well as of getting. The Indies have not made   14
Spain rich, because her outgoes are greater than her incomes.

"Away then with your expensive follies, and you will not then have so   15
much cause to complain of hard times, heavy taxes, and chargeable families; for

> Women and wine, game and deceit,   16
> Make the wealth small and the want great.

And further, *What maintains one vice would bring up two children.* You may think,   17
perhaps, that a little tea, or a little punch now and then, diet a little more costly, clothes a little finer, and a little entertainment now and then, can be no great

matter; but remember, *Many a little makes a mickle*. Beware of little expenses; *A small leak will sink a great ship*, as Poor Richard says; and again, *Who dainties love, shall beggars prove*; and moreover, *Fools make feasts, and wise men eat them*.

"Here you are all got together at this sale of fineries and knick-knacks. You call them *goods*; but, if you do not take care, they will prove *evils* to some of you. You expect they will be sold cheap, and perhaps they may for less than they cost; but, if you have no occasion for them, they must be dear to you. Remember what Poor Richard says; *Buy what thou hast no need of, and ere long thou shalt sell thy necessaries*. And again, *At a great pennyworth pause a while*. He means, that perhaps the cheapness is apparent only, and not real; or the bargain, by straitening thee in thy business, may do thee more harm than good. For in another place he says, *Many have been ruined by buying good pennyworths*. Again, *It is foolish to lay out money in a purchase of repentance*; and yet this folly is practised every day at auctions, for want of minding the Almanac. Many a one, for the sake of finery on the back, have gone with a hungry belly and half-starved their families. *Silks and satins, scarlet and velvets, put out the kitchen fire*, as Poor Richard says.

"These are not the necessaries of life; they can scarcely be called the conveniences; and yet, only because they look pretty, how many want to have them! these, and other extravagances, the genteel are reduced to poverty, and forced to borrow of those whom they formerly despised, but who, through industry and frugality, have maintained their standing; in which case it appears plainly, that *A ploughman on his legs is higher than a gentleman on his knees*, as Poor Richard says. Perhaps they have had a small estate left them, which they knew not the getting of; they think, *It is day, and will never be night*; that a little to be spent out of so much is not worth minding; but *Always taking out of the meal-tub, and never putting in, soon comes to the bottom*, as Poor Richard says; and then, *When the well is dry, they know the worth of water*. But this they might have known before, if they had taken his advice. *If you would know the value of money, go and try to borrow some; for he that goes a borrowing goes a sorrowing*, as Poor Richard says; and indeed so does he that lends to such people, when he goes to get it in again. Poor Dick further advises, and says,

> *Fond pride of dress is sure a very curse;*
> *Ere fancy you consult, consult your purse.*

And again, *Pride is as loud a beggar as Want, and a great deal more saucy*. When you have bought one fine thing, you must buy ten more, that your appearance may

18

19

20

21

be all of a piece; but Poor Dick says, *It is easier to suppress the first desire, than to satisfy all that follow it*. And it is as truly folly for the poor to ape the rich, as for the frog to swell in order to equal the ox.

> *Vessels large may venture more,*   22
> *But little boats should keep near shore.*

It is, however, a folly soon punished; for, as Poor Richard says, *Pride that dines on*   23
vanity, sups on contempt. Pride breakfasted with Plenty, dined with Poverty, and supped with Infamy. And, after all, of what use is this pride of appearance, for which so much is risked, so much is suffered? It cannot promote health, nor ease pain; it makes no increase of merit in the person; it creates envy; it hastens misfortune.

"But what madness must it be to *run in debt* for these superfluities? We are   24
offered by the terms of this sale, six months' credit; and that, perhaps, has induced some of us to attend it, because we cannot spare the ready money, and hope now to be fine without it. But, ah! think what you do when you run in debt; you give to another power over your liberty. If you cannot pay at the time, you will be ashamed to see your creditor; you will be in fear when you speak to him; you will make poor, pitiful, sneaking excuses, and, by degrees, come to lose your veracity, and sink into base, downright lying; for *The second vice is lying, the first is running in debt*, as Poor Richard says; and again, to the same purpose, *Lying rides upon Debt's back*; whereas a free-born Englishman ought not to be ashamed nor afraid to see or speak to any man living. But poverty often deprives a man of all spirit and virtue. *It is hard for an empty bag to stand upright*.

"What would you think of that prince, or of that government, who should   25
issue an edict forbidding you to dress like a gentleman or gentlewoman, on pain of imprisonment or servitude? Would you not say that you were free, have a right to dress as you please, and that such an edict would be a breach of your privileges, and such a government tyrannical? And yet you are about to put yourself under such tyranny, when you run in debt for such dress! Your creditor has authority, at his pleasure, to deprive you of your liberty, by confining you in gaol till you shall be able to pay him. When you have got your bargain, you may, perhaps, think little of payment; but, as Poor Richard says, *Creditors have better memories than debtors; creditors are a super stitious sect, great observers of set days and times*. The day comes round before you are aware, and the demand is made before you are prepared to satisfy it; or, if you bear your debt in mind, the term, which at first

seemed so long, will, as it lessens, appear extremely short. Time will seem to have added wings to his heels as well as his shoulders. *Those have a short Lent, who owe money to be paid at Easter.* At present, perhaps, you may think yourselves in thriving circumstances, and that you can bear a little extravagance without injury; but

> *For age and want save while you may;*   26
> *No morning sun lasts a whole day.*

Gain may be temporary and uncertain, but ever, while you live, expense is con-   27
stant and certain; and *It is easier to build two chimneys, than to keep one in fuel,* as Poor Richard says; so, *Rather go to bed supperless, than rise in debt.*

> *Get what you can, and what you get hold;*   28
> *'Tis the stone that will turn all your lead into gold.*

And, when you have got the Philosopher's stone*, sure you will no longer com-   29
plain of bad times, or the difficulty of paying taxes.

"IV. This doctrine, my friends, is reason and wisdom; but after all, do not   30
depend too much upon your own industry, and frugality, and prudence, though excellent things; for they may all be blasted, without the blessing of Heaven; and, therefore, ask that blessing humbly, and be not uncharitable to those that at present seem to want it, but comfort and help them. Remember, Job suffered, and was afterwards prosperous.

"And now, to conclude, *Experience keeps a dear school, but fools will learn in*   31
no other, as Poor Richard says, and scarce in that; for, it is true, *We may give advice, but we cannot give conduct.* However, remember this, *They that will not be counselled, cannot be helped;* and further, that, *If you will not hear Reason, she will surely rap your knuckles,* as Poor Richard says."

Thus the old gentleman ended his harangue. The people heard it, and   32
approved the doctrine; and immediately practised the contrary, just as if it had been a common sermon; for the auction opened, and they began to buy extravagantly. I found the good man had thoroughly studied my Almanacs, and digested all I had dropped on these topics during the course of twenty-five years. The frequent mention he made of me must have tired any one else; but my vanity was wonderfully delighted with it, though I was conscious that not a tenth part of the wisdom was my own, which he ascribed to me, but rather the gleanings that I

---

* The term "Philosopher's stone" is usually used metaphorically to refer to the precious intellectual ore that philosophers attempt to mine through rigorous thinking. Finding the stone supposedly brought the finder wisdom and a life of freedom from physical care, but no real philosopher has ever achieved this goal. Franklin is implying here that wisdom provides greater wealth than material goods do.

had made of the sense of all ages and nations. However, I resolved to be the better for the echo of it; and, though I had at first determined to buy stuff for a new coat, I went away resolved to wear my old one a little longer. Reader, if thou wilt do the same, thy profit will be as great as mine. I am, as ever, thine to serve thee,

Richard Saunders

Questions for Discussion

1. How should right-minded people live, according to Franklin/Poor Richard?
2. What might a twenty-first century reader find irritating about Poor Richard's advice?
3. Taken as a whole, what do Poor Richard's adages tell us about what colonial Americans desired and what they considered important?
4. What are Poor Richard's views on wealth? Is wealth mainly harmful or mainly beneficial? How should wealth be managed?
5. What place does industry have in colonial America? Why might Franklin have given so much space to discussing industry and idleness?
6. How are the virtues that Franklin highlights still relevant today? How are they part of the American identity?
7. Why does the letter format make an appropriate conveyance for the advice of Poor Richard? What creative freedoms does the fictitious character of Poor Richard allow Franklin?

Questions for Reflection and Writing

1. Which of Poor Richard's adages do you like best? Which do you like least? Why?
2. Write a Poor Richard-style "essay" of your own, making it a serious version of Poor Richard's almanac, updated for the current age, or a humorous or parody version, updating for the current age but in a more "realistic" way.
3. Read about Franklin's life as a leading citizen in Philadelphia. What kind of man was he? What were his greatest achievements and failures? How closely did he follow Poor Richard's advice?

Bill McKibben (1960–   ) was born in Palo Alto, California, and received a B.A. degree from Harvard in 1982. He first became a staff writer for the *New Yorker*, and later became an editor. Since 1987 he has been a regular writer for the magazine, working out of his home in the Adirondack Mountains of upstate New York. His book *The End of Nature* (1989) was an immediate bestseller. It urged readers to change their habits of consumption and materialism; if they did not, McKibben warned, the result would be ecological disaster. This is a recurring theme of McKibben's essays and books of nonfiction, which include *The Age of Missing Information* (1992); *Hope, Human and Wild: True Stories of Living Lightly on the Earth* (1995); and *Maybe One: An Environmental and Personal Argument for Single-Child Families* (1998).

A Modest Proposal to Destroy Western Civilization as We Know It: The $100 Christmas

Bill McKibben

I know what I'll be doing on Christmas Eve. My wife, my 4-year-old daughter, 1 my dad, my brother, and I will snowshoe out into the woods in late afternoon, ready to choose a hemlock or a balsam fir and saw it down—I've had my eye on three or four likely candidates all year. We'll bring it home, shake off the snow, decorate it, and then head for church, where the Sunday school class I help teach will gamely perform this year's pageant. (Last year, along with the usual shepherds and wise people, it featured a lost star talking on a cell phone.) And then it's home to hang stockings, stoke the fire, and off to bed. As traditional as it gets, except that there's no sprawling pile of presents under the tree.

Several years ago, a few of us in the northern New York and Vermont con- 2 ference of the United Methodist Church started a campaign for what we called "Hundred Dollar Holidays." The church leadership voted to urge parishioners not to spend more than $100 per family on presents, to rely instead on simple homemade gifts and on presents of services—a back rub, stacking a cord of firewood. That first year I made walking sticks for everyone. Last year I made spicy chicken sausage. My mother has embraced the idea by making calendars illustrated with snapshots she's taken.

The $100 figure was a useful anchor against the constant seductions of the 3 advertisers, a way to explain to children why they weren't getting everything on

Mother Jones, November/December 1997.

their list. So far, our daughter, Sophie, does fine at Christmas. Her stocking is exciting to her; the tree is exciting; skating on the pond is exciting. It's worth mentioning, however, that we don't have a television, so she may not understand the degree of her impoverishment.

This holiday idea may sound modest. It is modest. And yet at the same time it's pretty radical. Christmas, it turns out, is a bulwark of the nation's economy. Many businesses—bookstores, for instance, where I make my living—do one-third of their volume in the months just before December 25th. And so it hits a nerve to question whether it all makes sense, whether we should celebrate the birth of a man who said we should give all that we have to the poor by showering each other with motorized tie racks.   4

It's radical for another reason, too. If you believe that our consumer addiction represents our deepest problem—the force that keeps us from reaching out to others, from building a fair society, the force that drives so much of our environmental degradation—then Christmas is the nadir. Sure, advertising works its powerful dark magic year-round. But on Christmas morning, with everyone piling downstairs to mounds of presents, consumption is made literally sacred. Here, under a tree with roots going far back into prehistory, here next to a crèche with a figure of the infant child of God, we press *stuff* on each other, stuff that becomes powerfully connected in our heads to love, to family, and even to salvation. The 12 days of Christmas— and in many homes the eight nights of Hanukkah—are a cram course in consumption, a kind of brainwashing.   5

When we began the $100 campaign, merchants, who wrote letters to the local papers, made it clear to us what a threatening idea it was. Newspaper columnists thought it was pretty extreme, too—one said church people should stick to religion and leave the economy alone. Another said that while our message had merit, it would do too much damage to business.   6

And he was right, or at least not wrong. If we all backed out of Christmas excess this year, we would sink many a gift shop; if we threw less lavish office parties, caterers would suffer—and florists and liquor wholesalers and on down the feeding chain. But we have to start somewhere, if we're ever to climb down from the unsustainable heights we've reached, and Christmas might as well be it.   7

When we first began to spread this idea about celebrating Christmas in a new way, we were earnest and sober. Big-time Christmas was an environmental *disgrace*—all that wrapping paper, all those batteries. The money could be so much better spent: The price of one silk necktie could feed a village for a day; the cost of a big-screen television could vaccinate more than 60 kids. And strug-   8 gling to create a proper Christmas drives poor families into debt. Where I live, which is a poor and cold place, January finds many people cutting back on heat to pay off their bills.

Those were all good reasons to scale back. But as we continued our cam-   9
paign, we found we weren't really interested in changing Christmas because we wanted fewer batteries. We wanted more joy. We felt cheated by the Christmases we were having—so rushed, so busy, so full of mercantile fantasy and catalog hype that we couldn't relax and enjoy the season.

Our growing need to emphasize joy over guilt says a great deal about the   10
chances for Christian radicalism, for religious radicalism in general. At its truest, religion represents the one force in our society that can postulate some goal other than accumulation. In an I-dolatrous culture, religion can play a subversive role. Churches, mosques, and synagogues almost alone among our official institutions can say, It's not the economy, stupid. It's your life. It's learning that there's some other center to the universe.

Having that other center can change the way we see the world around us.   11
It's why devoted clergy and laypeople occasionally work small miracles in inner cities and prisons; it's why alcoholics talk about a Higher Power. If we're too big, then perhaps the solution lies in somehow making ourselves a little smaller.

You may be too late for this Christmas. You may already have bought your   12
pile of stuff, or perhaps it's too late to broach the subject with relatives who will gather with you for the holidays, bearing (and therefore expecting) great stacks of loot. Our local Methodist ministers begin in September, preaching a skit ser-mon about the coming holiday. Many in our church community now participate. So do some of our neighbors and friends around the country.

None of us is under any illusions; we know that turning the focus of   13
Christmas back to Christ is a long and patient effort, one that works against every force that consumer culture can muster. But to judge from our own holi-days in recent years, it's well worth the effort. I know what we'll be doing Christmas morning: After we open our stockings and exchange our few home-made gifts, we'll go out for a hike. Following the advice of St. Francis of Assisi, who said that even the birds deserve to celebrate this happy day, we'll spread seed hither and yon—and for one morning the chickadees and the jays will have it easy.

And then we'll head back inside to the warm and fragrant kitchen and start   14
basting the turkey, shaping the rolls, mashing the potatoes.

Some things are sacred.   15

Questions for Discussion

1. What is "radical" (paragraph 4) about McKibben's proposal?
2. What, in McKibben's opinion, is wrong with how people usually celebrate Christmas?
3. What things does McKibben consider "sacred" (paragraph 15)? What is the meaning of the line "consumption is made literally sacred" (paragraph 5)? Why might McKibben have chosen the word "sacred"? Why is consumption *literally* sacred?
4. How practical do you think this proposal is? Would people in your area be able or want to do what McKibben suggests? Why or why not? To what other holidays or events could McKibben's proposal apply?
5. McKibben addresses his words directly to "you." How did you react to this direct address? Is the strategy effective?
6. What is meant by the word "Destroy" in the title? Do you think that McKibben's proposal would destroy civilization?
7. How does McKibben structure his argument? What is the sequence of points that he makes?

Questions for Reflection and Writing

1. Describe your own family's attitude toward consumption during a holiday such as Christmas, events such as birthdays, or in general. Is there anything you definitely would or would not change about the attitude?
2. Write a "modest proposal" of your own to correct what you see as a serious problem in society.
3. McKibben takes his title from an earlier work, the famous satire "A Modest Proposal" written in 1714 by Jonathan Swift, who "proposed" that starvation in Ireland (caused by English policy toward the Irish) be solved by eating the children. Find a copy of Swift's satire, and write a comparison of the two "modest proposals," looking at the structure of the argument and the use of satire and irony in each of the two essays.

Gloria Steinem (1934–   ), writer, feminist, and social reformer, earned a B.A. at Smith College, then studied at the University of Delhi and the University of Calcutta in India. She stayed briefly in India to write newspaper articles and a guidebook. She returned to the United States to become a journalist and worked for two years for the Independent Research Service, leaving when she discovered that it was funded by the CIA. She moved to New York City, where she worked as a freelancer and as a television newswriter for NBC's *That Was the Week That Was*. Steinem went undercover for *Show* magazine in 1963 to write "I Was a Playboy Bunny," an article that brought her instant fame. She went on to write for a number of America's most important magazines, including *Vogue*, *Life*, *Cosmopolitan*, and *Glamour*, and she served as an editorial consultant to *Seventeen* and *Show*. In 1968 she was invited to write a column, "The City Politic," for *New York*. She soon became affiliated with a radical women's group, the Redstockings, and published her first overtly feminist article, "After Black Power, Women's Liberation" (1968). In 1971, with other feminists, Steinem formed the National Women's Political Caucus and launched *Ms.* magazine, which she edited until 1987. Today, she is among the most influential women in American public life, and her work has brought her numerous awards and honors, including the United Nations Ceres Medal and the Front Page Award. Among her full-length works are *Outrageous Acts and Everyday Rebellions* (1983), *Marilyn: Norma Jean* (1986), *A Revolution from Within: A Book of Self-Esteem* (1992), and *Moving Beyond Words* (1994).

The Importance of Work

Gloria Steinem

Toward the end of the 1970s, *The Wall Street Journal* devoted an eight-part, front-page series to "the working woman"—that is, the influx of women into the paid-labor force—as the greatest change in American life since the Industrial Revolution.   1

Many women readers greeted both the news and the definition with cynicism. After all, women have always worked. If all the productive work of human maintenance that women do in the home were valued at its replacement cost, the gross national product of the United States would go up by 26 percent. It's just that we are now more likely than ever before to leave our poorly rewarded, low-security, high-risk job of homemaking (though we're still trying to explain that it's a perfectly good one and that the problem is male society's refusal both   2

to do it and to give it an economic value) for more secure, independent, and bet-
ter-paid jobs outside the home.

Obviously, the real work revolution won't come until all productive work
is rewarded—including child rearing and other jobs done in the home—and
men are integrated into so-called women's work as well as vice versa. But the radical change being touted by the *Journal* and other media is one part of that long
integration process: the unprecedented flood of women into salaried jobs, that is,
into the labor force as it has been male-defined and previously occupied by men.
We are already more than 41 percent of it—the highest proportion in history.
Given the fact that women also make up a whopping 69 percent of the "discouraged labor force" (that is, people who need jobs but don't get counted in the
unemployment statistics because they've given up looking), plus an official
female unemployment rate that is substantially higher than men's, it's clear that
we could expand to become fully half of the national work force by 1990.

Faced with this determination of women to find a little independence and
to be paid and honored for our work, experts have rushed to ask: "Why?" It's a
question rarely directed at male workers. Their basic motivations of survival and
personal satisfaction are taken for granted. Indeed, men are regarded as "odd"
and therefore subjects for sociological study and journalistic reports only when
they *don't* have work, even if they are rich and don't need jobs or are poor and
can't find them. Nonetheless, pollsters and sociologists have gone to great
expense to prove that women work outside the home because of dire financial
need, or if we persist despite the presence of a wage-earning male, out of some
desire to buy "little extras" for our families, or even out of good old-fashioned
penis envy.

Job interviewers and even our own families may still ask salaried women
the big "Why?" If we have small children at home or are in some job regarded as
"men's work," the incidence of such questions increases. Condescending or accu-
satory versions of "What's a nice girl like you doing in a place like this?" have not
disappeared from the workplace.

How do we answer these assumptions that we are "working" out of some
pressing or peculiar need? Do we feel okay about arguing that it's as natural for us
to have salaried jobs as for our husbands—whether or not we have young children at home? Can we enjoy strong career ambitions without worrying about
being thought "unfeminine"? When we confront men's growing resentment of
women competing in the work force (often in the form of such guilt-producing

accusations as "You're taking men's jobs away" or "You're damaging your children"), do we simply state that a decent job is a basic human right for everybody?

I'm afraid the answer is often no. As individuals and as a movement, we tend to retreat into some version of a tactically questionable defense: "Womenworkbecausewehaveto." The phrase has become one word, one key on the typewriter—an economic form of the socially "feminine" stance of passivity and self-sacrifice. Under attack, we still tend to present ourselves as creatures of economic necessity and familial devotion. "Womenworkbecausewehaveto" has become the easiest thing to say.

7

Like most truisms, this one is easy to prove with statistics. Economic need *is* the most consistent work motive—for women as well as men. In 1976, for instance, 43 percent of all women in the paid-labor force were single, widowed, separated, or divorced, and working to support themselves and their dependents. An additional 21 percent were married to men who had earned less than $10,000 in the previous year, the minimum then required to support a family of four. In fact, if you take men's pensions, stocks, real estate, and various forms of accumulated wealth into account, a good statistical case can be made that there are more women who "have" to work (that is, who have neither the accumulated wealth, nor husbands whose work or wealth can support them for the rest of their lives) than there are men with the same need. If we were going to ask one group "Do you really need this job?" we should ask men.

8

But the first weakness of the whole "have to work" defense is its deceptiveness. Anyone who has ever experienced dehumanized life on welfare or any other confidence-shaking dependency knows that a paid job may be preferable to the dole, even when the handout is coming from a family member. Yet the will and selfconfidence to work on one's own can diminish as dependency and fear increase. That may explain why—contrary to the "have to" rationale—wives of men who earn less than $3000 a year are actually *less* likely to be employed than wives whose husbands make $10,000 a year or more.

9

Furthermore, the greatest proportion of employed wives is found among families with a total household income of $25,000 to $50,000 a year. This is the statistical underpinning used by some sociologists to prove that women's work is mainly important for boosting families into the middle or upper middle class. Thus, women's incomes are largely used for buying "luxuries" and "little extras": a neat doublewhammy that renders us secondary within our families, and makes our jobs expendable in hard times. We may even go along with this interpretation (at least, up to the point of getting fired so a male can have our job). It pre-

10

serves a husbandly egoneed to be seen as the primary breadwinner, and still allows us a safe "feminine" excuse for working.

But there are often rewards that we're not confessing. As noted in *The Two-Career Couple*, by Francine and Douglas Hall: "Women who hold jobs by choice, even blue-collar routine jobs, are more satisfied with their lives than are the full-time housewives." 11

In addition to personal satisfaction, there is also society's need for all its members' talents. Suppose that jobs were given out on only a "have to work" basis to both women and men—one job per household. It would be unthinkable to lose the unique abilities of, for instance, Eleanor Holmes Norton, the distinguished chair of the Equal Employment Opportunity Commission. But would we then be forced to question the important work of her husband, Edward Norton, who is also a distinguished lawyer? Since men earn more than twice as much as women on the average, the wife in most households would be more likely to give up her job. Does that mean the nation could do as well without millions of its nurses, teachers, and secretaries? Or that the rare man who earns less than his wife should give up his job? 12

It was this kind of waste of human talents on a society-wide scale that traumatized millions of unemployed or underemployed Americans during the Depression. Then, a one-job-per-household rule seemed somewhat justified, yet the concept was used to displace women workers only, create intolerable dependencies, and waste female talent that the country needed. That Depression experience, plus the energy and example of women who were finally allowed to work during the manpower shortage created by World War II, led Congress to reinterpret the meaning of the country's full-employment goal in its Economic Act of 1946. Full employment was officially defined as "the employment of those who want to work, without regard to whether their employment is, by some definition, necessary. This goal applies equally to men and to women." Since bad economic times are again creating a resentment of employed women—as well as creating more need for women to be employed—we need such a goal more than ever. Women are again being caught in a tragic double bind: We are required to be strong and then punished for our strength. 13

Clearly, anything less than government and popular commitment to this 1946 definition of full employment will leave the less powerful groups, whoever they may be, in danger. Almost as important as the financial penalty paid by the powerless is the suffering that comes from being shut out of paid and recognized work. Without it, we lose much of our self-respect and our ability to prove that 14 we are alive by making some difference in the world. That's just as true for the suburban woman as it is for the unemployed steel worker.

But it won't be easy to give up the passive defense of "weworkbecausewe-   15
haveto."

When a woman who is struggling to support her children and grandchil-   16
dren on welfare sees her neighbor working as a waitress, even though that neighbor's husband has a job, she may feel resentful; and the waitress (of course, not
the waitress' husband) may feel guilty. Yet unless we establish the obligation to
provide a job for everyone who is willing and able to work, that welfare woman
may herself be penalized by policies that give out only one public-service job per
household. She and her daughter will have to make a painful and divisive decision about which of them gets that precious job, and the whole household will
have to survive on only one salary.

A job as a human right is a principle that applies to men as well as women.   17
But women have more cause to fight for it. The phenomenon of the "working
woman" has been held responsible for everything from an increase in male
impotence (which turned out, incidentally, to be attributable to medication for
high blood pressure) to the rising cost of steak (which was due to high energy
costs and beef import restrictions, not women's refusal to prepare the cheaper,
slower-cooking cuts). Unless we see a job as part of every citizen's right to autonomy and personal fulfillment, we will continue to be vulnerable to someone else's
idea of what "need" is, and whose "need" counts the most.

In many ways, women who do not have to work for simple survival, but   18
who choose to do so nonetheless, are on the frontier of asserting this right for all
women. Those with well-to-do husbands are dangerously easy for us to resent
and put down. It's easier still to resent women from families of inherited wealth,
even though men generally control and benefit from that wealth. (There is no
Rockefeller Sisters Fund, no J. P. Morgan & Daughters, and sons-in-law may be
the ones who really sleep their way to power.) But to prevent a woman whose
husband or father is wealthy from earning her own living, and from gaining the
self-confidence that comes with that ability, is to keep her needful of that
unearned power and less willing to disperse it. Moreover, it is to lose forever her
unique talents.

Perhaps modern feminists have been guilty of a kind of reverse snobbism   19
that keeps us from reaching out to the wives and daughters of wealthy men; yet
it was exactly such women who refused the restrictions of class and financed the
first wave of feminist revolution.

For most of us, however, "womenworkbecausewehaveto" is just true   20
enough to be seductive as a personal defense.

If we use it without also staking out the larger human right to a job, how-   21
ever, we will never achieve that right. And we will always be subject to the false
argument that independence for women is a luxury affordable only in good economic times. Alternatives to layoffs will not be explored, acceptable unemployment will always be used to frighten those with jobs into accepting low wages,
and we will never remedy the real cost, both to families and to the country, of
dependent women and a massive loss of talent.

Worst of all, we may never learn to find productive, honored work as a nat-   22
ural part of ourselves and as one of life's basic pleasures.

Questions for Discussion

1. Why would women be cynical about *The Wall Street Journal*'s articles about
   working women?
2. Why is work important?
3. What does Steinem find erroneous about the comparisons that have been
   made between men and women and between men's work and women's
   work?
4. What is wrong with the "Womenworkbecausewehaveto" (Paragraph 7) reason for working?
5. Why should a "decent job" be a "basic human right" (Paragraph 6)?
6. How would you describe Steinem's tone? Is it angry or energetic? Resentful
   or frustrated? Optimistic or pessimistic? Or . . . ? What leads you to describe
   her tone as you do?
7. How does Steinem use statistics? What kinds of statistics does she use? For
   what purpose?

Questions for Reflection and Writing

1. Write about your own family, either the one you had growing up or the one
   you have now. Were there clear gender differences in the chores done,
   and/or in the jobs held by your parents or siblings? How was or is "work"
   defined in your family? What importance does work have in your family?
2. How plausible is Steinem's proposal "to provide a job for everyone who is
   willing and able to work" (Paragraph 16)? Write an essay in which you discuss what obstacles such a proposal would face and how the obstacles might
   be overcome (or would be impossible to overcome).
3. Research the legislative history of women's rights in the United States,
   Canada, or some other country. As an alternative, research the history of
   women's work.

Chapter 6
PHILOSOPHY

Plato (427–347 B.C.), ancient Greek philosopher, studied under Socrates and used Socratic dialogues to teach and write his philosophy. Legend has it that Plato (Greek for "broad" or "wide") was the nickname given to Aristocles for his broad shoulders. Plato witnessed the apex of Athenian culture and its decline after its defeat by Sparta in the Peloponnesian War. Athens eventually returned to democracy, but, ironically, it was a democratic government that condemned and executed Socrates, leaving Plato with the conviction that rulers must be philosophers, or vice versa, in order for society to achieve justice and virtue.

At about forty years of age, Plato founded his Academy, an institution of higher learning and communal living that flourished for over 900 years until it was shut down in A.D. 529 by the Roman Emperor Justinian I. Believing interpersonal instruction and the spoken word superior to book-based education and the written word, Plato nevertheless left provocative evidence for his views in his dialogues, such as *Apologia Socratis (Apology)*, *Euthyphro*, and *Gorgias* (all 399–390 B.C.); *Meno*, *Symposium*, *Republic*, and *Theaetetus* (388–366 B.C.); *Philebus*, and *Nomoi or Laws* (360–347 B.C.).

His work progressed from expressing Socrates's views in his earlier works to expressing his own in his later work. Plato claimed that there are pure "forms" or "ideas" outside the material realm on which material forms are based that are superior to their material counterparts. Plato considered knowledge to be a sort of bridge between reason and forms; conversely, the human senses can lead to belief but cannot provide true knowledge. Reason plays an important role in human life, according to Plato, who characterized humans as rational, irrational, and passionate. Plato opposed the Greek teachers, called Sophists, who traveled about, teaching public speaking, for Plato believed that the Sophists taught superficial skills while the philosopher could help a human improve his or her soul. Plato also contended that men and women had equal ability to serve as philosophers and leaders.

The Allegory of the Cave

Plato

And now, I said, let me show in a figure how far our nature is enlightened or   1
unenlightened: —Behold! human beings living in an underground den, which
has a mouth open towards the light and reaching all along the den; here they
have been from their childhood, and have their legs and necks chained so that
they cannot move, and can only see before them, being prevented by the chains
from turning round their heads. Above and behind them a fire is blazing at a distance, and between the fire and the prisoners there is a raised way; and you will
see, if you look, a low wall built along the way, like the screen which marionette

players have in front of them, over which they show the puppets.

I see. 2

And do you see, I said, men passing along the wall carrying all sorts of ves- 3
sels, and statues and figures of animals made of wood and stone and various materials, which appear over the wall? Some of them are talking, others silent.

You have shown me a strange image, and they are strange prisoners. 4

Like ourselves, I replied; and they see only their own shadows, or the shad- 5
ows of one another, which the fire throws on the opposite wall of the cave?

True, he said; how could they see anything but the shadows if they were 6
never allowed to move their heads?

And of the objects which are being carried in like manner they would only 7
see the shadows?

Yes, he said. 8

And if they were able to converse with one another, would they not sup- 9
pose that they were naming what was actually before them?

Very true. 10

And suppose further that the prison had an echo which came from the 11
other side, would they not be sure to fancy when one of the passers-by spoke that
the voice which they heard came from the passing shadow?

No question, he replied. 12

To them, I said, the truth would be literally nothing but the shadows of the 13
images.

That is certain. 14

And now look again, and see what will naturally follow if the prisoners are 15
released and disabused of their error. At first, when any of them is liberated and
compelled suddenly to stand up and turn his neck round and walk and look
towards the light, he will suffer sharp pains; the glare will distress him, and he will
be unable to see the realities of which in his former state he had seen the shadows; and then conceive some one saying to him, that what he saw before was an
illusion, but that now, when he is approaching nearer to being and his eye is
turned towards more real existence, he has a clearer vision—what will be his
reply? And you may further imagine that his instructor is pointing to the objects
as they pass and requiring him to name them,— will he not be perplexed? Will
he not fancy that the shadows which he formerly saw are truer than the objects
which are now shown to him?

Far truer. 16

And if he is compelled to look straight at the light, will he not have a pain   17
in his eyes which will make him turn away to take refuge in the objects of vision
which he can see, and which he will conceive to be in reality clearer than the
things which are now being shown to him?

True, he said.   18

And suppose once more, that he is reluctantly dragged up a steep and   19
rugged ascent, and held fast until he is forced into the presence of the sun himself, is he not likely to be pained and irritated? When he approaches the light his
eyes will be dazzled, and he will not be able to see anything at all of what are now
called realities.

Not all in a moment, he said.   20

He will require to grow accustomed to the sight of the upper world. And   21
first he will see the shadows best, next the reflections of men and other objects
in the water, and then the objects themselves; then he will gaze upon the light
of the moon and the stars and the spangled heaven; and he will see the sky and
the stars by night better than the sun or the light of the sun by day?

Certainly.   22

Last of all he will be able to see the sun, and not mere reflections of him in   23
the water, but he will see him in his own proper place, and not in another; and
he will contemplate him as he is.

Certainly.   24

He will then proceed to argue that this is he who gives the season and the   25
years, and is the guardian of all that is in the visible world, and in a certain way
the cause of all things which he and his fellows have been accustomed to behold?

Clearly, he said, he would first see the sun and then reason about him.   26

And when he remembered his old habitation, and the wisdom of the den   27
and his fellow prisoners, do you not suppose that he would felicitate himself on
the change, and pity them?

Certainly, he would.   28

And if they were in the habit of conferring honors among themselves on   29
those who were quickest to observe the passing shadows and to remark which of
them went before, and which followed after, and which were together; and who
were therefore best able to draw conclusions as to the future, do you think that
he would care for such honors and glories, or envy the possessors of them? Would
he not say with Homer,

Better to be the poor servant of a poor master,

and to endure anything, rather than think as they do and live after their manner?

Yes, he said, I think that he would rather suffer anything than entertain these false notions and live in this miserable manner.   30

Imagine once more, I said, such an one coming suddenly out of the sun to be replaced in his old situation; would he not be certain to have his eyes full of darkness?   31

To be sure, he said.   32

And if there were a contest, and he had to compete in measuring the shadows with the prisoners who had never moved out of the den, while his sight was still weak, and before his eyes had become steady (and the time which would be needed to acquire this new habit of sight might be very considerable), would he not be ridiculous? Men would say of him that up he went and down he came without his eyes; and that it was better not even to think of ascending; and if any one tried to loose another and lead him up to the light, let them only catch the offender, and they would put him to death.   33

No question, he said.   34

This entire allegory, I said, you may now append, dear Glaucon, to the previous argument; the prison house is the world of sight, the light of the fire is the sun, and you will not misapprehend me if you interpret the journey upwards to be the ascent of the soul into the intellectual world according to my poor belief, which, at your desire, I have expressed—whether rightly or wrongly God knows. But, whether true or false, my opinion is that in the world of knowledge the idea of good appears last of all, and is seen only with an effort; and, when seen, is also inferred to be the universal author of all things beautiful and right, parent of light and of the lord of light in this visible world, and the immediate source of reason and truth in the intellectual; and that this is the power upon which he who would act rationally either in public or private life must have his eye fixed.   35

I agree, he said, as far as I am able to understand you.   36

Moreover, I said, you must not wonder that those who attain to this beatific vision are unwilling to descend to human affairs; for their souls are ever hastening into the upper world where they desire to dwell; which desire of theirs is very natural, if our allegory may be trusted.   37

Yes, very natural.   38

And is there anything surprising in one who passes from divine contemplations to the evil state of man, misbehaving himself in a ridiculous manner; if, while his eyes are blinking and before he has become accustomed to the sur-   39 rounding darkness, he is compelled to fight in courts of law, or in other places, about the images or the shadows of images of justice, and is endeavoring to meet the conceptions of those who have never yet seen absolute justice?

Anything but surprising, he replied.   40

Anyone who has common sense will remember that the bewilderments of   41
the eyes are of two kinds, and arise from two causes, either from coming out of the light or from going into the light, which is true of the mind's eye, quite as much as of the bodily eye; and he who remembers this when he sees anyone whose vision is perplexed and weak, will not be too ready to laugh; he will first ask whether that soul of man has come out of the brighter life, and is unable to see because unaccustomed to the dark, or having turned from darkness to the day is dazzled by excess of light. And he will count the one happy in his condition and state of being, and he will pity the other; or, if he have a mind to laugh at the soul which comes from below into the light, there will be more reason in this than in the laugh which greets him who returns from above out of the light into the den.

That, he said, is a very just distinction.   42

But then, if I am right, certain professors of education must be wrong when   43
they say that they can put a knowledge into the soul which was not there before, like sight into blind eyes.

They undoubtedly say this, he replied.   44

Whereas, our argument shows that the power and capacity of learning   45
exists in the soul already; and that just as the eye was unable to turn from dark-ness to light without the whole body, so too the instrument of knowledge can only be the movement of the whole soul be turned from the world of becoming into that of being, and learn by degrees to endure the sight of being, and of the brightest and best of being, or in other words, of the good.

Very true.   46

And must there not be some art which will effect conversion in the easiest   47
and quickest manner; not implanting the faculty of sight, for that exists already, but has been turned in the wrong direction, and is looking away from the truth?

Yes, he said, such an art may be presumed.   48

And whereas the other so-called virtues of the soul seem to be akin to bod-   49
ily qualities, for even when they are not originally innate they can be implanted later by habit and exercise, the virtue of wisdom more than anything else con-tains a divine element which always remains, and by this conversion is rendered useful and profitable; or, on the other hand, hurtful and useless. Did you never

observe the narrow intelligence flashing from the keen eye of a clever rogue—how eager he is, how clearly his paltry soul sees the way to his end; he is the reverse of blind, but his keen eyesight is forced into the service of evil, and he is mischievous in proportion to his cleverness?

Very true, he said.   50

But what if there had been a circumcision of such natures in the days of   51
their youth; and they had been severed from those sensual pleasures, such as eating and drinking, which, like leaden weights, were attached to them at their birth, and which drag them down and turn the vision of their souls upon the things that are below— if, I say, they had been released from these impediments and turned in the opposite direction, the very same faculty in them would have seen the truth as keenly as they see what their eyes are turned to now.

Very likely.   52

Yes, I said; and there is another thing which is likely, or rather a necessary   53
inference from what has preceded, that neither the uneducated and uninformed of the truth, nor yet those who never make an end of their education, will be able ministers of State; not the former, because they have no single aim of duty which is the rule of all their actions, private as well as public; nor the latter, because they will not act at all except upon compulsion, fancying that they are already dwelling apart in the islands of the blessed.

Very true, he replied.   54

Then, I said, the business of us who are the founders of the State will be to   55
compel the best minds to attain that knowledge which we have already shown to be the greatest of all—they must continue to ascend until they arrive at the good; but when they have ascended and seen enough we must not allow them to do as they do now.

What do you mean?   56

I mean that they remain in the upper world: but this must not be allowed;   57
they must be made to descend again among the prisoners in the den, and partake of their labors and honors, whether they are worth having or not.

But is not this unjust? he said; ought we to give them a worse life, when   58
they might have a better?

You have again forgotten, my friend, I said, the intention of the legislator,   59
who did not aim at making any one class in the State happy above the rest; the happiness was to be in the whole State, and he held the citizens together by persuasion and necessity, making them benefactors of the State, and therefore bene-

factors of one another; to this end he created them, not to please themselves, but to be his instruments in binding up the State.

True, he said, I had forgotten.   60

Observe, Glaucon, that there will be no injustice in compelling our   61
philosophers to have a care and providence of others; we shall explain to them that in other States, men of their class are not obliged to share in the toils of politics: and this is reasonable, for they grow up at their own sweet will, and the government would rather not have them. Being self-taught, they cannot be expected to show any gratitude for a culture which they have never received. But we have brought you into the world to be rulers of the hive, kings of yourselves and of the other citizens, and have educated you far better and more perfectly than they have been educated, and you are better able to share in the double duty. Wherefore each of you, when his turn comes, must go down to the general underground abode, and get the habit of seeing in the dark. When you have acquired the habit, you will see ten thousand times better than the inhabitants of the den, and you will know what the several images are, and what they represent, because you have seen the beautiful and just and good in their truth. And thus our State, which is also yours, will be a reality, and not a dream only, and will be administered in a spirit unlike that of other States, in which men fight with one another about shadows only and are distracted in the struggle for power, which in their eyes is a great good. Whereas the truth is that the State in which the rulers are most reluctant to govern is always the best and most quietly governed, and the State in which they are most eager, the worst.

Quite true, he replied.   62

And will our pupils, when they hear this, refuse to take their turn at the   63
toils of State, when they are allowed to spend the greater part of their time with one another in the heavenly light?

Impossible, he answered; for they are just men, and the commands which   64
we impose upon them are just; there can be no doubt that every one of them will take office as a stern necessity, and not after the fashion of our present rulers of State.

Yes, my friend, I said; and there lies the point. You must contrive for your   65
future rulers another and a better life than that of a ruler, and then you may have a wellordered State; for only in the State which offers this, will they rule who are truly rich, not in silver and gold, but in virtue and wisdom, which are the true blessings of life. Whereas if they go to the administration of public affairs, poor and hungering after their own private advantage, thinking that hence they are

to snatch the chief good, order there can never be; for they will be fighting about office, and the civil and domestic broils which thus arise will be the ruin of the rulers themselves and of the whole State.

Most true, he replied.   66

And the only life which looks down upon the life of political ambition is   67
that of true philosophy. Do you know of any other?

Indeed, I do not, he said.   68

Questions for Discussion

1. What does the cave represent? To what is the cave analogous?
2. Who would be the "instructor" (Paragraph 15) who accompanies the released prisoners? Why would the instructor bother instructing these people?
3. Why would a released prisoner's first reaction be perplexity upon coming out of the shadows?
4. How are Socrates and Glaucon, the speakers of this dialogue, also trapped in the cave's world of shadows?
5. To what is Plato alluding in Paragraph 30 when Socrates says that honors were given to "those who were the quickest to observe the passing shadows"?
6. What is the relationship of the questioner to the answerer? What image of each person does the question-and-answer format create?
7. Is the Socratic dialogue format an effective one to make the point?

Questions for Reflection and Writing

1. Choose the one element of the allegory (cave, sun, chains, fire, vessels, shadows, etc.) that most intrigues you. Explain what the element represents.
2. Explain how "The Allegory of the Cave" applies to the government of classical Greece, and how it could be applied to government now.
3. Read more of *The Republic*, from which "The Allegory of the Cave" is taken. Summarize Plato's ideas, and speculate about how they could apply to the world now.

Josef Pieper was born in 1904 in Elte, Germany. He studied at the University of Berlin and University of Muenster from 1923 to 1928, when he received his Ph.D. in philosophy from Muenster with a dissertation on the ethical theory of Thomas Aquinas. Pieper taught at Muenster from 1928 to 1931 and then worked as a free-lance writer for seven years. After serving in the German Army during World War II, he taught for a brief time at Teachers College in Essen and then returned in 1946 to the University of Muenster, where he remained until his retirement from teaching in 1972. During his tenure at Muenster, he came to the United States to be a visiting professor at the University of Notre Dame (1950) and Stanford University (1956, 1962). Pieper has been awarded honorary degrees from the University of Munich (1964), the University of Muenster (1974), and the University of Eichstaett (1985).

Pieper's numerous books include the following, all of which have been translated into English: *Leisure, the Basis of Culture* (1948), *Reality and the Good* (1949), *Guide to Thomas Aquinas* (1958), *The Four Cardinal Virtues* (1964), *About Love* (1972), *The End of Time: A Meditation on the Philosophy of History* (1980), and *In Search of the Sacred* (1988).

Our reading is from "The Philosophical Act," an essay published separately in German in 1948 and published in English together with *Leisure, the Basis of Culture*. In this essay, building on the classical Western philosophical tradition of Plato, Aristotle, and Thomas Aquinas, Pieper sets forth his view of the nature of philosophizing. To philosophize means "to act in such a way that one steps out of the workaday world"; it is to leave behind, at least for a moment, life's practical concerns and simply to contemplate reality. To contemplate, Pieper explains, is to look at a being purely receptively, without a desire to change it or use it. Pieper argues that the human mind has the potential to contemplate not only particular beings, but the whole of being; this is what the tradition means when it says human beings have "spirit." Pieper maintains that philosophy begins in wonder—wonder about the ultimate nature of things. For example, we might wonder what justice really is. According to Pieper, the only way to grasp the true nature of something is to see it in relation to all of reality.

The Philosophical Act

Josef Pieper

I

When a physicist sets out to define his science and asks what physics is, he is posing a preliminary question; in asking it he is plainly not at the experimental stage—not yet, or perhaps, no longer. But for anyone to ask, "What does philosophizing mean?" is quite certainly philosophy. The question is neither a preliminary one, nor is it just a postscript, one to be raised after the task has been accomplished—in some such form as: "What have we been doing?" The question occurs   1 in the very midst of the undertaking. More precisely, I can say nothing whatsoever about philosophy without simultaneously saying something about man and his nature—and that, after all, is one of the central matters of philosophy. The opening question, "What does philosophizing mean?" is certainly philosophical.

But like all philosophical questions, it cannot be answered with complete finality. The answers to philosophical questions cannot, of their nature, be what Parmenides called "neatly rounded truths"[1] and they cannot be picked and held in the hand like apples. The whole structure of philosophy and of philosophizing is different. . . .   2

As a preliminary approach, however, it may be said that to philosophize is to act in such a way that one steps out of the workaday world. The next thing to do is to define what is meant by the workaday world, and then what is meant by going beyond that sphere.   3

The workaday world is the world of work, the utilitarian world, the world of the useful, subject to ends, open to achievement and subdivided according to functions; it is the world of demand and supply, of hunger and satiety. It is dominated by a single end: the satisfaction of the common need; it is the world of work in so far as work is synonymous with doing things for useful ends (so that effort and activity are characteristic of the workaday world). Work is "common need"—an expression that is by no means synonymous with the notion of "common good." The common need is an essential part of the common good; but the notion of common good is far more comprehensive. For example, the common good requires . . . that there should be men who devote themselves to the "useless" life of contemplation, and, equally, that some men should philosophize—whereas it could not be said that contemplation or philosophy helps to satisfy the common need.   4

More and more, at the present time, common good and common need are identified; and (what comes to the same thing) the world of work is becoming our entire world; it threatens to engulf us completely, and the demands of the world of work become greater and greater, till at last they make a "total" claim upon the whole of human nature.   5

If, then, it is true to say that in the act of philosophizing we transcend the world of work and are carried beyond the world of work, it becomes plain that the question "What does philosophizing mean?," which sounds so innocent at first, so "theoretical," so abstract, is a very pressing and "actual" question at the present time. . . .   6

The incommensurability of the philosophical act and the sphere of the workaday world needs, however, to be seen in its concrete aspects. It does not require any great effort of imagination to bring vividly to mind the things that dominate everyday life: we are plunged drastically in their midst. For so many people there is the   7 daily struggle for a bare physical existence, for food, warmth, clothing and a roof over their head. In addition to our private worries and anxieties . . . there is the struggle of nations for the goods of the earth. Everywhere there is a feeling of strain, of being overwrought and overdone—and this fatigue is only relieved in appearance by the breathless amusements or the brief pauses that punctuate its course: newspapers, a cinema, a cigarette. I do not have to detail what everyone knows. But there is no need either to concentrate on the present-day crisis and on the exaggerations which that involves. I mean quite simply the ordinary everyday world in which we live and play our part, with its very concrete ends to be achieved and realized, and which have to be squarely faced. Nothing, in fact, is further from my intention than in any way whatsoever to denigrate this world as though from some supposedly superior "philosophical" standpoint. Not a word need be wasted on that subject; that world is of course essentially part of man's world, being the very ground of his physical existence—without which, obviously, no one could philosophize!

But all the same, just try to imagine that all of a sudden, among the myri-   8
ad voices in the factories and on the market square ("Where can we get this, that or the other?")—that all of a sudden among those familiar voices and questions another voice were to be raised, asking: "Why, after all, should there be such a thing as being? Why not just nothing?"—the age-old, philosophical cry of wonder that Heidegger calls the basic metaphysical question![2] Is it really necessary to emphasize how incommensurable philosophical enquiry and the world of work are? Anyone who asked that question without warning in the company of people whose minds hinge on necessities and material success would most likely be regarded as crazy. It is, however, in extreme cases such as this that the whole extent of the contrast comes to light: and then it is clear that the question transcends the workaday world and leads beyond it.

A properly philosophical question always pierces the dome that encloses   9
the bourgeois workaday world, though it is not the only way of taking a step beyond that world. Poetry no less than philosophy is incommensurable with it.

> How sweet I roam'd from field to field
> And tasted all the summer's pride,
> Till I the Prince of Love beheld
> Who in the sunny beams did glide![3]

Surely the sudden effect of poetry in the realm of means and ends comes as   10
strange and remote as a philosophical question. Nor is it otherwise with prayer. Perhaps it is still understandable that men should say: "Give us this day our daily bread." But what of the words of the Gloria: *Gratias agimus tibi propter magnam gloriam tuam?*[4] Can words such as these be understood in the context of the "rational-useful" and of a utilitarian organization? Man also steps beyond the

chain of ends and means, that binds the world of work, in love, or when he takes a step towards the frontier of existence, deeply moved by some existential experience, for this, too, sends a shock through the world of relationships, whatever the occasion may be—perhaps the close proximity of death. The act of philosophizing, genuine poetry, any aesthetic encounter, in fact, as well as prayer, springs from some shock. And when such a shock is experienced, man senses the non-finality of this world of daily care; he transcends it, takes a step beyond it.

The philosophical act, the religious act, the aesthetic act, as well as the   11
existential shocks of love and death, or any other way in which man's relation to the world is convulsed and shaken—all these fundamental ways of acting belong naturally together, by reason of the power which they have in common of enabling a man to break through and transcend the workaday world.

When the Thracian maid saw Thales of Miletus, the stargazer, fall into the   12
cistern she laughed;[5] and Plato accepted her laughter as the answer of hardheaded common sense to philosophy. The history of European philosophy might be said to begin with that legend. Ever and again, so we are told in the *Theaetetus*, "ever and again" the philosopher is the occasion of laughter. [6] "Not only the maids of Thrace, but the many laugh at him because, a stranger to the world, he falls into a cistern and into many another embarrassment." [7] . . .

But that is only the negative aspect of the incommensurability in question;   13
the other aspect is: freedom. Philosophy is "useless" and unusable in matters of everyday life where things are to be turned to account and results achieved: that is one point. It is quite another thing, however, to say that it serves no purpose whatsoever beyond itself and its own end or that it can never be used apart from its own end. Philosophy is not functional knowledge but, as Newman said, "the knowledge of a gentleman"; not a useful knowledge, but a "free" knowledge.[8] Freedom, here, means that philosophical knowledge is not legitimized by its usefulness or usableness, or by virtue of its social function, or with reference to the common need. . . .

To philosophize is the purest form of *speculari*, of *the͞orein;*[9] it means to look   14
at reality purely receptively—in such a way that things are the measure and the soul is exclusively receptive. Whenever we look at being philosophically, we discourse purely "theoretically" about it—in a manner, that is to say, untouched in any way whatsoever by practical considerations, by the desire to change it; and it is in this sense that philosophy is said to be above any and every "purpose." . . . Man's real wealth consists, not in satisfying his needs, not in becoming "the master and owner of nature," but in seeing what is and the whole of what is, in seeing things not as useful or useless, serviceable or not, but simply as being. The basis of this conception of philosophy is the conviction that the greatness of man consists in his being *capax universi.*[10]

The ultimate perfection attainable to us, in the minds of the philosophers   15
of Greece, was this: that the order of the whole of existing things should be
inscribed in our souls.

II

. . . In the tradition of Western philosophy, the capacity for spiritual knowledge has   16
always been understood to mean the power of establishing relations with the whole
of reality, with all things existing; that is how it has been defined, and it is conceived as a definition more than as a description. *Spirit*, it might be said, is not only
defined as incorporeal, but as the power and capacity to relate itself to the totality
of being. Spirit, in fact, is a capacity for relations of such all-embracing power that
its field of relations transcends the frontiers of all and any "environment."

In summing up what he has said about the soul in the *De anima*, Aristotle   17
says: "The soul is, fundamentally, everything that is."[11] . . . The spiritual soul,
Aquinas says in his considerations on truth, is meant to fit in with all being.[12]
. . . "Every other being takes only a limited part in being," whereas the spiritual
being is "capable of grasping the whole of being."[13] And "because there is spirit,
it is possible for the perfection of the whole of being to exist in one being."[14]

That is the tradition of Western philosophy: to have spirit, or to be spirit,   18
means to exist in the midst of the whole of reality and before the whole of being,
the whole of being, *vis-à-vis de l'univers*.[15] Spirit does not exist in "a" world, nor
in "its" world, but in "the" world. . . .

Philosophizing . . . means to experience the fact that our immediate sur-   19
roundings, prescribed as they are by the aims and needs of life, not only can be,
but must be broken in upon (not only once but ever and again) by the disturbing call of "the world," of the whole world and the everlasting and essential
images of things mirrored by reality. To philosophize . . . means to step beyond
the sectional, partial environment of the workaday world into a position *vis-à-
vis de l'univers*: a step that takes one into the open, for the heavens are not a roof
over a man's head—though one ought always to leave the door open behind one,
for a man cannot live like that continuously. Who, in fact, would want to emi-
grate for good and all out of the Thracian maid's world or think it possible to do
so?—for it would mean leaving the human world altogether . . . .

III

. . . A man philosophizing does not look away from his environment in the   20
process of transcending it; he does not turn away from the ordinary things of the
workaday world, from the concrete, useful handy things of everyday life; he does
not have to look in the opposite direction to perceive the universal world of
essences. On the contrary, it is the same tangible, visible world that lies before

him upon which a genuine philosophical reflection is trained. But this world of things in their interrelationships has to be questioned in a specific manner: things are questioned regarding their ultimate nature and their universal essence, and as a result the horizon of the question becomes the horizon of reality as a whole. A philosophical question is always about some quite definite thing, straight in front of us; it is not concerned with something beyond the world or beyond our experience of everyday life. Yet, it asks what "this" really *is*, ultimately. The philosopher, Plato says,[16] does not want to know whether I have been unjust to you in this particular matter, or you to me, but what justice really is, and injustice; not whether a king who owns great wealth is happy or not, but what authority is, and happiness and misery—in themselves and ultimately.

Philosophical questions, then, are certainly concerned with the everyday   21
things that are before our very eyes. But to anyone raising such a question, the things "before his eyes" become, all at once, transparent; they lose their density and solidity and their apparent finality—they can no longer be taken for granted. Things then assume a strange, new, and deeper aspect. Socrates, who questioned men in this way, so as to strip things of their everyday character, compared himself for that reason to an electric fish that gives a paralysing shock to anyone who touches it. All day and every day we speak of "my" friend, of "my" wife, of "my" house taking for granted that we "have" or "own" such things; then all of a sudden we are brought to a halt; do we really "have" or "own" all these things? Can *anyone* have such things? And anyway, what do we mean here by "having" and "owning" something? To philosophize means to withdraw—not from the things of everyday life, but from the currently accepted meaning attached to them; or to question the value placed upon them. This does not, of course, take place by virtue of some decision to differentiate our attitude from that of others and to see things "differently," but because, quite suddenly, things themselves assume a different aspect. Really the situation is this: the deeper aspects of reality are apprehended in the ordinary things of everyday life and not in a sphere cut off and segregated from it, the sphere of the "essential" or whatever it may be called. It is in the things we come across in the experience of everyday life that the unusual emerges, and we no longer take them for granted—and that situation corresponds with the inner experience which has always been regarded as the beginning of philosophy: the act of "marvelling."

"By all the gods, Socrates, I really cannot stop marvelling at the signifi-   22
cance of these things, and at moments I grow positively giddy when I look at them," as the young mathematician Theaetetus impulsively declares, after Socrates has brought him to the point of admitting his ignorance, with his shrewd and kindly, but staggering and astonishing questions—questions that stagger and astonish one with wonder. And then follows Socrates's ironical

answer: "Yes, that is the very frame of mind that constitutes the philosopher; that and nothing else is the beginning of philosophy."[17] There, for the first time, in the *Theaetetus*, without solemnity or ceremony, almost "by the way," though fresh as dawn, appears the thought that has become a commonplace in the history of philosophy: the beginning of philosophy is wonder.

The unique and original relation to being that Plato calls *theoria* can only   23
be realized in its pure state through the sense of wonder, in that purely receptive attitude to reality, undisturbed and unsullied by the interjection of the will. *Theoria* is only possible in so far as man is not blind to the wonderful fact that things are. For our sense of wonder, in the philosophical meaning of the word, is not aroused by enormous, sensational things—though that is what a dulled sensibility requires to provoke it to a sort of ersatz experience of wonder. A man who needs the unusual to make him "wonder" shows that he has lost the capacity to find the true answer to the wonder of being.

Notes

1. Parmenides, fragment 1. Parmenides (born about 515 B.C.E.) was a Greek philosopher. [D.C.A., ed.]
2. Martin Heidegger, *Was Ist Metaphysik* (Frankfurt, Germany: Klostermann, 1943), p. 22. [J.P.]
3. William Blake, "The Prince of Love." [J.P.] Blake (1757–1827) was an English artist and poet. [D.C.A.]
4. The Gloria is a prayer in the Roman Catholic Mass. The line of the Gloria quoted here means, "We give You thanks for Your great glory" (Latin). [D.C.A.]
5. Pieper here refers to the legend (related by Plato) that once when the Greek philosopher Thales (about 625–547 B.C.E.) was looking up to study the stars, he fell into a cistern and was laughed at by a maid from Thrace for being so impractical. [D.C.A.]
6. Plato, *Theaetetus*, Stephanus p. 174. [J.P.]
7. Ibid. [J.P.]
8. John Henry Newman, *The Idea of a University*, Part I, Discourse V, section 6. [J.P.]
9. *Speculari* and *the ōrein* are the Latin and Greek words, respectively, for "to look at, to observe." [D.C.A.]
10. Thomas Aquinas, *Disputed Questions on Truth*, Question 2, Article 2. [J.P.] *Capax universi* means "capable of (grasping) the whole (the whole of being, the universe)" (Latin). [D.C.A.]
11. Aristotle, *De anima (On the Soul)*, Book III, Chapter 8. [J.P.]
12. Aquinas, *Disputed Questions on Truth*, Question 1, Article 1. [J.P.]
13. Aquinas, *Summa Contra Gentiles*, Book III, Chapter 112. [J.P.]
14. Aquinas, *Disputed Questions on Truth*, Question 2, Article 2. [J.P.]
15. *vis-à-vis de l'univers*: face-to-face with the universe (French) [D.C.A.]
16. Plato, *Theaetetus*, Stephanus p. 175. [J.P.]
17. Ibid., p. 155. [J.P.]

Bertrand Russell was born in Trelleck, Wales, in 1872. Both his parents died when he was young, and he and his older brother were raised by their paternal grandmother. Bertrand received his initial education from governesses and tutors. In 1890 he enrolled in Cambridge University, where he studied mathematics and then philosophy, receiving his degree in 1894. Russell was a fellow at Cambridge from 1895 to 1901 and a lecturer in philosophy from 1910 to 1916. In 1908 he became a member of the Royal Society. After his lectureship at Cambridge, Russell supported himself by writing and giving public lectures. On the death of his brother in 1931, he became Earl Russell. He moved to the United States in 1938, teaching first at the University of Chicago and then at the University of California at Los Angeles. He lectured at the Barnes Foundation in Philadelphia from 1941 to 1943. The following year he returned to England, having been invited to become a fellow again at Cambridge. In 1949 he became an honorary member of the British Academy and received the Order of Merit. The following year he was awarded the Nobel Prize for Literature. Russell died in 1970 near Penryndeudraeth, Wales, at the age of ninety-seven.

Russell's numerous works include *The Principles of Mathematics* (1903), *Principia Mathematica* (coauthored with Alfred North Whitehead; 3 volumes, 1910, 1912, 1913), *The Problems of Philosophy* (1912), *Our Knowledge of the External World* (1914), *The Conquest of Happiness* (1930), *An Inquiry into Meaning and Truth* (1940), and *A History of Western Philosophy* (1945). Our reading is from the final chapter of *The Problems of Philosophy*, "The Value of Philosophy." Russell argues that, although philosophy does not enhance our physical well-being, it greatly enriches our mental lives. This enrichment does not come from providing definitive answers to philosophical questions, for practically all philosophical questions remain undecided. For example, no one has ever proved—or is likely ever to prove—that the universe has or does not have a purpose. For Russell, the uncertainty in philosophy is an asset rather than a liability: By teaching us to inquire about the universe and to question our ordinary beliefs, philosophy liberates us from the prejudices of common sense, culture, and custom. Although philosophy does not provide definite answers about how things *are*, it broadens our mind by showing us many different ways that they *might* be.

A further value of philosophy, according to Russell, is its ability to free us from our instinctive tendency to interpret everything in terms of self. By attempting to see the universe as it is, rather than simply how it affects us, we enlarge our self by leaving behind (as much as is possible) our hopes and fears, our preconceptions and prejudices. And when we enlarge our self, we also enlarge the sphere of our actions and affections.

The Problems of Philosophy

Bertrand Russell

Chapter 15: The Value of Philosophy

Having now come to the end of our brief and very incomplete review of the problems of philosophy, it will be well to consider, in conclusion, what is the value of philosophy and why it ought to be studied. It is the more necessary to consider this question, in view of the fact that many men, under the influence of science or of practical affairs, are inclined to doubt whether philosophy is anything better than innocent but useless trifling, hair-splitting distinctions, and controversies on matters concerning which knowledge is impossible.

1

This view of philosophy appears to result, partly from a wrong conception 2
of the ends of life, partly from a wrong conception of the kind of goods which philosophy strives to achieve. Physical science, through the medium of inventions,
is useful to innumerable people who are wholly ignorant of it; thus the study of
physical science is to be recommended, not only, or primarily, because of the
effect on the student, but rather because of the effect on mankind in general. This
utility does not belong to philosophy. If the study of philosophy has any value at
all for others than students of philosophy, it must be only indirectly, through its
effects upon the lives of those who study it. It is in these effects, therefore, if anywhere, that the value of philosophy must be primarily sought.

But further, if we are not to fail in our endeavour to determine the value of 3
philosophy, we must first free our minds from the prejudices of what are wrongly
called "practical" men. The "practical" man, as this word is often used, is one who
recognises only material needs, who realises that men must have food for the
body, but is oblivious of the necessity of providing food for the mind. If all men
were well off, if poverty and disease had been reduced to their lowest possible
point, there would still remain much to be done to produce a valuable society;
and even in the existing world the goods of the mind are at least as important as
the goods of the body. It is exclusively among the goods of the mind that the
value of philosophy is to be found; and only those who are not indifferent to these
goods can be persuaded that the study of philosophy is not a waste of time.

Philosophy, like all other studies, aims primarily at knowledge. The knowledge 4
it aims at is the kind of knowledge which gives unity and system to the body of the sciences, and the kind which results from a critical examination of the grounds of our
convictions, prejudices, and beliefs. But it cannot be maintained that philosophy has
had any very great measure of success in its attempts to provide definite answers to its
questions. If you ask a mathematician, a mineralogist, a historian, or any other man of
learning, what definite body of truths has been ascertained by his science, his answer
will last as long as you are willing to listen. But if you put the same question to a
philosopher, he will, if he is candid, have to confess that his study has not achieved
positive results such as have been achieved by other sciences. It is true that this is partly accounted for by the fact that, as soon as definite knowledge concerning any subject becomes possible, this subject ceases to be called philosophy, and becomes a separate science. The whole study of the heavens, which now belongs to astronomy, was
once included in philosophy; Newton's great work was called "the mathematical principles of natural philosophy." Similarly, the study of the human mind, which was,
until very lately, a part of philosophy, has now been separated from philosophy and has
become the science of psychology. Thus, to a great extent, the uncertainty of philosophy is more apparent than real: those questions which are already capable of definite
answers are placed in the sciences, while those only to which, at present, no definite
answer can be given, remain to form the residue which is called philosophy.

This is, however, only a part of the truth concerning the uncertainty of philosophy. There are many questions—and among them those that are of the profoundest interest to our spiritual life—which, so far as we can see, must remain insoluble to the human intellect unless its powers become of quite a different order from what they are now. Has the universe any unity of plan or purpose, or is it a fortuitous concourse of atoms? Is consciousness a permanent part of the universe, giving hope of indefinite growth in wisdom, or is it a transitory accident on a small planet on which life must ultimately become impossible? Are good and evil of importance to the universe or only to man? Such questions are asked by philosophy, and variously answered by various philosophers. But it would seem that, whether answers be otherwise discoverable or not, the answers suggested by philosophy are none of them demonstrably true. Yet, however slight may be the hope of discovering an answer, it is part of the business of philosophy to continue the consideration of such questions, to make us aware of their importance, to examine all the approaches to them, and to keep alive that speculative interest in the universe which is apt to be killed by confining ourselves to definitely ascertainable knowledge.

Many philosophers, it is true, have held that philosophy could establish the truth of certain answers to such fundamental questions. They have supposed that what is of most importance in religious beliefs could be proved by strict demonstration to be true. In order to judge of such attempts, it is necessary to take a survey of human knowledge, and to form an opinion as to its methods and its limitations. On such a subject it would be unwise to pronounce dogmatically; but if the investigations of our previous chapters have not led us astray, we shall be compelled to renounce the hope of finding philosophical proofs of religious beliefs. We cannot, therefore, include as part of the value of philosophy any definite set of answers to such questions. Hence, once more, the value of philosophy must not depend upon any supposed body of definitely ascertainable knowledge to be acquired by those who study it.

The value of philosophy is, in fact, to be sought largely in its very uncertainty. The man who has no tincture of philosophy goes through life imprisoned in the prejudices derived from common sense, from the habitual beliefs of his age or his nation, and from convictions which have grown up in his mind without the cooperation or consent of his deliberate reason. To such a man the world tends to become definite, finite, obvious; common objects rouse no questions, and unfamiliar possibilities are contemptuously rejected. As soon as we begin to philosophize, on the contrary, we find . . . that even the most everyday things lead to problems to which only very incomplete answers can be given. Philosophy, though unable to tell us with certainty what is the true answer to the doubts which it raises, is able to suggest many possibilities which enlarge our thoughts and free them from the tyranny of custom. Thus, while diminishing our feeling of certainty as to what things are, it greatly increases our knowledge as to what they may be; it removes the somewhat arrogant dogmatism of those who have never travelled into the region of liberating doubt, and it keeps alive our sense of wonder by showing familiar things in an unfamiliar aspect.

Apart from its utility in showing unsuspected possibilities, philosophy has a   8
value—perhaps its chief value—through the greatness of the objects which it contemplates, and the freedom from narrow and personal aims resulting from this contemplation. The life of the instinctive man is shut up within the circle of his private interests: family and friends may be included, but the outer world is not regarded except as it may help or hinder what comes within the circle of instinctive wishes. In such a life there is something feverish and confined, in comparison with which the philosophic life is calm and free. The private world of instinctive interests is a small one, set in the midst of a great and powerful world which must, sooner or later, lay our private world in ruins. Unless we can so enlarge our interests as to include the whole outer world, we remain like a garrison in a beleaguered fortress, knowing that the enemy prevents escape and that ultimate surrender is inevitable. In such a life there is no peace, but a constant strife between the insistence of desire and the powerlessness of will. In one way or another, if our life is to be great and free, we must escape this prison and this strife.

One way of escape is by philosophic contemplation. Philosophic contempla-   9
tion does not, in its widest survey, divide the universe into two hostile camps—friends and foes, helpful and hostile, good and bad—it views the whole impartially. Philosophic contemplation, when it is unalloyed, does not aim at proving that the rest of the universe is akin to man. All acquisition of knowledge is an enlargement of the Self, but this enlargement is best attained when it is not directly sought. It is obtained when the desire for knowledge is alone operative, by a study which does not wish in advance that its objects should have this or that character, but adapts the Self to the characters which it finds in its objects. This enlargement of Self is not obtained when, taking the Self as it is, we try to show that the world is so similar to this Self that knowledge of it is possible without any admission of what seems alien. The desire to prove this is a form of self-assertion, and like all self-assertion, it is an obstacle to the growth of Self which it desires, and of which the Self knows that it is capable. Self-assertion, in philosophic speculation as elsewhere, views the world as a means to its own ends; thus it makes the world of less account than Self, and the Self sets bounds to the greatness of its goods. In contemplation, on the contrary, we start from the not-Self, and through its greatness the boundaries of Self are enlarged; through the infinity of the universe the mind which contemplates it achieves some share in infinity.

For this reason greatness of soul is not fostered by those philosophies which   10
assimilate the universe to Man. Knowledge is a form of union of Self and not-Self; like all union, it is impaired by dominion, and therefore by any attempt to force the universe into conformity with what we find in ourselves. There is a widespread philosophical tendency towards the view which tells us that man is the measure of all things, that truth is manmade, that space and time and the world of universals[1] are properties of the mind, and that, if there be anything not created by the mind, it is unknowable and of no account for us. This view . . . is untrue; but in addition to being untrue, it has the effect of robbing philosophic contem-

plation of all that gives it value, since it fetters contemplation to Self. What it calls knowledge is not a union with the not-Self, but a set of prejudices, habits, and desires, making an impenetrable veil between us and the world beyond. The man who finds pleasure in such a theory of knowledge is like the man who never leaves the domestic circle for fear his word might not be law.

The true philosophic contemplation, on the contrary, finds its satisfaction in **11** every enlargement of the not-Self, in everything that magnifies the objects contemplated, and thereby the subject contemplating. Everything, in contemplation, that is personal or private, everything that depends upon habit, self-interest, or desire, distorts the object, and hence impairs the union which the intellect seeks. By thus making a barrier between subject and object, such personal and private things become a prison to the intellect. The free intellect will see as God might see, without a *here* and *now*, without hopes and fears, without the trammels of customary beliefs and traditional prejudices, calmly, dispassionately, in the sole and exclusive desire of knowledge— knowledge as impersonal, as purely contemplative, as it is possible for man to attain. Hence also the free intellect will value more the abstract and universal knowledge into which the accidents of private history do not enter, than the knowledge brought by the senses, and dependent, as such knowledge must be, upon an exclusive and personal point of view and a body whose sense-organs distort as much as they reveal.

The mind which has become accustomed to the freedom and impartiality of **12** philosophic contemplation will preserve something of the same freedom and impartiality in the world of action and emotion. It will view its purposes and desires as parts of the whole, with the absence of insistence that results from seeing them as infinitesimal fragments in a world of which all the rest is unaffected by any one man's deeds. The impartiality which, in contemplation, is the unalloyed desire for truth, is the very same quality of mind which, in action, is justice, and in emotion is that universal love which can be given to all, and not only to those who are judged useful or admirable. Thus contemplation enlarges not only the objects of our thoughts, but also the objects of our actions and our affections: it makes us citizens of the universe, not only of one walled city at war with all the rest. In this citizenship of the universe consists man's true freedom, and his liberation from the thraldom of narrow hopes and fears.

Thus, to sum up our discussion of the value of philosophy: Philosophy is to be **13** studied, not for the sake of any definite answers to its questions, since no definite answers can, as a rule, be known to be true, but rather for the sake of the questions themselves; because these questions enlarge our conception of what is possible, enrich our intellectual imagination, and diminish the dogmatic assurance which closes the mind against speculation; but above all because, through the greatness of the universe which philosophy contemplates, the mind also is rendered great, and becomes capable of that union with the universe which constitutes its highest good.

Note

1. *universals:* realities corresponding to general concepts or terms [D.C.A., ed.]

Thomas D. Davis was born in New York City in 1941. He attended the University of Michigan, where he received his B.A. in philosophy in 1963 and his Ph.D. in 1975. Davis has held teaching positions at Michigan, Grinnell College, and the University of Redlands. He is currently teaching at De Anza College and writing fiction. Davis is the author of two mystery novels with philosophical themes: *Suffer Little Children*, which received a Shamus award from the Private Eye Writers of America for best first mystery of 1991, and *Murdered Sleep*. The selection below is taken from his McGraw-Hill text, *Philosophy: An Introduction through Original Fiction, Discussion, and Readings*.

"Why Don't You Just Wake Up?" dramatizes the idea that the world is only a dream: "Walking across campus, I see the world ripple again and suddenly I realize what it all looks like. It's like when you are watching a movie in class, and the movie screen ripples, distorting the image, and suddenly you're aware that it wasn't a world in front of you at all, but just an illusion, a not-very-large-piece of material. I put my arm out to feel the ripple, only my arm ripples too because it's part of the movie."

Why Don't You Just Wake Up?

Thomas D. Davis

I'm in the living room at home, and Dad's there, all serious, saying, "John,   1
where's your mind these days—you've got to wake up," and I think I wake up,
and I'm at my desk at home. I straighten up and yawn and pick up my history
book, and just then Mom comes in, saying, "Johnny, you're just not concentrating—you've got to wake up," and I think I wake up, and I'm sitting in class. I look
around, and Teresa's sitting next to me looking all upset, saying, "John, what's
with you these days—why don't you just wake up," and I think I wake up, and
I'm lying in bed in my dorm room.

It was all dreams within dreams within dreams, and what I thought was   2
waking was just more dreaming. I lie in my dorm bed and wonder who is going
to come in next and wake me from this, only no one comes in, and the digital
clock blinks slowly toward seven-thirty, and I guess this must be real.

It doesn't seem real, though. Nothing does these days. Everything that hap-   3
pens seems sort of vague somehow and out of focus and not all that important. I
have trouble concentrating—taking things seriously—and everybody's on my
case. That's the reason, I think, for all those dreams about dreaming and waking.

One reason, anyway. The other is that philosophy class and all that talk   4
about Descartes and whether all reality could be a dream. That's not helping
much either.

I'm late picking up Teresa again, and she's had to wait, and there won't be   5
time for us to get coffee together. She gives me that exasperated look I see a lot
these days, and we walk across campus without talking. Finally, she says:

"I don't know why I took that stupid philosophy class. I can't wait 'til it's   6
over."

I know it's not really the class she's annoyed at. It's me and the way I've   7
been lately. I know I should say something nice. But I'm feeling pushed and kind
of cranky.

"I like the class," I say, to be contrary.   8

"You do not."   9

"I do. It's kind of interesting."   10

"Interesting. Right. Like I really want to sit around all day wondering   11
whether I'm dreaming everything in the world."

"Maybe you are."   12

"Sure." She shakes her head. "That's so stupid."   13

"Just because you say 'stupid' doesn't make it wrong. How do you know you   14
aren't just dreaming this all up?"

She glares at me, but her eyes begin to dart the way they always do when   15
she's thinking hard. She's not in the mood for this, but I've gotten her mad.

"Because . . . I know what dreams look like. They're all hazy. Not like the   16
world looks now."

"You mean what you can see of it through the smog."   17

"Funny."   18

I know what she means, though. A few weeks back I would have said that   19
being awake looked a lot different from dreaming. But the guy in class is right.
That's just a matter of how things look. It doesn't prove how things are.

"Look," I say, "nobody's denying that what we call 'dreaming' looks differ-   20
ent from what we call 'being awake.' But is it really different? Maybe 'being
awake' is just a different kind of dream."

"Yeah, well, if I'm making all this up, how come we're talking about some-   21
thing I don't want to talk about?"

"Because you're not in control of this dream any more than you are your   22
dreams at night. It's your unconscious doing it."

"This is so much bullsh. . . ."   23

"Why?"   24

"It's crazy. You're standing here trying to convince me that everything is my   25
dream while you know you're real. That doesn't make any sense."

"Yeah, it does. I'm saying you can't know that I really exist, I can't know   26
that you . . ."

I stop suddenly, because something scary is happening. It's like a ripple   27
moving through the whole world, coming from the horizon to my left, but moving fast as if the world is really much smaller than it appears. And where the ripple is, everything becomes elongated and out of focus. The ripple passes over
Teresa, distorting her for a moment, like a fun house mirror. Then it's gone, and
everything's back to normal.

"John, are you okay?" says Teresa, giving me a worried look. "You look   28
white as a sheet."

"I don't know. I just got the weirdest feeling. I guess I'm okay."   29

"John, are you on something?"   30

"No. I told you. Really."   31

She looks at me for a moment and decides I'm telling the truth.   32

"Come on," she says, taking my hand. "The last thing you need right now   33
is philosophy class. Let's go get something to eat and then sit in the sun for
awhile. I bet you'll feel better."

"Hey, Ter, I'm sorry I'm being such a jerk. I . . ."   34

"Don't worry about it, John. It's okay. Come on."   35

Later I do feel better. I feel like things are almost back to normal. But my   36
night is full of dreams within dreams, and the next day the world seems full of
unreality once again. And then, at midday, the world ripples again.

I go to the university health service, and of course the doctor thinks it's   37
drugs, and we go round and round on that until I insist that he test me and then
he begins to believe I'm not lying. He becomes nicer then, and more concerned,
and schedules some tests and an appointment with a specialist he'd like me to
see, though he's "sure it's nothing, just exhaustion."

Walking across campus, I see the world ripple again and suddenly I realize   38
what it all looks like. It's like when you are watching a movie in class, and the
movie screen ripples, distorting the image, and suddenly you're aware that it was-
n't a world in front of you at all, but just an illusion on a not-very-large piece of
material. I put my arm out to feel the ripple, only my arm ripples too because it's
part of the movie.

I don't know what's happening, and I'm afraid. At night I keep myself from 39
sleeping because the idea of dreaming is something I suddenly find disturbing. In
the morning I'm exhausted, but I stumble off to class because I want something
to divert my attention, but once there I have trouble paying attention. I guess
the professor must have asked me something I didn't hear because I feel Teresa
nudging me in the ribs, and hear her say, "Come on, John, wake up."

I look up then at the professor standing behind his lectern, and just above 40
and in back of him a dark line seems to appear in the wall. It looks like the slow
fissure of an earthquake, except that the edges fold back against the surface of the
wall like the edges of torn paper, and I see that behind the tearing there is nothing at all, just darkness. Then I see that the tear isn't in the wall at all but in my
field of vision because as it reaches the professor he begins to split apart and then
the lectern and then the head of the student in the front row. On both sides of
the tear the world distorts and folds and collapses. The fissure moves downward
through the students and then, as I glance down, through my own body. No one
is moving or screaming—they take no more notice than movie characters on a
torn movie screen would. In a panic I reach out and touch Teresa, then watch as
she and my hand distort, as everything, absolutely everything, falls away.

* * * * * *

It is night. It's always night. A night without stars, without anything— just 41
an infinite emptiness falling away on every side. And so I float, an invisible being
in a nonexistent world.

How long have I been like this? I don't know. It feels like years, but that's 42
just a feeling because there is nothing here by which to mark the time.

I try to remember how it was, but my memories are such pale things, and 43
they grow more pale as time drags on.

I would pray, but there is nothing to pray to. And so I hope, for hope is all 44
I have: that one day, as inexplicably as once I did, I will begin to dream the world
again.

Thomas D. Davis was born in New York City in 1941. He attended the University of Michigan, where he received his B.A. in philosophy in 1963 and his Ph.D. in 1975. Davis has held teaching positions at Michigan, Grinnell College, and the University of Redlands. He is currently teaching at De Anza College and writing fiction. Davis is the author of two mystery novels with philosophical themes: *Suffer Little Children*, which received a Shamus award from the Private Eye Writers of America for best first mystery of 1991, and *Murdered Sleep*. The selection below is taken from his McGraw-Hill text, *Philosophy: An Introduction through Original Fiction, Discussion, and Readings*.

In "Please Don't Tell Me How The Story Ends" a prisoner who has undergone weeks of mental and physical testing is placed in a library-like cell. One huge set of books puzzles him: Every time he opens one of the volumes, it correctly describes what he has just thought and done. He comes to realize that he is part of an experiment testing the theory of determinism—that all events, including human choices, are governed by causal laws and are predictable given sufficient knowledge. The prisoner is horrified by the thought that he might be just a "puppet" of the universe and desperately sets out to prove that he has free will.

Please Don't Tell Me How the Story Ends

Thomas D. Davis

The heavy door closed behind him, and he glanced quickly at this new deten-   1
tion room. He was startled, almost pleasantly surprised. This was not like the drab cell in which he had spent the first days after his arrest, nor like the hospital rooms, with the serpentine carnival machines, in which he had been tested and observed for the last two months—though he assumed that he was being observed here as well. This was more like a small, comfortable library that had been furnished like a first-class hotel room. Against the four walls were fully stocked bookcases that rose ten feet to the white plaster ceiling; in the ceiling was a small skylight. The floor was covered with a thick green carpet, and in the middle of the room were a double bed with a nightstand, a large bureau, a desk, an easy chair with a side table, and several lamps. There were large gaps in the bookcases to accommodate two doors, including the one through which he had just entered, and also a traylike apparatus affixed to the wall. He could not immediately ascertain the purpose of the tray, but the other door, he quickly learned, led to a spacious bathroom complete with toilet articles. As he searched the main room, he found that the desk contained writing paper, pens, a clock, and a

calendar; the bureau contained abundant clothing in a variety of colors and two pairs of shoes. He glanced down at the hospital gown and slippers he was wearing, then quickly changed into a rust-colored sweater and a pair of dark brown slacks. The clothing, including the shoes, fitted him perfectly. It would be easier to face his situation, to face whatever might be coming, looking like a civilized human being.

But what was his situation? He wanted to believe that the improvement in 2 his living conditions meant an improvement in his status, perhaps even an imminent reprieve. But all the same he doubted it. Nothing had seemed to follow a sensible progression since his arrest, and it would be foolhardy to take anything at face value now. But what were they up to? At first, when he had been taken to the hospital, he had expected torture, some hideous pseudo-medical experiment, or a brainwashing program. But there had been no operation and no pain. He had been tested countless times: the endless details of biography; the responses to color, scent, sound, taste, touch; the responses to situation and ideas; the physical examination. But if these constituted mind-altering procedures, they had to be of the most subtle variety. Certainly he felt the same; at least no more compliant than he had been in the beginning. What were they after?

As his uncertainty grew to anxiety, he tried to work it off with whatever 3 physical exercise he could manage in the confines of the room: running in place, isometrics, sit-ups, and push-ups. He knew that the strength of his will would depend in part on the strength of his body, and since his arrest he had exercised as much as he could. No one had prevented this.

He was midway through a push-up when a loud buzzer sounded. He leaped 4 to his feet, frightened but ready. Then he saw a plastic tray of food on the metal tray that extended from the wall and a portion of the wall closing downward behind the tray. So this was how he would get his meals. He would see no one. Was this some special isolation experiment?

The question of solitude quickly gave way to hunger and curiosity about 5 the food. It looked delicious and plentiful; there was much more than he could possibly eat. Was it safe? Could it be drugged or poisoned? No, there could be no point to their finishing him in such an odd, roundabout fashion. He took the tray to the desk and ate heartily, but still left several of the dishes barely sampled or untouched.

That evening—the clock and the darkened skylight told him it was 6 evening—he investigated the room further. He was interrupted only once by the buzzer. When it continued to sound and nothing appeared, he realized that the buzzer meant he was to return the food dishes. He did so, and the plastic tray disappeared into the wall.

The writing paper was a temptation. He always thought better with a pen   7
in hand. Writing would resemble a kind of conversation and make him feel a little less alone. With a journal, he could construct some kind of history from what threatened to be days of dulling sameness. But he feared that they wanted him to write, that his doing so would somehow play into their hands. So he refrained.

Instead, he examined a portion of the bookshelf that contained paperback   8
volumes in a great variety of sizes and colors. The books covered a number of fields—fiction, history, science, philosophy, politics—some to his liking and some not. He selected a political treatise and put it on the small table next to the easy chair. He did not open it immediately. He washed up and then went to the bureau, where he found a green plaid robe and a pair of light yellow pajamas. As he lifted out the pajamas, he noticed a small, black, rectangular box and opened it.

Inside was a revolver. A quick examination showed that it was loaded and   9
operative. Quickly he shut the box, trembling. He was on one knee in front of the open drawer. His first thought was that a former inmate had left the gun to help him. He was sure that his body was blocking the contents of the drawer from the view of any observation devices in the room. He must not give away the secret. He forced himself to close the drawer casually, rise, and walk to the easy chair.

Then the absurdity of his hypothesis struck him. How could any prisoner   10
have gotten such a thing past the tight security of this place? And what good would such a weapon do him in a room to which no one came? No, the gun must be there because the authorities wanted it there. But why? Could it be they wanted to hide his death under the pretense of an attempted escape? Or could it be that they were trying to push him to suicide by isolating him? But again, what was the point of it? He realized that his fingerprints were on the gun. Did they want to use that as some kind of evidence against him? He went to the bureau again, ostensibly to switch pajamas, and, during the switch, opened the box and quickly wiped his prints off the gun. As casually as he could, he returned to the chair.

He passed the evening in considerable agitation. He tried to read but could   11
not. He exercised again, but it did not calm him. He tried to analyze his situation, but his thoughts were an incoherent jumble. Much later, he lay down on the bed, first pushing the easy chair against the door of the room. He recognized

the absurdity of erecting this fragile barrier, but the noise of their pushing it away would give him some warning. For a while, he forced his eyes open each time he began to doze, but eventually he fell asleep.

In the morning, he found everything unchanged, the chair still in place at   12 the door. Nothing but the breakfast tray had intruded. After he had exercised, breakfasted, bathed, and found himself still unmolested, he began to feel more calm. He read half the book he had selected the night before, lunched, and then dozed in his chair.

When he awoke, his eyes scanned the room and came to rest on one of the   13 bookshelves filled with a series of black, leatherbound volumes of uniform size, marked only by number. He had noticed them before but had paid little attention, thinking they were an encyclopedia. Now he noticed what a preposterous number of volumes there were, perhaps two hundred in all, filling not only one bookcase from floor to ceiling but filling parts of others as well. His curiosity piqued, he pulled down Volume XLIV, and opened it at random to page 494.

The page was filled with very small print, with a section at the bottom in   14 even smaller print that appeared to be footnotes. The heading of the page was large enough to be read at a glance. "RE: PRISONER 7439762 (referred to herein as 'Q')." He read on: "3/07/06. 14:03. Q entered room on 3/06/06 at 4:52. Surprised at pleasantness of room. Glanced at furniture, then bookcase, then ceiling. Noted metal tray and second door, puzzled by both. Entered bathroom, noting toilet articles. Lifted shaver and touched cologne." He skipped down the page: "Selected brown slacks, rust sweater, and tan shoes. Felt normal clothing made him more equal to his situation."

It seemed that they were keeping some sort of record of his activities here.   15 But what was the purpose of having the record here for him to read? And how had they gotten it in here? It was easy to figure out how they knew of his activities: they were watching him, just as he had suspected. They must have printed this page during the night and placed it here as he slept. Perhaps his food had been drugged to guarantee that he wouldn't awake.

He glanced toward the door of his cell and remembered the chair he had   16 placed against it. In a drugged sleep, he wouldn't have heard them enter. They could have pulled the chair back as they left. But all the way? Presumably there was some hidden panel in the door. Once the door was shut, they had merely to open the panel and pull the chair the last few inches.

Suddenly he remembered the matter of the gun. He glanced down the page   17 and there it was, a description of how he had handled the gun twice. There was no warning given nor any hint of an explanation as to why the gun was there. There was just the clipped, neutral-toned description of his actions and impressions. It described his hope that the gun might have been left by another prisoner, his rejection of that supposition, his fear that the gun might be used against him in some way, his desire to remove the fingerprints. But how on earth could they have known what he was feeling and thinking? He decided that he had acted and reacted as any normal person would have done, and they had simply drawn the obvious conclusions from his actions and facial expressions.

He glanced further down the page and read: "On 3/07/06, Q awoke at   18
8:33." And further ". . . selected *The Future of Socialism* by Felix Berofsky . . . ."
And further: ". . . bent the corner of page 206 to mark his place and put the book.
. . ." All his activities of that morning had already been printed in the report!

He began turning the book around in his hands and pulled it away from the   19
shelf. Was this thing wired in some way? Could they print their reports onto these pages in minutes without removing the books from the shelves? Perhaps they had some new process whereby they could imprint specially sensitized pages by electronic signal.

Then he remembered that he had just awakened from a nap, and he   20
slammed the volume shut in disgust. Of course: they had entered the room again during his nap. He placed the volume back on the shelf and started for his chair. How could they expect him to be taken in by such blatant trickery? But then a thought occurred to him. He had picked out a volume and page at random. Why had the description of yesterday and this morning been on that particular page? Were all the pages the same? He returned to the shelf and picked up the same volume, this time opening it to page 531. The heading was the same. He looked down the page: "Q began to return to his chair but became puzzled as to why the initial description of his activities should have appeared on page 494 of this volume." He threw the book to the floor and grabbed another, Volume LX, opening it to page 103: ". . . became more confused by the correct sequential description on page 531, Volume LXIV."

"What are you trying to do to me!" he screamed, dropping the second   21
book.

Immediately he was ashamed at his lack of self-control.   22

"What an absurd joke," he said loudly to whatever listening devices there   23
might be.

He picked up the two volumes he had dropped and put them back in place   24
on the bookshelf. He walked across the room and sat in the chair. He tried to
keep his expression neutral while he thought.

There was no possibility that observations were being made and immedi-   25
ately transmitted to the books by some electronic process. It all happened too
fast. Perhaps it was being done through some kind of mind control. Yet he was
certain that no devices of any kind had been implanted in his brain. That would
have involved anesthetizing him, operating, leaving him unconscious until all
scars had healed, and then reviving him with no sense of time lost. No doubt
they had ability, but not that much. It could be something as simple as hypnosis,
of course. This would require merely writing the books, then commanding him
to perform certain acts in a certain order, including the opening of the books. Yet
that would be such a simple, familiar experiment that it would hardly seem worth
doing. And it would hardly require the extensive testing procedures that he had
undergone before being placed in this room.

He glanced at the books again, and his eye fell on Volume I. If there was   26
an explanation anywhere in this room, it would be there, he thought. The page
would probably say only, "Q hoped for an explanation," and in that case he
would have to do without one. But it was worth taking a look.

He took Volume I from the shelf, opened it to the first page, and glanced   27
at the first paragraph: "Q hoped to find an explanation." He started to laugh, but
stopped abruptly. The explanation seemed to be there after all. He read on:
"Experiment in the Prediction of Human Behavior within a Controlled
Environment, No. 465, Variant No. 8, Case 2: Subject Aware of Behavior
Prediction."

He read through the brief "explanation" several times. (Of course, this in   28
itself might be trickery.) Obviously, these unknown experimenters considered all
human behavior to be theoretically predictable. They first studied a subject for a
number of weeks and then attempted to predict how that subject would behave
within a limited, controlled environment. In his case, they were attempting to
predict, in addition to all else, his reactions to the "fact" that his behavior was
predictable and being predicted. They had placed those volumes here as proof to
him that each prior series of acts had been successfully predicted.

He didn't believe they could do it; he didn't want to believe it. Of course,   29
much of what occurred in the universe, including much of human behavior, was
predictable in theory. The world wasn't totally chaotic, after all, and science had
had its successes in foreseeing certain events. But he refused to believe that there

was no element of chance in the world, that every event happened just as it did out of necessity. He had some freedom, some causal autonomy, some power to initiate the new. He was not merely a puppet of universal laws. Each of his choices was not simply a mathematical function of those laws together with the state of himself and the external world at the moment just prior to the choice. He would not believe that.

Nothing was written on page 1 to indicate how the other experiments had   30 turned out—not that he would have believed such a report anyway. No doubt the indication that his experience was a more complex "variant" of the experiment was meant to imply that the preceding experiments had been successful. But there had to have been mistakes, even if they claimed that the errors could eventually be overcome. As long as there were mistakes, one could continue to believe in human freedom. He *did* believe in human freedom.

His thoughts were interrupted by the buzzer. His dinner emerged from the   31 wall. He looked at it with anger, remembering how the first page to which he had turned had listed, perhaps even predicted, exactly what foods he would eat. But he didn't reject the meal. He needed his wits about him, and for that he needed strength. He must try to get his mind off all this for tonight, at least. He would eat, read, and then sleep.

For several hours, he was fairly successful in diverting his attention from   32 the books. Then, in bed with the lights out, he recalled the phrase "Variant No. 8, Case 2." That made him feel more hopeful. This was only the second time that this particular version of the experiment was being tried. Surely, the likelihood of error was great.

He found himself thinking about Case 1. What kind of man had he been,   33 and how had he fared? Had he worn green pajamas one day when the book said "yellow," or remained contemptuous when the book said "hysterical," and then laughed in their faces as they led him from the room? That would have been a triumph.

Suddenly, he thought of the gun and had an image of a man, seated on the   34 edge of the bed, looking at those volumes on the wall, slowly raising the gun to his head. ". . . To predict . . . his reactions to the 'fact' that his behavior was predictable and being predicted." God, was that the purpose of the gun? Had it been put there as one of his options? Had that been the ignominious ending of Case 1, and not the departure in triumph he had pictured a moment ago? He had a vision of himself lying dead on the floor and men in white robes grinning as they opened a volume to a page that described his death. Would he hold out, or would he die? The answer was somewhere in those thousands of pages—if he could only find it.

He realized that he was playing into their hands by supposing that they could do what he knew they could not. Anyway, even if one assumed that they could accurately predict his future, they were not forcing him to do anything. There were no mind-controlling devices; he wasn't being programmed by them. If they were to predict correctly, they must predict what he wanted to do. And he didn't want to die.

In spite of these reflections, he remained agitated. When he finally slept, he slept fitfully. He dreamed that he was a minuscule figure trapped in a maze on the scale of a dollhouse. He watched himself from a distance and watched the life-sized doctors who peered over the top of the maze. There were two exits from the maze, one to freedom and one to a black pit that he knew to be death. "Death," the doctors kept saying to one another, and he watched his steady progression in the maze toward death. He kept shouting instructions to himself. "No, not that way! Go to the left there!" But the doomed figure couldn't hear him.

When he awoke in the morning, he felt feverish and touched only the fruit and coffee on his breakfast tray. He lay on the bed for much of the morning, his thoughts obsessed with the black volumes on the wall. He knew that he must try to foil the predictions, but he feared failure. I am too upset and weak, he thought. I must ignore the books until I am better. I must turn my mind to other things.

But as he tried to divert himself, he became aware of an agonizing echo in his head. He would turn in bed and think: "Q turns onto left side." Or scratch: "Q scratches left thigh." Or mutter "damn them": "Q mutters, 'damn them.'" Finally, he could stand it no longer and stumbled to one of the bookshelves. He pulled two volumes from the shelves, juggled them in his hands, dropped one, then flipped the pages several times before picking a page.

"3/08/06. 11:43. At 15:29 on 3/07/06, Q opened Volume I to page 1 and read explanation of experiment."

He slammed the book.

"Damn you," he said aloud. "I'm a man, not a machine. I'll show you. I'll show you."

He took another volume and held it in his hand. "Two and two are five," he thought. "When I was six, I lived in China with the Duke of Savoy. The earth is flat." He opened the book.

"Q wants to confuse prediction. Thinks: Two and two are five. . . ."

He looked around the room as he tried to devise some other line of attack.   44
He noticed the clock and the calendar. Each page of the book gave the date and
time at which each page opened, the date and time of each event. He rushed to
the desk, flipped the pages of the calendar, and turned the knob that adjusted the
hands on the clock. He opened another book and read: "3/08/06. 12:03." He
yelled out:

"See? You're wrong. The calendar says June, and the time is 8:04. That's my   45
date and my time. Predict what you think if you want. This is what I think. And
I think you're wrong."

He had another idea. The first page he had looked at had been page 494,   46
Volume LXIV. He would open that volume to the same page. Either it must say
the same thing or it must be new. Either way they would have failed, for a new
entry would show them to be tricksters. He grabbed the volume and found the
page. "3/07/06. 14:03. Q entered room on 3/06/06 at 4:52." Once again, he spoke
aloud:

"Of course, but that's old news. I don't see anything here about my turning   47
to the page a second time. My, we do seem to be having our problems, don't we?"

He laughed in triumph and was about to shut the book when he saw the   48
fine print at the bottom. He licked his lips and stared at the print for a long time
before he pulled down another volume and turned to the page that had been
indicated in the footnote: ". . . then Q reopened Volume LXIV, page 494, hoping. . . ."

He ripped out the page, then another, and another. His determination gave   49
way to a fury, and he tore apart one book, then another, until twelve of them lay
in tatters on the floor. He had to stop because of dizziness and exhaustion.

"I'm a man," he muttered, "not a machine."   50

He started for his bed, ignoring the buzzer announcing the tray of food. He   51
made it only as far as the easy chair. He sank into it, and his eyelids seemed to
close of their own weight.

"I'm a. . . ."   52

Asleep, he dreamed again. He was running through the streets of a   53
medieval town, trying desperately to escape from a grotesque, devil-like creature.
"At midnight you die," it said. No matter where he ran, the devil kept reappear-
ing in front of him. "It doesn't matter where you go. I will be there at midnight."
Then a loud bell began to sound twelve chimes slowly. He found himself in a
huge library, swinging an axe at the shelves, which crumbled under his blows. He

felt great elation until he saw that everything he had destroyed had been reassembled behind him. He dropped the axe and began to scream.

When he awoke, he thought for a moment he was still dreaming. On the   54 floor, he saw twelve volumes, all intact. Then he turned his head and saw the twelve torn volumes where he had left them. The new ones were on the floor near the metal tray. His lunch had been withdrawn, and the books had been pushed through the opening in the wall while he had slept.

He moved to the bed, where he slept fitfully through the evening and   55 night, getting up only once to sip some tea from the dinner tray.

In the morning he remained in bed. He was no longer feverish, but he felt   56 more exhausted than he could remember ever having been. The breakfast tray came and went untouched. He didn't feel like eating. He didn't feel like doing anything.

At about eleven o'clock, he got out of bed just long enough to find the gun;   57 then he fingered it on his chest as he lay back, staring at the ceiling. There was no point in going on with it. They would have their laughs, of course. But they would have them in any case, since, no matter what he did, it would be in their books. And ultimately it wasn't their victory at all, but the victory of the universal laws that had dictated every event in this puppet play of a world. A man of honor must refuse to play his part in it. He, certainly, refused.

And how could the experimenters delight in their achievement? They   58 were not testing a theory about their prisoners but about all human beings, including themselves. Their success showed that they themselves had no control over their own destinies. What did it matter if his future was written in the books and their futures were not? There would always be the invisible books in the nature of things, books that contained the futures of everyone. Could they help seeing that? And when they saw that, if they too didn't reach for guns, could they help feeling degraded to the core of their souls? No, they had not won. Everyone had lost.

Eventually he sat up on the bed. His hand shook, but he was not surprised.   59 Whatever he might will, there would be that impulse for survival. He forced the hand up and put the barrel of the gun in his mouth.

The buzzer startled him, and the hand with the gun dropped to his side.   60 The lunch tray appeared, and suddenly he was aware of being ravenously hungry. He laughed bitterly. Well, he wouldn't be hungry for long. Still, wasn't the condemned man entitled to a last meal? Surely honor did not forbid that. And the food looked delicious. He put the gun on his pillow and took the tray to his desk.

While he was savoring his mushroom omelet, he glanced at the political 61 treatise that had remained half read by the easy chair for the last two days. God, had it been only two days? It was a shame that he would not be able to finish it; it was an interesting book. And there were other books on the shelves—not the black volumes, of course—that he had been meaning to read for some time and would have enjoyed.

As he sampled some artichokes, he glanced at the formidable black vol- 62 umes on the shelves. Somewhere there was a page that read: "After completing lunch, Q put the gun to his head and pulled the trigger." Of course, if he changed his mind and decided to finish reading the political treatise first, it would say that instead. Or if he waited a day more, it would register that fact. What were the possibilities? Could it ever say "reprieved"? He did not see how. They would never let him go free with the information he had about their experiments. Unless, of course, there was a change of regime. But that was the barest of possibilities. Could a page say that he had been returned to the regular cells? God, how he would like to talk to another human being. But that would pose the same problem for the experimenters as releasing him. Presumably, they would kill him eventually. Still, that was no worse than what he was about to do to himself. Perhaps they would continue the experiment a while longer. Meantime, he could live comfortably, eat well, read, exercise.

There were indeed possibilities other than immediate suicide, not all of 63 them unpleasant. But could he countenance living any longer? Didn't honor dictate defiance? Yet—defiance of whom? It wasn't as if the laws of the world had a lawmaker in whose face he might shake his fist. He had never believed in a god; rather, it was as if he were trapped inside some creaky old machine, unstarted and uncontrolled, that had been puttering along a complex but predictable path forever. Kick a machine when you're angry, and you only get a sore foot. Anyway, how could he have claimed credit for killing himself, since it would have been inevitable that he do so?

The black volumes stretched out like increments of time across the brown 64 bookshelves. Somewhere in their pages was this moment, and the next, and perhaps a tomorrow, and another, perhaps even a next month or a next year. He would never be able to read those pages until it was already unnecessary, but there might be some good days there; in any case, it would be interesting to wait and see.

After lunch he sat at his desk for a long time. Eventually, he got up and   65
replaced the gun in its case in the bureau drawer. He placed the lunch dishes
back on the metal tray and, beside the dishes, heaped the covers and torn pages
of the books he had destroyed. He then put the new volumes on the shelves. As
he started back to the chair, his eye was caught by the things on the desk. He
took a volume from the bookshelf, carried it to the desk, and opened it. He read
only the heading at the top: "3/09/06. 13:53." He adjusted the clock and the calendar accordingly. If he was going to live a while longer, he might as well know
the correct day and time.

The Grand Inquisitor

Fyodor Dostoyevksy

You see, even here we can't get by without a preface—a literary preface, that is, con-   1
found it! Ivan said, laughing. 'And what kind of an author am I? Look, the action of
my poem takes place in the sixteenth century, and back then—as a matter of fact,
this ought still to be familiar to you from your days at school—back then it was the
custom in works of poetry to bring the celestial powers down to earth. Dante I need
hardly mention. In France the magistrates' clerks and also the monks in the monasteries used to give entire dramatic spectacles in which they brought on to the stage
the Madonna, the angels, the saints, Christ and even God Himself. Back in those
days it was all very unsophisticated. In Victor Hugo's *Nôtre Dame de Paris*, under the
reign of Louis XI, an edifying spectacle is given to the people free of charge in the
auditorium of the Paris Town Hall, to celebrate the birthday of the French Dauphin,
under the title *Le bon jugement de la très sainte et gracieuse Vièrge Marie*, in which she
herself appears in person and pronounces her *bon jugement*. In our own country, in
the Moscow of pre-Petrine antiquity, dramatic spectacles of almost the same kind
especially of stories from the Old Testament, also took place from time to time; but,
in addition to dramatic spectacles, there passed throughout all the world a large number of tales and "verses" in which when necessary the saints, the angels, and all the
powers of heaven wrought their influence. The monks in our monasteries also occupied themselves with the translation, copying and even the composition of such
poems, and in such times, too: under the Tartar yoke. There is, for example, a certain
little monastic poem (from the Greek, of course) entitled *The Journey of the Mother
of God Through the Torments*, with scenes and with a boldness that are not inferior
to those of Dante. The Mother of god visits hell, and her guide through the "torments" is the Archangel Michael. She beholds the sinners and their sufferings. This
hell, incidentally, contains a most entertaining category of sinners in a burning lake:
those of them who sink into this lake so deep that they are unable to swim to its surface again are "forgotten by God"—a phrase of exceptional force and profundity. And
lo, the shocked and seeping Mother of God falls down before God's throne and
appeals to him to grant forgiveness to all who are in hell, all whom she has seen there,

without distinction. Her entreaty with God is of colossal interest. She implores him, she will not depart, and when God draws her attention to the nailed hands and feet of His Son and asks her: "How can I forgive his torturers?" she commands all the saints, all the martyrs, all the angels and archangels to fall down together with her and pray for the forgiveness of all without discrimination. The upshot of it is that she coaxes from God a respite from the torments each year, from Good Friday to Whit Sunday, and out of hell the sinners at once thank the Lord and loudly cry unto Him: "Just and true art thou, O Lord, that thou has judgèd thus." Well, my little poem would have been in similar vein, had it appeared in those days. He appears on my proscenium; to be sure, in my poem. He does not say anything, only makes his appearance and goes on his way. Fifteen centuries have now passed since He made his vow to come in his kingdom, fifteen centuries since his prophet wrote: "Behold, I come quickly." "But of that day and that hour knoweth no man, not even the Son, but only my Father in heaven," as He himself prophesied while yet on the earth. But human kind awaits him with its earlier faith and its earlier tender emotion. Oh, with even greater faith, for fifteen centuries have now passed since the pledges have ceased to be lent to man from the heavens:

Thou must have faith in what the heart saith,
For the heavens no pledges lend.

'And only faith in that which is said by the heart! To be sure, there were many 2 miracles back in those days. There were saints who effected miraculous healings; to some righteous men, according to their life chronicles, the Queen of heaven herself came down. But the Devil does not slumber, and in humankind there had already begun to grow a doubt in the genuineness of these miracles. Just at that time there appeared in the north, in Germany, a terrible new heresy. An enormous star, "burning as it were a lamp" (that's the church, you see), "fell upon the fountains of the waters, and they were made bitter". These heresies began blasphemously to contradict the miracles. But all the more ardent was the faith of those who remained true believers. The tears of humankind ascended to Him as before, He was awaited, loved, trusted in, people thirsted to suffer and die for him, as before . . . And for how many centuries had humankind prayed with faith and ardour: "O god the Lord, show us light", for how many centuries had it appealed to Him that He, in His immeasurable compassion, should deign to come down among His supplicants. He had been known to condescend before and had visited certain men of righteousness, martyrs and holy cenobites while yet they lived on earth, as it is written in their "Lives".

Among us Tyutchev, who believed profoundly in the truth of His words, announced that

> Weighed down by the Cross's burden,
> All of you, my native land,
> Heaven's Tsar in servile aspect
> Trudged while blessing, end to end.

Which really was the case, I do assure you, and so it happens that He conceives the desire to manifest Himself, if only for an instant, to His people—to His struggling, suffering, stinkingly sinful people that none the less childishly love Him. My poem is set in Spain, at the most dreadful period of the Inquisition, when bonfires glowed throughout the land every day to the glory of god and

> In resplendent *autos-da-fé*
> Burned the wicked heretics.

Oh, this is not, of course, that coming in which He will appear, according to His promise, at the end of days in the clouds of heaven with power and great glory and which will take place suddenly, "as the lightning cometh out of the east, and shineth even unto the west". No. He has conceived the desire to visit his children at least for an instant and precisely in those places where the bonfires of heretics had begun to crackle. In His boundless mercy He passes once more among men in that same human form in which for three years He walked among men fifteen centuries earlier. He comes down to the "hot streets and squares" of the southern town in which only the previous day, in a "resplendent *auto-da-fé*, in the presence of the king, the court, the knights, the cardinals and the loveliest ladies of the court, in the presence of the numerous population of all Seville, there have been burned by the Cardinal Grand Inquisitor very nearly a good hundred heretics all in one go, *ad majorem gloriam Dei*.

He has appeared quietly, unostentatiously, and yet—strange, this—everyone recognizes Him. That could have been one of the best bits in my poem—I mean, the question of why it is that everyone recognizes him. The people rush towards him with invincible force, surround him, mass around him, follow him. Saying nothing, He passes among them with a quiet smile of infinite compassion. The sun of love burns in his heart, the beams of Light, Enlightenment and Power flow from his eyes and, as they stream over people, shake their hearts with answering love. He stretches out His arms to them, blesses them, and from one touch of Him, even of His garments, there issues a healing force. Then from the crowd and old man, blind since the years of childhood, exclaims: "O Lord, heal me, that I may behold thee," and lo, it is as though the scales fall from the blind man's eyes, and he sees Him. The people weep and kiss the ground on which He walks. The children throw flowers in his path, singing and crying to Him: "Hossanah!" "It's Him, it's Him," they all repeat, "it must be Him, it can't be anyone but Him." He stops in the parvis of Seville Cathedral just at the moment a white, open child's coffin is being borne with weeping into the place of worship: in it is a seven-year-old girl, the only daughter of a certain noble and distinguished citizen. The dead child lies covered in flowers. "He will raise up your child," voices cry from the crowd to the weeping mother. The cathedral *pater* who has come out to meet the coffin looks bewildered and knits his brows. But then the mother of the dead child utters a resounding wail. She grows herself at his feet: "If it is You, then raise up my child!" she exclaims, stretching out her arms to him. The procession stops, the coffin is lowered to the parvis floor, to his feet. He gazes with compassion, and his lips softly pronounce again: *"Talitha cumi"* —Damsel, I say unto thee, arise." The girl rises in her coffin, sits up and looks around her, smiling, with astonished, wide-open eyes. In her arms is the bouquet of white roses with which she had lain in the coffin.

Among the people there are confusion, shouts, sobbing, and then suddenly, at that very moment, on his way past the cathedral comes the Cardinal Grand Inquisitor himself. He is an old man of almost ninety, tall and straight, with a withered face and sunken eyes, in which, however, there is still a fiery, spark-like gleam. Oh, he is not dressed in his resplendent cardinal's attire, the attire in which yesterday he showed himself off before the people as the enemies of the Roman faith were being burned—no, at this moment he wears only his old, coarse monkish cassock. Behind him at certain distance follow his surly assistants and servants and the "Holy" Guard. He stops before the crowd and observes from a distance. He has seen it all, has seen the coffin being put down at His feet, has seen the damsel rise up, and a shadow has settled on his face. He knits his thick, grey brows, and his eyes flash with an ill-boding fire. He extends his index finger and orders the guards to arrest Him. And lo, such is his power and so accustomed, submissive and tremblingly obedient to him are the people that the crowd immediately parts before the guards, and they, amidst the sepulchral silence that has suddenly fallen, place their hands on Him and march Him away. Instantly, the crowd, almost as one man, bow their heads to the ground before the Elder—Inquisitor, and without uttering a word he blesses the people and passes on his way. The Guard conduct the Captive to a narrow and murky vaulted prison in the ancient building of the Ecclesiastical Court and lock Him up in it. The day goes by, and the dark, passionate and "unbreathing" Seville night begins.

The air "of lemon and of laurel reeks." In the midst of the deep murk the prison's iron door is suddenly opened and the old Grand Inquisitor himself slowly enters the prison with a lamp in his hand. He is alone, the door instantly locks again behind him. He pauses in the entrance and for a long time, a minute or two, studies His face. At last he quietly goes up to Him, places the lamp on the table and says to Him:

"Is it you? You?" Receiving no answer, however, he quickly adds: "No, do not reply, keep silent. And in any case, what could you possibly say? I know only too well what you would say. And you have no right to add anything to what was said by you in former times. Why have you come to get in our way? For you have come to get in our way, and you yourself know it. But do you know what will happen tomorrow? I do not know who you are, and I do not want to know; you may be He or you may be only His likeness, but tomorrow I shall find you guilty and burn you at the stake as the most wicked of heretics, and those same people who today kissed your feet will tomorrow at one wave of my hand rush to rake up the embers on your bonfire, do you know that? Yes, I dare say you do," he added in heartfelt reflection, not for one moment removing his gaze from his Captive.'   5

'I don't quite understand this part of it, Ivan,' Aloyosha smiled; all the time he had listened in silence. 'Is it simply an immense fantasy, or is it some mistake on the part of an old man, some impossible *quiproquo?*'   6

'Why don't you assume it's the latter.' Ivan burst out laughing. 'If you've been so spoiled by contemporary realism that you can't endure anything fantastic and you want it to be a quiproquo, then so be it. It certainly can't be denied,' he laughed again, 'that the old man is ninety, and might easily have long ago been driven insane by the idea that is in his mind. On the other hand, the Captive might have struck him by His appearance. Or it might simply have been a hallucination, the vision of a ninety-year-old man on the threshold of death, given added feverish intensity by the previous day's *auto-da-fé* of a hundred burned heretics. Is it not, however, a matter of indifference to us whether it's a *quiproquo*, or whether it's a colossal fantasy? The point is merely that the old man wants to speak his mind, to finally say out loud the things he has kept silent about for ninety years.'   7

'And the Captive says nothing either? Gazes at him, but says no word?'   8

'But that is how it must be in all such instances,' Ivan laughed again. 'The old man himself remarks to Him that he has not the right to add anything to what has already been said by Him in former times. If one cares to, one can see in that statement the most basic characteristic of Roman Catholicism, in my opinion, at least; it's as if they were saying: "It was all told by you to the Pope and so it is now all of it in the Pope's possession, and now we should appreciate it if you would stay away alto-   9 gether and refrain from interfering for the time being, at any rate." That is the sense in which they not only speak but also write, the jesuits, at least. I've read such things in the works of their theologians. "Do you have the right to divulge to us so much as one of the mysteries of the world from which you have come?" my old man asks Him, supplying the answer himself: "no, you do not, lest you add anything to what has already been said by you, and lest you take away from people the freedom you so stood up for when you were upon the earth. Anything new that you divulge will encroach upon people's freedom to believe, for it will look like a miracle and their freedom to believe was what mattered to you most even back then, fifteen hundred years ago. Was it not you who so often used to say back then: 'I want to make you free'? Well, but now you have seen those 'free' people" the old man suddenly adds with a thoughtful and ironic smile. "Yes, this task has cost us dearly," he continues, looking at him sternly, "but we have at last accomplished it in your name. For fifteen centuries we have struggled with that freedom, but now it is all over, and over for good. You don't believe that it is over for good? You look at me meekly and do not even consider me worthy of indignation? Well, I think you ought to be aware that now, and particularly in the days we are currently living through, those people are even more certain than ever that they are completely free, and indeed they themselves have brought us their freedom and have laid it humbly at our feet. But we were the ones who did that, and was that what you desired, that kind of freedom?"'

'Once again I don't understand,' Alyosha broke in. 'Is he being ironic, is he   10
laughing?'

'Not at all. What he is doing is claiming the credit for himself and his kind for   11
at last having conquered freedom and having done so in order to make people happy. "For only now" (he is talking about the Inquisition, of course) "has it become possible to think for the first time about people's happiness. Man is constituted as a mutineer; can mutineers ever be happy? You were given warnings," he says to Him, "you had plenty of warnings and instructions, but you did not obey them, you rejected the only path by which people could have been made happy, but fortunately when you left you handed over the task to us. You gave your promise, you sealed it with your word, you gave us the right to bind and loose, and so of course you cannot even dream of taking that right from us now. So why have you come to get in our way?"'

'I wonder if you could explain the meaning of that phrase: "you had plenty of   12
warnings and instructions"?' Alyosha asked.

'Yes, well, that is exactly the point on which the old man wants to speak his   13
mind.'

"'The terrible and clever Spirit, the Spirit of self-annihilation and non-exis-   14
tence," the old man continues, "that great Spirit spoke with you in the wilderness,
and we are told in the Scriptures that it 'tempted' you. Is that so? And would it be
possible to say anything more true than those things which he made known to you
in three questions and which you rejected, and which in the Scriptures are called
'temptations'? Yet at the same time, if ever there took place on the earth a truly thun-
derous miracle, it was on that day, the day of those three temptations. Precisely in the
emergence of those three questions did the miracle lie. Were one to imagine, just for
the sake of experiment and as an example, that those three questions put by the terrible Spirit had been lost without trace from the Scriptures and that it was necessary
to reconstruct them, invent and compose them anew so they could again be entered
in the Scriptures, and for this purpose to gather all the sages of the earth—the rulers,
the high priests, the scholars, the philosophers, the poets, and give them the task of
inventing, composing three questions, but of such a kind that would not only correspond to the scale of the event but would also express, in three words, in but three
human phrases, the entire future history of the world and mankind—then do you
suppose that all the great wisdom of the earth, having united together, would be able
to invent anything at all even remotely equivalent in power and depth to those three
questions that were actually put to you that day by the mighty and clever Spirit in
the wilderness? Why, by those very questions alone, by the sheer miracle of their
emergence it is possible to gain the realization that one is dealing not with fleeting
human intelligence, but with one that is eternal and absolute. For it is as if in those
three questions there is conjoined into a single whole and prophesied the entire subsequent history of mankind, there are manifested the three images in which all the
unresolved historical contradictions of human nature throughout all the earth will
coincide. Back then this was not as yet evident for the future was unknown, but now
after the passage of fifteen centuries we can see that everything in those three questions was the product of such foresight and foreknowledge and was so reasonable that
it is no longer possible to add anything to them or to remove anything from them.

"'Decide for yourself who was right: You or the One who questioned You that   15
day? Remember the first question, though not in literal terms, its sense was this: 'You
want to go into the world and are going there with empty hands, with a kind of promise of freedom which they in their simplicity and inborn turpitude are unable even to
comprehend, which they go in fear and awe of—for nothing has ever been more
unendurable to man and human society than freedom! Look, you see those stones in
that naked, burning hot wilderness? Turn them into loaves and mankind will go trot-
ting after you like a flock, grateful and obedient, though ever fearful that you may

take away your hand and that your loaves may cease to come their way.' But you did not want to deprive man of freedom and rejected the offer, for what kind of freedom is it, you reasoned, if obediences is purchased with loaves? You retorted that man lives not by bread alone, but are you aware that in the name of that same earthly bread the Earth Spirit will rise up against you and fight with you and vanquish you, and everyone will follow it, crying: 'Who is like unto this beast, he has given us fire from heaven!' Are you aware that centuries will pass, and mankind will proclaim with the lips of its wisdom and science that there is no crime and consequently no sin either, but only the hungry. 'Feed them, and then ask virtue of them!'—that is what will be inscribed upon the banner they will raise against you and before which your temple will come crashing down. In the place of your temple there will be erected a new edifice, once again a terrible Tower of Babel will be erected, and even though this one will no more be completed than was the previous one, but even so you would be able to avoid that new Tower and abbreviate the sufferings of the human beings by a thousand years, for after all, it is to us that they will come, when they have suffered for a thousand years with their Tower! Then they will track us down again under the ground, in the catacombs, hiding (for we shall again be persecuted and tortured), they will find us and cry to us: 'Feed us, for those who promised us fire from heaven have not granted it.' And then we shall complete their Tower, for it is he that feeds them who will complete it, and it is only we that shall feed them, in your name, and lie that we do it in your name. Oh, never, never will they feed themselves without us! No science will give them bread while yet they are free, but the end of it will be that they will bring us their freedom and place it at our feet and say to us: 'Enslave us if you will, but feed us.' At last they themselves will understand that freedom and earthly bread in sufficiency for all are unthinkable together, for never, never will they be able to share between themselves! They will also be persuaded that they will never be able to be free, because they are feeble, depraved, insignificant and mutinous. You promised them the bread of heaven, but, I repeat again, can it compare in the eyes of a weak, eternally depraved and eternally dishonourable human race with the earthly sort? And if in the name of the break of heaven thousands and tens of thousands follow you, what will become of the millions and tens of thousand millions of creatures who are not strong enough to disdain the earthly bread for the heavenly sort? Or are the only ones you care about the tens of thousands of the great and the strong, while the remaining millions, numerous as the grains of sand in the sea, weak, but loving you, must serve as mere raw material for the great and the strong? No, we care about the weak, too. They are depraved and mutineers, but in the end they too will grow obedient. They will marvel at us and will consider us gods because we, in standing at their head, have consented to endure freedom and rule over them—so terrible will being free appear to them at last! But we shall say that we are obedient to you and that we rule in your name. We shall deceive them again for we shall not let you near us any more. In that deception will be our suffering, for we shall be compelled to lie.

That is the significance of the first question that was asked in the wilderness, 16 and that is what you rejected in the name of freedom, which you placed higher than anything else. Yet in that question lay the great secret of this world. Had you accepted the 'loaves', you would have responded to the universal and age-old anguish of man, both as an individual creature and as the whole of mankind, namely the question: 'Before whom should one bow down?' There is for man no preoccupation more constant or more nagging than, while in a condition of freedom, quickly to find someone to bow down before. But man seeks to bow down before that which is already beyond dispute, so far beyond dispute that all human beings will instantly agree to a universal bowing-down before it. For the preoccupation of these miserable creatures consists not only in finding something that everyone can come to believe in and bow down before, and that it should indeed be *everyone*, and that they should do it *all together*. It is this need for a *community* of bowing-down that has been the principal torment of each individual person and of mankind as a whole since the earliest ages. For the sake of a universal bowing-down they have destroyed one another with the sword. They have created gods and challenged one another: 'Give up your gods and come and worship ours or else death to you and to your gods!' And so it will be until the world's end, when even gods will vanish from the world: whatever happens, they will fall down before idols. You knew, you could not fail to know that peculiar secret of human nature, but you rejected the only absolute banner that was offered to you and that would have compelled everyone to bow down before you without dispute—the banner of earthly bread, and you rejected in in the name of freedom and the bread of heaven. Just take a look at what you did after that. And all of it again in the name of freedom! I tell you, man has no preoccupation more nagging than to find the person to whom that unhappy creature may surrender the gift of freedom with which he is born. But only he can take mastery of people's freedom who is able to set their consciences at rest. With bread you were given an undisputed banner: give bread and man will bow down, for nothing is more undisputed than bread, but if at the same time someone takes mastery of his conscience without your knowledge—oh, then he will even throw down your bread and follow the one who seduces his conscience. In that you were right. For the secret of human existence does not consist in living, merely, but in what one lives for. Without a firm idea of what he is to live for, man will not consent to live and will sooner destroy himself than remain on the earth, even though all around him there be loaves. That is so, but how has it worked out? Instead of taking mastery of people's freedom, you have increased that freedom even further! Or did you forget that peace of mind and even death are dearer to man than free choice and the cognition of good and evil? There is nothing more seductive for man than the freedom of his conscience, but there is nothing more tormenting for him, either. And so then in place of a firm foundation for the easing of the human conscience once and for all—you took everything that was exceptional, enigmatic and indeterminate, took everything that was beyond people's capacity to bear, and therefore acted as though you did not love them at all—and who was this? The one who had come to sacrifice his life for them! Instead of taking mastery of people's freedom, you augmented it and saddled the spiritual kingdom of man with it for ever. You desired that man's love should be free, that he should follow you freely, enticed and captivated by you. Henceforth, in place of the old, firm law, man was himself to decide with a free heart what is good and what is evil, with only your image before him to guide him—but surely you never dreamed that he would at last reject and call into question even your image and your truth were he to be oppressed by so terrible a burden as freedom of choice? They will exclaim at last that the truth is not in you, for it would have been impossible to leave them in more confusion and torment that you did when you left them so many worries and unsolvable problems.

Thus, you yourself laid the foundation for the destruction of your own kingdom, and no one else should be blamed for it. And yet is that really what was offered you? There are three powers, only three powers on earth that are capable of eternally vanquishing and ensnaring the consciences of those feeble mutineers, for their happiness—those powers are: miracle, mystery and authority. You rejected the first, the second and the third, and yourself gave the lead in doing so. When the wise and terrible Spirit set you on a pinnacle of the temple and said to you: 'If you would know whether you are the Son of God, then cast yourself down from hence, for it is written that the angels will take charge of him and bear him up, and he will not fall and dish himself to pieces—and then you will know if you are the Son of god, and will prove how much faith you have in your Father.' But having heard him through, you rejected his offer and did not give way and did not cast yourself down. Oh, of course, in that you acted proudly and magnificently, like God, but people, that weak, mutinying tribe—are they gods? Oh, that day you understood that by taking only one step, the step of casting yourself down, you would instantly have tempted the Lord and would have lost all faith in him, and would have dashed yourself to pieces against the earth which you had come to save, and the clever Spirit which had tempted you would rejoice. But, I repeat, are there many such as you? And could you really have

17

supposed, even for a moment, that people would have the strength to resist such a temptation? Is human nature really of a kind as to be able to reject the miracle, and to make do, at such terrible moments of life, moments of the most terrible fundamental and tormenting spiritual questions, with only a free decision of the heart? Oh, you knew that your great deed would be preserved in the Scriptures, would attain to the depth of the ages and to the outermost limits of the earth, and you hoped that, in following you, man too would make do with God, not requiring a miracle. But you did not know that no sooner did man reject the miracle than he would at once reject God also, for man does not seek God so much as miracles. And since man is not strong enough to get by without the miracle, he creates new miracles for himself, his own now, and bows down before the miracle of the quack and the witchcraft of the peasant woman, even though he is a mutineer, heretic and atheist a hundred times over. You did not come down from the Cross when they shouted to you, mocking and teasing you: 'Come down from the Cross and we will believe that it is You.' You did not come down because again you did not want to enslave man with a miracle and because you thirsted for a faith that was free, not miraculous. You thirsted for a love that was free, not for the servile ecstasies of the slave before the might that has inspired him with dread once and for all. But even here you had too high an opinion of human beings, for of course, they are slaves, though they are created mutineers. Look around you and judge, now that fifteen centuries have passed, take a glance at them: which of them have you borne up to yourself? Upon my word, man is created weaker and more base than you supposed! Can he, can he perform the deeds of which you are capable? In respecting him so much you acted as though you had ceased to have compassion for him, because you demanded too much of him—and yet who was this? The very one you had loved more than yourself! Had you respected him less you would have demanded of him less, and the would have been closer to love, for his burden would have been lighter. He is weak and dishonourable. So what if now he mutinies against your power and is proud of his mutiny? This is the pride of a small boy, a schoolboy. These are little children, mutinying in class and driving out their teacher. But the ecstasy of the little boys will come to an end, and it will cost them dearly. They will overthrow the temples and soak the earth in blood. But at last the stupid children will realize that even though they are mutineers, they are feeble mutineers, who are unable to sustain their mutiny. In floods of stupid tears they will at last recognize that the intention of the one who created them mutineers was undoubtedly to make fun of them. They will say this in despair and their words will be blasphemy, which will make them even more unhappy, for human nature cannot endure blasphemy and in the end invariably takes revenge for it. Thus, restlessness, confusion and unhappiness——those ar the lot of human beings now, after all that you underwent for the sake of their freedom! Your great prophet says in allegorical vision that he saw all those who took part in the first resurrection and that of each tribe there were twelve thousand. But if there were so many of them, they cannot have been human beings, but gods. They had borne your Cross, they had borne decades in the hungry and barren wilderness, living on roots and locust—and of course, it goes without saying that you may point with pride to those children of freedom, of a love that is free, of the free and magnificent sacrifice they have made in your name. Remember, however, that there were only a few thousand of them, and those were gods—but what about the rest? And in what way are the other weak human beings to blame for not having been able to bear the same things as the mighty? In what way is the weak soul to blame for not having the strength to accommodate such terrible gifts? And indeed, did you really only come to the chosen ones and for the chosen ones? But if that is so, then there is a mystery there and it is not for us to comprehend it. And if there is a mystery, then we were within our rights to propagate that mystery and teach them that it was not the free decision of their hearts and not love that mattered, but the mystery, which they must obey blindly, even in opposition to their consciences. And that we what we did. We corrected your great deed and founded it upon *miracle, mystery* and *authority*. And people were glad that they had once been brought together into a flock and that at last from their hearts had been removed such a terrible gift, which had brought them so much torment. Were we right, to teach and act thus, would you say? Did we not love mankind, when we so humbly admitted his helplessness, lightening his burden with love and allowing his feeble nature even sin, but with your permission? Why have you come to get in our way now? And why do you gaze at me so silently and sincerely with those meek eyes of yours? Why do you not get angry? I do not want your love, because I myself do not love you. And what is there I can conceal from you? Do you think I don't know who I'm talking to? What I have to say to you is all familiar to you already, I can read it in your eyes. And do you think I would conceal our secret from you? Perhaps it is my own lips that you want to hear it from—then listen: we are not with you, but with *him*, there is our secret! It is now just eight centuries since we took from him that which you in indignation rejected, that final gift he offered you, when he showed you all the kingdoms of the world: we took from him Rome and the sword of Caesar and announced that we alone were the kings of the world, the only kings, even though to this day we have not succeeded in bringing our task to its complete fulfillment. But whose is the blame for that? Oh, this task is as yet only at its beginning, but it has begun. The world will have to wait for its accomplishment for a long time yet, and it will have to suffer much, but we shall reach our goal and shall be Caesars and then we shall give thought to the universal happiness of human beings. And yet even back then you could have taken the sword of Caesar. Why did you reject that final gift? Had you accepted that third counsel of the mighty Spirit, you would have supplied everything that man seeks in the world, that is: someone to bow down before, someone to entrust one's conscience to, and a way of at last uniting everyone into an undisputed, general and consensual ant-heap, for the need of universal union is the third and final torment of human beings. Invariably mankind as a whole has striven to organize itself on a universal basis. Many great peoples have there been, and peoples with great histories, but the loftier those peoples, the more unhappy, for more acutely than others have they been conscious of the need for a universal union of human beings. The great conquerors, the Tamburlaines and Genghis Khans, hurtled like a whirlwind through the world, striving to conquer the universe, but even they, though they did so unconsciously, expressed the same great need of mankind for universal and general union. Had you accepted the world and the purple of Caesar, you would have founded a universal kingdom and given men universal peace. For who shall reign over human beings if not those who reign over their consciences and in whose hands are their loaves? Well, we took the sword of Caesar, and, of course, in taking it rejected you and followed *him*. Oh, centuries yet will pass of the excesses of the free intellect, of their science and anthropophagy, because, having begun to erect their Tower of Babel without us, they will end in anthropophagy. But then the beast will come crawling to our feet and lick them and sprinkle them with the bloody tears from his eyes. And we will sit upon the beast and raise the cup, and on it will begin the kingdom of peace and happiness. You are proud of your chosen ones, but all you have are chosen ones, and we shall bring rest to all. And there is more: how many of those chosen ones, of the mighty, who might have become chosen ones, at last grew tired of waiting for you, and have transferred and will yet transfer the energies of their spirits and the fervor of their hearts to a different sphere and end by raising their *free* banner against you. But it was you yourself who raised that banner. In our hands, though, everyone will be happy and will neither mutiny nor destroy one another any more, as they do in your freedom, wherever one turns. Oh, we shall persuade them that they will only become free when they renounce their freedom for us and submit to us. And what does it matter whether we are right or whether we are telling a lie? They themselves will be persuaded we are right, for they will remember to what horrors of slavery and confusion your freedom has brought them. Freedom, the free intellect and science will lead them into such labyrinths and bring them up against such miracles and unfathomable mysteries that some of them, the disobedient and ferocious ones, will destroy themselves; others, disobedient and feeble, will destroy one another, while a third group, those who are left, the feeble and unhappy ones, will come crawling to our feet, and will cry out to us: 'Yes, you were right, you alone were masters of his secret, and we are returning to you, save us from ourselves.'

Receiving loaves from us, of course, they will clearly see the what we have done   18 is to take from them the loaves they one with their own hands in order to distribute it to them without any miracles, they will see that we have not turned stones into loaves, but truly, more than of the bread, they will be glad of the fact that they are receiving it from our hands! For they will be only too aware that in former times, when we were not there, the very loaves they won used merely to turn to stones in their hands, and yet now they have returned to us those very same stones have turned back to loaves again. All too well, all too well will they appreciate what it means to subordinate themselves to us once and for all! And until human beings understand that, they will be unhappy. Who contributed most of all to that lack of understanding, tell me? Who split up the flock and scattered it over the unknown ways? But the flock will once more gather and once more submit and this time it will be for ever. Then we shall give them a quiet, reconciled happiness, the happiness of feeble creatures, such as they were created. Oh, we shall persuade them at last not to be proud, for you bore them up and by doing so taught them to be proud; we shall prove to them that they are feeble, that they are merely pathetic children, but that childish behavior but that childish happiness is sweeter than all others. They will grow fearful and look at us and press themselves to us in their fear, like nestlings to their mother. They will marvel at us and regard us with awe and be proud that we are so powerful and so clever as to be able to pacify such a turbulent, thousand-million-headed flock. They will feebly tremble with fright before our wrath, their minds will grow timid, their eyes will brim with tears, like those of women and children, but just as lightly at a nod from us will they pass over into cheerfulness and laughter, radiant joy and happy children's songs. Yes, we shall make them work, but in their hours of freedom from work we shall arrange their lives like a childish game, with childish songs, in chorus, with innocent dances. Oh, we shall permit them sin, too, they are weak and powerless, and they will love us like children for letting them sin. We shall tell them that every sin can be redeemed as long as it is committed with our leave; we are allowing them to sin because we love them, and as for the punishment for those sins, very well, we shall take it upon ourselves. And we shall take it upon ourselves, and they will worship us as benefactors who have assumed responsibility for their sins before God. And they shall have no secrets from us. We shall permit them or forbid them to live with their wives or paramours, to have or not to have children—all according to the degree of their obedience—and they will submit to us with cheer-fulness and joy. The most agonizing secrets of their consciences—all, all will they bring to us, and we shall resolve it all, and they will attend our decision with joy, because it will deliver them from the great anxiety and fearsome present torments of free and individual decision. And all will be happy, all the millions of beings except for the hundred thousand who govern for them. For only we, we, who preserve the mystery, only we shall be unhappy. There will be thousands upon millions of happy babes, and a hundred thousand martyrs who have taken upon themselves the curse of the knowledge of good and evil. Quietly they will die, quietly they will fade away in your name and beyond the tomb will find only death. But we shall preserve the secret and for the sake of their happiness will lure them with a heavenly and eternal reward. For if there were anything in the other world, it goes without saying that it would not be for the likes of them. It is said and prophesied that you will come and prevail anew, will come with your chosen, your proud mighty ones, but we will say that they have saved only themselves, while we have saved all. It is said the the whore who sits on the beast holding her MYSTERY will be disgraced, that the weak will rise up in mutiny again, that they will tear her purple and render naked her 'des-olate' body. But then I shall arise and draw your attention to the thousands upon mil-lions of happy babes who know not sin. And we, who for the sake of their happiness have taken their sins upon us, we shall stand before you and say: 'Judge us if you can and dare.' You may as well know that I am not afraid of you. You may as well know that I too was in the wilderness, that I too nourished myself on roots and locusts, that I too blessed the freedom with which you have blessed human beings, I too prepared myself to join the number of your chosen ones, the number of the strong and the mighty, with a yearning to 'fulfill the number'. But I came to my senses again and was unwilling to serve madness. I returned and adhered to the crowd of those who have *corrected your great deed.* I left the proud and returned to the humble for the sake of their happiness. What I say to you will come to pass, and our kingdom shall be accomplished. I tell you again: tomorrow you will see the obedient flock, which at the first nod of my head will rush to rake up the hot embers to the bonfire on which I am going to burn you for having come to get in our way. For if there ever was one who deserved our bonfire more than anyone else, it is you. Tomorrow I am going to burn you. *Dixi.*'"

Ivan paused. He had grown flushed from talking, and talking with passion; now   19
that he had stoped, however, he suddenly smiled.

Alyosha, who had listened to him all this time without saying anything,   20
though towards the end, in a state of extreme agitation, he had several times attempt-

ed to interrupt the flow of his brother's speech, but had evidently held himself in check, suddenly began to speak as though he had leapt into motion.

'But . . . that is preposterous!' he exclaimed, turning red. 'Your poem is a eulo-   21
gy to Jesus, not a vilification of him, as you intended it. And who will listen to you on the subject of freedom? That is a fine way, a fine way to understand it! That is not how it's understood in the Orthodox faith. That's Rome, and not even Rome completely, either, that isn't true—it's the worse elements in Catholicism, the inquisitors, the Jesuits! . . . And in any case, a fantastic character like your Inquisitor could not possibly have existed. What are these sins of human beings that have been taken by others upon themselves? Who are these bearers of mystery who have taken upon themselves some kind of curse for the sake of human happiness? Whoever heard of such people? We know the Jesuits, bad things are said of them, but they're not as they appear in your poem, are they? They're not at all like that, in no way like that . . . They are simply a Roman army for a future universal earthly kingdom, with an emperor—the Pontiff of Rome at their head . . . That is their ideal but without any mysteries or exalted melancholy. The most straightforward desire for power, for sordid earthly blessings, for enslavement . . . like a future law of serf-ownership, with themselves as the owners . . . that's all they care about. Why they probably don't even believe in God. Your suffering Inquisitor is only a fantasy . . .'

'Hold on, hold on,' Ivan said, laughing. 'What a temper you're in. A fantasy,   22
you say—very well! All right, it's a fantasy. But wait a moment; do you really suppose that the whole of that Catholic movement of recent centuries is nothing but a desire for power in order to attain earthly comfort? That wouldn't be something Father Paisy taught you, would it?'

'No, no, on the contrary, Father Paisy did actually once say something that was   23
slightly similar to your idea . . . but of course it wasn't the same, not the same at all,' Alyosha suddenly remembered.

'A valuable piece of information, nevertheless, in spite of your, "not the same   24
at all". The question I want to ask you is why have your Jesuits and inquisitors joined together for the sole purpose of attaining wretched material comfort? Why may there not be among them a single martyr, tormented by a great *Weltschmerz* and loving mankind? Look: suppose that out of all those who desire nothing but sordid material comfort there is just one—like my aged Inquisitor—who has himself eaten roots in the wilderness and raged like one possessed as he conquered his flesh in order to make himself free and perfect, though all his life he has loved mankind and has suddenly had his eyes opened and seen that there is not much moral beatitude in attaining perfect freedom if at the same time one is convinced that millions of the rest of

God's creatures have been stitched together as a mere bad joke, that they will never have the strength to cope with their freedom, that from pathetic mutineers there will never grow giants to complete the building of the Tower, that not for such geese did the great idealist dream of his harmony. Having understood all that, he returned and joined forces with . . . the clever people. Could that really not happen?

'A fine lot of people he joined! How can one call them clever?' Alyosha   25 exclaimed, almost reckless in his passion. 'They have no intelligence, nor do they have any mysteries or secrets . . . Except perhaps atheism—that is their only secret. Your Inquisitor doesn't believe in God, that's his whole secret!'

'So what if even that is true? At last you've realized it! And indeed it is true,   26 that is indeed the only secret, but is that not suffering, even for a man such as he, who has wasted his entire life on a heroic feat in the wilderness, and has not been cured of his love for mankind? In the decline of his days he becomes clearly persuaded that only the counsel of the terrible Spirit could in any way reconstitute in tolerable order the feeble mutineers, "imperfect, frail creatures, who were created as a bad joke". And lo, persuaded of this, he sees that it is necessary to proceed according to the indication of the clever Spirit, the terrible Spirit of death and destruction, and to such end accept deceit and falsehood and lead people consciously to death and destruction and deceive them moreover all of the way, so that they do not notice whither they are being led, so that at least on the way those pathetic blind creatures shall believe themselves happy. And note that it is deceit in the name of the One in whose ideal the old man had all his life so passionately believed! Is that not a misfortune? And even if there were only one such man at the head of this entire army, "thirsting for power for the sake of mere sording earthly blessings", then would not one such man be enough to produce a tragedy? Not only that: one such man, standing at their head, would be enough in order to establish at last the whole guiding idea of the Roman cause with all its armies and Jesuits, the loftiest idea of that cause. I declare to you outright that I firmly believe that these unique men even among the Roman pontiffs? Who can say—perhaps that accursed old man who loved mankind with such a stubborn, original love exists even now in the form of a whole crowd of such unique old men and not by mere accident but as a secret alliance, formed long ago for the preservation of the mystery, for its preservation, from feeble and unhappy human beings, in order to make them happy. That is certainly the case, and must be so. I fancy that even among the Masons there is something of the same sort of mystery at the basis of their movement and that the Catholics hate the Freemasons so much because they see them as rivals, a division of the unity of the idea, while there must be one flock and one shepherd . . . . As a matter of fact, in defending my thesis like this, I feel like an author who is unable to withstand your criticism. Enough of this.'

'I think you are a Freemason yourself!' Alyosha suddenly let out, "You don't   27
believe in God,' he added, this time with extreme sorrow. It seemed to him, morev-
er, that his brother we gazing at him with mockery. 'How does your poem end?' he
asked suddenly, looking at the ground. 'Or have we already had the end?'

'I was going to end it like this: when the Inquisitor falls silent, he waits for a   28
certain amount of time to hear what his Captive will say in response. He finds his
silence difficult to bear. He has seen that the Prisoner has listened to him all this time
with quiet emotion, gazing straight into his eyes and evidently not wishing to raise
any objection. The old man would like the Other to say something to him, even if it
is bitter, terrible. But He suddenly draws near to the old man without saying anything
and quietly kisses him on his bloodless, ninety-year-old lips. That is His only
response. The old man shudders. Something has stirred at the corners of his mouth;
he goes to the door, opens it and says to Him: "Go and do not come back . . . do not
come back at all . . . ever . . . ever!" And he releases him into "the town's dark streets
and squares." The Captive departs.'

'And the old man?'   29

'The kiss burns within his heart, but the old man remains with his former idea.'   30

'And you along with him, you too?' Alyosha exclaimed sadly. Ivan laughed.   31

'Oh, Alyosha, why, you know, it's nonsense—it's just an incoherent poema by   32
an incoherent student who has never so much as put two lines of verse to paper. Why
are you taking it so seriously? Surely you don't think that now I shall go straight there,
to the Jesuits, in order to join the crowd of people who are correcting His great deed?
Oh Lord, what do I care about that? I mean, I told you: all I want to do is to hold out
until I'm thirty, and then—dash the cup to the floor!'

'And the sticky leaf-buds, and the beloved tombs, and the blue sky, and the   33
woman you love? How are you doing to live, what are you going to love them with?'
Alyosha exclaimed sadly. 'With a hell like that in your breast and your head, is it possible? No, of course you're going to join them . . . and if you don't, you'll kill yourself,
you won't be able to endure!'

'There is a power that can endure everything!' Ivan said, with a cold, ironic   34
smile now.

'What power?'   35

'The Karamazovian power . . . the power of Karamazovian baseness.'   36

"You mean, to drown in depravity, to crush the life from your soul in corrup-   37
tion, is the it, is that it?'

'Possibly that too . . . Only perhaps when I'm thirty, I shall escape, and then . . .'   38

'But how will you escape? With what means will you escape? With your ideas   39
it's impossible.'

'Again, the Karamazovian way.'   40

"So that "all things are lawful"? All things are lawful, is that what you mean,   41
is that it?"

Ivan frowned and suddenly turned strangely pale.   42

'Ah, you've got hold of the little remark I made yesterday at which Miusov   43
took such offense . . . and which brother Dmitry was so naive as to butt in and repeat?'
he said, smiling a crooked smile. 'Yes, perhaps: "all things are lawful", since the
remark has been made. I do not disown it. And dear Mitya's version of it is not so
bad, either.'

Alyosha stared at him without saying anything.   44

'In leaving, brother, I had imagined that in all the world I have only you,' Ivan   45
said suddenly, with unexpected emotion, 'but now I see that in your heart there is no
room for me, my dear hermit. I do not disown the formula "all things are lawful", but,
I mean, are you going to disown me because of it—eh? eh?'

Alyosha rose, walked over to him, and without saying anything kissed him qui-   46
etly on the lips.

'Literary thieving!' Ivan exclaimed, suddenly passing into a kind of ecstasy. 'You   47
stole that from my *poema*! But never mind, I thank you. Come on, Alyosha, let us go,
it is time for both you and for me.'

They went outside, but paused by the entrance to the inn.   48

'Look, Alyosha,' Ivan pronounced in a resolute voice. 'If I am indeed capable   49
of loving the sticky leaf-buds, then I shall love them at the mere memory of you. It
is enough for me that you are somewhere here, and I shan't yet lose my will to live.
Is that enough for you? If you like, you may take it as a confession of love. But now
you must go to the right, and I to the left—and enough, do you hear, enough. That
is to say that if it proves that I do not leave tomorrow (though it seems to me that I
most certainly shall) and we were again to meet somehow, then I want you not to say
another word to me on all these subjects. I earnestly request you. And concerning
brother Dmitry I also particularly request that you not even so much as mention him
to me ever again,' he added in sudden irritation. 'It's all settled and decided, isn't it?
and in exchange for that, I for my part will also give you a certain promise: when I
attain the age of thirty and want to "dash the cup to the floor" then, wherever you
are, I shall come once again to discuss things with you . . . even if it's from America,
I shall have you know. I shall come specially. It will be very interesting to set eyes on

you at that time: what will you be like? You see, it's quite a solemn sort of promise. And indeed it may well be that we are saying goodbye for seven, for ten years. Well, go to your *Pater Seraphicus* now, after all, he is dying; if he dies in your absence you may well be angry at me for having kept you back. Goodbye, kiss me once more—like that—and go . . .'

Ivan suddenly turned and went his way, without looking round this time. It resembled the manner in which brother Dmitry had left Alyosha the day before, though then the mood had been quite different. This strange little observation flashed, like an arrow, through Alyosha's sad mind, sad and sorrowful at the moment. He waited for a bit as he watched his brother go. For some reason he suddenly noticed that brother Ivan walked with a kind of sway and that, seen from behind, his right shoulder looked lower than his left. Never had he observed this previously. Suddenly, however, he also turned and set off almost at a run in the direction of the monastery. It was by now getting very dark, and he felt a sense that was almost one of fear; something new was growing within him, something he was unable to account for. The wind rose again, as it had done yesterday, and the ancient pine trees soughed darkly around him as he entered the hermitage woods. He was almost running. 'Pater Seraphicus'—that name, he had taken it from somewhere—where?—flashed through Alyosha's brain. 'Ivan, poor Ivan, and when will I see you again . . . Here is the hermitage, O Lord! Yes, yes, it is him, it is *Pater Seraphicus,* he will save me . . . from him and for ever!"

Later on, several times in his life, he recollected that moment with great bewilderment, wondering how he could suddenly, having only just parted with Ivan, so completely forget his brother Dmitry, who that morning, only a few hours ago, he had determined to track down, vowing not to return without having done so, even if it meant he could not go back to the monastery that night.

Nietzsche was born in Röcken, Prussia, in 1844. After graduating from the Lutheran boarding school at Pforta in 1864, he enrolled in the University of Bonn to study theology. There he began to doubt his Christian faith (he eventually became an atheist and harsh critic of Christianity) and in 1865 transferred to the University of Leipzig to study classical philology (Greek and Latin language and literature) and music. He was recognized as a brilliant student of philology, and at the age of twentyfour, before he had even finished his doctorate, he was offered the chair of classical philology at the University of Basel in Switzerland. The University of Leipzig quickly granted his degree, and Nietzsche assumed the professorship at Basel in 1869. Ten years later, because of his increasingly bad health, Nietzsche resigned his position. For the next ten years, half blind and in unremitting pain, he wandered through Switzerland, Germany, and Italy in search of a cure. His mental health began to deteriorate as well; in 1889 he collapsed on the streets of Turin, Italy, completely insane. He died in Weimar in 1900.

Nietzsche's principal works are *The Birth of Tragedy out of the Spirit of Music* (1872), *Human, All Too Human* (1878), *The Gay Science* (1882), *Thus Spoke Zarathustra* (1883–1885), *Beyond Good and Evil* (1886), and *On the Genealogy of Morals* (1887).

Our selection is from *Beyond Good and Evil*, a book consisting of about three hundred aphorisms on various subjects. The topic of Chapter 9, from which our reading comes, is "What Is Noble?" According to Nietzsche, to be noble means to see oneself as the center and origin of all value. In fact, the terms "good" and "bad" originally designated simply what the aristocracy did and did not value. For Nietzsche, "life *is* precisely the will to power," and historically members of the aristocracy exercised their will to power by exploiting common people and using them as they saw fit. Nietzsche calls the morality of the ruling aristocracy a "master morality." He contrasts this kind of morality with "slave morality," which arose when common people tried to make their inferior and despicable lives more bearable by exalting as virtues such qualities as kindness, sympathy, selflessness, patience, and humility (the cornerstones of Christian morality). Slave morality gave rise to the pair of terms "good" and "evil," which Nietzsche contrasts with the "good" and "bad" of master morality. In slave morality, "good" refers to the slaves' (false) values, and "evil" to the (legitimate and noble) values of the rulers. Since rulers are not in the inferior position of slaves, they need not subscribe to slave values and are "beyond good and evil."

Nietzsche bemoans the fact that modern civilization, with its democratic and egalitarian tendencies, is replacing life-affirming master morality with life-denying slave morality. Yet there are still elements of master morality in some souls, and it is to these souls that Nietzsche's praise of "what is noble" is addressed.

Beyond Good and Evil

Friedrich Nietzsche

Chapter 9: What Is Noble?

257 Every elevation of the type "man" has hitherto been the work of an aristocratic society—and so will it always be—a society believing in a long scale of gra-   1 dations of rank and differences of worth among human beings, and requiring slavery in some form or other. Without the *pathos of distance*, such as grows out of the incarnated difference of classes, out of the constant outlooking and down-looking of the ruling caste on subordinates and instruments, and out of their equally constant practice of obeying and commanding, of keeping down and keeping at a distance—that other more mysterious pathos could never have aris-en, the longing for an ever new widening of distance within the soul itself, the formation of ever higher, rarer, further, more extended, more comprehensive states—in short, just the elevation of the type "man," the continued "self-sur-mounting of man," to use a moral formula in a supermoral sense. To be sure, one must not resign oneself to any humanitarian illusions about the history of the ori-gin of an aristocratic society (that is to say, of the preliminary condition for the elevation of the type "man"): the truth is hard. Let us acknowledge unpreju-dicedly how every higher civilisation hitherto has *originated!* Men with a still nat-ural nature—barbarians in every terrible sense of the word, men of prey, still in possession of unbroken strength of will and desire for power—threw themselves upon weaker, more moral, more peaceful races (perhaps trading or cattle-rearing communities), or upon old mellow civilisations in which the final vital force was flickering out in brilliant fireworks of wit and depravity. At the commencement, the noble caste was always the barbarian caste. Their superiority did not consist first of all in their physical, but in their psychical power—they were more *com-plete* men (which at every point also implies the same as "more complete beasts").

258 Corruption—as the indication that anarchy threatens to break out among the instincts, and that the foundation of the emotions, called "life," is con-vulsed—is something radically different according to the organisation in which it manifests itself. When, for instance, an aristocracy like that of France at the beginning of the Revolution flung away its privileges with sublime disgust and sacrificed itself to an excess of its moral sentiments, it was corruption—it was really only the closing act of the corruption which had existed for centuries, by virtue of which that aristocracy had abdicated step by step its lordly prerogatives and lowered itself to a *function* of royalty (in the end even to its decoration and parade-dress). The essential thing, however, in a good and healthy aristocracy is that it should *not* regard itself as a function either of the kingship or the com-monwealth, but as the *significance* and highest justification [of it]—that it should therefore accept with a good conscience the sacrifice of a legion of individuals who, *for its sake*, must be suppressed and reduced to imperfect men, to slaves and instruments. Its fundamental belief must be precisely that society is *not* allowed to exist for its own sake, but only as a foundation and scaffolding by means of which a select class of beings may be able to elevate themselves to their higher duties, and in general to a higher *existence*—like those sun-seeking climbing plants in Java (they are called *Sipo matador*), which encircle an oak so long and so often with their arms, until at last, high above it, but supported by it, they can unfold their tops in the open light and exhibit their happiness.

259 To refrain mutually from injury, from violence, from exploitation, and to put   3
one's will on a par with that of others—this may result in a certain rough sense in good conduct among individuals when the necessary conditions are given (namely, the actual similarity of the individuals in amount of force and degree of worth, and their co-relation within one organisation). As soon, however, as one wished to take this principle more generally, and if possible even as *the fundamental principle of society*, it would immediately disclose what it really is—namely, a will to the *denial* of life, a principle of dissolution and decay. Here one must think profoundly to the very basis and resist all sentimental weakness: life itself is *essentially* appropriation, injury, conquest of the strange and weak, suppression, severity, obtrusion of peculiar forms, incorporation, and at the least (putting it most mildly), exploitation. But why should one forever use precisely these words on which for ages a disparaging purpose has been stamped? Even the organisation within which, as was previously supposed, the individuals treat each other as equal—it takes place in every healthy aristocracy—must itself, if it be a living and not a dying organisation, do all that towards other bodies, which the individuals within it refrain from doing to each other: it will have to be the incarnated will to power, it will endeavour to grow, to gain ground, attract to itself and acquire ascendency—not owing to any morality or immorality, but because it *lives*, and because life *is* precisely will to power. On no point, however, is the ordinary consciousness of Europeans more unwilling to be corrected than on this matter; people now rave everywhere, even under the guise of science, about coming conditions of society in which "the exploiting character" is to be absent. That sounds to my ears as if they promised to invent a mode of life which should refrain from all organic functions. "Exploitation" does not belong to a depraved, or imperfect and primitive society: it belongs to the *nature* of the living being as a primary organic function; it is a consequence of the intrinsic will to power, which is precisely the will to life. Granting that as a theory this is a novelty—as

a reality it is the *fundamental fact* of all history: let us be so far honest towards ourselves!

260 In a tour through the many finer and coarser moralities which have hither-   4
to prevailed or still prevail on the earth, I found certain traits recurring regularly
together and connected with one another, until finally two primary types
revealed themselves to me, and a radical distinction was brought to light. There
is *master morality* and *slave morality*—I would at once add, however, that in all
higher and mixed civilisations, there are also attempts at the reconciliation of
the two moralities; but one finds still oftener the confusion and mutual misunderstanding of them, indeed, sometimes their close juxtaposition—even in the
same man, within one soul. The distinctions of moral values have either originated in a ruling caste, pleasantly conscious of being different from the ruled—
or among the ruled class, the slaves and dependents of all sorts. In the first case,
when it is the rulers who determine the conception "good," it is the exalted,
proud disposition which is regarded as the distinguishing feature, and that which
determines the order of rank. The noble type of man separates from himself the
beings in whom the opposite of this exalted, proud disposition displays itself: he
despises them. Let it at once be noted that in this first kind of morality the
antithesis "good" and "bad" means practically the same as "noble" and "despicable"—the antithesis "good" and *"evil"* is of a different origin. The cowardly, the
timid, the insignificant, and those thinking merely of narrow utility are despised;
also the distrustful, with their constrained glances, the self-abasing, the dog-like
kind of men who let themselves be abused, the mendicant flatterers, and above
all the liars—it is a fundamental belief of all aristocrats that the common people
are untruthful. "We truthful ones" the nobility in ancient Greece called themselves. It is obvious that everywhere the designations of moral value were at first
applied to *men* and were only derivatively and at a later period applied to *actions*;
it is a gross mistake, therefore, when historians of morals start with questions like,
"Why have sympathetic actions been praised?" The noble type of man regards
himself as a determiner of values; he does not require to be approved of; he passes the judgment, "What is injurious to me is injurious in itself"; he knows that it
is he himself only who confers honour on things; he is a *creator of values*. He honours whatever he recognises in himself: such morality is self-glorification. In the
foreground there is the feeling of plenitude, of power, which seeks to overflow,
the happiness of high tension, the consciousness of a wealth which would give
and bestow. The noble man also helps the unfortunate, but not—or scarcely—

out of pity, but rather from an impulse generated by the superabundance of power. The noble man honours in himself the powerful one, him also who has power over himself, who knows how to speak and how to keep silence, who takes pleasure in subjecting himself to severity and hardness, and has reverence for all that is severe and hard. "Wotan placed a hard heart in my breast," says an old Scandinavian saga: it is thus rightly expressed from the soul of a proud Viking. Such a type of man is even proud of *not* being made for sympathy; the hero of the saga therefore adds warningly: "He who has not a hard heart when young, will never have one." The noble and brave who think thus are the furthest removed from the morality which sees precisely in sympathy, or in acting for the good of others, or in *désintéressement*,[1] the characteristic of the moral; faith in oneself, pride in oneself, a radical enmity and irony towards "selflessness," belong as definitely to noble morality as do a careless scorn and precaution in presence of sympathy and the "warm heart." It is the powerful who *know* how to honour; it is their art, their domain for invention. The profound reverence for age and for tradition (all law rests on this double reverence), the belief and prejudice in favour of ancestors and unfavourable to newcomers, is typical in the morality of the powerful. And if, reversely, men of "modern ideas" believe almost instinctively in "progress" and the "future" and are more and more lacking in respect for old age, the ignoble origin of these "ideas" has complacently betrayed itself thereby. A morality of the ruling class, however, is more especially foreign and irritating to present-day taste in the sternness of its principle that one has duties only to one's equals, that one may act towards beings of a lower rank, towards all that is foreign, just as seems good to one, or "as the heart desires," and in any case "beyond good and evil." It is here that sympathy and similar sentiments can have a place. The ability and obligation to exercise prolonged gratitude and prolonged revenge (both only within the circle of equals), artfulness in retaliation, *raffinement*[2] of the idea in friendship, a certain necessity to have enemies (as outlets for the emotions of envy, quarrelsomeness, arrogance—in fact, in order to be a good *friend*): all these are typical characteristics of the noble morality, which, as has been pointed out, is not the morality of "modern ideas" and is therefore at present difficult to realise, and also to unearth and disclose. It is otherwise with the second type of morality, *slave morality*. Supposing that the abused, the oppressed, the suffering, the unemancipated, the weary, and those uncertain of themselves, should moralise; what will be the common element in their moral estimates? Probably a pessimistic suspicion with regard to the entire situation of man will find expression, perhaps a condemnation of man, together with his situation.

The slave has an unfavourable eye for the virtues of the powerful; he has a scepticism and distrust, a refinement of distrust of everything "good" that is there honoured —he would persuade himself that the very happiness there is not genuine. On the other hand, those qualities which serve to alleviate the existence of sufferers are brought into prominence and flooded with light; it is here that sympathy, the kind, helping hand, the warm heart, patience, diligence, humility, and friendliness attain to honour; for here these are the most useful qualities and almost the only means of supporting the burden of existence. Slave morality is essentially the morality of utility. Here is the seat of the origin of the famous antithesis "good" and "*evil*"—power and dangerousness are assumed to reside in the evil, a certain dreadfulness, subtlety, and strength, which do not admit of being despised. According to slave morality, therefore, the "evil" man arouses fear; according to master morality, it is precisely the "good" man who arouses fear and seeks to arouse it, while the bad man is regarded as the despicable being. The contrast attains its maximum when, in accordance with the logical consequences of slave morality, a shade of depreciation—it may be slight and well-intentioned—at last attaches itself even to the "good" man of this morality; because, according to the servile mode of thought, the good man must in any case be the *safe* man: he is good-natured, easily deceived, perhaps a little stupid, *un bonhomme*.[3] Everywhere that slave morality gains the ascendency, language shows a tendency to approximate the significations of the words "good" and "stupid." A last fundamental difference: the desire for *freedom*, the instinct for happiness and the refinements of the feeling of liberty belong as necessarily to slave morals and morality, as artifice and enthusiasm in reverence and devotion are the regular symptoms of an aristocratic mode of thinking and estimating. Hence we can understand without further detail why love *as a passion*—it is our European speciality—must absolutely be of noble origin. As is well known, its invention is due to the Provençal poet-cavaliers, those brilliant ingenious men of the *"gai saber,"*[4] to whom Europe owes so much, and almost owes itself.

261 Vanity is one of the things which are perhaps most difficult for a noble man   5
to understand: he will be tempted to deny it, where another kind of man thinks he sees it self-evidently. The problem for him is to represent to his mind beings who seek to arouse a good opinion of themselves which they themselves do not possess—and consequently also do not "deserve" —and who yet *believe* in this good opinion afterwards. This seems to him on the one hand such bad taste and so self-disrespectful, and on the other hand so grotesquely unreasonable, that he

would like to consider vanity an exception and is doubtful about it in most cases when it is spoken of. He will say, for instance: "I may be mistaken about my value, and on the other hand may nevertheless demand that my value should be acknowledged by others precisely as I rate it—that, however, is not vanity (but selfconceit, or, in most cases, that which is called 'humility,' and also 'modesty')." Or he will even say: "For many reasons I can delight in the good opinion of others, perhaps because I love and honour them and rejoice in all their joys, perhaps also because their good opinion endorses and strengthens my belief in my own good opinion, perhaps because the good opinion of others, even in cases where I do not share it, is useful to me, or gives promise of usefulness—all this, however, is not vanity." The man of noble character must first bring it home forcibly to his mind, especially with the aid of history, that, from time immemorial, in all social strata in any way dependent, the ordinary man *was* only that which he *passed for*; not being at all accustomed to fix values, he did not assign even to himself any other value than that which his master assigned to him (it is the peculiar *right of masters* to create values). It may be looked upon as the result of an extraordinary atavism[5] that the ordinary man, even at present, is still always *waiting* for an opinion about himself, and then instinctively submitting himself to it; yet by no means only to a "good" opinion, but also to a bad and unjust one (think, for instance, of the greater part of the self-appreciations and self-depreciations which believing women learn from their confessors, and which in general the believing Christian learns from his church). In fact, conformably to the slow rise of the democratic social order (and its cause, the blending of the blood of masters and slaves), the originally noble and rare impulse of the masters to assign a value to themselves and to "think well" of themselves will now be more and more encouraged and extended. But it has at all times an older, ampler, and more radically ingrained propensity opposed to it—and in the phenomenon of "vanity" this older propensity overmasters the younger. The vain person rejoices over *every* good opinion which he hears about himself (quite apart from the point of view of its usefulness, and equally regardless of its truth or falsehood), just as he suffers from every bad opinion: for he subjects himself to both, he *feels* himself subjected to both, by that oldest instinct of subjection which breaks forth in him. It is "the slave" in the vain man's blood, the remains of the slave's craftiness—and how much of the "slave" is still left in woman, for instance!—which seeks to *seduce* to good opinions of itself; it is the slave, too, who immediately afterwards falls prostrate himself before these opinions, as though he had not called them forth. And to repeat it again: vanity is an atavism. . . .

265 At the risk of displeasing innocent ears, I submit that egoism belongs to the   6
essence of a noble soul—I mean the unalterable belief that to a being such as
"we," other beings must naturally be in subjection, and have to sacrifice themselves. The noble soul accepts the fact of his egoism without question, and also
without consciousness of harshness, constraint, or arbitrariness therein, but
rather as something that may have its basis in the primary law of things. If he
sought a designation for it, he would say: "It is justice itself." He acknowledges
under certain circumstances, which made him hesitate at first, that there are
other equally privileged ones; as soon as he has settled this question of rank, he
moves among those equals and equally privileged ones with the same assurance,
as regards modesty and delicate respect, which he enjoys in intercourse with
himself—in accordance with an innate heavenly mechanism which all the stars
understand. It is an *additional* instance of his egoism, this artfulness and self-lim-
itation in intercourse with his equals (every star is a similar egoist). He honours
himself in them; and in the rights which he concedes to them, he has no doubt
that the exchange of honours and rights, as the *essence* of all intercourse, belongs
also to the natural condition of things. The noble soul gives as he takes, prompted by the passionate and sensitive instinct of requital, which is at the root of his
nature. The notion of "favour" has, *inter pares*,[6] neither significance nor good
repute; there may be a sublime way of letting gifts, as it were, light upon one from
above, and of drinking them thirstily like dewdrops; but for those arts and displays the noble soul has no aptitude. His egoism hinders him here: in general, he
looks "aloft" unwillingly —he looks either *forward*, horizontally and deliberately, or downwards; *he knows that he is on a height. . . .*

272 Signs of nobility: never to think of lowering our duties to the rank of duties   7
for everybody; to be unwilling to renounce or to share our responsibilities; to
count our prerogatives, and the exercise of them, among our *duties. . . .*

287 What is noble? What does the word "noble" still mean for us nowadays?   8
How does the noble man betray himself, how is he recognised under this heavy
overcast sky of the commencing plebeianism, by which everything is rendered
opaque and leaden? It is not his actions which establish his claim (actions are
always ambiguous, always inscrutable); neither is it his "works." One finds nowadays among artists and scholars plenty of those who betray by their works that a
profound longing for nobleness impels them; but this very *need of* nobleness is
radically different from the needs of the noble soul itself, and is in fact the elo-

quent and dangerous sign of the lack thereof. It is not the works, but the *belief* which is here decisive and determines the order of rank—to employ once more an old religious formula with a new and deeper meaning. It is some fundamental certainty which a noble soul has about itself, something which is not to be sought, is not to be found, and perhaps, also, is not to be lost. *The noble soul has reverence for itself.*

Notes

1. *désintéressement:* unselfishness (French) [D.C.A., ed.]
2. *raffinement:* refinement (French) [D.C.A.]
3. *un bonhomme:* a simple-minded person; literally, "a good person" (French) [D.C.A.]
4. *gai saber:* the art of the troubadours (a fourteenth-century French term that means, literally, "the merry science") [D.C.A.]
5. *atavism:* recurrence of a trait that appeared in one's remote ancestors [D.C.A.]
6. *inter pares:* among equals (Latin) [D.C.A.]

Albert Camus (1913–1966), born in what was then the French colony of Algeria, studied philosophy at the University of Algeria. He began his career as an actor and a playwright, but he soon gave up the theater for journalism and began writing for *Alger Republican* and for *Paris- Soir* in France. During World War II, Camus was very active in the French Resistance and was coeditor (with Jean Paul Sartre) of *Combat,* an important underground newspaper. He is remembered as a leading existentialist, defining the individual as free and totally responsible for his or her own destiny, and considering the world to be devoid of meaning except for that which the individual is able to create. This is clearly evident in his famous novels, *The Stranger* (1942), *The Plague* (1947), and *The Rebel* (1951). Camus won the Nobel Prize for Literature in 1957.

The Myth of Sisyphus

Albert Camus

The gods had condemned Sisyphus to ceaselessly rolling a rock to the top of a   1
mountain, whence the stone would fall back of its own weight. They had thought with some reason that there is no more dreadful punishment than futile and hopeless labor.

   If one believes Homer, Sisyphus was the wisest and most prudent of mor-   2
tals. According to another tradition, however, he was disposed to practice the profession of highwayman. I see no contradiction in this. Opinions differ as to the reasons why he became the futile laborer of the underworld. To begin with, he is accused of a certain levity in regard to the gods. He stole their secrets. Aegina, the daughter of Aesopus, was carried off by Jupiter. The father was shocked by that disappearance and complained to Sisyphus. He, who knew of the abduction, offered to tell about it on condition that Aesopus would give water to the citadel of Corinth. To the celestial thunderbolts he preferred the benediction of water. He was punished for this in the under-world. Homer tells us also that Sisyphus had put Death in chains. Pluto could not endure the sight of his deserted, silent empire. He dispatched the god of war, who liberated Death from the hands of her conqueror.

It is said also that Sisyphus, being near to death, rashly wanted to test his   3
wife's love. He ordered her to cast his unburied body into the middle of the public square. Sisyphus woke up in the underworld. And there, annoyed by an obedience so contrary to human love, he obtained from Pluto permission to return
to earth in order to chastise his wife. But when he had seen again the face of this
world, enjoyed water and sun, warm stones and the sea, he no longer wanted to
go back to the infernal darkness. Recalls, signs of anger, warnings were of no
avail. Many years more he lived facing the curve of the gulf, the sparkling sea,
and the smiles of earth. A decree of the gods was necessary. Mercury came and
seized the impudent man by the collar and, snatching him from his joys, led him
forcibly back to the underworld, where his rock was ready for him.

You have already grasped that Sisyphus is the absurd hero. He *is*, as much   4
through his passions as through his torture. His scorn of the gods, his hatred of
death, and his passion for life won him that unspeakable penalty in which the
whole being is exerted toward accomplishing nothing. This is the price that must
be paid for the passions of this earth. Nothing is told us about Sisyphus in the
underworld. Myths are made for the imagination to breathe life into them. As
for this myth, one sees merely the whole effort of a body straining to raise the
huge stone, to roll it and push it up a slope a hundred times over; one sees the
face screwed up, the cheek tight against the stone, the shoulder bracing the clay-
covered mass, the foot wedging it, the fresh start with arms outstretched, the
wholly human security of two earth-clotted hands. At the very end of his long
effort measured by skyless space and time without depth, the purpose is achieved.
Then Sisyphus watches the stone rush down in a few moments toward that lower
world whence he will have to push it up again toward the summit. He goes back
down to the plain.

It is during that return, that pause, that Sisyphus interests me. A face that   5
toils so close to stones is already stone itself! I see that man going back down with
a heavy yet measured step toward the torment of which he will never know the
end. That hour like a breathing-space which returns as surely as his suffering,
that is the hour of consciousness. At each of those moments when he leaves the
heights and gradually sinks toward the lairs of the gods, he is superior to his fate.
He is stronger than his rock.

If this myth is tragic, that is because its hero is conscious. Where would his   6
torture be, indeed, if at every step the hope of succeeding upheld him? The workman of today works every day in his life at the same tasks, and this fate is no less
absurd. But it is tragic only at the rare moments when it becomes conscious.

Sisyphus, proletarian of the gods, powerless and rebellious, knows the whole extent of his wretched condition: it is what he thinks of during his descent. The lucidity that was to constitute his torture at the same time crowns his victory. There is no fate that cannot be surmounted by scorn.

If the descent is thus sometimes performed in sorrow, it can also take place   7
in joy. This word is not too much. Again I fancy Sisyphus returning toward his rock, and the sorrow was in the beginning. When the images of earth cling too tightly to memory, when the call of happiness becomes too insistent, it happens that melancholy rises in man's heart: this is the rock's victory, this is the rock itself. The boundless grief is too heavy to bear. These are our nights of Gethsemane. But crushing truths perish from being acknowledged. Thus, Oedipus at the outset obeys fate without knowing it. But from the moment he knows, his tragedy begins. Yet at the same moment, blind and desperate, he realizes that the only bond linking him to the world is the cool hand of a girl. Then a tremendous remark rings out: "Despite so many ordeals, my advanced age and the nobility of my soul make me conclude that all is well." Sophocles' Oedipus, like Dostoyevsky's Kirilov, thus gives the recipe for the absurd victory. Ancient wisdom confirms modern heroism.

One does not discover the absurd without being tempted to write a manu-   8
al of happiness. "What! by such narrow ways–?" There is but one world, howev-er. Happiness and the absurd are two sons of the same earth. They are insepara-ble. It would be a mistake to say that happiness necessarily springs from the absurd discovery. It happens as well that the feeling of the absurd springs from happiness. "I conclude that all is well," says Oedipus, and that remark is sacred. It echoes in the wild and limited universe of man. It teaches that all is not, has not been, exhausted. It drives out of this world a god who had come into it with dissatisfaction and a preference for futile sufferings. It makes of fate a human mat-ter, which must be settled among men.

All Sisyphus' silent joy is contained therein. His fate belongs to him. His   9
rock is his thing. Likewise, the absurd man, when he contemplates his torment, silences all the idols. In the universe suddenly restored to its silence, the myriad wondering little voices of the earth rise up. Unconscious, secret calls, invitations from all the faces, they are the necessary reverse and price of victory. There is no sun without shadow, and it is essential to know the night. The absurd man says yes and his effort will henceforth be unceasing. If there is a personal fate, there is no higher destiny, or at least there is but one which he concludes is inevitable and despicable. For the rest, he knows himself to be the master of his days. At

that subtle moment when man glances backward over his life, Sisyphus returning toward his rock, in that slight pivoting he contemplates that series of unrelated actions which becomes his fate, created by him, combined under his memory's eye and soon sealed by his death. Thus, convinced of the wholly human origin of all that is human, a blind man eager to see who knows that the night has
no end, he is still on the go. The rock is still rolling.

I leave Sisyphus at the foot of the mountain! One always finds one's bur-   10
den again. But Sisyphus teaches the higher fidelity that negates the gods and raises rocks. He too concludes that all is well. This universe henceforth without a
master seems to him neither sterile nor futile. Each atom of that stone, each mineral flake of that night-filled mountain, in itself forms a world. The struggle itself
toward the heights is enough to fill a man's heart. One must imagine Sisyphus
happy.

Questions for Discussion

1. Why is this particular Greek myth useful to explain the human condition?
   Why is Sisyphus such an apt representative of a twentieth-century human?
   Why is perpetually pushing a rock up a hill the most appropriate punishment for him?
2. What might have motivated Camus to write this essay? What might Camus
   have wanted to teach his readers?
3. How are absurdity and happiness related? Why must we imagine Sisyphus
   happy? What happens if we do not?
4. Camus equates Sisyphus with the "workman of today" (Paragraph 6). Does
   Sisyphus have to be a laborer? Besides a laborer, what other professions
   could be represented by Sisyphus?
5. What makes the myth of Sisyphus a tragic one? Is there anything comic
   about it? Is there a place in tragedy for comedy?
6. What does consciousness have to do with the "tragedy" of being human?
7. Is Camus pessimistic or optimistic? How do you know?

Questions for Reflection and Writing

1. "Myths are made for the imagination to breathe life into them," Camus
   writes in Paragraph 4. What is meant by this? Explain and respond to the
   statement.
2. What do the rock and pushing the rock up the hill symbolize for the twen-
   ty-firstcentury person? Apply Camus' essay to the future human condition.

3. Look up "absurd hero" in a dictionary of literary terms. Write an essay in which you define the idea of the absurd hero, explain when and by whom the term was first used, and say to what fictional characters is it usually applied. To what in your own reading can the term be applied?

Confucius (551–479 B.C.), a Chinese philosopher, is believed to have had an impoverished childhood, living with his mother after his father's death. He learned archery and charioteering, and studied ancient texts. As a young man, he became a bookkeeper and royal herdsman. In his thirties he considered problems of state, but he is best known as a philosopher, the occupation he took up when he was in his fifties. Although Confucius's teachings had few followers in his own day, China made Confucianism the official state philosophy in the second century b.c. While Confucianism ceased to be the dominant influence in China in the early twentieth century, it still wields a strong influence in eastern Asia.

Confucius' moral teachings in the *Lun-yu* (*Analects*) primarily take the form of dialogues. Confucius valued loyalty and feudal order in the face of the murderous and deceitful Chou Dynasty of his day. Confucius taught that virtue required the individual to live according to standards dictated by his or her social role, thereby setting an example that enhances social stability. "The Way" (*Tao*), or harmony with the human order, is achieved through virtue (*Te*), or proper living. Although he was not interested in concepts of divinity or soul, he acknowledged a life force called "Heaven" (*t'ien*).

Perfect Virtue

Confucius

Yen Yuan asked about perfect virtue. The Master said, "To subdue one's self and   1
return to propriety, is perfect virtue. If a man can for one day subdue himself and
return to propriety, an under heaven will ascribe perfect virtue to him. Is the
practice of perfect virtue from a man himself, or is it from others?"

Yen Yuan said, "I beg to ask the steps of that process." The Master replied,   2
"Look not at what is contrary to propriety; listen not to what is contrary to propriety; speak not what is contrary to propriety; make no movement which is contrary to propriety." Yen Yuan then said, "Though I am deficient in intelligence
and vigor, I will make it my business to practice this lesson."

Chung-kung asked about perfect virtue. The Master said, "It is, when you   3
go abroad, to behave to every one as if you were receiving a great guest; to
employ the people as if you were assisting at a great sacrifice; not to do to others
as you would not wish done to yourself; to have no murmuring against you in the
country, and none in the family." Chung-kung said, "Though I am deficient in
intelligence and vigor, I will make it my business to practice this lesson."

Sze-ma Niu asked about perfect virtue.   4

The Master said, "The man of perfect virtue is cautious and slow in his   5
speech."

"Cautious and slow in his speech!" said Niu;—"is this what is meant by per-   6
fect virtue?" The Master said, "When a man feels the difficulty of doing, can he
be other than cautious and slow in speaking?"

Sze-ma Niu asked about the superior man. The Master said, "The superior   7
man has neither anxiety nor fear."

"Being without anxiety or fear!" said Nui; "does this constitute what we call   8
the superior man?"

The Master said, "When internal examination discovers nothing wrong,   9
what is there to be anxious about, what is there to fear?"

Sze-ma Niu, full of anxiety, said, "Other men all have their brothers, I only   10
have not."

Tsze-hsia said to him, "There is the following saying which I have heard'   11
Death and life have their determined appointment; riches and honors depend
upon Heaven."

"Let the superior man never fail reverentially to order his own conduct,   12
and let him be respectful to others and observant of propriety:—then all within
the four seas will be his brothers. What has the superior man to do with being
distressed because he has no brothers?"

Tsze-chang asked what constituted intelligence. The Master said, "He with   13
whom neither slander that gradually soaks into the mind, nor statements that
startle like a wound in the flesh, are successful may be called intelligent indeed.
Yea, he with whom neither soaking slander, nor startling statements, are successful, may be called farseeing."

Tsze-kung asked about government. The Master said, "The requisites of   14
government are that there be sufficiency of food, sufficiency of military equipment, and the confidence of the people in their ruler."

Tsze-kung said, "If it cannot be helped, and one of these must be dispensed   15
with, which of the three should be foregone first?" "The military equipment,"
said the Master.

Tsze-kung again asked, "If it cannot be helped, and one of the remaining   16
two must be dispensed with, which of them should be foregone?" The Master
answered, "Part with the food. From of old, death has been the lot of an men; but
if the people have no faith in their rulers, there is no standing for the state."

Chi Tsze-ch'ang said, "In a superior man it is only the substantial qualities   17
which are wanted;—why should we seek for ornamental accomplishments?"

Tsze-kung said, "Alas! Your words, sir, show you to be a superior man, but   18
four horses cannot overtake the tongue. Ornament is as substance; substance is
as ornament. The hide of a tiger or a leopard stripped of its hair, is like the hide
of a dog or a goat stripped of its hair."

The Duke Ai inquired of Yu Zo, saying, "The year is one of scarcity, and   19
the returns for expenditure are not sufficient;—what is to be done?"

Yu Zo replied to him, "Why not simply tithe the people?"   20

"With two tenths, said the duke, "I find it not enough;—how could I do   21
with that system of one tenth?"

Yu Zo answered, "If the people have plenty, their prince will not be left to   22
want alone. If the people are in want, their prince cannot enjoy plenty alone."

Tsze-chang having asked how virtue was to be exalted, and delusions to be   23
discovered, the Master said, "Hold faithfulness and sincerity as first principles,
and be moving continually to what is right,—this is the way to exalt one's virtue.

"You love a man and wish him to live; you hate him and wish him to die.   24
Having wished him to live, you also wish him to die. This is a case of delusion.
'It may not be on account of her being rich, yet you come to make a difference.'"

The Duke Ching, of Ch'i, asked Confucius about government. Confucius   25
replied, "There is government, when the prince is prince, and the minister is
minister; when the father is father, and the son is son."

"Good!" said the duke; "if, indeed, the prince be not prince, the not min-   26
ister, the father not father, and the son not son, although I have my revenue, can
I enjoy it?"

The Master said, "Ah! it is Yu, who could with half a word settle litiga-   27
tions!"

Tsze-lu never slept over a promise.   28

The Master said, "In hearing litigations, I am like any other body. What is   29
necessary, however, is to cause the people to have no litigations."

Tsze-chang asked about government. The Master said, "The art of govern-   30
ing is to keep its affairs before the mind without weariness, and to practice them
with undeviating consistency."

The Master said, "By extensively studying all learning, and keeping him-   31
self under the restraint of the rules of propriety, one may thus likewise not err
from what is right."

The Master said, "The superior man seeks to perfect the admirable quali-   32
ties of men, and does not seek to perfect their bad qualities. The mean man does
the opposite of this."

Chi K'ang asked Confucius about government. Confucius replied, "To govern means to rectify. If you lead on the people with correctness, who will dare not to be correct?"   33

Chi K'ang, distressed about the number of thieves in the state, inquired of Confucius how to do away with them. Confucius said, "If you, sir, were not covetous, although you should reward them to do it, they would not steal."   34

Chi K'ang asked Confucius about government, saying, "What do you say to killing the unprincipled for the good of the principled?" Confucius replied, "Sir, in carrying on your government, why should you use killing at all? Let your evinced desires be for what is good, and the people will be good. The relation between superiors and inferiors is like that between the wind and the grass. The grass must bend, when the wind blows across it."   35

Tsze-chang asked, "What must the officer be, who may be said to be distinguished?"   36

The Master said, "What is it you call being distinguished?"   37

Tsze-chang replied, "It is to be heard of through the state, to be heard of throughout his clan.   38

" The Master said, "That is notoriety, not distinction.   ·   39

"Now the man of distinction is solid and straightforward, and loves righteousness. He examines people's words, and looks at their countenances. He is anxious to humble himself to others. Such a man will be distinguished in the country; he will be distinguished in his clan.   40

"As to the man of notoriety, he assumes the appearance of virtue, but his actions are opposed to it, and he rests in this character without any doubts about himself. Such a man will be heard of in the country; he will be heard of in the clan."   41

Fan Ch'ih rambling with the Master under the trees about the rain altars, said, "I venture to ask how to exalt virtue, to correct cherished evil, and to discover delusions."   42

The Master said, "Truly a good question!   43

"If doing what is to be done be made the first business, and success a secondary consideration:—is not this the way to exalt virtue? To assail one's own wickedness and not assail that of others;—is not this the way to correct cherished evil? For a morning's anger to disregard one's own life, and involve that of his parents;—is not this a case of delusion?"   44

Fan Ch'ih asked about benevolence. The Master said, "It is to love all men." He asked about knowledge. The Master said, "It is to know all men."   45

Fan Ch'ih did not immediately understand these answers.   46

The Master said, "Employ the upright and put aside all the crooked; in this   47
way the crooked can be made to be upright."

Fan Ch'ih retired, and, seeing Tsze-hsia, he said to him, "A Little while ago,   48
I had an interview with our Master, and asked him about knowledge. He said,
'Employ the upright, and put aside all the crooked;—in this way, the crooked will
be made to be upright.' What did he mean?"

Tsze-hsia said, "Truly rich is his saying!   49

"Shun, being in possession of the kingdom, selected from among all the   50
people, and employed Kai-yao-on which all who were devoid of virtue disappeared. T'ang, being in possession of the kingdom, selected from among all the
people, and employed I Yin-and an who were devoid of virtue disappeared."

Tsze-kung asked about friendship. The Master said, "Faithfully admonish   51
your friend, and skillfully lead him on. If you find him impracticable, stop. Do
not disgrace yourself."

The philosopher Tsang said, "The superior man on grounds of culture   52
meets with his friends, and by friendship helps his virtue."

Questions for Discussion

1. What is perfect virtue? What makes it perfect? What are intelligence and
    proper government, and how does the superior man manifest these quali-
    ties?

2. How does a person obtain perfect virtue? Can anyone attain it?

3. Why does the Master give a different answer to the first three disciples?
    What is different about each definition? How do the definitions work in
    concert?

4. What makes a man "superior"?

5. What are the three requisites of government? What is the most important
    requisite? Do you agree? Does what Confucius describe fit your country at
    present?

6. Does the Master have all the answers? Is he the only expert? Who shares
    authority with him?

7. Why is the teacher-student dialogue a useful one by which to convey moral
    principles?

Questions for Reflection and Writing

1. How might Confucius' definition of virtue apply to today, especially to politics? Write about one case in which "perfect virtue" would apply, or would obviously not apply.

2. How should a person live life? In your opinion, what constitutes perfect virtue, intelligence, and superiority? Describe the qualities for which one should strive. Refer to this piece by Confucius where appropriate.

3. Research Confucius' life. What is known about him? What have been his influences on historical and modern Chinese culture? Choose one aspect of Chinese culture— such as education, religion, domestic life, government, foreign affairs—and explain how Confucius' philosophy has shaped it.

David A. Hoekema (1950–   ), Professor of Philosophy at Calvin College, served previously as academic dean and as interim vice-president of student life at Calvin. He taught at St. Olaf College from 1977 until 1984, when he joined the philosophy faculty at the University of Delaware and was appointed executive director of the American Philosophical Association, a position he held until 1992. His published books include *Rights and Wrongs: Coercion, Punishment, and the State* (1986); *Handbook for Administrators of Learned Societies, Campus Rules and Moral Community* (1994); and an anthology edited with Bobby Fong, *Christianity and Culture in the Crossfire* (1997). His articles on issues of political philosophy, religious and academic freedom, and Christian ethics have appeared in *Israel Law Review*, *Teaching Philosophy*, *Christian Scholars' Review*, *Social Philosophy and Policy*, *Criminal Justice Ethics*, *Art Journal*, *Christian Century*, *Academe*, and *Commonweal*.

Capital Punishment: The Question of Justification

David Hoekema

In 1810 a bill introduced in the British Parliament sought to abolish capital pun-   1
ishment for the offense of stealing five shillings or more from a shop. Judges and magistrates unanimously opposed the measure. In the House of Lords, the chief justice of the King's Bench, Lord Ellenborough, predicted that the next step would be abolition of the death penalty for stealing five shillings from a house; thereafter no one could "trust himself for an hour without the most alarming apprehension that on his return, every vestige of his property [would] be swept away by the hardened robber" (quoted by Herbert B. Ehrmann in "The Death Penalty and the Administration of Justice," in *The Death Penalty in America*, edited by Hugo Adam Bedau [Anchor, 1967], p. 415).

During the same year Parliament abolished the death penalty for picking   2
pockets, but more than 200 crimes remained punishable by death. Each year in Great Britain more than 2000 persons were being sentenced to die, though only a small number of these sentences were actually carried out.

In this regard as in many others, the laws of the English colonies in North   3
America were much less harsh than those of the mother country. At the time of the Revolution, statutes in most of the colonies prescribed hanging for about a

dozen offenses—among them murder, treason, piracy, arson, rape, robbery, burglary, sodomy and (in some cases) counterfeiting, horse theft and slave rebellion. But by the early nineteenth century a movement to abolish the death penalty was gaining strength.

The idea was hardly new: czarist Russia had eliminated the death penalty   4
on religious grounds in the eleventh century. In the United States the movement had been launched by Benjamin Rush in the eighteenth century, with the support of such other distinguished citizens of Philadelphia as Benjamin Franklin and Attorney General William Bradford. By the 1830s, bills calling for abolition of capital punishment were being regularly introduced, and defeated, in several state legislatures. In 1846 Michigan voted effectively to abolish the death penalty—the first English-speaking jurisdiction in the world to do so.

In the years since, twelve states have abolished capital punishment entire-   5
ly. Although statutes still in effect in some states permit the death penalty to be imposed for a variety of offenses—ranging from statutory rape to desecration of a grave to causing death in a duel—murder is virtually the only crime for which it has been recently employed. There are about 400 persons in U.S. prisons under sentence of death, but only one execution (Gary Gilmore's) has been carried out in this country in the past eleven years.

However, the issue of whether capital punishment is justifiable is by no   6
means settled. Since the Supreme Court, in the case of *Furman v. Georgia* in 1972, invalidated most existing laws permitting capital punishment, several states have enacted new legislation designed to meet the court's objections to the Georgia law. And recent public-opinion surveys indicate that a large number, possibly a majority, of Americans favor imposing the death penalty for some crimes. But let us ask the ethical question: Ought governments to put to death persons convicted of certain crimes?

First, let us look at grounds on which capital punishment is defended. Most   7
prominent is the argument from *deterrence*. Capital punishment, it is asserted, is necessary to deter potential criminals. Murderers must be executed so that the lives of potential murder victims may be spared.

Two assertions are closely linked here. First, it is said that convicted mur-   8
derers must be put to death in order to protect the rest of us against those individuals who might kill others if they were at large. This argument, based not strictly on deterrence but on incapacitation of known offenders, is inconclusive, since there are other effective means of protecting the innocent against convict-

ed murderers—for example, imprisonment of murderers for life in high-security institutions.

Second, it is said that the example of capital punishment is needed to deter those who would otherwise commit murder. Knowledge that a crime is punishable by death will give the potential criminal pause. This second argument rests on the assumption that capital punishment does in fact reduce the incidence of capital crimes—a presupposition that must be tested against the evidence. Surprisingly, none of the available empirical data shows any significant correlation between the existence or use of the death penalty and the incidence of capital crimes.   9

When studies have compared the homicide rates for the past fifty years in states that employ the death penalty and in adjoining states that have abolished it, the numbers have in every case been quite similar: the death penalty has had no discernible effect on homicide rates. Further, the shorter-term effects of capital punishment have been studied by examining the daily number of homicides reported in California over a ten-year period to ascertain whether the execution of convicts reduced the number. Fewer homicides were reported on days immediately following an execution, but this reduction was matched by an increase in the number of homicides on the day of execution and the preceding day. Executions had no discernible effect on the weekly total of homicides. (Cf. "Death and Imprisonment as Deterrents to Murder," by Thorsten Sellin, in Bedau, op. cit., pp. 274–284, and "The Deterrent Effect of Capital Punishment in California," by William F. Graves, in Bedau, op. cit., pp. 322–332.)   10

The available evidence, then, fails to support the claim that capital punishment deters capital crime. For this reason, I think, we may set aside the deterrence argument. But there is a stronger reason for rejecting the argument—one that has to do with the way in which supporters of that argument would have us treat persons.   11

Those who defend capital punishment on grounds of deterrence would have us take the lives of some—persons convicted of certain crimes—because doing so will discourage crime and thus protect others. But it is a grave moral wrong to treat one person in a way justified solely by the needs of others. To inflict harm on one person in order to serve the purposes of others is to use that person in an immoral and inhumane way, treating him or her not as a person with rights and responsibilities but as a means to other ends. The most serious flaw in the deterrence argument, therefore, is that it is the wrong *kind* of argu-   12 ment. The execution of criminals cannot be justified by the good which their deaths may do the rest of us.

A second argument for the death penalty maintains that some crimes, chief 13 among them murder, *morally require* the punishment of death. In particular, Christians frequently support capital punishment by appeal to the Mosaic code, which required the death penalty for murder. "The law of capital punishment," one writer has concluded after reviewing relevant biblical passages, "must stand as a silent but powerful witness to the sacredness of God-given life" ("Christianity and the Death Penalty," by Jacob Vellenga, in Bedau, op. cit., pp. 123–130.).

In the Mosaic code, it should be pointed out, there were many capital 14 crimes besides murder. In the book of Deuteronomy, death is prescribed as the penalty for false prophecy, worship of foreign gods, kidnapping, adultery, deception by a bride concerning her virginity, and disobedience to parents. To this list the laws of the book of Exodus add witchcraft, sodomy, and striking or cursing a parent.

I doubt that there is much sentiment in favor of restoring the death penal- 15 ty in the United States for such offenses. But if the laws of Old Testament Israel ought not to govern our treatment of, say, adultery, why should they govern the penalty for murder? To support capital punishment by an appeal to Old Testament law is to overlook the fact that the ancient theocratic state of Israel was in nearly every respect profoundly different from any modern secular state. For this reason, we cannot simply regard the Mosaic code as normative for the United States today.

But leaving aside reference to Mosaic law, let me state more strongly the 16 argument we are examining. The death penalty, it may be urged, is the only just penalty for a crime such as murder, it is the only fair *retribution*. Stated thus, the argument at hand seems to be the right *kind* of argument for capital punishment. If capital punishment can be justified at all, it must be on the basis of the *seriousness of the offense* for which it is imposed. Retributive considerations *should* govern the punishment of individuals who violate the law, and chief among these considerations are the principle of proportionality between punishment and offense and the requirement that persons be punished only for acts for which they are truly responsible. I am not persuaded that retributive considerations are sufficient to set a particular penalty for a given offense, but I believe they do require that in comparative terms we visit more serious offenses with more severe punishment.

Therefore, the retributive argument seems the strongest one in support of capital punishment. We ought to deal with convicted offenders not as we want to, but as they deserve. And I am not certain that it is wrong to argue that a person who has deliberately killed another person deserves to die.   17

But even if this principle is valid, should the judicial branch of our governments be empowered to determine whether individuals deserve to die? Are our procedures for making laws and for determining guilt sufficiently reliable that we may entrust our lives to them? I shall return to this important question presently. But consider the following fact: During the years from 1930 to 1962, 466 persons were put to death for the crime of rape. Of these, 399 were black. Can it seriously be maintained that our courts are administering the death penalty to all those and only to those who deserve to die?   18

Two other arguments deserve brief mention. It has been argued that, even if the penalty of life imprisonment were acceptable on other grounds, our society could not reasonably be asked to pay the cost of maintaining convicted murderers in prisons for the remainder of their natural lives.   19

This argument overlooks the considerable costs of retaining the death penalty. Jury selection, conduct of the trial, and the appeals process become extremely timeconsuming and elaborate when death is a possible penalty. On the other hand, prisons should not be as expensive as they are. At present those prisoners who work at all are working for absurdly low wages, frequently at menial and degrading tasks. Prisons should be reorganized to provide meaningful work for all able inmates; workers should be paid fair wages for their work and charged for their room and board. Such measures would sharply reduce the cost of prisons and make them more humane.   20

But these considerations—important as they are—have little relevance to the justification of capital punishment. We should not decide to kill convicted criminals only because it costs so much to keep them alive. The cost to society of imprisonment, large or small, cannot justify capital punishment.   21

Finally, defenders of capital punishment sometimes support their case by citing those convicted offenders—for example, Gary Gilmore—who have asked to be executed rather than imprisoned. But this argument, too, is of little relevance. If some prisoners would prefer to die rather than be imprisoned, perhaps we should oblige them by permitting them to take their own lives. But this con-   22 sideration has nothing to do with the question of whether we ought to impose the punishment of death on certain offenders, most of whom would prefer to live.

Let us turn now to the case *against* the death penalty. It is sometimes argued that   23 capital punishment is unjustified because those guilty of crimes cannot help acting as they do: the environment, possibly interacting with inherited characteristics, causes some people to commit crimes. It is not moral culpability or choice that divides lawabiding citizens from criminals—so Clarence Darrow argued—eloquently—but the accident of birth or social circumstances.

If determinism of this sort were valid, not only the death penalty but all   24 forms of punishment would be unjustified. No one who is compelled by circumstances to act deserves to be punished. But there is little reason to adopt this bleak view of human action. Occasionally coercive threats compel a person to violate the law; and in such cases the individual is rightly excused from legal guilt. Circumstances of deprivation, hardship and lack of education—unfortunately much more widely prevalent—break down the barriers, both moral and material, which deter many of us from breaking the law. They are grounds for exercising extreme caution and for showing mercy in the application of the law, but they are not the sole causes of crimes: they diminish but do not destroy the responsibility of the individual. The great majority of those who break the law do so deliberately, by choice and not as a result of causes beyond their control.

Second, the case against the death penalty is sometimes based on the view   25 that the justification of punishment lies in the reform which it effects. Those who break the law, it is said, are ill, suffering either from psychological malfunction or from maladjustment to society. Our responsibility is to treat them, to cure them of their illness, so that they become able to function in socially acceptable ways. Death, obviously, cannot reform anyone.

Like the deterrence argument for capital punishment, this seems to be the   26 wrong *kind* of argument. Punishment is punishment and treatment is treatment, and one must not be substituted for the other. Some persons who violate the law are, without doubt, mentally ill. It is unreasonable and inhumane to punish them for acts which they may not have realized they were doing; to put such a person to death would be an even more grievous wrong. In such cases treatment is called for.

But most persons who break the law are not mentally ill and do know what   27 they are doing. We may not force them to undergo treatment in place of the legal penalty for their offenses. To confine them to mental institutions until those put in authority over them judge that they are cured of their criminal tendencies is far more cruel than to sentence them to a term of imprisonment. Voluntary programs of education or vocational training, which help prepare prisoners for non-criminal careers on release, should be made more widely available. But compulsory treatment for all offenders violates their integrity as persons; we need only look to the Soviet Union to see the abuses to which such a practice is liable.

Let us examine a third and stronger argument, a straightforward moral assertion: 28
the state ought not to take life unnecessarily. For many reasons—among them the example which capital punishment sets, its effect on those who must carry out death sentences and, above all, its violation of a basic moral principle—the state ought not to kill people.

The counterclaim made by defenders of capital punishment is that in cer-   29
tain circumstances killing people is permissible and even required, and that capital punishment is one of those cases. If a terrorist is about to throw a bomb into a crowded theater, and a police officer is certain that there is no way to stop him except to kill him, the officer should of course kill the terrorist. In some cases of grave and immediate danger, let us grant, killing is justified.

But execution bears little resemblance to such cases. It involves the   30
planned, deliberate killing of someone in custody who is not a present threat to human life or safety. Execution is not necessary to save the lives of future victims, since there are other means to secure that end.

Is there some vitally important purpose of the state or some fundamental   31
right of persons which cannot be secured without executing convicts? I do not believe there is. And in the absence of any such compelling reason, the moral principle that it is wrong to kill people constitutes a powerful argument against capital punishment.

Of the arguments I have mentioned in favor of the death penalty, only one has   32
considerable weight. That is the retributive argument that murder, as an extremely serious offense, requires a comparably severe punishment. Of the arguments so far examined against capital punishment, only one, the moral claim that killing is wrong, is, in my view, acceptable.

There is, however, another argument against the death penalty which I   33
find compelling—that based on the imperfection of judicial procedure. In the case of *Furman v. Georgia*, the Supreme Court struck down existing legislation

because of the arbitrariness with which some convicted offenders were executed and others spared. Laws enacted subsequently in several states have attempted to meet the court's objection, either by making death mandatory for certain offenses or by drawing up standards which the trial jury must follow in deciding, after guilt has been established, whether the death penalty will be imposed in a particular case. But these revisions of the law diminish only slightly the discretion of the jury. When death is made the mandatory sentence for first-degree murder, the question of death or imprisonment becomes the question of whether to find the accused guilty as charged or guilty of a lesser offense, such as second-degree murder.

When standards are spelled out, the impression of greater precision is often   34
only superficial. A recent Texas statute, for example, instructs the jury to impose a sentence of death only if it is established "beyond a reasonable doubt" that "there is a probability that the defendant would commit criminal acts of violence that would constitute a continuing threat to society" (Texas Code of Criminal Procedure, Art. 37.071; quoted in *Capital Punishment: The Inevitability of Caprice and Mistake,* by Charles L. Black, Jr. [Norton, 1974], p. 58). Such a law does not remove discretion but only adds confusion.

At many other points in the judicial process, discretion rules, and arbitrary   35
or incorrect decisions are possible. The prosecutor must decide whether to charge the accused with a capital crime, and whether to accept a plea of guilty to a lesser charge. (In most states it is impossible to plead guilty to a charge carrying a mandatory death sentence.) The jury must determine whether the facts of the case as established by testimony in court fit the legal definition of the offense with which the defendant is charged—a definition likely to be complicated at best, incomprehensible at worst. From a mass of confusing and possibly conflicting testimony the jury must choose the most reliable. But evident reliability can be deceptive: persons have been wrongly convicted of murder on the positive identification of eyewitnesses.

Jurors must also determine whether at the time of the crime the accused   36
satisfied the legal definition of insanity. The most widely used definition—the McNaghten Rules formulated by the judges of the House of Lords in 1843—states that a person is excused from criminal responsibility if at the time of his act he suffered from a defect of reason which arose from a disease of the mind and as a result of which he did not "know the nature and quality of his act," or "if he did know it . . . he did not know he was doing what was wrong" (quoted in *Punishment and Responsibility,* by H. L. A. Hart [Oxford University Press, 1968],

p. 189). Every word of this formula has been subject to legal controversy in interpretation, and it is unreasonable to expect that juries untrained in law will be able to apply it consistently and fairly. Even after sentencing, some offenders escape the death penalty as a result of appeals, other technical legal challenges, or executive clemency.

Because of all these opportunities for arbitrary decision, only a small num-   37
ber of those convicted of capital crimes are actually executed. It is hardly surprising that their selection has little to do with the character of their crimes but a great deal to do with the skill of their legal counsel. And the latter depends in large measure on how much money is available for the defense. Inevitably, the death penalty has been imposed most frequently on the poor, and in this country it has been imposed in disproportionate numbers on blacks.

To cite two examples in this regard: All those executed in Delaware   38
between 1902 and the (temporary) abolition of the state's death penalty in 1958 were unskilled workers with limited education. Of 3860 persons executed in the United States between 1930 and the present, 2066, or 54 percent, were black. Although for a variety of reasons the per capita rate of conviction for most types of crime has been higher among the poor and the black, that alone cannot explain why a tenth of the population should account for more than half of those executed. Doubtless prejudice played a part. But no amount of goodwill and fair-mindedness can compensate for the disadvantage to those who cannot afford the highly skilled legal counsel needed to discern every loophole in the judicial process.

Even more worrisome than the discriminatory application of the death penalty   39
is the possibility of mistaken conviction and its ghastly consequences. In a sense, any punishment wrongfully imposed is irrevocable, but none is so irrevocable as death. Although we cannot give back to a person mistakenly imprisoned the time spent or the self-respect lost, we can release and compensate him or her. But we cannot do anything for a person wrongfully executed. While we ought to minimize the opportunities for capricious or mistaken judgments throughout the legal system, we cannot hope for perfect success. There is no reason why our mistakes must be fatal.

Numerous cases of erroneous convictions in capital cases have been docu-   40
mented; several of those convicted were put to death before the error was discovered. However small their number, it is too large. So long as the death penalty exists, there are certain to be others, for every judicial procedure—however

meticulous, however compassed about with safeguards—must be carried out by fallible human beings.

One erroneous execution is too many, because even lawful executions of the indisputably guilty serve no purpose. They are not justified by the need to protect the rest of us, since there are other means of restraining persons dangerous to society, and there is no evidence that executions deter the commission of crime. A wrongful execution is a grievous injustice that cannot be remedied after the fact. Even a legal and proper execution is a needless taking of human life. Even if one is sympathetic—as I am—to the claim that a murderer deserves to die, there are compelling reasons not to entrust the power to decide who shall die to the persons and procedures that constitute our judicial system. 41

Questions for Discussion

1. What are the claims made for capital punishment? What is the evidence for these claims?
2. What are the claims made against capital punishment? What is the evidence for these claims?
3. Is evidence for and against capital punishment evenly presented?
4. Where does Hoekema ask questions? Why does he ask these particular questions?
5. Hoekema uses transitions, such as "first," "second," and so on, that help divide the complex information into smaller pieces. What other transitions does he use?
6. Can you tell whether Hoekema is himself for or against capital punishment? Or does he take a purely neutral stance? How can you tell?
7. What does the historical background add to your understanding of the issue? Does the historical information change your opinion about the issue?

Questions for Reflection and Writing

1. Choose one of the questions that Hoekema asks; respond to it, adding your own ideas to those of Hoekema's.
2. State your own opinion about capital punishment, using Hoekema as a source of statistics and quotes.
3. Find other cases that could be used as evidence for either side of the debate on capital punishment. Explain how these other cases support that side's argument.

Chapter 7
RELIGION AND ETHICS

At the Start: Genesis Made New

Mary Phil Korsak

Chapter 1

1   At the start Elohim created the skies and the earth

2   —the earth was tohu-bohu
       darkness on the face of the deep
       and the breath of Elohim
       hovering on the face of the waters—

3   Elohim said
       Let light be
       Light was
4   Elohim saw the light How good!
       Elohim separated the light from the darkness
5   Elohim called to the light "Day"
       To the darkness he called "Night"
       It was evening, it was morning
       One day

6   Elohim said
       Let a vault be in the middle of the waters
       it shall separate waters from waters
7   Elohim made the vault
       It separated the waters under the vault
       from the waters above the vault
       It was so
8   Elohim called to the vault "Skies"
       It was evening, it was morning
       A second day

9   Elohim said
Let the waters under the skies be massed to one place
Let the dry be seen
It was so

10   Elohim called to the dry "Earth"
To the massing of the waters he called "Seas"
Elohim saw. How good!

11   Elohim said
Let the earth grow grass
plants seeding seed
fruit-tree making fruit of its kind
with its seed in it on the earth
It was so

12   The earth brought forth grass
plants seeding seed of their kind
and tree making fruit with its seed in it of its kind
Elohim saw How good!

13   It was evening, it was morning
A third day

14   Elohim said
Let lights be in the vault of the skies
to separate the day from the night
They shall be signs for set times, for days and years

15   They shall be lights in the vault of the skies
to light upon the earth
It was so

16   Elohim made the two great lights
the great light for ruling the day
the small light for ruling the night
and the stars

17   Elohim gave them to the vault of the skies
to light upon the earth

18   to rule the day and the night
and to separate the light from the darkness
Elohim saw How good!

19   It was evening, it was morning

A fourth day

20   Elohim said
      Let the waters swarm with a swarm of living souls
      and let fowl fly above the earth
      upon the face of the vault of the skies
21   Elohim created the great monsters
      all living souls that creep
      with which the waters swarm of their kind
      and every winged fowl of its kind
      Elohim saw How good!
22   Elohim blessed them, saying
      'Be fruitful, increase, fill the waters in the seas
      Let the fowl increase on the earth
23   It was evening, it was morning
      A fifth day

24   Elohim said
      Let the earth bring forth living souls of their kind
      cattle, creeper and beast of the earth of its kind
      It was so
25   Elohim made the beast of the earth of its kind
      the cattle of their kind
      and every creeper of the ground of its kind
      Elohim saw How good!

26   Elohim said
      We will make a groundling (Adam)
      in our image, after our likeness
      Let them govern the fish of the sea
      the fowl of the skies, the cattle, all the earth
      every creeper that creeps on the earth
27   Elohim created the groundling in his image
      created it in the image of Elohim
      male and female created them
28   Elohim blessed them
      Elohim said to them

Be fruitful, increase, fill the earth, subject it
Govern the fish of the sea, the fowl of the skies
every beast that creeps on the earth
29   Elohim said, here I give you
all plants seeding seed upon the face of all the earth
and every tree with tree-fruit in it seeding seed
It shall be for you for eating
30   And for every beast of the earth
for every fowl of the skies
for all the creeps on the earth with living soul in it
all green of plants for eating
It was so
31   Elohim saw all he had made Here! it was very good
It was evening, it was morning
The sixth day

Chapter 2

1   They were finished, the skies, the earth
and all their company
2   Elohim had finished on the seventh day
his work that he had done
He ceased on the seventh day
from all his work that he had done
3   Elohim blessed the seventh day and made it holy
for on it he ceased from all his work
that Elohim had created and done

4   These are the breedings of the skies and the earth
at their creation
5   On the day YHWH Elohim made earth and skies
no shrub of the field was yet in the earth
no plant of the field had yet sprouted
for YHWH Elohim had not made it rain on the earth
and there was no groundling to serve the ground
6   But a surge went up from the earth
and gave drink to all the face of the ground

7   YHWH Elohim formed the groundling, soil of the ground
He blew into its nostrils the blast of life
and the groundling became a living soul

8   YHWH Elohim planted a garden in Eden in the east
There he set the groundling he had formed
9   YHWH Elohim made sprout from the ground
all trees attractive to see and good for eating
the tree of live in the middle of the garden
and the tree of the knowing of good and bad

10   A river goes out in Eden to give drink to the garden
From there it divides and becomes four heads
11   The name of the first is Pishon
It winds through all the land of Havilah
where there is gold
12   The gold of that land is good
Bdellium is there and onyx stone
13   The name of the second river is Gihon
It winds through all the land of Cush
14   The name of the third river is Tigris
It goes east of Asshur
The fourth river is Euphrates

15   YHWH Elohim took the groundling
and set it to rest in the garden of Eden
to serve it and keep it
16   YHWH Wlohim commanded the groundling, saying
Of every tree of the garden eat! you shall eat

17   but of the tree of knowing of good and bad
you shall not eat
for on the day you eat of it
die! you shall die

[4]YHWH: the personal name of the God of the Hebrews is not pronounced. Read Adonai, or Yahweh, or the Lord.

18   YHWH Elohim said
It is not good for the groundling to be alone
I will make for it a help as its counterpart

19   YHWH Elohim formed out of the ground
all beasts of the field, all fowl of the skies
and brought them to the groundling
to see what it would call them
Whatever the groundling called to each living soul
that is its name
20   The groundling called names for all the cattle
for all fowl of the skies, for all beasts of the field
But for a groundling it found no help as its counterpart
21   YHWH Elohim made a swoon fall upon the groundling
it slept
He took one of its sides
and closed up the flesh in its place
22   YHWH Elohim built the side
he had taken from the groundling into woman
He brought her to the groundling
23   The groundling said
This one this time
is bone from my bones
flesh from my flesh
This one shall be called wo-man
for from man
she has been taken this one
24   So a man will leave his father and his mother
he will cling to his wo-man
and they will become one flesh

25   The two of them were naked
the groundling and his woman
they were not ashamed

Chapter 3

1   The serpent was the most shrewd
    of all the beasts of the field
    that YHWH Elohim had made
    It said to the woman, So Elohim said
    You shall not eat of all the trees of the garden . . .

2   The woman said to the serpent
    We will eat the fruit of the trees of the garden

3   but of the fruit of the tree
    in the middle of the garden, Elohim said
    You shall not eat of it, you shall not touch it
    lest you die

4   The serpent said to the woman
    Die! you shall not die

5   No, Elohim knows that the day you eat of it
    your eyes will be opened
    and you will be as Elohim knowing good and bad

6   The woman saw that the tree was good for eating
    yes, an allurement to the eyes
    and that the tree was attractive to get insight
    She took of its fruit and ate
    She also gave to her man with her and he ate

7   The eyes of the two of them were opened
    they knew that they were naked
    They sewed fig leaves together
    and made themselves loin clothes

8   They heard the voice of YHWH Elohim
    walking in the garden in the breeze of the day
    The groundling and his woman hid from YHWH Elohim
    in the middle of the tree of the garden

9   YHWH Elohim called to the groundling and said to him
    Where are you?

10 He said, I heard your voice in the garden

and I was afraid for I was naked
and I hid
11 He said, Who told you that you were naked?
Did you eat of the tree
I commanded you not to eat of?
12 The groundling said
The woman you gave to be with me,
she, she gave me of the tree and I ate
13 YHWH Elohim said to the woman
What have you done?
The woman said
The serpent enticed me and I ate

14 YHWH Elohim said to the serpent
As you have done this
you are banned from all the cattle
of all the beasts of the field
You shall go on your stomach
and you shall eat soil
all the days of your life
15 I will put enmity between you and the woman
between your seed and her seed
It, it shall strike at your head
and you, you shall strike at its heel

16 To the woman he said
Increase! I will increase
your pains and your conceivings
With pains you shall breed sons
For your man your longing
and he, he shall rule you
17 To the groundling he said
As you have heard your woman's voice
and have eaten of the tree
of which I commanded you, saying
You shall not eat of it!
cursed is the ground for you

With pains you shall eat of it
all the days of your life
18   Thorn and thistle it shall sprout for you
You shall eat the plants of the field
19   With the sweat of your face you shall eat bread
till you return to the ground
for from it you were taken
for soil you are and to the soil you shall return

20   The groundling called his woman's name Life (Eve)
for she is the mother of all that lives

21   YHWH Elohim made for the groundling and his woman
robes of skin and clothed them
22   YHWH Elohim said
Here, the groundling has become one of us
knowing good and bad
Now, let it not put out its hand
to take from the tree of life also
and eat and live for ever!
23   YHWH Elohim sent it away from the garden of Eden
to serve the ground from which it was taken
24   He cast out the groundling
and made dwell east of the garden of Eden
the Cherubim and the scorching, turning sword
to keep the road to the tree of life

The Upanishads

The term "the Upanishads" designates a large collection of Hindu texts (originally oral in form) written in Sanskrit. Each individual text is a Upanishad and has its own name—for example, the *Kena* Upanishad. The earliest Upanishads were composed between 800 and 400 B.C.E.; others were written as late as the fifteenth century C.E. The word "Upanishad" is a compound of three Sanskrit words: *upa* ("near"), *ni* ("down"), and *shad* ("sit"). A Upanishad is a "sitting down near" in the sense of being a secret doctrine that a student could hear if he or she sat down very close to the teacher. Some Upanishads are in verse and some in prose, but all of them are highly poetic.

The Upanishads are the final sections of each of the four *Vedas* (the Hindu scriptures; *veda* means, literally, "wisdom, knowledge")—the *Rg Veda*, the *Jajur Veda*, the *Sama Veda*, and the *Atharva Veda*. Some scholars consider the Upanishads commentaries on the Vedas, rather than parts of the Vedas themselves. The Upanishads vary greatly in length, from a single page to over a hundred pages. Our selections are excerpts from the two earliest Upanishads, the *Brihad-Aranyaka* (about 800 B.C.E.) and the *Chandogya* (about 750 B.C.E.); excerpts from two other ancient Upanishads, the *Kena* and the *Isa*; and the complete text of another ancient Upanishad, the succinct *Mandukya*.

These Upanishads discuss the human soul, Brahman, and the relation between the two. The soul (*atman*) is our spirit, our inner reality, that which makes us who we are and remains the same through all the changes in our lives—our permanent self. Brahman (a transliteration of the Sanskrit word) is Reality, Being, the Absolute—the ground of all reality and of all things. The highest wisdom, according to the Upanishads, is to realize that our soul *is* Brahman, and that Brahman is our soul. Brahman, accordingly, is called Soul, Self. When we attain this highest wisdom, we attain liberation from the cycle of rebirth.

Rebirth (reincarnation, transmigration of the soul) is a basic assumption of Hindu thought. According to Hinduism, the form that our next incarnation takes is determined by the *law of karma*, which states that our good and bad actions in our current life (*karma* means "action") bear fruit in our next incarnation. The inexorable law of cause and effect means that good actions will lead to benefits in our next life, and bad actions will lead to suffering. We can progress to better and better lives from one incarnation to the next, but the ultimate goal is to escape the reincarnation cycle altogether. The Upanishads teach that emancipation from the cycle of birth, death, and rebirth occurs when I gain the insight that my soul is Soul (Brahman), that my self is Self.

Our selection from the *Brihad-Aranyaka* Upanishad (literally, "The Great Forest Text") begins with a brief instruction of Gargya by Ajatasatru, and then gives a series of teachings by Yajnavalkya, who imparts his wisdom to Maitreyi, Ushasta Cakrayana, Kahola Kaushitakeya, Uddalaka Aruni, and Janaka. The *Chandogya* Upanishad (literally, "pertaining to the *chando-gas*," the priests who intone hymns) presents the instruction Uddalaka gave to his son Svetaketu about the relation of soul to Brahman, and a story about how the god Indra and the devil Virocana became disciples of the sage Prajapati in order to learn to satisfy all their desires. The *Kena* Upanishad (named from its first word, *kena*, "by whom") begins with a poem about Brahman and then tells a story about how the gods came to know Brahman. The *Isa* Upanishad (named from its first word, *isa*, "lord") is a poem about the wondrous nature of Brahman, the Lord. Our readings conclude with the *Mandukya* Upanishad, which is a hymn to the word *om*, which is "the Self indeed."

The Thirteen Principal Upanishads, trans. Robert Ernest Hume. London, England: Oxford University Press, 1921 (updated stylistically).

Brihad-Aranyaka Upanishad

Second Adhyaya

First Brahmana . . . Gargya said: "Let me come to you as a pupil."   1
Ajatasatru said: "Verily, it is contrary to the course of things that a   2
Brahmin[1] should come to a Kshatriya,[2] thinking 'He will tell me [about]
Brahman.' However, I shall cause you to know him clearly."

He took him by the hand and rose. The two went up to a man who was   3
asleep. They addressed him with these words: "Great white-robed King Soma!"
He did not rise. Ajatasatru woke him by rubbing him with his hand. That one
arose.

Ajatasatru said: "When this man fell asleep thus, where then was the per-   4
son who consists of intelligence? From where did he thus come back?"

And this also Gargya did not know.   5

Ajatasatru said: "When this man has fallen asleep thus, then the person   6
who consists of intelligence, having by his intelligence taken to himself the
intelligence of these senses, rests in that place which is the space within the
heart. When that person restrains the senses, that person is said to be asleep.
Then the breath is restrained, the voice is restrained, the eye is restrained, the
ear is restrained, the mind is restrained.

"When he goes to sleep, these worlds are his. Then he becomes a great   7
king, as it were. Then he becomes a great Brahmin, as it were. He enters the high
and the low, as it were. As a great king, taking with him his people, moves
around in his own country as he pleases, even so here this one, taking with him
his senses, moves around in his own body as he pleases.

"Now when one falls sound asleep (when one knows nothing whatsoever,   8
having crept out through the seventy-two thousand veins which lead from the
heart to the pericardium), one rests in the pericardium. Verily, as a youth or a
great king or a great Brahmin might rest when he has reached the summit of
bliss, so this one now rests.

"As a spider might come out with his thread, as small sparks come forth   9
from the fire, even so from this Soul come forth all vital energies, all worlds, all
gods, all beings. The mystic meaning of this is 'the Real of the real.' Breathing
creatures, verily, are the real. He is their Real." . . .

Fourth Brahmana . . . "Maitreyi," said Yajnavalkya, "verily, I am about to go   10
forth from this state.[3] Behold, let me make a final settlement for you and
Katyayani." .

Then Maitreyi said: "If now, sir, this whole earth filled with wealth were   11
mine, would I be immortal thereby?"

"No," said Yajnavalkya. "As the life of the rich, even so would your life be.   12
Of immortality, however, there is no hope through wealth."

Then said Maitreyi: "What should I do with that through which I may not   13
be immortal? What you know, sir—that, indeed, tell me." Then said
Yajnavalkya: "Ah, as you are dear to us, dear is what you say. Come, sit down; I
will explain it to you. But while I am expounding, do you seek to ponder on it."

Then he said: "Lo, verily, not for love of the husband is a husband dear, but   14
for love of the Soul a husband is dear.

"Verily, not for love of the wife is a wife dear, but for love of the Soul a wife   15
is dear.

"Verily, not for love of the sons are sons dear, but for love of the Soul sons   16
are dear.

"Verily, not for love of the wealth is wealth dear, but for love of the Soul   17
wealth is dear.

"Verily, not for love of Brahminhood[4] is Brahminhood dear, but for love of   18
the Soul Brahminhood is dear.

"Verily, not for love of Kshatrahood[5] is Kshatrahood dear, but for love of   19
the Soul Kshatrahood is dear.

"Verily, not for love of the worlds are the worlds dear, but for love of the   20
Soul the worlds are dear.

"Verily, not for love of the gods are the gods dear, but for love of the Soul   21
the gods are dear.

"Verily, not for love of the beings are beings dear, but for love of the Soul   22
beings are dear.

"Verily, not for love of all is all dear, but for love of the Soul all is dear.   23

"Verily, it is the Soul that should be seen, that should be hearkened to, that   24
should be thought on, that should be pondered on, O Maitreyi. Verily, with the
seeing of, with the hearkening to, with the thinking of, and with the understanding of the Soul, this world-all is known.

"Brahminhood has deserted him who knows Brahminhood in anything   25
other than the Soul.

"Kshatrahood has deserted him who knows Kshatrahood in anything other   26
than the Soul.

"The worlds have deserted him who knows the worlds in anything other   27
than the Soul.

"The gods have deserted him who knows the gods in anything other than   28
the Soul.

"Beings have deserted him who knows beings in anything other than the   29
Soul.

"Everything has deserted him who knows everything in anything other   30
than the Soul.

"This Brahminhood, this Kshatrahood, these worlds, these gods, these   31
beings, everything here is what this Soul is.

"It is—as when a drum is being beaten, one would not be able to grasp the   32
external sounds, but by grasping the drum or the beater of the drum the sound is
grasped.

"It is—as when a conch shell is being blown, one would not be able to   33
grasp the external sounds, but by grasping the conch shell or the blower of the
conch shell the sound is grasped.

"It is—as when a lute is being played, one would not be able to grasp the   34
external sounds, but by grasping the lute or the player of the lute the sound is
grasped. . . .

"It is—as a lump of salt cast in water would dissolve right into the water;   35
there would not be any of it to seize, as it were, but [whatever water] one may
take, it is salty indeed—so, verily, this great Being, infinite, limitless, is just a mass
of knowledge.

"Arising out of these elements, into them also one vanishes away. After   36
death there is no consciousness. Thus I say." Thus spoke Yajnavalkya.

Then Maitreyi spoke: "Here, indeed, you have bewildered me, sir—in say-   37
ing: 'After death there is no consciousness.'"

Then Yajnavalkya spoke: "Verily, I speak not bewilderment. Sufficient,   38
verily, is this for understanding. For where there is a duality, as it were, there one
sees another, there one smells another, there one hears another, there one speaks
to another, there one thinks of another, there one understands another. Where,
verily, everything has become just one's own Self, then whereby and whom
would one smell? Then whereby and whom would one see? Then whereby and
whom would one hear? Then whereby and to whom would one speak? Then
whereby and on whom would one think? Then whereby and whom would one

understand? Whereby would one understand him by whom one understands this All? Whereby would one understand the understander?" . . .

Third Adhyaya

Fourth Brahmana Then Ushasta Cakrayana questioned [Yajnavalkya]. 39 "Yajnavalkya," he said, "explain to me him who is the Brahman present and not beyond our ken, him who is the Soul in all things."

"He is your soul, which is in all things." 40

"Which one, O Yajnavalkya, is in all things?" 41

"He who breathes in with your breathing in, is the Soul of yours, which is 42 in all things. He who breathes out with your breathing out, is the Soul of yours, which is in all things. He who breathes about with your breathing about, is the Soul of yours, which is in all things. He who breathes up with your breathing up is the Soul of yours, which is in all things. He is your Soul, which is in all things."

Ushasta Cakrayana said: "This has been explained to me just as one might 43 say, 'This is a cow. This is a horse.' Explain to me him who is just the Brahman present and not beyond our ken, him who is the Soul in all things."

"He is your Soul, which is in all things." 44

"Which one, O Yajnavalkya, is in all things?" 45

"You could not see the seer of seeing. You could not hear the hearer of hear- 46 ing. You could not think the thinker of thinking. You could not understand the understander of understanding. He is your Soul, which is in all things. Anything other than him is wretched."

Thereupon Ushasta Cakrayana held his peace. 47

Fifth Brahmana Now Kahola Kaushitakeya questioned him. "Yajnavalkya," he 48 said, "explain to me him who is just the Brahman present and not beyond our ken, him who is the Soul in all things."

"He is your Soul, which is in all things." 49

"Which one, O Yajnavalkya, is in all things?" 50

"He who passes beyond hunger and thirst, beyond sorrow and delusion, 51 beyond old age and death—Brahmins who know such a Soul overcome desire for sons, desire for wealth, desire for worlds, and live the life of [beggars]. For desire for sons is desire for wealth, and desire for wealth is desire for worlds, for both these are merely desires. Therefore let a Brahmin become disgusted with learning and desire to live as a child. When he has become disgusted both with the state of childhood and with learning, then he becomes an ascetic. When he has become disgusted both with the nonascetic state and with the ascetic state, then he becomes a Brahmin."

"By what means would he become a Brahmin?"   52

"By that means by which he does become such a one. Anything other than   53
this Soul is wretched."

Thereupon Kahola Kaushitakeya held his peace. . . .   54

Seventh Brahmana . . . Then Uddalaka Aruni questioned him. . . . "O   55
Yajnavalkya, declare the Inner Controller."

"He who, dwelling in the earth, yet is other than the earth, whom the earth   56
does not know, whose body the earth is, who controls the earth from within—
He is your Soul, the Inner Controller, the Immortal.

"He who, dwelling in the waters, yet is other than the waters, whom the   57
waters do not know, whose body the waters are, who controls the waters from
within—He is your Soul, the Inner Controller, the Immortal.

"He who, dwelling in the fire, yet is other than the fire, whom the fire does   58
not know, whose body the fire is, who controls the fire from within— He is your
Soul, the Inner Controller, the Immortal.

"He who, dwelling in the atmosphere, yet is other than the atmosphere,   59
whom the atmosphere does not know, whose body the atmosphere is, who controls the atmosphere from within—He is your Soul, the Inner Controller, the
Immortal.

"He who, dwelling in the wind, yet is other than the wind, whom the wind   60
does not know, whose body the wind is, who controls the wind from within—
He is your Soul, the Inner Controller, the Immortal.

"He who, dwelling in the sky, yet is other than the sky, whom the sky does   61
not know, whose body the sky is, who controls the sky from within— He is your
Soul, the Inner Controller, the Immortal.

"He who, dwelling in the sun, yet is other than the sun, whom the sun does   62
not know, whose body the sun is, who controls the sun from within— He is your
Soul, the Inner Controller, the Immortal.

"He who, dwelling in the quarters of heaven, yet is other than the quarters   63
of heaven, whom the quarters of heaven do not know, whose body the quarters
of heaven are, who controls the quarters of heaven from within—He is your
Soul, the Inner Controller, the Immortal.

"He who, dwelling in the eye, yet is other than the eye, whom the eye does 64
not know, whose body the eye is, who controls the eye from within— He is your
Soul, the Inner Controller, the Immortal.

"He who, dwelling in the ear, yet is other than the ear, whom the ear does 65
not know, whose body the ear is, who controls the ear from within— He is your
Soul, the Inner Controller, the Immortal.

"He who, dwelling in the mind, yet is other than the mind, whom the 66
mind does not know, whose body the mind is, who controls the mind from within—He is your Soul, the Inner Controller, the Immortal.

"He who, dwelling in the understanding, yet is other than the understand- 67
ing, whom the understanding does not know, whose body the understanding is,
who controls the understanding from within—He is your Soul, the Inner
Controller, the Immortal.

"He is the unseen Seer, the unheard Hearer, the unthought Thinker, the 68
understood Understander. Other than He there is no seer. Other than He
there is no hearer. Other than He there is no thinker. Other than He there is no
understander. He is your Soul, the Inner Controller, the Immortal."

Thereupon Uddalaka Aruni held his peace. . . . 69

Fourth Adhyaya
Third Brahmana . . . Once when Janaka, King of Videha, and Yajnavalkya were 70
discussing together at an Agnihotra,[6] Yajnavalkya granted the former a boon. He
chose to ask whatever question he wished. Yajnavalkya granted it to him. So the
king asked him:

"Yajnavalkya, what light does a person here have?" 71

"He has the light of the sun, O king," he said. "For with the sun indeed as 72
his light, one sits, moves around, does his work, and returns."

"Quite so, Yajnavalkya. But when the sun has set, Yajnavalkya, what light 73
does a person here have?"

"The moon indeed is his light," he said, "for with the moon indeed as his 74
light one sits, moves around, does his work, and returns."

"Quite so, Yajnavalkya. But when the sun has set and the moon has set, 75
what light does a person here have?"

"Fire indeed is his light," he said, "for with fire indeed as his light, one sits, 76
moves around, does his work, and returns."

"Quite so, Yajnavalkya. But when the sun has set, Yajnavalkya, and the 77
moon has set and the fire has gone out, what light does a person here have?"

"Speech indeed is his light," he said, "for with speech indeed as his light,   78
one sits, moves around, does his work, and returns. Therefore, verily, O king,
where one does not discern even his own hands, when a voice is raised, then one
goes straight towards it."

"Quite so, Yajnavalkya. But when the sun has set, Yajnavalkya, and the   79
moon has set and the fire has gone out and speech is hushed, what light does a
person here have?"

"The soul indeed is his light," he said, "for with the soul indeed as his light,   80
one sits, moves around, does his work, and returns." . . .

Fourth Brahmana [Yajnavalkya said:] "Now the man who does not desire, who   81
is without desire, who is freed from desire, whose desire is satisfied, whose desire
is the Soul—his breaths do not depart. Being verily Brahman, he goes to
Brahman.

"On this point there is this verse: 82

When are liberated all   83
The desires that lodge in one's heart,
Then a mortal becomes immortal!
Therein he reaches Brahman!

"As the slough of a snake lies on an anthill, dead, cast off—even so lies this   84
body. But this incorporeal, immortal Life is Brahman indeed, is light indeed."
"I will give you, noble sir, a thousand [cows]," said Janaka, king of Videha.   85
[Yajnavalkya continued:] "On this point there are these verses: 86

The ancient narrow path that stretches far away   87
Has been touched by me, has been found by me.
By it the wise, the knowers of Brahman, go up
Hence to the heavenly world, released.

On it, they say, is white and blue   88
And yellow and green and red.
That was the path by Brahman found;
By it goes the knower of Brahman, the doer of right and every shining one.

Into blind darkness enter they   89

That worship ignorance;
Into darkness greater than that, as it were, they
That delight in knowledge.

Joyless are those worlds called,   90
Covered with blind darkness.
To them after death go those
People that have not knowledge, that are not awakened.

If a person knew the Soul   91
With the thought "I am he,"
With what desire, for love of what
Would he cling unto the body?

He who has found and has awakened to the Soul   92
That has entered this conglomerate abode—
He is the maker of everything, for he is the creator of all;
The world is his: indeed, he is the world itself.

Verily, while we are here we may know this.   93
If you have known it not, great is the destruction,
Those who know this become immortal,
But others go only to sorrow.
. . . .
They who know the breathing of the breath,   94
The seeing of the eye, the hearing of the ear,
The food of food, the thinking of the mind—
They have recognized the ancient, primeval Brahman.
. . . .
As a unity only is It to be looked upon—   95
This indemonstrable, enduring Being,
Spotless, beyond space,
The unborn Soul, great, enduring.

By knowing Him only, a wise   96
Brahmin should get for himself intelligence;
He should not meditate upon many words,

For that is a weariness of speech.

". . . That Soul is not this, it is not that. It is unseizable, for it cannot be   97
seized. It is indestructible, for it cannot be destroyed. It is unattached, for it does
not attach itself. It is unbound. It does not tremble. It is not injured.

"Therefore, having this knowledge, having become calm, subdued, quiet,   98
patiently enduring, and collected, one sees the Soul just in the soul. One sees
everything as the Soul. Evil does not overcome him; he overcomes all evil. Evil
does not burn him; he burns all evil. Free from evil, free from impurity, free from
doubt, he becomes a Brahmin. . . .

"Verily, that great, unborn Soul, undecaying, undying, immortal, fearless, is   99
Brahman. Verily, Brahman is fearless. He who knows this becomes the fearless
Brahman."

Chandogya Upanishad

Third Prapathaka
Thirteenth Khanda . . . The light which shines higher than this heaven, on the   100
backs of all, on the backs of everything, in the highest worlds, than which there
are no higher—verily, that is the same as this light which is here within a person.

There is this seeing of it—when one perceives by touch this heat here in   101
the body. There is this hearing of it—when one closes his ears and hears as it
were a sound, as it were a noise, as of a fire blazing. One should reverence that
light as something that has been seen and heard. He becomes one beautiful to
see, one heard of in renown, who knows this—yea, who knows this!

Fourteenth Khanda Verily, this whole world is Brahman. Tranquil, let one wor-   102
ship It as that from which he came forth, as that into which he will be dissolved,
as that in which he breathes.

Now, verily, a person consists of purpose. According to the purpose which   103
a person has in this world, thus does he become on departing hence. So let him
form for himself a purpose.

He who consists of mind, whose body is life, whose form is light, whose   104
conception is truth, whose soul is space, containing all works, containing all
desires, containing all odors, containing all tastes, encompassing this whole
world, the unspeaking, the unconcerned—this Soul of mine within the heart is

smaller than a grain of rice, or a barleycorn, or a mustard seed, or a grain of millet, or the kernel of a grain of millet; this Soul of mine within the heart is greater than the earth, greater than the atmosphere, greater than the sky, greater than these worlds.

Containing all works, containing all desires, containing all odors, contain- 105 ing all tastes, encompassing this whole world, the unspeaking, the unconcerned—this is the Soul of mine within the heart, this is Brahman. Into him I shall enter on departing hence. . . .

Sixth Prapathaka

Ninth Khanda [Uddalaka said to his son Svetaketu:] "As the bees, my dear, pre- 106 pare honey by collecting the essences of different trees and reducing the essence to a unity, as they are not able to discriminate 'I am the essence of this tree,' 'I am the essence of that tree'—even so, indeed, my dear, all creatures here, though they reach Being, know not 'We have reached Being.'

"Whatever they are in this world—whether tiger, or lion, or wolf, or boar, 107 or worm, or fly, or gnat, or mosquito—that they become.

"That which is the finest essence—this whole world has that as its soul. 108 That is Reality. That is Soul. That you are, Svetaketu."

"Do you, sir, cause me to understand even more." 109

"So be it, my dear," he said. 110

Tenth Khanda "These rivers, my dear, flow—the eastern toward the east, the 111 western toward the west. They go just from the ocean to the ocean. They become the ocean itself. As there they know not I am this one, I am that one— even so, indeed, my dear, all creatures here, though they have come forth from Being, know not 'We have come forth from Being.' Whatever they are in this world—whether tiger, or lion, or wolf, or boar, or worm, or fly, or gnat, or mosquito—that they become.

"That which is the finest essence—this whole world has that as its soul. 112 That is Reality. That is Soul. That you are, Svetaketu."

"Do you, sir, cause me to understand even more."

"So be it, my dear," he said.

Eleventh Khanda "Of this great tree, my dear, if someone should strike at the 113 root, it would bleed but still live. If someone should strike at its middle, it would bleed but still live. If someone should strike at its top, it would bleed but still live.

Being pervaded by Soul, it continues to stand, eagerly drinking in moisture and rejoicing.

"If the life leaves one branch of it, then [that branch] dries up. It leaves a   114 second, then that dries up. It leaves a third, then that dries up. It leaves the whole, the whole dries up. Even so, indeed, my dear, understand," he said.

"Verily, indeed, when life has left it, this body dies. The life does not die.   115

"That which is the finest essence—this whole world has that as its soul.   116 That is Reality. That is Soul. That you are, Svetaketu."

"Do you, sir, cause me to understand even more."   117

"So be it, my dear," he said.   118

Twelfth Khanda "Bring here a fig from there."   119

"Here it is, sir."   120

"Divide it."   121

"It is divided, sir."   122

"What do you see there?"   123

"These rather fine seeds, sir."   124

"Of these, please divide one."   125

"It is divided, sir."   126

"What do you see there?"   127

"Nothing at all, sir."   128

Then he said to him: "Verily, my dear, that finest essence which you do not   129 perceive—verily, my dear, from that finest essence this great sacred fig tree thus arises. Believe me, my dear, that which is the finest essence— this whole world has that as its soul. That is Reality. That is Soul. That you are, Svetaketu." "

'Do you, sir, cause me to understand even more."   130

"So be it, my dear," he said.   131

Thirteenth Khanda "Place this salt in the water. In the morning come unto   132 me."

Then he did so.   133

Then he said to him: "That salt you placed in the water last evening—   134 please, bring it here."

Then he grasped for it but did not find it, as it was completely dissolved.   135

"Please take a sip of it from this end," he said. "How is it?"   137

"Salt."   138

"Take a sip from the middle," he said. "How is it?"   139

"Salt." 140

"Take a sip from that end," he said. "How is it?" 141

"Salt." 142

"Set it aside. Then come to me." 143

He did so, saying, "It is always the same." 144

Then he said to him: "Verily, my dear, you do not perceive Being here. 145 Verily, it is here. That which is the finest essence—this whole world has that as its soul. That is Reality. That is Soul. That you are, Svetaketu." . . .

Eighth Prapathaka

Seventh Khanda "The Self, which is free from evil, ageless, deathless, sorrowless, 146 hungerless, thirstless, whose desire is the Real, whose conception is the Real— he should be searched out, him one should desire to understand. He obtains all worlds and all desires who has found out and who understands that Self." Thus spoke Prajapati.

Both the gods and the devils heard it. Then they said: "Come, let us search 147 out that Self, the Self by searching out whom one obtains all worlds and all desires!"

Then Indra from among the gods went forth to him, and Virocana from 148 among the devils. Then, without communicating with each other, the two came into the presence of Prajapati, fuel in hand.[7]

Then for thirty-two years the two lived the chaste life of a student of sacred 149 knowledge.

Then Prajapati said to the two: "Desiring what have you been living?" 150

Then the two said: "'The Self, which is free from evil, ageless, deathless, 151 sorrowless, hungerless, thirstless, whose desire is the Real, whose conception is the Real—he should be searched out, him one should desire to understand. He obtains all worlds and all desires who has found out and who understands that Self.' Such do people declare to be your words, sir. We have been living desiring him."

Then Prajapati said to the two: "That Person who is seen in the eye— He 152 is the Self of whom I spoke. That is the immortal, the fearless. That is Brahman."

"But this one, sir, who is observed in water and in a mirror—which one is 153 he?"

"The same one, indeed, is observed in all these," he said. 154

Eighth Khanda "Look at yourself in a pan of water. Anything that you do 155
not understand of the Self, tell me."

Then the two looked in a pan of water.   156

Then Prajapati said to the two: "What do you see?"   157

Then the two said: "We see everything here, sir, a Self corresponding   158
exactly, even to the hair and fingernails."

Then Prajapati said to the two: "Make yourselves well-ornamented, well-   159
dressed, adorned, and look in a pan of water."

Then the two made themselves well-ornamented, well-dressed, adorned,   160
and looked in a pan of water.

Then Prajapati said to the two: "What do you see?"   161

Then the two said: "Just as we ourselves are here, sir, well-ornamented,   162
well-dressed, adorned—so there, sir, well-ornamented, well-dressed, adorned."

"That is the Self," said he. "That is the immortal, the fearless. That is   163
Brahman."

Then with tranquil heart the two went forth.   164

Then Prajapati glanced after them and said: "They go without having com-   165
prehended, without having found the Self. Whoever shall have such a mystic
doctrine, be they gods or be they devils, they shall perish."

Then with tranquil heart Virocana came to the devils. To them he then   166
declared this mystic doctrine: "Oneself is to be made happy here on earth.
Oneself is to be waited upon. He who makes his own self happy here on earth,
who waits upon himself—he obtains both worlds, both this world and the yonder."

Therefore even now here on earth they say of one who is not a giver, who   167
is not a believer, who is not a sacrificer, "Oh, devilish!" For such is the doctrine
of the devils. They adorn the body of one deceased with what they have begged,
with dress—with ornament, as they call it—for they think that thereby they will
win yonder world.

Ninth Khanda But then Indra, even before reaching the gods, saw this danger: 168
"Just as, indeed, that one [the bodily self] is well-ornamented when this body is
well-ornamented, well-dressed when this is well-dressed, adorned when this is
adorned—even so that one is blind when this is blind, lame when this is lame,
maimed when this is maimed. It perishes immediately upon the perishing of this
body. I see nothing enjoyable in this."

Fuel in hand, he came back again. Then Prajapati said to him: "Desiring 169
what, O Maghavan ['Munificent One'], have you come back again, since you
along with Virocana went forth with tranquil heart?"

Then he said: "Just as, indeed, that one [the bodily self] is wellornamented 170
when this body is well-ornamented, well-dressed when this is well-dressed,
adorned when this is adorned—even so it is blind when this is blind, lame when
this is lame, maimed when this is maimed. It perishes immediately upon the perishing of this body. I see nothing enjoyable in this."

"He is even so, O Maghavan," he said. "However, I will explain this further 171
to you. Live with me thirty-two years more."

Then he lived with him thirty-two years more.   172

To him [Indra] Prajapati then said: 173

Tenth Khanda "He who moves about happy in a dream—he is the Self," he said. 174
"That is the immortal, the fearless. That is Brahman."

Then with tranquil heart Indra went forth.   175

Then, even before reaching the gods, he saw this danger: "Now, even if this 176
body is blind, that one [the Self] is not blind. If this is lame, he is not lame.
Indeed, he does not suffer defect through defect of this. He is not slain with one's
murder. He is not lame with one's lameness. Nevertheless, as it were, they kill
him; as it were, they unclothe him; as it were, he comes to experience what is
unpleasant; as it were, he even weeps. I see nothing enjoyable in this."

Fuel in hand, he came back again. Then Prajapati said to him: "Desiring 177
what, O Maghavan, have you come back again, since you went forth with tranquil heart?"

Then Indra said: "Now, sir, even if this body is blind, that one [the Self] is 178
not blind. If this is lame, he is not lame. Indeed, he does not suffer defect through
defect of this. He is not slain with one's murder. He is not lame with one's lameness. Nevertheless, as it were, they kill him; as it were, they unclothe him; as it
were, he comes to experience what is unpleasant; as it were, he even weeps. I see
nothing enjoyable in this."

"He is even so, O Maghavan," he said. "However, I will explain this further 179
to you. Live with me thirty-two years more."

Then he lived with him thirty-two years more.   180

To him [Indra] Prajapati then said: 181

Eleventh Khanda "Now when one is sound asleep, composed, serene, and 182
knows no dream—that is the Self," he said. "That is the immortal, the fearless.
That is Brahman."

Then with tranquil heart he went forth.   183

Then, even before reaching the gods, he saw this danger: "Assuredly, 184
indeed, this [self] does not exactly know himself with the thought 'I am he,' nor
indeed the things here. He becomes one who has gone to destruction. I see nothing enjoyable in this."

Fuel in hand, back again he came. Then Prajapati said to him: "Desiring 185
what, O Maghavan, have you come back again, since you went forth with tranquil heart?"

Then Indra said: "Assuredly, this [self] does not exactly know himself with 186
the thought 'I am he,' nor indeed the things here. He becomes one who has gone
to destruction. I see nothing enjoyable in this."

"He is even so, O Maghavan," he said. "However, I will explain this fur- 187
ther to you, and there is nothing else besides this. Live with me five years more."

Then he lived with him five years more; that makes one hundred and one 188
years. Thus it is that people say, "Verily, for one hundred and one years
Maghavan lived the chaste life of a student of sacred knowledge with Prajapati."

To him [Indra] Prajapati then said: 189

Twelfth Khanda "O Maghavan, verily, this body is mortal. It has been appropri- 190
ated by Death. But it is the standing-ground of that deathless, bodiless Self.
Verily, he who is [embodied] has been appropriated by pleasure and pain. Verily,
there is no freedom from pleasure and pain for one while he is [embodied]. Verily,
while one is bodiless, pleasure and pain do not touch him.

"The wind is bodiless. Clouds, lightning, thunder—these are bodiless. Now 191
as these, when they arise from yonder space and reach the highest light, appear
each with its own form, even so that serene one, when he rises up from this body
and reaches the highest light, appears with his own form. Such a one is the
supreme person. There such a one goes around laughing, sporting, having enjoyment with women or chariots or friends, not remembering the appendage of this
body. As a draft animal is yoked in a wagon, even so this spirit is yoked in this
body.

"Now when the eye is directed thus toward space, that is the seeing Person; 192
the eye is [the instrument] for seeing. Now he who knows 'Let me smell this,'
that is the Self; the nose is [the instrument] for smelling. Now he who knows 'Let

me utter this,' that is the Self; the voice is [the instrument] for utterance. Now, he who knows 'Let me hear this,' that is the Self; the ear is [the instrument] for hearing.

"Now he who knows 'Let me think this,' that is the Self; the mind is his 193 divine eye. He, verily, with that divine eye the mind, sees desires here and experiences enjoyment.

"Verily, those gods who are in the Brahman-world[8] reverence that Self. 194 Therefore all worlds and all desires have been appropriated by them. He obtains all worlds and all desires who has found out and who understands that Self."

Thus spoke Prajapati—yea, thus spoke Prajapati! 195

Kena Upanishad
First Khanda

By whom impelled soars forth the mind projected? 196
By whom enjoined goes forth the earliest breathing?
By whom impelled this speech do people utter?
The eye, the ear—what god, pray, them enjoins?

That which is the hearing of the ear, the thought of the mind, 197
The voice of speech, as also the breathing of the breath,
And the sight of the eye! Past these escaping, the wise,
On departing from this world, become immortal.

There the eye goes not; 198
Speech goes not, nor the mind.
We know not, we understand not
How one would teach It.

Other, indeed, is It than the known, 199
And moreover above the unknown.
Thus have we heard from the ancients
Who to us have explained It.

That which is unexpressed with speech, 200
That with which speech is expressed—
That indeed know as Brahman,
Not this that people worship as this.

That which one thinks not with thought,   201
That with which they say thought is thought—
That indeed know as Brahman,
Not this that people worship as this.

That which one sees not with sight,   202
That with which one sees sights—
That indeed know as Brahman,
Not this that people worship as this.

That which one hears not with hearing,   203
That with which hearing here is heard—
That indeed know as Brahman,
Not this that people worship as this.

That which one breathes not with breathing,   204
That with which breathing is conducted—
That indeed know as Brahman,
Not this that people worship as this.

Second Khanda

If you think "I know well," only very slightly now do you know. . . .   205

It is conceived of by him by whom It is not conceived of.   206
He by whom It is conceived of, knows It not.
It is not understood by those who say they understand It.
It is understood by those who say they understand It not.

When known by an awakening, It is conceived of;   207
Truly it is immortality one finds.
With the Soul one finds power;
With knowledge one finds the immortal.

If one has known It here, then there is truth.   208
If one has known It not here, great is the destruction.
Discerning It in every single being, the wise,
On departing from this world, become immortal.

Third Khanda

Now Brahman won a victory for the gods. Now in the victory of this Brahman 209 the gods were exulting. They thought to themselves: "Ours indeed is this victory! Ours indeed is this greatness!"

Now It understood this about them. It appeared to them. They did not 210 understand It. "What wonderful being is this?" they said.

They said to Agni:[9] "Jatavedas,[10] find out this—what this wonderful being 211 is."

"So be it."   212

He ran unto It.   213

It spoke to him: "Who are you?"   214

"Verily, I am Agni," he said. "Verily, I am Jatavedas."   215

"In such as you what power is there?"   216

"Indeed, I might burn everything here, whatever there is here in the 217 earth!"

It put down a straw before him. "Burn that!" He went forth at it with all 218 speed.

He was not able to burn it.   219

Thereupon indeed he returned [to the gods], saying: "I have not been able 220 to find out this—what this wonderful being is."

Then they said to Vayu:[11] "Vayu, find out this—what this wonderful being 221 is."

"So be it."   222

He ran unto It.   223

It spoke to him: "Who are you?"   224

"Verily, I am Vayu," he said. "Verily, I am Matarisvan."[12]   225

"In such as you what power is there?"   226

"Indeed, I might carry off everything here, whatever there is here in the 227 earth."

It put down a straw before him. "Carry that off!"   228

He went at it with all speed. He was not able to carry it off. Thereupon 229 indeed he returned [to the gods], saying: "I have not been able to find out this— what this wonderful being is."

Then they said to Indra: "Maghavan, find out this—what this wonderful 230 being is."

"So be it."   231

He ran unto It. It disappeared from him.   232

In that very space he came upon a woman exceedingly beautiful—Uma, 233
daughter of the Snowy Mountain.

He said to her: "What is this wonderful being?" 234

Fourth Khanda

"It is Brahman," she said. "In that victory of Brahman, verily, exult." 235

Thereupon indeed he knew it was Brahman. 236

Therefore, verily, these gods—namely Agni, Vayu, and Indra—are above 237
the other gods, as it were. For these touched It nearest, for these and [especially]
Indra, first knew It was Brahman.

Therefore, verily, Indra is above the other gods, as it were. For he touched 238
It nearest, for he first knew It was Brahman.

Isa Upanishad

By the Lord enveloped must this all be— 239
Whatever moving thing there is in the moving world.
With this renounced, you may enjoy.
Covet not the wealth of any one at all.

. . . .

Devilish are those worlds called, 240
With blind darkness covered o'er!
Unto them, on deceasing, go
Whatever folk are slayers of the Self.

Unmoving, the One is swifter than the mind. 241
The sense powers reached not It, speeding on before.
Past others running, This goes standing.
In It Matarisvan places action.

It moves. It moves not. 242
It is far, and It is near.
It is within all this,
And It is outside of all this.

Now, he who on all beings 243
Looks as just in the Self
And on the Self as in all beings—

He does not shrink away from Him.

In whom all beings 244
Have become just the Self of the discerner—
Then what delusion, what sorrow is there,
Of him who perceives the unity!

He has [encircled]—the bright, the bodiless, the scatheless, 245
The sinewless, the pure, unpierced by evil,
Wise, intelligent, encompassing, self-existent,
Appropriately he distributed objects through the eternal years.

Into blind darkness enter they 246
That worship ignorance;
Into darkness greater than that, as it were, they
That delight in knowledge.

Other indeed, they say, than knowledge; 247
Other, they say, than non-knowledge—
Thus we have heard from the wise
Who have explained It to us.

Knowledge and non-knowledge— 248
He who this pair conjointly knows,
With non-knowledge passing over death,
With knowledge wins the immortal.

Into blind darkness enter they 249
Who worship non-becoming;
Into darkness greater than that, as it were, they
Who delight in becoming.

Other indeed, they say, than origin; 250
Other, they say, than non-origin—
Thus have we heard from the wise
Who have explained It to us.

Becoming and destruction—   251
He who this pair conjointly knows,
destruction passing over death,
With becoming wins the immortal.
. . . .

O Agni, by a goodly path to prosperity lead us,   252
You who know all the ways.
Keep far from us crooked-going sin.
Most ample expression of adoration to you would we render.

Mandukya Upanishad

Om. This syllable is this whole world. Its further explanation is: the past, the   253
present, the future—everything is just the word *om*. And whatever else that
transcends threefold time—that, too, is just the word *om*.

For truly, everything here is Brahman; this self is Brahman. This same self   254
has four fourths.

The waking state—outwardly cognitive, having seven limbs, having nine-   255
teen mouths, enjoying the gross, the common-to-all-men—is the first fourth.

The dreaming state—inwardly cognitive, having seven limbs, having   256
nineteen mouths, enjoying the exquisite, the brilliant—is the second fourth.

If one asleep desires no desire whatsoever, sees no dream whatsoever— that   257
is deep sleep.

The deep-sleep state—unified, just a cognition-mass consisting of bliss,   258
enjoying bliss, whose mouth is thought, the cognitional—is the third fourth.

This is the lord of all. This is the all-knowing. This is the inner controller.   259
This is the source of all, for this is the origin and the end of beings.

Not inwardly cognitive, not outwardly cognitive, not both; not a cogni-   260
tion-mass, not cognitive, not non-cognitive; unseen, with which there can be no
dealing, ungraspable, having no distinctive mark, non-thinkable; that cannot be
designated, the essence of the assurance of which is the state of being one with
the Self; the cessation of development, tranquil, benign, without a second—such
they think is the fourth. He is the Self. He should be discerned.

This is the Self with regard to the word *om*, with regard to its elements.   261
The elements are the fourths; the fourths, the elements: the letter *a*, the letter *u*,
the letter *m*.[13]

The waking state, the common-to-all-men, is the letter *a*, the first element, 262
from *apli* ("obtaining") or from *adimatva* ("being first"). He obtains, verily,
indeed, all desires, he becomes first—he who knows this.

The sleeping state, the brilliant, is the letter *u*, the second element, from 263
utkarsa ("exaltation") or from *ubhayatva* ("intermediateness"). He exalts, verily,
indeed, the continuity of knowledge; and he becomes equal—no one ignorant of
Brahman is born in the family of him who knows this.

The deep-sleep state, the cognitional, is the letter *m*, the third element, 264
from *miti* ("erecting") or from *apiti* ("immersing"). He, verily, indeed, erects this
whole world, and he becomes its immersing—he who knows this.

The fourth is without an element, with which there can be no dealing, the 265
cessation of development, benign, without a second. Thus *om* is the Self indeed.
He who knows this, with his self enters the Self—yea, he who knows this!

Notes

1. *Brahmin:* a member of the highest Hindu class, the priests. [D.C.A., ed.]
2. *Kshatriya:* a member of the second highest Hindu class, the warriors. [D.C.A.]
3. *this state:* the state of being a householder. Yajnavalkya is about to go from being a householder to the next state of ideal Hindu life, a hermit living in the forest. [D.C.A., after R.E.H., trans.]
4. *Brahminhood:* the Brahmin class (priests). [D.C.A., after R.E.H.]
5. *Kshatrahood:* the Kshatriya class (warriors). [D.C.A., after R.E.H.]
6. *Agnihotra:* a sacrificial rite. [D.C.A.]
7. Fuel was a traditional gift of a disciple to the teacher. [D.C.A., after R.E.H.]
8. *those gods who are in the Brahman-world:* namely, those gods who were instructed by Prajapati, through Indra. [D.C.A., after R.E.H.]
9. *Agni:* the fire god. [D.C.A.]
10. *Jatavedas:* meaning either "All-Knower" or "All-Possessor." [R.E.H.]
11. *Vayu:* the wind god. [D.C.A.]
12. *Matarisvan:* a name for Vayu. [D.C.A.]
13. *Om* can be considered as having three letters, since the sound *o* is a combination of the sounds *a* and *u*. The letters *a*, *u*, and *m* constitute the first three elements of *om*. The "fourth," with regard to *om*, is not an additional element but the silence that follows the utterance of *om* (*a*, *u*, and *m*). As the final paragraph of the *Mandukya* Upanishad explains, "The fourth is without an element." [D.C.A.]

Does Morality Need Religion?

YES: C. Stephen Layman, from *The Shape of the Good: Christian Reflections on the Foundations of Ethics* (University of Notre Dame Press, 1991)

NO: John Arthur, from "Religion, Morality, and Conscience," in John Arthur, ed., *Morality and Moral Controversies*, 4th ed. (Prentice Hall, 1996)

Issue Summary

YES: Philosopher C. Stephen Layman that morality makes the most sense from a theistic perspective and that a purely secular perspective is insufficient. The secular perspective, Layman asserts, does not adequately deal with secret violations, and it does not allow for the possibility of fulfillment of people's deepest needs in an afterlife.

NO: Philosopher John Arthur counters that morality is logically independent of religion, although there are historical connections. Religion, he believes, is not necessary for moral guidance or moral answers; morality is social.

There is a widespread feeling that morality and religion are connected. One view   1
is that religion provides a ground for morality, so without religion there is no
morality. Thus, a falling away from religion implies a falling away from morality.

Such thoughts have troubled many people. The Russian novelist Dos-   2
toyevsky (1821-1881) wrote, "If there is no God, then everything is permitted."
Many Americans today also believe that religious faith is important. They often
maintain that even if doctrines and dogmas cannot be known for certain, religion nevertheless leads to morality and good behavior. President Dwight D.
Eisenhower is reputed to have said that everyone should have a religious faith
but that it did not matter what that faith was. And many daily newspapers

throughout the country advise their readers to attend the church or synagogue of their choice. Apparently, the main reason why people think it is important to subscribe to a religion is that only in this way will one be able to attain morality. If there is no God, then everything is permitted and there is moral chaos. Moral chaos can be played out in societies and, on a smaller scale, within the minds of individuals. Thus, if you do not believe in God, then you will confront moral chaos; you will be liable to permit (and permit yourself to do) anything, and you will have no moral bearings at all.

Such a view seems to face several problems, however. For example, what   3
are we to say of the morally good atheist or of the morally good but completely nonreligious person? A true follower of the view that morality derives from religion might reply that we are simply begging the question if we believe that such people *could* be morally good. Such people might do things that are morally right and thus might *seem* good, the reply would go, but they would not be acting for the right reason (obedience to God). Such people would not have the same anchor or root for their seemingly moral attitudes that religious persons do.

Another problem for the view that links morality with religion comes from   4
the following considerations: If you hold this view, what do you say of devoutly religious people who belong to religious traditions and who support moralities that are different from your own? If morality is indeed derived from religion, if different people are thus led to follow different moralities, and if the original religions are not themselves subject to judgment, then it is understandable how different people arrive at different moral views. But the views will still be different and perhaps even incompatible. If so, the statement that morality derives from religion must mean that one can derive *a* morality from a religion (and not that one derives morality itself from religion). The problem is that by allowing this variation among religions and moralities back into the picture, we seem to allow moral chaos back in, too.

The view that what God commands is good, what God prohibits is evil,   5
and without divine commands and prohibitions nothing is either good or bad in itself is called the *divine command theory*, or the *divine imperative view*. This view resists the recognition of any source of good or evil that is not tied to criteria or standards of God's own creation. Such a recognition is thought to go against the idea of God's omnipotence. A moral law that applied to God but was not of God's own creation would seem to limit God in a way in which he cannot be limited. But, on the other hand, this line of thought (that no moral law outside of God's own making should apply to him) seems contrary to the orthodox

Christian view that God is good. For if good means something in accordance
with God's will, then when we say that God is good, we are only saying that he
acts in accordance with his own will-and this just does not seem to be enough.

In the following selections, C. Stephen Layman argues that a religious per-   6
spective makes better sense of moral commitment than a secular perspective.
Indeed, in his view, it is not even clear that a secular individual who followed the
dictates of morality would be rational. John Arthur asserts that morality does not
need a religious foundation at all and that morality is social.

YES
Ethics and the Kingdom of God

C. Stephen Layman

Why build a theory of ethics on the assumption that there is a God? Why not   7
simply endorse a view of ethics along... secular lines...? I shall respond to these
questions in [two] stages. First, I contrast the secular and religious perspectives on
morality. Second, I explain why I think the moral life makes more sense from the
point of view of theism [belief in God] than from that of atheism....

As I conceive it, the modern secular perspective on morality involves at   8
least two elements. First, there is no afterlife; each individual human life ends at
death. It follows that the only goods available to an individual are those he or
she can obtain this side of death.[1]

Second, on the secular view, moral value is an emergent phenomenon.   9
That is, moral value is "a feature of certain effects though it is not a feature of
their causes" (as wetness is a feature of H_2O, but not of hydrogen or oxygen).[2]
Thus, the typical contemporary secular view has it that moral value emerges only
with the arrival of very complex nervous systems (viz., human brains), late in the
evolutionary process. There is no Mind "behind the scenes" on the secular view,
no intelligent Creator concerned with the affairs of human existence. As one
advocate of the secular view puts it, "Ethics, though not consciously created
[either by humans or by God], is a product of social life which has the function
of promoting values common to the members of society."[3]

By way of contrast, the religious point of view (in my use of the phrase)   10
includes a belief in God and in life after death. God is defined as an eternal be-

From C. Stephen Layman, *The Shape of the Good: Christian Reflections on the Foundations of Ethics* (University of Notre Dame Press, 1991).
Copyright © 1991 by University of Notre Dame Press. Reprinted by permission

ing who is almighty and perfectly morally good. Thus, from the religious point of view, morality is not an emergent phenomenon, for God's goodness has always been in existence, and is not the product of nonmoral causes. Moreover, from the religious point of view, there are goods available after death. Specifically, there awaits the satisfaction of improved relations with God and with redeemed creatures.

It is important to note that, from the religious perspective, *the existence of* 11 *God and life after death* are not independent hypotheses. If God exists, then at least two lines of reasoning lend support to the idea that death is not final. While I cannot here scrutinize these lines of reasoning, I believe it will be useful to sketch them.[4] (1) It has often been noted that we humans seem unable to find complete fulfillment in the present life. Even those having abundant material possessions and living in the happiest of circumstances find themselves, upon reflection, profoundly unsatisfied.... [I]f this earthly life is the whole story, it appears that our deepest longings will remain unfulfilled. But if God is good, He surely will not leave our deepest longings unfulfilled provided He is able to fulfill them-at least to the extent that we are willing to accept His gracious aid. So, since our innermost yearnings are not satisfied in this life, it is likely that they will be satisfied after death.

(2) Human history has been one long story of injustice, of the oppression 12 of the poor and weak by the rich and powerful. The lives of relatively good people are often miserable, while the wicked prosper. Now, if God exists, He is able to correct such injustices, though He does not correct all of them in the present life, But if God is also good, He will not leave such injustices forever unrectified. It thus appears that He will rectify matters at some point after death. This will involve benefits for some in the afterlife-it may involve penalties for others. (However, the... possibility of post-mortem punishment does not necessarily imply the possibility of hell as *standardly conceived.*)

We might sum up the main difference between the secular and religious 13 views by saying that the only goods available from a secular perspective are *earthly* goods. Earthly goods include such things as physical health, friendship, pleasure, self-esteem, knowledge, enjoyable activities, an adequate standard of living, etc. The religious or theistic perspective recognizes these earthly goods *as good*, but it insists that there are non-earthy or *transcendent* goods. These are goods available only if God exists and there is life after death for humans. Transcendent goods include harmonious relations with God prior to death as well as the joys of the afterlife-right relations with both God and redeemed creatures.

[One secular] defense of the virtues amounts to showing that society can-   14
not function well unless individuals have moral virtue. If we ask, "Why should
we as individuals care about society?", the answer will presumably be along the
following lines: "Individuals cannot flourish apart from a well-functioning society, *so morality pays for the individual.*"

This defense of morality raises two questions we must now consider. First,   15
is it misguided to defend morality by an appeal to self-interest? Many people feel
that morality and self-interest are fundamentally at odds: "If you perform an act
because you see that it is in your interest to do so, then you aren't doing the right
thing *just because it's right.* A successful defense of morality must be a defense of
duty for duty's sake. Thus, the appeal to self-interest is completely misguided."
Second, *does* morality really pay for the individual? More particularly, does
morality always pay in terms of earthly goods? Let us take these questions up in
turn.

(1) Do we desert the moral point of view if we defend morality on the   16
grounds that it pays? Consider an analogy with etiquette. Why should one bother with etiquette? Should one do the well-mannered thing simply for its own
sake? Do we keep our elbows off the table or refrain from belching just because
these things are "proper"?

To answer this question we must distinguish between the *justification of an*   17
institution and the *justification of a particular act within that institution.* (By 'institution' I refer to any system of activities specified by rules.) This distinction can be
illustrated in the case of the game (institution) of baseball. If we ask a player why
he performs a particular act during a game, he will probably give an answer such
as, "To put my opponent out" or "To get a home run." These answers obviously
would not be relevant if the question were, "Why play baseball at all?" Relevant
answers to this second question would name some advantage for the individual
player, e.g., "Baseball is fun" or "It's good exercise." Thus, a justification of the
institution of baseball (e.g., "It's good exercise") is quite different from a justification of a particular act within the institution (e.g., "To get a home run").

Now let's apply this distinction to our question about etiquette. If our ques-   18
tion concerns the justification of a particular act within the institution of etiquette, then the answer may reasonably be, in effect, "This is what's proper. This
is what the rules of etiquette prescribe.". . .

But plainly there are deeper questions we can ask about etiquette. Who   19
hasn't wondered, at times, what the point of the institution of etiquette is? Why
do we have these quirky rules, some of which seem to make little sense? When

these more fundamental questions concerning the entire institution of etiquette are being asked, it makes no serve to urge etiquette for etiquette's sake. What is needed is a description of the human *ends* the institution fulfills ?ends which play a justificatory role similar to fun or good exercise in the case of baseball. And it is not difficult to identify some of these ends. For example, the rules of etiquette seem designed, in part, to facilitate social interaction; things just go more smoothly if there are agreed upon ways of greeting, eating, conversing, etc.

If anyone asks, "Why should I as an individual bother about etiquette?", an initial reply might be: "Because if you frequently violate the rules of etiquette, people will shun you." If anyone wonders why he should care about being shunned, we will presumably reply that good social relations are essential to human flourishing, and hence that a person is jeopardizing his own best interests if he places no value at all on etiquette. Thus, in the end, a defense of the institution of etiquette seems to involve the claim that the institution of etiquette *pays* for those who participate in it it would not be illuminating to answer the question, "Why bother about etiquette?" by saying that etiquette is to be valued for its own sake.

Now, just as we distinguish between justifying the institution of etiquette (or baseball) and justifying a particular act within the institution, so we must distinguish between justifying the institution of morality and justifying a particular act within the institution. When choosing a particular course of action we may simply want to know what's right. But a more ultimate question also cries out for an answer: "What is the point of the institution of morality, anyway? Why should one bother with it?" It is natural to respond by saying that society cannot function well without morality, and individuals cannot flourish apart from a well-functioning society. In short, defending the institution of morality involves claiming that morality pays for the individual in the long run. It seems obscurantist to preach duty for duty's sake, once the more fundamental question about the point of the institution of morality has been raised.

But if morality is defended on the grounds that it pays, doesn't this distort moral motivation? Won't it mean that we no longer do things because they are right, but rather because they are in our self-interest? No. We must bear in mind our distinction between the reasons that justify a particular act within an institution and the reasons that justify the institution itself. A baseball player performs a given act in order to get on base or put an opponent out; he does not calculate whether this particular swing of the bat (or throw of the ball) is fun or good exercise. A well-mannered person is not constantly calculating whether a given act will improve her relations with others, she simply does "the proper thing." Similarly, even if we defend morality on the grounds that it pays, it does not follow that the motive for each moral act becomes, "It will pay" for we are not constantly thinking of the philosophical issues concerning the justification of the entire system of morality; for the most part we simply do things because they are right, honest, fair, loving, etc. Nevertheless, our willingness to plunge wholeheartedly into "the moral game" is apt to be vitiated should it become clear to us that the game does not pay.

At this point it appears that the institution of morality is justified only if it   23
pays for the individuals who participate in it. For if being moral does not pay for individuals, it is difficult to see why they should bother with it. The appeal to duty for duty's sake is irrelevant when we are asking for a justification of the institution of morality itself.

(2) But we must now ask, "Does morality in fact pay?" There are at least   24
four reasons for supposing that morality does not pay from a *secular* perspective. (a) One problem for the secular view arises from the fact that the moral point of view involves a concern for *all* human beings—or at least for all humans affected by one's actions. Thus, within Christian theology, the parable of the good Samaritan is well known for its expansion of the category of "my neighbor." But human societies seem able to get along well without extending full moral concern to all outsiders; this is the essence of tribal morality. Thus, explorers in the 1700s found that the Sioux Indians followed a strict code in dealing with each other, but regarded themselves as free to steal horses from the Crow. Later on, American whites repeatedly broke treaties with the American Indians in a way that would not have been possible had the Indians been regarded as equals. It is no exaggeration to say that throughout much of human history tribal morality has been the morality humans lived by.

And so, while one must agree... that the virtues are necessary for the exis-   25
tence of society, it is not clear that this amounts to anything more than a defense of tribal morality.... From a purely secular point of view, it is unclear why the scope of moral concern must extend beyond one's society—or, more precisely, why one's concern must extend to groups of people outside of one's society *who are powerless and stand in the way of things one's society wants.* Why should the members of a modern industrial state extend full moral consideration to a tiny Amazonian tribe? . . .

(b) A second problem for secular views concerns the possibility of secret   26
violations of moral rules. What becomes of conscientiousness when one can

break the rules in secret, without anyone knowing? After all, if I can break the rules in secret, I will not cause any social disharmony. Of course, there can be no breaking of the rules in secret if there is a God of the Christian type, who knows every human thought as well as every human act. But there are cases in which it is extraordinarily unlikely that any *humans* will discover one's rule breaking. Hence, from a secular perspective, there are cases in which secret violations of morality are possible.

Consider the following case. Suppose A has borrowed some money from B, 27 but A discovers that B has made a mistake in his records. Because of the mistake, B believes that A has already paid the money back. B even goes out of his way to thank A for prompt payment on the loan. Let us further suppose that B is quite wealthy, and hence not in need of the money. Is it in A's interest to pay the money back? Not paying the money back would be morally wrong; but would it be irrational, from a secular point of view? Not necessarily. Granted, it might be irrational in some cases, e.g., if A would have intense guilt feelings should he fail to repay the loan. But suppose A will not feel guilty because he really needs the money (and knows that B does not need it), and because he understands that secret violations belong to a special and rare category of action. Then, from a secular point of view, it is doubtful that paying the loan would be in A's interest.

The point is not that theists never cheat or lie. Unfortunately they do. The 28 point is rather that secret violations of morality arguably pay off from a secular point of view. And so, once again, it seems that there is a "game" that pays off better (in terms of earthly goods) than the relatively idealistic morality endorsed by the great ethicists, viz., one allowing secret "violations."

(c) Even supposing that morality pays for some people, does it pay for *ev-* 29 *eryone* on the secular view? Can't there be well-functioning societies in which some of the members are "moral freeloaders"? In fact, don't all actual societies have members who maintain an appearance of decency, but are in fact highly manipulative of others? How would one show, on secular grounds, that it is in the interest of these persons to be moral? Furthermore, according to psychiatrists, some people are highly amoral, virtually without feelings of guilt or shame. Yet in numerous cases these amoral types appear to be happy. These "successful egoists" are often intelligent, charming, and able to evade legal penalties for their unconventional behavior.[5] How could one show, on secular grounds, that it is in the interests of such successful egoists to be moral? They seem to find their amoral lives amply rewarding.

(d) Another problem from the secular perspective stems from the fact that   30
in some cases morality demands that one risk death. Since death cuts one off
from all earthly goods, what sense does it make to be moral (in a given case) if
the risk of death is high?

This point must be stated with care. In many cases it makes sense, from a   31
secular point of view, to risk one's life. For example, it makes sense if the risk is
small and the earthly good to be gained is great; after all, one risks one's life driving to work. Or again, risking one's life makes sense from a secular point of view
if failing to do so will probably lead to profound and enduring earthly unhappiness. Thus, a woman might take an enormous risk to save her child from an
attacker. She might believe that she would be "unable to live with herself" afterward if she stood by and let the attacker kill or maim her child. Similarly, a man
might be willing to die for his country, because he could not bear the dishonor
resulting from a failure to act courageously.

But failing to risk one's life does not always lead to profound and enduring   32
earthly unhappiness. Many soldiers play it safe in battle when risk taking is essential for victory; they may judge that victory is not worth the personal risks. And
many subjects of ruthless tyrants entirely avoid the risks involved in resistance
and reform. Though it may be unpleasant for such persons to find themselves
regarded as cowards, this unpleasantness does not necessarily lead to profound
and enduring earthly unhappiness. It seems strained to claim that what is commonly regarded as moral courage always pays in terms of earthly goods.

At this point it appears that the institution of morality cannot be justified   33
from a secular point of view. For, as we have seen, the institution of morality is
justified only if it pays (in the long run) for the individuals who participate in it.
But if by "morality" we mean the relatively idealistic code urged on us by the
great moralists, it appears that the institution of morality does not pay, according
to the secular point of view. This is not to say that no moral code could pay off
in terms of earthly goods; a tribal morality of some sort might pay for most people, especially if it were to include conventions which skirt the problems inherent in my "secret violation" and "risk of death" cases. But such a morality would
be a far cry from the morality most of us actually endorse.

Defenders of secular morality may claim that these difficulties evaporate if   34
we look at morality from an evolutionary point of view. The survival of the
species depends on the sacrifice of individuals in some cases, and the end of
morality is the survival of the species. Hence, it is not surprising that being highly moral will not always pay off for individuals.

This answer is confused for two reasons. First, even if morality does have   35
survival value for the species, we have seen that this does not by itself justify the
individual's involvement in the institution of morality. In fact, it does not justify such involvement if what is best for the species is not what is best for the individual member of the species. And I have been arguing that, from a secular point
of view, the interests of the species and the individual diverge.

Second, while evolution might explain why humans *feel* obligated to make   36
sacrifices, it is wholly unable to account for genuine moral obligation. If we did
not feel obligated to make sacrifices for others, it might be that the species would
have died out long ago. So, moral *feelings* may have survival value. However, *feeling obligated* is not the same thing as *being obligated*.... Thus, to show that moral
feelings have survival value is not to show that there are any actual moral obligations at all.... The point is, the evolutionary picture does not require the existence of real obligations; it demands only the existence of moral feelings or
beliefs. Moral feelings or beliefs would motivate action even if there were in actuality no moral obligations. For example, the belief that human life is sacred may
very well have survival value even if human life is not sacred. Moral obligation,
as opposed to moral feeling, is thus an unnecessary postulate from the standpoint
of evolution.

At this point defenders of the secular view typically make one of two   37
moves: (i) They claim that even if morality does not pay, there remain moral
truths which we must live up to; or (ii) they may claim that morality pays in subtle ways which we have so far overlooked. Let us take these claims up in turn.

(i) It may be claimed that moral obligation is just a fact of life, woven into   38
the structure of reality. Morality may not always pay, but certain moral standards
remain true, e.g., "Lying is wrong" or "Human life is sacred." These are not made
true by evolution or God, but are necessary truths, independent of concrete existence, like "1 + 1 = 2" or "There are no triangular circles."

There are at least three difficulties with this suggestion. First, assuming that   39
there are such necessary truths about morality, why should we care about them
or pay them any attention? We may grant that an act is correct from the moral
point of view and yet wonder whether we have good reason to participate in the
institution of morality. So, even if we grant that various statements of the form
"One ought to do X" are necessarily true, this does not show that the institution
of morality pays off. It just says that morality is a "game" whose rules are necessary truths.... To defend the institution of morality simply on the grounds that

certain moral statements are necessarily true is to urge duty for duty's sake. And... this is not an acceptable defense of the institution of morality.

Second, the idea that some moral truths are necessary comports poorly   40 with the usual secular account. As Mavrodes points out, necessary moral truths seem to be what Plato had in mind when he spoke about the Form of the Good. And Plato's view, though not contradicted by modern science, receives no sup- port from it either. Plato's Form of the Good is not an emergent phenomenon, but is rather woven into the very structure of reality, independently of physical processes such as evolution. So, Plato's view is incompatible with the typically modern secular view that moral value is an emergent phenomenon, coming into existence with the arrival of the human nervous system. For this reason, Plato's views have "often been taken to be congenial... to a religious understanding of the world."[6]

Third, it is very doubtful that there are any necessary truths of the form   41 "One ought to do X." We have seen that the institution of morality stands unjus- tified if participation in it does not pay (in the long run) for individuals. And why should we suppose that there are *any* necessary moral truths if the institution of morality is unjustified? . . . [S]tatements of the form "One ought to do X" are not *necessary* truths, though they may be true *if* certain conditions are met.... Hence, if there are any necessary moral truths, they appear to be conditional (if-then) in form: If certain conditions exist, one ought to do X. Among the conditions, as we have seen, is the condition that doing X pays for the individual in the long run. So, it is very doubtful that there are any necessary moral truths of the form "One ought to do X."[7] The upshot is that morality is partly grounded in those features of reality which guarantee that morality pays; and the secular view lacks the metaphysical resources for making such a guarantee....

(ii) But some have claimed that, if we look closely at human psychology,   42 we can see that morality does pay *in terms of earthly goods*. For example, Plato sug- gested that only a highly moral person could have harmony between the various elements of his soul (such as reason and desire). Others have claimed that being highly moral is the only means to inner satisfaction. We humans are just so con- stituted that violations of morality never leave us with a net gain. Sure, we may gain earthly goods of one sort or another by lying, stealing, etc., but these are always outweighed by inner discord or a sense of dissatisfaction with ourselves.

There are several problems with this. First, some may doubt that moral   43 virtue is the best route to inner peace. After all, one may experience profound inner discord when one has done what is right. It can be especially upsetting to stand up for what is right when doing so is unpopular; indeed, many people avoid "making waves" precisely because it upsets their inner peace....

Second, how good is the evidence that inner peace *always* outweighs the 44 benefits achievable through unethical action? Perhaps guilt feelings and inner discord are a reasonable price to pay for certain earthly goods. If a cowardly act enables me to stay alive, or a dishonest act makes me wealthy, I may judge that my gains are worth the accompanying guilt feelings. A quiet conscience is not everything.

Third, if inner discord or a sense of dissatisfaction stems from a feeling of 45 having done wrong, why not reassess my standards? Therapists are familiar with the phenomenon of false guilt. For example, a married woman may feel guilty for having sex with her spouse. The cure will involve enabling the patient to view sex as a legitimate means of expressing affection. The point is that just because I feel a certain type of act is wrong, it does not follow that the only route to inner peace is to avoid the action. I also have the option of revising my standards, which may enable me to pursue self-interested goals in a less inhibited fashion. Why drag along any unnecessary moral baggage? How could it be shown, on secular grounds, that it is in my interest to maintain the more idealistic standards endorsed by the great moralists? Certainly, some people have much less idealistic standards than others, and yet seem no less happy.

By way of contrast with the secular view, it is not difficult to see how moral- 46 ity might pay if there is a God of the Christian type. First, God loves all humans and wants all included in his kingdom. So, a tribal morality would violate his demands, and to violate his demands is to strain one's most important personal relationship. Second, there are no secret violations of morality if God exists. Since God is omniscient, willful wrongdoing of any sort will estrange the wrongdoer from God. Third, while earthly society may be able to function pretty well even though there exists a small number of "moral freeloaders," the freeloaders themselves are certainly not attaining harmonious relations with God. Accordingly, their ultimate fulfillment is in jeopardy. Fourth, death is the end of earthly life, but it is not the end of conscious existence, according to Christianity. Therefore, death does not end one's opportunity for personal fulfillment; indeed, if God is perfectly good and omnipotent, we can only assume that the afterlife will result in the fulfillment of our deepest needs—unless we willfully reject God's efforts to supply those needs.

So, it seems to me that the moral life makes more sense from a theistic per- 47 spective than from a secular perspective. Of course, I do not claim that I have proved the existence of God, and a full discussion of this metaphysical issue would take us too far from matters at hand.[8] But if I have shown that the moral life makes more sense from a theistic perspective than from a secular one, then I have provided an important piece of evidence in favor of the rationality of belief in God. Moreover, I believe that I have turned back one objection to the Christian teleological view, namely, the allegation that theism is unnecessary metaphysical baggage.

Notes

1. It can be argued that, even from a secular perspective, some benefits and harms are available after death. For example, vindicating the reputation of a deceased person may be seen as benefiting that person. See, for example, Thomas Nagel, *Mortal Questions* (London: Cambridge University Press, 1979), pp. 1-10. But even if we grant that these are goods for the deceased, it is obvious that, from the secular point of view, such post-mortem goods cannot be consciously enjoyed by the deceased. They are not available in the sense that he will never take pleasure in them.

2. George Mavrodes, "Religion and the Queerness of Morality," in *Rationality, Religious Belief, and Moral Commitment*, ed. Robert Audi and William J. Wainwright (Ithaca, N.Y.: Cornell University Press, 1986), p. 223.

3. Peter Singer, *Practical Ethics*, (London: Cambridge University Press, 1970), p. 209.

4. For an excellent discussion of arguments for immortality, see William J. Wainwright, *Philosophy of Religion* (Belmont, Calif.: Wadsworth, 1988), pp. 99-111.

5. My source for these claims about "happy psychopaths" is Singer, Practical Ethics, pp. 214-216. Singer in turn is drawing from Hervey Cleckley, *The Mask of Sanity*, (*An Attempt to Clarify Some Issues About the So-Called Psychopathic Personality*), 5th ed. (St. Louis, Mo.: E. S. Cleckley, 1988).

6. Mavrodes, "Religion and the Queerness of Morality," p. 224. I am borrowing from Mavrodes throughout this paragraph.

7. Those acquainted with modal logic may have a question here. By a principle of modal logic, if p is a necessary truth and p necessarily implies q, then q is a necessary truth. So, if it is necessarily true that "certain conditions are met" and necessarily true that "If they are met, one ought to X," then, "One ought to do X" is a necessary truth. But I assume it is not necessarily true that "certain conditions are met." In my judgment it would be most implausible to suppose, e.g., that "Morality pays for humans" is a necessary truth.

8. Two fine discussions of moral arguments for theism are Robert Merrihew Adams, "Moral Arguments for Theistic Belief," in *Rationality and Religious Belief*, ed. C. F. Delaney (Notre Dame, Ind.: University of Notre Dame Press, 1979), pp. 116-140, and J. L. Mackie, *The Miracle of Theism* (Oxford: Oxford University Press, 1982), pp. 102-118.

NO
Religion, Morality, and Conscience

John Arthur

My first and prime concern in this paper is to explore the connections, if any,   48
between morality and religion. I will argue that in fact religion is not necessary for morality. Yet despite the lack of any logical or other necessary connection, I will claim, there remain important respects in which the two are related. In the concluding section I will discuss the notion of moral conscience, and then look briefly at the various respects in which morality is "social" and the implications of that idea for moral education. First, however, I want to say something about the subjects: just what are we referring to when we speak of morality and of religion?

Morality and Religion
A useful way to approach the first question—the nature of morality—is to ask   49
what it would mean for a society to exist without a social moral code. How would such people think and behave? What would that society look like? First, it seems clear that such people would never feel guilt or resentment. For example, the notions that I ought to remember my parent's anniversary, that he has a moral responsibility to help care for his children after the divorce, that she has a right to equal pay for equal work, and that discrimination on the basis of race is unfair would be absent in such a society. Notions of duty, rights, and obligations would not be present, except perhaps in the legal sense; concepts of justice and fairness would also be foreign to these people. In short, people would have no tendency to evaluate or criticize the behavior of others, nor to feel remorse about their own behavior. Children would not be taught to be ashamed when they steal or hurt

From John Arthur, "Religion, Morality, and Conscience," in John Arthur, ed., *Morality and Moral Controversies*, 4th ed. (Prentice Hall, 1996).

others, nor would they be allowed to complain when others treat them badly. (People might, however, feel regret at a decision that didn't turn out as they had hoped; but that would only be because their expectations were frustrated, not because they feel guilty.)

Such a society lacks a moral code. What, then, of religion? Is it possible 50
that a people lacking a morality would nonetheless have religious beliefs? It seems clear that it is possible. Suppose every day these same people file into their place of worship to pay homage to God (they may believe in many gods or in one all-powerful creator of heaven and earth). Often they can be heard praying to God for help in dealing with their problems and thanking Him for their good fortune. Frequently they give sacrifices to God, sometimes in the form of money spent to build beautiful temples and churches, other times by performing actions they believe God would approve such as helping those in need. These practices might also be institutionalized, in the sense that certain people are assigned important leadership roles. Specific texts might also be taken as authoritative, indicating the ways God has acted in history and His role in their lives or the lives of their ancestors.

To have a moral code, then, is to tend to evaluate (perhaps without even 51
expressing it) the behavior of others and to feel guilt at certain actions when we perform them. Religion, on the other hand, involves beliefs in supernatural power(s) that created and perhaps also control nature, the tendency to worship and pray to those supernatural forces or beings, and the presence of organizational structures and authoritative texts. The practices of morality and religion are thus importantly different. One involves our attitudes toward various forms of behavior (lying and killing, for example), typically expressed using the notions of rules, rights, and obligations. The other, religion, typically involves prayer, worship, beliefs about the supernatural, institutional forms and authoritative texts.

We come, then, to the central question: What is the connection, if any, 52
between a society's moral code and its religious practices and beliefs? Many people have felt that morality is in some way dependent on religion or religious truths. But what sort of "dependence" might there be? In what follows I distinguish various ways in which one might claim that religion is necessary for morality, arguing against those who claim morality depends in some way on religion. I will also suggest, however, some other important ways in which the two are related, concluding with a brief discussion of conscience and moral education.

Religious Motivation and Guidance

One possible role that religion might play in morality relates to motives people 53
have. Religion, it is often said, is necessary so that people will DO right.
Typically, the argument begins with the important point that doing what is right
often has costs: refusing to shoplift or cheat can mean people go without some
good or fail a test; returning a billfold means they don't get the contents. Religion
is therefore said to be necessary in that it provides motivation to do the right
thing. God rewards those who follow His commands by providing for them a
place in heaven or by insuring that they prosper and are happy on earth. He also
punishes those who violate the moral law. Others emphasize less self-interested
ways in which religious motives may encourage people to act rightly. Since God
is the creator of the universe and has ordained that His plan should be followed,
they point out, it is important to live one's life in accord with this divinely
ordained plan. Only by living a moral life, it is said, can people live in harmony
with the larger, divinely created order.

The first claim, then, is that religion is necessary to provide moral motiva- 54
tion. The problem with that argument, however, is that religious motives are far
from the only ones people have. For most of us, a decision to do the right thing
(if that is our decision) is made for a variety of reasons: "What if I get caught?
What if somebody sees me what will he or she think? How will I feel afterwards?
Will I regret it?" Or maybe the thought of cheating just doesn't arise. We were
raised to be a decent person, and that's what we are Period. Behaving fairly and
treating others well is more important than whatever we might gain from stealing or cheating, let alone seriously harming another person. So it seems clear that
many motives for doing the right thing have nothing whatsoever to do with religion. Most of us, in fact, do worry about getting caught, being blamed, and being
looked down on by others. We also may do what is right just because it's right, or
because we don't want to hurt others or embarrass family and friends. To say that
we need religion to act morally is mistaken; indeed it seems to me that many of
us, when it really gets down to it, don't give much of a thought to religion when
making moral decisions. All those other reasons are the ones which we tend to
consider, or else we just don't consider cheating and stealing at all. So far, then,
there seems to be no reason to suppose that people can't be moral yet irreligious
at the same time.

A second argument that is available for those who think religion is nec- 55
essary to morality, however, focuses on moral guidance and knowledge rather
than on people's motives. However much people may want to do the right thing,

according to this view, we cannot ever know for certain what is right without the guidance of religious teaching. Human understanding is simply inadequate to this difficult and controversial task; morality involves immensely complex problems, and so we must consult religious revelation for help.

Again, however, this argument fails. First, consider how much we would   56
need to know about religion and revelation in order for religion to provide moral guidance. Besides being sure that there is a God, we'd also have to think about which of the many religions is true. How can anybody be sure his or her religion is the right one? But even if we assume the Judeo-Christian God is the real one, we still need to find out just what it is He wants us to do, which means we must think about revelation.

Revelation comes in at least two forms, and not even all Christians agree   57
on which is the best way to understand revelation. Some hold that revelation occurs when God tells us what he wants by providing us with His words: The Ten Commandments are an example. Many even believe, as evangelist Billy Graham once said, that the entire *Bible* was written by God using 39 secretaries. Others, however, doubt that the "word of God" refers literally to the words God has spoken, but believe instead that the *Bible* is an historical document, written by human beings, of the events or occasions in which God revealed Himself. It is an especially important document, of course, but nothing more than that. So on this second view revelation is not understood as *statements* made by God but rather as His *acts* such as leading His people from Egypt, testing Job, and sending His son as an example of the ideal life. The *Bible* is not itself revelation, it's the historical account of revelatory actions.

If we are to use revelation as a moral guide, then, we must first know what   58
is to count as revelation—words given us by God, historical events, or both? But even supposing that we could somehow answer those questions, the problems of relying on revelation are still not over since we still must interpret that revelation. Some feel, for example, that the *Bible* justifies various forms of killing, including war and capital punishment, on the basis of such statements as "An eye for an eye." Others, emphasizing such sayings as "Judge not lest ye be judged" and "Thou shalt not kill," believe the *Bible* demands absolute pacifism. How are we to know which interpretation is correct? It is likely, of course, that the answer people give to such religious questions will be influenced in part at least by their own moral beliefs: if capital punishment is thought to be unjust, for example, then an interpreter will seek to read the *Bible* in a way that is consistent with that moral truth. That is not, however, a happy conclusion for those wishing to rest

morality on revelation, for it means that their understanding of what God has revealed is itself dependent on their prior moral views. Rather than revelation serving as a guide for morality, morality is serving as a guide for how we interpret revelation.

So my general conclusion is that far from providing a short-cut to moral 59 understanding, looking to revelation for guidance often creates more questions and problems. It seems wiser under the circumstances to address complex moral problems like abortion, capital punishment, and affirmative action directly, considering the pros and cons of each side, rather than to seek answers through the much more controversial and difficult route of revelation.

The Divine Command Theory

It may seem, however, that we have still not really gotten to the heart of the mat- 60 ter. Even if religion is not necessary for moral motivation or guidance, it is often claimed, religion is necessary in another more fundamental sense. According to this view, religion is necessary for morality because without God there could BE no right or wrong. God, in other words, provides the foundation or bedrock on which morality is grounded. This idea was expressed by Bishop R. C. Mortimer:

"God made us and all the world. Because of that He has an absolute claim 61 on our obedience.... From [this] it follows that a thing is not right simply because we think it is. It is right because God commands it."[1]

What Bishop Mortimer has in mind can be seen by comparing moral rules 62 with legal ones. Legal statutes, we know, are created by legislatures; if the state assembly of New York had not passed a law limiting speed people can travel, then there would be no such legal obligation. Without the statutory enactments, such a law simply would not exist. Mortimer's view, the *divine command theory*, would mean that God has the same sort of relation to moral law as legislature has to statutes it enacts: without God's commands there would be no moral rules, just as without a legislature there would be no statutes.

Defenders of the divine command theory often add to this a further claim, 63 that only by assuming God sits at the foundation of morality can we explain the objective difference between right and wrong. This point was forcefully argued by F. C. Copleston in a 1948 British Broadcasting Corporation radio debate with Bertrand Russell.

Copleston: . . . The validity of such an interpretation of man's conduct depends   64
on the recognition of God's existence, obviously.... Lees take a look at the
Commandant of the [Nazi] concentration camp at Belsen. That appears to you
as undesirable and evil and to me too. To Adolf Hitler we suppose it appeared as
something good and desirable. I suppose you'd have to admit that for Hitler it
was good and for you it is evil.

Russell: No, I shouldn't go so far as that. I mean, I think people can make mis-   65
takes in that as they can in other things. If you have jaundice you see things yellow that are not yellow. You're making a mistake.

Copleston: Yes, one can make mistakes, but can you make a mistake if it's simply   66
a question of reference to a feeling or emotion? Surely Hitler would be the only
possible judge of what appealed to his emotions.

Russell: . . . You can say various things about that; among others, that if that sort   67
of thing makes that sort of appeal to Hitler's emotions, then Hitler makes quite
a different appeal to my emotions.

Copleston: Granted. But there's no objective criterion outside feeling then for   68
condemning the conduct of the Commandant of Belsen, in your view.... The
human being's idea of the content of the moral law depends certainly to a large
extent on education and environment, and a man has to use his reason in assessing the validity of the actual moral ideas of his social group. But the possibility of
criticizing the accepted moral code presupposes that there is an objective standard, that there is an ideal moral order, which imposes itself.... It implies the existence of a real foundation of God.[2]

  Against those who, like Bertrand Russell, seek to ground morality in feel-   69
ings and attitudes, Copleston argues that there must be a more solid foundation
if we are to be able to claim truly that the Nazis were evil. God, according to
Copleston, is able to provide the objective basis for the distinction, which we all
know to exist, between right and wrong. Without divine commands at the root
of human obligations, we would have no real reason for condemning the behavior of anybody, even Nazis. Morality, Copleston thinks, would then be nothing
more than an expression of personal feeling.

  To begin assessing the divine command theory, let's first consider this last   70
point. Is it really true that only the commands of God can provide an objective
basis for moral judgments? Certainly many philosophers have felt that morality
rests on its own perfectly sound footing, be it reason, human nature, or natural

sentiments. It seems wrong to conclude, automatically, that morality cannot rest on anything but religion. And it is also possible that morality doesn't have any foundation or basis at all, so that its claims should be ignored in favor of whatever serves our own self-interest.

In addition to these problems with Copleston's argument, the divine com-   71
mand theory faces other problems as well. First, we would need to say much more about the relationship between morality and divine commands. Certainly the expressions "is commanded by God" and "is morally required" do not mean the same thing. People and even whole societies can use moral concepts without understanding them to make any reference to God. And while it is true that God (or any other moral being for that matter) would tend to want others to do the right thing, this hardly shows that being right and being commanded by God are the same thing. Parents want their children to do the right thing, too, but that doesn't mean parents, or anybody else, can make a thing right just by commanding it!

I think that, in fact, theists should reject the divine command theory. One   72
reason is what it implies. Suppose we were to grant (just for the sake of argument) that the divine command theory is correct, so that actions are right just because they are commanded by God. The same, of course, can be said about those deeds that we believe are wrong. If God hadn't commanded us not to do them, they would not be wrong.

But now notice this consequence of the divine command theory. Since   73
God is all-powerful, and since right is determined solely by His commands, is it not possible that He might change the rules and make what we now think of as wrong into right? It would seem that according to the divine command theory the answer is "yes": it is theoretically possible that tomorrow God would decree that virtues such as kindness and courage have become vices while actions that show cruelty and cowardice will henceforth be the right actions. (Recall the analogy with a legislature and the power it has to change law.) So now rather than it being right for people to help each other out and prevent innocent people from suffering unnecessarily, it would be right (God having changed His mind) to create as much pain among innocent children as we possibly can! To adopt the divine command theory therefore commits its advocate to the seemingly absurd position that even the greatest atrocities might be not only acceptable but morally required if God were to command them.

Plato made a similar point in the dialogue *Euthyphro*. Socrates is asking   74
Euthyphro what it is that makes the virtue of holiness a virtue, just as we have

been asking what makes kindness and courage virtues. Euthyphro has suggested that holiness is just whatever all the gods love.

Socrates: Well, then, Euthyphro, what do we say about holiness? Is it not loved   75
by all the gods, according to your definition?

Euthyphro: Yes.   76

Socrates: Because it is holy, or for some other reason?   77

Euthyphro: No, because it is holy.   78

Socrates: Then it is loved by the gods because it is holy: it is not holy because   79
it is loved by them?

Euthyphro: It seems so.   80

Socrates. . . . Then holiness is not what is pleasing to the gods, and what is   81
pleasing to the gods is not holy as you say, Euthyphro. They are different things.

Euthyphro: And why, Socrates?   82

Socrates: Because we are agreed that the gods love holiness because it is holy: 83
and that it is not holy because they love it.[3]

This raises an interesting question: Why, having claimed at first that   84
virtues are merely whit is loved (or commanded) by the gods, would Euthyphro
so quickly contradict this and agree that the gods love holiness because it's holy,
rather than the reverse? One likely possibility is that Euthyphro believes that
whenever the gods love something they do so with good reason, not without justification and arbitrarily. To deny this, and say that it is merely the gods' love that
makes holiness a virtue, would mean that the gods have no basis for their attitudes, that they are arbitrary in what they love. Yet—and this is the crucial
point—it's far from clear that a religious person would want to say that God is
arbitrary in that way. If we say that it is simply God's loving something that
makes it right, then what sense would it make to say God wants us to do right?
All that could mean, it seems, is that God wants us to do what He wants us to
do; He would have no reason for wanting it. Similarly "God is good" would mean
little more than "God does what He pleases." The divine command theory therefore leads us to the results that God is morally arbitrary, and that His wishing us
to do good or even God's being just mean nothing more than that God does
what He does and wants whatever He wants. Religious people who reject that
consequence would also, I am suggesting, have reason to reject the divine com-

mand theory itself, seeking a different understanding of morality.

This now raises another problem, however. If God approves kindness be- 85
cause it is a virtue and hates the Nazis because they were evil, then it seems that
God discovers morality rather than inventing it. So haven't we then identified a
limitation on God's power, since He now, being a good God, must love kindness
and command us not to be cruel? Without the divine command theory, in other
words, what is left of God's omnipotence?

But why, we may ask, is such a limitation on God unacceptable? It is not 86
at all clear that God really can do anything at all. Can God, for example, destroy
Himself? Or make a rock so heavy that He cannot lift it? Or create a universe
which was never created by Him? Many have thought that God cannot do these
things, but also that His inability to do them does not constitute a serious limitation on His power since these are things that cannot be done at all: to do them
would violate the laws of logic. Christianity's most influential theologian,
Thomas Aquinas, wrote in this regard that "whatever implies contradiction does
not come within the scope of divine omnipotence, because it cannot have the
aspect of possibility. Hence it is more appropriate to say that such things cannot
be done than that God cannot do them."[4]

How, then, ought we to understand God's relationship to morality if we 87
reject the divine command theory? Can religious people consistently maintain
their faith in God the Creator and yet deny that what is right is right because He
commands it? I think the answer to this is "yes." Making cruelty good is not like
making a universe that wasn't made, of course. It's a moral limit on God rather
than a logical one. But why suppose that God's limits are only logical?

One final point about this. Even if we agree that God loves justice or kind- 88
ness because of their nature, not arbitrarily, there still remains a sense in which
God could change morality even having rejected the divine command theory.
That's because if we assume, plausibly I think, that morality depends in part on
how we reason, what we desire and need, and the circumstances in which we
find ourselves, then morality will still be under God's control since God could
have constructed us or our environment very differently. Suppose, for instance,
that he created us so that we couldn't be hurt by others or didn't care about freedom. Or perhaps our natural environment were created differently, so that all we
have to do is ask and anything we want is given to us. If God had created either
nature or us that way, then it seems likely our morality might also be different in
important ways from the one we now think correct. In that sense, then, morality depends on God whether or not one supports the divine command theory.

"Morality Is Social"

I have argued here that religion is not necessary in providing moral motivation   89
or guidance, and against the divine command theory's claim that God is necessary for there to be morality at all. In this last section, I want first to look briefly
at how religion and morality sometimes *do* influence each other. Then I will consider the development of moral conscience and the important ways in which
morality might correctly be thought to be "social."

Nothing I have said so far means that morality and religion are indepen-   90
dent of each other. But in what ways are they related, assuming I am correct in
claiming morality does not *depend* on religion? First, of course, we should note
the historical influence religions have had on the development of morality as
well as on politics and law. Many of the important leaders of the abolitionist and
civil rights movements were religious leaders, as are many current members of
the pro-life movement. The relationship is not, however, one sided: morality has
also influenced religion, as the current debate within the Catholic church over
the role of women, abortion, and other social issues shows. In reality, then, it
seems clear that the practices of morality and religion have historically each
exerted an influence on the other.

But just as the two have shaped each other historically, so, too, do they   91
interact at the personal level. I have already suggested how people's understanding of revelation, for instance, is often shaped by morality as they seek the best
interpretations of revealed texts. Whether trying to understand a work of art, a
legal statute, or a religious text, interpreters regularly seek to understand them in
the best light—to make them as good as they can be, which requires that they
bring moral judgment to the task of religious interpretation and understanding.

The relationship can go the other direction as well, however, as people's   92
moral views are shaped by their religious training and beliefs. These relationships
between morality and religion are often complex, hidden even from ourselves,
but it does seem clear that our views on important moral issues, from sexual
morality and war to welfare and capital punishment, are often influenced by our
religious outlook. So not only are religious and moral practices and understandings historically linked, but for many religious people the relationship extends to
the personal level—to their understanding of moral oblogations as well as their
sense of who they are and their vision of who they wish to be.

Morality, then, is influenced by religion (as is religion by morality), but   93
morality's social character extends deeper even than that, I want to argue. First,
of course, we possess a socially acquired language within which we think about

our various choices and the alternatives we ought to follow, including whether a possible course of action is the right thing to do. Second, morality is social in that it governs relationships among people, defining our responsibilities to others and theirs to us. Morality provides the standards we rely on in gauging our interactions with family, lovers, friends, fellow citizens, and even strangers. Third, morality is social in the sense that we are, in fact, subject to criticism by others for our actions. We discuss with others what we should do, and often hear from them concerning whether our decisions were acceptable. Blame and praise are a central feature of morality.

While not disputing any of this, John Dewey has stressed another, less   94
obvious aspect of morality's social character. Consider then the following comments regarding the origins of morality and conscience in an article he titled "Morality Is Social":

In language and imagination we rehearse the responses of others just as we   95
dramatically enact other consequences. We foreknow how others will act, and the foreknowledge is the beginning of judgment passed on action. We know with them; there is conscience. An assembly is formed within our breast which discusses and appraises proposed and performed acts. The community without becomes an forum and tribunal within, a judgment-seat of charges, assessments and exculpations. Our thoughts of our own actions are saturated with the ideas that others entertain about them.... Explicit recognition of this fact is a prerequisite of improvement in moral education.... Reflection is morally indispensable.[5]

To appreciate fully the role of society in shaping morality and influencing   96
people's sense of responsibility, Dewey is arguing, requires appreciating the fact that to think from the moral point of view, as opposed to the selfish one, for instance, means rejecting our private, subjective perspective in favor of the view of others, envisioning how they might respond to various choices we might make. Far from being private and unrelated to others, moral conscience is in that sense "public." To consider a decision from the moral perspective, says Dewey, requires that we envision an "assembly of others" that is "formed within our breast." In that way, our moral conscience cannot be sharply distinguished from our nature as social beings since conscience invariably brings with it, or constitutes, the perspective of the other. "Is this right?" and "What would this look like were I to have to defend it to others?" are not entirely separable questions.[6]

It is important not to confuse Dewey's point here, however. He is not say-   97
ing that what is right is finally to be determined by the reactions of actually existing other people, or even by the reaction of society as a whole. What is right or
fair can never be finally decided by a vote, and might not meet the approval of
any specific others. But what then might Dewey mean in speaking of such an
"assembly of others" as the basis of morality? The answer is that rather than actual people or groups, the assembly Dewey envisions is hypothetical or "ideal." The
"community without" is thus transformed into a "forum and tribunal within, a
judgment seat of charges, assessments and exculpations." So it is through the
powers of our imagination that we can meet our moral responsibilities and exercise moral judgment, using these powers to determine what morality requires by
imagining the reaction of Dewey's "assembly of others."

Morality is therefore *inherently* social, in a variety of ways. It depends on   98
socially learned language, is learned from interactions with others, and governs
our interactions with others in society. But it also demands, as Dewey put it, that
we know "with" others, envisioning for ourselves what their points of view would
require along with our own. Conscience demands we occupy the positions of
others.

Viewed in this light, God would play a role in a religious person's moral   99
reflection and conscience since it is unlikely a religious person would wish to
exclude God from the "forum and tribunal" that constitutes conscience. Rather,
for the religious person conscience would almost certainly include the imagined
reaction [of] God along with the reactions of others who might be affected by the
action. Other people are also important, however, since it is often an open question just what God's reaction would be; revelation's meaning, as I have argued,
is subject to interpretation. So it seems that for a religious person morality and
God's will cannot be separated, though the connection between them is not the
one envisioned by defenders of the divine command theory.

Which leads to my final point, about moral education. If Dewey is correct,   100
then it seems clear there is an important sense in which morality not only can
be taught but must be. Besides early moral training, moral thinking depends on
our ability to imagine others' reactions and to imaginatively put ourselves into
their shoes. "What would somebody (including, perhaps, God) think if this got
out?" expresses more than a concern with being embarrassed or punished; it is

also the voice of conscience and indeed of morality itself. But that would mean, thinking of education, that listening to others, reading about what others think and do, and reflecting within ourselves about our actions and whether we could defend them to others are part of the practice of morality itself. Morality cannot exist without the broader, social perspective introduced by others, and this social nature ties it, in that way, with education and with public discussion, both actual and imagined. "Private" moral reflection taking place independent of the social world would be no moral reflection at all; and moral education is not only possible, but essential.

Notes

1. R. C. Mortimer, *Christian Ethics* (London: Hutchinson's University Library, 1950), pp. 7–8.

2. This debate was broadcast on the "Third Program " of the British Broadcasting Corporation in 1948.

3. Plato, *Euthyphro*, tr. H. N. Fowler (Cambridge MA: Harvard University Press,1947).

4 Thomas Aquinas, *Summa Theologica*, Part I, Q. 25, Art. 3.

5. John Dewey, "Morality Is Social" in The *Moral Writings of John Dewey*, revised edition, ed. James Gouinlock (Amherst, NY: Prometheus Books, 1994), pp. 182–4.

6. Obligations to animals raise an interesting problem for this conception of morality. Is it wrong to torture animals only because other *people* could be expected to disapprove? Or is it that the animal itself would disapprove? Or, perhaps, duties to animals rest on sympathy and compassion while human moral relations are more like Dewey describes, resting on morality's inherently social nature and on the dictates of conscience viewed as an assembly of others?

Postscript
Does Morality Need Religion?

As Arthur notes, some of the earliest—and indeed some of the best—arguments 101 on this issue can be found in Plato's dialogue *Euthyphro*, which was written in the fourth century B.C. His arguments were in terms of Greek religious practices and Greek gods, but we can reformulate the points and elaborate on the arguments in monotheistic terms.

One key dilemma in the original Greek version asks us to consider whether   102
holy things (i) are holy because they please the gods or (ii) please the gods
because they are holy. In monotheistic terms, the dilemma would be whether
holy things (i) are holy because they please God or (ii) please God because they
are holy. The question can then be broadened and the dilemma posed in terms
of good things in general. We then ask whether good things are (i) good because
God wills them or (ii) willed by God because they are good.

Plato believed that the gods love what is holy because it is holy (i.e., he   103
believed the second option above), just as Christians have traditionally believed
that God wills good things because they are good. Traditionally, a contrast is
drawn between God, an infinite and all-good being who always wills the good,
and humans, finite beings who are not all-good and do not always will the good.
We might also consider a parallel dilemma concerning truths. Are things true
because God knows them, or does God know them because they are true? The
traditional view is that God is all-knowing. God knows all truths because they
are truths (and no truths lie outside divine knowledge), whereas people do not
know all truths (and many truths lie outside human knowledge).

Nevertheless, there has also been in Christianity a tradition that the al-   104
mighty power of God is not to be constrained by anything—even if we imagine
that what constrains God are good things. This view holds that God creates not
only good things but the very fact that a good thing (such as honesty) is good
while another thing (such as false witness against your neighbor) is not. Thus, in
this view, God in his power determines what is good and what is bad.

These topics are further discussed in Glenn Tinder, "Can We Be Good   105
Without God? On the Political Meaning of Christianity," *The Atlantic Monthly*
(December 1989); Richard J. Mouw, *The God Who Commands: A Study in Divine
Command Ethics* (University of Notre Dame Press, 1990); E. M. Adams, *Religion
and Cultural Freedom* (Temple University Press, 1993); D. Z. Phillips, ed., *Religion
and Morality* (St. Martin's Press, 1996); and Paul Chamberlain, *Can We Be Good
Without God? A Conversation About Truth, Morality, Culture, and a Few Other
Things That Matter* (InterVarsity Press, 1996).

Walter Wink is Professor of Biblical Interpretation at Auburn Theological Semi-
nary in New York City. He has also taught at Union Theological Seminary and
Hartford Seminary, and has been a visiting professor at Columbia and Drew universities.
In 1989-1990 he was a Peace Fellow at the United States Institute of Peace in Washing-
ton, D.C. His published works include a trilogy on the Powers: *Naming the Powers* (1984),
Unmasking the Powers (1986), and *Engaging the Powers* (1992), all from Forress Press.
Engaging the Powers received three "Religious Book of the year" awards in 1993. Double-
day Books will publish a condensed version of the Powers trilogy in 1998 under the title
The Powers That Be. He is also the author of *The Bible in Human Transformation* (Fortress,
1973), *Transforming Bible Study* (Abingdon, second edition, 1990), and other works,
including over 140 articles. He is a member of the American Academy of Religion, the
Society of Biblical Literature, Studiorum Novi Testamenti Societas, and the Fellowship of
Reconciliation, and has lectured at over seventy universities. He has led workshops on
nonviolence and other themes all over North america, as well as in South Africa, Northern Ireland, East Germany, South Korea, New Zealand, and South and Central America.

He is a United Methodist minister, works for a Presbyterian seminary, and attends
Quaker meeting. For five years he served as pastor of a church in southeast Texas.

Homosexuality and the Bible

Walter Wink

Sexual issues are tearing our churches apart today as never before. The issue of   /
homosexuality threatens to fracture whole denominations, as the issue of slavery
did one hundred and fifty years ago. We naturally turn to the Bible for guidance,
and find ourselves mired in interpretative quicksand. Is the Bible able to speak to
our confusion on this issue?

The debate over homosexuality is a remarkable opportunity, because it rais-   2
es in an especially acute way how we interpret the Bible, not in this case only, but
in numerous others as well. The real issue here, then, is not simply homosexuality, but how Scripture informs our lives today.

Some passages that have been advanced as pertinent to the issue of homo-   3
sexuality are, in fact, irrelevant. One is the attempted gang rape in Sodom (Gen.
19:1-29). That was a case of ostensibly heterosexual males intent on humiliating
strangers by treating them "like women," thus demasculinizing them. (This is also
the case in a similar account in Judges 19-21.) Their brutal behavior has nothing

to do with the problem of whether genuine love expressed between consenting adults of the same sex is legitimate or not. Likewise, Deut. 23:17-18 must be pruned from the list, since it most likely refers to a heterosexual prostitute involved in Canaanite fertility rites that have infiltrated Jewish worship; the King James Version inaccurately labeled him a "sodomite."

Several other texts are ambiguous. It is not clear whether 1 Cor. 6:9 and 1   4
Tim. 1:10 refers to the "passive" and "active partners in homosexual relationships, or to homosexual and heterosexual male prostitutes. In short, it is unclear whether the issue is homosexuality alone, or promiscuity and "sex-for-hire."

Unequivocal Condemnations

Putting these texts to the side, we are left with three references, all of which   5
unequivocally condemn same-sex sexual behavior. Lev. 18:22 states the principle: "You (masculine) shall not lie with a male as with a woman; it is an abomination." The second (Lev. 20:13) add the penalty: "If a man lies with a male as with a woman, both of them have committed an abomination; they shall be put to death; their blood is upon them."

Such an act was regarded as an "abomination" for several reasons. The   6
Hebrew prescientific understanding was that male semen contained the whole of nascent life. With no knowledge of eggs and ovulation, it was assumed that the woman provided only the incubating space. Hence, the spilling of semen for any non-procreative purpose—in coitus interruptus (Gen. 38:1-11), male homosexual acts, or male masturbation—was considered tantamount to abortion or murder. Female homosexual acts were consequently not so seriously regarded, and are not mentioned at all in the Old Testament (but see Rom. 1:26). One can appreciate how a tribe struggling to populate a country in which its people were outnumbered would value procreation highly, but such values are rendered questionable in a world facing uncontrolled overpopulation.

In addition, when a man acted like a woman sexually, male dignity was com-   7
promised. It was a degradation, not only in regard to himself, but for every other male. The patriarchalism of Hebrew culture shows its hand in the very formulation of the commandment, since no similar stricture was formulated to forbid homosexual acts between females. And the repugnance felt toward homosexuality was not just that it was deemed unnatural but also that it was considered unJewish, representing yet one more incursion of pagan civilization into Jewish life. On top of that is the more universal repugnance heterosexuals tend to feel for acts and orientations foreign to them. (Left-handedness has evoked something of the same response in many cultures.)

Whatever the rationale for their formulation, however, the texts leave no   8
room for maneuvering. Persons committing homosexual acts are to be executed.
This is the unambiguous command of the Scripture. The meaning is clear: anyone who wishes to base his or her beliefs on the witness of the Old Testament
must be completely consistent and demand the death penalty for everyone who
performs homosexual acts. (That may seem very extreme, but there actually are
some "Christians" urging this very thing today.) It is unlikely that any American
court will ever again condemn a homosexual to death, even though Scripture
clearly commands it.

Old Testament texts have to be weighed against the New. Consequently,   9
Paul's unambiguous condemnation of homosexual behavior in Rom. 1:26-27
must be the centerpiece of any discussion.

> For this reason God gave them up to degrading passions.   10
> Their women exchanged natural intercourse for unnatural,
> and in the same way also the men, giving up natural inter-
> course with women, were consumed with passion for one
> another. Men committed shameless acts with men and
> received in their own persons the due penalty for their error.

No doubt Paul was unaware of the distinction between sexual orientation,   11
over which one has apparently very little choice, and sexual behavior, over which
one does. He seemed to assume that those whom he condemned were heterosexuals who were acting contrary to nature, "leaving," "giving up," or "exchanging" their regular sexual orientation for that which was foreign to them. Paul
knew nothing of the modern psychosexual understanding of homosexuals as persons whose orientation is fixed early in life, or perhaps even genetically in some
cases. For such persons, having heterosexual relations would be acting contrary
to nature, "leaving," "giving up" or "exchanging" their natural sexual orientation
for one that was unnatural to them.

In other words, Paul really thought that those whose behavior he con-   12
demned were "straight," and that they were behaving in ways that were unnatural to them. Paul believed that everyone was "straight." He had no concept of
homosexual orientation. The idea was not available in his world. There are people that are genuinely homosexual by nature (whether genetically or as a result
of upbringing no one really knows, and it is irrelevant). For such a person it
would be acting contrary to nature to have sexual relations with a person of the
opposite sex.

Likewise, the relationships Paul describes are heavy with lust; they are not   13
relationships between consenting adults who are committed to each other as
faithfully and with as much integrity as any heterosexual couple. That was something Paul simply could not envision. Some people assume today that venereal
disease and AIDS are divine punishment for homosexual behavior; we know it
as a risk involved in promiscuity of every stripe, homosexual and heterosexual. In
fact, the vast majority of people with AIDS the world around are heterosexuals.
We can scarcely label AIDS a divine punishment, since non-promiscuous lesbians are at almost no risk.

And Paul believes that homosexual behavior is contrary to nature, whereas   14
we have learned that it is manifested by a wide variety of species, especially (but
not solely) under the pressure of overpopulation. It would appear then to be a
quite natural mechanism for preserving species. We cannot, of course, decide
human ethical conduct solely on the basis of animal behavior or the human sciences, but Paul here is arguing from nature, as he himself says, and new knowledge of what is "natural" is therefore relevant to the case.

Hebrew Sexual Mores

Nevertheless, the Bible quite clearly takes a negative view of homosexual activ-   15
ity, in those few instances where it is mentioned at all. But this conclusion does
not solve the problem of how we are to interpret Scripture today. For there are
other sexual attitudes, practices and restrictions which are normative in Scripture
but which we no longer accept as normative:

• Old Testament law strictly forbids sexual intercourse during the seven days   16
of the menstrual period (Lev. 18:19; 15:19-24), and anyone in violation was to
be "extirpated," or "cut off from their people" (kareth, Lev. 18:29, a term referring
to execution by stoning, burning, strangling, or to flogging or expulsion; Lev.
15:24 omits this penalty). Today many people on occasion have intercourse during menstruation and think nothing of it. Should they be "extirpated"? The
Bible says they should.

• The punishment for adultery was death by stoning for both the man and   17
the woman (Deut. 22:22), but here adultery is defined by the marital status of the
woman. In the Old Testament, a man could not commit adultery against his own
wife; he could only commit adultery against another man be sexually using the
other's wife. And a bride who is found not to be a virgin is to be stoned to death
(Deut. 22:13-21), but male virginity at marriage is never mentioned. It is one of
the curiosities of the current debate on sexuality that adultery, which creates far

more social havoc, is considered less "sinful" than homosexual activity. Perhaps this is because there are far more adulterers in our churches. Yet no one, to my knowledge, is calling for their stoning, despite the clear command of Scripture. And we ordain adulterers.

• Nudity, the characteristic of paradise, was regarded in Judaism as reprehen- 18 sible (2 Sam. 6:20; 1:4, Isa. 20:2-4; 47:3). When one of Noah's sons beheld his father naked, he was cursed (Gen. 9:20-27). To a great extent this nudity taboo probably even inhibited the sexual intimacy of husbands and wives (this is still true of a surprising number of people reared in the Judeo-Christian tradition). We may not be prepared for nude beaches, but are we prepared to regard nudity in the locker room or at the old swimming hole or in the privacy of one's home as an accursed sin? The Bible does.

• Polygamy (many wives) and concubinage (a woman living with a man to 19 whom she is not married) were regularly practiced in the Old Testament. Nei- ther is ever condemned by the New Testament (with the questionable exceptions of 1 Tim. 3:2, 12 and Titus 1:6). Jesus' teaching about marital union in Mark 10:6-8 is no exception, since he quotes Gen. 2:24 as his authority (the man and the woman will become "one flesh"), and this text was never understood in Israel as excluding polygamy. A man could become "one flesh" with more than one woman, through the act of sexual intercourse. We know from Jewish sources that polygamy continued to be practiced within Judaism for centuries following the New Testament period. So if the Bible allowed polygamy and concubinage, why don't we?

• A form of polygamy was the levirate marriage. When a married man in 20 Israel died childless, his widow was to have intercourse with each of his brothers in turn until she bore him a male heir. Jesus mentions this custom without crit- icism (Mark 12:18-27 par.). I am not aware of any Christians who still obey this unambiguous commandment of Scripture. Why is this law ignored, and the one against homosexual behavior preserved?

• The Old Testament nowhere explicitly prohibits sexual relations between 21 unmarried consenting heterosexual adults, as long as the woman's economic value (bride price) is not compromised, that is to say, as long as she is not a vir- gin. There are poems in the Song of Sons that eulogize a love affair between two unmarried persons, though commentators have often conspired to cover up the fact with heavy layers of allegorical interpretation. In various parts of the Chris- tian world, quite different attitudes have prevailed about sexual intercourse before marriage. In some Christian communities, proof of fertility (that is, pregnancy) was required for marriage. This was especially the case in farming areas where the inability to produce children-workers could mean economic hardship. Today, many single adults, the widowed, and the divorced are reverting to "biblical" practice, while others believe that sexual intercourse belongs only within marriage. Both views are Scriptural. Which is right?

• The Bible virtually lacks terms for the sexual organs, being content with   22
such euphemisms as "foot" or "thigh" for genitals, and using other euphemisms to describe coitus, such as "he knew her." Today most of us regard such language as "puritanical" and contrary to a proper regard for the goodness of creation. In short, we don't follow Biblical practice.

• Semen and menstrual blood rendered all who touched them unclean (Lev.   23
15:16). Intercourse rendered one unclean until sundown; menstruation rendered the woman unclean for seven days. Today most people would regard semen and menstrual fluid as completely natural and only at times "messy," not "unclean."

• Social regulations regarding adultery, incest, rape and prostitution are, in   24
the Old Testament, determined largely by considerations of the males' property rights over semen. Prostitution was considered quite natural and necessary as a safeguard of the virginity of the unmarried and the property rights of husbands (Gen. 38:12-19; Josh. 2:1-7). A man was not guilty of sin for visiting a prostitute, though the prostitute herself was regarded as a sinner. Paul must appeal to reason in attacking prostitution (1 Cor. 6:12-20); he cannot lump it in the category of adultery (vs. 9). Today we are moving with great social turbulence and at a high but necessary cost, toward a more equitable, non-patriarchal set of social arrangements in which women are no longer regarded as the chattel of men. We are also trying to move beyond the double standard. Love, fidelity and mutual respect replace property rights. We have, as yet, made very little progress in changing the double standard in regard to prostitution. As we leave behind patriarchal gender relations, what will we do with the patriarchalism in the Bible?

• Jews were supposed to practice endogamy—that is, marriage within the   25
twelve tribes of Israel. Until recently a similar rule prevailed in the American south, in laws against interracial marriage (miscegenation). We have witnessed, within the lifetime of many of us, the nonviolent struggle to nullify state laws against intermarriage and the gradual change in social attitudes toward interracial relationships. Sexual mores can alter quite radically even in a single lifetime.

• The law of Moses allowed for divorce (Deut. 24:1-4); Jesus categorically   26
forbids it (Mark 10:1-12; Matt. 19:9 softens his severity). Yet many Christians, in clear violation of a command of Jesus, have been divorced. Why, then, do some

of these very people consider themselves eligible for baptism, church membership, communion, and ordination, but not homosexuals? What makes the one so
much greater a sin that the other, especially considering the fact that Jesus never
even mentioned homosexuality but explicitly condemned divorce? Yet we ordain
divorcees. Why not homosexuals?

• The Old Testament regarded celibacy as abnormal, and 1 Tim. 4:1-3 calls   27
compulsory celibacy a heresy. Yet the Catholic Church has made it mandatory for
priests and nuns. Some Christian ethicists demand celibacy of homosexuals,
whether they have a vocation for celibacy or not. But this legislates celibacy by
category, not by divine calling. Others argue that since God made men and
women for each other in order to be fruitful and multiply, homosexuals reject
God's intent in creation. But this would mean that childless couples, single persons, priests and nuns would be in violation of God's intention in their creation.
Those who argue thus must explain why the apostle Paul never married. And are
they prepared to charge Jesus with violating the will of God by remaining single?
Certainly heterosexual marriage is normal, else the race would die out. But it is
not normative. God can bless the world through people who are married and
through people who are single, and it is false to generalize from the marriage of
most people to the marriage of everyone. In 1 Cor. 7:7, Paul goes so far as to call
marriage a "charisma," or divine gift, to which not everyone is called. He preferred that people remain as he was—unmarried. In an age of overpopulation,
perhaps a gay orientation is especially sound ecologically!

• In many other ways we have developed different norms from those explic-   28
itly laid down by the Bible. For example, "If men get into a fight with one another, and the wife of one intervenes to rescue her husband from the grip of his opponent by reaching out and seizing his genitals, you shall cut off her hand: show no
pity" (Deut. 25:11f.). We, on the contrary, might very well applaud her for trying
to save her husband's life!

• The Old and New Testaments both regarded slavery as normal and   29
nowhere categorically condemned it. Part of that heritage was the use of female
slaves, concubines and captives as sexual toys, breeding machines, or involuntary
wives by their male owners, which 2 Sam. 5:13, Judges 19-21, and Num. 31:18
permitted—and as many American slave owners did some 150 years ago, citing
these and numerous other Scripture passages as their justification.

The Problem of Authority

These cases are relevant to our attitude toward the authority of Scripture. They   30
are not cultic prohibitions from the Holiness Code that are clearly superseded in
Christianity, such as rules about eating shellfish or wearing clothes made of two
different materials. They are rules concerning sexual behavior, and they fall
among the moral commandments of Scripture. Clearly, we regard certain rules,
especially in the Old Testament, as no longer binding. Other things we regard as
binding, including legislation in the Old Testament that is not mentioned at all
in the New. What is our principle of selection here?

For example, virtually all modern readers would agree with the Bible in rejecting: 31

incest

rape

adultery

intercourse with animals.

But we disagree with the Bible on most other sexual mores. The Bible con-   32
demned the following behaviors which we generally allow:

intercourse during menstruation

celibacy

exogamy (marriage with non-Jews)

naming sexual organs

nudity (under certain conditions)

masturbation (some Christians still condemn this)

birth control (some Christians still forbid this).

And the Bible regarded semen and menstrual blood as unclean, which most of us   33
do not.

Likewise, the Bible permitted behaviors that we today condemn: 34

prostitution

polygamy

levirate marriage

sex with slaves

concubinage

treatment of women as property

very early marriage (for the girl, age 11-13).

And while the Old Testament accepted divorce, Jesus forbade it. In short, of the   35
sexual mores mentioned here, we only agree with the Bible on four of them and
disagree with it on sixteen!

Surely no one today would recommend reviving the levirate marriage. So   36
why do we appeal to proof texts in Scripture in the case of homosexuality alone,
when we feel perfectly free to disagree with Scripture regarding most other sexual practices? Obviously, many of our choices in these matters are arbitrary. Mormon polygamy was outlawed in this country, despite the constitutional protection
of freedom of religion, because it violated the sensibilities of the dominant Christian culture. Yet no explicit biblical prohibition against polygamy exists.

If we insist on placing ourselves under the old law, as Paul reminds us, we are   37
obligated to keep every commandment of the law (Gal. :3). But if Christ is the
end of the law (Rom. 10:4), if we have been discharged from the law to serve, not
under the old written code but in the new life of the Spirit (Rom. 7:6), then all
of these biblical sexual mores come under the authority of the Spirit. We cannot
then take even what Paul himself says as a new Law. Christians reserve the right
to pick and choose which sexual mores they will observe, though they seldom
admit to doing just that. And this is as true of evangelicals and fundamentalists
as it is of liberals and mainliners.

Judge for Yourselves

The crux of the matter, it seems to me, is simply that the Bible has no sexual   38
ethic. There is no Biblical sex ethic. Instead, it exhibits a variety of sexual mores,
some of which changed over the thousand-year span of biblical history. Mores
are unreflective customs accepted by a given community. Many of the practices
that the Bible prohibits, we allow, and many that it allows, we prohibit. The
Bible knows only a love ethic, which is constantly being brought to bear on whatever sexual mores are dominant in any given country, or culture, or period.

The very notion of a "sex ethic" reflects the materialism and splitness of   39
modern life, in which we increasingly define our identity sexually. Sexuality cannot be separated off from the rest of life. No sex act is "ethical" in and of itself,
without reference to the rest of a person's life, the patterns of the culture, the special circumstances faced, and the will of God. What we have are simply sexual
mores, which change, sometimes with startling rapidity, creating bewildering
dilemmas. Just within one lifetime we have witnessed the shift from the ideal of
preserving one's virginity until marriage, to couples living together for several
years before getting married. The response of many Christians is merely to long
for the hypocrisies of an earlier era.

I agree that rules and norms are necessary; that is what sexual mores are. But   40
rules and norms also tend to be impressed into the service of the Domination System, and to serve as a form of crowd control rather than to enhance the fullness
of human potential. So we must critique the sexual mores of any given time and
clime by the love ethic exemplified by Jesus. Such a love ethic is non-exploita-
tive (hence, no sexual exploitation of children, no using of another to their loss),
it does not dominate (hence, no patriarchal treatment of women as chattel), it is
responsible, mutual, caring, and loving. Augustine already dealt with this in his
inspired phrase, "Love God, and do as you please."

Our moral task, then, is to apply Jesus' love ethic to whatever sexual mores   41
are prevalent in a given culture. This doesn't mean everything goes. It means
that everything is to be critiqued by Jesus' love commandment. We might
address younger teens, not with laws and commandments whose violation is a sin,
but rather with the sad experiences of so many of our own children who find too
much early sexual intimacy overwhelming, and who react by voluntary celibacy
and even the refusal to date. We can offer reasons, not empty and unenforceable
orders. We can challenge both gays and straights to question their behaviors in
the light of love and the requirements of fidelity, honesty, responsibility, and genuine concern for the best interests of the other and of society as a whole.

Christian morality, after all, is not an iron chastity belt for repressing urges,   42
but a way of expressing the integrity of our relationship with God. It is the
attempt to discover a manner of living that is consistent with who God created
us to be. For those of same-sex orientation, as for heterosexuals, being moral
means rejecting sexual mores that violate their own integrity and the of others,
and attempting to discover what it would mean to live by the love ethic of Jesus.
Morton Kelsey goes so far as to argue that homosexual orientation has nothing
to do with morality, any more than left-handedness does. It is simply the way
some people's sexuality is configured. Morality enters the picture when that pre-
disposition is enacted. If we saw it as a God-given gift to those for whom it is normal, we could get beyond the acrimony and brutality that have so often characterized the unchristian behavior of Christians toward gays.

Approached from the point of view of love rather than that of law, the issue   43
is at once transformed. Now the question is not "What is permitted?", but, rather,
"What does it mean to love my homosexual neighbor?" Approached from the
point of view of faith rather than works, the question ceases to be "What constitutes a breach of divine law in the sexual realm?", and becomes, instead "What
constitutes integrity before the God revealed in the cosmic lover, Jesus Christ?"

Approached from the point of view of the Spirit rather than the letter, the question ceased to be "What does Scripture command?", and becomes "What is the Word that the Spirit speaks to the churches now, in the light of Scripture, tradition, theology, and, yes, psychology, genetics, anthropology, and biology? We can't continue to build ethics on the basis of bad science.

In a little-remembered statement, Jesus said, "Why do you not judge for 44 yourselves what is right?" (Luke 12:57). Such sovereign freedom strikes terror in the hearts of many Christians; they would rather be under law and be told what is right. Yet Paul himself echoes Jesus' sentiment when he says, "Do you not know that we are to judge angels? How much more, matters pertaining to this life!" (1 Cor. 6:3 RSV. The last thing Paul would want is for people to respond to his ethical advice as a new law engraved on tablets of stone. He is himself trying to "judge for himself what is right." If now new evidence is in on the phenomenon of homosexuality, are we not obligated—no, free—to reevaluate the whole issue in the light of all the available data and decide what is right, under God, for ourselves? Is this not the radical freedom for obedience in which the gospel establishes us?

Where the Bible mentions homosexual behavior at all, it clearly condemns 45 it. I freely grant that. The issue is precisely whether that Biblical judgment is correct. The Bible sanctioned slavery as well, and nowhere attacked it as unjust. Are we prepared to argue today that slavery is biblically justified? One hundred and fifty years ago, when the debate over slavery was raging, the Bible seemed to be clearly on the slaveholders' side. Abolitionists were hard pressed to justify their opposition to slavery on biblical grounds. Yet today, if you were to ask Christians in the South whether the Bible sanctions slavery, virtually everyone would agree that it does not. How do we account for such a monumental shift?

What happened is that the churches were finally driven to penetrate beyond 46 the legal tenor of Scripture to an even deeper tenor, articulated by Israel out of the experience of the Exodus and the prophets and brought to sublime embodiment in Jesus' identification with harlots, tax collectors, the diseased and maimed and outcast and poor. It is that God suffers with the suffering and groans toward the reconciliation of all things. Therefore, Jesus went out of his way to declare forgiven, and to reintegrate into society in all details, those who were identified as "sinners" by virtue of the accidents of birth, or biology, or economic desperation. In the light of that supernal compassion, whatever our position on gays, the gospel's imperative to love, care for, and be identified with their sufferings is unmistakably clear.

In the same way, women are pressing us to acknowledge the sexism and patri-   47
archalism that pervades Scripture and has alienated so many women from the
church. The way out, however, is not to deny the sexism in Scripture, but to
develop an interpretive theory that judges even Scripture in the light of the revelation in Jesus. What Jesus gives us is a critique of domination in all its forms, a
critique that can be turned on the Bible itself. The Bible thus contains the principles of its own correction. We are freed from bibliolatry, the worship of the
Bible. It is restored to its proper place as witness to the Word of God. And that
word is a Person, not a book.

With the interpretive grid provided by a critique of domination, we are able   48
to filter out the sexism, patriarchalism, violence, and homophobia that are very
much a part of the Bible, thus liberating it to reveal to us in fresh ways the in
breaking, in our time, of God's domination-free order.

An Appeal for Tolerance

What most saddens me in this whole raucous debate in the churches is how sub-   49
Christian most of it has been. It is characteristic of our time the the issues most
difficult to assess, and issues on which the Bible can be interpreted as supporting
either side. I am referring to abortion and homosexuality.

We need to take a few steps back and be honest with ourselves. I am deeply   50
convinced of the rightness of what I have said in this essay. But I must acknowledge that it is not an airtight case. You can find weaknesses in it, just as I can in
others'. The truth is, we are not given unequivocal guidance in either area, abortion or homosexuality. Rather than tearing at each others' throats, therefore, we
should humbly admit our limitations. How do I know I am correctly interpreting
God's word for us today? How do you? Wouldn't it be wiser for Christians to lower
the decibels by 95 percent and quietly present our beliefs, knowing full well that
we might be wrong?

I know a couple, both well known Christian authors in their own right, who   51
have both spoken out on the issue of homosexuality. She supports gays, passionately; he opposes their behavior, strenuously. So far as I can tell, this couple still
enjoy each other's company, eat at the same table, and, for all I know, sleep in the
same bed.

We in the church need to get our priorities straight. We have not reached a   52
consensus about who is right on the issue of homosexuality. But what is clear,

utterly clear, is that we are commanded to love one another. Love not just our gay sisters and brothers, who are often sitting beside us, unacknowledged, in church, but all of us who are involved in this debate. These are issues about which we should amiably agree to disagree. We don't have to tear whole denominations to shreds in order to air our differences on this point. If that couple I mentioned can continue to embrace across this divide, surely we can do so as well.

Symbols of Faith

Paul Tillich

I. The Meaning of Symbol

Man's ultimate concern must be expressed symbolically, because symbolic language   1
alone is able to express the ultimate. This statement demands explanation in several respects. In spite of the manifold research about the meaning and function of symbols which is going on in contemporary philosophy, every writer who uses the term "symbol" must explain his understanding of it.

Symbols have one characteristic in common with signs; they point beyond   2
themselves to something else. The red sign at the street corner points to the order to stop the movements of cars at certain intervals. A red light and the stopping of cars have essentially no relation to each other, but conventionally they are united as long as the convention lasts. The same is true of letters and numbers and partly even words. They point beyond themselves to sounds and meanings. They are given this special function by convention within a nation or by international conventions, as the mathematical signs. Sometimes such signs are called symbols; but this is unfortunate because it makes the distinction between signs and symbols more difficult. Decisive is the fact that signs do not participate in the reality of that to which they point, while symbols do. Therefore, signs can be replaced for reasons of expediency or convention, while symbols cannot.

This leads to the second characteristic of the symbol: It participates in that to   3
which it points: the flag participates in the power and dignity of the nation for which it stands. Therefore, it cannot be replaced except after an historic catastrophe that changes the reality of the nation which it symbolizes. An attack on the flag is felt as an attack on the majesty of the group in which it is acknowledged. Such an attack is considered blasphemy.

The third characteristic of a symbol is that it opens up levels of reality which   4
otherwise are closed for us. All arts create symbols for a level of reality which cannot be reached in any other way. A picture and a poem reveal elements of reality which cannot be approached scientifically. In the creative work of art we encounter reality in a dimension which is closed for us without such works. The symbol's fourth char-

acteristic not only opens up dimensions and elements of reality which otherwise would remain unapproachable but also unlocks dimensions and elements of our soul which correspond to the dimensions and elements of reality. A great play gives us not only a new vision of the human scene, but it opens up hidden depths of our own being. Thus we are able to receive what the play reveals to us in reality. There are within us dimensions of which we cannot become aware except through symbols, as melodies and rhythms in music.

Symbols cannot be produced intentionally—this is the fifth characteristic. 5 They grow out of the individual or collective unconscious and cannot function without being accepted by the unconscious dimension of our being. Symbols which have an especially social function, as political and religious symbols, are created or at least accepted by the collective unconscious of the group in which they appear.

The sixth and last characteristic of the symbol is a consequence of the fact that 6 symbols cannot be invented. Like living beings, they grow and they die. They grow when the situation is ripe for them, and they die when the situation changes. The symbol of the "king" grew in a special period of history, and it died in most parts of the world in our period. Symbols do not grow because people are longing for them, and they do not die because of scientific or practical criticism. They die because they can no longer produce response in the group where they originally found expression.

These are the main characteristics of every symbol. Genuine symbols are cre- 7 ated in several spheres of man's cultural creativity. We have mentioned already the political and the artistic realm. We could add history and, above all, religion, whose symbols will be our particular concern.

2. Religious Symbols

We have discussed the meaning of symbols generally because, as we said, man's ulti- 8 mate concern must be expressed symbolically! One may ask: Why can it not be expressed directly and properly? If money, success or the nation is someone's ultimate concern, can this not be said in a direct way without symbolic language? Is it not only in those cases in which the content of the ultimate concern is called "God" that we are in the realm of symbols? The answer is that everything which is a matter of unconditional concern is made into a god. If the nation is someone's ultimate concern, the name of the nation becomes a sacred name and the nation receives divine qualities which far surpass the reality of the being and functioning of the nation. The nation then stands for and symbolizes the true ultimate, but in an idolatrous way. Success as ultimate concern is not the natural desire of actualizing potentialities, but is a readiness to sacrifice all other values of life for the sake of a position of power and social predominance. The anxiety about not being a success is an idolatrous form of the anxiety about divine condemnation. Success is grace; lack of success, ultimate judgment. In this way concepts designating ordinary realities become idolatrous symbols of ultimate concern.

The reason for this transformation of concepts into symbols is the character of   9
ultimacy and the nature of faith. That which is the true ultimate transcends the realm of finite reality infinitely. Therefore, no finite reality can express it directly and properly. Religiously speaking, God transcends his own name. This is why the use of his name easily becomes an abuse or a blasphemy. Whatever we say about that which concerns us ultimately, whether or not we call it God, has a symbolic meaning. It points beyond itself while participating in that to which it points. In no other way can faith express itself adequately. The language of faith is the language of symbols. If faith were what we have shown that it is not, such an assertion could not be made. But faith, understood as the state of being ultimately concerned, has no language other than symbols. When saying this I always expect the question: Only a symbol? He who asks this question shows that he has not understood the difference between signs and symbols nor the power of symbolic language, which surpasses in quality and strength the power of any nonsymbolic language. One should never say "only a symbol," but one should say "not less than a symbol." With this in mind we can now describe the different kinds of symbols of faith.

The fundamental symbol of our ultimate concern is God. It is always present   10
in any act of faith, even if the act of faith includes the denial of God. Where there is ultimate concern, God can be denied only in the name of God. One God can deny the other one. Ultimate concern cannot deny its own character as ultimate. Therefore, it affirms what is meant by the word "God." Atheism, consequently, can only mean the attempt to remove any ultimate concern—to remain unconcerned about the meaning of one's existence. Indifference toward the ultimate question is the only imaginable form of atheism. Whether it is possible is a problem which must remain unsolved at this point. In any case, he who denies God as a matter of ultimate concern affirms God, because he affirms ultimacy in his concern. God is the fundamental symbol for what concerns us ultimately. Again it would be completely wrong to ask: So God is nothing but a symbol? Because the next question has to be: A symbol for what? And then the answer would be: For God! God is symbol for God. This means that in the notion of God we must distinguish two elements: the element of ultimacy, which is a matter of immediate experience and not symbolic in itself, and the element of concreteness, which is taken from our ordinary experience and symbolically applied to God. The man whose ultimate concern is a sacred tree

has both the ultimacy of concern and the concreteness of the tree which symbolizes his relation to the ultimate. The man who adores Apollo is ultimately concerned, but not in an abstract way. His ultimate concern is symbolized in the divine figure of Apollo. The man who glorifies Jahweh, the God of the Old Testament, has both an ultimate concern and a concrete image of what concerns him ultimately. This is the meaning of the seemingly cryptic statement that God is the symbol of God. In this qualified sense God is the fundamental and universal content of faith.

It is obvious that such an understanding of the meaning of God makes the dis- 11 cussions about the existence or nonexistence of God meaningless. It is meaningless to question the ultimacy of an ultimate concern. This element in the idea of God is in itself certain. The symbolic expression of this element varies endlessly through the whole history of mankind. Here again it would be meaningless to ask whether one or another of the figures in which an ultimate concern is symbolized does "exist." If "existence" refers to something which can be found within the whole of reality, no divine being exists. The question is not this, but: which of the innumerable symbols of faith is most adequate to the meaning of faith? In other words, which symbol of ultimacy expresses the ultimate without idolatrous elements? This is the problem, and not the so-called "existence of God"—which is in itself an impossible combination of words. God as the ultimate in man's ultimate concern is more certain that any other certainty, even that of oneself. God as symbolized in a divine figure is a matter of daring faith, of courage and risk.

God is the basic symbol of faith, but not the only one. All the qualities we 12 attribute to him, power, love, justice, are taken from finite experiences and applied symbolically to that which is beyond finitude and infinity. If faith calls God "almighty," it uses the human experience of power in order to symbolize the content of its infinite concern, but it does not describe a highest being who can do as he pleases. So it is with all the other qualities and with all the actions, past, present and future, which men attribute to God. They are symbols taken from our daily experience, and not information about what god did once upon a time or will do sometime in the future. Faith is not the belief in such stories, but it is the acceptance of symbols that express our ultimate concern in terms of divine actions.

Another group of symbols of faith are manifestations of the divine in things 13 and events, in persons and communities, in words and documents. This whole realm of sacred objects is a treasure of symbols. Holy things are not holy in themselves, but they point beyond themselves to the source of all holiness, that which is of ultimate concern.

3. Symbols and Myths

The symbols of faith do not appear in isolation. They are united in "stories of the   14
gods," which is the meaning of the Greek word "mythos"—myth. The gods are individualized figures, analogous to human personalities, sexually differentiated, descending from each other, related to each other in love and struggle, producing world and
man, acting in time and spaced. They participate in human greatness and misery, in
creative and destructive works. They give to man cultural and religious traditions,
and defend these sacred rites. They help and threaten the human race, especially
some families, tribes or nations. They appear in epiphanies and incarnations, establish sacred places, rites and persons, and thus create a cult. But they themselves are
under the command and threat of a fate which is beyond everything that is. This is
mythology as developed most impressively in ancient Greece. But many of these
characteristics can be found in every mythology. Usually the mythological gods are
not equals. There is a hierarchy, at the top of which is a ruling god, as in Greece; or
a trinity of them, as in India; or a duality of them, as in Persia. There are savior-gods
who mediate between the highest gods and man, sometimes sharing the suffering and
death of man in spite of their essential immortality. This is the world of the myth,
great and strange, always changing but fundamentally the same: man's ultimate concern symbolized in divine figures and actions. Myths are symbols of faith combined
in stories about divine-human encounters.

Myths are always resent in every act of faith, because the language of faith is   15
the symbol. They are also attacked, criticized and transcended in each of the great
religions of mankind. The reason for this criticism is the very nature of the myth. It
uses material from our ordinary experience. It put the stories of the gods into the
framework of time and space although it belongs to the nature of the ultimate to be
beyond time and space. Above all, it divides the divine into several figures, removing ultimacy from each of them without removing their claim to ultimacy. This
inescapably leads to conflicts of ultimate claims, able to destroy life, society, and consciousness.

The criticism of the myth first rejects the division of the divine and goes   16
beyond it to one God, although in different ways according to the different types of
religion. Even one God is an object of mythological language, and if spoken about is
drawn into the framework of time and space. Even he loses his ultimacy if made to
be the content of concrete concern. Consequently, the criticism of the myth does not
end with the rejection of the polytheistic mythology.

Monotheism also falls under the criticism of the myth. It needs, as one says   17
today, "demythologization." This word has been used in connection with the elabo-

ration of the mythical elements in stories and symbols of the Bile, both of the Old and the New Testaments—stories like those of the Paradise, of the fall of Adam, of the great Flood, of the Exodus from Egypt, of the virgin birth of the Messiah, of many of his miracles, of his resurrection and ascension, of his expected return as the judge of the universe. In short, all the stories in which divine-human interactions are told are considered as mythological in character, and objects of demythologization. What does this negative and artificial term mean? It must be accepted and supported if it points to the necessity of recognizing a symbol as a symbol and a myth as a myth. It must be attacked and rejected if it means the removal of symbols and myths altogether. Such an attempt which never can be successful, because symbol and myth are forms of the human consciousness which are always present. One can replace one myth by another, but one cannot remove the myth from man's spiritual life. For the myth is the combination of symbols of our ultimate concern.

A myth which is understood as a myth, but not removed or replaced, can be called a "broken myth." Christianity denies by its very nature any unbroken myth, because its presupposition is the first commandment: the affirmation of the ultimate as ultimate and the rejection of any kind of idolatry. All mythological elements in the Bible, and doctrine and liturgy should be recognizes as mythological, but they should be maintained in their symbolic form and not be replaced by scientific substitutes. For there is no substitute for the use of symbols and myths: they are the language of faith.   18

The radical criticism of the myth is due to the fact that the primitive mythological consciousness resists the attempt to interpret the myth of myth. It is afraid of every act of demythologization. It believes that the broken myth is deprived of its truth and of its convincing power. Those who live in an unbroken mythological world feel safe and certain. They resist, often fanatically, any attempt to introduce an element of uncertainty by "breaking the myth," namely, by making conscious its symbolic character. Such resistance is supported by the authoritarian systems, religious or political, in order to give security to the people under their control. The resistance against demythologization expresses itself in "literalism." The symbols and myths are understood in their immediate meaning. The material, taken from nature and history, is used in its proper sense. The character of the symbol to point beyond itself to something else is disregarded. Creation is taken as a magic act which happened once upon a time. The fall of Adam is localized on a special geographical point and attributed to a human individual. The virgin birth of the Messiah is understood in biological terms, resurrection and ascension as physical events, the second coming of the Christ as a telluric, or cosmic, catastrophe. The presupposition of such literal-   19 ism is that God is a being, acting in time and space, dwelling in a special place, affecting the course of events and being affected by them like any other being in the universe. Literalism deprives God of his ultimacy and, religiously speaking, of his majesty. It draws him down to the level of that which is not ultimate, the finite and conditional. In the last analysis it is not rational criticism of the myth which is decisive but the inner religious criticism. Faith, if it takes its symbols literally, becomes idolatrous! It calls something ultimate which is less than ultimate. Faith, conscious of the symbolic character of its symbols, gives God the honor which is due him.

One should distinguish two stages of literalism, the natural and the reactive. 20 The natural stage of literalism is that in which the mythical and the literal are indistinguishable. The primitive period of individuals and groups consists in the inability to separate the creations of symbolic imagination from the facts which can be verified through observation and experiment. This stage has a full right of its own and should not be disturbed, either in individuals or in groups, up to the moment when man's questioning mind breaks the natural acceptance of the mythological visions as literal. If, however, this moment has come, two ways are possible. The one is to replace the unbroken by the broken myth. It is the objectively demanded way, although it is impossible for many people who prefer the repression of their questions to the uncertainty which appears with the breaking of the myth They are forced into the second stage of literalism, the conscious one, which is aware of the questions but represses them, half consciously, half unconsciously. The tool of repression is usually an acknowledged authority with sacred qualities like the Church or the Bible, to which one owes unconditional surrender. This stage is still justifiable, if the questioning power is very weak and can easily be answered. It is unjustifiable if a mature mind is broken in its personal center by political or psychological methods, split in his unity, and hurt in his integrity. The enemy of a critical theology is not natural literalism but conscious literalism with repression of and aggression toward autonomous thought.

Symbols of faith cannot be replaced by other symbols, such as artistic ones, and 21 they cannot be removed by scientific criticism. They have a genuine standing in the human mind, just as science and art have. Their symbolic character is their truth and their power. Nothing less than symbols and myths can express our ultimate concern.

One more question arises, namely, whether myths are able to express every 22 kind of ultimate concern. For example, Christian theologians argue that the word "myth" should be reserved for natural myths in which repetitive natural processes, such as the seasons, are understood in their ultimate meaning. They believe that if the world is seen as a historical process with beginning, end and center, as in

Christianity and Judaism, the term "myth" should not be used. This would radically reduce the realm in which the term would be applicable. Myth could not be understood as the language of our ultimate concern, but only as a discarded idiom of this language. Yet history roves that there are not only natural myths but also historical myths. If the earth is seen as the battleground of two divine powers, as in ancient Persia, this is an historical myth. If the God of creation selects and guides a nation through history toward an end which transcends all history, this is an historical myth. If the Christ—a transcendent, divine being—appears in the fullness of time, lives, dies and is resurrected, this is an historical myth. Christianity is superior to those religions which are bound to a natural myth. But Christianity speaks the mythological language like every other religion. It is a broken myth, but it is a myth; otherwise Christianity would not be an expression of ultimate concern.

Martin Luther King, Jr. (1929–1968) had at first planned to become a doctor or a

lawyer, but when he graduated from Morehouse College in Atlanta at the age of nineteen, he abandoned these ambitions and went into the seminary. After seminary, he went to
Boston University, where he received his Ph.D. in 1955. He was ordained as a Baptist minister
in his father's church, the Ebenezer Baptist Church in Atlanta, a church he copastored with
his father from 1960 to 1968. He was also founder and director of the Southern Christian
Leadership Conference from 1957 to 1968, and a member of the Montgomery Improvement
Association, an activist group protesting racial segregation. Inspired by Mahatma Gandhi's
principles of nonviolent protest, King led this group in several demonstrations. In May 1963,
he was arrested and imprisoned in Birmingham for demonstrating against segregation in hotels
and restaurants. It was while in jail that he wrote his famous "Letter from Birmingham Jail," a
work that was published in 1963 and expanded and republished in 1968. It was also in 1963
that King made the speech entitled "I Have a Dream" to over 200,000 people at the March on
Washington. King received numerous awards for his work for human rights, including the
Nobel Prize for Peace in 1964. On April 4, 1968, while talking with other human rights
activists on a motel balcony in Memphis, King was assassinated.

Loving Your Enemies

Martin Luther King Jr.

*Ye have heard that it hath been said, Thou shalt, love thy neighbour, and hate
thine enemy, But I say unto you, Love your enemies, bless them that curse you,
do good to them that hate you, and pray for them which despitefully use you, and
persecute you; that ye may be children of your Father which is in heaven.*

Matthew 5:43–45

Probably no admonition of Jesus has been more difficult to follow than the com-   1
mand to "love your enemies." Some men have sincerely felt that its actual practice is not possible. It is easy, they say, to love those who love you, but how can
one love those who openly and insidiously seek to defeat you? Others, like the
philosopher Nietzsche, contend that Jesus' exhortation to love one's enemies is
testimony to the fact that the Christian ethic is designed for the weak and cowardly, and not for the strong and courageous. Jesus, they say, was an impractical
idealist.

    In spite of these insistent questions and persistent objections, this command   2
of Jesus challenges us with new urgency. Upheaval after upheaval has reminded

us that modern man is traveling along a road called hate, in a journey that will bring us to destruction and damnation. Far from being the pious injunction of a Utopian dreamer, the command to love one's enemy is an absolute necessity for our survival. Love even for enemies is the key to the solution of the problems of our world. Jesus is not an impractical idealist: he is the practical realist.

I am certain that Jesus understood the difficulty inherent in the act of lov-   3
ing one's enemy. He never joined the ranks of those who talk glibly about the easiness of the moral life. He realized that every genuine expression of love grows out of a consistent and total surrender to God. So when Jesus said "Love your enemy," he was not unmindful of its stringent qualities. Yet he meant every word of it. Our responsibility as Christians is to discover the meaning of this command and seek passionately to live it out in our daily lives.

I

Let us be practical and ask the question, *How do we love our enemies?*   4

First, we must develop and maintain the capacity to forgive. He who is   5
devoid of the power to forgive is devoid of the power to love. It is impossible even to begin the act of loving one's enemies without the prior acceptance of the necessity, over and over again, of forgiving those who inflict evil and injury upon us. It is also necessary to realize that the forgiving act must always be initiated by the person who has been wronged, the victim of some great hurt, the recipient of some tortuous injustice, the absorber of some terrible act of oppression. The wrongdoer may request forgiveness. He may come to himself, and, like the prodigal son, move up some dusty road, his heart palpitating with the desire for forgiveness. But only the injured neighbour, the loving father back home, can really pour out the warm waters of forgiveness.

Forgiveness does not mean ignoring what has been done or putting a false   6
label on an evil act. It means, rather, that the evil act no longer remains as a bar-rier to the relationship. Forgiveness is a catalyst creating the atmosphere necessary for a fresh start and a new beginning. It is the lifting of a burden or the canceling of a debt. The words "I will forgive you, but I'll never forget what you've done" never explain the real nature of forgiveness. Certainly one can never forget, if that means erasing it totally from his mind. But when we forgive, we forget in the sense that the evil deed is no longer a mental block impeding a new relationship. Likewise, we can never say, "I will forgive you, but I won't have anything further to do with you." Forgiveness means reconciliation, a coming together again. Without this, no man can love his enemies. The degree to which we are able to forgive determines the degree to which we are able to love our enemies.

Second, we must recognize that the evil deed of the enemy-neighbour, the   7
thing that hurts, never quite expresses all that he is. An element of goodness may
be found even in our worst enemy. Each of us is something of a schizophrenic
personality, tragically divided against ourselves. A persistent civil war rages within all of our lives. Something within us causes us to lament with Ovid, the Latin
poet, "I see and approve the better things, but follow worse," or to agree with
Plato that human personality is like a charioteer having two headstrong horses,
each wanting to go in a different direction, or to repeat with the Apostle Paul,
"The good that I would I do not: but the evil which I would not, that I do."

This simply means that there is some good in the worst of us and some evil   8
in the best of us. When we discover this, we are less prone to hate our enemies.
When we look beneath the surface, beneath the impulsive evil deed, we see
within our enemy-neighbour a measure of goodness and know that the viciousness and evilness of his acts are not quite representative of all that he is. We see
him in a new light. We recognize that his hate grows out of fear, pride, ignorance,
prejudice, and misunderstanding, but in spite of this, we know God's image is
ineffably etched in his being. Then we love our enemies by realizing that they
are not totally bad and that they are not beyond the reach of God's redemptive
love.

Third, we must not seek to defeat or humiliate the enemy but to win his   9
friendship and understanding. At times we are able to humiliate our worst
enemy. Inevitably, his weak moments come and we are able to thrust in his side
the spear of defeat. But this we must not do. Every word and deed must contribute to an understanding with the enemy and release those vast reservoirs of
goodwill which have been blocked by impenetrable walls of hate.

The meaning of love is not to be confused with some sentimental outpour-   10
ing. Love is something much deeper than emotional bosh. Perhaps the Greek
language can clear our confusion at this point. In the Greek New Testament are
three words for love. The word *eros* is a sort of aesthetic or romantic love. In the
Platonic dialogues *eros* is a yearning of the soul for the realm of the divine. The
second word is *philia*, a reciprocal love and the intimate affection and friendship
between friends. We love those whom we like, and we love because we are loved.
The third word is *agape*, understanding and creative, redemptive goodwill for all
men. An overflowing love which seeks nothing in return, *agape* is the love of
God operating in the human heart. At this level, we love men not because we
like them, nor because their ways appeal to us, nor even because they possess
some type of divine spark; we love every man because God loves him. At this

level, we love the person who does an evil deed, although we hate the deed that he does.

Now we can see what Jesus meant when he said, "Love your enemies." We   11
should be happy that he did not say, "Like your enemies." It is almost impossible to like some people. "Like" is a sentimental and affectionate word. How can we be affectionate toward a person whose avowed aim is to crush our very being and place innumerable stumbling blocks in our path? How can we like a person who is threatening our children and bombing our homes? That is impossible. But Jesus recognized that *love* is greater than *like*. When Jesus bids us to love our enemies, he is speaking neither of *eros* nor *philia*; he is speaking of *agape*, understanding and creative, redemptive goodwill for all men. Only by following this way and responding with this type of love are we able to be children of our Father who is in heaven.

II

Let us move now from the practical *how* to the theoretical *why: Why should we*   12
love our enemies? The first reason is fairly obvious. Returning hate multiplies hate, adding deeper darkness to a night already devoid of stars. Darkness cannot drive out darkness; only light can do that. Hate cannot drive out hate; only love can do that. Hate multiplies hate, violence multiplies violence, and toughness multiplies toughness in a descending spiral of destruction. So when Jesus says "Love your enemies," he is setting forth a profound and ultimately inescapable admonition. Have we not come to such an impasse in the modern world that we must love our enemies—or else? The chain reaction of evil—hate begetting hate, wars producing more wars—must be broken, or we shall be plunged into the dark abyss of annihilation.

Another reason why we must love our enemies is that hate scars the soul   13
and distorts the personality. Mindful that hate is an evil and dangerous force, we too often think of what it does to the person hated. This is understandable, for hate brings irreparable damage to its victims. We have seen its ugly consequences in the ignominious deaths brought to six million Jews by a hate-obsessed madman named Hitler, in the unspeakable violence inflicted upon Negroes by bloodthirsty mobs, in the dark horrors of war, and in the terrible indignities and injustices perpetrated against millions of God's children by unconscionable oppressors.

But there is another side which we must never overlook. Hate is just as   14
injurious to the person who hates. Like an unchecked cancer, hate corrodes the

personality and eats away its vital unity. Hate destroys a man's sense of values and his objectivity. It causes him to describe the beautiful as ugly and the ugly as beautiful, and to confuse the true with the false and the false with the true.

Dr. E. Franklin Frazier, in an interesting essay entitled "The Pathology of   15
Race Prejudice," included several examples of white persons who were normal, amiable, and congenial in their day-to-day relationships with other white persons but when they were challenged to think of Negroes as equals or even to discuss the question of racial injustice, they reacted with unbelievable irrationality and an abnormal unbalance. This happens when hate lingers in our minds. Psychiatrists report that many of the strange things that happen in the subconscious, many of our inner conflicts, are rooted in hate. They say, "Love or perish." Modern psychology recognizes what Jesus taught centuries ago: hate divides the personality and love in an amazing and inexorable way unites it.

A third reason why we should love our enemies is that love is the only force   16
capable of transforming an enemy into a friend. We never get rid of an enemy by meeting hate with hate; we get rid of an enemy by getting rid of enmity. By its very nature, hate destroys and tears down; by its very nature, love creates and builds up. Love transforms with redemptive power.

Lincoln tried love and left for all history a magnificent drama of reconcili-   17
ation. When he was campaigning for the presidency one of his archenemies was a man named Stanton. For some reason Stanton hated Lincoln. He used every ounce of his energy to degrade him in the eyes of the public. So deep rooted was Stanton's hate for Lincoln that he uttered unkind words about his physical appearance, and sought to embarrass him at every point with the bitterest diatribes. But in spite of this Lincoln was elected President of the United States. Then came the period when he had to select his cabinet which would consist of the persons who would be his most intimate associates in implementing his programme. He started choosing men here and there for the various secretaryships. The day finally came for Lincoln to select a man to fill the all-important post of Secretary of War. Can you imagine whom Lincoln chose to fill this post? None other than the man named Stanton. There was an immediate uproar in the inner circle when the news began to spread. Adviser after adviser was heard saying, "Mr. President, you are making a mistake. Do you know this man Stanton? Are you familiar with all of the ugly things he said about you? He is your enemy. He will seek to sabotage your programme. Have you thought this through, Mr. President?" Mr. Lincoln's answer was terse and to the point: "Yes, I know Mr. Stanton. I am aware of all the terrible things he has said about me. But after look-

ing over the nation, I find he is the best man for the job." So Stanton became Abraham Lincoln's Secretary of War and rendered an invaluable service to his nation and his President. Not many years later Lincoln was assassinated. Many laudable things were said about him. Even today millions of people still adore him as the greatest of all Americans. H. G. Wells selected him as one of the six great men of history. But of all the great statements made about Abraham Lincoln, the words of Stanton remain among the greatest. Standing near the dead body of the man he once hated, Stanton referred to him as one of the greatest men that ever lived and said "he now belongs to the ages." If Lincoln had hated Stanton both men would have gone to their graves as bitter enemies. But through the power of love Lincoln transformed an enemy into a friend. It was this same attitude that made it possible for Lincoln to speak a kind word about the South during the Civil War when feeling was most bitter. Asked by a shocked bystander how he could do this, Lincoln said, "Madam, do I not destroy my enemies when I make them my friends?" This is the power of redemptive love.

We must hasten to say that these are not the ultimate reasons why we should love our enemies. An even more basic reason why we are commanded to love is expressed explicitly, in Jesus' words, "Love your enemies . . . *that ye may be children of your Father which is in heaven.*" We are called to this difficult task in order to realize a unique relationship with God. We are potential sons of God. Through love that potentiality becomes actuality. We must love our enemies, because only by loving them can we know God and experience the beauty of his holiness.   18

The relevance of what I have said to the crisis in race relations should be readily apparent. There will be no permanent solution to the race problem until oppressed men develop the capacity to love their enemies. The darkness of racial injustice will be dispelled only by the light or forgiving love. For more than three centuries American Negroes have been battered by the iron rod of oppression, frustrated by day and bewildered by night by unbearable injustice, and burdened with the ugly weight of discrimination. Forced to live with these shameful conditions, we are tempted to become bitter and to retaliate with a corresponding hate. But if this happens, the new order we seek will be little more than a duplicate of the old order. We must in strength and humility meet hate with love.   19

Of course, this is not practical. Life is a matter of getting even, of hitting back, of dog eat dog. Am I saying that Jesus commands us to love those who hurt and oppress us? Do I sound like most preachers—idealistic and impractical?   20

Maybe in some distant Utopia, you say, that idea will work, but not in the hard, cold world in which we live.

My friends, we have followed the socalled practical way for too long a time   21 now, and it has led inexorably to deeper confusion and chaos. Time is cluttered with the wreckage of communities which surrendered to hatred and violence. For the salvation of our nation and the salvation of mankind, we must follow another way. This does not mean that we abandon our righteous efforts. With every ounce of our energy we must continue to rid this nation of the incubus of segregation. But we shall not in the process relinquish our privilege and our obligation to love. While abhorring segregation, we shall love the segregationist. This is the only way to create the beloved community.

To our most bitter opponents we say: "We shall match your capacity to   22 inflict suffering by our capacity to endure suffering. We shall meet your physical force with soul force. Do to us what you will, and we shall continue to love you. We cannot in all good conscience obey your unjust laws, because non-cooperation with evil is as much a moral obligation as is cooperation with good. Throw us in jail, and we shall still love you. Send your hooded perpetrators of violence into our community at the midnight hour and beat us and leave us half dead, and we shall still love you. But be ye assured that we will wear you down by our capacity to suffer. One day we shall win freedom, but not only for ourselves. We shall so appeal to your heart and conscience that we shall win you in the process, and our victory will be a double victory."

Love is the most durable power in the world. This creative force, so beau-   23 tifully exemplified in the life of our Christ, is the most potent instrument available in mankind's quest for peace and security. Napoleon Bonaparte, the great military genius, looking back over his years of conquest, is reported to have said: "Alexander, Caesar, Charlemagne and I have built great empires. But upon what did they depend? They depended on force. But centuries ago Jesus started an empire that was built on love, and even to this day millions will die for him." Who can doubt the veracity of these words. The great military leaders of the past have gone, and their empires have crumbled and burned to ashes. But the empire of Jesus, built solidly and majestically on the foundation of love, is still growing. It started with a small group of dedicated men, who, through the inspiration of their Lord, were able to shake the hinges from the gates of the Roman Empire, and carry the gospel into all the world. Today the vast earthly kingdom of Christ numbers more than 900,000,000 and covers every land and tribe. Today we hear again the promise of victory:

Jesus shall reign where'er the sun
Does his successive journeys run;
His kingdom stretch from shore to shore,
Till moon shall wax and wane no more.

Another choir joyously responds:

In Christ there is no East or West,
In Him no South or North,
But one great Fellowship of Love
Throughout the whole wide earth.

Jesus is eternally right. History is replete with the bleached bones of nations 24
that refused to listen to him. May we in the twentieth century hear and follow
his words—before it is too late. May we solemnly realize that we shall never be
true sons of our heavenly Father until we love our enemies and pray for those
who persecute us.

Martin Luther King, Jr. (1929–1968) had at first planned to become a doctor or a lawyer, but when he graduated from Morehouse College in Atlanta at the age of nineteen, he abandoned these ambitions and went into the seminary. After seminary, he went to Boston University, where he received his Ph.D. in 1955. He was ordained as a Baptist minister in his father's church, the Ebenezer Baptist Church in Atlanta, a church he copastored with his father from 1960 to 1968. He was also founder and director of the Southern Christian Leadership Conference from 1957 to 1968, and a member of the Montgomery Improvement Association, an activist group protesting racial segregation. Inspired by Mahatma Gandhi's principles of nonviolent protest, King led this group in several demonstrations. In May 1963, he was arrested and imprisoned in Birmingham for demonstrating against segregation in hotels and restaurants. It was while in jail that he wrote his famous "Letter from Birmingham Jail," a work that was published in 1963 and expanded and republished in 1968. It was also in 1963 that King made the speech entitled "I Have a Dream" to over 200,000 people at the March on Washington. King received numerous awards for his work for human rights, including the Nobel Prize for Peace in 1964. On April 4, 1968, while talking with other human rights activists on a motel balcony in Memphis, King was assassinated.

On Being a Good Neighbour

Martin Luther King, Jr.

> *And who is my neighbour?*
> Luke 10:29

I should like to talk with you about a good man, whose exemplary life will always be a   1
flashing light to plague the dozing conscience of mankind. His goodness was not found in
a passive commitment to a particular creed, but in his active participation in a life-saving
deed; not in a moral pilgrimage that reached its destination point, but in the love ethic by
which he journeyed life's highway. He was good because he was a good neighbour.

The ethical concern of this man is expressed in a magnificent little story, which   2
begins with a theological discussion on the meaning of eternal life and concludes in
a concrete expression of compassion on a dangerous road. Jesus is asked a question by
a man who had been trained in the details of Jewish law: "Master, what shall I do to
inherit eternal life?" The retort is prompt: "What is written in the law? how readest
thou?" After a moment the lawyer recites articulately: "Thou shalt love the Lord thy
God with all thy heart, and with all thy soul, and with all thy strength, and with all
thy mind; and thy neighbour as thyself." Then comes the decisive word from Jesus:
"Thou hast answered right: this do, and thou shalt live."

The lawyer was chagrined. "Why," the people might ask, "would an expert in   3
the law raise a question that even the novice can answer?" Desiring to justify himself
and to show that Jesus' reply was far from conclusive, the lawyer asks, "And who is
my neighbour?" The lawyer was now taking up the cudgels of debate that might have
turned the conversation into an abstract theological discussion. But Jesus, determined not to be caught in the "paralysis of analysis," pulls the question from mid-air
and places it on a dangerous curve between Jerusalem and Jericho.

He told the story of "a certain man" who went down from Jerusalem to Jericho   4
and fell among robbers who stripped him, beat him, and, departing, left him half dead.
By chance a certain priest appeared, but he passed by on the other side, and later a
Levite also passed by. Finally, a certain Samaritan, a half-breed from a people with
whom the Jews had no dealings, appeared. When he saw the wounded man, he was
moved with compassion, administered first aid, placed him on his breast, "and
brought him to an inn, and took care of him."

Who is my neighbour? "I do not know his name," says Jesus in essence. "He is   5
anyone toward whom you are neighbourly. He is anyone who lies in need at life's
roadside. He is neither Jew nor Gentile; he is neither Russian nor American; he is
neither Negro nor white. He is 'a certain man'—any needy man—on one of the
numerous Jericho roads of life." So Jesus defines a neighbour, not in a theological definition, but in a life situation.

What constituted the goodness of the good Samaritan? Why will he always be   6
an inspiring paragon of neighbourly virtue? It seems to me that this man's goodness
may be described in one word—altruism. The good Samaritan was altruistic to the
core. What is altruism? The dictionary defines altruism as "regard for, and devotion
to, the interest of others." The Samaritan was good because he made concern for others the first law of his life.

I

The Samaritan had the capacity for a *universal altruism*. He had a piercing insight   7
into that which is beyond the eternal accidents of race, religion, and nationality. One
of the great tragedies of man's long trek along the highway of history has been the limiting of neighbourly concern to tribe, race, class, or nation. The God of early Old
Testament days was a tribal god and the ethic was tribal. "Thou shalt not kill" meant
"Thou shalt not kill a fellow Israelite, but for God's sake, kill a Philistine." Greek
democracy embraced a certain aristocracy, but not the hordes of Greek slaves whose
labours built the city-states. The universalism at the centre of the Declaration of
Independence has been shamefully negated by America's appalling tendency to sub-

stitute "some" for "all." Numerous people in the North and South still believe that the affirmation, "All men are created equal," means "All white men are created equal." Our unswerving devotion to monopolistic capitalism makes us more concerned about the economic security of the captains of industry than for the labouring men whose sweat and skills keep industry functioning.

What are the devastating consequences of this narrow, group-centred attitude?   8
It means that one does not really mind what happens to the people outside his group. If an American is concerned only about his nation, he will not be concerned about the peoples of Asia, Africa, or South America. Is this not why nations engage in the madness of war without the slightest sense of penitence? Is this not why the murder of a citizen of your own nation is a crime, but the murder of the citizens of another nation in war is an act of heroic virtue? If manufacturers are concerned only in their personal interests, they will pass by on the other side while thousands of working people are stripped of their jobs and left displaced on some Jericho road as a result of automation, and they will judge every move toward a better distribution of wealth and a better life for the working man to be socialistic. If a white man is concerned only about his race, he will casually pass by the Negro who has been robbed of his personhood, stripped of his sense of dignity, and left dying on some wayside road.

A few years ago, when an automobile carrying several members of a Negro col-   9
lege basketball team had an accident on a Southern highway, three of the young men were severely injured. An ambulance was immediately called, but on arriving at the place of the accident, the driver, who was white, said without apology that it was not his policy to service Negroes, and he drove away. The driver of a passing automobile graciously drove the boys to the nearest hospital, but the attending physician belligerently said, "We don't take niggers in this hospital." When the boys finally arrived at a "coloured" hospital in a town some fifty miles from the scene of the accident, one was dead and the other two died thirty and fifty minutes later respectively. Probably all three could have been saved if they had been given immediate treatment. This is only one of thousands of inhuman incidents that occur daily in the South, an unbelievable expression of the barbaric consequences of any tribal-centred, national-centred, or racial-centred ethic.

The real tragedy of such narrow provincialism is that we see people as entities or   10
merely as things. Too seldom do we see people in their true *humanness*. A spiritual myopia limits our vision to external accidents. We see men as Jews or Gentiles, Catholics or Protestants, Chinese or American, Negroes or whites. We fail to think of them as fellow human beings made from the same basic stuff as we, moulded in the same divine image. The priest and the Levite saw only a bleeding body, not a human being like themselves. But the good Samaritan will always remind us to remove the

cataracts of provincialism from our spiritual eyes and see men as men. If the Samaritan had considered the wounded man as a Jew first, he would not have stopped, for the Jews and the Samaritans had no dealings. He saw him a human being first, who was a Jew only by accident. The good neighbour looks beyond the external accidents and discerns those inner qualities that make all men human and, therefore, brothers.

II

The Samaritan possessed the capacity for a *dangerous altruism*. He risked his life to save a   11 brother. When we ask why the priest and the Levite did not stop to help the wounded man, numerous suggestions come to mind. Perhaps they could not delay their arrival at an important ecclesiastical meeting. Perhaps religious regulations demanded that they touch no human body for several hours prior to the performing of their temple functions. Or perhaps they were on their way to an organizational meeting of a Jericho Road Improvement Association. Certainly this would have been a real need, for it is not enough to aid a wounded man on the Jericho Road; it is also important to change the conditions which make robbery possible. Philanthropy is commendable, but it must not cause the philanthropist to overlook the circumstances of economic injustice which make philanthropy necessary. Maybe the priest and the Levite believed that it is better to cure injustice at the causal source than to get bogged down with a single individual effect.

These are probable reasons for their failure to stop, yet there is another possibil-   12 ity, often overlooked, that they were afraid. The Jericho Road was a dangerous road. When Mrs. King and I visited the Holy Land, we rented a car and drove from Jerusalem to Jericho. As we travelled slowly down that meandering, mountainous road, I said to my wife, "I can now understand why Jesus chose this road as the setting for his parable." Jerusalem is some two thousand feet above and Jericho one thousand feet below sea level. The descent is made in less than twenty miles. Many sudden curves provide likely places for ambushing and expose the traveller to unforseen attacks. Long ago the road was known as the Bloody Pass. So it is possible that the priest and the Levite were afraid that if they stopped, they too would be beaten. Perhaps the robbers were still nearby. Or maybe the wounded man on the ground was a faker, who wished to draw passing travellers to his side for quick and easy seizure. I imagine that the first question which the priest and the Levite asked was: "If I stop to help this man, what will happen to me?" But by the very nature of his concern, the good Samaritan reversed the question: "If I do not stop to help this man, what will happen to him?" The good Samaritan engaged in a dangerous altruism.

We so often ask, "What will happen to my job, my prestige, or my status if I take   13 a stand on this issue? Will my home be bombed, will my life be threatened, or will I be jailed?" The good man always reverses the question. Albert Schweitzer did not ask,

"What will happen to my prestige and security as a university professor and to my status as a Bach organist, if I work with the people of Africa?" but rather he asked, "What will happen to these millions of people who have been wounded by the forces of injustice, if I do not go to them?" Abraham Lincoln did not ask, "What will happen to me if I issue the Emancipation Proclamation and bring an end to chattel slavery?" but he asked, "What will happen to the Union and to millions of Negro people, if I fail to do it?" The Negro professional does not ask, "What will happen to my secure position, my middle-class status, or my personal safety, if I participate in the movement to end the system of segregation?" but "What will happen to the cause of justice and the masses of Negro people who have never experienced the warmth of economic security, if I do not participate actively and courageously in the movement?"

The ultimate measure of a man is not where he stands in moments of comfort   14
and convenience, but where he stands at times of challenge and controversy. The true neighbour will risk his position, his prestige, and even his life for the welfare of others. In dangerous valleys and hazardous pathways, he will lift some bruised and beaten brother to a higher and more noble life.

III

The Samaritan also possessed *excessive altruism*. With his own hands he bound the   15
wounds of the man and then set him on his own breast. It would have been easier to pay an ambulance to take the unfortunate man to the hospital, rather than risk having his neatly trimmed suit stained with blood.

True altruism is more than the capacity to pity; it is the capacity to sympathize.   16
Pity may represent little more than the impersonal concern which prompts the mailing of a cheque, but true sympathy is the personal concern which demands the giving of one's soul. Pity may arise from interest in an abstraction called humanity, but sympathy grows out of a concern for a particular needy human being who lies at life's roadside. Sympathy is fellow feeling for the person in need—his pain, agony, and burdens. Our missionary efforts fail when they are based on pity, rather than true compassion. Instead of seeking to do something *with* the African and Asian peoples, we have too often sought only to do something *for* them. An expression of pity devoid of genuine sympathy, leads to a new form of paternalism which no self-respecting person can accept. Dollars possess the potential for helping wounded children of God on life's Jericho Road, but unless those dollars are distributed by compassionate fingers they will enrich neither the giver nor the receiver. Millions of missionary dollars have gone to Africa from the hands of church people who would die a million deaths before they would permit a single African the privilege of worshipping in their con-

gregation. Millions of Peace Corps dollars are being invested in Africa because of the votes of some men who fight unrelentingly to prevent African ambassadors from holding membership in their diplomatic clubs or establishing residency in their particular neighbourhoods. The Peace Corps will fail if it seeks to do something *for* the underprivileged people of the world; it will succeed if it seeks creatively to do something *with* them. It will fail as a negative gesture to defeat Communism; it will succeed only as a positive effort to wipe poverty, ignorance, and disease from the earth. Money devoid of love is like salt devoid of savour, good for nothing except to be trodden under the foot of men. True neighbourliness requires personal concern. The Samaritan used his hands to bind up the wounds of the robbed man's body, and he also released an overflowing love to bind up the wounds of his broken spirit.

Another expression of the excessive altruism on the part of the Samaritan was   17 his willingness to go far beyond the call of duty. After tending to the man's wounds, he put him on his breast, carried him to an inn, and left money for his care, making clear that if further financial needs arose he would gladly meet them. "Whatsoever thou spendest more, when I come again, I will repay thee." Stopping short of this, he would have more than fulfilled any possible rule concerning one's duty to a wounded stranger. He went beyond the second mile. His love was complete.

Dr. Harry Emerson Fosdick has made an impressive distinction between   18 enforceable and unenforceable obligations. The former are regulated by the codes of society and the vigorous implementation of law-enforcement agencies. Breaking these obligations, spelled out on thousands of pages in law books, has filled numerous prisons. But unenforceable obligations are beyond the reach of the laws of society. They concern inner attitudes, genuine person-to-person relations, and expressions of compassion which law books cannot regulate and jails cannot rectify. Such obligations are met by men's commitment to an inner law, written on the heart. Man-made laws assure justice, but a higher law produces love. No code of conduct ever persuaded a father to love his children or a husband to show affection to his wife. The law court may force him to provide bread for the family, but it cannot make him provide the bread of love. A good father is obedient to the unenforceable. The good Samaritan represents the conscience of mankind because he also was obedient to that which could not be enforced. No law in the world could have produced such unalloyed compassion, such genuine love, such thorough altruism.

In our nation today a might struggle is taking place. It is a struggle to conquer   19 the reign of an evil monster called segregation and its inseparable twin called discrimination—a monster that has wandered through this land for well-nigh one hundred years, stripping millions of Negro people of their sense of dignity and robbing them of their birthright of freedom.

Let us never succumb to the temptation of believing that legislation and judi-   20
cial decrees play only minor roles in solving the problem. Morality cannot be legis-
lated, but behaviour can be regulated. Judicial decrees may not change the heart, but
they can restrain the heartless. The law cannot make an employer love an employee,
but it can prevent him from refusing to hire me because of the colour of my skin. The
habits, if not the hearts, of people have been and are being altered every day by legislative acts, judicial decisions, and executive orders. Let us not be misled by those
who argue that segregation cannot be ended by the force of law.

But acknowledging this, we must admit that the ultimate solution to the race   21
problem lies in the willingness of men to obey the unenforceable. Court orders and
federal enforcement agencies are of inestimable value in achieving desegration, but
desegregation is only a partial, though necessary, step toward the final goal which we
seek to realize, genuine intergroup and interpersonal living. Desegregation will break
down the legal barriers and bring men together physically, but something must touch
the hearts and souls of men so that they will come together spiritually because it is
natural and right. A vigorous enforcement of civil rights laws will bring an end to segregated public facilities which are barriers to a truly desegregated society, but it cannot bring an end to fears, prejudice, pride, and irrationality, which are the barriers to
a truly integrated society. These dark and demonic responses will be removed only as
men are possessed by the invisible, inner law which etches on their hearts the conviction that all men are brothers and that love is mankind's most potent weapon for-
personal and social transformation. True integration will be achieved by true neighbors who are willingly obedient to unenforceable obligations.

More than ever before, my friends, men of all races and nations are today chal-   22
lenged to be neighbourly. The call for a worldwide good-neighbour policy is more
than an ephemeral shibboleth; it is the call to a way of life which will transform our
imminent cosmic elegy into a psalm of creative fulfillment. No longer can we afford
the luxury of passing by on the other side. Such folly was once called moral failure;
today it will lead to universal suicide. We cannot long survive spiritually separated in
a world that is geographically together. In the final analysis, I must not ignore the
wounded man on life's Jericho road, because he is a part of me and I am a part of him.
His agony diminishes me, and his salvation enlarges me.

In our quest to make neighbourly love a reality, we have, in addition to the   23
inspiring example of the good Samaritan, the magnanimous life of our Christ to guide
us. His altruism was universal, for he thought of all men, even publicans and sinners,
as brothers. His altruism was dangerous, for he willingly travelled hazardous roads in
a cause he knew was right. His altruism was excessive, for he chose to die on Calvary,
history's most magnificent expression of obedience to the unenforceable.

The Good Samaritan

Luke 10: 25-37

On one occasion, a legal expert stood up to put him to the test with a question: 1
"Teacher, what do I have to do to inherit eternal life?"

He said to him, "How do you read what is written in the Law?" 2

And he answered, "You are to love the Lord your God with all your heart, 3
with all your soul, with all your energy, and with all your mind; and your neighbor as yourself."

Jesus said to him, "You have given the correct answer; do this and you will 4
have life."

But with a view to justifying himself, he said to Jesus, "But who is my neighbor?" 5

Jesus replied: 6

This fellow was on his way from Jerusalem down to Jericho when he fell 7
into the hands of robbers. They stripped him, beat him up, and went off,
leaving him half dead. Now by coincidence a priest was going down that
road; when he caught sight of him, he went out of his way to avoid him.
In the same way, when a Levite came to the place, he took one look at him
and crossed the road to avoid him. But this Samaritan who was traveling
that way came to where he was and was moved to pity at the sight of him.
He went up to him and bandaged his wounds, pouring olive oil and wine
on them. He hoisted him onto his own animal, brought him to an inn, and
looked after him.

The next day he took out two silver coins, which he gave to the 8
innkeeper, and said, "Look after him, and on my way back I'll reimburse
you for any extra expense you have had."

"Which of these three, in your opinion, acted like a neighbor to the man 9
who fell into the hands of robbers?"

He said, "The one who showed him compassion." 10

Jesus said to him, "Then go and do the same yourself." 11

The Buddha

The Buddha (literally, "the awakened one" or "the enlightened one") is a title that was given to Siddhatta Gotama (this is the Pali form of his name; the Sanskrit form is Siddhartha Gautama) after he achieved supreme spiritual enlightenment. Gotama was born in about 563 B.C.E. among the Sakya people, who lived in the lowlands of what is now Nepal. The son of the king and queen, he was probably born in the Sakyas' capital city of Kapilavatthu (now Lumbini). He spent his early years in pleasure and luxury, but he later renounced his princely life and became a wandering ascetic. According to legend, when he was twenty-nine he became suddenly aware of the suffering that pervades human life and abruptly left his home in the middle of the night (while his wife and infant son were still sleeping) to begin his quest for the solution to human suffering. Gotama wandered among the forests and cities and along the Ganges River, learning the doctrines and following the practices—including the self-infliction of severe bodily austerities—of several noted spiritual masters. Finding no solution to the problem of suffering, he resolved to find his own answer. Tradition states that one night, at the age of thirty-five, while seated in deep meditation under a fig tree (the species now known as the *bodhi* ["enlightenment"] or bo tree), he achieved supreme spiritual awakening. The Buddha then gathered disciples and formed communities of monks and nuns. In about 483, after forty-five years of teaching his doctrine and training disciples, the Buddha died in the village of Kusinara (now Kasia).

The Buddha did not write down his teachings, but for several centuries after his death they were recorded by his disciples. The Buddhist scriptures are written in several languages and fill many volumes. Our reading is taken from a work of about the first century B.C.E., written in Pali, called *The Questions of King Milinda*. Milinda was the ruler of Sagala, a city in Bactria, a region northeast of India that was settled by Greeks from Ionia. In *The Questions of King Milinda*, Milinda invites the learned Buddhist monk Nagasena, who lives in a monastery in the Himalaya Mountains, to Sagala so he can inquire about all the principal doctrines of the Buddha.

Our selection from *The Questions of King Milinda* begins with a "secular narrative" that introduces Milinda and Nagasena and sets the stage for their dialogue. Nagasena then answers Milinda's questions about the Buddhist doctrines of no permanent self (permanent individuality), reincarnation (reindividualization), karma (a force generated by one's deeds that carries over into one's next incarnation), and nirvana (the extinction of desire, which brings complete liberation from suffering).

The Questions of King Milinda

Buddhist Scriptures

Book I. The Secular Narrative

There is in the country of the Yonakas[1] a great center of trade, a city that is called   1
Sagala, situated in a delightful country well-watered and hilly, abounding in

The Questions of King Milinda, trans. T. W. Rhys Davids. 2 vols. Oxford, England: Clarendon Press, 1890, 1894 (updated stylistically).

parks, gardens, groves, lakes, and [lotus pools]—a paradise of rivers and mountains and woods. . . .

The king of the city of Sagala in India, Milinda by name, [was] learned, eloquent, wise, and able—and a faithful observer, and at the right time, of all the various acts of devotion and ceremony enjoined by his own sacred hymns concerning things past, present, and to come. Many were the arts and sciences he knew. . . .

As a disputant he was hard to equal, harder still to overcome—the acknowledged superior of all the founders of the various schools of thought. And as in wisdom, so in strength of body, swiftness, and valor, there was found none equal to Milinda in all India. He was rich too, mighty in wealth and prosperity, and the number of his armed hosts knew no end. . . .

Now at that time the city of Sagala had for twelve years been devoid of learned men, whether Brahmans,[2] Samanas,[3] or laymen. But wherever the king heard that such persons dwelt, there he would go and put his questions to them. But they all alike, being unable to satisfy the king by their solution of his problems, departed hither and thither, or if they did not leave for some other place, were at all events reduced to silence. And the brethren of the Order[4] went, for the most part, to the Himalaya Mountains.

Now at that time there dwelt, in the mountain region of the Himalayas, on the Guarded Slope, an innumerable company of arahants.[5]

The innumerable company of the arahants at the Guarded Slope in the Himalaya mountains sent a message to [Nagasena] to come, for they were anxious to see him. And when he heard the message, the venerable Nagasena vanished from the Asoka Park and appeared before them. And they said: "Nagasena, that King Milinda is in the habit of harassing the brethren by knotty questions and by argumentations this way and that. Nagasena, go and master him."

[Nagasena replied:] "Not only let King Milinda, holy ones, but let all the kings of India, come and propound questions to me. I will break all those puzzles up and solve them. You may go fearlessly to Sagala."

Then all the elders went to the city of Sagala, lighting it up with their yellow robes like lamps, and bringing down upon it the breezes from the heights where the sages dwell. . . .

Devamantiya[6] said to King Milinda: ". . . There is an elder named Nagasena, learned, able, and wise, of subdued manners, yet full of courage, versed in the traditions, a master of language, and ready in reply—one who understands alike the spirit and the letter of the law, and can expound its difficulties and

2

3

4

5

6

7

8

9

refute objections to perfection. He is staying at present at the Sankheyya hermitage. You should go, great king, and put your questions to him. He is able to discuss things with you, and dispel your doubts."

Then when Milinda the king heard the name Nagasena, thus suddenly   10 introduced, he was seized with fear and with anxiety, and the hairs of his body stood on end.[7] But he asked Devamantiya: "Is that really so?"

And Devamantiya replied: "He is capable, sire, of discussing things with   11 the guardians of the world—with Indra, Yama, Varuna, Kuvera, Prajapati, Suyama, and Santushita[8]—and even with the great Brahma[9] himself, the progenitor of mankind, how much more then with a mere human being!"

"Do you then, Devamantiya," said the king, "send a messenger to say I am   12 coming."

And he did so. And Nagasena sent word back that he might come. And   13 the king, attended by the five hundred Yonakas, mounted his royal chariot and proceeded with a great retinue to the Sankheyya hermitage, and to the place where Nagasena dwelt. . . .

Book II. The Distinguishing Characteristics of Ethical Qualities
Chapter 1
Now Milinda the king went up to where the venerable Nagasena was, and   14 addressed him with the greetings and compliments of friendship and courtesy, and took his seat respectfully apart. And Nagasena reciprocated his courtesy, so that the heart of the king was propitiated.

And Milinda began by asking, "How is Your Reverence known, and what,   15 sir, is your name?"

"I am known as Nagasena, O king, and it is by that name that my brethren   16 in the faith address me. But although parents, O king, give such a name as 'Nagasena,' 'Surasena,' 'Virasena,' or 'Sihasena,' yet this [name], sire, is only a generally understood term, a designation in common use. For there is no permanent individuality[10] involved in the matter."

Then Milinda called upon the Yonakas and the brethren to witness: "This   17 Nagasena says there is no permanent individuality implied in his name. Is it now even possible to approve him in that?" And turning to Nagasena, he said: "If, most reverend Nagasena, there be no permanent individuality involved in the matter, who is it, pray, who gives to you members of the Order your robes and food and lodging and necessaries for the sick? Who is it who enjoys such things when given? Who is it who lives a life of righteousness? Who is it who devotes himself to meditation? Who is it who attains to the goal of the Excellent Way, to the nirvana of arahatship? And who is it who destroys living creatures? Who is it who takes what is not his own? Who is it who lives an evil life of worldly lusts, who speaks lies, who drinks strong drink, who (in a word) commits any one of the five sins which work out their bitter fruit even in this life? If that be so, there is neither merit nor demerit; there is neither doer nor causer of good or evil deeds; there is neither fruit nor result of good or evil karma.[11] If, most reverend Nagasena, we are to think that were a man to kill you there would be no murder, then it follows that there are no real masters or teachers in your Order, and that your ordinations are void. You tell me that your brethren in the Order are in the habit of addressing you as 'Nagasena.' Now what is that Nagasena? Do you mean to say that the hair is Nagasena?"

"I don't say that, great king."   18

"Or the hairs on the body, perhaps?"   19

"Certainly not."   20

"Or is it the nails, the teeth, the skin, the flesh, the nerves, the bones, the   21 marrow, the kidneys, the heart, the liver, the abdomen, the spleen, the lungs, the larger intestines, the lower intestines, the stomach, the feces, the bile, the phlegm, the pus, the blood, the sweat, the fat, the tears, the serum, the saliva, the mucus, the oil that lubricates the joints, the urine, or the brain—or any or all of these—that is Nagasena?"

And to each of these he answered no.   22

"Is it the outward form then, that is Nagasena, or the sensations, or the   23 ideas, or the constituent elements of character, or the consciousness, that is Nagasena?"

And to each of these also he answered no.   24

"Then is it all these skandhas[12] combined that are Nagasena?"   25

"No, great king."   26

"But is there anything outside the five skandhas that is Nagasena?"   27

And still he answered no.   28

"Then thus, ask as I may, I can discover no Nagasena. Nagasena is a mere   29 empty sound. Who then is the Nagasena that we see before us? It is a falsehood that Your Reverence has spoken, an untruth!"

And the venerable Nagasena said to Milinda the king: "You, sire, have   30 been brought up in great luxury, as beseems your noble birth. If you were to walk [at noon] on the hot and sandy ground, trampling under foot the gritty, gravelly grains of the hard sand, your feet would hurt you. And as your body would be in pain, your mind would be disturbed and you would experience a sense of bodily suffering. How then did you come, on foot or in a chariot?"

"I did not come, sir, on foot; I came in a carriage."   31

"Then if you came, sire, in a carriage, explain to me what that is. Is it the   32
pole that is the chariot?"

"I did not say that."   33

"Is it the axle that is the chariot?"   34

"Certainly not."   35

"Is it the wheels, or the framework, or the ropes, or the yoke, or the spokes   36
of the wheels, or the goad, that are the chariot?"

And to all these he still answered no.   37

"Then is it all these parts of it that are the chariot?"   38

"No, sir."   39

"But is there anything outside them that is the chariot?"   40

And still he answered no.   41

"Then thus, ask as I may, I can discover no chariot. Chariot is a mere empty   42
sound. What then is the chariot you say you came in? It is a falsehood that Your Majesty has spoken, an untruth! There is no such thing as a chariot! You are king over all India, a mighty monarch. Of whom then are you afraid, that you speak untruth?"

And he called upon the Yonakas and the brethren to witness, saying: 43
"Milinda the king here has said that he came by carriage. But when asked in that case to explain what the carriage was, he is unable to establish what he averred. Is it possible to approve him in that?"

When he had thus spoken, the five hundred Yonakas shouted their   44
applause, and said to the king: "Now let Your Majesty get out of that if you can!"

And Milinda the king replied to Nagasena and said: "I have spoken no   45
untruth, reverend sir. It is on account of its having all these things—the pole, and the axle, the wheels, and the framework, the ropes, the yoke, the spokes, and the goad—that it comes under the generally understood term, the designation in common use, of 'chariot.'"

"Very good! Your Majesty has rightly grasped the meaning of 'chariot.' And   46
just even so it is on account of all those things you questioned me about—the thirty-two kinds of organic matter in a human body and the five constituent elements of being[13]—that I come under the generally understood term, the designation in common use, of 'Nagasena.' For it was said, sire, by [the nun] Vajira in the presence of the Blessed One:[14] 'Just as it is by . . . the coexistence of its var-

ious parts that the word *chariot* is used, just so is it that, when the skandhas are there, we talk of a *being*.'"

"Most wonderful, Nagasena, and most strange. Well has the puzzle put to   47
you—most difficult though it was—been solved. Were the Buddha himself here, he would approve your answer. Well done, well done, Nagasena!". . .

The king said: "Nagasena, is there anyone who, after death, is not reindividual-   48
ized?" [15]

> "Some are, and some not."   49
>
> "Who are they?"   50
>
> "A sinful being is reindividualized, a sinless one is not."   51
>
> "Will you be reindividualized?"   52
>
> "If when I die, I die with craving for existence in my heart, yes; but if not,   53
> no."
>
> "Very good, Nagasena!"   54

The king said: "Nagasena, he who escapes reindividualization—is it by reason-   55
ing that he escapes it?"

> "By reasoning, your Majesty, and by wisdom, and by other good qualities."   56
>
> "But are not reasoning and wisdom surely much the same?"   57
>
> "Certainly not. Reasoning is one thing, wisdom another. Sheep and goats,   58
> oxen and buffaloes, camels and asses have reasoning, but wisdom they have not."
>
> "Well put, Nagasena!"   59

The king said: "What is the characteristic mark of reasoning, and what of wis-   60
dom?"

> "Reasoning has always comprehension as its mark; but wisdom has cutting   61
> off."
>
> "But how is comprehension the characteristic of reasoning, and cutting off   62
> of wisdom? Give me an illustration."
>
> "Do you [know about] barley reapers?"   63
>
> "Yes, certainly."   64
>
> "How do they reap the barley?"   65
>
> "With the left hand they grasp the barley into a bunch; and taking the sick-   66
> le into the right hand, they cut it off with that."

"Just so, O king, does the recluse by his thinking grasp his mind, and by his   67
wisdom cut off his failings. In this way is it that comprehension is the characteristic of reasoning, but cutting off of wisdom."

"Well put, Nagasena!"   68

The king said: "When you said just now, 'and by other good qualities,' to which   69
did you refer?"

"Good conduct, great king, and faith, perseverance, mindfulness, and med-   70
itation." . . .

Chapter 2

The king said: "He who is reborn, Nagasena, does he remain the same or become   71
another?"

"Neither the same nor another."   72

"Give me an illustration."   73

"Now what do you think, O king? You were once a baby, a tender thing and   74
small in size, lying flat on your back. Was that the same as you who are now
grown up?"

"No. That child was one; I am another."   75

"If you are not that child, it will follow that you have had neither mother   76
nor father nor teacher. You cannot have been taught either learning or behavior
or wisdom. What, great king! Is the mother of the embryo in the first stage different from the mother of the embryo in the second stage, or the third, or the
fourth? Is the mother of the baby a different person from the mother of the
grown-up man? Is the person who goes to school one, and, when he has finished
his schooling, another? Is it one who commits a crime, another who is punished
by having his hands or feet cut off?"

"Certainly not. But what would you, sir, say to that?"   77

The Elder[16] replied: "I should say that I am the same person, now that I am   78
grown up, as I was when I was a tender tiny baby, flat on my back. For all these
states are included in one by means of this body."

"Give me an illustration."   79

"Suppose a man, O king, were to light a lamp. Would it burn the night   80
through?"

"Yes, it might do so."   81

"Now, is it the same flame that burns in the first watch of the night, sir, and   82
in the second?"

"No."　83

"Or the same that burns in the second watch and in the third?"　84

"No."　85

"Then is there one lamp in the first watch, and another in the second, and　86
another in the third?"

"No. The light comes from the same lamp all the night through."　87

"Just so, O king, is the continuity of a person or thing maintained. One　88
comes into being, another passes away; and the rebirth is, as it were, simultaneous. Thus neither as the same nor as another does a man go on to the last phase
of his self-consciousness."

"Give me a further illustration."　89

"It is like milk which, when once taken from the cow, turns, after a lapse　90
of time, first to curds, and then from curds to butter, and then from butter to
ghee. Now would it be right to say that the milk was the same thing as the curds,
or the butter, or the ghee?"

"Certainly not; but they are produced out of it."　91

"Just so, O king, is the continuity of a person or thing maintained. One　92
comes into being, another passes away; and the rebirth is, as it were, simultaneous. Thus neither as the same nor as another does a man go on to the last phase
of his self-consciousness."

"Well put, Nagasena!" . . .　93

The king said: "What is it, Nagasena, that is reborn?"　94

"Name-and-form is reborn."　95

"What, is it this same name-and-form that is reborn?"　96

"No. But by this name-and-form deeds are done, good or evil—and by　97
these deeds another name-and-form is reborn."

"If that be so, sir, would not the new being be released from its evil karma?"　98

The Elder replied: "Yes, if it were not reborn. But just because it is reborn,　99
O king, it is therefore not released from its evil karma."

"Give me an illustration."　100

"Suppose, O king, some man were to steal a mango from another man, and　101
the owner of the mango were to seize him, bring him before the king, and charge
him with the crime. And suppose the thief were to say: 'Your Majesty, I have not
taken away this man's mangoes. Those that he put in the ground are different
from the ones I took. I do not deserve to be punished.' How then? Would he be
guilty?"

"Certainly, sir. He would deserve to be punished."   102

"But on what grounds?"   103

"Because, in spite of whatever he may say, he would be guilty in respect to 104
the last mango which resulted from the first one."

"Just so, great king, deeds good or evil are done by this name-andform and 105
another is reborn. But that other is not thereby released from its deeds."

"Give me a further illustration."   106

"It is like rice or sugar so stolen, of which the same might be said as of the 107
mango. Or it is like the fire which a man in the cold season might kindle and,
when he had warmed himself, leave still burning, and go away. Then if that fire
were to set another man's field on fire, and the owner of the field were to seize
him and bring him before the king and charge him with the injury, and he were
to say: 'Your Majesty, it was not I who set this man's field on fire. The fire I left
burning was a different one from that which burned his field. I am not guilty.
Now would the man, O king, be guilty?"

"Certainly, sir."   108

"But why?"   109

"Because, in spite of whatever he might say, he would be guilty in respect 110
to the subsequent fire that resulted from the previous one."

"Just so, great king, deeds good or evil are done by this name-andform and 111
another is reborn. But that other is not thereby released from its deeds." . . .

"Very good, Nagasena!" . . .   112

The king said: "You were talking just now of name-and-form. What does 'name' 113
mean in that expression, and what 'form'?"

"Whatever is gross therein, that is form; whatever is subtle, mental, that is 114
name."

"Why is it, Nagasena, that name is not reborn separately, or form separate- 115
ly?"

"These conditions, great king, are connected one with the other, and 116
spring into being together."

"Give me an illustration."   117

"As a hen, great king, would not [produce] a yolk or an eggshell separately, 118
but both would arise in one (the two being intimately dependent one on the
other)—just so, if there were no name, there would be no form. What is meant
by 'name' in 'name-and-form' is intimately dependent on what is meant by

'form'; they spring up together. And this is, through time immemorial, their nature."

"You are ready, Nagasena, in reply." . . .   119

Book III. The Removal of Difficulties
Chapter 4

The king said: "Why is it, Nagasena, that all men are not alike, but some are 120 short-lived and some long-lived, some sickly and some healthy, some ugly and some beautiful, some without influence and some of great power, some poor and some wealthy, some lowborn and some highborn, some stupid and some wise?"

The Elder replied: "Why is it that all vegetables are not alike, but some 121 sour, some salty, some acidic, some astringent, and some sweet?"

"I fancy, sir, it is because they come from different kinds of seeds."   122

"And just so, great king, are the differences you have mentioned among 123 men to be explained. For it has been said by the Blessed One: 'Beings, O Brahmans, have each their own karma, are inheritors of karma, belong to the tribe of their karma, are relatives by karma, have each their karma as their protecting overlord. It is karma that divides them up into low and high and the like divisions."

"Very good, Nagasena!" . . .   124

The king said: "Is cessation nirvana?"[17]   125

"Yes, your Majesty."   126

"How is that, Nagasena?"   127

"All foolish individuals, O king, take pleasure in the senses and in the 128 objects of sense, find delight in them, continue to cleave to them. Hence are they carried down by that flood [of human passions]. They are not set free from birth, old age, and death, from grief, lamentation, pain, sorrow, and despair— they are not set free, I say, from suffering. But the wise individual, O king, the disciple of the noble ones, neither takes pleasure in those things, nor finds delight in them, nor continues cleaving to them. And inasmuch as he does not, in him craving ceases; and by the cessation of craving, grasping ceases; and by the cessation of grasping, becoming ceases; and when becoming has ceased, birth ceases; and with its cessation birth, old age, and death, grief, lamentation, pain, sorrow, and despair cease to exist. Thus is the cessation brought about the end of all that aggregation of pain. Thus is it that cessation is nirvana."

"Very good, Nagasena!"   129

The king said: "Venerable Nagasena, do all men receive nirvana?"   130
    "Not all, O king. But he who walks righteously, who admits those condi- 131
tions which ought to be admitted, perceives clearly those conditions which
ought to be perceived clearly, abandons those conditions which ought to be
abandoned, practices himself in those conditions which ought to be practiced,
realizes those conditions which ought to be realized —he receives nirvana."
    "Very good, Nagasena!"   132

The king said: "Venerable Nagasena, does he who does not receive nirvana 133
know how happy a state nirvana is?"
    "Yes, he knows it."   134
    "But how can he know that without receiving nirvana?"   135
    "Now what do you think, O king? Do those whose hands and feet have not 136
been cut off know how sad a thing it is to have them cut off?"
    "Yes, sir, that they know."   137
    "But how do they know it?"   138
    "By hearing the sound of the lamentation of those whose hands and feet 139
have been cut off, they know it."
    "Just so, great king, it is by hearing the glad words of those who have seen 140
nirvana, that they who have not received it know how happy a state it is."
    "Very good, Nagasena!"   141

Chapter 5
. . . The king said: "Where there is no transmigration, Nagasena, can there be 142
rebirth?"
    "Yes, there can."   143
    "But how can that be? Give me an illustration."   144
    "Suppose a man, O king, were to light a lamp from another lamp. Can it 145
be said that the one lamp transmigrates from, or to, the other?"
    "Certainly not."   146
    "Just so, great king, is rebirth without transmigration."   147
    "Give me a further illustration."   148
    "Do you recollect, great king, having learned, when you were a boy, some 149
verse or other from your teacher?"
    "Yes, I recollect that."   150

"Well then, did that verse transmigrate from your teacher?"   151

"Certainly not."   152

"Just so, great king, is rebirth without transmigration."   153

"Very good, Nagasena!" . . .   154

Chapter 6

The king said: "Is the body, Nagasena, dear to you recluses?"   155

"No, we do not love the body."   156

"Then why do you nourish it and lavish attention upon it?"   157

"In all the times and places, O king, that you have gone down to battle, did 158
you never get wounded by an arrow?"

"Yes, that has happened to me."   159

"In such cases, O king, is not the wound anointed with salve, smeared with 160
oil, and bound up in a bandage?"

"Yes, such things are done to it."   161

"What then? Is the wound dear to you, that you treat it so tenderly and lav- 162
ish such attention upon it?"

"No, it is not dear to me in spite of all that which is done that the flesh may 163
grow again."

"Just so, great king, with the recluses and the body. Without cleaving to it, 164
they bear the body about for the sake of righteousness of life. The body, O king,
has been declared by the Blessed One to be like a wound. And therefore merely
as a sore—without cleaving to it—do the recluses bear the body about. For it has
been said by the Blessed One:

Covered with clammy skin, an impure thing and foul,   165
Nine-apertured, it oozes like a sore,

"Well answered, Nagasena!" . . .

The king said: "When you speak of transmigration, Nagasena, what does 166
that mean?"

"A being born here, O king, dies here. Having died here, it springs up else- 167
where. Having been born there, there it dies. Having died there, it springs up
elsewhere. That is what is meant by transmigration."

"Give me an illustration."   168

"It is like the case of a man who, after eating a mango, should set the seed   169
in the ground. From that a great tree would be produced and give fruit. And
there would be no end to the succession, in that way, of mango trees."

"Very good, Nagasena!" . . .   170

Book IV. The Solving of Dilemmas
Chapter 6 . . .

"Venerable Nagasena, you say: 'There is one kind of pain only which an arahant   171
suffers—bodily pain, that is, and not mental pain.' How is this, Nagasena? The
arahant keeps his mind going by means of the body. Has the arahant no lordship,
no mastery, no power over the body?"

"No, he has not, O king."   172

"That, sir, is not right—that over the body, by which he keeps his mind   173
going, he should have neither lordship nor mastery nor power. Even a bird, sir, is
lord and master and ruler over the nest in which he dwells."

"There are ten qualities, O king, inherent in the body, which run after it,   174
as it were, and accompany it from existence to existence. And what are the ten?
Cold and heat, hunger and thirst, the necessity of voiding excreta, fatigue and
sleepiness, old age, disease, and death. And in respect to these, the arahant is
without lordship, without mastery, without power."

"Venerable Nagasena, what is the reason why the commands of the ara-   175
hant have no power over his body, and he has no mastery over it? Tell me that."

"Just, O king, as whatever beings are dependent on the land walk, dwell,   176
and carry on their business in dependence upon it. But do their commands have
force, does their mastery extend over it?"

"Certainly not, sir!"   177

"Just so, O king, the arahant keeps his mind going through the body. And   178
yet his commands have no authority over it, nor power."

"Venerable Nagasena, why is it that the ordinary man suffers both bodily   179
and mental pain?"

"By reason, O king, of the untrained state of his mind. Just, O king, as an   180
ox when trembling with starvation might be tied up with a weak and fragile and
tiny rope of grass or creeper. But if the ox were excited, then would he escape,
dragging the fastening with him. Just so, O king, when pain comes upon him
whose mind is untrained, then is his mind excited, and the mind so excited
bends his body this way and that and makes it grovel on the ground. And he,

being thus untrained in mind, trembles and cries and gives forth terrible groans. This is why the ordinary man, O king, suffers pain as well in body as in mind."

"Then why, sir, does the arahant only suffer one kind of pain—bodily, that   181 is, and not mental?"

"The mind of the arahant, O king, is trained, well practiced, tamed,   182 brought into subjection, and obedient, and it hearkens to his word. When affected with feelings of pain, he grasps firmly the idea of the impermanence of all things, so ties his mind, as it were, to the post of contemplation. And his mind, bound to the post of contemplation, remains unmoved, unshaken, becomes steadfast, wanders not—though his body meanwhile may bend this way and that and roll in agony by the disturbing influence of the pain. This is why it is only one kind of pain that the arahant suffers—bodily pain, that is, and not mental."

"Venerable Nagasena, that verily is a most marvelous thing that, when the   183 body is trembling, the mind should not be shaken. Give me a reason for that."

"Suppose, O king, there were a noble tree, mighty in trunk and branches   184 and leaves. When agitated by the force of the wind, its branches should wave. Would the trunk also move?"

"Certainly not, sir."   185

"Well, O king, the mind of the arahant is as the trunk of that noble tree."   186

"Most wonderful, Nagasena, and most strange! Never before have I seen a   187 lamp of the law that burned so brightly through all time." . . .

Chapter 7

"Venerable Nagasena, there are found beings in the world who have come into   188 existence through karma, others who are the result of a cause, and others produced by [forces of nature]. Tell me, is there anything that does not fall under one of these three heads?"

"There are two such things, O king. And what are the two? Space, O king,   189 and nirvana."

"Now do not spoil the word of the Conqueror,[18] Nagasena, nor answer a   190 question without knowing what you say."

"What, pray, is it I have said, O king, that you should address me thus?"   191

"Venerable Nagasena, what you said is right in respect to space. But with   192 hundreds of reasons did the Blessed One proclaim to his disciples the way to the realization of nirvana. And yet you say that nirvana is not the result of any cause!"

"No doubt, O king, the Blessed One gave hundreds of reasons for our   193
entering on the way to the realization of nirvana. But he never told us of a cause
out of which nirvana could be said to be produced."

"Now in this, Nagasena, we have passed from darkness into greater dark-   194
ness, from a jungle into a denser jungle, from a thicket into a deeper thicket—
inasmuch as you say there is a cause for the realization of nirvana, but no cause
from which it can arise. If, Nagasena, there be a cause of the realization of nirvana, then we must expect to find a cause of the origin of nirvana. Just as,
Nagasena, because the son has a father, therefore, we ought to expect that that
father had a father—or because the pupil has a teacher, therefore we ought to
expect that the teacher had a teacher—or because the plant came from a seed,
therefore we ought to expect that the seed too had come from a seed—so,
Nagasena, if there be a reason for the realization of nirvana, we ought to expect
that there is a reason too for its origin—just as, if we saw the top of a tree or of a
creeper, we should conclude that it had a middle part and a root."

"Nirvana, O king, is unproducible, and no cause for its origin has been   195
declared."

"Come now, Nagasena, give me a reason for this. Convince me by argu-   196
ment, so that I may know how it is that, while there is a cause that will bring
about the realization of nirvana, there is no cause that will bring about nirvana
itself."

"Then, O king, give ear attentively, and listen well, and I will tell you what   197
the reason is. Could a man, O king, by his ordinary power go up from here to a
Himalaya, the king of mountains?"

"Yes, sir, he could."   198

"But could a man, by his ordinary power, bring a Himalaya mountain   199
here?"

"Certainly not, sir."   200

"Well, therefore is it that while a cause for the realization of nirvana can be   201
declared, the cause of its origin cannot. And could a man, O king, by his ordinary power cross over the great ocean in a ship, and so go to the further shore of
it?"

"Yes, sir, he could."   202

"But could a man by his ordinary power bring the further shore of the   203
ocean here?"

"Certainly not, sir."   204

"Well, so is it that while a cause for the realization of nirvana can be 205 declared, the cause of its origin cannot. And why not? Because nirvana is not put together of any qualities."

"What, sir? Is it not put together?" 206

"No, O king. It is uncompounded, not made of anything. Of nirvana, O 207 king, it cannot be said that it has been produced, or not been produced, or can be produced; that it is past or future or present; that it is perceptible by the eye or the ear or the nose or the tongue or the sense of touch."

"But if so, Nagasena, then you are only showing us how nirvana is a condi- 208 tion that does not exist. There can be no such thing as nirvana."

"Nirvana exists, O king. And it is perceptible to the mind. By means of his 209 pure heart—refined and straight, free from the obstacles,19 free from low crav- ings—the disciple of the noble ones who has fully attained can see nirvana."

"Then what, sir, is nirvana—such a nirvana, I mean, as can be explained 210 by similes? Convince me by argument, as far as the fact of its existence can be explained by similes."

"Is there such a thing, O king, as wind?" 211

"Yes, of course." 212

"Show it to me then, I pray you, O king—whether by its color or its form, 213 whether as thin or thick, short or long."

"But wind, Nagasena, cannot be pointed out in that way. It is not of such 214 a nature that it can be taken into the hand or squeezed. But it exists all the same."

"If you can't show me the wind, then there can't be such a thing." 215

"But I know there is, Nagasena. I am convinced that wind exists, though I 216 cannot show it to you."

"Well, just so, O king, does Nirvana exist, though it cannot be shown to 217 you in color or in form."

"Very good, Nagasena! That is so, and I accept it as you say." 218

"Venerable Nagasena, what are they who are said, in this connection, to be 219 karma-born, and cause-born, and [natural-forces]-born? And what is it that is none of these?"

"All beings, O king, that are conscious, are karma-born. Fire, and all things 220 growing out of seeds,20 are cause-born. The earth, and the hills, water, and wind—all these are [natural-forces]-born. Space and nirvana exist independent- ly of karma, cause, and [forces of nature]. Of nirvana, O king, it cannot be said that it is karma-born or cause-born or [naturalforces]- born; that it has been or has not been or can be produced; that it is past or future or present; that it is perceptible by the eye or the nose or the ear or the tongue or the sense of touch. But it is perceptible, O king, by the mind. By means of his pure heart—refined and straight, free from the obstacles, free from low cravings—the disciple of the noble ones who has fully attained can see nirvana."

"Well has this delightful puzzle, venerable Nagasena, been examined into,   221 cleared of doubt, brought into certitude. My perplexity has been put to an end as soon as I consulted you, O best of the best of the leaders of schools!" . . .

Chapter 8

. . . "Venerable Nagasena, I will grant you that nirvana is bliss unalloyed, and yet   222 that is impossible to make clear, either by simile or explanation, by reason or by argument, either its form or its figure, either its duration or its size. But is there no quality of nirvana which is inherent also in other things, and is such that it can be made evident by metaphor?"

"Though there is nothing as to its form which can be so explained, there is   223 something, O king, as to its qualities which can."

"O happy word, Nagasena! Speak then, quickly, that I may have an expla-   224 nation of even one point in the characteristics of nirvana. Appease the fever of my heart. Allay it by the cool sweet breezes of your words."

"There is one quality of the lotus, O king, inherent in nirvana, and two   225 qualities of water, and three of medicine." . . .

"Venerable Nagasena, that one quality of the lotus which you said was   226 inherent in nirvana—which is that?"

"As the lotus, O king, is untarnished by the water,[21] so is nirvana untar-   227 nished by any evil dispositions. This is the one quality of the lotus inherent in nirvana."

"Venerable Nagasena, those two qualities of water which you said were   228 inherent in nirvana—which are they?"

"As water, O king, is cool and assuages heat, so also is nirvana cool and   229 assuages the fever arising from all evil dispositions. This is the first quality of water inherent in nirvana. And again, O king, as water allays the thirst of men and beasts when they are exhausted, anxious, craving for drink, and tormented by thirst—so does nirvana allay the thirst of the craving after lusts, the craving after future life, and the craving after worldly prosperity. This is the second quality of water inherent in nirvana."

"Venerable Nagasena, those three qualities of medicine, which you said 230 were inherent in nirvana—which are they?"

"As medicine, O king, is the refuge of beings tormented by poison, so is nir- 231 vana the refuge of beings tormented with the poison of evil dispositions. This is the first quality of medicine inherent in nirvana. And again, O king, as medicine puts an end to diseases, so does nirvana put an end to griefs. This is the second quality of medicine inherent in nirvana. And again, O king, as medicine is ambrosia,[22] so also is nirvana ambrosia. This is the third quality of medicine inherent in nirvana." . . .

. . . "Venerable Nagasena, does there exist the spot—in the direction of the east, 232 the south, the west, or the north; either above or below or on the horizon— where nirvana is stored up?" . . .

"There is no spot, O king, where nirvana is [stored up], and yet nirvana *is*— 233 and he who orders his life right will, by careful attention, realize nirvana. Just so, fire exists, and yet there is no place where fire is stored up. But if a man rubs two sticks together the fire comes. Just so, O king, nirvana exists, though there is no spot where it is stored up—and he who orders his life aright will, by careful atten- tion, realize nirvana." . . .

"Venerable Nagasena, let it be granted that there is no place where nirvana 234 is stored up. But is there any place on which a man may stand and, ordering his life aright, realize nirvana?"

"Yes, O king, there is such a place."   235

"Which then, Nagasena, is that place?"   236

"Virtue, O king, is the place. For if grounded in virtue, and careful in atten- 237 tion—whether in the land of the Scythians or the Greeks, whether in China or Tartary, whether in Alexandria[23] or in Nikumba, whether in Benares or in Kosala, whether in Kashmir or in Gandhara, whether on a mountaintop or in the highest heavens—wheresoever he may be, the man who orders his life aright will realize nirvana. O king, as the man who has eyes, wherever he may be . . . will be able to behold the expanse of heaven and to see the horizon facing him— just so, O king, will he who orders his conduct aright and is careful in attention . . . wheresoever he may be, attain to the realization of nirvana."

"Very good, Nagasena!"   238

Notes

1. *Yonakas:* Ionian Greeks who settled in Bactria, a region northeast of India. [D.C.A., ed.]
2. *Brahmans:* Hindus of the highest, priestly caste. [D.C.A.]
3. *Samanas:* wandering ascetics. [D.C.A.]
4. *Order:* the Order of Buddhist monks. [D.C.A.]
5. *arahants:* perfected ones. [D.C.A.]
6. Devamantiya is an attendant of King Milinda. [D.C.A.]
7. The name itself, which means "chief of the Naga snakes," is terrible enough, especially as the Nagas were looked on as supernatural beings. But it is no doubt also intended that the king had heard of his fame. [T.W.R.D., trans.]
8. These are the names of Hindu gods. [D.C.A.]
9. Brahma is the creator god of Hinduism. [D.C.A.]
10. *permanent individuality (puggala):* something unchanging that makes someone the same, identical person through changes in time; permanent self. *Puggala* is similar to what other Buddhist scriptures call *atta* (Pali form; *atman* in Sanskrit). [D.C.A.]
11. *karma:* literally, "action, deed"; the force generated by a person's good or evil actions, which carries over into the person's next incarnation. [D.C.A.]
12. *skandhas:* literally, "bundles"; the five aggregates of ever-changing forces (outward form, sensations, ideas, elements of character, and consciousness—which Nagesena has just enumerated) that contain nothing permanent. [D.C.A.]
13. *five constituent elements of being:* the five skandhas. [D.C.A.]
14. *the Blessed One:* a title of the Buddha. [D.C.A.]
15. *reindividualized:* reincarnated. [D.C.A.]
16. *The Elder:* Nagesena. [D.C.A.]
17. *nirvana:* literally, "extinction"; the complete extinction of desire, which produces permanent liberation from suffering. [D.C.A.]
18. *the Conqueror:* the Buddha. [D.C.A.]
19. *the obstacles:* namely, lust, malice, pride, sloth, and doubt. [T.W.R.D.]
20. *things growing out of seeds:* things originating from a preexisting material being. [D.C.A.]
21. That is, no drop of water adheres to the lotus, though it is surrounded by water and water may fall on it. [T.W.R.D.]
22. *ambrosia (amata):* food of the gods. [D.C.A.]
23. *Alexandria:* a city in Asia, on the Indus River (not the city in Egypt with the same name). [D.C.A., after T.W.R.D.]

Kwasi Wiredu, a professor of philosophy at the University of South Florida, was formerly professor and head of the Department of Philosophy at the University of Ghana. Educated at the universities of Ghana and Oxford, he has been a visiting professor at the University of California, Los Angeles, and has received fellowships from the Woodrow wilson Center and the National Humanities Center. His publications are primarily in the areas of philosophy of logic and African philosophy and includes his book, *Philosophy and an African Culture* (Cambridge University Press, 1980). In the selection that follows, he explains that the word *religion* may not be properly applicable to most traditional African thought.

Religion from an African Perspective

Kwasi Wiredu

Two assumptions that may safely be made about the human species are one, that the   1
entire race shares some fundamental categories and criteria of thought in common and two, that, nevertheless, there are some very deep disparities among the different tribes of humankind in regard to their modes of conceptualization in some sensitive areas of thought. The first accounts for the possibility of communication among different peoples, the second for the difficulties and complications that not infrequently beset that interaction.

Is religion a field of convergence or divergence of though among the people   2
and cultures of the world? The obvious answer, in alignment with our opening reflection, is that religion is both. There is also an obvious question: What are the specifics? But here an obvious answer is unavailable, at lest, as concerns Africa vis-à-vis, for instance, the West. In fact, it is not at all obvious in what sense the English word "religion" is applicable to any aspect of African life and thought.

This last remark, of course, amounts to discounting the frequent affirmations,   3
in the literature of African studies, of the immanent religiosity of the African mind. What exactly are the features of life and thought that are appealed to in that characterization? In investigating this issue I am going to have to be rather particularistic. I am going to have particular, though not exclusive, recourse to the Akans of West africa, for the considerations to be adduced pre-suppose a level of cultural and linguistic insight to which I cannot pretend in regard to any African peoples except that particular ethnic group which I know through birth, upbringing, reading and

deliberate reflective observation. This particularism, has, at least, the logical potential of all counter-examples against universal claims.

Let us return to the word "religion". It has been suggested, even by some   4
authors by whose reckoning African life is full of religion, that there is no word in
many African languages which translates this word.[1] Whether this is true of all
African languages or not I do not know, but it is certainly true of Akan, in the traditional use of that language, that is. Not only is there no single word for religion but
there is also no periphrastic equivalent. There is, indeed, the word "Anyamesom"
which many translators might be tempted to proffer. But the temptation ought to be
resisted. The word is a Christian invention by which the missionaries distinguished,
in Akan speech, between their own religion and what they perceived to be the religion of the indigenous "pagans". Thus, it means, not religion, pure and simple, but
Christianity. Ironically, in this usage the Christian missionaries were constrained by
linguistic exigencies to adapt a word which the Akans use for the Supreme Being.
"Onyame" is one among several names for the Supreme Being in Akan. Another
very frequent one is "Onyankopon" which literally means The Being That Is Alone
Great, in other words, That Than Which a Greater Cannot Be Conceived (with
apologies to Saint Anselm). The remaining component of the word "Anyamesom"
is "som" which means "to serve", so that the whole word means, literally, "the service of the Supreme Being" or, if you follow Christian methods of translation, "the
service of God". In turn, this was taken to mean the worship of God.

By what of a designation for what they saw as indigenous religion, the   5
Christians used the word "Abosomsom". This is a combination of two words
"Obosom" and "Som". Etymologically, "obsom" means the service of stones. Thus,
literally, the barbarism means the service of stone service! Still, it served its Christian
purpose. But why stones? That is an allusion to the fact that the Akans traditionally believe that various objects, such as certain special rocks, trees and rivers, are the
abode of extra-human forces and being of assorted grades.

Having gathered from the foregoing remarks that the Akans, in fact, believe in   6
the existence of a supreme being and a variety of extra-human forces and being, the
reader might be disposed to wonder why I make any issue of the sense in which "religion" might be applied to any aspect of Akan culture. If so, let him or her attend to
the following considerations. To begin with, religion, however it is defined, involves
a certain kind of attitude. If a given religion postulates a supra-human supreme
being, that belief must, on any common showing, necessarily be joined to an attitude
not only of unconditional reverence but also of worship. Some will go as far as to
insist that this worshipful attitude will have to be given practical expression through

definite rituals, especially if the being in question is supposed to be the determiner or controller of human destiny. There is a further condition of the utmost importance; it is one which introduces an ethical dimension into the definition. Essential to any religion in the primary sense is a conception of moral uprightness. If it involves supra-human beliefs, the relevant ethic will be based logically or psychologically on the "supra" being or beings concerned. Typically, but by no means invariably, a religion will have a social framework. In that case, it will have organized hortatory and other procedures for instilling or revivifying the commitment to moral virtue.

Consider, now, the character of the Akan belief in the Supreme Being. There   7
is, indeed, generally among the Akans a confirmed attitude of unconditional reverence for Onyankopon, the Supreme Being. However, there is, most assuredly, no attitude or ritual of worship directed to that being either at a social or an individual level. They regard Him as good, wise and powerful in the highest. He is the determiner of human destiny as of everything else. But in all this they see no rational for worship. Neither is the akan conception or practice of morality based logically or even psychologically on the belief of the Supreme Being. Being good in the highest, He disapproves of evil; but, to the Akan mind, the reason why people should not do evil is not because he disapproves of it but rather because it is contrary to human well-being, which is why He disapproves of it, in the first place.[2] The early European visitors to Africa, especially the missionaries, were quick to notice the absence of any worship of God[3] among the Akans and various other African peoples. They were hardly less struck by the fact that god was not the foundation of Akan morals. On both grounds they deduced a spiritual and intellectual immaturity in the African. Notice the workings here of a facile universalism. It seems to have been assumed that belief in God must move every sound mind to worship. Perhaps, even now, such an assumption might sound plausible to many Western ears. It is, of course, not likely in this day and age that many can be found to suppose that any person of a sound mind must necessarily embrace belief in God. But given the prevailing tendencies in Western and even some non-Western cultures, it might be tempting to think that if people believe in God, then the natural thing for them to do is to worship Him. Yet, consider the notion of a perfect being. Why would he (she, it) need to be worshiped? What would be the point of it? It is well-known that the Judeo-Christian God *jealously* demands to be worshiped—witness The Ten Commandments—but, from an Akan point of view,[4] such clamoring for attention must be paradoxical in the extreme in a perfect being, and I confess to being an unreconstructed Akan in this regard.

There is, in their resort to the word "Abosomsom" (the worship of stones) to   8
name what they took to be Akan religion, an odd manifestation of the special importance that the Christian missionaries attached to worship. Having seen that the
Akans did not worship God, they were keen to find out what it was that they worshiped, for surely a whole people must worship something. They quickly settled on
the class of what I have called extra-human forces and beings, which, as I have
already hinted, is a feature of the Akan worldview. There is, indeed, a great variety
of such entities postulated in the Akan ontology (as in any other African ontology
that I know of). Some are relatively person-like; others somewhat automatic in their
operation. The former can, it is believed, be communicated with through some special procedures, and are credited with a moral sense. Commonly, a being of this sort
would be believed to be localized at a household "shrine" from where it would protect the given group from evil forces. More person-like still are the ancestors who are
thought to live in a realm closely linked with the world of the living.

Actually, the ancestors are conceived of as persons who continue to be mem-   9
bers of their pre-mortem families, watching over their affairs and generally helping
them. They are regarded as persons, but not as mortal persons; for they have tasted
death and transcended it. Accordingly, they are considered to be more irreversibly
moral than any living mortal. All these attributes are taken to entitle the ancestors
to genuine reverence. Not quite the same deference is accorded to the first group of
beings, but in view of their presumed power to promote human well-being, they are
approached with considerable respect.

More types of extra-human forces and beings are spoken of in the Akan ontol-   10
ogy than we have mentioned, but these are among the most relevant, and they will
suffice for the impending point; which is this: The Akan attitude to the beings in
question bears closer analogy to secular esteem than religious worship. The reverence given to the ancestors is only a higher degree of the respect that in Akan society is considered to be due to the earthly elders. For all their post-mortem ontolog-
ic transformation, the ancestors are, let it be repeated, regarded as members of their
families. The libations that are poured to them on a ceremonial and other important
occasions are simply invitations to them to come and participate in family events.
Moreover, everybody hopes eventually to become an ancestor, but this is not seen as
a craving for self-apotheosis. Ancestorship is simply the crowning phase of human
existence.

The non-religious character of the Akan attitude to the non-ancestral forces is   11
even more clear. Real religious devotion to a being must be unconditional. But that
is the one thing that the Akan approach to those beings is not; it is purely utilitari-

an: if they bring help, praise be to them, and other beings besides. On the other hand, if they fail, particularly if that happens consistently, they can fall into disrepute or worse. K. A. Busia and J. B. Danquah, the two most celebrated expositors of Akan thought, have borne unambiguous and, as it seems to me, reliable testimony to this fact. Busia says, "The gods are treated with respect if they deliver the goods, and with contempt if they fail . . . .Attitudes to [the gods] depend upon their success, and vary from healthy respect to sneering contempt."[5] Danquah goes somewhat further: ". . . the general tendency is to sneer at and ridicule the fetish and its priest',[6] There is an even more radical consideration. According to popular belief, these "gods" are capable of dying. Of a "god" who is finished the Akans say *nano atro*, that is, its powers have become totally blunted. This may happen through unknown causes, but it may also happen through human design. People can cause the demise of "god" simply by permanently depriving it of attention. Or, for more rapid results, apply an antithetical substance to its "shrine". Such antidotes are known for at least some of thee "gods", according to popular belief. It ought, perhaps, to be emphasized that in this matter the thought is not that a "god" has betaken itself elsewhere, but rather that it has ceased to be a force to be reckoned with at all. In light of all this, it is somewhat of a hyperbole to call the procedures designed for establishing satisfactory relations with the beings in question religious worship.

The considerations rehearsed so far should be enough, I think, to suggest the   12 need for a review of the enthusiastic, not to say indiscriminate, attributions of religiosity to African peoples. But there are deeper reasons of the same significance. And in studying them we will see the role which the hasty universalization of certain Western categories of though have played in the formation of the misapprehensions under scrutiny. Take, then, the Akan belief in the Supreme Being. In English discourse about Akan thought the word "God" is routinely used to refer to this being. This has led, or has been due, to the supposition that both the Akans and the Christians are talking of the same being when they speak of the Supreme Being, notwithstanding any divergences of cultural perception. This supposed identity of reference has come in handy to Christianized Africans wishing to demonstrate that they can profess Christianity and still remain basically true to their indigenous religions: There is, after all, only one god, and we are all trying to reach Him.[7]

Yet, in spite of any apparent similarities, such as the postulation of That Than   13 Which a Greater Cannot Be Conceived in both traditions of thought, the Akan supreme being is profoundly different from the Christian one. the Christian God is a creator of the world out of nothing. In further philosophical characterization, He is said to be transcendent, supernatural and spiritual in the sense of immaterial, non-physical. In radical contrast, the Akan supreme being is a kind of cosmic architect, a fashioner of the world order, who occupies the apex of the same hierarchy of being which accommodates, in its intermediate ranges, the ancestors and living mortals and, in its lower reaches, animals, plants and inanimate objects. This universe of being is ontologically homogenous. In other words, everything that exists exists in exactly the same sense as everything else. And this sense is empirical, broadly speaking. In the Akan language to exist is to "wo ho" which, in literal translation, means to be at some place. There is no equivalent, in Akan, of the existential "to be" or "is" of English, and there is no way of pretending in that medium to be speaking of the existence of something which is not in space. This locative connotation[8] of the Akan concept of existence is irreducible except metaphorically. Thus you might speak of there existing an explanation for something *(ne nkyerease wo ho)* without incurring any obligation of spatial specification, because an explanation is not an object in any but a metaphorical sense; and to a metaphorical object corresponds only a metaphorical kind of space. The same applies to the existence of all so-called abstract entities.[9] In the Akan conceptual framework, then, existence is spatial. Now, since, whatever transcendence means in this context, it implies existence beyond space, it follows that talk of any transcendent being is not just false, but unintelligible, from an Akan point of view.

But not only transcendence goes by the board. Neither the notion of the super-   14 natural nor that of the spiritual can convey any coherent meaning to an Akan understanding in its traditional condition.[10] No line is drawn in the Akan worldview demarcating one area of being corresponding to nature from another corresponding to supernature. Whatever is real belongs to one or another of the echelons of being postulated in that worldview. In that context it has all the explanation that is appropriate to it. An important axiom of Akan thought is that everything has its explanation, *biribiara wo nenkyerease*—a kind of principle of sufficient reason; and a clear presupposition of Akan explanations of phenomena is that there are interactions among all the orders of existents in the world. Accordingly, if an event in human affairs, for instance, does not appear explicable in human terms, there is no hesitation in invoking extra-human causality emanating from the higher or even the lower rungs of the hierarchy of beings. In doing this there is no sense of crossing an ontological chasm; for the idea is that there is only one universe of many strata wherein God, the ancestors, humans, animals, plants and all the rest of the furniture of the world have their being.

In this last connection, it might, perhaps, enhance understanding to regiment   15 our terminology a little. Suppose we use the term "the world" to designate the totality of ordered existents fashioned out by God in the process of "creation", then, of course, God, being the author of the world, is not a part of it, in the Akan scheme of things. But we might, then, reserve the term "universe" for the totality of absolutely all existents. In this sense God would be part of the universe. Apart from regimenting our terminology, this gives us the opportunity to reinforce the point regarding the Akan sense of the inherent law-likeness of reality. And the crucial consideration is that god's relationship with the rest of the universe, that is, the world, is also conceived to be inherently law-like. This is the implication of the Akan saying that "The Creator created Death and Death killed the Creator", *Odomankoma boo Owuo na Owuo kum Odomankoma*, which, in my opinion, is one of the profoundest in the Akan corpus of metaphysical aphorisms.

But though God's relation with the world is conceived to be law-like, He is not 16 made the basis of the explanation of any specific phenomenon, for since everything is ultimately traceable to Him, *Biribiara ne Nyame*, references to Him are incapable of helping to explain why any particular thing is what it is and not another thing. Divine law-likeness only ensures that there will be no arbitrary interferences in the course of the world-process. Thus the reason why Akan explanations of specific things do not invoke God is not because He is thought to be transcendent or supernatural or anything like that, but rather because He is too immanently implicated in the nature and happening of things to have an explanatory value.

Still, however, in facing the cognitive problems of this world all the mundane 17 theaters of being, human and extra-human, are regarded as *equally* legitimate sources of explanation. Thus, if an Akan explains a mysterious malady in terms of, say, the wrath of the ancestors, it makes a little sense to ascribe to him or her a belief in the supernatural. That characterization is intelligible only in a conceptual framework in which the natural/supernatural dichotomy has a place. But the point is that it has no place in the Akan system of thought. We may be sure, then, that the widespread notion that Africans are given to supernatural explanations is the result of the superimposition of alien categories of thought on African thought-structures, in the Akan instance, at least. There is nothing particularly insidious in the fact that Western writers on African thought have generally engaged in this practice; for, after all, one thinks most naturally in terms of the conceptual framework of one's intellectual upbringing, and the natural/supernatural distinction is very endemic, indeed, in Western though. I do not mean by this, of course, that there is a universal belief in the supernatural in the West. The suggestion is only that this concept together with its logical complement is a customary feature of Western conceptualizations; so much so, that even the Western philosophical naturalist, in denying the existence of anything supernatural, does not necessarily dispute the coherence of that concept. It is a more striking fact that many contemporary African expositors of their own traditional systems of thought yield no ground to their Western colleagues in stressing the role of belief in the supernatural in African thinking.[11] It is hard not to see this as evidence of the fact that in some ways Christian proselytization and Western education have been over-successful in Africa.

But an interesting and important question arises. Suppose it granted that, as I have been arguing, the natural/supernatural dichotomy has no place in Akan and, perhaps, African thought generally. Does that not still leave the question of its objective validity intact? And, if it should turn out to be objectively valid, would it not be reasonable to think that it would be a good thing for Africans to learn to think along that line? My answer to both questions is affirmative; which implies a rejection of relativism. This disavowal is fully premeditated and is foreshadowed in the opening paragraph of this essay. However, for reasons of the division of preoccupation, I cannot try to substantiate my anti-relativism here.[12]   18

Stated baldly, my thesis is that there is such a thing as the objective validity of an idea. Were it not for the recent resurgence of relativism in Philosophy, this would have been too platitudinous for any words. Furthermore, and rather less obviously, if an idea is objectively valid (or invalid or even incoherent) in any given language or conceptual framework, both the idea and its status can, in principle, be *represented* in, if not necessarily translated into, any other language or conceptual framework.   19

A corollary of the foregoing contention is that, however natural it may be to think in one's native framework of concepts, it is possible for human beings to think astride conceptual frameworks. In the absence of extended argumentation for this general claim, I will content myself with an illustration with respect to the idea of the supernatural. A relevant question, then, is: "Do the Akans need to incorporate the natural/supernatural distinction into their modes of thought?" I think not; for not only is Akan thought inhospitable to this distinction but also the distinction is, in my opinion, objectively incoherent. If this is so, it follows from our principle that it ought to be demonstrable (to the extent that such speculative matters are susceptible of demonstration) in any language and, in particular, in English. In fact, a simple argument suffices for this purpose.   20

In the sense pertinent to our discussion, the supernatural is that which surpasses the order of nature. In other words, a supernatural event is one whose occurrence is contrary to the laws of nature. But if the event actually happens, then any law that fails to reckon with its possibility is inaccurate and is in need of some modification, at least. However, if the law is suitably amended, even if only by means of an excep-   21 tive rider, the event is no longer contrary to natural law. Hence no event can be consistently described as supernatural.

What of the notion of the spiritual? Again, I begin with a disclaimer on behalf 22
of Akan ontological thinking. As can be expected from the spatial character of the Akan concept of existence, the radical dualism of the material and the spiritual can find no home in the Akan scheme of reality. All the extra-human beings and powers, even including God, are spoken of in language irreducibly charged with spatial imagery. It is generally recognized by students of African eschatology that the *place* of the dead, the *abode* of the ancestors, is almost completely modeled on the world of living mortals.[13] If the replication is not complete, it is only because the ancestors are not thought of as having *fully* material bodies. Some analogue of material bodies they surely must be supposed to have, given the sorts of things that are said about them. For example, a postulated component of a person that is supposed to survive death and eventually become an ancestor, all things being equal, is believed soon after death to travel *by land and by river* before arriving at the abode of the ancestors. For this reason in traditional times coffins were stuffed with travel needs such as clothing and money for the payment of ferrying charges. I have never heard it suggested in traditional circles that this practice was purely symbolic. If it were a purely symbolic gesture, that, certainly, would have been carrying symbolism rather far. But, in any case, the practice as of a piece with the conception, and the conception is decidedly quasi-material.

I use the term "quasi-material" to refer to any being or entity conceived as spa- 23
tial but lacking some of the properties of material objects. The ancestors, for instance, although they are thought of as occupying space, are believed to be invisible to the naked eye and inaudible to the normal ear, except rarely when they choose to *manifest* themselves to particular persons for special reasons. On such occasions the can, according to very widely received conceptions among the Akans, appear and disappear at will unconstrained by those limitations of speed and impenetrability to which the gross bodies of the familiar world are subject. This is held to be generally true of all the relatively personalized forms of extra-human phenomena.

It is apparent from what has just been said that if the extra-human beings of 24
the Akan worldview are not fully material, they are not fully immaterial either. Further, to confirm this last point, we might note that, although the beings in question are not supposed to be generally visible to the *naked* eye, they are widely believed to be perceivable to the superior eyes of certain persons of special gift or training. People reputed to be of this class will sometimes tell you, "If you but had eyes to see, you would be amazed at what is going on right here around where you are standing".

And here imagery tends to be so lustily spatial that, but for their selective invisibility, one would be hard put to distinguish between the quasi-material apparitions and the garden variety objects of the material world. Descriptions of human-like creatures gyrating on their heads are not unknown in such contexts. Whatever one may thing of such claims, the conceptual point itself is clear, namely, that the extra-human existents of the Akan ontology do not belong to the category of the spiritual in the Cartesian sense of non-spatial, unextended. The category itself is conceptually inadmissible in this system of thought. Should the reader be curious at this stage as to whether mind too is quasi-material in the Akan way of thinking, the short answer[14] is that mind is not thought of as an entity at all but rather simply as the *capacity*, supervenient upon the brain states and processes, to do various things. Hence the question whether mind is a spiritual or material or quasi-material entity does not arise.

The Akan worldview, then, involves no sharp ontological cleavages such as   25 the Cartesian dichotomy of the material and the spiritual; what difference in nature there is between ordinary material things and those extra-human beings and forces so often called "spirits" in the literature is the difference between the fully material and the partially material. I ought, by the way, to stress that the absence of spiritual in the metaphysical sense, for the Akan conceptual framework does not imply the absence of spirituality, in the popular sense, from Akan life. In the latter sense spirituality is sensitivity to the less gross aspects of human experience.

But let us return to the class of quasi-material entities. A legitimate question is   26 whether there is adequate evidence that such entities exist. Actually, this is not a question which faces Akan thought alone. All cultures, East, West and Central, abound in stories of quasi-material goings-on. In the West investigating the veridity and theoretical explicability of such stories is one of the main concerns of Parapsychology. In Africa there are any number of people who would be willing to bet their lives on the reality of such things, on the basis, reputedly, of first hand experience. Basically, the issue is an empirical one, though probably not completely; for if such phenomena were to be definitively confirmed, there explanation would be likely to have conceptual reverberations. Speaking for myself, I would say that neither in Africa nor elsewhere have I seen compelling evidence of such things; though dogmatism would be ill-advised. At all events, it is worth noting that the plausibility of specific quasi-material claims tends to dwindle in the face of advancing scientific knowledge, a consideration which any contemporary African would need to take to heart.

It is, however, interesting to note that the waning, in Africa, of belief in extra-   27 material entities and forces would leave the indigenous orientation thoroughly empirical; for the African worldview, at any rate, the Akan one, makes room for only material and quasi-material existents. The contrary seems to be the case in the West. Here any reduction in quasi-material beliefs has not automatically resulted in gains for empirical thinking in the minds of a large mass of people; for in addition to the categories of material and quasi-material, there is that of the spiritual, i.e. the immaterial, which exercises the profoundest influence in philosophic and quasi-philosophic speculation. Not only is actual belief in immaterial entities widespread in the West but also the intelligibility of the material/immaterial contrast seems to be taken for granted even more widely. Moreover, in spite of the fact that, to say the least, quasi-material beliefs are not at all rare in the West, the tendency is for thinking to be governed by an exclusive disjunction of the material with the immaterial. Thus, for many, though, of course, not everybody, in the West, if a thing is not supposed to be material, it is necessarily immaterial. The Europeans who imposed on themselves the "burden" of bringing "salvation" to the souls of the peoples of Africa certainly had this particular either-or fixation. Consequently, those of them who made sympathetic, though not necessarily empathetic, studies of African thought could not but formulate their results in terms of that and cognate schemes of thought. A visible outcome of their assiduous evangelism is the great *flock* of faithful African converts who think in the same language, proudly attributing to their own peoples belief in sundry things spiritual and supernatural.

 Yet, not only is the notion of the spiritual unintelligible within a thought system such as that of the Akans, but also it is objectively a very problematic one. One searches in vain for a useful definition of the spiritual. The sum total of the information available from Cartesian and many other spiritually dedicated sources is that the spiritual is that which is non-material. But, definition by pure negation, such as this, brings little enlightenment. The word "that" in the definition suggests that one is envisaging some *sort* of a referent, but this possibility of reference is given absolutely no grounding. How are we to differentiate between the spiritual and the void, for instance? Some negative definitions can be legitimate, but only if their context provides suitable information. In the present case the context seems to be a veritable void!

 An even more unfortunate definition of the spiritual than the foregoing is sometimes encountered.[15] It is explained that the spiritual is the unperceivable, the invisible or, to adapt a phrase of Saint Paul's, the unseen. The problem with this definition is not its apparent negativeness, for the conditions of unperceivability are concrete enough; the problems is that it is so broad as to make gravity, for example, spiritual. It is, of course, not going to help to protest that although gravity is unseen,

28

29

its effects are seen and felt; for exactly the same is what is claimed for the spiritual. Nor would it be of greater avail to add the condition of non-spatiality to that of invisibility, for something like the square root of four is neither spatial nor visible, and yet one wonders how spiritual it is.

Of the material/spiritual (immaterial) dichotomy, then, we can say the follow-   30
ing. It is not a universal feature of human thinking, since the Akans, at least, do not use it. And, in any case, its coherence is questionable. It is not to be assumed, though, that if a mode of conceptualization is universal among humankind, then it is, for that reason, objectively valid. Belief in quasi-material entities, for example, seems to be universal among cultures (though not among all individuals) but the chances are that the concepts involved denote nothing.

After all the foregoing the reader is unlikely to be surprised to learn that the   31
idea of creation out of nothing too does not make sense in the Akan framework of thinking. Avenues to that concept are blocked in Akanland from the side both of the concept of creation and that of nothingness. To take the latter first: Nothingness in the Akan language is relative to location. The idea is expressed as the absence of anything at a given location, *se whee mni ho*, literally, the circumstance of there not being something there. Note here the reappearance of the locative conception of existence. If you subtract the locative connotation from this and that of, say, the Christian religion, since, even if the Akan Nyame is not thought of as supernatural, he is still regarded as in some sense the author of the world and determiner of its destiny. But conceptions or beliefs that do not dovetail into the fabric of practical life can hardly constitute a religion in the primary sense.

That the belief in Nyame has no essential role in the conduct of Akan life can   32
be seen from a little exercise of the imagination. Imagine the belief in Nyame to be altogether removed from the Akan consciousness. What losses will be incurred in terms of sustenance for any institutions or procedures of practical life? The answer is, "Exactly zero." Customs and moral rules relating to the critical (or even non-critical) stages and circumstances in the lives of individuals do not have their basis in the belief in Nyame. The same is true of the institutions of traditional Akan public life. Thus neither the pursuit of moral virtue and noble ideals by individuals nor the cooperative endeavors of the community towards the common good can be said to stand or fall with the belief in Nayme; they all have a sold enough basis in considerations of human well-being, considerations, in other words, which are completely "This-worldly".

To elaborate a little on this last point: to the traditional Akan what gives   33
meaning to life is usefulness to self, family, community and the species.[16] Nothing

transcending life in human society and its empirical conditions enters into the constitution of the meaning of life. In particular, there is not, in Akan belief, in contrast, for instance, to Christian belief, any notion of an afterlife of possible salvation and eternal bliss; what afterlife there is thought to be is envisaged very much on the model of this life, as previously hinted. More importantly, that afterlife is not pictured as a life of eternal fun for the immortals but rather as one of eternal vigilance—vigilance over the affairs of the living with the sole purpose of promoting their well-being within the general constraints of Akan ethics. Indeed, this is what is taken to give meaning to their survival. From everything said (to my knowledge) about the ancestors, they are generally believed never to relent in this objective; which is one reason why they are held in such high esteem. the inhabitants of the world of the dead, then, are themselves thoroughly "this-worldly" in their orientation, according to Akan traditional conceptions.

Basically the same considerations would seem to discourage attributing to the Akans any sort of non-supernaturalistic religiosity. One great difficulty would be how to articulate such a notion within the Akan conceptual framework. Suppose we construe religion as life and thought impregnated by a sense of the sacred. Then, since the primary meaning of the word "sacred" presupposes some conception of deity, we would be in duty bound to give some notification of a broadening of meaning. Accordingly, the sacred might be understood as that in ethical life most worthy of respect, reverence and commitment. But this, in turn, would presuppose a system of values and ideals, and, in the case of the Akans, would bring us back to their irreducibly "this-worldly" ethic. Now, the remarkable thing is that in this ethic a demonstrated basic commitment to the values and ideals of the society is a component of the very concept of a person. An individual is not a person in the fullest sense unless he or she has shown a responsiveness to those ideals in confirmed habits of life. Not, of course, that an individual failing this test is denuded of human rights; for every individual, simply on the grounds of being human, is regarded as a center of quite extensive rights.[17] On the other hand, there is a prestige attached to the status of personhood, or more strictly, superlative personhood—for indeed the status is susceptible of degrees—to which all Akans of sound mind aspire. But this is simply the aspiration to become a responsible individual in society, an individual who, through intelligent thinking, judicious planning and hard work, is able to carve out an adequate livelihood for himself and family and make significant contributions to the well-being of the community. The problem, now, is that if this is what, in the specific context of Akan culture, living a life informed by a sense of the sacred means, then applying the concept of religion to it would scarcely pick out anything in the culture corresponding to what in, say, Western culture might be called a non-supernaturalistic religion. In Western society there are historical as well as conceptual reasons why one might want to organize one's life on the lines of what might be called a non-supernaturalist religion. In Akan society there are really none. In the West, loss of the belief in God, for example, usually results in disengagement from certain well-known institutions and practices. The consequent psychological or social void might be filled for some by a "non-theistic" religion. In the Akan situation, on the other hand, no such void is to be anticipated from a comparable belief mutation. Speaking from my own experience, failure to retain the belief in *Nyame*—I make no mention here of the Christian God, the conception of whom registers no coherent meaning upon my understanding—has caused me not the slightest alienation from any of the institutions or practices of Akan culture.

Not unexpectedly, what has cost me some dissonance with the culture is my 35 skepticism regarding the continued existence of our ancestors. The pouring of libation, for example, is a practice in which, as previously hinted, the Akans call upon the ancestors to come and participate in important functions and lend their good auspices to any enterprise launched. This is a significant and not infrequent ceremony in Akan life. But obviously, if one does not believe that the ancestors are actually there, one cannot pretend to do so. I cannot personally, therefore, participate in a custom like this with any total inwardness. In this, by the way, I do not stand alone. Any Akan Christian—and there are great numbers of them—is logically precluded from believing such things as the Akan doctrine of ancestors, for it does not cohere with Christian eschatology. As far as I am concerned, however, there is a saving consideration. This custom of libation, and many other customs of a like quasi-material basis, can be retained by simply reinterpreting the reference to the ancestors as commemoration rather than invocation. That, of course, would entail obvious verbal reformulations, but it should present no problem. What of customs that prove not to be susceptible to such revisions in the face of advancing skepticism? One hopes that they would eventually be abandoned. The culture is rich enough not to suffer any real existential deficit from such a riddance. Nor is the atrophy of custom under the pressure of changing times at all rare in the history of culture.

Be that as it may, the fact remains that as already argued, the Akan belief in 36 the existence and power of such being as the ancestors, and the procedures associated with that belief do not constitute a religion in any reliable sense. We are not, therefore, brought to the following conclusion: The concept of religion is not unproblematically applicable within all cultures, and Akan culture is a case in point.[18] Nevertheless, there may be some justification for speaking of Akan religion in a broadened sense of the word "religion."[19] In this sense the word would refer simply to the fact that the Akans believe in Nyame, a being regarded as the architect of the world order. Certainly, this is an extremely attenuated concept of religion. As pointed out already, religion in the fullest sense, whether it be supernaturalistic or not, is not just a set of beliefs and conceptions but also a way of life based on those ideas. What we have seen, however, is that the Akan way of life is not based on the belief in Nyame. Hence, if we do not use the word "religion" in the Akan context on the grounds of the belief in Nyame, we should evince some consciousness of the fact that we have made a considerable extension of meaning; otherwise we propagate a subtle misunderstanding of Akan and cognate cultures under the apparently widespread illusion that religion is a cultural universal.

Yet, surely, something must be universal. Consider the ease with which Christian missionaries have been able to convert large masses of Africans to Christianity by relaying to them "tidings" which are in some important parts most likely conceptually incoherent, or, at any rate, incongruous with categories deeply embedded in indigenous ways of thinking. To be sure, it cannot be assumed that in the large majority of cases conversion has been total in terms of moral and cosmological outlook. Still there are impressive enough numbers of African converts, some in the high reaches of ecclesiastical authority, whose understanding of and dedication to the christian religion challenges the severest comparisons among the most exalted practitioners of the same faith in the West. I take this as testimony to the malleability of the human mind which enables the various people of the world to share not only their insights but also their incoherences. This characteristic of the mind, being fundamental to the human status, makes our common humanity the one universal which potentially transcends all cultural particularities.

Endnotes
1. See, for example, John S. Mbiti, *African Religions and Philosophy*. London: Heinemann, 1969, p. 2.
2. On this see further Kwasi Wiredu, "Morality and Religion in Akan Thought", in H. Odera Oruka and D. A. Masolo, *Philosophy and Cultures*. Nairobi: Bookwise Limited, 1983.
3. For convenience, I am using the word "God" here. But this is subject to a rider to be entered below.
4. Abraham asserts, correctly, I think, that "if a distinction can be drawn between worship and serving, then the Akans never had a word for worship. Worship is

a concept that had no place in Akan thought", (W. E. Abraham, *The Mind of Africa*. Chicago: The University of Chicago Press, 1962, p. 52.)

5. K. A. Busia, "The Ashanti" in Daryll Forde (ed.), *African Worlds*, Oxford, 1954, p. 205.

6. J. B. Danquah, "Obligation in Akan Society", *West African Affairs*, No. 89, published by the Bureau of Current Affairs, London, 1952, for the Department of Extra-Mural Studies, University of the Gold Coast (now the University of Ghana), p. 6. (I commented on this quote from Danquah along with that from Busia cited in note 5 in my "Morality and Religion in Akan Thought" op. cit.)

7. See, for example, E. Bolaji Idowu, *African Traditional Religion: A Definition*. London: SCM Press, 1973, p. 146.

8. Kwame Gyekye insists very spiritedly on the locative connotation of the Akan concept of existence, but he does not draw the empirical implications. See his *An Essay on African Philosophical Thought*. New York: Cambridge University Press, 1987, p. 179.

9. My own explication of the concepts of existence and objecthood is essentially in conformity with Akan conception of existence. In this connection see my "Logic and Ontology" series in *Second Order: An African Journal of Philosophy*, January 1973, July 1973, July 1974, and January 1975. The definition of an object which emerged from those discussions was that an object is what can be the non-conceptual referent of a symbol. It should not strain human resources to show that any such referent will have to be in space.

10. As will become clear below, my own conceptual orientation is decidedly Akan in this respect.

11. K. A. Busia, for example, speaks of "the belief held among African communities that the supernatural powers and deities operate in every sphere and activity of life". *Africa in Search of Democracy*. London: Routledge and Kegan Paul, 1967, p. 9. This is in spite of the fact that in his earlier work *The Challenge of Africa* (New York: Frederick A. Praeger, 1962, p. 36) he had remarked on "the apparent absence of any conceptual cleavage between the natural and the supernatural" in Akan thought. Gyekye also says that "the Akan universe is a spiritual universe, one in which supernatural beings play significant roles in the thought and action of the people," *An Essay on African Philosophical Thought*. New York: Cambridge University Press, 1987, p. 69.

12. I argue against relativism in "Are There Cultural Universals?", paper presented at a Symposium of the XVIII World Congress of Philosophy, Brighton, England, August 1988.

13. See further Kwasi Wiredu, "Death and the Afterlife in African Culture" presented at Symposium on "Death and Afterlife" at the Woodrow Wilson International Center for Scholars, Washington, D.C., June 1988. Published in Arthur S. Berger et al., eds., *Perspectives on Death and Dying: Cross-Cultural and Multi-disciplinary Views*. Philadelphia: The Charles Press, 1989.

14. For a longer answer see Kwasi Wiredu, "The Akan Concept of Mind", *The Ibadan Journal of Humanistic Studies*, October 1983 (University of Ibadan, Nigeria). Also in Guttorm Floistad, ed., *Contemporary Philosophy, A New Survey, Vol. 5: African Philosophy*. Dordrecht: Martinus Nijhoff Publishers (Boston: Kluwer Academic, 1987).

15. Gyekye in attributing spiritual beliefs to the Akans uses a definition of this sort: "The Supreme Being, the deities, and the ancestors are spiritual entities. They are considered invisible and unperceivable to the naked eye: This is in fact the definition of the word 'spiritual' . . ." (*An Essay on African Philosophical Thought*, p. 69.)

16. The species-wide dimensions of the Akan sense of solidarity is explicit in a number of traditional maxims. When the Akans say, for example, that *onipa hyia mmoa*, which literally means a human being needs help but is more strictly to be rendered in some such wise as "a human being, simply in virtue of being human, is deserving of help"—when the Akans say this, they mean absolutely and explicitly *any* human being. If you add to this sense of human fellowship the acute sense of the vulnerability of an individual in a strange place—the Akans say *okwantufo ye mmobo*, meaning the plight of a traveller is pitiable—then you begin to understand the ideology behind the hospitality to strangers, black or white, for which the Akans, and actually, Chanaians generally, are famous.

17. On this see further, Kwasi Wiredu, "An Akan Perspective on Human Rights," in Francis Deng, et al., eds., *Human Rights in Africa: Cross-Cultural Perspectives*, Washington, D.C.: Brookings Institution, forthcoming.

18. Akan culture may not be unique in this regard. It is, for example, an open question how appropriate it is to describe the early Greek beliefs about their motley collection of gods and goddesses as a religion. It is no less an open question whether Theraveda Buddhism is a religion or a non-religious philosophy of life translated into a way of life.

19. This does not mean, however, that the concept of religion corresponds to anything in the Akans' conceptualizations of their own experience or external existence. As one might expect from the fact, noted earlier on, that they do not, rightly, as I think, make a sharp distinction between the material and the spiri-

tual, they do not operate with anything like the distinction between the secular and the religious. Many students of African "religion" have noted this, but have strangely drawn from it, or deduced it from, the inverted impression that in African life everything is religious. Thus Mbiti, speaking of African ways of thought, remarks that "there is no formal distinction between the sacred and the secular, between the religious and the non-religious, between the spiritual and the material areas of life". (*African Religions and Philosophy*, p. 2.) But he supposes that this is because "traditional religions permeate all the departments of life" (loc. cit). And he goes on to say things like "religion is their whole system of being" (*ibid.*, p. 3). See also K. A. Busia, *Africa in Search of Democracy*, New York, Frederick A. Praeger, 1967, chap. 1: "The Religious Heritage": Kofi Asare Opoku, *West African Traditional Religion*, London: F.E.P. International Private Ltd., 91978, chap. 1: "African Traditional Religion: A General Introduction"; Kwesi A. Dickson, *Theology in Africa*, New York: Orbis Book, 1984, chap. 2: "The African Religio-Cultural Reality". Since all these writers are Africans—actually they are all Ghanaians except Mbiti, who is an Ugandan—it might have been hoped that they would have stopped to ponder how the blanket attributions of religiosity to their peoples might be expressed within the indigenous languages. The difficulty of the experiment might well have bred caution. In any case, logic alone should have inspired doubt as to the conceptual significance of the idea of being religious in the thought of a people who, by general admission, do not have the distinction between the secular and the religious in their framework of categories.

Chapter 8
MEDIA AND THE ARTS

Ingmar Bergman (1918–   ) is a filmmaker and stage director known for his sophisti-cation, symbolism, and dark vision. He was born July 14, 1918, in Uppsala, Sweden, the son of a Lutheran minister. He attended the University of Stockholm, where he became involved in theater, and was appointed to the Swedish Royal Opera in 1942. In 1945 he directed his first film, *Crisis*, about a miserable love affair resulting in suicide. In 1956 he directed the acclaimed symbolic film *The Seventh Seal*, a medieval morality play about a knight who challenges Death to a chess game. He shifted gears to make *Wild Strawberries* in 1957, a film that maintains a warm tone as it contrasts youth with age. He returned to symbolism in *The Magician* (1959), and returned to a medieval setting in *The Virgin Spring* (1960). In 1961 he began a trilogy of films about the philosophical problem of isolation in a godless world with *Through the Glass Darkly*, about domestic violence. He continued the trilogy with *Winter Light* in 1962, which focuses on loss of faith, and ended with *The Silence* in 1963, a surrealistic film which takes up the theme of the fear of silence. He made more films in the 1960s, but tax problems forced him to spend much of the 1970s producing television work in Norway and Germany. Some of his noted later films include *Cries and Whispers* (1971); *Scenes from a Marriage* (1973, made for tel-evision); and *The Magic Flute* (1973, made for television). His most accessible film, which some have called his best, was *Fanny and Alexander* (1982) and was announced as his final film. In the late 1980s Bergman turned to writing, producing an autobiography in 1988 entitled *The Magic Lantern* and a novel in 1989, *Best Intentions*. Bergman continues to write and direct for Swedish television and theater.

What Is 'Film-Making'?

Ingmar Bergman

"Film-making" is for me a necessity of nature, a need comparable to hunger and   1
thirst. For some, self-expression involves writing books, climbing mountains, beating one's children or dancing the samba. In my case, I express myself in mak-ing films.

In *The Blood of a Poet*, the great Jean Cocteau shows us his alter ego stum-   2
bling down the corridors of a nightmare hotel and gives us a glimpse, behind each one of the doors, of one of the factors of which he is composed and which form his ego.

Without attempting here to equate my personality with Cocteau's, I   3
thought I would take you on a guided tour of my internal studios where, invisi-

bly, my films take form. This visit, I am afraid, will disappoint you; the equipment is always in disorder because the owner is too absorbed in his affairs to have time to straighten it up. Furthermore, the lighting is rather bad in certain spots, and on the door of certain rooms, you will find the word "Private" written in large letters. Finally, the guide himself is not always sure of what is worth the trouble of showing.

Whatever the case may be, we will open a few doors a crack. I won't guarantee that you will find precisely the answer to the questions you are wondering about, but perhaps, in spite of everything, you will be able to put together a few pieces of the complicated puzzle that the forming of a film represents.   4

If we consider the most fundamental element of the cinematographic art, the perforated film, we note that it is composed of a number of small, rectangular images—fifty-two per meter—each of which is separated from the other by a thick, black line. Looking more closely, we discover that these tiny rectangles, which at first glance seem to contain exactly the same picture, differ from each other by an almost imperceptible modification of this picture. And when the feeding mechanism of the projector causes the images in question to succeed each other on the screen so that each one is seen only for a twentieth of a second, we have the illusion of movement.   5

Between each of these small rectangles the shutter closes and plunges us into total darkness, only to return us to full light with the next rectangle. When I was ten years old and working with my first apparatus, a shaky lantern made of sheet metal— with its chimney, its gas lamp and its perpetual films which repeated themselves indefinitely—I used to find the above-mentioned phenomenon exciting and full of mystery. Even today, I feel myself quiver as I did when I was a child when I think of the fact that, in reality, I am creating illusion; for the cinema would not exist but for an imperfection of the human eye, namely its inability to perceive separately a series of images which follow each other rapidly and which are essentially identical.   6

I have calculated that if I see a film that lasts an hour, I am in fact plunged for twenty minutes in total darkness. In making a film, therefore, I am making myself guilty of a fraud; I am using a device designed to take advantage of a physical imperfection of man, a device by means of which I can transport my audience from a given feeling to the feeling that is diametrically opposed to it, as if each spectator were on a pendulum; I can make an audience laugh, scream with terror, smile, believe in legends, become indignant, take offense, become enthusiastic, lower itself or yawn from boredom. I am, then, either a deceiver or—   7 when the audience is aware of the fraud—an illusionist. I am able to mystify, and I have at my disposal the most precious and the most astounding magical device that has ever, since history began, been put into the hands of a juggler.

There is in all this, or at least there should be, the source of an insoluble   8
moral conflict for all those who create films or work on them.

As for our commercial partners, this is not the place to bring out the mis-   9
takes they have made from year to year, but it would certainly be worthwhile someday for a scientist to discover some unit of weight or measure which one could use to "calculate" the quantity of natural gifts, initiatives, genius and creative forces that the film industry has ground through its formidable mills. Obviously, anyone entering into the game must accept the rules in advance, and there is no reason why work in the cinematographic branch should be more respected than anywhere else. The difference is due to the fact that, in our specialty, brutality is manifested more overtly, but this is actually rather an advantage.

Loss of balance offers consequences that are even more grave for the film-   10
maker than for a tightrope walker or an acrobat who performs his tricks beneath a circus tent and without a net. For the film-maker as well as for the equilibrist, the danger is of the same order: falling and being killed. No doubt you think I am exaggerating; making a film isn't as dangerous as all that! I maintain my point, however; the risk is the same. Even if, as I mentioned, one is a bit of a magician, no one can mystify the producers, the bank directors, the movie-theatre owners or the critics when the public abstains from going to see a film and from paying out the obol from which producers, bank directors, movie-theatre owners, critics and magicians must draw their subsistence!

I can give you as an example a very recent experience, the memory of   11
which still makes me shudder—an experience in which I myself risked losing my balance. A singularly bold producer invested money in one of my films which, after a year of intense activity, appeared under the title of *The Naked Night* (*Gycklarnas afton*). The reviews were, in general, destructive, the public stayed away, the producer added up his losses, and I had to wait several years before trying again.

If I make two or three more films which fail financially, the producer will   12
quite justifiably consider it a good idea not to bet on my talents.

At that point, I will become, suddenly, a suspect individual, a squanderer,   13
and I will be able to reflect at my leisure on the usefulness of my artistic gifts, for
the magician will be deprived of his apparatus.

When I was younger, I didn't have these fears. Work for me was an excit-   14
ing game and, whether the results succeeded or failed, I was delighted with my
work like a child with his castles of sand or clay. The equilibrist was dancing on
his rope, oblivious and therefore unconcerned about the abyss beneath him and
the hardness of the ground of the circus-ring.

The game has changed into a bitter combat. The walk on the rope is now   15
performed in full awareness of the danger, and the two points where the rope is
attached are now called "fear" and "incertitude." Each work to be materialized
mobilizes all of the resources of one's energy. The act of creation has become,
under the effect of causes that are as much interior as they are exterior and economic, an exacting duty. Failure, criticism, coldness on the part of the public
today cause more sensitive wounds. These wounds take longer to heal and their
scars are deeper and more lasting.

Before undertaking a work or after having begun it, Jean Anouilh has the   16
habit of playing a little mental game in order to exorcise his fear. He says to himself, "My father is a tailor. He intimately enjoys creating with his hands, and the
result is a beautiful pair of pants or an elegant overcoat. This is the joy and the
satisfaction of the artisan, the pride of a man who knows his profession."

This is the same practice I follow. I recognize the game, I play it often and   17
I succeed in duping myself—and a few others—even if this game is in fact nothing but a rather poor sedative: "My films are fine pieces of work, I am enthusiastic, conscientious and extremely attentive of details. I create for my contemporaries and not for eternity; my pride is the pride of an artisan."

I know however that, if I speak this way, it is in order to deceive myself, and   18
an irrepressible anxiety cries out to me, "What have you done that can last? Is
there in any of your movies a single foot of film worthy of being passed on to posterity, a single line of dialogue, a single situation which is really and indisputably
true? "

And to this question I am forced to answer—perhaps still under the effect   19
of a disloyalty which is ineradicable even in the most sincere people—"I don't
know, I hope so."

You must excuse me for having described at such length and with so much   20
commentary the dilemma which those who create films are forced to confront.

I wanted to try to explain to you why so many of those who are devoted to the realization of cinematographic works give in to a temptation which cannot really be expressed and which is invisible; why we are afraid; why we sometimes lose our enthusiasm for the works we are doing; why we become fools and allow ourselves to be annihilated by colorless and vile compromises.

I would still, however, like to dwell a bit longer on one of the aspects of the   21 problem, the aspect that is the most important and difficult to comprehend—the public.

The creator of films is involved in a means of expression which concerns   22 not only himself but also millions of other people, and more often than not he feels the same desire as other artists: "I want to succeed today. I want celebrity now. I want to please, to delight, to move people immediately."

Midway between this desire and its realization is found the public, who   23 demands but one thing of the film: "I've paid, I want to be distracted, swept off my feet, involved; I want to forget my troubles, my family, my work, I want to get away from myself. Here I am, seated in the darkness, and, like a woman about to give birth, I want deliverance."

The film-maker who is aware of these demands and who lives on the   24 money of the public is placed in a situation which is difficult and which creates obligations for him. In making his film, he must always take the reaction of the public into account. On my part, personally, I am forever asking myself this question: "Can I express myself more simply, more purely, more briefly? Will everybody understand what I want to say now? Will the simplest mind be able to follow the course of these events? And, even more importantly, this question: up to what point do I have the right to admit compromise and where do my obligations to myself begin? "

Any experimentation necessarily involves a great risk, for it always keeps   25 the public at a distance, and keeping the public at a distance can lead to sterility and to isolation in an ivory tower.

It would be quite desirable, then, for producers and other technical direc-   26 tors of the cinema to put laboratories at the disposition of the creators. But this is scarcely the case today. The producers have confidence only in the engineers and stupidly imagine that the salvation of the film industry depends on inventions and technical complications.

Nothing is easier than frightening a spectator. One can literally terrify him,   27 for most people have in some part of their bearing a fear that is all ready to blossom. It is much more difficult to make people laugh, and to make them *laugh* in the right way. It is easy to put a spectator in a state worse than the one he was in when he entered the theater; it is difficult to put him in a better state; it is precisely this, however, that he desires each time he sits down in the darkness of a movie-theater. Now, how many times and by what means do we give him this satisfaction?

This is the way I reason; but at the same time I know with an absolute evi- 28
dence that this reasoning is dangerous, since it involves the risk of condemning all failures, of confusing the ideal with pride, and of considering as absolute the frontiers that the public and the critics establish, whereas you neither recognize these frontiers nor consider them your own, since your personality is perpetually in the process of becoming. On the one hand, I am tempted to adapt myself and to make myself what the public wants me to be; but on the other hand, I feel that this would be the end of everything, and that this would imply a total indifference on my part. Thus, I am delighted to have not been born with exactly as many brains as feelings, and it has never been written anywhere that a filmmaker must be contented, happy, or satisfied. Who says you can't make noise, cross frontiers, battle against windmills, send robots to the moon, have visions, play with dynamite or tear pieces of flesh from one's self or others? Why not frighten film producers? It is their job to be afraid, and they are paid to have stomach ulcers!

But *"film-making"* is not always confronting problems, dilemmas, econom- 29
ic worries, responsibilities and fear. There are also games, dreams, secret memories.

Often it begins with an image: a face which is suddenly and strongly illu- 30
minated; a hand which rises; a square at dawn where a few old ladies are seated on a bench, separated from each other by sacks of apples. Or it may be a few words that are exchanged; two people who, suddenly, say something to each other in a completely personal tone of voice—their backs are perhaps turned from me, I can't even see their faces, and yet I am forced to listen to them, to wait for them to repeat the same words which are without any particular meaning but which are pregnant with a secret tension, with a tension of which I am not yet even fully conscious but which acts like a crafty potion. The illuminated face, the hand raised as if for an incantation, the old ladies at the square, the few banal words, all of these images come and attach themselves like silvery fish to my net, or more precisely, I myself am trapped in a net, the texture of which I am not aware of—fortunately!

Quite rapidly, even before the motive has been entirely designed in my   31
mind, I submit the game of my imagination to the test of reality. I place, as if I'm
playing a game, my sketch, which is still very rough and fragile, on an easel in
order to judge it from the point of view of all the technical resources of the studios. This imaginary test of "viability" constitutes for the motive an effective fer-
ruginous bath. Will it suffice? Will the motive keep its value when it is plunged
into the daily, murderous routine of the studios, far from the shadows of sunrises,
which are quite propitious for the games of the imagination?

A few of my films mature very quickly and are finished rapidly. These are   32
the ones that meet the general expectations, like children that are still undisciplined but in good health and about whom one can predict immediately: "They
are the ones who will support the family."

And then there are other films, films which come slowly, which take years,   33
which refuse to be imprisoned in a formal or technical solution, and which, in
general, refuse any concrete solution. They remain in a shadowy zone; if I want
to find them, I have to follow them there and find a context, characters and situation. There, faces that are turned aside begin to speak, the streets are strange,
a few, scattered people glance out through window-panes, an eye glistens at dusk
or changes into a carbuncle and then bursts with a noise of breaking crystal. The
square, this autumn morning, is a sea; the old ladies are transformed into ancient
trees and the apples are children building cities of sand and stone near the foam
of the waves.

The tension is there, ever present, and it appears again, either in the writ-   34
ten word, or in the visions, or in the excess of energy, which bends like the arch
of a bridge, ready to rise up by its own forces, by these forces which are the most
important element, once the manuscript is finished, in setting in motion the
immense wheel which the work required in shooting a film represents.

What is "shooting a film," then? If I were to ask this question of everybody,   35
I would no doubt obtain quite different responses, but perhaps you would all
agree on one point: shooting a film is doing what is necessary in order to transport the contents of the manuscript onto a piece of film. In doing so, you would
be saying quite a lot and yet not nearly enough. For me, shooting a film represents days of inhumanly relentless work, stiffness of the joints, eyes full of dust,
the odors of makeup, sweat and lamps, an indefinite series of tensions and relax-
ations, an uninterrupted battle between volition and duty, between vision and
reality, conscience and laziness. I think of early risings, of nights without sleep, of
a feeling keener than life, of a sort of fanaticism centered about a single task, by

which I myself become, finally, an integral part of the film, a ridiculously tiny piece of apparatus whose only fault is requiring food and drink.

It sometimes happens—in the middle of all this excitement, when the studios are humming with a life and a labor that seem as if they should make the studios explode—that, suddenly, I find the idea for my next film. You would be wrong, however, if you thought that the activity of a film-maker supposes, at this moment, a kind of ecstatic vertigo, an uncontrolled excitement and a frightening disorganization. To shoot a film is to undertake the taming of a wild beast that is difficult to handle and very valuable; you need a clear mind, meticulousness, stiff and exact calculations. Add to this a temper that is always even and a patience that is not of this world. 36

Shooting a film is organizing an entire universe, but the essential elements are industry, money, construction, shooting, developing and copying, a schedule to follow but which is rarely followed, a battle plan minutely prepared where the irrational factors occur the most often. The star has too much black around her eyes—a thousand dollars to start the scene over again. One day, the water in the pipes has too much chlorine in it and the negatives got spotted—let's start again! Another day, death plays a dirty trick on you by taking away an actor—let's start with another—and there are several thousand more dollars swallowed up. It starts to thunder, the electric transformer breaks down, and there we are, all made up and waiting in the pale light of the day, the hours flying by and money with them. 37

Idiotic examples, chosen at random. But they have to be idiotic, since they touch that great and sublime idiocy, the transforming of dreams into shadows, the chopping up of a tragedy into five hundred small pieces, the experimentation with each of these pieces, and finally the putting back together of these pieces so that they constitute again a unity which will once more be the tragedy. It is the idiocy of fabricating a tapeworm 8,000 feet long which will nourish itself on the life and mind of the actors, producers, and creators. Shooting a film is all that, but it is still something else, and it is much worse. 38

Film-making is also plunging with one's deepest roots back into the world of childhood. Let's descend, if you wish, into this interior studio, located in the most intimate recesses of the life of the creator. Let's open up for a moment the most secret of these rooms so that we can look at a painting of Venice, an old windowblind, and a first apparatus for showing "action films." 39

At Upsala, my grandmother had a very old apartment. While I was there, I once slipped beneath the dining-room table; I was wearing an apron with a 40 pocket in front of it; from my vantage point I listened to the voice of the sun-beams which entered through the immensely high windows. The rays moved continually; the bells of the cathedral chimed out, the rays moved, and their movement generated a sort of special sound. It was one of those days between winter and spring; I had the measles and I was five years old. In the neighboring apartment, somebody was playing the piano—it was always waltzes—and on the wall hung a big painting of Venice. While the rays of sun and the shadows were passing like waves across the painting, the water of the canal began to flow, the pigeons flew up from the pavement of the square, people spoke to each other noiselessly, making movements with their hands and heads. The sound of the bells wasn't coming from the cathedral but rather from the painting, as were the strains from the piano. There was something very strange about this painting of Venice. Almost as strange as the fact that the sunbeams in my grandmother's liv-ing-room were not silent but had a sound. Perhaps it was all those bells—or per-haps the enormous pieces of furniture which were conversing uninterruptedly.

I seem to remember, however, an experience even more distant than the   41
one of the year I had measles: the perception—impossible to date—of the move-ment of a window-blind.

It was a black window-blind of the most modern variety, which I could see,   42
in my nursery, at dawn or at dusk, when everything becomes living and a bit frightening, when even toys transform into things that are either hostile or sim-ply indifferent and curious. At that moment the world would no longer be the everyday world with my mother present, but a vertiginous and silent solitude. It wasn't that the blind moved; no shadow at all appeared on it. The forms were on the surface itself; they were neither little men, nor animals, nor heads, nor faces, but *things for which no name exists!* In the darkness, which was interrupted here and there by faint rays of light, these forms freed themselves from the blind and moved toward the green folding-screen or toward the bureau, with its pitcher of water. They were pitiless, impassive and terrifying; they disappeared only after it became completely dark or light, or when I fell asleep.

Anyone who, like myself, was born in the family of a pastor, learns at an   43
early age to look behind the scenes in life and death. Whenever Father has a bur-ial, a marriage, a baptism, a mediation, he writes a sermon. You make an early acquaintance with the devil and, like all children, you need to give him a con-crete form. Here is where the magic lantern comes in, a little sheetmetal box with a gas lamp (I can still smell the odor of the heated metal) and which pro-jected colored pictures. Among others, there was Little Red Ridinghood and the

wolf. The wolf was the devil, a devil without horns but with a tail and vivid red mouth, a curiously palpable and yet elusive devil, the emissary of evil and persecution on the flowered wallpaper of the nursery.

The first film I ever owned was about ten feet long and brown. It pictured a young girl asleep in a prairie; she woke up, stretched, arose and, with outstretched arms, disappeared at the right side of the picture. That was all. Drawn on the box the film was kept in was a glowing picture with the words, "Frau Holle." Nobody around me knew who Frau Holle was, but that didn't matter; the film was quite successful, and we showed it every evening until it got torn so badly we couldn't repair it. 44

This shaky bit of cinema was my first sorcerer's bag, and, in fact, it was pretty strange. It was a mechanical plaything; the people and things never changed, and I have often wondered what could have fascinated me so much and what, even today, still fascinates me in exactly the same way. This thought comes to me sometimes in the studio, or in the semidarkness of the editing room, while I am holding the tiny picture before my eyes and while the film is passing through my hands; or else during that fantastic childbirth that takes place during the recomposition as the finished film slowly finds its own face. I can't help thinking that I am working with an instrument so refined that with it, it would be possible for us to illuminate the human soul with an infinitely more vivid light, to unmask it even more brutally and to annex to our field of knowledge new domains of reality. Perhaps we would even discover a crack that would allow us to penetrate into the *chiaroscuro* of surreality, to tell tales in a new and overwhelming manner. At the risk of affirming once more something I cannot prove, let me say that, the way I see it, we film-makers utilize only a minute part of a frightening power—we are moving only the little finger of a giant, a giant who is far from not being dangerous. 45

But it is equally possible that I am wrong. It might be that the cinema has attained the high point of its evolution, that this instrument, by its very nature, can no longer conquer new teritory, that we are stuck with our noses to the wall, since the road ends in a dead end. Many people are of this opinion, and it is true that we are treading water in a marsh, our noses just rising above the surface of the water, and paralyzed by economic problems, conventions, stupidity, fear, incertitude and disorder. 46

I am asked sometimes what I am trying to attain in my films, what my goal is. The question is difficult and dangerous, and I usually answer it by lying or hedging: "I am trying to tell the truth about the condition of men, the truth as I 47 see it." This answer always satisfies people, and I often wonder how it happens that nobody notices my bluff, because the true response should be, "I feel an incoercible need to express through film that which, in a completely subjective way, takes form some place in my consciousness. This being the case, I have no other goal but myself, my daily bread, the amusement and respect of the public, a kind of truth that I feel precisely at that moment. And if I try to sum up my second answer, the formula I end up with is not terribly exciting: 'An activity without much meaning.'"

I am not saying that this conclusion doesn't distress me inordinately. I am   48
in the same situation as most artists of my generation; the activity of each one of us doesn't have much meaning. Art for art's sake. My personal truth, or three-quarters of a truth, or no truth at all, except that it has a value for me.

I realize that this way of looking at things is quite unpopular, particularly   49
today. Let me hasten, then, to form the question in a different way: "What would be your goal in making your films?"

The story is told that, a long time ago, the cathedral of Chartres was struck   50
by lightning and burned from top to bottom. It is said that thousands of people rushed there from the four corners of the world, people of all conditions; they crossed Europe like lemmings in migration; together, they began to rebuild the cathedral upon its old foundations. They stayed there until the immense edifice was completed, all of them, architects, workers, artists, jugglers, nobles, priests and the bourgeoisie, but their names were unknown, and, even today, nobody knows the names of those who built the cathedral of Chartres.

Without letting that give you any preconceived ideas about my beliefs or   51
doubts—which, furthermore, have nothing to do with what we are discussing here—I think that any art loses its essential potency the moment it becomes separated from the "cult." It has cut the umbilical cord and it lives its own separate life, a life that is astonishingly sterile, dim, and degenerate. Creative collectivity, humble anonymity are forgotten and burried relics, deprived of any value. Little wounds of the ego and moral colics are examined under a microscope *sub specie aeternitatis*. The fear of the dark which characterizes subjectivism and scrupulous consciences has become quite stylish, and ultimately we are all running around in a big enclosure where we argue with one another about our solitude without listening to each other or even noticing that we are pushing ourselves mutually to the point of dying of suffocation from all this. It is in such a way that individualists look each other in the eye, deny the existence of those they see and invoke omnipotent obscurity without ever having once felt the saving force of

the joys of community. We are so poisoned by our own vicious circles, so closed in by our own anguish that we are becoming incapable of distinguishing true from false, the ideality of gangsters and sincere unaffectedness.

To the question concerning the goal of my films, I could therefore answer: 52 "I want to be one of the artists of the cathedral that stands above the plains. I want to occupy myself making from stone a dragon's head, an angel or a devil, or perhaps a saint, it doesn't really matter; I feel the same enjoyment in each case. Whether I am a believer or an unbeliever, a Christian or a pagan, I am working along with everybody else to construct a cathedral, because I am an artist and an artisan, and because I have learned to extract faces, limbs, and bodies from stone. I never have to worry about the judgment of posterity or of my contemporaries; my first and last names are engraved nowhere, and they will disappear with me. But a small part of my self will survive in the anonymous and triumphant totality. A dragon or a devil, or perhaps a saint, what does it matter!"

Questions for Discussion

1. What *is* film-making?
2. What lies beyond the art of making a film? What other factors are involved, besides creativity?
3. How is film-making a "game"?
4. What anxieties does Bergman feel when he makes a film? Would these anxieties be felt by any artist? In what ways are film-makers and other artists alike?
5. What creates the tension between film-maker and film viewer? How does Bergman resolve this tension?
6. What are some of the ways Bergman describes film-making, beginning with his question "What is 'shooting a film,' then?" in paragraph 35? What other comparisons can you think of?
7. Bergman uses the personal pronoun ("I") and writes this essay as a personal narrative interlaced with commentary about art, marketing, audiences, and so forth. Why is this approach effective?

Questions for Reflection and Writing

1. Summarize Bergman's process for making a film.
2. What does Bergman mean with his statement in paragraph 27 that "It is easy to put a spectator in a state worse than the one he was in when he entered the theater; it is difficult to put him in a better state . . ."? Find

examples of films, Bergman's or those of other film-makers, that illustrate this statement, and write an essay in which you explain the statement in the context of those films.

3. See a film by Bergman. Write a review of it, using as a model the film reviews of a national newspaper. If you have time, watch the film more than once in order to pick up more details to include in your review, or see more than one film by Bergman and compare the films in your review.

George Orwell (1903–1950) is the pseudonym of Eric Blair. He was born in India, where his father served in the British colonial government, but he was sent to Eton, in England, to be educated. He started his career as a policeman in the Indian Imperial Police, in Burma, and wrote about his experiences there in *Burmese Days* (1934), a novel about the political injustices of imperialism. Back in England, he lived as a beggar in the East End of London, an experience which he wrote about in *Down and Out in Paris and London* (1933). He was also busy writing other novels, including *A Clergyman's Daughter* (1935) and *Keep the Aspidestra Flying* (1936). Later, he was wounded while fighting for the loyalists in the Spanish Civil War, the subject of *Homage to Catalonia* (1938). Orwell despised the "Big Brother" mentalities of both the fascists and the communists, who backed opposing sides in that war; however, he also condemned corrupt and bureaucratic democracies, a stance reinforced by his work as a war correspondent during World War II. He is best remembered for his political satires *Animal Farm* (1946) and *1984* (1949).

Politics and the English Language

George Orwell

Most people who bother with the matter at all would admit that the English language is in a bad way, but it is generally assumed that we cannot by conscious action do anything about it. Our civilization is decadent and our language—so the argument runs—must inevitably share in the general collapse. It follows that any struggle against the abuse of language is a sentimental archaism, like preferring candles to electric light or hansom cabs to aeroplanes. Underneath this lies the half-conscious belief that language is a natural growth and not an instrument which we shape for our own purposes.   1

Now, it is clear that the decline of a language must ultimately have political and economic causes: it is not due simply to the bad influence of this or that individual writer. But an effect can become a cause, reinforcing the original cause and producing the same effect in an intensified form, and so on indefinitely. A man may take to drink because he feels himself to be a failure, and then fail all the more completely because he drinks. It is rather the same thing that is happening to the English language. It becomes ugly and inaccurate because our thoughts are foolish, but the slovenliness of our language makes it easier for us to   2 have foolish thoughts. The point is that the process is reversible. Modern English, especially written English, is full of bad habits which spread by imitation and which can be avoided if one is willing to take the necessary trouble. If one gets rid of these habits one can think more clearly, and to think clearly is a necessary first step towards political regeneration: so that the fight against bad English is not frivolous and is not the exclusive concern of professional writers. I will come back to this presently, and I hope that by that time the meaning of what I have said here will have become clearer. Meanwhile, here are five specimens of the English language as it is now habitually written.

These five passages have not been picked out because they are especially bad— I could have quoted far worse if I had chosen—but because they illustrate various of the mental vices from which we now suffer. They are a little below the average, but are fairly representative samples. I number them so that I can refer back to them when necessary:

3

1. I am not, indeed, sure whether it is not true to say that the Milton who once seemed not unlike a seventeenth-century Shelley had not become, out of an experience ever more bitter in each year, more alien [sic] to the founder of that Jesuit sect which nothing could induce him to tolerate.

4

Professor Harold Laski (Essay in *Freedom of Expression*)

2. Above all, we cannot play ducks and drakes with a native battery of idioms which prescribes such egregious collocations of vocables as the Basic *put up with* for *tolerate* or *put at a loss* for *bewilder*.

5

Professor Lancelot Hogben (*Interglossa*)

3. On the one side we have the free personality: by definition it is not neurotic, for it has neither conflict nor dream. Its desires, such as they are, are transparent, for they are just what institutional approval keeps in the forefront of consciousness; another institutional pattern would alter their number and intensity; there is little in them that is natural, irreducible, or culturally dangerous. But *on the other side*, the social bond itself is noticing but the mutual reflection of these self-secure integrities. Recall the definition of love. Is not this the very picture of a small academic? Where is there a place in this hall of mirrors for either personality or fraternity?

6

Essay on Psychology in *Politics* (New York)

4. All the "best people" from the gentlemen's clubs, and all the frantic fascist   7
captains, united in common hatred of Socialism and bestial horror of the rising tide of the mass revolutionary movement, have turned to acts of provocation, to foul incendiarism, to medieval legends of poisoned wells, to legal-
ize their own destruction of proletarian organizations, and rouse the agitated petty-bourgeoisie to chauvinistic fervor on behalf of the fight against the
revolutionary way out of the crisis.

Communist Pamphlet

5. If a new spirit *is* to be infused into this old country, there is one thorny and   8
contentious reform which must be tackled, and that is the humanization
and galvanization of the B.B.C. Timidity here will bespeak canker and atrophy of the soul. The heart of Britain may be sound and of strong beat, for
instance, but the British lion's roar at present is like that of Bottom in
Shakespeare's *Midsummer Night's Dream*—as gentle as any sucking dove. A
virile new Britain cannot continue indefinitely to be traduced in the eyes or
rather ears, of the world by the effete languors of Langham Place, brazenly
masquerading as "standard English." When the voice of Britain is heard at
nine o'clock, better far and infinitely less ludicrous to hear aitches honestly
dropped than the present priggish, inflated, inhibited, school-ma'amish
arch braying of blameless bashful mewing maidens!

Letter in *Tribune*

Each of these passages has faults of its own, but, quite apart from avoidable   9
ugliness, two qualities are common to all of them. The first is staleness of
imagery; the other is lack of precision. The writer either has a meaning and cannot express it, or he inadvertently says something else, or he is almost indifferent
as to whether his words mean anything or not. This mixture of vagueness and
sheer incompetence is the most marked characteristic of modern English prose,
and especially of any kind of political writing. As soon as certain topics are raised,
the concrete melts into the abstract and no one seems able to think of turns of
speech that are not hackneyed: prose consists less and less of *words* chosen for the
sake of their meaning, and more and more of *phrases* tacked together like the sections of a prefabricated henhouse. I list below, with notes and examples, various
of the tricks by means of which the work of prose-construction is habitually
dodged:

Dying Metaphors

A newly invented metaphor assists thought by evoking a visual image, while on   10
the other hand a metaphor which is technically "dead" (e.g., *iron resolution*) has
in effect reverted to being an ordinary word and can generally be used without
loss of vividness. But in between these two classes there is a huge dump of worn-
out metaphors which have lost all evocative power and are merely used because
they save people the trouble of inventing phrases for themselves. Examples are:
*Ring the changes on, take up the cudgels for, toe the line, ride roughshod over, stand
shoulder to shoulder with, play into the hands of, no axe to grind, grist to the mill, fishing in troubled waters, on the order of the day, Achilles' heel, swan song, hotbed.* Many
of these are used without knowledge of their meaning (what is a "rift," for
instance?), and incompatible metaphors are frequently mixed, a sure sign that
the writer is not interested in what he is saying. Some metaphors now current
have been twisted out of their original meaning without those who use them
even being aware of the fact. For example, *toe the line* is sometimes written *tow
the line.* Another example is *the hammer and the anvil,* now always used with the
implication that the anvil gets the worst of it. In real life it is always the anvil
that breaks the hammer, never the other way about: a writer who stopped to
think what he was saying would be aware of this, and would avoid perverting the
original phrase.

Operators or Verbal False Limbs

These save the trouble of picking out appropriate verbs and nouns, and at the   11
same time pad each sentence with extra syllables which give it an appearance of
symmetry. Characteristic phrases are *render inoperative, militate against, make contact with, be subjected to, give rise to, give grounds for, have the effect of, play a leading part (role) in, make itself felt, take effect, exhibit a tendency to, serve the purpose
of,* etc., etc. The keynote is the elimination of simple verbs. Instead of being a
single word, such as *break, stop, spoil, mend, kill,* a verb becomes *a phrase,* made
up of a noun or adjective tacked on to some general-purpose verb such as *prove,
serve, form, play, render.* In addition, the passive voice is wherever possible used
in preference to the active, and noun constructions are used instead of gerunds
(*by examination of* instead of *by examining*). The range of verbs is further cut down
by means of the *-ize* and *de-* formations, and the banal statements are given an
appearance of profundity by means of the *not un-* formation. Simple conjunctions
and prepositions are replaced by such phrases as *with respect to, having regard to,
the fact that, by dint of, in view of, in the interests of, on the hypothesis that;* and the

ends of sentences are saved from anticlimax by such resounding common-places as *greatly to be desired, cannot be left out of account, a development to be expected in the near future, deserving of serious consideration, brought to a satisfactory conclusion,* and so on and so forth.

Pretentious Diction

Words like *phenomenon, element, individual* (as noun), *objective, categorical, effec-*   12
tive, virtual, basic, primary, promote, constitute, exhibit, exploit, utilize, eliminate, liquidate, are used to dress up simple statements and give an air of scientific impartiality to biased judgments. Adjectives like *epoch-making, epic, historic, unforgettable, triumphant, age-old, inevitable, inexorable, veritable,* are used to dignify the sordid processes of international politics, while writing that aims at glorifying war usually takes on an archaic color, its characteristic words being: *realm, throne, chariot, mailed fist, trident, sword, shield, buckler, banner, jackboot, clarion.* Foreign words and expressions such as *cul de sac, ancien régime, deus ex machina, mutatis mutandis, status quo, gleichschaltung, weltanschauung,* are used to give an air of culture and elegance. Except for the useful abbreviations *i.e., e.g.,* and *etc.,* there is no real need for any of the hundreds of foreign phrases now current in English. Bad writers, and especially scientific, political and sociological writers, are nearly always haunted by the notion that Latin or Greek words are grander than Saxon ones, and unnecessary words like *expedite, ameliorate, predict, extraneous, deracinated, clandestine, subaqueous* and hundreds of others constantly gain ground from their Anglo-Saxon opposite numbers.[1] The jargon peculiar to Marxist writing (*hyena, hangman, cannibal, petty bourgeois, these gentry, lacquey, flunkey, mad dog, White Guard,* etc.) consists largely of words and phrases translated from Russian, German or French; but the normal way of coining a new word is to use a Latin or Greek root with the appropriate affix and, where necessary, the *-ize* formation. It is often easier to make up words of this kind (*deregionalize, impermissible, extramarital, nonfragmentary* and so forth) than to think up the English words that will cover one's meaning. The result, in general, is an increase in slovenliness and vagueness.

Meaningless Words

In certain kinds of writing, particularly in art criticism and literary criticism, it is   13
normal to come across long passages which are almost completely lacking in meaning.[2] Words like *romantic, plastic, values, human, dead, sentimental, natural, vitality,* as used in art criticism, are strictly meaningless, in the sense that they not

only do not point to any discoverable object, but are hardly ever expected to do so by the reader. When one critic writes, "The outstanding feature of Mr. X's work is its living quality," while another writes, "the immediately striking thing about Mr. X's work is its peculiar deadness," the reader accepts this as a simple difference of opinion. If words like *black* and *white* were involved, instead of the jargon words *dead* and *living*, he would see at once that language was being used in an improper way. Many political words are similarly abused. The word *Fascism* has now no meaning except in so far as it signifies "something not desirable." The words *democracy, socialism, freedom, patriotic, realistic, justice*, have each of them several different meanings which cannot be reconciled with one another. In the case of a word like *democracy*, not only is there no agreed definition, but the attempt to make one is resisted from all sides. It is almost universally felt that when we call a country democratic we are praising it: consequently the defenders of every kind of régime claim that it is a democracy, and fear that they might have to stop using the word if it were tied down to any one meaning. Words of this kind are often used in a consciously dishonest way. That is, the person who uses them has his own private definition, but allows his hearer to think he means something quite different. Statements like *Marshal Pétain was a true patriot, The Soviet Press is the freest in the world, The Catholic Church is opposed to persecution,* are almost always made with intent to deceive. Other words used in variable meanings, in most cases more or less dishonestly, are: *class, totalitarian, science, progressive, reactionary, bourgeois, equality.*

Now that I have made this catalogue of swindles and perversions, let me   14
give another example of the kind of writing that they lead to. This time it must of its nature be an imaginary one. I am going to translate a passage of good English into modern English of the worst sort. Here is a well-known verse from *Ecclesiastes:*

I returned and saw under the sun, that the race is not to the swift, nor the   15
battle to the strong, neither yet bread to the wise, nor yet riches to men of understanding, nor yet favour to men of skill; but time and chance happeneth to them all.

Here it is in modern English:

Objective consideration of contemporary phenomena compels the conclu-   16
sion that success or failure in competitive activities exhibits no tendency to

be commensurate with innate capacity, but that a considerable element of the unpredictable must invariably be taken into account.

This is a parody, but not a very gross one. Exhibit (3), above, for instance,   17
contains several patches of the same kind of English. It will be seen that I have not made a full translation. The beginning and ending of the sentence follow the original meaning fairly closely, but in the middle the concrete illustrations— race, battle, bread— dissolve into the vague phrase "success or failure in competitive activities." This had to be so, because no modern writer of the kind I am discussing—no one capable of using phrases like "objective consideration of contemporary phenomena"—would ever tabulate his thoughts in that precise and detailed way. The whole tendency of modern prose is away from concreteness. Now analyze these two sentences a little more closely. The first contains fortynine words but only sixty syllables, and all its words are those of everyday life. The second contains thirty-eight words of ninety syllables: eighteen of its words are from Latin roots, and one from Greek. The first sentence contains six vivid images, and only one phrase ("time and chance") that could be called vague. The second contains not a single fresh, arresting phrase, and in spite of its ninety syllables it gives only a shortened version of the meaning contained in the first. Yet without a doubt it is the second kind of sentence that is gaining ground in modern English. I do not want to exaggerate. This kind of writing is not yet universal, and outcrops of simplicity will occur here and there in the worstwritten page. Still, if you or I were told to write a few lines on the uncertainty of human fortunes, we should probably come much nearer to my imaginary sentence than to the one from *Ecclesiastes*.

As I have tried to show, modern writing at its worst does not consist in   18
picking out words for the sake of their meaning and inventing images in order to make the meaning clearer. It consists in gumming together long strips of words which have already been set in order by someone else, and making the results presentable by sheer humbug. The attraction of this way of writing is that it is easy. It is easier—even quicker, once you have the habit—to say *In my opinion it is not an unjustifiable assumption that* than to say *I think*. If you use ready-made phrases, you not only don't have to hunt about for words; you also don't have to bother with the rhythms of your sentences, since these phrases are generally so arranged as to be more or less euphonious. When you are composing in a hurry— when you are dictating to a stenographer, for instance, or making a public speech—it is natural to fall into a pretentious, Latinized style. Tags like *a consid-*

eration which we should do well to bear in mind or a conclusion to which all of us would readily assent will save many a sentence from coming down with a bump. By using stale metaphors, similes and idioms, you save much mental effort, at the cost of leaving your meaning vague, not only for your reader but for yourself. This is the significance of mixed metaphors. The sole aim of a metaphor is to call up a visual image. When these images clash—as in *The Fascist octopus has sung its swan song, the jackboot is thrown into the melting pot*—it can be taken as certain that the writer is not seeing a mental image of the objects he is naming; in other words he is not really thinking. Look again at the examples I gave at the beginning of this essay. Professor Laski (1) uses five negatives in fifty-three words. One of these is superfluous, making nonsense of the whole passage, and in addition there is the slip *alien* for *akin*, making further nonsense, and several avoidable pieces of clumsiness which increase the general vagueness. Professor Hogben (2) plays ducks and drakes with a battery which is able to write prescriptions, and while, disapproving of the everyday phrase *put up with*, is unwilling to look *egregious* up in the dictionary and see what it means; (3), if one takes an uncharitable attitude towards it, is simply meaningless: probably one could work out its intended meaning by reading the whole of the article in which it occurs. In (4), the writer knows more or less what he wants to say, but an accumulation of stale phrases chokes him like tea leaves blocking a sink. In (5), words and meaning have almost parted company. People who write in this manner usually have a general emotional meaning—they dislike one thing and want to express solidarity with another—but they are not interested in the detail of what they are saying. A scrupulous writer, in every sentence that he writes, will ask himself at least four questions, thus: What am I trying to say? What words will express it? What image or idiom will make it clearer? Is this image fresh enough to have an effect? And he will probably ask himself two more: Could I put it more shortly? Have I said anything that is avoidably ugly? But you are not obliged to go to all this trouble. You can shirk it by simply throwing your mind open and letting the ready-made phrases come crowding in. They will construct your sentences for you— even think your thoughts for you, to a certain extent—and at need they will perform the important service of partially concealing your meaning even from yourself. It is at this point that the special connection between politics and the debasement of language becomes clear.

In our time it is broadly true that political writing is bad writing. Where it 19 is not true, it will generally be found that the writer is some kind of rebel, expressing his private opinions and not a "party line." Orthodoxy, of whatever color, seems to demand a lifeless, imitative style. The political dialects to be found in pamphlets, leading articles, manifestos, White Papers and the speeches of under-secretaries do, of course, vary from party to party, but they are all alike in that one almost never finds in them a fresh, vivid, home-made turn of speech. When one watches some tired hack on the platform mechanically repeating the familiar phrases—*bestial atrocities, iron heel, bloodstained tyranny, free peoples of the world, stand shoulder to shoulder*—one often has a curious feeling that one is not watching a live human being but some kind of dummy: a feeling which suddenly becomes stronger at moments when the light catches the speaker's spectacles and turns them into blank discs which seem to have no eyes behind them. And this is not altogether fanciful. A speaker who uses that kind of phraseology has gone some distance towards turning himself into a machine. The appropriate noises are coming out of his larynx, but his brain is not involved as it would be if he were choosing his words for himself. If the speech he is making is one that he is accustomed to make over and over again, he may be almost unconscious of what he is saying, as one is when one utters the responses in church. And this reduced state of consciousness, if not indispensable, is at any rate favorable to political conformity.

In our time, political speech and writing are largely the defense of the inde-   20
fensible. Things like the continuance of British rule in India, the Russian purges and deportations, the dropping of the atom bombs on Japan, can indeed be defended, but only by arguments which are too brutal for most people to face, and which do not square with the professed aims of political parties. Thus political language has to consist largely of euphemism, question-begging and sheer cloudy vagueness. Defenseless villages are bombarded from the air, the inhabitants driven out into the countryside, the cattle machine-gunned, the huts set on fire with incendiary bullets: this is called *pacification*. Millions of peasants are robbed of their farms and sent trudging along the roads with no more than they can carry: this is called *transfer of population* or *rectification of frontiers*. People are imprisoned for years without trial, or shot in the back of the neck or sent to die of scurvy in Arctic lumber camps: this is called *elimination of unreliable elements*. Such phraseology is needed if one wants to name things without calling up mental pictures of them. Consider for instance some comfortable English professor defending Russian totalitarianism. He cannot say outright, "I believe in killing off your opponents when you can get good results by doing so." Probably, therefore, he will say something like this:

While freely conceding that the Soviet regime exhibits certain features   21
which the humanitarian may be inclined to deplore, we must, I think,
agree that a certain curtailment of the right to political opposition is an
unavoidable concomitant of transitional periods, and that the rigors which
the Russian people have been called upon to undergo have been amply justified in the sphere of concrete achievement.

The inflated style is itself a kind of euphemism. A mass of Latin words falls   22
upon the facts like soft snow, blurring the outlines and covering up all the details.
The great enemy of clear language is insincerity. When there is a gap between
one's real and one's declared aims, one turns as it were instinctively to long words
and exhausted idioms, like a cuttlefish squirting out ink. In our age there is no
such thing as "keeping out of politics." All issues are political issues, and politics
itself is a mass of lies, evasions, folly, hatred and schizophrenia. When the general atmosphere is bad, language must suffer. I should expect to find—this is a guess
which I have not sufficient knowledge to verify—that the German, Russian and
Italian languages have all deteriorated in the last ten to fifteen years, as a result
of dictatorship.

But if thought corrupts language, language can also corrupt thought. A bad   23
usage can spread by tradition and imitation, even among people who should and
do know better. The debased language that I have been discussing is in some
ways very convenient. Phrases like *a not unjustifiable assumption*, *leaves much to be
desired*, *would serve no good purpose*, *a consideration which we should do well to bear
in mind*, are a continuous temptation, a packet of aspirins always at one's elbow.
Look back through this essay, and for certain you will find that I have again and
again committed the very faults I am protesting against. By this morning's post I
have received a pamphlet dealing with conditions in Germany. The author tells
me that he "felt impelled" to write it. I open it at random, and here is almost the
first sentence that I see: "[The Allies] have an opportunity not only of achieving
a radical transformation of Germany's social and political structure in such a way
as to avoid a nationalistic reaction in Germany itself, but at the same time of laying the foundations of cooperative and unified Europe." You see, he "feels
impelled" to write—feels, presumably, that he has something new to say—and
yet his words, like cavalry horses answering the bugle, group themselves automatically into the familiar dreary pattern. This invasion of one's mind by ready-
made phrases (*lay the foundations*, *achieve a radical transformation*) can only be pre-

vented if one is constantly on guard against them, and every such phrase anaesthetizes a portion of one's brain.

I said earlier that the decadence of our language is probably curable. Those 24 who deny this would argue, if they produced an argument at all, that language merely reflects existing social conditions, and that we cannot influence its development by any direct tinkering with words and constructions. So far as the general tone or spirit of a language goes, this may be true, but it is not true in detail. Silly words and expressions have often disappeared, not through any evolutionary process but owing to the conscious action of a minority. Two recent examples were *explore every avenue* and *leave no stone unturned*, which were killed by the jeers of a few journalists. There is a long list of flyblown metaphors which could similarly be got rid of if enough people would interest themselves in the job; and it should also be possible to laugh the not un- formation out of existence,3 to reduce the amount of Latin and Greek in the average sentence, to drive out foreign phrases and strayed scientific words, and, in general, to make pretentiousness unfashionable. But all these are minor points. The defense of the English language implies more than this, and perhaps it is best to start by saying what it does *not* imply.

To begin with it has nothing to do with archaism, with the salvaging of 25 obsolete words and turns of speech, or with the setting up of a "standard English" which must never be departed from. On the contrary, it is especially concerned with the scrapping of every word or idiom which has outworn its usefulness. It has nothing to do with correct grammar and syntax, which are of no importance so long as one makes one's meaning clear, or with the avoidance of Americanisms, or with having what is called a "good prose style." On the other hand it is not concerned with fake simplicity and the attempt to make written English colloquial. Nor does it even imply in every case preferring the Saxon word to the Latin one, though it does imply using the fewest and shortest words that will cover one's meaning. What is above all needed is to let the meaning choose the word, and not the other way about. In prose, the worst thing one can do with words is to surrender to them. When you think of a concrete object, you think wordlessly, and then, if you want to describe the thing you have been visualizing you probably hunt about till you find the exact words that seem to fit in. When you think of something abstract you are more inclined to use words from the start, and unless you make a conscious effort to prevent it, the existing dialect will come rushing in and do the job for you, at the expense of blurring or even changing your meaning. Probably it is better to put off using words as long as possible and get one's meaning as clear as one can through pictures or sensations. Afterwards one can choose—not simply *accept*—the phrases that will best cover the meaning, and then switch round and decide what impression one's words are likely to make on another person. This last effort of the mind cuts out all stale or mixed images, all prefabricated phrases, needless repetitions, and humbug and vagueness generally. But one can often be in doubt about the effect of a word or a phrase, and one needs rules that one can rely on when instinct fails. I think the following rules will cover most cases:

(i)   Never use a metaphor, simile or other figure of speech which you are used   26
      to seeing in print.

(ii) Never use a long word where a short one will do.   27

(iii) If it is possible to cut a word out, always cut it out.   28

(iv) Never use the passive where you can use the active.   29

(v)   Never use a foreign phrase, a scientific word or a jargon word if you can   30
      think of an everyday English equivalent.

(vi) Break any of these rules sooner than say anything outright barbarous.   31

These rules sound elementary, and so they are, but they demand a deep change   32
of attitude in anyone who has grown used to writing in the style now fashionable. One could keep all of them and still write bad English, but one could not write the kind of stuff that I quoted in those five specimens at the beginning of this article.

I have not here been considering the literary use of language, but merely   33
language as an instrument for expressing and not for concealing or preventing thought. Stuart Chase and others have come near to claiming that all abstract words are meaningless, and have used this as a pretext for advocating a kind of political quietism. Since you don't know what Fascism is, how can you struggle against Fascism? One need not swallow such absurdities as this, but one ought to recognize that the present political chaos is connected with the decay of language, and that one can probably bring about some improvement by starting at the verbal end. If you simplify your English, you are freed from the worst follies of orthodoxy. You cannot speak any of the necessary dialects, and when you make a stupid remark its stupidity will be obvious, even to yourself. Political language—and with variations this is true of all political parties, from Conservatives to Anarchists—is designed to make lies sound truthful and murder respectable, and to give an appearance of solidity to pure wind. One cannot change this all

in a moment, but one can at least change one's own habits, and from time to time one can even, if one jeers loudly enough, send some worn-out and useless phrase—some *jackboot, Achilles' heel, hotbed, melting pot, acid test, veritable inferno* or other lump of verbal refuse—into the dustbin where it belongs.

Endnotes

1. An interesting illustration of this is the way in which the English flower names which were in use till very recently are being ousted by Greek ones, snapdragonbecoming antirrhinum, forget-me-notbecoming myosotis,etc. It is hard to see any practical reason for this change of fashion: it is probably due to an instinctive turning-away from the more homely word and a vague feeling that the Greek word is scientific.

2. Example: "Comfort's catholicity of perception and image, strangely Whitmanesque in range, almost the exact opposite in aesthetic compulsion, continues to evoke that trembling atmospheric accumulative hinting at a cruel, an inexorably serene timelessness. . . . Wrey Gardiner scores by aiming at simple bull's-eyes with precision. Only they are not simple, and through this contented sadness runs more than the surface bitter-sweet of resignation." (Poetry Quarterly.)

3. One can cure oneself of the not un-formation by memorizing this sentence: A not unblack dog was chasing a not unsmall rabbit across a not ungreen field.

Questions for Discussion

1. What is the connection between a language and politics? How does a language decline?

2. What are the "mental vices" (Paragraph 3) that Orwell holds up for vilification? In particular, what are verbal false limbs, and how do they function in a piece of prose?

3. Does language used poorly lead to sloppy thinking, or does sloppy thinking lead to poorly used language? What is Orwell's answer? What is your answer (if it's different from his)?

4. What would be the simple English words that would clearly state the terms listed in Paragraph 12, especially the terms "deregionalize," "impermissible," "extramarital," and non "fragmentary"? What other recently created terms can you think of that fall into the pretentious diction category?

5. Which of the "mental vices" does Orwell himself use in this essay? Why does he tell you, in Paragraph 23, that he has done the same thing that he faults in others?

6. Why is Orwell so bothered by what he sees as the decline of English? Where is his irritation most apparent in the essay?

7. Why is classification such a good organizational strategy for this essay?

Questions for Reflection and Writing

1. Summarize the cause-effect relationship explained in this essay? What has caused what? What has the potential to cause what? As an alternative, try writing intentionally bad prose, using Orwell's list of vices and his "translation" of the verse from *Ecclesiastes* to guide you. How easy was it to write this prose? As an alternative, apply the six questions that a "scrupulous writer" should ask (Paragraph 18) to your own writing.

2. As Orwell has done, select passages of poorly written prose and explain what makes them poorly written. Refer to Orwell's categories of faults, but invent more categories as needed. You can limit the project by selecting passages from particular genres, such as children's literature, textbooks, or newspaper journalism.

3. Research what other professional writers and educators say about the state of the English language currently or at some point in the past. Do they agree that the English language is "in a bad way" (Paragraph 1)?

S **usan Sontag** (1933-   ), a writer and a critic, earned a B.A. in philosophy from the University of Chicago (1951) and an M.A. in English (1954) and an M.A. in philosophy (1955) from Harvard University, where she also did work toward a Ph.D. Later, she did post-graduate study at Oxford University. From Oxford she moved to Paris, and thence to New York City, where she took a job in 1959 as an editor at *Commentary*, a neoconservative journal. That same year she taught at City College and Sarah Lawrence College, and from 1960 to 1963 she taught at Columbia University. Her reputation as a cultural critic was made with her essay "Notes on Camp" in 1964 and her book *Against Interpretation* in 1966. Although she has written novels, directed films, and written screenplays, she is best known for her nonfiction writing on aesthetics, including *Styles of Radical Will* (1969) and *On Photography* (1976). Two books on how society thinks about and treats illness are *Illness as Metaphor* (1978), a book inspired by her (metaphorical) battle with breast cancer, and *AIDS and Its Metaphors* (1988).

The Image-World

Susan Sontag

Reality has always been interpreted through the reports given by images; and   1
philosophers since Plato have tried to loosen our dependence on images by evoking the standard of an image-free way of apprehending the real. But when, in the mid-nineteenth century, the standard finally seemed attainable, the retreat of old religious and political illusions before the advance of humanistic and scientific thinking did not—as anticipated—create mass defections to the real. On the contrary, the new age of unbelief strengthened the allegiance to images. The credence that could no longer be given to realities understood *in the form of* images was now being given to realities understood *to be* images, illusions. In the preface to the second edition (1843) of *The Essence of Christianity*, Feuerbach observes about "our era" that it "prefers the image to the thing, the copy to the original, the representation to the reality, appearance to being"—while being aware of doing just that. And his premonitory complaint has been transformed in the twentieth century into a widely agreed-on diagnosis: that a society becomes "modern" when one of its chief activities is producing and consuming images, when images that have extraordinary powers to determine our demands upon reality and are themselves coveted substitutes for firsthand experience become

indispensable to the health of the economy, the stability of the polity, and the pursuit of private happiness.

Feuerbach's words—he is writing a few years after the invention of the   2
camera—seem, more specifically, a presentiment of the impact of photography. For the images that have virtually unlimited authority in a modern society are mainly photographic images; and the scope of that authority stems from the properties peculiar to images taken by cameras.

Such images are indeed able to usurp reality because first of all a photo-   3
graph is not only an image (as a painting is an image), an interpretation of the real; it is also a trace, something directly stenciled off the real, like a footprint or a death mask. While a painting, even one that meets photographic standards of resemblance, is never more than the stating of an interpretation, a photograph is never less than the registering of an emanation (light waves reflected by objects)—a material vestige of its subject in a way that no painting can be. Between two fantasy alternatives, that Holbein the Younger had lived long enough to have painted Shakespeare or that a prototype of the camera had been invented early enough to have photographed him, most Bardolators would choose the photograph. This is not just because it would presumably show what Shakespeare really looked like, for even if the hypothetical photograph were faded, barely legible, a brownish shadow, we would probably still prefer it to another glorious Holbein. Having a photograph of Shakespeare would be like having a nail from the True Cross.

Most contemporary expressions of concern that an image-world is replac-   4
ing the real one continue to echo, as Feuerbach did, the Platonic depreciation of the image: true insofar as it resembles something real, sham because it is no more than a resemblance. But this venerable naïve realism is somewhat beside the point in the era of photographic images, for its blunt contrast between the image ("copy") and the thing depicted (the "original")—which Plato repeatedly illustrates with the example of a painting—does not fit a photograph in so simple a way. Neither does the contrast help in understanding image-making at its origins, when it was a practical, magical activity, a means of appropriating or gaining power over something. The further back we go in history, as E. H. Gombrich has observed, the less sharp is the distinction between images and real things; in primitive societies, the thing and its image were simply two different, that is, physically distinct, manifestations of the same energy or spirit. Hence, the supposed efficacy of images in propitiating and gaining control over powerful presences. Those powers, those presences were present in *them*.

For defenders of the real from Plato to Feuerbach to equate image with 5
mere appearance—that is, to presume that the image is absolutely distinct from
the object depicted—is part of that process of desacralization which separates us
irrevocably from the world of sacred times and places in which an image was
taken to participate in the reality of the object depicted. What defines the originality of photography is that, at the very moment in the long, increasingly secular history of painting when secularism is entirely triumphant, it revives—in
wholly secular terms—something like the primitive status of images. Our irrepressible feeling that the photographic process is something magical has a genuine basis. No one takes an easel painting to be in any sense co-substantial with
its subject; it only represents or refers. But a photograph is not only like its subject, a homage to the subject. It is part of, an extension of that subject; and a
potent means of acquiring it, of gaining control over it.

Photography is acquisition in several forms. In its simplest form, we have 6
in a photograph surrogate possession of a cherished person or thing, a possession
which gives photographs some of the character of unique objects. Through photographs, we also have a consumer's relation to events, both to events which are
part of our experience and to those which are not—a distinction between types
of experience that such habit-forming consumership blurs. A third form of acquisition is that, through image-making and image-duplicating machines, we can
acquire something as information (rather than experience). Indeed, the importance of photographic images as the medium through which more and more
events enter our experience is, finally, only a by-product of their effectiveness in
furnishing knowledge disassociated from and independent of experience.

This is the most inclusive form of photographic acquisition. Through being 7
photographed, something becomes part of a system of information, fitted into
schemes of classification and storage which range from the crudely chronological order of snapshot sequences pasted in family albums to the dogged accumu-
lations and meticulous filing needed for photography's uses in weather forecast-
ing, astronomy, microbiology, geology, police work, medical training and diagnosis, military reconnaissance, and art history. Photographs do more than redefine
the stuff of ordinary experience (people, things, events, whatever we see—albeit,
differently, often inattentively— with natural vision) and add vast amounts of
material that we never see at all. Reality as such is redefined—as an item for
exhibition, as a record for scrutiny, as a target for surveillance. The photographic exploration and duplication of the world fragments continuities and feeds the
pieces into an interminable dossier, thereby providing possibilities of control that

could not even be dreamed of under the earlier system of recording information: writing.

That photographic recording is always, potentially, a means of control was   8
already recognized when such powers were in their infancy. In 1850, Delacroix noted in his *Journal* the success of some "experiments in photography" being made at Cambridge, where astronomers were photographing the sun and the moon and had managed to obtain a pinhead-size impression of the star Vega. He added the following "curious" observation:

> Since the light of the star which was daguerreotyped took twenty years to   9
> traverse the space separating it from the earth, the ray which was fixed on the plate had consequently left the celestial sphere a long time before Daguerre had discovered the process by means of which we have just gained control of this light.

Leaving behind such puny notions of control as Delacroix's, photography's   10
progress has made ever more literal the senses in which a photograph gives control over the thing photographed. The technology that has already minimized the extent to which the distance separating photographer from subject affects the precision and magnitude of the image; provided ways to photograph things which are unimaginably small as well as those, like stars, which are unimaginably far; rendered picture-taking independent of light itself (infrared photography) and freed the picture-object from its confinement to two dimensions (holography); shrunk the interval between sighting the picture and holding it in one's hands (from the first Kodak, when it took weeks for a developed roll of film to be returned to the amateur photographer, to the Polaroid, which ejects the image in a few seconds); not only got images to move (cinema) but achieved their simultaneous recording and transmission (video)—this technology has made photography an incomparable tool for deciphering behavior, predicting it, and interfering with it.

Photography has powers that no other image-system has ever enjoyed   11
because, unlike the earlier ones, it is *not* dependent on an image maker. However carefully the photographer intervenes in setting up and guiding the image-making process, the process itself remains an optical-chemical (or electronic) one, the workings of which are automatic, the machinery for which will inevitably be modified to provide still more detailed and, therefore, more useful maps of the real. The mechanical genesis of these images, and the literalness of the powers

they confer, amounts to a new relationship between image and reality. And if photography could also be said to restore the most primitive relationship—the partial identity of image and object—the potency of the image is now experienced in a very different way. The primitive notion of the efficacy of images presumes that images possess the qualities of real things, but our inclination is to attribute to real things the qualities of an image.

As everyone knows, primitive people fear that the camera will rob them of some part of their being. In the memoir he published in 1900, at the end of a very long life, Nadar reports that Balzac had a similar "vague dread" of being photographed. His explanation, according to Nadar, was that

12

> every body in its natural state was made up of a series of ghostly images superimposed in layers to infinity, wrapped in infinitesimal films. . . . Man never having been able to create, that is to make something material from an apparition, from something impalpable, or to make from nothing, an object—each Daguerreian operation was therefore going to lay hold of, detach, and use up one of the layers of the body on which it focused.

It seems fitting for Balzac to have had this particular brand of trepidation—"Was Balzac's fear of the Daguerreotype real or feigned?" Nadar asks. "It was real . . ."—since the procedure of photography is a materializing, so to speak, of what is most original in his procedure as a novelist. The Balzacian operation was to magnify tiny details, as in a photographic enlargement, to juxtapose incongruous traits or items, as in a photographic layout: made expressive in this way, any one thing can be connected with everything else. For Balzac, the spirit of an entire milieu could be disclosed by a single material detail, however paltry or arbitrary-seeming. The whole of a life may be summed up in a momentary appearance.[1] And a change in appearances is a change in the person, for he refused to posit any "real" person ensconced behind these appearances. Balzac's fanciful theory, expressed to Nadar, that a body is composed of an infinite series of "ghostly images," eerily parallels the supposedly realistic theory expressed in his novels, that a person is an aggregate of appearances, appearances which can be made to yield, by proper focusing, infinite layers of significance. To view reality as an endless set of situations which mirror each other, to extract analogies from the most dissimilar things, is to anticipate the characteristic form of perception stimulated by photographic images. Reality itself has started to be understood as a kind of writing, which has to be decoded—even as photographed images were themselves first

13

compared to writing. (Niepce's name for the process whereby the image appears on the plate was heliography, sun-writing; Fox Talbot called the camera "the pencil of nature.")

The problem with Feuerbach's contrast of "original" with "copy" is its sta-   14
tic definitions of reality and image. It assumes that what is real persists, unchanged and intact, while only images have changed: shored up by the most tenuous claims to credibility, they have somehow become more seductive. But the notions of image and reality are complementary. When the notion of reality changes, so does that of the image, and vice versa. "Our era" does not prefer images to real things out of perversity but partly in response to the ways in which the notion of what is real has been progressively complicated and weakened, one of the early ways being the criticism of reality as facade which arose among the enlightened middle classes in the last century. (This was of course the very opposite of the effect intended.) To reduce large parts of what has hitherto been regarded as real to mere fantasy, as Feuerbach did when he called religion "the dream of the human mind" and dismissed theological ideas as psychological projections; or to inflate the random and trivial details of everyday life into ciphers of hidden historical and psychological forces, as Balzac did in his encyclopedia of social reality in novel form—these are themselves ways of experiencing reality as a set of appearances, an image.

Few people in this society share the primitive dread of cameras that comes   15
from thinking of the photograph as a material part of themselves. But some trace of the magic remains: for example, in our reluctance to tear up or throw away the photograph of a loved one, especially of someone dead or far away. To do so is a ruthless gesture of rejection. In *Jude the Obscure* it is Jude's discovery that Arabella has sold the maple frame with the photograph of himself in it which he gave her on their wedding day that signifies to Jude "the utter death of every sentiment in his wife" and is "the conclusive little stroke to demolish all sentiment in him." But the true modern primitivism is not to regard the image as a real thing; photographic images are hardly that real. Instead, reality has come to seem more and more like what we are shown by cameras. It is common now for people to insist about their experience of a violent event in which they were caught up—a plane crash, a shoot-out, a terrorist bombing—that "it seemed like a movie." This is said, other descriptions seeming insufficient, in order to explain how real it was. While many people in non-industrialized countries still feel apprehensive when being photographed, divining it to be some kind of trespass, an act of disrespect, a sublimated looting of the personality or the culture, peo-

ple in industrialized countries seek to have their photographs taken—feel that they are images, and are made real by photographs.

A steadily more complex sense of the real creates its own compensatory fervors   16 and simplifications, the most addictive of which is picture-taking. It is as if photographers, responding to an increasingly depleted sense of reality, were looking for a transfusion —traveling to new experiences, refreshing the old ones. Their ubiquitous activities amount to the most radical, and the safest, version of mobility. The urge to have new experiences is translated into the urge to take photographs: experience seeking a crisis-proof form.

As the taking of photographs seems almost obligatory to those who travel   17 about, the passionate collecting of them has special appeal for those confined— either by choice, incapacity, or coercion—to indoor space. Photograph collections can be used to make a substitute world, keyed to exalting or consoling or tantalizing images. A photograph can be the starting point of a romance (Hardy's Jude had already fallen in love with Sue Bridehead's photograph before he met her), but it is more common for the erotic relation to be not only created by but understood as limited to the photographs. In Cocteau's *Les Enfants Terribles*, the narcissistic brother and sister share their bedroom, their "secret room," with images of boxers, movie stars, and murderers. Isolating themselves in their lair to live out their private legend, the two adolescents put up these photographs, a private pantheon. On one wall of cell No. 426 in Fresnes Prison in the early 1940s Jean Genet pasted the photographs of twenty criminals he had clipped from newspapers, twenty faces in which he discerned "the sacred sign of the monster," and in their honor wrote *Our Lady of the Flowers*; they served as his muses, his models, his erotic talismans. "They watch over my little routines," writes Genet—conflating reverie, masturbation, and writing—and "are all the family I have and my only friends." For stay-at-homes, prisoners, and the selfimprisoned, to live among the photographs of glamorous strangers is a sentimental response to isolation and an insolent challenge to it.

J. G. Ballard's novel *Crash* (1973) describes a more specialized collecting of   18 photographs in the service of sexual obsession: photographs of car accidents which the narrator's friend Vaughan collects while preparing to stage his own death in a car crash. The acting out of his erotic vision of car death is anticipated and the fantasy itself further eroticized by the repeated perusal of these photographs. At one end of the spectrum, photographs are objective data; at the other end, they are items of psychological science fiction. And as in even the most dreadful, or neutral-seeming, reality a sexual imperative can be found, so even the most banal photograph-document can mutate into an emblem of desire. The mug shot is a clue to a detective, an erotic fetish to a fellow thief. To Hofrat Behrens, in *The Magic Mountain*, the pulmonary X-rays of his patients are diagnostic tools. To Hans Castorp, serving an indefinite sentence in Behrens' sanatorium, and made lovesick by the enigmatic, unattainable Clavdia Chauchat, "Clavdia's X-ray portrait, showing not her face, but the delicate bony structure of the upper half of her body, and the organs of the thoracic cavity, surrounded by the pale, ghostlike envelope of flesh," is the most precious of trophies. The "transparent portrait" is a far more intimate vestige of his beloved than the Hofrat's painting of Clavdia, that "exterior portrait," which Hans had once gazed at with such longing.

Photographs are a way of imprisoning reality, understood as recalcitrant, 19 inaccessible; of making it stand still. Or they enlarge a reality that is felt to be shrunk, hollowed out, perishable, remote. One can't possess reality, one can possess (and be possessed by) images—as, according to Proust, most ambitious of voluntary prisoners, one can't possess the present but one can possess the past. Nothing could be more unlike the self-sacrificial travail of an artist like Proust than the effortlessness of picture-taking, which must be the sole activity resulting in accredited works of art in which a single movement, a touch of the finger, produces a complete work. While the Proustian labors presuppose that reality is distant, photography implies instant access to the real. But the results of this practice of instant access are another way of creating distance. To possess the world in the form of images is, precisely, to reexperience the unreality and remoteness of the real.

The strategy of Proust's realism presumes distance from what is normally 20 experienced as real, the present, in order to reanimate what is usually available only in a remote and shadowy form, the past—which is where the present becomes in his sense real, that is, something that can be possessed. In this effort photographs were of no help. Whenever Proust mentions photographs, he does so disparagingly: as a synonym for a shallow, too exclusively visual, merely voluntary relation to the past, whose yield is insignificant compared with the deep discoveries to be made by responding to cues given by all the senses—the technique he called "involuntary memory." One can't imagine the Overture to *Swann's Way* ending with the narrator's coming across a snapshot of the parish church at Combray and the savoring of *that* visual crumb, instead of the taste of the humble madeleine dipped in tea, making an entire part of his past spring into view. But this is not because a photograph cannot evoke memories (it can, depending on the quality of the viewer rather than of the photograph) but because of what Proust makes clear about his own demands upon imaginative recall, that it be not just extensive and accurate but give the texture and essence of things. And by considering photographs only so far as he could use them, as an instrument of memory, Proust somewhat misconstrues what photographs are: not so much an instrument of memory as an invention of it or a replacement.

It is not reality that photographs make immediately accessible, but images. 21 For example, now all adults can know exactly how they and their parents and grandparents looked as children—a knowledge not available to anyone before the invention of cameras, not even to that tiny minority among whom it was customary to commission paintings of their children. Most of these portraits were less informative than any snapshot. And even the very wealthy usually owned just one portrait of themselves or any of their forebears as children, that is, an image of one moment of childhood, whereas it is common to have many photographs of oneself, the camera offering the possibility of possessing a complete record, at all ages. The point of the standard portraits in the bourgeois household of the eighteenth and nineteenth centuries was to confirm an ideal of the sitter (proclaiming social standing, embellishing personal appearance); given this purpose, it is clear why their owners did not feel the need to have more than one. What the photograph-record confirms is, more modestly, simply that the subject exists; therefore, one can never have too many.

The fear that a subject's uniqueness was leveled by being photographed was 22 never so frequently expressed as in the 1850s, the years when portrait photography gave the first example of how cameras could create instant fashions and durable industries. In Melville's *Pierre*, published at the start of the decade, the hero, another fevered champion of voluntary isolation,

> considered with what infinite readiness now, the most faithful portrait of any one could be taken by the Daguerreotype, whereas in former times a faithful portrait was only within the power of the moneyed, or mental aristocrats of the earth. How natural then the inference, that instead of, as in old times, immortalizing a genius, a portrait now only *dayalized* a dunce. Besides, when every body has his portrait published, true distinction lies in not having yours published at all.

But if photographs demean, paintings distort in the opposite way: they make   23
grandiose. Melville's intuition is that all forms of portraiture in the business civilization are compromised; at least, so it appears to Pierre, a paragon of alienated
sensibility. Just as a photograph is too little in a mass society, a painting is too
much. The nature of a painting, Pierre observes, makes it

> better entitled to reverence than the man; inasmuch as nothing belittling
> can be imagined concerning the portrait, whereas many unavoidably belit-
> tling things can be fancied as touching the man.

Even if such ironies can be considered to have been dissolved by the complete-   24
ness of photography's triumph, the main difference between a painting and a
photograph in the matter of portraiture still holds. Paintings invariably sum up;
photographs usually do not. Photographic images are pieces of evidence in an
ongoing biography or history. And one photograph, unlike one painting, implies
that there will be others.

"Ever—the Human Document to keep the present and the future in touch   25
with the past," said Lewis Hine. But what photography supplies is not only a
record of the past but a new way of dealing with the present, as the effects of the
countless billions of contemporary photograph-documents attest. While old
photographs fill out our mental image of the past, the photographs being taken
now transform what is present into a mental image, like the past. Cameras establish an inferential relation to the present (reality is known by its traces), provide
an instantly retroactive view of experience. Photographs give mock forms of possession: of the past, the present, even the future. In Nabokov's *Invitation to a
Beheading* (1938), the prisoner Cincinnatus is shown the "photohoroscope" of a
child cast by the sinister M'sieur Pierre: an album of photographs of little Emmie
as an infant, then a small child, then pre-pubescent, as she is now, then—by
retouching and using photographs of her mother—of Emmie the adolescent, the
bride, the thirty-year-old, concluding with a photograph at age forty, Emmie on
her deathbed. A "parody of the work of time" is what Nabokov calls this exemplary artifact; it is also a parody of the work of photography.

Photography, which has so many narcissistic uses, is also a powerful instru-   26
ment for depersonalizing our relation to the world; and the two uses are complementary. Like a pair of binoculars with no right or wrong end, the camera makes
exotic things near, intimate; and familiar things small, abstract, strange, much
farther away. It offers, in one easy, habit-forming activity, both participation and

alienation in our own lives and those of others—allowing us to participate, while confirming alienation. War and photography now seem inseparable, and plane crashes and other horrific accidents always attract people with cameras. A society which makes it normative to aspire never to experience privation, failure, misery, pain, dread disease, and in which death itself is regarded not as natural and inevitable but as a cruel, unmerited disaster, creates a tremendous curiosity about these events—a curiosity that is partly satisfied through picture-taking. The feeling of being exempt from calamity stimulates interest in looking at painful pictures, and looking at them suggests and strengthens the feeling that one is exempt. Partly it is because one is "here," not "there," and partly it is the character of inevitability that all events acquire when they are transmuted into images. In the real world, something *is* happening and no one knows what is *going* to happen. In the image-world, it *has* happened, and it *will* forever happen in that way.

Knowing a great deal about what is in the world (art, catastrophe, the beauties of nature) through photographic images, people are frequently disappointed, surprised, unmoved when they see the real thing. For photographic images tend to subtract feeling from something we experience at first hand and the feelings they do arouse are, largely, not those we have in real life. Often something disturbs us more in photographed form than it does when we actually experience it. In a hospital in Shanghai in 1973, watching a factory worker with advanced ulcers have nine-tenths of his stomach removed under acupuncture anesthesia, I managed to follow the threehour procedure (the first operation I'd ever observed) without queasiness, never once feeling the need to look away. In a movie theater in Paris a year later, the less gory operation in Antonioni's China documentary *Chung Kuo* made me flinch at the first cut of the scalpel and avert my eyes several times during the sequence. One is vulnerable to disturbing events in the form of photographic images in a way that one is not to the real thing. That vulnerability is part of the distinctive passivity of someone who is a spectator twice over, spectator of events already shaped, first by the participants and second by the image maker. For the real operation I had to get scrubbed, don a surgical gown, then stand alongside the busy surgeons and nurses with my roles to play: inhibited adult, well-mannered guest, respectful witness. The movie operation precludes not only this modest participation but whatever is active in spectatorship. In the operating room, I am the one who changes focus, who makes the close-ups and the medium shots. In the theater, Antonioni has already chosen what parts of the operation I can watch; the camera looks for

27

me—and obliges me to look, leaving as my only option not to look. Further, the movie condenses something that takes hours to a few minutes, leaving only interesting parts presented in an interesting way, that is, with the intent to stir or shock. The dramatic is dramatized, by the didactics of layout and montage. We turn the page in a photo magazine, a new sequence starts in a movie, making a contrast that is sharper than the contrast between successive events in real time.

Nothing could be more instructive about the meaning of photography for 28 us— as, among other things, a method of hyping up the real—than the attacks on Antonioni's film in the Chinese press in early 1974. They make a negative catalogue of all the devices of modern photography, still and film.[2] While for us photography is intimately connected with discontinuous ways of seeing (the point is precisely to see the whole by means of a part—an arresting detail, a striking way of cropping), in China it is connected only with continuity. Not only are there proper subjects for the camera, those which are positive, inspirational (exemplary activities, smiling people, bright weather), and orderly, but there are proper ways of photographing, which derive from notions about the moral order of space that preclude the very idea of photographic seeing. Thus Antonioni was reproached for photographing things that were old, or old-fashioned—"he sought out and took dilapidated walls and blackboard newspapers discarded long ago"; paying "no attention to big and small tractors working in the fields, [he] chose only a donkey pulling a stone roller"—and for showing undecorous moments—"he disgustingly filmed people blowing their noses and going to the latrine"—and undisciplined movement—"instead of taking shots of pupils in the classroom in our factory-run primary school, he filmed the children running out of the classroom after a class." And he was accused of denigrating the right subjects by his way of photographing them: by using "dim and dreary colors" and hiding people in "dark shadows"; by treating the same subject with a variety of shots—"there are sometimes long-shots, sometimes close-ups, sometimes from the front, and sometimes from behind"—that is, for not showing things from the point of view of a single, ideally placed observer; by using high and low angles— "The camera was intentionally turned on this magnificent modern bridge from very bad angles in order to make it appear crooked and tottering"; and by not taking enough full shots—"He racked his brain to get such close-ups in an attempt to distort the people's image and uglify their spiritual outlook."

Besides the mass-produced photographic iconography of revered leaders, 29 revolutionary kitsch, and cultural treasures, one often sees photographs of a private sort in China. Many people possess pictures of their loved ones, tacked to the wall or stuck under the glass on top of the dresser or office desk. A large number of these are the sort of snapshots taken here at family gatherings and on trips; but none is a candid photograph, not even of the kind that the most unsophisticated camera user in this society finds normal—a baby crawling on the floor, someone in midgesture. Sports photographs show the team as a group, or only the most stylized balletic moments of play: generally, what people do with the camera is assemble for it, then line up in a row or two. There is no interest in catching a subject in movement. This is, one supposes, partly because of certain old conventions of decorum in conduct and imagery. And it is the characteristic visual taste of those at the first stage of camera culture, when the image is defined as something that can be stolen from its owner; thus, Antonioni was reproached for "forcibly taking shots against people's wishes," like "a thief." Possession of a camera does not license intrusion, as it does in this society whether people like it or not. (The good manners of a camera culture dictate that one is supposed to pretend not to notice when one is being photographed by a stranger in a public place as long as the photographer stays at a discreet distance—that is, one is supposed neither to forbid the picture-taking nor to start posing.) Unlike here, where we pose where we can and yield when we must, in China taking pictures is always a ritual; it always involves posing and, necessarily, consent. Someone who "deliberately stalked people who were unaware of his intention to film them" was depriving people and things of their right to pose, in order to look their best.

Antonioni devoted nearly all of the sequence in *Chung Kuo* about Peking's 30 Tien An Men Square, the country's foremost goal of political pilgrimage, to the pilgrims waiting to be photographed. The interest to Antonioni of showing Chinese performing that elementary rite, having a trip documented by the camera, is evident: the photograph and being photographed are favorite contemporary subjects for the camera. To his critics, the desire of visitors to Tien An Men Square for a photograph souvenir

is a reflection of their deep revolutionary feelings. But with bad intentions, Antonioni, instead of showing this reality, took shots only of people's clothing, movement, and expressions: here, someone's ruffled hair; there, people peering, their eyes dazzled by the sun; one moment, their sleeves; another, their trousers. . . .

The Chinese resist the photographic dismemberment of reality. Closeups are not   31
used. Even the postcards of antiquities and works of art sold in museums do not show part of something; the object is always photographed straight on, centered, evenly lit, and in its entirety.

We find the Chinese naïve for not perceiving the beauty of the cracked   32
peeling door, the picturesqueness of disorder, the force of the odd angle and the significant detail, the poetry of the turned back. We have a modern notion of embellishment—beauty is not inherent in anything; it is to be found, by another way of seeing—as well as a wider notion of meaning, which photography's many uses illustrate and powerfully reinforce. The more numerous the variations of something, the richer its possibilities of meaning: thus, more is said with photographs in the West than in China today. Apart from whatever is true about *Chung Kuo* as an item of ideological merchandise (and the Chinese are not wrong in finding the film condescending), Antonioni's images simply mean *more* than any images the Chinese release of themselves. The Chinese don't want photographs to mean very much or to be very interesting. They do not want to see the world from an unusual angle, to discover new subjects. Photographs are supposed to display what has already been described. Photography for us is a double-edged instrument for producing clichés (the French word that means both trite expression and photographic negative) and for serving up "fresh" views. For the Chinese authorities, there are only clichés—which they consider not to be clichés but "correct" views.

In China today, only two realities are acknowledged. We see reality as   33
hopelessly and interestingly plural. In China, what is defined as an issue for debate is one about which there are "two lines," a right one and a wrong one. Our society proposes a spectrum of discontinuous choices and perceptions. Theirs is constructed around a single, ideal observer; and photographs contribute their bit to the Great Monologue. For us, there are dispersed, interchangeable "points of view"; photography is a polylogue. The current Chinese ideology defines reality as a historical process structured by recurrent dualisms with clearly outlined, morally colored meanings; the past, for the most part, is simply judged as bad. For us, there are historical processes with awesomely complex and sometimes contradictory meanings; and arts which draw much of their value

from our consciousness of time as history, like photography. (This is why the passing of time adds to the aesthetic value of photographs, and the scars of time make objects more rather than less enticing to photographers.) With the idea of history, we certify our interest in knowing the greatest number of things. The only use the Chinese are allowed to make of their history is didactic: their interest in history is narrow, moralistic, deforming, uncurious. Hence, photography in our sense has no place in their society.

The limits placed on photography in China only reflect the character of 34 their society, a society unified by an ideology of stark, unremitting conflict. Our unlimited use of photographic images not only reflects but gives shape to this society, one unified by the denial of conflict. Our very notion of the world—the capitalist twentieth century's "one world"—is like a photographic overview. The world is "one" not because it is united but because a tour of its diverse contents does not reveal conflict but only an even more astounding diversity. This spurious unity of the world is affected by translating its contents into images. Images are always compatible, or can be made compatible, even when the realities they depict are not.

Photography does not simply reproduce the real, it recycles it—a key pro- 35 cedure of a modern society. In the form of photographic images, things and events are put to new uses, assigned new meanings, which go beyond the distinctions between the beautiful and the ugly, the true and the false, the useful and the useless, good taste and bad. Photography is one of the chief means for producing that quality ascribed to things and situations which erases these distinctions: "the interesting." What makes something interesting is that it can be seen to be like, or analogous to, something else. There is an art and there are fashions of seeing things in order to make them interesting; and to supply this art, these fashions, there is a steady recycling of the artifacts and tastes of the past. Clichés, recycled, become meta-clichés. The photographic recycling makes clichés out of unique objects, distinctive and vivid artifacts out of clichés. Images of real things are interlayered with images of images. The Chinese circumscribe the uses of photography so that there are no layers or strata of images, and all images reinforce and reiterate each other.3 We make of photography a means by which, precisely, anything can be said, any purpose served. What in reality is discrete, images join. In the form of a photograph the explosion of an A-bomb can be used to advertise a safe.

To us, the difference between the photographer as an individual eye and 36 the photographer as an objective recorder seems fundamental, the difference often regarded, mistakenly, as separating photography as art from photography as document. But both are logical extensions of what photography means: note-taking on, potentially, everything in the world, from every possible angle. The same Nadar who took the most authoritative celebrity portraits of his time and did the first photo-interviews was also the first photographer to take aerial views; and when he performed "the Daguerreian operation" on Paris from a balloon in 1855 he immediately grasped the future benefit of photography to warmakers.

Two attitudes underlie this presumption that anything in the world is mate-   37
rial for the camera. One finds that there is beauty or at least interest in every-thing, seen with an acute enough eye. (And the aestheticizing of reality that makes everything, anything, available to the camera is what also permits the coopting of any photograph, even one of an utterly practical sort, as art.) The other treats everything as the object of some present or future use, as matter for estimates, decisions, and predictions. According to one attitude, there is nothing that should not be *seen*; according to the other, there is nothing that should not be *recorded*. Cameras implement an aesthetic view of reality by being a machine-toy that extends to everyone the possibility of making disinterested judgments about importance, interest, beauty. ("*That* would make a good picture.") Cameras implement the instrumental view of reality by gathering information that enables us to make a more accurate and much quicker response to whatev-er is going on. The response may of course be either repressive or benevolent: military reconnaissance photographs help snuff out lives, X-rays help save them.

Though these two attitudes, the aesthetic and the instrumental, seem to   38
produce contradictory and even incompatible feelings about people and situa-tions, that is the altogether characteristic contradiction of attitude which mem-bers of a society that divorces public from private are expected to share in and live with. And there is perhaps no activity which prepares us so well to live with these contradictory attitudes as does picture-taking, which lends itself so bril-liantly to both. On the one hand, cameras arm vision in the service of power—of the state, of industry, of science. On the other hand, cameras make vision expressive in that mythical space known as private life. In China, where no space is left over from politics and moralism for expressions of aesthetic sensibility, only some things are to be photographed and only in certain ways. For us, as we become further detached from politics, there is more and more free space to fill up with exercises of sensibility such as cameras afford. One of the effects of the newer camera technology (video, instant movies) has been to turn even more of what is done with cameras in private to narcissistic uses—that is, to self-surveil-

lance. But such currently popular uses of image-feedback in the bedroom, the therapy session, and the weekend conference seem far less momentous than video's potential as a tool for surveillance in public places. Presumably, the Chinese will eventually make the same instrumental uses of photography that we do, except, perhaps, this one. Our inclination to treat character as equivalent to behavior makes more acceptable a widespread public installation of the mechanized regard from the outside provided by cameras. China's far more repressive standards of order require not only monitoring behavior but changing hearts; there, surveillance is internalized to a degree without precedent, which suggests a more limited future in their society for the camera as a means of surveillance.

China offers the model of one kind of dictatorship, whose master idea is 39 "the good," in which the most unsparing limits are placed on all forms of expression, including images. The future may offer another kind of dictatorship, whose master idea is "the interesting," in which images of all sorts, stereotyped and eccentric, proliferate. Something like this is suggested in Nabokov's *Invitation to a Beheading*. Its portrait of a model totalitarian state contains only one, omnipresent art: photography—and the friendly photographer who hovers around the hero's death cell turns out, at the end of the novel, to be the headsman. And there seems no way (short of undergoing a vast historical amnesia, as in China) of limiting the proliferation of photographic images. The only question is whether the function of the image-world created by cameras could be other than it is. The present function is clear enough, if one considers in what contexts photographic images are seen, what dependencies they create, what antagonisms they pacify—that is, what institutions they buttress, whose needs they really serve.

A capitalist society requires a culture based on images. It needs to furnish 40 vast amounts of entertainment in order to stimulate buying and anesthetize the injuries of class, race, and sex. And it needs to gather unlimited amounts of information, the better to exploit natural resources, increase productivity, keep order, make war, give jobs to bureaucrats. The camera's twin capacities, to subjectivize reality and to objectify it, ideally serve these needs and strengthen them. Cameras define reality in the two ways essential to the workings of an advanced industrial society: as a spectacle (for masses) and as an object of surveillance (for rulers). The production of images also furnishes a ruling ideology. Social change is replaced by a change in images. The freedom to consume a plurality of images and goods is equated with freedom itself. The narrowing of free political choice to free economic consumption requires the unlimited production and consumption of images.

The final reason for the need to photograph everything lies in the very logic of   41
consumption itself. To consume means to burn, to use up—and, therefore, to
need to be replenished. As we make images and consume them, we need still
more images; and still more. But images are not a treasure for which the world
must be ransacked; they are precisely what is at hand wherever the eye falls. The
possession of a camera can inspire something akin to lust. And like all credible
forms of lust, it cannot be satisfied: first, because the possibilities of photography
are infinite; and, second, because the project is finally self-devouring. The
attempts by photographers to bolster up a depleted sense of reality contribute to
the depletion. Our oppressive sense of the transience of everything is more acute
since cameras gave us the means to "fix" the fleeting moment. We consume
images at an ever faster rate and, as Balzac suspected cameras used up layers of
the body, images consume reality. Cameras are the antidote and the disease, a
means of appropriating reality and a means of making it obsolete.

The powers of photography have in effect de-Platonized our understanding   42
of reality, making it less and less plausible to reflect upon our experience according to the distinction between images and things, between copies and originals.
It suited Plato's derogatory attitude toward images to liken them to shadows—
transitory, minimally informative, immaterial, impotent co-presences of the real
things which cast them. But the force of photographic images comes from their
being material realities in their own right, richly informative deposits left in the
wake of whatever emitted them, potent means for turning the tables on reality—
for turning *it* into a shadow. Images are more real than anyone could have supposed. And just because they are an unlimited resource, one that cannot be
exhausted by consumerist waste, there is all the more reason to apply the conservationist remedy. If there can be a better way for the real world to include the
one of images, it will require an ecology not only of real things but of images as
well.

Endnotes

1. I am drawing on the account of Balzac's realism in Erich Auerbach's
    Mimesis. The passage that Auerbach analyzes from the beginning of Le Père
    Goriot(1834)—Balzac is describing the dining room of the Vauquer pension at seven in the morning and the entry of Madame Vauquer—could

hardly be more explicit (or proto-Proustian). "Her whole person," Balzac writes, "explains the pension, as the pension implies her person. . . . The short-statured woman's blowsy embonpoint is the product of the life here, as typhoid is the consequence of the exhalations of a hospital. Her knitted wool petticoat, which is longer than her outer skirt (made of an old dress), and whose wadding is escaping by the gaps in the splitting material, sums up the drawing-room, the dining room, the little garden, announces the cook-ing and gives an inkling of the boarders. When she is there, the spectacle is complete."

2.   See *A Vicious Motive, Despicable Tricks—A Criticism of Antonioni's Anti-China Film "China"*(Peking: Foreign Languages Press, 1974), an eighteen-page pamphlet (unsigned) which reproduces an article that appeared in the paper Renminh Ribao on January 30, 1974; and "Repudiating Antonioni's Anti-China Film," Peking Review,No. 8 (February 22, 1974), which supplies abridged versions of three other articles published that month. The aim of these articles is not, of course, to expound a view of photography—their interest on that score is inadvertent—but to construct a model ideological enemy, as in other mass educational cam-paigns staged during this period. Given this purpose, it was as unnecessary for the tens of millions mobilized in meetings held in schools, factories, army units, and communes around the country to "Criticize Antonioni's Anti-China Film" to have actually seen Chung Kuoas it was for the participants in the "Criticize Lin Piao and Confucius" campaign of 1976 to have read a text of Confucius.

3.   The Chinese concern for the reiterative function of images (and of words) inspires the distributing of additional images, photographs that depict scenes in which, clearly, no photographer could have been present; and the continuing use of such photographs suggests how slender is the population's understanding of what photographic images and picture-taking imply. In his book Chinese Shadows, Simon Leys gives an example from the "Movement to Emulate Lei Feng," a mass campaign of the mid-1960s to inculcate the ideals of Maoist citizenship built around the apotheosis of an Unknown Citizen, a conscript named Lei Feng who died at twenty in a banal accident. Lei Feng Exhibitions organized in the large cities included "photographic documents, such as 'Lei Feng helping an old woman to cross the street,' 'Lei Feng secretly [sic] doing his comrade's washing,' 'Lei Feng giving his lunch to a comrade who forgot his lunch box,' and so forth," with, apparently,

nobody questioning "the providential presence of a photographer during the various incidents in the life of that humble, hitherto unknown soldier." In China, what makes an image true is that it is good for people to see it.

Questions for Discussion

1. What is the "image-world"?
2. How does photography strengthen or challenge the need for images?
3. According to Sontag, what is the impact of photography on society?
4. How is photography different from painting, and why does that difference make photography more influential than painting?
5. What do photographs do? In other words, what is their function, for good or evil?
6. What prior knowledge does this essay require in order to read its difficult language and ideas with ease?
7. Who are the ideal readers of this essay?

Questions for Reflection and Writing

1. Where did you have difficulty reading this essay, and where did you readily understand it? Why? Write a list of questions that you wish you could ask Sontag. Reread the essay and see if she answers your questions.
2. In her introductory paragraph, Sontag asserts that "a society becomes 'modern' when one of its chief activities is producing and consuming images." Write a reflective essay on this statement, agreeing or disagreeing with it and linking it to your own experiences and observations. Do your experiences and observations support the statement?
3. Read more about photography: its history, famous photographers or photographs, critics' and theorists' commentary on photography. Just how influential has photography been?

John Berger (1926–   ), British art critic and fiction writer, is also a poet, an essayist, a playwright, a screenwriter, and a translator. Beginning his career as a teacher and artist, John (Peter) Berger exhibited at important London galleries and also worked as an art critic for such major publications as *New Statesman, Punch,* and the *Sun Times.* Literary reviewers have described Berger's work as being interested in the relationship between art and politics without being influenced by fashion in either literature or politics.

His work includes original photography books, such as *Another Way of Telling,* which devalues linear sequence as symbolic of political processes that threaten privacy and free choice. Later in his career, Berger became more engaged with the visual and cognitive processes. In this period, he produced nonfiction works such as *The Sense of Sight: Writings,* which features his impressions of several world cities, peasant art, and renowned artists such as Goya and Rembrandt.

The essays, meditations, and poems that compose *Keeping a Rendezvous* (1991) contextualize their artistic subjects in various ways, including sexuality, geography, and the collapse of communism. In 1996, Berger published *Photocopies,* a collection of autobiographical vignettes.

Berger's fiction includes *A Painter of Our Time* (1958; expanded ed., 1989); *Corker's Freedom* (1964); *G—* (1972); a trilogy published as *Into Their Labours* in 1991, consisting of *Pig Earth* (1979, reprint 1992), *Once in Europa* (1987), and *Lilac and Flag: An Old Wives' Tale of a City* (1990). Berger's most recent novel is *King: A Street Story* (1999).

On Visibility/Painting and Time

John Berger

On Visibility

To look: 1

at everything which overflows the outline, the contour, the category, the name of what it is.

All appearances are continually changing one another: visually everything is   2
interdependent. Looking is submitting the sense of sight to the experience of
that interdependence. To look *for* something (a pin that has dropped) is the
opposite of this looking. Visibility is a quality of light. Colours are the faces of
light. This is why looking is to recognize, enter a whole. Identity of an object or
colour or form is what visibility *reveals:* it is a conclusion of visibility; but it has

nothing to do with the *process* of visibility which is as uncontainable, which is as much a form of energy as light itself. Light which is the source of all life. The visible is a feature of that life; it cannot exist without it. In a dead universe nothing is visible.

Visibility is a form of growth.   3

Aim: to see the appearance of a thing (even an inanimate thing) as a stage in its   4
growth—or as a stage in a growth of which it is part. To see its visibility as a kind of flowering.

Clouds gather visibility, and then disperse into invisibility. All appearances are   5
of the nature of clouds.

The hyacinth grows into visibility. But so does the garnet or sapphire.   6

Not to say that *behind* appearances is the truth, the Platonic way. It is very possi-   7
ble that visibility *is* the truth and that what lies outside visibility are only the 'traces' of what has been or will become visible.

To look at light.   8
To recognize that outlines are an invention.
To transcend scale: a few blades of grass as large as the sky looks: the ant visibly coexistent with the mountain: in its *visibility* comparable with the mountain. Perhaps that's the point. The fact is visibility (inseparable from light) is greater than its categories of measurement (small, big, distant, near, dark, light, blue, yellow, etc.). To look is to rediscover, over and beyond these measurements, the primacy of visibility itself.

The eye receiving.   9
But also the eye intercepting. The eye intercepts the continual intercourse between light and the surfaces which reflect and absorb it. Separate objects are like isolated words. Meaning is only to be found in the relation between them. What is the meaning to be found in the visible? A form of energy, continually transforming itself.

Exercise.   10
Look:
White transparent curtains across the window.
Light coming from the right.
Shadows of folds, hanging folds, darker than clouds.
Suddenly sunlight.
The window frames now cast shadows across the curtains. The shadows are con-
voluted following the folds: the window frames are straight and rectangular.
Between the curtains and the window: a space like the lines on which music is
written: but three-dimensional, and the notes of light, rather than sound. The
space between the rectangular window frames and their shadows convoluted
because the curtains hang in folds half-transparently.

Looking through the curtain, a cloud crossing the sky, its upper edge yellowy sil-   11
ver and undulating—with almost exactly the same rhythm as the convolutions
of the shadows (now disappeared because the sun has gone in). The cloud is
moving fast.
Almost at gale speed.
On the houses opposite the wrought-iron balconies are absolutely still. For an
instant the sun comes out again.

Snake shadow—gone.   12

Clouds moving.   13

Sea swelling.   14

Charlie's van comes back.   15

A heavy swell at sea.   16

A memory. Visual.   17

Tall cliffs. White. With straight horizontal lines of dark flashing grey flint.   18
Between the lines centuries of chalk deposit.
The fringe of the cliffs against the sky, grass hanging over.

The thickness of the turf in relation to the height of the cliffs like the thickness of an animal's fur. At the height of the grass gulls wheeling. Figures of eight cut off by the cliff. The shadows of the cliffs on the sea (the tide is in, almost up to the cliffs.) The shadow of the cliffs on the sea, lying on the sea, from the water's edge to eighty metres out: the length of the coast. In the shadow of the cliff the sea is almost brown. Further out, just beyond the shadow of the grass fringe, the sea is a green mixed with a little white. The green that oxidized copper goes, but with sun. As I write this very sentence, the sun comes out above Noel Road, casts the shadow of the window frame on the curtains, the curtains stir in the window, my pen casts a shadow on this paper and the sun goes in.

To look: 19
at everything which overflows the outline, the contour, the category, the name of what it is.

Painting and Time

Paintings are static. The uniqueness of the experience of looking at a painting   1
repeatedly —over a period of days or years—is that, in the midst of flux, the image remains changeless. Of course the significance of the image may change, as a result of either historical or personal developments, but what is depicted is unchanging: the same milk flowing from the same jug, the waves on the sea with exactly the same formation unbroken, the smile and the face which have not altered.

One might be tempted to say that paintings preserve a moment. Yet on   2
reflection this is obviously untrue. For the moment of a painting, unlike a moment photographed, never existed as such. And so a painting cannot be said to preserve it.

If a painting 'stops' time, it is not, like a photograph, preserving a moment   3
of the past from the supersession of succeeding moments. I am thinking of the image within the frame, the scene which is depicted. Clearly if one considers an artist's life-work or the history of art, one is treating paintings as being, partly, records of the past, evidence of what has been. Yet this historical view, whether used within a Marxist or idealist tradition, has prevented most art experts from considering—or even noticing— the problem of how time exists (or does not) *within* painting.

In early Renaissance art, in paintings from non-European cultures, in cer-   4
tain modern works, the image implies a passage of time. Looking at it, the spec-

tator sees *before, during* and *after*. The Chinese sage takes a walk from one tree to another, the carriage runs over the child, the nude descends the staircase. And this of course has been analysed and commented upon. Yet the ensuing image is still static whilst referring to the dynamic world beyond its edges, and this poses the problem of what is the meaning of that strange contrast between static and dynamic. Strange because it is both so flagrant and so taken for granted.

Painters themselves practise a partial answer, even if it remains unformu-   5
lated in words. When is a painting finished? Not when it finally corresponds to something already existing—like the second shoe of a pair—but when the *fore-seen* ideal moment of it being looked at is filled as the painter feels or calculates it should be filled. The long or short process of painting a picture is the process of constructing the future moments when it will be looked at. In reality, despite the painter's ideal, these moments cannot be entirely determined. They can never be entirely filled by the painting. Nevertheless the painting is entirely addressed to these moments.

Whether the painter is a hack or a master makes no difference to the   6
'address' of the painting. The difference is in what a painting delivers: in how closely the moment of its being looked at, as foreseen by the painter, corresponds to the interests of the actual moments of its being looked at later by other peo-ple, when the circumstances surrounding its production (patronage, fashion, ide-ology) have changed.

Some painters when working have a habit of studying their painting, when   7
it has reached a certain stage, in a mirror. What they then see is the image reversed. If questioned about why this helps, they say that it allows them to see the painting anew, with a fresher eye. What they glimpse in the mirror is some-thing like the content of the future moment to which the painting is being addressed. The mirror allows them to half-forget their own present vision as a painter, and to borrow something of the vision of a future spectator.

What I am saying can perhaps be made sharper by again making a compar-   8
ison with photographs. Photographs are records of the past. (The importance of the role of the photographer and his subjectivity in this recording does not change the fact that photographs are records.) Paintings are prophecies received from the past, prophecies about *what the spectator is seeing in front of the painting at that moment.* Some prophecies are quickly exhausted—the painting loses its address; others continue.

Cannot the same be said about other art forms? Are not poems, stories,   9
music addressed to the future in a similar way? Often in their written forms they
are. Nevertheless painting and sculpture are distinct.

First because, even in their origin, they were not spontaneous performanc-   10
es. There is a sense in which a poem or story being spoken, or music being played,
emphasizes the *presence* of the speaker or player. Whereas a visual image, so long
as it is not being used as a mask or disguise, is always a comment on an *absence*.
The depiction comments on the absence of what is being depicted. Visual
images, based on appearances, always speak of *dis*appearance.

Secondly because, whereas verbal and musical language have a symbolic   11
relation to what they signify, painting and sculpture have a mimetic one, and this
means that their static character is all the more flagrant.

Stories, poetry, music, belong to time and play within it. The static visual   12
image denies time within itself. Hence its prophecies across and through time are
the more startling.

We can now ask what would have seemed at first an arbitrary question.   13
Why is it that the still imagery of painting interests us? What prevents painting
being patently inadequate—just because it is static?

To say that paintings prophesy the experience of their being looked at, does   14
not answer the question. Rather one has to say that such prophecy assumes a
continuing interest in the static image. Why, at least until recently, was such an
assumption justified? The conventional answer has been that, because painting
is static, it has the power to establish a visually 'palpable' harmony. Only something which is still can be so instantaneously composed, and therefore so complete. A musical composition, since it uses time, is obliged to have a beginning
and an end. A painting only has a beginning and an end insofar as it is a physical object: within its imagery there is neither beginning nor end. All this is what
was meant by composition, pictorial harmony, significant form and so on.

The terms of this explanation are both too restrictive and too aesthetic.   15
There has to be a virtue in that flagrant contrast: the contrast between the
unchanging painted form and the dynamic living model.

What I have so far argued can now help us to locate this virtue. The still-   16
ness of the image was symbolic of timelessness. The fact that paintings were
prophecies of themselves being looked at had nothing to do with the perspective
of modern avant-gardism whereby the future vindicates the misunderstood
prophet. What the present and the future had in common, and to which painting through its very stillness referred, was a substratum, a ground of timelessness.

Until the nineteenth century all world cosmologies—even including that 17
of the European Enlightenment—conceived of time as being in one way or
another surrounded or infiltrated by timelessness. This timelessness constituted
a realm of refuge and appeal. It was prayed to. It was where the dead went. It was
intimately but invisibly related to the living world of time through ritual, stories
and ethics.

Only during the last hundred years—since the acceptance of the 18
Darwinian theory of evolution—have people lived in a time that contains everything and sweeps everything away, and for which there is no realm of timelessness. In the galactic perspective proposed by such a cosmology, a hundred years
are less than an instant. Even in the perspective of the history of man they cannot yet be considered more than an aberration.

When we consider this history of man we are faced by change and recur- 19
rence. History is change. What recurs are the subjects (and objects) of history:
the lives of conscious women and men. What such consciousness works upon is
subject to change and is part of the material of history. The character of such
consciousness also changes. Yet some of its structures since the birth of language
have probably not changed. Consciousness is pegged to certain constants of the
human condition: birth, sexual attraction, social cooperation, death. The list is
by no means exhaustive: one could add contingencies such as hunger, pleasure,
fear.

The nineteenth-century discovery of history as the terrain of human free- 20
dom inevitably led to an underestimation of the ineluctable and the continuous.
It deposited the continuous within the flow of history—i.e. the continuous was
that which had a longer duration than the ephemeral. Previously, the continuous was thought of as the unchanging or timeless existing outside the flow of history.

The language of pictorial art, because it was static, became the language of 21
such timelessness. Yet what it spoke about—unlike geometry—was the sensuous,
the particular and the ephemeral. Its mediation between the realm of the timeless and the visible and tangible was more total and poignant than that of any
other art. Hence its iconic function, and special power.

We can all still discover through introspection a vestige of this power. 22
Consider a photograph. I have emphasized that photographs, unlike paintings,
are records. This is why they only work iconically if the record is personal and
there is a continuity within that personal life which reanimates the photograph.
But, having said that, photographs *are* static images and they do refer to the

ephemeral. Take an old family photograph. And you will find your imagination bifurcating: reconstructing the occasion, finding the date; and, at the same time, grappling with the question: where is that moment now? This bifurcation is a vestige of the response to the iconic power of painting when, cosmologically and philosophically, a realm of timelessness was acceptable.

Needless to say the iconic power of pictorial art was used for diverse social   23 and historical purposes, and the ideological function of art in a class society is part of that class history. Needless to say, too, that during the secularization of art its iconic power was often forgotten. Yet whenever a painting provoked deep emotion, something of this power reasserted itself. Indeed had pictorial art not possessed this power—the power to speak with the language of timelessness about the ephemeral—neither priesthoods nor ruling classes would have had any use for it.

During the second half of the nineteenth century, as the Darwinian pro-   24 posal about time became more and more dominant in all fields, the mediation of painting between the timeless and the ephemeral became more and more prob- lematic, more and more difficult to sustain. On one hand, the represented moment of the ephemeral became briefer and briefer; the Impressionists set out to represent one hour, the Expressionists an instant of subjective feeling; on the other hand, the Pointillists and Futurists tried to abolish the static and timeless. Other artists like Mondrian insisted upon a geometry from which the ephemer- al was banished altogether. Only the Cubists, as painters, sketched out a new cos- mology in which relativity might have accorded the timeless a new place. But the Cubist sketch was destroyed by the First World War.

After the war, the Surrealists made the unresolved problematic of time the   25 constant theme of all their work; all Surrealist paintings conjure up the time of dreams; dreams being by then the only realm of the timeless left intact.

During the last forty years transatlantic painting has demonstrated how   26 there is no longer anything left to mediate and therefore anything left to paint. The timeless —as Rothko so intensely showed us—had been emptied. The ephemeral has become the sole category of time. Banalized by pragmatism and consumerism, the ephemeral was excluded from abstract art, or fetishized as short-lived fashion in pop art and its derivatives. The ephemeral, no longer appealing to the timeless, becomes as trivial and instant as the fashionable. Without an acknowledged coexistence of the ephemeral and the timeless, there is nothing of consequence for pictorial art to do. Conceptual art is merely a dis- cussion of this fact.

An acknowledgment of the coexistence of the timeless and the ephemer- 27
al need not necessarily imply are turn to earlier religious forms. It does, however,
presume a radical questioning of something which most recent European thinking, including revolutionary theory, has ignored: the view of time developed by,
and inherited from the culture of nineteenth-century European capitalism.

This questioning becomes more urgent if one realizes that the problem of 28
time has not been, and can never be, solved scientifically. On the question of
time, science is bound to be solipsist. The problem of time is a problem of choice.

Questions for Discussion

1. What is meant by the statement "All appearances are continually changing
    one another" (Paragraph 2 of "On Visibility")? How is everything "visually
    . . . interdependent"?
2. In "On Visibility," what is Berger saying about the act of interpretation? Is
    misinterpretation impossible, or inevitable?
3. "When is a painting finished?" How does Berger answer this question,
    which he asks in Paragraph 5 of "Painting and Time"? What would you add
    to his answer?
4. How are paintings and sculptures different from other art forms? How is a
    painting different from a photograph?
5. What is the "ideological function of art" (Paragraph 23 of "Painting and
    Time")?
6. Why might Berger have chosen the unusual format of the first section, "On
    Visibility," with pithy sayings, poetic fragments, academic explanations, and
    even an exercise blended together? How does the format force you to read
    differently from the way you would normally read?
7. How would you account for the differences in style and format of the two
    sections from the one source, *The Sense of Sight*?

Questions for Reflection and Writing

1. Choose any one of Berger's sentences in "On Visibility" and explain it,
    reflect on it, and apply it to your own life.
2. Do the "exercise" in "On Visibility" by applying it to a window at your
    house, apartment, or dormitory. Describe what you see, and then write a
    comment about doing the exercise. Did doing the exercise lead you to a dif-
    ferent way of seeing or interpreting the window view?
3. Summarize "Painting and Time," and then apply what Berger says to a
    painting at your school's or your community's art gallery.

Holly Brubach (1953–   ), a writer, educator, and choreographer, was born in Pittsburgh on December 7 and received her B.A. from Duke University in 1975. She has worked for *Mademoiselle*, *Vogue*, Henri Bendel, and *Atlantic Monthly*. A choreographer for the Smithsonian Institution, Ynternal Amateur Ballet, and the American Dance Festival, Brubach has also written scripts for WNET-TV. She has contributed to various periodicals, including the *Saturday Review* and the *New York Times Book Review*. She has also collaborated on memoirs by Alexandra Danilova. Brubach claims to have become a writer "by accident" after an injury prevented her from pursuing a career in dance: "I'm a good example of someone who got into writing by the back door."

Rock-and-Roll Vaudeville

Holly Brubach

The first video shown on MTV, or Music Television, when it began three years   1
ago was a song called "Video Killed the Radio Star," by the Buggles. The title was wishful thinking, a prophecy that rock-and-roll singers who couldn't hold the camera's attention would go the way of silent-movie actors with cartoon character voices. Anyone who took the lyrics at their word and assumed that this new form posed a threat to pure music had only to look at the video itself, which showed the Buggles in an airless, all-white TV studio, surrounded by a lot of futuristic-looking synthesizers and state-of-the-art equipment, lipsynching their hearts out. Every now and again a girl in a tight skirt and spike heels (all the women in music videos wear spike heels) wandered across the screen. That was it. Radio stars had nothing to fear here.

Since then music videos have come a long way, though not nearly far   2
enough. Videos now play a large part in selling records, and singers are under pressure from their record companies to make videos, just as fifteen years ago they were obliged to go on tour. Even Dean Martin has gotten into the act, sitting poolside in his tuxedo and singing "Since I Met You Baby."

"Beat It," made in 1983, wasn't the first good video, but it may have been   3
the first great one. Michael Jackson epitomizes the form at its best—intense and brief. "Beat It" is one of the few videos that actually improve on their songs, which is what a video ought to do, and the song is pretty good to begin with. But

the music alone lacks the breakneck momentum that the video has. Where the song is merely agitated, the video is all worked up. The lyrics are about macho pride and territorial rights, and Jackson grunts and whoops between the lines, accompanying himself. We watch members of two rival gangs leave their hangouts, a sleazy luncheonette and a pool hall, and head for the scene of a fight, a warehouse loading dock. The video cuts back and forth from one gang to the other to Jackson. He stops by the luncheonette, slams the doors open—empty— does a little dance at the counter, a preview of what's to come, and then heads on out. The camera cuts pick up speed and the suspense builds until we finally arrive at the big number. When Jackson comes bouncing down a flight of stairs, snapping his fingers double time, breaking up a knife fight like an agent of divine intervention through dance, we feel like cheering. He parts the gangs, steps to the front, and bursts out dancing, and the tough guys fall in behind, in a finale that goes to show how much better a place the world would be if everybody danced.

"Beat It" was a breakthrough. Slick and well made, dramatic, concise, it   4
showed everybody how good music videos could be and inspired a long line of imitations. Suddenly all the people on MTV were dancing, whether they could or not. There was "Uptown Girl," with Billy Joel and the Lockers, set in a garage. Stevie Nicks galumphed her way through "If Anyone Falls." A big finale was part of the formula. Donna Summer belted "She Works Hard for the Money" from a fire escape overlooking the street, where a squadron of waitresses, nurses, cleaning ladies, and lady cops rolled their hips and churned a dance routine in unison. Bob Giraldi, who directed "Beat It," went on to make Pat Benatar's "Love Is a Battlefield," another video with a miniature plot that culminates in a big dance finish. Benatar leaves home, in what looks like a small town in New Jersey, and rides the bus into Manhattan, where she walks 42nd Street and winds up a hooker—though you would think that she had joined a sorority: the other girls look on indulgently as she writes a letter to her little brother. The finale takes place in a bar, where a sinisterlooking Latin type (Gary Chryst, formerly of the Joffrey Ballet) stares Benatar down and provokes her into dancing with him, to no real avail. Benatar is not what you would call a natural dancer. She's concentrating so hard that you can read the choreography as it crosses her mind: shimmy two three four, walk, walk, turn . . .

Even Michael Jackson went on to plagiarize his own performance in "Beat   5
It" with "Thriller," in which he leads a phalanx of dancing ghouls. Weird Al

Yankovic has done a "Beat It" parody, called "Eat It," in which the tough guys wear Happy Face T-shirts and he reproduces Michael Jackson's moves, verbatim.

Aside from "Beat It" and its sequels, there is a certain sameness to music   6
videos. Most are set in a new-wave never-never land, where logic and the law of gravity don't apply. Now that acid rock has given way to coke rock, the corresponding images have gone from psychedelic to surrealistic. A sequence of pictures or events that makes no apparent sense teases the viewer, who keeps watching, waiting for the piece that will explain the entire puzzle; the piece is usually missing. Rooms furnished with a single chair, long billowing curtains, corridors with no exit, empty swimming pools, forests of old gas pumps in the middle of the desert—these are standard features of the landscape, typically lit by a single bare bulb, or a full moon, or the sun's flat brightness.

The women are long-stemmed, with sexy bodies and baby faces. They wear   7
lots of lipstick, leather clothes, and, when their clothes are off, lingerie that makes them look vaguely sadistic. The men are less attractive, but then they're the ones who write the songs.

The vast majority of videos look as if they had been directed by the same   8
two or three people, all of whom you would guess to be seventeen-year-old boys. The screen is overrun with fantasies of wide-open spaces and wicked girls. Parents get their comeuppance. Everyone drives sexy cars—stretch limos, Chevy convertibles, and Thunderbirds. "I'm in love with a working girl," the Members sing, wearing sleeveless black leather jackets and jeans, as they guzzle champagne paid for by gorgeous, expensively dressed career women. In Huey Lewis and the News' "I Want a New Drug" Lewis falls for a pretty fan in the front row, thereby staging his fantasy of what it's like to be a rock-and-roll star and every groupie's fantasy of what could happen at a concert.

Compare these predominantly male notions of a good time with Cyndi   9
Lauper's "Girls Just Want to Have Fun," a *Bye Bye Birdie*–style romp in which she dances up and down the street, sings on the phone to her friends, and throws a party in her room, and men begin to look like an awfully self-important, dull bunch. Whether or not girls just want to have fun, they appear to be the only ones who know how.

Videos divide fairly neatly into two broad categories. The first is perform-   10
ances— either in a studio, where the director has more control and can devise some fancy effects with lights and cameras, or in concert, where the band is seen in its full glory, at the height of an adrenalin rush, in front of a sellout audience going wild. These are some of the dullest, most gratuitous videos on the screen,

and they all tend to look alike, even when the monotonous frenzy of the performance is alleviated by intermittent glimpses of beautiful girls or exotic landscapes. Unfortunately, good singers are not necessarily interesting performers, and music videos consistently expose this in a way that concerts, which get by on being events, almost never do. Furthermore, there is probably nothing to redeem a concert video if you don't like the song in the first place. While Def Leppard, a heavy-metal band I am not fitted to appreciate, beats its music to a pulp, there is not much to look at, unless it's the drummer dressed in briefs made out of a Union Jack. The Scorpions sing "Rock You Like a Hurricane," a song that isn't bad, behind bars, surrounded by an audience. This scene, with the fans getting carried away and shaking the bars in time to the music, is intercut with images of girls in cages. The video ends with the girls and the band members lying down in glass boxes and the lids slamming shut. Despite its use of such loaded images, this video does not purport to mean anything.

Prince and David Bowie are better in concert situations. In "Little Red   11
Corvette" Prince curls his upper lip and half-closes his eyes, coming on to the camera in closeup. This is the kind of shot that a lot of singers attempt but few carry off, and the ones who don't look ludicrous. (David Lee Roth, the lead singer for Van Halen, flexing his pelvis and crawling on all fours toward the camera, should have been saved from himself.) David Bowie, in "Modern Love," doesn't even acknowledge the camera, but he's riveting to watch and sexy without trying to be. With his hollow-cheeked, hungry look and his loose-jointed restlessness he captures the song's nervous energy.

Videos that aren't performances are referred to as "concept" videos, which   12
may be giving a lot of directors the benefit of the doubt. Nearly all concept videos include shots of the singer singing, but they differ from performance videos in that there's something else going on and the goingson dominate the video. Some concepts are better than others, and some are pretty obscure. You wonder, for instance, why there is a gymnast vaulting over and around video monitors on which Asia is seen singing "Only Time Will Tell." A lot of the weakest videos on MTV seem to be the work of so-called visual people who are careful not to let their minds get in the way of their creativity.

The more successful concept videos are those that are based, however   13
loosely, on a plot: there are characters, a situation is established, and something happens. Bowie's "China Girl," a fairly straightforward love story, is a good example. One of the most common devices is to follow two parallel plots simultaneously, cutting from one to the other, until they come together in the final scene.

Elton John's "That's Why They Call It the Blues" does this, keeping track of a boy in boot camp and his girl back home; in the end the sweethearts are reunited. In the Rolling Stones' "Undercover" the action alternates between a suburban rec room, where a teenage couple sits watching TV, and some Central American-looking country in the throes of violent revolution, where a truck drives into a cathedral and a man is marched onto a bridge and shot. These two stories converge in the rec room when the girl's parents walk in on her and her boyfriend making out: the father is wearing an army general's uniform. In the alternative version of this two-track plot the camera cuts from a story or a dramatic situation to the band playing and in the end the band steps into the plot. Even when there's a story to be told, it seems, rock bands insist on being the stars of their own videos.

The few exceptions are notable. Bruce Springsteen's "Atlantic City" serves 14 as the soundtrack for a series of desolate black-and-white scenes in which no one, not even Springsteen, appears. One of the most inventive music videos to date is Barnes and Barnes's "Fish Heads," an offbeat, amusing, unpretentious sequence of events that dignifies a silly song ("You can ask fish heads anything you want to; They won't answer, they can't talk"). No description of these scenes of real fish heads dressed in miniature turtleneck sweaters, propped up in plush theater seats or gathered around a table at a birthday party, can do this bizarre gem justice. "Fish Heads" proves that imagination can take a video a long way, further than closeup shots of celebrity singers or an elaborate, high-budget production can.

Some videos are up to nothing more than entertainment, song-and-dance 15 sales pitches to the camera. ABC, a band with a reputation for inventive video productions, is mastering this form: in "Look of Love" its members roam around a bright-colored fantasyland version of Central Park—steep rolling hills, bridges, and lampposts squeezed onto a tiny sound stage—with such ingenuous conviction that you expect Danny Kaye to turn up and join in.

After watching a lot of music videos, it's hard to escape the conclusions 16 that no one has the nerve to say no to a rock-and-roll star and that most videos would be better if someone did. A lot of these people ought to be told that they're not irreistible, or that they can't dance, or that their concept is dumb. Culture Club, for instance, makes dopey videos that do its music, which is pleasant and intelligent, a disservice.

Good videos work for various reasons. Despite the conventions that exist 17 already, there is no surefire formula, but the fact remains that dancing can make a video take off. This happens when the choreography is decent and well shot, the performance is good, and the images are edited according to the rhythm of the song. But it doesn't happen often enough. Judging from most music videos, you would think that dance on television hadn't come very far. Toni Basil is considered one of the best rock-androll choreographers, but her cheerleading routine in "Mickey" doesn't look any better than my memories of *Shindig* and *Hullabaloo*.

The mystery is why music videos aren't enlisting the best talents in dance   18 today. We know that more interesting possibilities for choreography to rock music exist and that they are surprisingly varied, because we've seen them on stage, in works by Twyla Tharp, William Forsythe, Marta Renzi, Karole Armitage, and others. Twyla Tharp's choreography for *The Golden Section*, set to the marked rhythms of David Byrne's music, has a jittery lyricism. In *Love Songs*, at the Joffrey Ballet, William Forsythe lays bare the obsession and violence inherent in love relations, with highly dramatic choreography that alternates between tender gestures and brutal attacks, set to a score of songs by Aretha Franklin and Dionne Warwick. By comparison the choreography in music videos looks tame and stale.

If this new form is going to justify itself, it might well be by giving us dance   19 performances that we can't see anywhere else. Though it looks to me as if there is more dancing in recent music videos, it's astonishing how slow directors have been to catch on to the thrill of watching somebody like Mick Jagger or Michael Jackson cut loose to a good song.

In "Going to a Go-Go" Mick Jagger makes a spectacle of himself, and it's   20 the spectacle that is impossible to turn away from. You marvel at how he manages to look so magnificently peculiar and ridiculous. He slithers along, sticking his neck out, jerking his knees in a hyperactive, Egyptian-looking style of movement. It's hard to believe that anyone can be so completely uninhibited in front of an audience. Jagger furthers his songs by losing himself in his music.

Michael Jackson never lets go the way Mick Jagger does, but watching him   21 is a more kinesthetic experience. The audience gets keyed up, waiting for the dancing that is his release. Unlike Fred A staire or Peter Martins, Michael Jackson doesn't feign effortlessness. He has taken the concertgoer's urge to tap his foot in response to good music and the willpower it takes to keep that urge in check and magnified the tug-of-war between them, so that you can see it all over his body: this is the basis of his performance. When he can't contain the music inside him any longer, be blurts out the steps that have been building up for the past eight or sixteen bars.

It looks as if Michael Jackson has only ten or twelve steps in his repertory   22
and the rest are variations on those. Even so, his ten steps are better than most
dancers' whole vocabularies. One is a staccato kick, a chest-high punch with his
foot. Another is a special way of snapping his fingers, with a sideways flick of the
wrist, as if he were dealing cards. Another is a high-speed spin: he crosses his
knees, wraps one foot around the other, and turns to unwind his legs. His dancing owes something to break dancing, robotics, and mime, but his style is more
sophisticated than any of these.

Performances like his are all too rare. You tune in to MTV for a few min-   23
utes and you're still there two hours later, seduced by the rapid turnover into hoping that the next video will be a good one. It isn't long before you've grown weary
of the innumerable scenes that feature a rock-and-roll singer lying on a psychia-
trist's couch, intended as an excuse for the fantasies that follow. On the evidence
of music videos, most people's wildest dreams come down to the same few basic
themes—vanity, greed, debauchery, retaliation, and sex—and the forms they
take are disappointingly similar.

Questions for Discussion

1. What should music videos add to the original song? How should they do
   this?

2. What does Brubach like best about music videos? In other words, what does
   she think videos do that the song alone cannot?

3. What does Brubach dislike about music videos? In other words, how can
   videos harm the original song? What happens when a video is poorly done?

4. What are the two broad categories of music videos? What categories and
   examples would you add to Brubach's?

5. Is Brubach being too gentle on the poorly done videos she describes? Is she
   being too kind to the videos she thinks are well done?

6. Why might Brubach have attached the term "vaudeville" to "rock-and-
   roll"? What is "vaudeville" and why is it appropriate for the title of this
   essay?

7. Where does Brubach reveal a bias toward a particular kind of music? Does
   her bias harm her credibility, or help it?

Questions for Reflection and Writing

1. In your opinion, what do videos bring to the world of the performing arts? You can apply this question to rock music, to another kind of music, or to another performing art.

2. What are the typical elements of music videos, according to Brubach, and how have they changed since she wrote this in 1984, according to you? Write an essay in which you summarize Brubach's elements and add your own comments about the way music videos have changed over the years.

3. Write a review of a recent music (or other performing art) video. Include your criteria for judging it, then use your criteria to evaluate the elements of the video. If you have space, compare the video to others of its type.

Basic Issues in Aesthetics: Defining the Issues: An Overview

Marcia Muelder Eaton

Quite lately, my noble friend, when I was condemning as ugly some things in certain compositions, and praising others as beautiful, somebody threw me in confusion by interrogating me in a most offensive manner, rather to this effect: "You, Socrates, pray how do you know what things are beautiful and what are ugly/ Come now, can you tell me what beauty is?" In my incompetence I was confounded, and could find no proper answer to give him—so leaving the company, I was filled with anger and reproaches against myself, and promised myself that the first time I met with one of you wise men, I would listen to him and learn, and when I had mastered my lesson thoroughly, I would go back to my questioner and join battle with him again. So you see that you have come at a beautifully appropriate moment, and I ask you to teach me properly what is beauty by itself, answering my question with the utmost precision you can attain: I do not want to be made to look a fool a second time, by another cross-examination.

Socrates, *Greater Hippias*

Defining 'Beauty', 'Art', and 'Aesthetic'

Theories of beauty and art go back at least as far as the ancient Greeks. Socrates was   1
confounded, as we will are today, by questions that most readers claim that something or someone is beautiful, but are thrown into a quandary when someone asks them to explain what they mean. One friend says that a film is exciting, another complains that she was bored. A song I am moved by is described by someone else as sickeningly sentimental.

How, if at all, can we support our judgments? When we try, sometimes we   2
become even more confused. We point to features of the film or song to prove its worth, only to have those same features used as evidence of its lack of value:

"What a movie—one car chase after another!"   3
"I know; I was bored to death."   4
"The lyrics were so romantic!"   5

"Yes, that's exactly why they were so sentimental."   6

The worry about how we can know is at the heart of aesthetics just as it is at   7
the heart of other branches of philosophy. Socrates believed that he could justify his
condemnation of things as *ugly* and his praising of things as *beautiful* only if he could
provide a definition for those terms. In philosophical aesthetics, as in other areas of
philosophy, attempts to define key terms have played a central role. So have questions about how we can know that the definitions are correct and how we can tell if
an object fits the definition.

When Socrates was asked, "Come now, can you tell me what beauty is?" he was   8
being asked to define 'beauty', and the question is still debated. It is easy to understand why definition has been elusive, for people simply do not agree about what
'beauty' means. Though philosophers have tried for centuries to define this terms, no
definition has seemed universally acceptable. Ask yourself what you mean when you
say a sunset or a car or a dance movement is beautiful. Do you mean the same thing
in each case, even though the things described as beautiful are so different from one
another? If you believe that something is a car, you can reasonably be confident that
others will share you belief. The same degree of confidence does not seem to attend
the belief that something is beautiful. It is precisely this lack of agreement that leads
to the old saying, "Beauty is in the eye of the beholder." If everyone uses the terms
'beauty' or 'beautiful' differently, no wonder they have escaped precise definition.
More than mere disagreement over words is at stake here. Understanding the very
nature of aesthetic activity, experience, and judgment demands explaining how communication is possible when key words seem to mean such different things to different people.

Because the experiences we identify as aesthetic are often connected with   9
works of art, aesthetics is sometimes identified as the 'philosophy of art'. But the
question "can you tell me what art is?" is as difficult as the question about the definition of 'beauty'.

Contemporary art in particular often leaves us at a loss. We do not know how   10
to approach it, let alone evaluate it. In a downtown public park in Hartford,
Connecticut, is a group of thirty-six boulders. They were put there under the supervision of the artist Carl Andre. (At least Andre calls himself an artist; we shall ask
ourselves in this book whether he is correct.) Andre called his creation *Stone Field*.
Although no local money was used to pay Andre, he received $87,000 from the
National Endowment for the Arts and the Hartford Foundation for Public Giving.
The total expense of materials, shipping, placement, and so on, has been estimated
at $2,000.[1] Thus Andre was paid well for his "work."

What are we to make of these rocks? Can we use the terms 'beautiful' or 'ugly'   11
to describe them? Is there one single work of art here of which the individual boulders are parts? Is there an artwork here at all? The frustration felt by Socrates at the
foot of the Acropolis in ancient Athens seems even more pronounced as we confront
such puzzling objects in our public spaces (and in our museums and concert halls as
well).

Socrates was thrown into confusion when he was asked to justify his claim that   12
some things are beautiful and others ugly. The boulders in Hartford caused confusion
for different reasons. Andre and the people who commissioned his work called something 'art' that others were unwilling (and remain unwilling) to accept as such. To
the latter an arrangement of rocks did not seem to demonstrate genuine *artistic* activity. Some critics have insisted that "little kids could do it"; others say that Andre has
ruined the city.[2] Many people have objected to the money spent on it; one person
described it as "another slap in the face for the poor and elderly."[3]

Some people, however, report that they love *Stone Field*. And Andre did   13
attempt to defend himself and explain his work. The group of boulders is located next
to a graveyard and, like it, uses stones quarried from nearby hills. The artist (if we can
at least provisionally call him that) said that he hoped to unite "natural history with
the smaller scale of human history."[4] Andre may also like many contemporary artists,
have wanted to make his audience think about the nature of art and artistic activity.
If that was his aim, he was surely successful! But does such success entitle Andre to
be called an 'artist'?

Just as troublesome as 'beauty' and 'art' is the term 'aesthetic'. What does it   14
mean to say that someone is having an 'aesthetic experience' or is 'responding aesthetically'?

The term 'aesthetic' did not appear until the eighteenth century, although the   15
history of issues that it refers to is as long as that of ethics, logic, metaphysics, and
epistemology. The philosopher Alexander Baumgarten coined it in 1750 to refer to
a special area of philosophy. Using the Greek word *aisthetikos* meaning "sensory perception," Baumgarten wanted to produce a science of beauty based upon sense perception. The shift of attention from *things* to *perception of things*, from object to subject, signaled by Baumgartgen's concentration on sensory experience, indicates that
the central position of the question "How can we know when things are beautiful or
ugly?" began to be taken over by the question "What happens when people respond
aesthetically?"

I attended college at a small, liberal arts college in the Midwest. Each spring   16
there was an Art Festival—a weekend filled with theatrical performances, concerts,

and an exhibit of students' artworks. Experts from Chicago, whose credentials showed that they knew a great deal about art, were hired to judge the works and award prizes. The grand prize my senior year went to a young man known by many locally because his father was a doctor. Many of the people attending the exhibit knew his family. The painting—done in dissonant purples and greens—was of a hideously ugly woman with numerous distorted breasts. It was titled *Mother*, and that year the festival happened to fall during Mother's Day weekend.

Philosophical debates are not always coolly objective. The one that took place 17 in my home following my family's visit to the art show nearly ruined our Mother's Day weekend. My mother knew and felt very sorry for the artist's mother She strongly believed that the Chicago experts should not have awarded the first prize to such an ugly painting. She further believed that the art professors were wrong to allow it to be displayed—particularly with such a title.

My father, a history professor, believed just as strongly that freedom of expres- 18 sion would have been abridged if the picture had not been hung with the artist's chosen title. My younger brother argued that outsiders could not have known that the artist's mother or her friends would be in the audience. My older brother thought it would have been irrelevant even if they had. I agreed, insisting that judgments of aesthetic merit alone counted—that moral considerations were not at issue. We accused each other of various sorts of insensitivity, but the main charge was that my mother was letting her emotions and moral principles get in the way—that she was not responding aesthetically.

Was this a fair charge? After all, my mother did say that the painting was 19 "ugly," and surely this is an aesthetic description. Doesn't using it indicate that one is responding aesthetically? Is it impossible to respond aesthetically and morally at the same time? How, in general, do we know if and when we and others are demonstrating *aesthetic* sensitivity? What counts as aesthetic activity? Is it enough to look at a painting? Or must we study it in a certain way? Does a special emotion, or repression of emotion, always characterize aesthetic experience? If someone creates a beautiful (or ugly) painting, can we be sure that he or she has had an aesthetic experience?

These questions, and others, will be addressed in this book. I shall not provide 20 a history of Aesthetics, but shall discuss current problems and some definitions and theories that have been formulated in an attempt to deal with them.

Aesthetic Theories

Questions about definitions of key terms such as 'beauty', 'art', and 'aesthetic' have   21
led philosophers to try to formulate theories to explain these difficult concepts. In
this section, I will briefly describe examples of aesthetic theories and consider a
philosopher who believes that theories of the aesthetic are impossible.

In contemporary aesthetics, 'art' is more often discussed than 'beauty'. For sev-   22
eral centuries art was considered a species of imitation. (Statues were thought to be
imitations of human beings, drama were considered imitations of human actions, and
music an imitation of the harmonies of the universe.) Theorists tried to explain art
by distinguishing it from other kinds of imitation in terms of the medium in and purpose for which it was produced. For example, Aristotle defined tragedy as the verbal
imitation of an action in which a noble hero suffers pitiful and fearful misfortunes and
through which an audience experiences pleasurable catharsis (working out) of pity
and fear. Some philosophers still hold imitation theories of art, but through the years
such theories have been overshadowed by other theories, many of which will be discussed in later chapters.

Theories of the aesthetic often take the form of presenting necessary and suffi-   23
cient conditions for asserting that something is an aesthetic object, activity, experience, or situation. A *necessary condition* is a condition that *must* be present in order
for something to occur. For example, a necessary condition of being a bachelor is that
a man is unmarried. Something is a *sufficient condition* if it is *all* that is required in
order for a thing to occur or be present. A temperature of -10° Fahrenheit is sufficient
for fresh water to freeze.

Ideally, aesthetic theories will allow one to distinguish the aesthetic from the   24
non-aesthetic by clearly stipulating what conditions or properties all and only those
things that are described as 'aesthetic' fulfill or have. Different components of what
we might call an "aesthetic situation" provide ways of grouping aesthetic theories
according to: (1) the maker (at least when the object of attention is an artifact), (2)
the viewer or audience, (3) the object or event, and (4) the circumstances or context in which the object, event, or performance is experienced. Aesthetic theories
often concentrate on one of these four elements, or upon ways in which these elements interact, and thus necessary and sufficient conditions are often laid out in such
terms.

Aesthetic theories concentrating on the artist explain such key terms as 'beau-   25
ty', 'art', or 'aesthetic' in terms of things thought to be special about about artistic psychology or activity. Such theories would answer the sorts of questions that arose in
connection with the *Mother* painting by referring to the artist's role. They might say

that what is necessary is a special purpose or intention that the artist has. Thus a definition might propose that something is an aesthetic response. Or some theories urge that the artist necessarily possesses creativity or imagination. Another kind of aesthetic theory highlights artistic expression or communication. Theories that center on the artist are the subject of Chapter 2.

Aesthetic theories that concentrate on the viewer emphasize the necessity of   26
a special kind of audience experience. These theorists believe that 'aesthetic' or 'art' or 'beauty' is best understood by examining viewers—by looking, for example, at the various ways in which members of my family reacted to *Mother*. A special response (one in which moral considerations are absent, for example) is often at the center of viewer theories. This response has variously been accounted for in terms of a particular kind of aesthetic experience, such as the exercise of taste or taking of a unique attitude. Other theories of viewers center on a special kind of emotional or mental operation. Viewer theories are the subject of Chapter 3.

Aesthetic theorists who believe that the object is most important try to distin-   27
guish aesthetic or artistic objects form non-aesthetic, non-artistic objects, without relying on some special quality of either the creator or the viewer. (The theories will be discussed in Chapters 4 and 5.) Such theories may insist on a particular property—beauty, for instance. Some theories focus on what are called "formal properties" (sound, color, or shape, for instance) and try to show that in aesthetic situations these are the only aesthetically relevant objects of attention. According to such views, only properties of *Mother* matter, not the artist or viewer's reaction. Some of the most important work in recent philosophic aesthetics has grown out of attempts to explain that a special kind of language is present in aesthetic objects. Works of art are considered symbols that only people familiar with the symbol system can grasp. (Some theorists would argue that the type of reaction my mother displayed shows that she does not know how to "read" a painting.)

Finally, there are theorists who believe that what really matters is whether or   28
not the context in which makers, viewers, and objects appear is ripe for aesthetic reception. Institutional theorists, for example, insist that certain sorts of institutions such as museums or conventions governing performance practices or reviewing procedures are necessary before we can make sense of the aesthetic. In the absence of Chicago experts, for example, *Mother* cannot be a painting, let alone a good painting. Nor without complex social practices could a bunch of rocks become a work entitled *Stone Field*. Other theorists point to historic or economic or social conditions that must exist in order for aesthetic experience to take place.

The Possibility of Aesthetic Theories

Although I have said that in later chapters we shall examine and evaluate various   29
definitions and theories, be aware that some people reject the possibility of defining
or theorizing about key aesthetic concepts altogether. Not all contemporary philosophers of aesthetics devote themselves to attempting to state the necessary and sufficient conditions that mark off the aesthetic. Indeed, many philosophers are quiet
skeptical about the possibility of defining key aesthetic terms such as 'beauty', 'art', or
'aesthetic' or of devising theories that explain what is special or unique about them.

One of the most articulate of these skeptics is Morris Weitz, who gives what   30
many consider a convincing argument for the indefinability of the word 'art'.
Agreeing with the philosopher Ludwig Wittgenstein that most basic words in our
vocabulary cannot be precisely defined, Weitz believes that 'art' names things that
bear at most a loose "family resemblance" to one another. He thinks that conditions
necessary and sufficient for its proper use cannot be given. For example, consider the
term *game*. Soccer, golf, Trivial Pursuit, Dungeons and Dragons, and I Spy are all
games. But try to specify anything that they and only they have in common; it cannot be done. What do Beethoven's Fifth Symphony, Leonardo da Vinci's Mona Lisa,
and Shakespeare's *Hamlet* have in common? The vast number of things and actions
correctly called 'art' seem to make defining 'art' at least as elusive as defining *game*.

The puzzle has intensified in the twentieth century. We have already looked   31
at the "work of art" commissioned for downtown Hartford. Other unlikely objects
and events have been displayed as art. Marcel Duchamp's work displayed in a museum and titled *Fountain by R. Mutt* is an ordinary urinal. John Cage has asked us to
"listen" to "4 Minutes and 33 Seconds of Silence." Some contemporary poetry
anthologies display blank pages as "poems." There are films lasting several minutes
that show nothing but an empty hallway and dances in which crowds of people just
walk back and forth across the stage. There seems to be no property or set of properties that all of these share with each other or with the "standard" works of art referred
to in the preceding paragraph.

Weitz believes that the creative nature of art demands indefinability: "The   32
very expansive, adventurous character of art, its ever-present changes and novel creations, make it logically impossible to insure any set of defining properties."[5] He distinguishes between "closed" and "open" concepts: *closed concepts* are concepts that
lend themselves to definitions stating necessary and sufficient conditions; *open concepts* are those that do not lend themselves to such definition. 'Urinal' or 'fountain'
may be closed; 'art' is open, he believes. If a philosopher says what 'art' is, the next

day an artist will create a counterexample—and would we really have it otherwise?

Some philosophers believe that we can have it both ways, that is, that we can   33
say what art is without denying or precluding its creativity. The philosopher Maurice Mandelbaum argues that Wittgenstein, and subsequently Weitz, failed to notice that family resemblance is a two fold relationship[6] In addition to physical features that members of the same family may or may not share (a broad jaw, for instance), family resemblance depends upon common ancestry. He suggests that there may be something analogous to this with respect to games and art. There may not be *manifest properties*—features that are directly perceivable, like a broad jaw or a goalpost or rhyming words—but there may be some property that cannot be directly perceived like a causal history of a special sort, or a distinctive purpose, that enables us to distinguish art from everything else. If you look only at my mother and me and have no knowledge about our causal relationship, you will not be able to tell whether we are related. Similarly, if you look only at an object, you may not be able to see how it came into being or what its purpose is, and thus you may not be able to say if it is art or not.

Mandelbaum thinks that because of Wittgenstein's emphasis on "directly   34
exhibited resemblances" and his failure to "consider other possible similarities," he failed to "provide an adequate clue as to what—in some cases at least—governs our use of common names."[7] The inclusion of photography as art, for example, has been tied to the fact that it "arises out of the same sorts of interest, and can satisfy the same sorts of interest, and our criticism of it employs the same sorts of standards, as is the case with respect to the other arts."[8] These features are not directly exhibited, but once we know bout them, we realize that photography has become an art form.

But, Weitz's supporters respond, Mandelbaum's statement implies that we   35
know what these interests and standards are when we do not. Just as there are not directly observable properties that all and only artworks have, so there are no special interests that art and only art serves (such as expressing emotion or providing pleasure) and no uniform, generally accepted set of standards for judging works of art or aesthetic objects. Mandelbaum assumes that we can say what the standards are that operate in recognized art forms, but his critics believe that doing this is as impossible as stating what the manifest properties are that all artworks share.

The frustration that accompanies this apparent discovery is manifest, and it is   36
not only directly perceivable in debates between philosophers. If we attend an exhibition of contemporary paintings or a performance of modern music, the audience's confusion is often obvious.

In Paris in May, 1913, the first performance of Igor Stravinsky's ballet *Rite of*   37
Spring was presented at the Théâtre de Champs-Elysees. As the music began to be
played, members of the audience shouted their disapproval. The music was considered revolutionary; it seemed to break all rules of melody and rhythm. The dancers
had had great difficulty with it from the beginning. The composer himself reported
that when he worked with Vaslav Nijinsky, the dancer-choreographer, Nijinsky suggested that he count aloud for the dancers while Stravinsky played the piano and that
they would just "see where we come out." The dancers continued to rely on
Nijinsky's counting (he stood offstage during the premiere), and as the audience's
heckling grew louder, it became harder and harder for the dancers to hear where they
were supposed to be. Fighting broke out in the hall between Stravinsky's supporters
and opponents, and the music could no longer be heard by anyone. In the end about
fifty combatants (some of whom had actually had their clothes torn off) were arrested.[9]

This is only one dramatic instance of a public thrown into confusion. The   38
mushrooming of explanatory aids in museums, lengthy written texts on the walls
next to paintings, and cassette players that can be rented at an exhibit (indicating
what one should look *for* and often *at* as well) signal that the problem of defining 'art'
and 'the aesthetic' is not one encountered solely in departments of philosophy.
Philosophic skepticism becomes public skepticism expressed in the statement, "I
guess art is whatever anybody says it is," an attitude that is clearly similar to one
expressed in its precursors, "Beauty is in the eye of the beholder."

The art-is-what-anybody-says-is-art attitude is articulated in a more sophisti-   39
cated fashion by some contemporary aestheticians. Others, though sympathetic to
it, find it unacceptable in certain respects and prefer a version that restricts the
"sayer" to certain authorities or experts. In other words, certain people are qualified
to say what art is. In both views, it is not manifest properties of objects that make
them art or some unique experience of beholders (see Chapter 5). Rather, something
special about the social context in which objects are created or displayed results in
their correctly or incorrectly being called 'art'. I shall present my own definition of
'art' later, and I hope it will help us to settle questions like those raised in connection
with *Stone Field* or *Mother.* I also hope to show that my definition successfully deals
with those who believe that defining 'art' is impossible.

Aesthetic Judgments and Policies

Another set of problems is raised in Socrates' speech when he asks how we *know*   40
when things are beautiful. In the history of aesthetics, particularly in our own cen-

tury, this question has been broadened to include not just *how* but also *whether* we can know if something has aesthetic value or not. Are statements made about works of art or aesthetic objects or expressions (both descriptions and evaluations) the kind of statement that can be *proved* to be true or false? If not, is there any way of justifying aesthetic claims or judgments?

When people describe works of art, to what extent can we trust what they say? 41 Are remarks about songs or plays, for example, as reliable as reports about the weather or baseball games? Consider the following paragraph from the *New York Times* theater section of August 5, 1984:

> *The Happiest Days of Your Life* is an utterly enjoyable post-war farce about 42
> boys and girls boarding schools forced to share the same quarters. John
> Dighton, the author, wrote such classic film comedies as *Kind Hearts and*
> *Coronets* and *The Man in the White Suit.* For all its outrageous puns and
> prim public school sexuality, the trifling *Happiest Days* remains endearing
> in its nostalgia-suffused Clifford Williams staging; Peggy Mount we born to
> play the headmistress originated by Margaret Rutherford on stage and film.
> When the cast leads the audience in a school-anthem singalong at the end,
> the joy seems more spontaneous than at any other London curtain call.

Frank Rich who wrote the review of this play in London, makes several claims, and it is illuminating to break some of them down.

1. *Happiest Days* is an enjoyable postwar farce. 43
   1.1 *Happiest Days* is a postwar play
   1.2 *Happiest Days* is a farce.
   1.3 *Happiest Days* is enjoyable.

2. John Dighton is the author of *Happiest Days* and of the film classics *Kind Hearts* 44
   and Coronets and *The Man in the White Suit.*
   2.1 John Dighton wrote H, K, and M.
   2.2 M and K are films.
   2.3 M and K are classics.

3. There are outrageous puns in *Happiest Days*. 45
   3.1 There are puns in *Happiest Days*.
   3.2 The puns in *Happiest Days* are outrageous.

4. The trifling *Happiest Days* remains endearing in its nostalgia-suffused Clifford   46
Williams staging.

4.1 Clifford Williams did the staging.

4.2 *Happiest Days* is nostalgically staged.

4.3 *Happiest Days* is trifling.

4.4 *Happiest Days* is endearing.

5. Peggy Mount was born to play the headmistress originated by Margaret   47
Rutherford.

5.1 Peggy Mount plays the headmistress.

5.2 Margaret Rutherford was the first to appear in the role of head-mistress

5.3 Peggy Mount was born to play the role.

I have ordered the substatements in such a way that the initial entrants seem   48
clearly to state facts. Perhaps Rich made a mistake; the play might have been written just before the war, for instance. But nonetheless, this and the other first substatements can easily be verified. As we proceed down the list, it becomes less and less
clear that Rich is giving us purely factual information about the play. "Objective"
data seem to give way to reports on his "subjective" response. *Objective statements*
make claims about objects in the world and their truth or falsity is at least potentially a matter of general agreement. A claim about the author of a play (2.1, for
instance) is objective. *Subjective statements* are reports incapable of general verification. Many people would classify the claim that the play is endearing or that the puns
are outrageous as subjective. (Interpreted literally, 5.3 seems obviously false. But fig-
uratively it fits into the subjective category—Rich thought that Mount was very good
in the part.)

But if Rich is simply giving us a report of his own idiosyncratic reactions, of   49
what possible interest can his article be to others? How can the activity known as
"criticism" be of any help to us? If, as many believe, "The play is endearing" is not a
statement of fact that can somehow be proven true or false, then including such
statements in newspaper articles should seem superfluous. We might believe that
Rich is someone like ourselves and that we are likely to react to plays in much the
way he does. Or we might believe that critics in general are more sensitive people
whose personal reactions are more trustworthy than our own. But since rich and
most critics are strangers to most of us, neither of these explanations accounts for the
interest readers take in how reviewers react. The inclusion of reviews in newspapers
must serve some purpose other than reportage of facts.

It is helpful, I think, to compare statements such as "The play is endearing" to   50
statements that most of us believe are clearly instances of simple reports of personal
reactions or preferences. "Oysters taste awful" is something I often say when my family gathers for Thanksgiving dinner. Buy my statement is certainly not of general or
public interest. When I say it, I don't expect anyone to ask me for my reasons, any
more than I would accuse my husband of being irrational for thinking that oysters,
even raw ones, are wonderful. Herein lies an important difference between pure preference statements (if we may call them that without attaching too much weight to
"pure") and critical statements. We do expect critics to be able to give reasons in support of their evaluations. Is this an irrational expectation? Or is there something significantly different about statements of aesthetic preference, so that reasons play a
role but not one of verification? I shall discuss these questions in Chapter 6 and shall
argue that aesthetic judgments can be viewed as claims that can be rationally supported or justified.

Philosophers have often compared and contrasted aesthetic and moral judg-   51
ments. (I will discuss some of these philosophers in Chapter 7.) In Plato's dialogue
The Republic, Socrates urges the deportation of all artists from the utopia he and other
characters propose on the ground that they distract people from what should be their
just goals. Morality does not thrive in an artistic atmosphere, he believed. But others—for example, Leo Tolstoy—have thought that morality is likely to thrive only in
a society in which true art (art in which sincere human emotion is communicated)
abounds. Still others, particularly in our own century, have insisted that it is a mistake to confuse aesthetic and moral value; the two values are, it is often claimed,
utterly distinct.

I have promised that I shall later present my own definition of 'art' and argue   52
for an objective basis for aesthetic evaluation. These proposals will, I hope, provide
a means for dealing with what I call "applied aesthetics." In recent years, philosophical ethics has become more and more relevant by addressing contemporary problems
in our society both inside and outside the academic classroom. Such applied courses
as medical ethics, business ethics, and ethics for engineers outside of the academy. For
a variety of reasons, applied aesthetics has been slower to develop. But there are several practical aesthetic problems that I shall discuss at the end of this book. For example, public money is spent in support of the arts (although the amount decreased in
the 1980s). In neighborhoods all over the United States and in many other parts of
the world, sculptures suddenly appear and poets can be heard reciting their latest
verses. National and local commissions have been established whose purpose is to
enrich the aesthetic lives of taxpayers. Yet the way in which funds are distributed for

such purposes remains a mystery to the average citizen. Questions of public policy and aesthetic judgments are thus connected.

Aesthetic issues are becoming more intertwined with other public decisions.   53
The Environmental Policy Act of 1969, for example, requires that environmental impact studies not only consider a proposed project's consequence for pollution or other social, safety, or health effects on the population but also that effects on "aesthetic amenities" be studied. How is such a study to be carried out? Four our purposes here, a more important question is Can philosophical aesthetics be of any use to the people engaged in such investigations? Questions of philosophic aesthetic's role in public policy will be discussed in the last chapter.

Throughout this book, I shall provide examples to clarify the various problems   54
and positions that are discussed. You as a reader are encouraged to consider examples from your own experience. At the risk of becoming, like Socrates, angry at being confused when unable to give completely satisfying answers, you should ask yourself if you know an artist when you see one, or if you know when you are having an aesthetic experience, or if you know when you are looking at something that is truly a work of art. If you believe that a song has been produced by a machine rather than a human voice, does that affect your belief about whether it is a work of art? Can you *prove* to a friend that your favorite musical group is good? Aesthetics, like other areas of philosophy, is as much a matter of asking questions as of answering them.

Notes

1. "Indentations in Space," *The New Yorker*, 21 November 1977, p. 51.
2. *New York Times*, 5 September 1977, 21: 1.
3. "Indentations in Space," p. 52.
4. *New York Times*, 2 September 1977, III, 16: 3.
5. Morris Weitz, "The Role of Theory in Aesthetics," *Journal of Aesthetics and Art Criticism* 15 (1956): 32.
6. Maurice mandelbaum, "Family Resemblances and Generalizations Concerning the Arts," *American Philosophical Quarterly* 2 (1965): 219-28.
7. Ibid., p. 222.
8. Ibid., p. 227.
9. For accounts of this incident, see Robert Siohan, *Stravinsky*, trans. Eric Walter White (London: Calder and Boyars, 1965), pp. 41-46 and Francis Routh, *Stravinsky* (London: J. M. Dent & Sons, 1975), pp. 10-13.

Mathematical Creation

Henri Poincaré

The Genesis of mathematical creation is a problem which should intensely interest   1
the psychologist. It is the activity in which the human mind seems to take least from
the outside world, in which it acts or seems to act only of itself and on itself, so that
in studying the procedure of geometric thought we may hope to reach what is most
essential in man's mind.

This has long been appreciated, and some time back the journal called   2
L'Enseignement Mathématique, edited by Lasaint and Fehr, began investigation of the
mental habits and methods of work of different mathematicians. I had finished the
main outlines of this article when the results of the inquiry were published, so I have
hardly been able to utilize them and shall confine myself to saying that the majority
of witnesses confirm my conclusions; I do not say all, for when the appeal is to universal suffrage unanimity is not to be hoped.

A first fact should surprise us, or rather would surprise us if we were not so used   3
to it. How does it happen there are people who do not understand mathematics? If
mathematics invokes only the rules of logic, such as are accepted by all normal minds;
if its evidence is based on principles common to all men, and that none could deny
without being mad, how does it come about that so many persons are here refracto-
ry?

That not every one can invent is nowise mysterious. That not every one can   4
retain a demonstration once learned may also pass. But that not everyone can understand mathematical reasoning when explained appears very surprising when we
think of it. And yet those who can follow this reasoning only with difficulty are in
the majority: that is undeniable, and will surely not be gainsaid by the experience of
secondary-school teachers.

And further: how is error possible in mathematics? A sane mind should not be   5
guilty of a logical fallacy, and yet there are very fine minds who do not trip in brief
reasoning such as occurs in the ordinary doings of life, and who are incapable of fol-

From "Mathematical Creation," by Henri Poincaré in *The Foundations of Science*, translated by George Bruce Halsted. By permission of the publishers: The Science Press, Lancaster, Pennsylvania, copyright 1915, reprinted 1921. First printed as "Le Raisonement Mathématique" in *Science et
méthode*. By permission of the French publishers: Ernest Flammarion, 1908, Paris.

lowing or repeating without error the mathematical demonstrations which are longer, but which after all are only an accumulation of brief reasonings wholly analogous to those they make so easily. Need we add that mathematicians themselves are   6
not infallible?

The answer seems to me evident. Imagine a long series of syllogisms, and that the conclusions of the first serve as premises of the following: we shall be able to catch each of these syllogisms, and it is not in passing from premises to conclusion that we are in danger of deceiving ourselves. But between the moment in which we first meet a proposition as conclusion of one syllogist, and that in which we reencounter it as a premise of another syllogist occasionally some time will elapse, several links of the chain will have unrolled; so it may happen that we have forgotten it, or worse, that we have forgotten its meaning. So it may happen that we replace it by a slightly different proposition, or that, while retaining the same enunciation, we attribute to it a   7
slightly different meaning, and thus it is that we are exposed to error.

Often the mathematician uses a rule. Naturally he begins by demonstrating this rule; and at the time when this proof is fresh in his memory he understands perfectly its meaning and its bearing, and he is no danger of changing it. But subsequently he trusts his memory and afterward only applies it in a mechanical way; and then if his memory fails him, he may apply it all wrong. Thus it is, to take a simple example, that we sometimes make slips in calculation because we have forgotten our mul-   8
tiplications table.

According to this, the special aptitude for mathematics would be due only to a very sure memory or to a prodigious force of attention. It would be a power like that of the whist-player who remembers the cards played; or, to go up a step, like that of the chess-player who can visualize a great number of combinations and hold them in his memory. Every good mathematician ought to be a good chess-player, and inversely; likewise he should be a good computer. Of course that sometimes happens; thus Gauss was at the same time a geometer of genius and a very precocious and accurate   9
computer.

But there are exceptions; or rather I err; I can not call them exceptions without the exceptions being more than the rule. Gauss it is, on the contrary, who was an exception. As for myself, I must confess, I am absolutely incapable even of adding without mistakes. In the same way I should be but a poor chess-player; I would perceive that by a certain play I should expose myself to a certain danger; I would pass in review several other plays, rejecting them for other reasons, and then finally I should make the move first examined, having meantime forgotten the danger I had foreseen.   10

In a word, my memory is not bad, but it would be insufficient to make me a good chess-player. Why then does it not fail me in a difficult piece of mathematical reasoning where most chess-players would lose themselves? Evidently because it is guided by the general march of the reasoning. A mathematical demonstration is not a simple juxtaposition of syllogisms, it is syllogisms *placed in a certain order*, and the order in which these elements are placed is much more important than the elements themselves. If I have the feeling, the intuition, so to speak, of this order, so as to perceive at a glance the reasoning as a whole, I need no longer fear lest I forget one of the elements, for each of them will take its allotted place in the array, and that without any effort of memory on my part.

It seems to me then, in repeating a reasoning learned, that I could have invent-   11
ed it. This is often only an illusion; but even then, even if I am not so gifted as to create it by myself, I myself re-invent it in so far as I repeat it.

We know that this feeling, this intuition of mathematical order, than makes us   12
divine hidden harmonies and relations, can not be possessed by every one. Some will not have either this delicate feeling so difficult to define, or a strength of memory and attention beyond the ordinary, and then they will be absolutely incapable of understanding higher mathematics. Such are the majority. Others will have this feeling only in a slight degree, but they will be gifted with an uncommon memory and a great power of attention. They will learn by heart the details one after another; they can understand mathematics and sometimes make applications, but they cannot create. Others, finally, will possess in a less or greater degree the special intuition referred to, and then not only can they understand mathematics even if their memory is nothing extraordinary, but they may become creators and try to invent with more or less success according as this intuition is more or less developed in them.

In fact, what is mathematical creation? It does not consist in making new com-   13
binations with mathematical entities already known. Any one could do that, but the combinations so made would be infinite in number and most of them absolutely without interest. To create consists precisely in not making useless combinations and in making those which are useful and which are only a small minority. Invention is discernment, choice.

How to make this choice I have before explained; the mathematical facts wor-   14
thy of being studied are those which, by their analogy with other facts, are capable of leading us to the knowledge of a mathematical law just as experimental facts lead us to the knowledge of a physical law. They are those which reveal to us unsuspected kinship between other facts, long known, but wrongly believed to be strangers to one another.

Among chosen combinations the most fertile will often be those formed of ele-   15
ments drawn from domains which are far apart. Not that I mean as sufficing for

invention the bringing together of objects as disparate as possible; most combinations so formed would be entirely sterile. But certain among them, very rare, are the most fruitful of all.

To invent, I have said, is to choose; but the word is perhaps not wholly exact.   16 It makes one think of a purchaser before whom are displayed a large number of samples, and who examines them, one after the other, to make a choice. Here the samples would be so numerous that a whole lifetime would not suffice to examine them. This is not the actual state of things. The sterile combinations do not even present themselves to the mind of the inventor. Never in the field of his consciousness do combinations appear that are not really useful, except some that he rejects but which have to some extent the characteristics of useful combinations. All goes on as if the inventor were an examiner for the second degree who would only have to question the candidates who had passed a previous examination.

But what I have hitherto said is what may be observed or inferred in reading   17 the writings of the geometers, reading reflectively.

It is time to penetrate deeper and to see what goes on in the very soul of the   18 mathematician. For this, I believe, I can do best by recalling memories of my own. But I shall limit myself to telling how I wrote my first memoir on Fuchsian functions. I beg the reader's pardon; I am about to use some technical expressions, but they need not frighten him, for he is not obliged to understand them. I shall say, for example, that I have found the demonstration of such a theorem under such circumstances. This theorem will have a barbarous name, unfamiliar to many, but that is unimportant; what is of interest for the psychologist is not the theorem but the circumstances.

For fifteen days I strove to prove that there could not be any functions like   19 those I have since called Fuchsian functions. I was then very ignorant; every day I seated myself at my work table, stayed an hour or two, tried a great number of combinations and reached no results. One evening, contrary to my custom, I drank black coffee and could not sleep. Ideas rose in crowds; I felt them collide until pairs interlocked, so to speak, making a stable combination. By the next morning I had established the existence of a class of Fuchsian functions, those which come from the hypergeometric series; I had only to write out the results, which took but a few hours.

Then I wanted to represent these functions by the quotient of two series; this   20 idea was perfectly conscious and deliberate, the analogy with elliptic functions guide me. I asked myself what properties these series must have if they existed, and I succeeded without difficulty in forming the series I have called theta-Fuchsian.

Just at this time I left Caen, where I was then living, to go on a geologic excur-   21 sion under the auspices of the school of mines. The changes of travel made me forget my mathematical work. Having reached Coutances, we entered an omnibus to go some place or other. At the moment when I put my foot on the step the idea came to me, without anything in my former thoughts seeming to have paved the way for it, that the transformations I had used to define the Fuchsian functions were identical with those of non-Euclidean geometry. I did not verify the idea; I should not have had time, as, upon taking my seat in the omnibus, I went on with a conversation already commenced, but I felt a perfect certainty. On my return to Caen, for conscience' sake I verified the result at my leisure.

Then I turned my attention to the study of some arithmetical questions apparently without much success and without a suspicion of any connection with my preceding researches. Disgusted with my failure, I went to spend a few days at the seaside, and thought of something else. One morning, walking on the bluff, the idea came to me, with just the same characteristics of brevity, suddenness and immediate certainty, that the arithmetic transformations of indeterminate ternary quadratic forms were identical with those of non-Euclidean geometry. 22

Returned to Caen, I meditated on this result and deduced the consequences. 23 The example of quadratic forms showed me that there were Fuchsian groups other than those corresponding to the hypergeometric series; I saw that I could apply to them the theory of theta-Fuchsian series and that consequently there existed Fuchsian functions other than those from the hypergeometric series, the ones I then knew. Naturally I set myself to form all these functions. I made a systematic attack upon them and carried all the outworks, one after another. There was one however that still held out, whose fall would involve that of the whole place. But all my efforts only served at first the better to show me the difficulty, which indeed was something. All this work was perfectly conscious.

Thereupon I left for Mont-Valérian, where I was to go through my military 24 service; so I was very differently occupied. One day, going along the street, the solution of the difficulty which had stopped me suddenly appeared to me. I did not try to go deep into it immediately, and only after my service did I again take up the question. I had all the elements and had only to arrange them and put them together. So I wrote out my final memoir at a single stroke and without difficulty.

I shall limit myself to this single example; it is useless to multiply them. In 25 regard to my other researches I would have to say analogous things, and the observations of other mathematicians given in *L'Enseignement Mathématique* would only confirm them.

Most striking at first is this appearance of sudden illumination, a manifest sign 26 of long, unconscious prior work. The role of this unconscious work in mathematical invention appears to me incontestable, and traces of it would be found in other cases where it is less evident. Often when one works at a hard question, nothing good is accomplished at the first attack. Then one takes a rest, longer or shorter, and sits down anew to the work. During the first half-hour, as before, nothing is found, and then all of a sudden the decisive idea presents itself to the mind. It might be said that the conscious work has been more fruitful because it has been interrupted and the rest has given back to the mind its force and freshness. But it is more probably that this rest has been filled out with unconscious work and that the results of this work has afterward revealed itself to the geometer just as in the cases I have cited; only the revelation, instead of coming during a walk or a journey, has happened during a period of conscious work, but independently of this work which plays at most a role of excitant, as if it were the goad stimulating the results already reached during rest, but remaining unconscious, to assume the conscious form.

There is another remark to be made about the conditions of this unconscious   27 work: it is possible, and of a certainty it is only fruitful, if it is on the one hand preceded and on the other hand followed by a period of conscious work. These sudden inspirations (and the examples already cited sufficiently prove this) never happen except after some days of voluntary effort which has appeared absolutely fruitless and whence nothing good seems to have come, where the way taken seems totally astray. These efforts then have not been as sterile as one thinks; they have set agoing the unconscious machine and without them it would not have moved and would have produced nothing.

The need for the second period of conscious work, after the inspiration, is still   28 easier to understand. It is necessary to put in shape the results of this inspiration, to deduce from them the immediate consequences, to arrange them, to word the demonstrations, but above all is verification necessary. I have spoken of the feeling of absolute certitude accompanying the inspiration; in the cases cited this feeling was no deceiver, nor is it usually. But do not think this is a rule without exception; often this feeling deceives us without being any the less vivid, and we only find it out when we seek to put on foot the demonstration. I have especially noticed this fact in regard to ideas coming to me in the morning or evening in bed while in a semi-hypnagogic state.

Such are the realities; now for the thoughts they force upon us. The uncon-   29 scious, or, as we say, the subliminal self plays an important role in mathematical creation; this follows from what we have said. But usually the subliminal self is considered as purely automatic. Now we have seen that mathematical work is not simply mechanical, that it could not be done by a machine, however perfect. It is not merely a question of applying rules, of making the most combinations possible according to certain fixed laws. The combinations so obtained would be exceedingly numerous, useless and cumbersome. The true work of the inventor consists in choosing among these combinations so as to eliminate the useless ones or rather to avoid the trouble of making them, and the rules which must guide this choice are extremely fine and delicate. It is almost impossible to state them precisely; they are felt rather than formulated. Under these conditions, how imagine a sieve capable of applying them mechanically?

A first hypothesis now presents itself: the subliminal self is in no way inferior   30
to the conscious self; it is not purely automatic; it is capable of discernment; it has tact, delicacy; it knows how to choose, to divine. What do I say? It knows better how to divine that the conscious self, since it succeeds where that has failed. In a word, is not the subliminal self superior to the conscious self? You recognize the full importance of this question. Boutroux in a recent lecture has shown how it came up on a very different occasion, and what consequences would follow an affirmative answer.

Is this affirmative answer forced upon us by the facts I have just given? I con-   31
fess that, for my part, I should hate to accept it. Re-examine the facts then and see if they are not compatible with another explanation.

It is certain that the combinations, which present themselves to the mind in a   32
sort of sudden illumination, after an unconscious working somewhat prolonged, are generally useful and fertile combinations, which seem the result of a first impression. Does it follow that the subliminal self, having divined by a delicate intuition that these combinations would be useful, has formed only these, or has it rather formed many others which were lacking in interest and have remained unconscious?

In this second way of looking at it, all the combinations would be formed in   33
consequence of the automatism of the subliminal self, but only the interesting ones would break into the domain of consciousness. And this is still very mysterious. What is the cause that, among the thousand products of our unconscious activity, some are called to pass the threshold, while others remain below? Is it a simple chance which confers this privilege? Evidently not; among all the stimuli of our senses, for example, only the most intense fix our attention, unless it has been drawn to them by other causes. More generally the privileged unconscious phenomena, those susceptible of becoming conscious, are those which, directly or indirectly, affect most profoundly our emotional sensibility.

It may be surprising to see emotional sensibility invoked à propos of mathemat-   34
ical demonstrations which, it would seem, can interest only the intellect. This would be to forget the feeling of mathematical beauty, of the harmony of numbers and

forms, of geometric elegance. This is a true esthetic feeling that all real mathematicians know, and surely it belongs to emotional sensibility.

Now, what are the mathematic entities to which we attribute this character of   35
beauty and elegance, and which are capable of developing in us a sort of esthetic emotion? They are those whose elements are harmoniously disposed so that the mind without effort can embrace their totality while realizing the details. This harmony is at once a satisfaction of our esthetic needs and an aid to the mind, sustaining and guiding. And at the same time, in putting under our eyes a well-ordered whole, it makes us foresee a mathematical law. Now, as we have said above, the only mathematical facts worthy of fixing our attention and capable of being useful are those which can teach us a mathematical law. So that we reach the following conclusion: The useful combinations are precisely the most beautiful, I mean those best able to charm this special sensibility that all mathematicians know, but of which the profane are so ignorant as often to be tempted to smile at it.

What happens then? Among the great numbers of combinations blindly   36
formed by the subliminal self, almost all are without interest and without utility; but just for that reason they are also without effect upon the esthetic sensibility. Consciousness will never know them; only certain ones are harmonious, and, consequently, at once useful and beautiful. They will be capable of touching this special sensibility of the geometer of which I have just spoken, and which, once aroused, will call our attention to them, and thus give them occasion to become conscious.

This is only a hypothesis, and yet here is an observation which may confirm it: 37
when a sudden illumination seizes upon the mind of the mathematician, it usually happens that it does not deceive him, but it also sometimes happens, as I have said, that it does not stand the test of verification; well, we almost always notice that this false idea, had it been true, would have gratified our natural feeling for mathematical elegance.

Thus it is this special aesthetic sensibility which plays the role of the delicate   38
sieve of which I spoke, and that sufficiently explains why the one lacking it will never be a real creator.

Yet all the difficulties have not disappeared. The conscious self is narrowly limited, and as for the subliminal self we know not its limitations, and this is why we are   39
not too reluctant in supposing that it has been able in a short time to make more different combinations than the whole life of a conscious being could encompass. yet these limitations exist. Is it likely that it is able to form all the possible combinations, whose number would frighten the imagination? Nevertheless that would seem necessary, because if it produces only a small part of these combinations, and if it makes

them at random, there would be small chance that the good, the one we should choose, would be found among them.

Perhaps we ought to seek the explanation in that preliminary period of con-   40
scious work which always precedes all fruitful unconscious labor. Permit me a rough comparison. Figure the future elements of our combinations as something like the hooked atoms of Epicurus. During the complete repose of the mind, these atoms are motionless, they are, so to speak, hooked to the wall; so this complete rest may be indefinitely prolonged without the atoms meeting, and consequently without any combination between them.

On the other hand, during a period of apparent rest and unconscious work, cer-   41
tain of them are detached from the wall and put in motion. They flash in every direc-tion through the space (I was about to say the room) where they are enclosed, as would, for example, a swarm of gnats or, if you prefer a more learned comparison, like the molecules of gas in the kinematic theory of gases. Then their mutual impacts may produce new combinations.

What is the role of the preliminary conscious work? It is evidently to mobilize   42
certain of these atoms, to unhook them from the wall and put them in swing. We think we have done no good, because we have moved these elements a thousand dif-ferent ways in seeking to assemble them, and have found no satisfactory aggregate. But, after this shaking up imposed upon them by our will, these atoms do not return to their primitive rest. They freely continue their dance.

Now, our will did not choose them at random; it pursued a perfectly deter-   43
mined aim. The mobilized atoms are therefore not any atoms whatsoever; they are those from which we might reasonably expect the desired solution. Then the mobi-lized atoms undergo impacts which make them enter into combinations among themselves or with other atoms at rest which they struck against in their course. Again I beg pardon, my comparison is very rough, but I scarcely know how otherwise to make my thought understood.

However it may be, the only combinations that have a chance of forming are   44
those where at least one of the elements is one of those atoms freely chosen by our will. Now, it is evidently among these that is found what I called the *good combina-tion*. Perhaps this is a way of lessening the paradoxical in the original hypothesis.

Another observation. It never happens that the unconscious work gives us the   45
result of a somewhat long calculation all *made*, where we have only to apply fixed rules. We might think the wholly automatic subliminal self particularly apt for this sort of work, which is in a way exclusively mechanical. It seems that thinking in the evening upon the factors of a multiplication we might hope to find the product ready

made upon our awakening, or again that an algebraic calculation, for example a verification, would be made unconsciously. Nothing of the sort, as observation proves. All one may hope from these inspirations, fruits of unconscious work, is a point of departure for such calculations. As for the calculations themselves, they must be made in the second period of conscious work, that which follow the inspiration, that in which one verifies the results of this inspiration and deduces their consequences. The rules of these calculations are strict and complicated. They require discipline, attention, will, and therefore consciousness. In the subliminal self, on the contrary, reigns what I should call liberty, if we might give this name to the simple absence of discipline and to the disorder born of chance. Only, this disorder itself permits unexpected combinations.

I shall make a last remark: when above I made certain personal observations, I   46
spoke of a night of excitement when I worked in spite of myself. Such cases are frequent, and it is not necessary that the abnormal cerebral activity be caused by a physical excitant as in that I mentioned. It seems, in such cases, that one is present at his own unconscious work, made partially perceptible to the over-excited consciousness, yet without having changed its nature. Then we vaguely comprehend what distinguishes the two mechanisms or, if you wish, the working methods of the two egos. And the psychologic observations I have been able thus to make seem to me to confirm in their general outlines the views I have given.

Surely they have need of it, for they are and remain in spite of all very hypo-   47
thetical: the interest of the questions is so great that I do not repent of having submitted them to the reader.

Translated by George Bruce Halsted

Aaron **Copland** (1900–1990), composer, conductor, pianist, author, and lecturer, was renowned for bringing an American sound to classical music, drawing upon rich American traditions such as cowboy songs, hymns, and folk songs. One of the most influential composers of the twentieth century, Copland was born in Brooklyn and died in North Tarrytown, New York. He began his career in 1920, composing for orchestra, ballet, stage, films, chamber music, and voice. He taught composition and poetry at Harvard University and was affiliated with Berkshire Music Center; he also delivered public lectures across the United States. He performed piano solos nationwide and conducted around the world, also promoting new music, organizing concerts, and serving as mentor to young composers. Copland founded the American Festival of Contemporary Music at Yaddo in 1932.

Copland was honored with the Pulitzer Prize in 1944 for his ballet score, *Appalachian Spring*; won an Academy Award in 1950 for his score for the film *The Heiress*; received the Presidential Medal of Freedom in 1964; and won the Kennedy Center Award for lifetime contributions to culture and the performing arts in 1979. His compositions include *Billy the Kid*, *Rodeo*, *El Salon Mexico*, *Lincoln Portrait*, and *Fanfare for the Common Man*. After 1970 Copland virtually gave up composing, turning to conducting, lecturing, and writing. His books include *What to Listen for in Music* (1939; rev. 1957); *Our New Music* (1941, rev. 1968); *Music and Imagination* (1952); *Copland on Music* (1960); and a two-volume autobiography written in collaboration with Vivian Perlis.

How We Listen to Music

Aaron Copland

We all listen to music according to our separate capacities. But, for the sake of   1
analysis, the whole listening process may become clearer if we break it up into its
component parts, so to speak. In a certain sense we all listen to music on three
separate planes. For lack of a better terminology, one might name these: (1) the
sensuous plane, (2) the expressive plane, (3) the sheerly musical plane. The only
advantage to be gained from mechanically splitting up the listening process into
these hypothetical planes is the clearer view to be had of the way in which we
listen.

The simplest way of listening to music is to listen for the sheer pleasure of   2
the musical sound itself. That is the sensuous plane. It is the plane on which we
hear music without thinking, without considering it in any way. One turns on

the radio while doing something else and absent-mindedly bathes in the sound. A kind of brainless but attractive state of mind is engendered by the mere sound appeal of the music.

You may be sitting in a room reading this book. Imagine one note struck   3 on the piano. Immediately that one note is enough to change the atmosphere of the room—proving that the sound element in music is a powerful and mysterious agent, which it would be foolish to deride or belittle.

The surprising thing is that many people who consider themselves quali-   4 fied music lovers abuse that plane in listening. They go to concerts in order to lose themselves. They use music as a consolation or an escape. They enter an ideal world where one doesn't have to think of the realities of everyday life. Of course they aren't thinking about the music either. Music allows them to leave it, and they go off to a place to dream, dreaming because of and apropos of the music yet never quite listening to it.

Yes, the sound appeal of music is a potent and primitive force, but you must   5 not allow it to usurp a disproportionate share of your interest. The sensuous plane is an important one in music, a very important one, but it does not constitute the whole story.

There is no need to digress further on the sensuous plane. Its appeal to   6 every normal human being is self-evident. There is, however, such a thing as becoming more sensitive to the different kinds of sound stuff as used by various composers. For all composers do not use that sound stuff in the same way. Don't get the idea that the value of music is commensurate with its sensuous appeal or that the loveliest sounding music is made by the greatest composer. If that were so, Ravel would be a greater creator than Beethoven. The point is that the sound element varies with each composer, that his usage of sound forms an integral part of his style and must be taken into account when listening. The reader can see, therefore, that a more conscious approach is valuable even on this primary plane of music listening.

The second plane on which music exists is what I have called the expres-   7 sive one. Here, immediately, we tread on controversial ground. Composers have a way of shying away from any discussion of music's expressive side. Did not Stravinsky himself proclaim that his music was an "object," a "thing," with a life of its own, and with no other meaning than its own purely musical existence? This intransigent attitude of Stravinsky's may be due to the fact that so many people have tried to read different meanings into so many pieces. Heaven knows it is difficult enough to say precisely what it is that a piece of music means, to say it definitely, to say it finally so that everyone is satisfied with your explanation. But that should not lead one to the other extreme of denying to music the right to be "expressive."

My own belief is that all music has an expressive power, some more and   8
some less, but that all music has a certain meaning behind the notes and that that meaning behind the notes constitutes, after all, what the piece is saying, what the piece is about. This whole problem can be stated quite simply by asking, "Is there a meaning to music?" My answer to that would be, "Yes." And "Can you state in so many words what the meaning is?" My answer to that would be, "No." Therein lies the difficulty.

Simple-minded souls will never be satisfied with the answer to the second   9
of these questions. They always want music to have a meaning, and the more concrete it is the better they like it. The more the music reminds them of a train, a storm, a funeral, or any other familiar conception the more expressive it appears to be to them. This popular idea of music's meaning—stimulated and abetted by the usual run of musical commentator—should be discouraged wherever and whenever it is met. One timid lady once confessed to me that she suspected something seriously lacking in her appreciation of music because of her inability to connect it with anything definite. That is getting the whole thing backward, of course.

Still, the question remains, how close should the intelligent music lover   10
wish to come to pinning a definite meaning to any particular work? No closer than a general concept, I should say. Music expresses, at different moments, serenity or exuberance, regret or triumph, fury or delight. It expresses each of these moods, and many others, in a numberless variety of subtle shadings and differences. It may even express a state of meaning for which there exists no adequate word in any language. In that case, musicians often like to say that it has only a purely musical meaning. They sometimes go farther and say that *all* music has only a purely musical meaning. What they really mean is that no appropriate word can be found to express the music's meaning and that, even if it could, they do not feel the need of finding it.

But whatever the professional musician may hold, most musical novices   11
still search for specific words with which to pin down their musical reactions. That is why they always find Tschaikovsky easier to "understand" than Beethoven. In the first place, it is easier to pin a meaning-word on a Tschaikovsky piece than on a Beethoven one. Much easier. Moreover, with the Russian composer, every time you come back to a piece of his it almost always

says the same thing to you, whereas with Beethoven it is often quite difficult to put your finger right on what he is saying. And any musician will tell you that that is why Beethoven is the greater composer—because music which always says the same thing to you will necessarily soon become dull music, but music whose meaning is slightly different with each hearing has a greater chance of remaining alive.

Listen, if you can, to the forty-eight fugue themes of Bach's *Well Tempered*   12
Clavichord. Listen to each theme, one after another. You will soon realize that each theme mirrors a different world of feeling. You will also soon realize that the more beautiful a theme seems to you the harder it is to find any word that will describe it to your complete satisfaction. Yes, you will certainly know whether it is a gay theme or a sad one. You will be able, in other words, in your own mind, to draw a frame of emotional feeling around your theme. Now study the sad one a little closer. Try to pin down the exact quality of its sadness. Is it pessimistically sad; is it fatefully sad or smilingly sad?

Let us suppose that you are fortunate and can describe to your own satis-   13
faction in so many words the exact meaning of your chosen theme. There is still no guarantee that anyone else will be satisfied. Nor need they be. The important thing is that each one feel for himself the specific expressive quality of a theme or, similarly, an entire piece of music. And if it is a great work of art, don't expect it to mean exactly the same thing to you each time you return to it.

Themes or pieces need not express only one emotion, of course. Take such   14
a theme as the first main one of the *Ninth Symphony*, for example. It is clearly made up of different elements. It does not say only one thing. Yet anyone hearing it immediately gets a feeling of strength, a feeling of power. It isn't a power that comes simply because the theme is played loudly. It is a power inherent in the theme itself. The extraordinary strength and vigor of the theme results in the listener's receiving an impression that a forceful statement has been made. But one should never try to boil it down to "the fateful hammer of life," etc. That is where the trouble begins. The musician, in his exasperation, says it means nothing but the notes themselves, whereas the nonprofessional is only too anxious to hang on to any explanation that gives him the illusion of getting closer to the music's meaning.

Now, perhaps, the reader will know better what I mean when I say that   15
music does have an expressive meaning but that we cannot say in so many words what that meaning is.

The third plane on which music exists is the sheerly musical plane. Besides   16
the pleasurable sound of music and the expressive feeling that it gives off, music
does exist in terms of the notes themselves and of their manipulation. Most listeners are not sufficiently conscious of this third plane.

Professional musicians, on the other hand, are, if anything, too conscious   17
of the mere notes themselves. They often fall into the error of becoming so
engrossed with their arpeggios and staccatos that they forget the deeper aspects
of the music they are performing. But from the layman's standpoint, it is not so
much a matter of getting over bad habits on the sheerly musical plane as of
increasing one's awareness of what is going on, in so far as the notes are concerned.

When the man in the street listens to the "notes themselves" with any   18
degree of concentration, he is most likely to make some mention of the melody.
Either he hears a pretty melody or he does not, and he generally lets it go at that.
Rhythm is likely to gain his attention next, particularly if it seems exciting. But
harmony and tone color are generally taken for granted, if they are thought of
consciously at all. As for music's having a definite form of some kind, that idea
seems never to have occurred to him.

It is very important for all of us to become more alive to music on its sheer-   19
ly musical plane. After all, an actual musical material is being used. The intelligent listener must be prepared to increase his awareness of the musical material
and what happens to it. He must hear the melodies, the rhythms, the harmonies,
the tone colors in a more conscious fashion. But above all he must, in order to
follow the line of the composer's thought, know something of the principles of
musical form. Listening to all of these elements is listening on the sheerly musical plane.

Let me repeat that I have split up mechanically the three separate planes   20
on which we listen merely for the sake of greater clarity. Actually, we never listen on one or the other of these planes. What we do is to correlate them—listening in all three ways at the same time. It takes no mental effort, for we do it
instinctively.

Perhaps an analogy with what happens to us when we visit the theater will   21
make this instinctive correlation clearer. In the theater, you are aware of the
actors and actresses, costumes and sets, sounds and movement. All these give
one the sense that the theater is a pleasant place to be in. They constitute the
sensuous plane in our theatrical reactions.

The expressive plane in the theater would be derived from the feeling that   22
you get from what is happening on the stage. You are moved to pity, excitement,
or gayety. It is this general feeling, generated aside from the particular words
being spoken, a certain emotional something which exists on the stage, that is
analogous to the expressive quality in music.

The plot and plot development is equivalent to our sheerly musical plane.   23
The playwright creates and develops a character in just the same way that a composer creates and develops a theme. According to the degree of your awareness
of the way in which the artist in either field handles his material will you become
a more intelligent listener.

It is easy enough to see that the theatergoer never is conscious of any of   24
these elements separately. He is aware of them all at the same time. The same is
true of music listening. We simultaneously and without thinking listen on all
three planes.

In a sense, the ideal listener is both inside and outside the music at the   25
same moment, judging it and enjoying it, wishing it would go one way and
watching it go another—almost like the composer at the moment he composes
it; because in order to write his music, the composer must also be inside and outside his music, carried away by it and yet coldly critical of it. A subjective and
objective attitude is implied in both creating and listening to music.

What the reader should strive for, then, is a more *active* kind of listening.   26
Whether you listen to Mozart or Duke Ellington, you can deepen your understanding of music only by being a more conscious and aware listener—not someone who is just listening, but someone who is listening *for* something.

Questions for Discussion

1. What are the three ways of listening to music, according to Copland?
    Which of the three do you usually use? Why?
2. Why should a person not listen to music solely for the pleasure of it? Why
    is the appeal of music on the sensuous plane "self-evident" (paragraph 6)?
3. How is the value of music determined?
4. What is the expressive plane, and why is it controversial?
5. If one must find some meaning in a piece of music, how should one listen
    to music in order to do that?
6. Why must we become more attuned to music on the sheerly musical plane?
    How might we go about this?

7.   What reasons does Copland give for breaking the way we listen to music into categories? What other reasons might there be that he does not mention? Why is division into categories a useful strategy for this type of essay?

Questions for Reflection and Writing

1.   Describe how you listen to music, using a specific piece or type of music as an example. You can describe the chronological process or define the way you listen.

2.   Summarize the expressive plane of listening to music, which Copland defines in paragraphs 7 through 15. Then apply this term and the questions it raises to a musical composition, or even to another art form such as literature, photography, sculpture, or painting.

3.   Apply what Copland is saying about classical music to another kind of music. For example, what are the criteria for evaluating rock music? Is the most pleasant-sounding rock song necessarily the best? List, define, and provide a rationale for your criteria, then apply them to the type of music you chose. Include examples of the best, average, and worst musical composition, based on your criteria.

Christopher Lasch (1932–), born on June 1 in Omaha, Nebraska, received a B.A. from Harvard University in 1954, an M.A. in 1955, and a Ph.D. in 1961. A resident of Pittsford, New York, Lasch is a professor of history at the University of Rochester. He has also taught at Williams College, Roosevelt University, the University of Iowa, and Northwestern University.

He has received honorary degrees and the 1980 American Book Award in current interest (paperback) for *The Culture of Narcissism: American Life in an Age of Diminishing Expectations* (1977). Some of his other works include *The New Radicalism in America, 1889–1963: The Intellectual as a Social Type* (1965), *The Agony of the American Left* (essays, 1969), *The World of Nations* (1973, 1974), *Haven in a Heartless World: The Timely Besieged* (1977), *The Minimal Self: Psychic Survival in Troubled Times* (1984), and *American Social Thought, 1890–1930*. Lasch is known for provocative and controversial writing that mourns a spiritual void in our culture that stems, he believes, from our obsession with materialism. Lasch has been called, on the one hand, a Jeremiah, a pessimist, and a Victorian in sensibility, and on the other hand, an original and scholarly intellectual.

The Degradation of Work and the Apotheosis of Art

Christopher Lasch

Like many amateur musicians, I cherish enthusiasms and strong opinions—   1
untested by professional experience or learned rebuttal—that I am always looking for a chance to inflict on anyone willing to listen. Beethoven's overuse of the
diminished seventh; his addiction to chords in root position; the canard that
Schumann couldn't orchestrate; the critical neglect of Ludwig Spohr; the
Brahms-Wagner controversy (I am an anti-Wagnerian); the need for more compositions featuring prominent but easy parts for the viola: I am ready to expound
on these topics whenever I can find a captive audience. Unfortunately no one
needs to hear about these things from me, when there are so many authoritative
commentators to choose from. Nor do they need to hear from me that music is
the queen of the arts; that it combines the most immediate kind of sensuous
pleasure with the most intellectual and abstract; that it provides the most compelling illustration of the possibility of disciplining feeling with form; that it uses
the simplest and most economical means, an alphabet consisting of only twelve
basic units, to achieve the most complex results; and that its capacity not merely to beguile time but to order experience and evoke its depths is inexhaustible.

How music does all these things is a mystery I will not attempt to elucidate.   2
I will content myself with a more prosaic question on which, as a student of
American society and culture, I can hope to shed some light: how does it happen that, in spite of all these riches, the great tradition of Western music remains
so little understood and appreciated in this country? Why do the arts in general
lead such a precarious existence in America? Why is the audience for good music
so limited, in spite of radio and records and all the other marvels of mass communication?

The fiscal crisis in education reminds us, in case we had forgotten during   3
the boom years after World War II, that the fine arts rank very low on the scale
of American priorities. In the expansive educational climate of the Fifties and
Sixties, the arts enjoyed a brief period of public favor. But the taxpayers' revolt,
the shrinking tax base out of which education is supported, the end of the baby
boom, and a series of deep cuts in federal spending have combined to force new
economies on the schools; and in this climate of retrenchment, luxuries and frills
are naturally the first to be dropped from the curriculum. It doesn't do much good
for friends of the arts to protest that they are a necessity, not a frill. Such arguments are likely to make little impression on hard-pressed school boards hoping
to rescue what they consider absolutely essential to the educational enterprise
and confronted, moreover, with a powerful if misguided movement demanding
a return to basics.

Even a cursory consideration of the current plight of music education leads   4
to the conclusion that the school system, especially in times when funds are
scarce, reflects the state of American culture as a whole. The crisis of music education forces us back to the question of why Americans continue to regard culture, with a capital "C," as a rather dubious and peripheral undertaking, something not quite serious, something incidental to the business of making a living
and getting ahead in the world.

This way of posing the question is a little misleading, as I will try to show   5
later on, but first let me outline some of the answers that have been offered and
explain what is wrong with them. The stock answer is that Americans are a
young and still somewhat crude people, preoccupied until recently with the conquest of a vast wilderness and with the establishment of the material foundations
on which a future civilization could hope to rise. According to this view of
things, the pioneer spirit lived on long after pioneering was completed, carrying
with it the cultural prejudices that art is not quite manly, that real men don't eat
quiche, and that although a real man may go to the opera occasionally to please

his wife, he won't enjoy it and shouldn't enjoy it and certainly shouldn't admit to enjoying it even if he does.

Another explanation of American cultural backwardness stresses the com-   6
mercial values long dominant in American society, themselves rooted in the pioneering ethic but endowed with the added prestige accorded in the twentieth century to business and everything connected with it. "The business of America is business," said Calvin Coolidge, and Charles Wilson, Eisenhower's secretary of defense, added that what's good for General Motors is good for the country. Such wisdom still commands widespread, almost automatic agreement.

Another feature of American society that has allegedly inhibited the   7
development of the arts is the country's cultural dependence on Europe, its cultural inferiority complex, its tendency to import culture instead of creating an indigenous culture of its own. The underdevelopment of American music offers a particularly good example of this cultural colonialism. Until recently, almost all of our conductors and opera singers came from Europe, American composers were held in very low esteem, and performing artists went to Europe for much of their training. Even today, the main tradition of Western music is for the most part a European tradition. American music may now be good enough to be judged by the highest standards, but the standards themselves, it can be argued, are still set in Europe.

The cultural legacy of Puritanism has been put forth as another influence   8
inhibiting the growth of the fine arts in America. In the early years of this century, when American culture seemed to be on the verge of its coming-of-age, in the words of Van Wyck Brooks's famous manifesto, it was common to blame the underdevelopment of American culture on Puritanical repression and the Puritanical fear of beauty. According to Brooks, Puritanism represented the other side of pioneering, the spiritual equivalent of pioneering. Together they divided the American mind between them, the one "spectral and aloof," "sterile and inhuman," the other obsessed with practical results. Divided between two extremes, "bare facts and metaphysics, the machinery of self-preservation and the mystery of life," American culture lacked the "genial middle ground of human tradition" on which a vigorous development of art and intellect depends.

A final line of explanation makes democracy itself the source of America's   9
failure to develop a tradition of high culture. American culture is the culture of the common man, in this view; it reflects a national commitment to social justice and to democratic standards of openness and sociability; and although it includes an admiration of art, it cannot generate the great art that is inherently

elitist and antisocial, "resistant to gregariousness," and dependent, in George Steiner's words, on a "cultivation of solitude verging on the pathological." In a 1980 essay in *Salmagundi*, "The Archives of Eden," Steiner maintains that the kind of culture that flourishes in the United States, in museums, concert halls, the record industry, the paperback-book industry, is a "custodial," not a creative or original culture: "Roger Sessions, Elliott Carter are composers of undoubted stature. Charles Ives is a most intriguing 'original.' Up to this point in its history, however, American music has been of an essentially provincial character. The great symphony of 'the new world' is by Dvořák."

The weakness of American music, according to Steiner, is the weakness of   10 American high culture as a whole. Rejecting the argument that the country is still young, he attributes the meagerness of the American contribution to world culture to the preference, "thoroughly justifiable in itself," of "democratic endeavor over authoritarian caprice, of an open society over one of creative hermeticism and censorship, of a general dignity of mass status over the perpetuation of an elite" that is often "inhumane" in its conduct and outlook but remains essential to the production of original works of art. The cultural price of democracy, Steiner says, can be seen most clearly in the "disaster of pseudo-literacy and pseudo-numeracy in the American high school and in much of what passes for so-called 'higher education.'" Here Steiner's scorn for American culture overflows and finds its most appropriate object: "The predigested trivia, the prolix and pompous didacticism, the sheer dishonesty of presentation which characterize the curriculum, the teaching, the administrative politics of daily life in the high school, in the junior college, in the open-admission 'university' (how drastically America has devalued this proud term), constitute the fundamental scandal in American culture."

In one form or another, all these explanations of American cultural inferi-   11 ority have been around for a long time, and all of them contain some truth. Yet all of them misconceive the problem by exaggerating the degree to which the plight of high culture is peculiar to the United States. In this respect, they are themselves symptoms of a national sense of cultural inferiority, which compares America unfavorably with Europe and ignores similar problems there. The crisis of high culture is not so much an American issue as a twentieth-century issue. The custodial attitude toward culture, the breakdown of the educational system, the attenuation of the creative spirit have now appeared in Europe as well, and not because Europe has been Americanized, as so many people complain, but because there is something intrinsic to industrial societies that is antagonistic to the fullest development of the artistic imagination.

If we look at contemporary music as a whole, what strikes us most forceful-   12
ly is not the vitality of European music as compared with American music but the hostility of audiences to modern music, in Europe just as in the United States; the selfconscious, self-referential, and academic quality of most of the music now being written; and the endless recycling of masterpieces composed in the eighteenth and nineteenth centuries. The European musical tradition has become as custodial in its orientation as the American tradition. The passage of time has given the lie to the modernist dogma that great works of art find a popular audience in the fullness of time. Except for the early works of Stravinsky and a few other isolated favorites, many of them written in earlier styles, the products of musical modernism have not established themselves in the symphonic repertory, and the recent attempt to revive the Romantic style once again, precisely because it is such a self-conscious, often ironic undertaking, seems equally unlikely to generate a permanent body of acknowledged masterpieces. We have to face the possibility that the musical tradition in the West has arrived, at least temporarily, at a dead end, and that the crisis of music education therefore derives from its attempt to disseminate a tradition that no longer has much life. If the Western musical tradition has become a dead language, then music teachers, like Latin teachers, will find themselves engaged in a rear-guard action not to win a broader following for their subject but to save it from academic extinction.

I said at the outset that the question of why Americans don't show more   13
interest in great art or support it more generously is misleading. It is misleading because it treats as a purely American problem what is actually a Western problem but also because it exaggerates society's indifference to art. The decline in the quality of artistic production has occurred at the very same time that art has come to be taken more seriously than ever before. In modern society, art is not an object of indifference. In some quarters, at least, it is an object of worship. It has come to enjoy the esteem formerly reserved for religion. Indeed, the difficulty may be not that art isn't taken seriously but that it is taken more seriously than is good for it. It has been cut off from the rest of life and put on a pedestal. It has been relegated to the museum and to the concert hall (and the concert hall, as has been pointed out, has become a museum in its own right), not because it is considered unimportant but because its adoration can best take place in an atmosphere uncontaminated by everyday concerns.

In earlier times, music often served as an accompaniment to other activi- 14
ties— dancing, socializing, religious worship. Only in the nineteenth century did
music come to be segregated from ordinary life and surrounded with an aura of
sanctity. This development coincided with the elevation of the performing artist
and, above all, the composer to heroic status. Formerly, composers, like other
musicians, had been regarded as craftsmen, as staff members of educational or
religious institutions, even as superior household servants. In the nineteenth
century, the artistic genius came to be seen as a heroic rebel, iconoclast, and
pathbreaker. (The cult of Wagner and of his "music of the future" played a central role in this glorification of the artist.) The flowering of music in the nineteenth century should not obscure the possibility that, in the long run, this deification of artistic genius had very bad effects, leading to the dead end of experimentation, the struggle for novelty and originality, and the defiance of established forms and constraints, or their reimposition in the most stifling manner,
that characterize the musical scene today. It looks now as if nineteenth-century
music represented the culmination of an earlier tradition rather than the dawn
of a golden age. It looks as if it owed at least part of its glory to a dependence on
its popular roots, to the persistence of dance forms and other reminders of the
historic associations between music, popular recreation, and religious ritual. Nor
is it a coincidence that it is the least pure of musical forms that have shown the
most life in our own century: opera, ballet, even religious music, the continuing
attraction of which, in an allegedly godless age, suggests that music is better off
when the spirit of veneration is directed away from music itself and toward a
more suitable object.

The best starting point for anyone who wants to understand the plight of 15
modern music and the plight of the arts in general is the great Dutch historian
Johan Huizinga's book *Homo Ludens*. Huizinga traces the decline of the "play-
element" in culture, as he calls it. "The great archetypal activities of human society are all permeated with play from the start," he argues. Language, myth, and
ritual, but also "law and order, commerce and profit, craft and art, poetry, wisdom
and science," are "rooted in the primaeval soil of play." Even those activities that
are carried on with an instrumental end in view, Huizinga says, have always contained an admixture of play, which enlists skill and intelligence, the utmost concentration of purpose, not in the service of utility but in the service of an arbitrary objective that has little importance in itself, compared with the arbitrary
forms and conventions and rituals that define its pursuit.

The serious business of life, in other words, has always been colored by an   16
attitude that is not serious in this sense and that finds more satisfaction in gratuitous difficulty than in the achievement of a given objective with a minimum of
effort. The playspirit, if you will, values maximum effort for minimal results. The
futility of play, and nothing else, explains its appeal—its artificiality, the obstacles it sets up for no other purpose than to challenge the players to surmount
them, the absence of any utilitarian or uplifting object. But the appeal of play is
so basic that it has always pervaded other activities as well lending to religion, to
law, even to warfare an element of free fantasy without which they quickly
degenerate into meaningless routine. This is precisely what has happened in our
time, according to Huizinga. The rationalization of warfare, politics, and work
has banished the play-element from the workaday world and forced it to take
refuge in sports, games, and art, which are collapsing under the weight now
imposed on them. Art has "lost rather than gained in playfulness," Huizinga says.
It has become a "substitute for religion," and this "apotheosis of art" has had pernicious effects, on the whole: "It was a blessing for art to be largely unconscious
of its high purpose and the beauty it creates. When art becomes self-conscious,
that is, conscious of its own grace, it is apt to lose something of its eternal child-
like innocence."

The most striking example of the process Huizinga was trying to analyze—   17
the decline of the play-element in culture—is one he himself paid no attention
to: the growing split between work and leisure. In most jobs, work long ago lost
the qualities of playfulness and craftsmanship. It no longer satisfies what John
Dewey called the "unconquerable impulse towards experiences enjoyable in
themselves." Today work is strictly a means to an end—profits for the capitalist,
wages for the worker. The taste for beauty and the instinct of workmanship no
longer find satisfaction in the workplace and are therefore forced to seek other
outlets. People who work at jobs deliberately divested of every challenge to ingenuity and imagination are encouraged to become consumers of beautiful objects,
to cultivate an appreciation of great art and great music, to surround themselves
with reproductions of great paintings and recordings of symphonic masterpieces.
If they prefer the deadening drumbeat of rock-and-roll, this is not necessarily
because serious music, so-called, is inherently unpopular but because it has
become so closely identified not just with leisure but with the leisure class. Great
works of art have increasingly taken on the quality of collectors' items, valued
because they advertise the wealth and leisure necessary for their consumption.

The emergence of the institutions that preserve high culture today dates   18
back, like the deification of art, to the nineteenth century. Opera houses, symphony orchestras, galleries, museums, the art market—these institutions monu-
mentalized the wealth and social aspirations of the same industrial capitalists
who were systematizing production, replacing skilled workers with machines,
and redesigning the workplace as an environment conceived along strictly utilitarian lines and deeply opposed to the spirit of play. Having banished art from
the factory, the captains of industry proceeded to glorify it and, incidentally, to
display their own munificence and connoisseurship in a setting carefully sealed
off from popular intrusion, uncontaminated by association with the workaday
world.

In industrial societies, art is doubly segregated from everyday life, in the first   19
place because it retains so few of its earlier associations with ritual, sociability,
and work, and in the second place because the glorification of art has gone hand
in hand with its definition as a leisure-time activity and specifically as an activity of the leisure class. "Culture in America," Thomas Hearn recently observed,
"is dangerously close to becoming strictly a class matter. If you drink beer, you
belong to the union and watch television. If you drink champagne, you belong
to the country club and go to the symphony." The democratization of leisure has
not democratized the consumption of high culture, and, even if it had, the creation of a broader audience for the arts would not restore the connections
between art and everyday life, on which the vitality of art depends. Works of art,
as Dewey put it, "idealize qualities found in common experience." When they
lose touch with common experience, they become hermetic and self-referential,
obsessed with originality at the expense of communicability, indifferent to anything beyond the artist's private, subjective, and idiosyncratic perception of reality.

Those who love the arts and deplore their marginal status in American   20
society need to rethink the task confronting them. The task is not to broaden the
market for the fine arts, not to create larger numbers of enlightened consumers
of culture, but to end the segregation of art and to achieve anew integration of
art and everyday life. Instead of encouraging people to make better use of their
leisure time, friends of the arts should think about making the workplace more
joyous and playful, even if this means challenging the basic premises of our society. I don't mean that employers should be encouraged to introduce free concerts
during coffee breaks. I have in mind something more fundamental: the restora-

tion of craftsmanship, the revival of the artistic dimension of practical activity, the unification of work and play.

In a period of fiscal retrenchment, justifying support for the arts assumes   21 great urgency. Unfortunately, the issue tends to present itself to educators as a choice between a hardheaded appeal to practical arguments that practical men and women can allegedly understand and a more principled and dignified defense of art based on appeals to its intrinsic value. The *Music Educators Journal* devoted its March 1983 issue to just such a controversy: "utilitarian vs. aesthetic rationales for arts education." One side stressed the industrial, nationalistic, and therapeutic value of music. A proponent of the utilitarian position went so far as to argue that "music is one of the few remaining places in the curriculum in which a feeling of national pride is built up." Another utilitarian insisted that a discipline that "believes in its own lack of utility is doomed." The other side held that music is valuable precisely because it resists assimilation into the "instrumental values" that are dominant in American society.

Instead of continuing this debate, educators might reformulate the ques-   22 tion. To state it as a choice between utilitarian and aesthetic defenses of the arts acquiesces in the divorce of art from practical life. This formulation accepts as the premise of debate the very condition that has led to the crisis of music and music education in the first place. Historically, the exaltation of art has been closely linked to the degradation of labor. Banished from the workplace, the artistic impulse has taken refuge in the rarefied realm of art for art's sake. It is no wonder that the fine arts have lost popular favor; nor are they likely to recover it by a last-minute attempt to make themselves useful. The issue is not how to make art useful but how to make useful activities artistic. This is not an issue that is likely to be settled in the schools. On the contrary, it will have to be settled in the workplace. But the schools will play an important part in its resolution, if only because they have the responsibility of training the work force and can therefore contribute to a public debate about the kind of work force that is needed. A debate on this issue is already taking shape, and it provides an opportunity to reexamine the relations between education and industry, culture and practical life.

The educational system has come under intense criticism, much of it justi-   23 fied. A number of recent reports have linked educational failure to the decline of American productivity and the weakening of America's position in the world market. The latest of these reports, issued by leaders of sixteen corporations and universities— including the presidents of Harvard, Radcliffe, Notre Dame, and the State University of New York—demands the integration of "domestic and foreign policies into aggressive, coordinated national strategies to meet the challenge of international competition." It calls for, among other things, a "displaced-worker program modeled after the GI Bill," improvements in the training of high-school mathematics and science teachers, "more competitive salaries for engineering faculties," and closer collaboration between industry and higher education in "problem-oriented research."

This is not a program likely to appeal to friends of the arts. But the debate over the connection between cultural decadence and economic decline creates an opportunity for those who reject this kind of program to offer a competing explanation of the crisis and a competing program for social and cultural renewal. They might point out, for example, that the schools are bad because our industrial system does not in fact need large numbers of skilled workers. As R. P. Blackmur once observed, it needs "only enough mind to create and tend the machines together with enough of the new illiteracy for other machines—those of our mass media—to exploit." 24

All the fashionable talk about the need to upgrade the work force through training in computer literacy, math, science, and engineering is based on a complete misreading of economic trends. The trend is toward a deskilled and degraded work force. The work force of the future will not consist of "information workers" and "data communicators." Skilled jobs will continue to be scarce. Already many industries dependent on skilled labor have exported production to places like Hong Kong and Taiwan, where skilled labor is cheap. Other industries are replacing skilled labor with capital. A careful student of employment patterns notes that the "major demand for workers in the next decade will not be for computer scientists and engineers but for janitors, nurses' aides, sales clerks, cashiers, nurses, fast-food preparers, secretaries, truck drivers, and kitchen helpers." 25

Since music educators have nothing to gain from the rage for computer literacy and the whole high-tech program, they ought to be the first to challenge it. But the best way to challenge it is to question its basic premises, not to conduct a halfhearted defense of music as an adjunct to a technical curriculum. I don't see why music educators, and all humanists, shouldn't be the first to point out that our society has little use for education in the arts, little use for education in general, because it provides most people with jobs that are repetitious, mechanical, and mindless. It gets the education system it deserves; indeed, it probably gets a better educational system than it needs to run the industrial machine. If Americans really believe in education, they had better think about 26 changing the system of production so as to provide people with work that is challenging and artistic, work that demands an education.

I don't think there is much hope for the arts and the humanities unless they   27
become serious critics of the educational system and the society behind it. We humanists won't get much of a hearing if we merely try to defend our own turf or seek to operate as one more pressure group in a political environment dominated by much stronger pressure groups. But if we join in a national debate on education and help give a clearer focus to the widespread public dissatisfaction, not just with education but with the industrial system in general, we can make our presence felt. Instead of debating on our adversaries' ground, we can force them to debate on ours. We know more about the good life than they do. We stand for the things America claims to believe in but disregards in practice: truth, beauty, the full development of human capacities. It is time we made our voices heard.

Questions for Discussion

1. How does the status of music education reflect "the state of American culture as a whole" (Paragraph 4)? Why are music and the other arts the first to be dropped from school curricula?
2. What are Lasch's answers to the questions in Paragraph 2? What are the five stock answers, and why does Lasch discount them?
3. What are George Steiner's criticisms of higher education in America? Do you agree with them?
4. According to Lasch, what should each of us do to change American attitudes toward the arts? What should educators and artists do?
5. How do work and industrialization affect the arts?
6. Why is play necessary for human creative development? How is play defined by Lasch and by Johan Huizinga?
7. What is an apotheosis, and why does Lasch assign it to art in the title?

Questions for Reflection and Writing

1. What is Lasch's answer to those who advocate more training in computers, math, and the sciences? What should Americans do, if they "really believe in education"? Summarize Lasch or state your own opinion.
2. Reread the five stock reasons that the fine arts have not been developed or properly appreciated in the United States. Summarize and respond to them.
3. Lasch's essay is based on the assumptions that there is a "decline in the quality of artistic production" and that "art has come to be taken more seriously than ever before" (Paragraph 13). Do you agree? Are his assumptions well founded? Research this issue, writing an essay that evaluates Lasch's assumptions.

Chapter 9
SCIENCE AND TECHNOLOGY

Charles Darwin (1809–1882) was born in Shrewsbury, England and studied medicine at Edinburgh University and theology at Cambridge. From 1831 to 1836 he served as a naturalist aboard the *H.M.S. Beagle*. Darwin's experiences on the voyage led to his world-changing book, *On the Origin of Species by Means of Natural Selection* (1859), which argued that life evolved over millions of years. Much of his other work, including *The Descent of Man* (1871) and *The Voyage of the Beagle* (1909), expanded upon his theory. "Natural Selection" is taken from *On the Origin of Species*.

Natural Selection

Charles Darwin

In order to make it clear how, as I believe, natural selection acts, I must beg per-   1
mission to give one or two imaginary illustrations. Let us take the case of a wolf,
which preys on various animals, securing some by craft, some by strength, and
some by fleetness; and let us suppose that the fleetest prey, a deer for instance, had
from any change in the country increased in numbers, or that other prey had
decreased in numbers, during that season of the year when the wolf is hardest
pressed for food. I can under such circumstances see no reason to doubt that the
swiftest and slimmest wolves would have the best chance of surviving, and so be
preserved or selected, provided always that they retained strength to master their
prey at this or at some other period of the year, when they might be compelled to
prey on other animals. I can see no more reason to doubt this, than that man can
improve the fleetness of his greyhounds by careful and methodical selection, or
by that unconscious selection which results from each man trying to keep the best
dogs without any thought of modifying the breed.

Even without any change in the proportional numbers of the animals on   2
which our wolf preyed, a cub might be born with an innate tendency to pursue
certain kinds of prey. Nor can this be thought very improbable; for we often
observe great differences in the natural tendencies of our domestic animals; one
cat, for instance, taking to catch rats, another mice; one cat, according to Mr. St.
John, bringing home winged game, another hares or rabbits, and another hunting on marshy ground and almost nightly catching woodcocks or snipes. The tendency to catch rats rather than mice is known to be inherited. Now, if any slight
innate change of habit or of structure benefited an individual wolf, it would have
the best chance of surviving and of leaving offspring. Some of its young would

probably inherit the same habits or structure, and by the repetition of this process, a new variety might be formed which would either supplant or coexist with the parent-form of wolf. Or, again, the wolves inhabiting a mountainous district, and those frequenting the lowlands, would naturally be forced to hunt different prey; and from the continued preservation of the individuals best fitted for the two sites, two varieties might slowly be formed. These varieties would cross and blend where they met; but to this subject of intercrossing we shall soon have to return. I may add, that, according to Mr. Pierce, there are two varieties of the wolf inhabiting the Catskill Mountains in the United States, one with a light greyhound-like form, which pursues deer, and the other more bulky, with shorter legs, which more frequently attacks the shepherd's flocks.

Let us now take a more complex case. Certain plants excrete a sweet juice, apparently for the sake of eliminating something injurious from their sap; this is effected by glands at the base of the stipules in some Leguminosæ, and at the back of the leaf of the common laurel. This juice, though small in quantity, is greedily sought by insects. Let us now suppose a little sweet juice or nectar to be excreted by the inner bases of the petals of a flower. In this case insects in seeking the nectar would get dusted with pollen, and would certainly often transport the pollen from one flower to the stigma of another flower. The flowers of two distinct individuals of the same species would thus get crossed; and the act of crossing, we have good reason to believe (as will hereafter be more fully alluded to), would produce very vigorous seedlings, which consequently would have the best chance of flourishing and surviving. Some of these seedlings would probably inherit the nectar-excreting power. Those individual flowers which had the largest glands or nectaries, and which excreted most nectar, would be oftenest visited by insects, and would be oftenest crossed; and so in the long-run would gain the upper hand. Those flowers, also, which had their stamens and pistils placed, in relation to the size and habits of the particular insects which visited them, so as to favor in any degree the transportal of their pollen from flower to flower, would likewise be favored or selected. We might have taken the case of insects visiting flowers for the sake of collecting pollen instead of nectar; and as pollen is formed for the sole object of fertilization, its destruction appears a simple loss to the plant; yet if a little pollen were carried, at first occasionally and then habitually, by the pollen-devouring insects from flower to flower, and a cross thus effected, although nine-tenths of the pollen were destroyed, it might still be a great gain to the plant; and those individuals which produced more and more pollen, and had larger and larger anthers, would be selected.

When our plant, by this process of the continued preservation or natural   4
selection of more and more attractive flowers, had been rendered highly attractive to insects, they would, unintentionally on their part, regularly carry pollen
from flower to flower; and that they can most effectually do this, I could easily
show by many striking instances. I will give only one—not as a very striking case,
but as likewise illustrating one step in the separation of the sexes of plants,
presently to be alluded to. Some holly-trees bear only male flowers, which have
four stamens producing rather a small quantity of pollen, and a rudimentary pistil; other holly-trees bear only female flowers; these have a full-sized pistil, and
four stamens with shrivelled anthers, in which not a grain of pollen can be detect-
ed. Having found a female tree exactly sixty yards from a male tree, I put the stig-
mas of twenty flowers, taken from different branches, under the microscope, and
on all, without exception, there were pollengrains, and on some a profusion of
pollen. As the wind had set for several days from the female to the male tree, the
pollen could not thus have been carried. The weather had been cold and boister-
ous, and therefore not favorable to bees; nevertheless every female flower which
I examined had been effectually fertilized by the bees, accidentally dusted with
pollen, having flown from tree to tree in search of nectar. But to return to our
imaginary case: as soon as the plant had been rendered so highly attractive to
insects that pollen was regularly carried from flower to flower, another process
might commence. No naturalist doubts the advantage of what has been called
the "physiological division of labor"; hence we may believe that it would be
advantageous to a plant to produce stamens alone in one flower or on one whole
plant, and pistils alone in another flower or on another plant. In plants under culture and placed under new conditions of life, sometimes the male organs and
sometimes the female organs become more or less impotent; now if we suppose
this to occur in ever so slight a degree under nature, then as pollen is already carried regularly from flower to flower, and as a more complete separation of the
sexes of our plant would be advantageous on the principle of the division of labor,
individuals with this tendency more and more increased, would be continually
favored or selected, until at last a complete separation of the sexes would be
effected.

Let us now turn to the nectar-feeding insects in our imaginary case: we may   5
suppose the plant of which we have been slowly increasing the nectar by continued selection, to be a common plant; and that certain insects depended in main
part on its nectar for food. I could give many facts, showing how anxious bees are
to save time; for instance, their habit of cutting holes and sucking the nectar at
the bases of certain flowers, which they can, with a very little more trouble, enter

by the mouth. Bearing such facts in mind, I can see no reason to doubt that an accidental deviation in the size and form of the body, or in the curvature and length of the proboscis, etc., far too slight to be appreciated by us, might profit a bee or other insect, so that an individual so characterized would be able to obtain its food more quickly, and so have a better chance of living and leaving descendants. Its descendants would probably inherit a tendency to a similar slight deviation of structure. The tubes of the corollas of the common red and incarnate clovers (Trifolium pratense and incarnatum) do not on a hasty glance appear to differ in length; yet the hive-bee can easily suck the nectar out of the incarnate clover, but not out of the common red clover, which is visited by humble-bees alone; so that the whole fields of the red clover offer in vain an abundant supply of precious nectar to the hive-bee. Thus it might be a great advantage to the hive-bee to have a slightly longer or differently constructed proboscis. On the other hand, I have found by experiment that the fertility of clover greatly depends on bees visiting and moving parts of the corolla, so as to push the pollen on to the stigmatic surface. Hence, again, if humble-bees were to become rare in any country, it might be a great advantage to the red clover to have a shorter or more deeply divided tube to its corolla, so that the hive-bee could visit its flowers. Thus I can understand how a flower and a bee might slowly become, either simultaneously or one after the other, modified and adapted in the most perfect manner to each other, by the continued preservation of individuals presenting mutual and slightly favorable deviations of structure.

I am well aware that this doctrine of natural selection, exemplified in the above imaginary instances, is open to the same objections which were at first urged against Sir Charles Lyell's noble views on "the modern changes of the earth, as illustrative of geology"; but we now very seldom hear the action, for instance, of the coast-waves, called a trifling and insignificant cause, when applied to the excavation of gigantic valleys or to the formation of the longest lines of inland cliffs. Natural selection can act only by the preservation and accumulation of infinitesimally small inherited modifications, each profitable to the preserved being; and as modern geology has almost banished such views as the excavation of a great valley by a single diluvial wave, so will natural selection, if it be a true principle, banish the belief of the continued creation of new organic beings, or of any great and sudden modification in their structure. 6

Questions for Discussion

1.   Why does Darwin start this piece with "imaginary illustrations"? Are they effective?
2.   How does the mention of Sir Charles Lyell function in this essay?

3. Explain the title of this essay.
4. Why does Darwin say that his example about plants is more complex than his example about wolves? Do you agree?
5. How would you characterize the tone of this essay? What evidence can you point to in order to support your answer?

Questions for Reflection and Writing

1. This piece was published in 1859. Did the language present any difficulties for you? Did the scientific material? If so, how did you overcome them? Was the struggle worth it?
2. Why do human beings not allow "survival of the fittest" to dictate who lives and who dies in human society—or do we? Provide examples of how we attempt to moderate the principles of natural selection in human society, or explain how we fool ourselves into thinking we do.
3. Some religious groups have fought against the teaching of evolution because the concept contradicts a literal reading of the Bible. (For many sites on both sides of the issue, type in + "Bible" +"evolution" +"teaching" in a search engine such as Google.com.) What do you make of this objection? Do your religious beliefs affect your answer? Explain.

Spirit in the Sky

Rex Graham

Astronomical discoveries of the past millennium have revolutionized our under-   1
standing of the universe, but the light of civilization has dimmed our visual connection to it. From Athens to Atlanta, light pollution has dulled all but a few
hundred of the brightest stars and planets from view.

Imagine for a moment we could see the Milky Way's full glory, a glittering   2
swath extending horizon to horizon. Imagine the awe our ancestors must have
felt as they gazed at the starry extravaganza 117,000 years ago. Our understanding of the night sky changes with each new discovery, bout our wonder remains
constant.

As the new millennium begins astronomers continue to probe the uni-   3
verse's farthest reaches. They hope their observations will answer questions that
occurred to worshippers at Stonehenge, philosophers at Athens, and authors of
the Old Testament. How did our universe begin? Where did we come from?
What is the fate of our universe?

As consummate stargazers, Paleolithic human knew the paths taken by the   4
sun, moon, and planets. A cave painting found in Lascaux, France, depicts their
first effort at astrology. German archaeoastronomer Michael A. Rappenglueck
says the image—a bison attacking a man who has the head of a bird and another bird head thrust on a stick—displays a pattern of stars that bears remarkable
resemblance to today's Summer Triangle, comprised of parts of the Swan, Lyre,
Dolphin and Eagle constellations. Rappenglueck says this bird-god symbol
aligned along such an axis represented shamans who traveled the skies as guides.
When the painting was made about 16,500 years ago, the Earth's slow preces-
sion of its rotational axis would have put the Summer Triangle near Polaris' current position.

Antiquity's oral histories contain mythic tales involving constellations,   5
probably devised to help each generation remember their positions. Stars and the
moon offered guidance for nomadic tribes traveling at night, but when they settled in the Nile valley about 10,000 years ago they began to worship the sun. The
first farmers realized that the spring rising of the river coincided with the first

sighting of Sirius—the brightest nighttime star—in the east at sunrise. That observation led them to begin numbering years when Sirius lined up with the sun, thereby creating a much-needed calendar to time crop planting.

Prehistoric sun worship flourished from Peru to Palestine. The Sumerians,   6
who settled nearby in Mesopotamia around 4000 BCE, worshipped the sun, moon, and Venus as gods. Astrologers, priests who could communicate with these gods, became the first rulers. These rulers felt pressured to predict the influence of heavenly bodies on humankind. Studying the night sky's patterns helped their Babylonian successors correctly predict Venus' appearances and disappearances.

"It was natural for Babylonians to believe in astrology when you consider   7
that things like the growth of plants were dependent upon the position of the sun," says Michael J. Crowe, a historian of science at the University of Notre Dame and author of *Theories of the World from Antiquity to the Copernican Revolution.* "They would tend to think that more things were dependent on the position of planets and the moons."

From spiritual relevance to scientific analysis

Before the rise of Muslim astronomers of the 12th century, China was home to   8
the most accurate and prolific astronomers in the world. As early as 2000 BCE, Chinese astronomers began predicting eclipses and recording comets, which they called broom stars, and supernovas, called guest stars. Rogue comets and eclipses were feared worldwide because they didn't fit the predictable clockwork of the cosmos, and ancient skywatchers viewed them as harbingers of doom. Those who could predict eclipses were highly regarded by kings and emperors.

Comets' reigns of terror persisted worldwide for millennia. Even 13th-cen-   9
tury English scientist Roger Bacon concluded that a comet sighted in 1264 pre-saged discord because it moved toward Mars, a planet viewed to have the warlike nature of its namesake.

The first astronomers believed Earth enjoyed special status among the   10
celestial bodies. Religious beliefs left no room to suggest that life existed elsewhere. Aristotle was one of many renowned scholars who believed an Earth-centered universe made the most sense. He argued that the moon, planets, sun, and stars revolved around the Earth in perfect circles. He and earlier Greek philosophers used theoretical models to explain their geocentric belief, trying to deduce the properties of their universe from philosophical reasoning. This required them to compare their beliefs to observation. In effect, they invented modern observational astronomy.

Aristotle's spheres fit around the Earth like onion layers, each with its own   11
motion. The model was elegant but flawed. Planets occasionally move backward
in relation to the stars. Five hundred years later, Greek astronomer Ptolemy proposed a model that accounted for the retrograde motion: He explained the moon
and planets move in small circles, or epicycles, centered on larger circles around
the Earth. Careful observation showed this couldn't possibly be true, yet geocentrism persisted 1,400 years.

A new celestial view

The Catholic Church adhered to the Aristotelian model until one of its own   12
clerics—16th-century Polish scientist Nicolaus Copernicus—persuaded his peers
that geocentrism didn't fit with observations. With the 1543 publication of *De
Revolutionibus Orbium Coelestium*, Copernicus put the sun firmly at the center of
the solar system. He shattered the view of sky as heaven and created breathing
room for the possibility of life elsewhere.

Astronomers' views have expanded with breathtaking speed during the past   13
century. In 1916, Albert Einstein revolutionized Isaac Newton's view of gravity
by proposing gravity is a geometrical distortion of space near masses such as planets, stars, and galaxies. Astronomers verified Einstein's theory by showing distant
starlight bends as it passes around celestial objects as if they were glass lenses—
making the connection between space and gravity, energy and matter.

By the next decade, American astronomer Edwin Hubble discovered that   14
many nebulae, or diffuse patches of light, actually were distant galaxies. He also
discovered, to his own disbelief, that the galaxies were receding from Earth. The
farther away they were, the faster they went.

The Big Ban theory was born in 1927, when Catholic priest and astronomer   15
Georges Lemaitre proposed the universe came into being after a superdense atom
exploded. Others soon proposed the Big Bang took place about 15 billion years
ago. Most astronomers now agree space has been expanding ever since.

During the past year, to theorists' astonishment, observations have suggest-   16
ed the universe's expansion is accelerating. Nobody know the force responsible
for it.

Life in the cosmos?

Where ancient observers saw mythical figures and influences on humanity in the   17
constellations, modern scientists search for Earth-like planets orbiting nearby
stars. Will we one day find life forms in Orion, Hydra, or Centaurus?

Astronomers agree that our galaxy is just one of hundreds of billions of   18
galaxies. Astrophysicists have shown everything in the visible universe—planets,
stars, solar systems, galaxies—amounts to only 10 percent of the universe's total
mass. Perhaps as surprising as learning Earth is not the center of the universe is
realizing the type of mass we are familiar with—made up of electrons, protons,
neutrons—does not even compromise the majority of the universe. The vast bulk
of the universe remains unknown.

Theorists also debate how life arose on Earth and the possibility that intel-   19
ligent life exists elsewhere. As our universe's geometry and physical limits come
into focus, some argue an infinite number of other universes may exist beyond our
ability to detect them. The multiverse theory gaining among theorists allows
each universe to have its own set of physical laws and mathematical constants.
Yet many scientists, such as Jill Tarter, an astronomer with the Search of Extraterrestrial Intelligence in Mountain View, California, remain more interested in
probing the universe we can see rather than discussing ones we can't.

"The changes in cosmological thinking over the past decade or so amount   20
to fine tuning," she says. "Obviously, our universe is suitable for life because we
exist in it. And this question—Are there multiple universes in which the important constants have different values and a lot of the physics may be different?—
doesn't affect my work because I live in this universe and I'm looking for intelligent civilizations that occupy this one."

The possibility for life to exist at all is regarded as highly unlikely and a tri-   21
umph over extremely long odds. Still, theorists continue to speculate about
whether life could exist in other universes.

"That is not very scientifically satisfactory because we can't observe those   22
other universes," says Charles Townes, a Nobel Prize-winning physicist at the
University of California at Berkeley. "It is another area where science is imping-
ing on the religious thought that this is a special world."

God may not fit into science's cosmological equations, but nonscientists   23
complain that what religion proposes, science disposes. Steven Weinberg, the
Nobel Prize-winning cosmologist at the University of Texas, considers what we
know about our universe and sees purposelessness. Other scientists have a radically different view.

"There is something very special about our world, and I have a strong feel-   24
ing of a presence," Townes says. "When you think about how our world is put
together and works, it is fantastic. Many scientists will agree that this place is very,
very special."

Stephen Jay Gould (1941–   ) was born in New York City and earned a Ph.D. from Columbia University in 1967. He's been a professor of zoology at Harvard University since 1967, specializing in evolutionary theory, geology, and the history of science. Among his numerous awards and honors is a MacArthur Foundation Prize Fellowship. His best-selling books include *Ever Since Darwin: Reflections in Natural History* (1977) and *The Mismeasure of Man* (1981). Gould also contributes frequently to periodicals, and has written a monthly column called "This View of Life" for *Natural History* since 1974. "The Terrifying Normalcy of AIDS" was first published in 1987 in *The New York Times* magazine.

The Terrifying Normalcy of AIDS

Stephen Jay Gould

Disney's Epcot Center in Orlando, Fla., is a technological tour de force and a conceptual desert. In this permanent World's Fair, American industrial giants have built their versions of an unblemished future. These masterful entertainments convey but one message, brilliantly packaged and relentlessly expressed: progress through technology is the solution to all human problems. G.E. proclaims from Horizons: "If we can dream it, we can do it." A.T.&T. speaks from on high within its giant golf ball: We are now "unbounded by space and time." United Technologies bubbles from the depths of Living Seas: "With the help of modern technology, we feel there's really no limit to what can be accomplished."   1

Yet several of these exhibits at the Experimental Prototype Community of Tomorrow, all predating last year's space disaster, belie their stated message from within by using the launch of the shuttle as a visual metaphor for technological triumph. The Challenger disaster may represent a general malaise, but it remains an incident. The AIDS pandemic, an issue that may rank with nuclear weaponry as the greatest danger of our era, provides a more striking proof that mind and technology are not omnipotent and that we have not canceled our bond to nature.   2

In 1984, John Platt, a biophysicist who taught at the University of Chicago for many years, wrote a short paper for private circulation. At a time when most of us were either ignoring AIDS, or viewing it as a contained and peculiar affliction of homosexual men, Platt recognized that the limited data on the origin of AIDS and its spread in America suggested a more frightening prospect: we   3

Stephen Jay Gould, "The Terrifying Normalcy of AIDS," 1987. With permission from Stephen Jay Gould, Agassiz Professor of Zoology, Harvard University.

are all susceptible to AIDS, and the disease has been spreading in a simple exponential manner.

Exponential growth is a geometric increase. Remember the old kiddy prob-   4
lem: if you place a penny on square one of a checkerboard and double the number of coins on each subsequent square—2, 4, 8, 16, 32 . . .—how big is the stack by the sixtyfourth square? The answer: about as high as the universe is wide. Nothing in the external environment inhibits this increase, thus giving to exponential processes their relentless character. In the real, noninfinite world, of course, some limit will eventually arise, and the process slows down, reaches a steady state, or destroys the entire system: the stack of pennies falls over, the bacterial cells exhaust their supply of nutrients.

Platt noticed that data for the initial spread of AIDS fell right on an expo-   5
nential curve. He then followed the simplest possible procedure of extrapolating the curve unabated into the 1990s. Most of us were incredulous, accusing Platt of the mathematical gamesmanship that scientists call "curve fitting." After all, aren't exponential models unrealistic? Surely we are not all susceptible to AIDS. Is it not spread only by odd practices to odd people? Will it not, therefore, quickly run its short course within a confined group?

Well, hello 1987—worldwide data still match Platt's extrapolated curve. This   6
will not, of course, go on forever. AIDS has probably already saturated the African areas where it probably originated, and where the sex ratio of afflicted people is 1-to-1, male-female. But AIDS still has far to spread, and may be moving exponentially, through the rest of the world. We have learned enough about the cause of AIDS to slow its spread, if we can make rapid and fundamental changes in our handling of that most powerful part of human biology—our own sexuality. But medicine, as yet, has nothing to offer as a cure and precious little even for palliation.

This exponential spread of AIDS not only illuminates its, and our, biology,   7
but also underscores the tragedy of our moralistic misperception. Exponential processes have a definite time and place of origin, an initial point of "inoculation"—in this case, Africa. We didn't notice the spread at first. In a population of billions, we pay little attention when one increases to two, or eight to sixteen, but when one million becomes two million, we panic, even though the rate of doubling has not increased.

The infection has to start somewhere, and its initial locus may be little more   8
than an accident of circumstance. For a while, it remains confined to those in close contact with the primary source, but only by accident of proximity, not by

intrinsic susceptibility. Eventually, given the power and lability of human sexuality, it spreads outside the initial group and into the general population. And now AIDS has begun its march through our own heterosexual community.

What a tragedy that our moral stupidity caused us to lose precious time, the   9
greatest enemy in fighting an exponential spread, by downplaying the danger because we thought that AIDS was a disease of three irregular groups of minorities: minorities of life style (needle users), of sexual preference (homosexuals), and of color (Haitians). If AIDS had first been imported from Africa into a Park Avenue apartment, we would not have dithered as the exponential march began.

The message of Orlando—the inevitability of technological solutions—is wrong,   10
and we need to understand why.

Our species has not won its independence from nature, and we cannot do   11
all that we can dream. Or at least we cannot do it at the rate required to avoid tragedy, for we are not unbounded from time. Viral diseases are preventable in principle, and I suspect that an AIDS vaccine will one day be produced. But how will this discovery avail us if it takes until the millennium, and by then AIDS has fully run its exponential course and saturated our population, killing a substantial percentage of the human race? A fight against an exponential enemy is primarily a race against time.

We must also grasp the perspective of ecology and evolutionary biology and   12
recognize, once we reinsert ourselves properly into nature, that AIDS represents the ordinary workings of biology, not an irrational or diabolical plague with a moral meaning. Disease, including epidemic spread, is a natural phenomenon, part of human history from the beginning. An entire subdiscipline of my profession, paleopathology, studies the evidence of ancient diseases preserved in the fossil remains of organisms. Human history has been marked by episodic plagues. More native peoples died of imported disease than ever fell before the gun during the era of colonial expansion. Our memories are short, and we have had a respite, really, only since the influenza pandemic at the end of World War I, but AIDS must be viewed as a virulent expression of an ordinary natural phenomenon.

I do not say this to foster either comfort or complacency. The evolutionary   13
perspective is correct, but utterly inappropriate for our human scale. Yes, AIDS is a natural phenomenon, one of a recurring class of pandemic diseases. Yes, AIDS may run through the entire population, and may carry off a quarter or more of us. Yes, it may make no *biological* difference to Homo sapiens in the long run: there will still be plenty of us left and we can start again. Evolution cares as little for its agents—organisms struggling for reproductive success—as physics cares for individual atoms

of hydrogen in the sun. But we care. These atoms are our neighbors, our lovers, our children and ourselves. AIDS is both a natural phenomenon and, potentially, the greatest natural tragedy in human history.

The cardboard message of Epcot fosters the wrong attitudes: we must both reinsert   14
ourselves into nature and view AIDS as a natural phenomenon in order to fight properly. If we stand above nature and if technology is all-powerful, then AIDS is a horrifying anomaly that must be trying to tell us something. If so, we can adopt one of two attitudes, each potentially fatal. We can either become complacent, because we believe the message of Epcot and assume that medicine will soon generate a cure, or we can panic in confusion and seek a scapegoat for something so irregular that it must have been visited upon us to teach us a moral lesson.

But AIDS is not irregular. It is part of nature. So are we. This should galva-   15
nize us and give us hope, not prompt the worst of all responses: a kind of "new-age" negativism that equates natural with what we must accept and cannot, or even should not, change. When we view AIDS as natural, and when we recognize both the exponential property of its spread and the accidental character of its point of entry into America, we can break through our destructive tendencies to blame others and to free ourselves of concern.

If AIDS is natural, then there is no message in its spread. But by all that sci-   16
ence has learned and all that rationality proclaims, AIDS works by a *mechanism*— and we can discover it. Victory is not ordained by any principle of progress, or any slogan of technology, so we shall have to fight like hell, and be watchful. There is no message, but there is a mechanism.

Questions for Discussion

1. Why do you think Gould begins this piece at Disney's Epcot Center? Is the device effective?

2. How, according to Gould, are the Challenger disaster and the AIDS pandemic alike? How are they different? What's gained in comparing them at all?

3. What does exponential growth have to do with this essay? How does the example about pennies and the checkerboard function?

4. The words "terrifying" and "normalcy" suggest an opposition. How does this opposition function in this essay?

5. The author uses the words "message" and "mechanism" as foils for each other. Trace the function of this dichotomy throughout the essay. Why should Gould rely so heavily on oppositions in his essay? How does this structure affect your reading of his piece?

Questions for Reflection and Writing

1. Has AIDS affected your life? If so, how? Whether you feel that it has or has not affected you personally, use Gould's piece as a jumping-off place for reflection on the impact of AIDS on our culture. Do you think it has changed our culture permanently?

2. Explain the phrase "moralistic misperception" within the context of this essay. According to the author, what did it lead to? What place, if any, do you think moral considerations have in the AIDS pandemic?

3. Gould writes that the human "species has not won its independence from nature" (paragraph 11). What does he mean by this? Respond to his claim. When else are we reminded of our dependence upon nature? Is the goal of "independence from nature" a valuable one?

Is Science a Faith?

YES: Daniel Callahan, from "Calling Scientific Ideology to Account," *Society* (May/June 1996)

NO: Richard Dawkins, from "Is Science a Religion?" *The Humanist* (January/February 1997)

Issue Summary

YES: Bioethicist Daniel Callahan argues that science's domination of the cultural landscape unreasonably excludes other ways of understanding nature and the world and sets it above any need to accept moral, social, and intellectual judgment from political, religious, and even traditional values.

NO: Biologist Richard Dawkins maintains that science "is free of the main vice of religion, which is faith" because it relies on evidence and logic instead of tradition, authority, and revelation.

Science and technology have come to play a huge role in human culture, largely   1
because they have led to vast improvements in nutrition, health care, comfort, communication, transportation, and mankind's ability to affect the world. However, science has also enhanced understanding of human behavior and of how the universe works, and in this it frequently contradicts what people have long thought they knew. Furthermore, it actively rejects any role of God in scientific explanation.

Many people therefore reject what science tells us. They see science as just   2
another way of explaining how the world and humanity came to be; in this view, science is no truer than religious accounts. Indeed, some say science is just another religion, with less claim on followers' allegiance than other religions that have been divinely sanctioned and hallowed by longer traditions. Certainly, they see little significant difference between the scientist's faith in reason, evidence, and skepticism as the best way to achieve truth about the world and the religious believer's faith in revelation and scripture.

The antipathy between science and religion has a long history. In 1616 the   3
Catholic Church attacked the Italian physicist Galileo Galilei (1564-1642) for
teaching Copernican astronomy and, thus, contradicting the teachings of the
Church; when invited to look through the telescope and see the moons of Jupiter
for themselves, the Church's representatives reportedly refused (Pope John Paul
II finally pardoned Galileo in 1983). On the other side of the conflict, the French
Revolution featured the destruction of religion in the name of rationality and sci-
ence, and the worship of God was officially abolished on November 10, 1793.

To many people, the conflict between science and religion is really a con-   4
flict between religions, or faiths, much like those between Muslims and Hindus
or between conservative and liberal Christians. This view often becomes explicit in the debates between creationists and evolutionists.

The rejection of science is also evident among those who see science as   5
denying both the existence of God and the importance of "human values"
(meaning behaviors that are affirmed by traditional religion). This leads to a basic
antipathy between science and religion, especially conservative religion, and
especially in areas-such as human origins-where science and scripture seem to be
talking about the same things but are contradicting each other. This has been
true ever since evolutionary theorist Charles Darwin first published *On the Origin of Species by Means of Natural Selection* in 1859.

Religious people are not the only ones who see in science a threat to   6
"human values." Science also contradicts people's preferences, which are often
based less on religion than on tradition and prejudice. For instance, science insists
that no race or gender is superior to another; that homosexuality is natural, not
wicked; that different ways of living deserve respect; and that it is possible to have
too many children and to cut down too many trees. It also argues that religious
proscriptions that may have once made sense are no longer relevant (the Jewish
practice of not eating pork, for example, is a good way to avoid trichinosis; however, says science, so are cooking the meat at higher temperatures and not feeding pigs potentially contaminated feed).

Many people feel that there is a baby in the bathwater that science pitches   7
out the window. Science, they say, neglects a very important side of human existence embodied in that "human values" phrase. Daniel Callahan sees this side as
the source of moral, political, and intellectual judgment, which science by its dominance of society tends to evade. Science, he argues in the following selection, has
become an ideology in its own right, as intolerant as any other, and it sorely needs
judgment or criticism to keep it from steamrollering the more human side of life.

In the second selection, Richard Dawkins maintains that science differs   8
profoundly from religion in its reliance on evidence and logic—not on tradition,
authority, and revelation—and is therefore to be trusted much more.

YES
Calling Scientific Ideology to Account

Daniel Callahan

I come to the subject of science and religion with some complex emotions and a   9
personal history not irrelevant to my own efforts to think about this matter. It
seems appropriate for me to lay this history out a bit to set the stage for the argument I want to make. For the fast half of my life, from my teens through my mid-
thirties, I was a serious religious believer, a church member (Roman Catholic),
and someone whose identity as both a person and as an intellectual had a belief
in God at its center. During that time I had little contact with the sciences; literature and philosophy caught my imagination. I was a fine example, for that matter, of the gap between the two cultures that C. P. Snow described, caught up as
I was in the humanities and generally ignorant about science. I spent most of my
time among humanists and religious believers (though believers of a generally liberal kind).

All of that changed in my late thirties. Two events happened simultane-   10
ously. The first was a loss of my religious faith, utterly and totally. I ceased to be a
theist, became an atheist, and so I remain today. I did not, however, have any
revolt against organized religion (as it is sometimes pejoratively called) or the
churches; nor did I lose respect for religious believers. They just seem to me wrong
in their faith and mistaken in their hope. The second event was my discovery of
the field of biomedical ethics, seemingly a fertile area for my philosophical training and an important window into the power of the biomedical sciences to
change the way we think about and live our lives. With this new interest I began
spending much of my time with physicians and bench scientists and worked hard
to understand the universe of science that I was now entering (through the side
door of biomedical ethics).

Meanwhile, as I was undergoing my own personal changes, the relationship   11
between science and religion was shifting in the country as well. When I was

From Daniel Callahan, "Calling Scientific Ideology to Account," *Society*, vol. 33, no. 4 (May/June 1996). Copyright 0 1996 by
Transaction Publishers. Reprinted by permission. All rights reserved.

growing up, there was still considerable debate about religion and science, with some believers arguing that there was a fundamental incompatibility between them and others holding that they were perfectly congenial. Some scientists, for their part, wrote books about religion, saying that they had found God in their science. Others, of a more positivistic bent, thought that science had forever expunged the notion of a God and that science would eventually offer an explanation of everything.

This debate seemed to subside significantly in the 1970s and 1980s. Science   12
came almost totally to win the minds and emotions of educated Americans, and technological innovation was endlessly promoted as the key to both human progress and economic prosperity, a most attractive combination of doing good and doing well. While public opinion polls and church attendance figures, not to mention the gestures of politicians, showed the continuing popularity of religion, it was science that had captured the academy, the corridors of economic power, and high-brow prestige in the media. There remained, to be sure, skirmishes here and there over such issues as the teaching of creationism in the schools, particularly in the Bible Belt, and mutterings about the "religious Right" and its opposition to abortion, embryo and fetal research, and the like. Although there had been some bursts of anti-technology sentiments as part of the fallout of the 1960s culture wars, they had little staying power. The "greening of America" soon ran into a drought.

Science, in short, finally gained the ascendancy, coming to dominate the   13
cultural landscape as much as the economic marketplace. This was the world of science I entered and in which I still remain enmeshed. My reaction to the news in May 1995 that a religious group, with the help of Jeremy Rifkin, was entering a challenge to the patenting of life was one of rueful bemusement: what a quixotic gesture, almost certainly doomed to failure but not, perhaps, before a round of media attention. Such battles make good copy, but that's about it.

The specific issue of the patenting of life deserves discussion, and someone   14
or other would have raised it. Yet it hardly signals a new struggle between science and religion. It is neither that central an issue, nor did it appear even to galvanize a serious follow-up response among most religious groups. Congress, moreover, has given no indication that it will take up the issue in any serious way. In other words, it appears to have sunk as an issue as quickly as it arose.

Yet I confess to a considerable degree of uneasiness here. Science should not   15
have such easy victories. It needs to have a David against its Goliath. This is only to say that scientific modernism—that is, the cultural dominance of science— desperately needs to have a serious and ongoing challenger. By that I mean the

challenge of a different way of looking at nature and the world, one capable of shaking scientific self-satisfaction and complacency and resisting its at-present overpowering social force. Science needs, so to speak, a kind of loyal opposition.

This kind of opposition need not and should not entail hostility to the sci-   16
entific method, to the investment of money in scientific research, or to the hope that scientific knowledge can make life better for us. Not at all. What it does entail is a relentless skepticism toward the view that science is the single and greatest key to human progress, that scientific knowledge is the only valid form of knowledge, and that some combination of science and the market is the way to increased prosperity and well-being for all. When religion can only fight science with the pea-shooters of creationism and antipatenting threats, it has little going for it. That response surely does not represent a thoughtful, developed, and articulate counterbalance to the hold of science on modern societies.

I say all of this because what I discovered upon entering the culture of sci-   17
ence-that is, scientism was something more than a simple commitment to the value and pursuit of scientific knowledge. That is surely present, but it is also accompanied socially by two other ingredients, science as ideology and science as faith.

Science as Ideology

By science as ideology I mean that constellation of values that, for many, con-   18
stitutes a more or less integrated way of interpreting life and nature, not only providing a sense of meaning but also laying out a path to follow in the living of a life. At the core of that ideology is a commitment to science as the most reliable source of knowledge about the nature of things and to technological innovation as the most promising way to improve human life. Closely related features of that ideology are an openness to untrammeled inquiry, limited by neither church nor state, skepticism toward all but scientifically verifiable claims, and a steady revision of all knowledge. While religion should be tolerated in the name of toleration rather than on grounds of credibility, it should be kept in the private sphere, out of the public space, public institutions, and public education. The ideology of scientism is all-encompassing, a way of knowing, and, culturally embodied, a way of living.

By science as faith I mean the ideology of science when it includes also a   19
kind of non-falsifiable faith in the capacity of science not simply to provide reliable knowledge but also to solve all or most human problems, social, political, and economic. It is non-falsifiable in the sense that it holds that any failure to date of science to find solutions to human problems says nothing at all about its

future capacity to do so; such solutions are only a matter of time and more refined knowledge. As for the fact that some of the changes science and technology have wrought are not all good, or have both good and bad features, science as faith holds that there is no reason in principle that better science and new knowledge cannot undo earlier harm and avoid future damage. In a word, no matter what science does, better science can do even better. No religious believer, trying to reconcile the evil in the world with the idea of a good and loving God, can be any more full of hope that greater knowledge will explain all than the scientific believer. And there is no evidence that is allowed to count against such a belief, and surely not religious arguments.

It is at just this point that I, the former religious believer, find it hard to con- 20 fidently swallow the ideology of science, much less the serene faith of many of its worshippers. I left one church but I was not looking to join another. Nonetheless, when I stepped into the territory of science that appeared to be exactly the demand: If you want to be one of us, have faith. Yet a perspective that aims to supply the kind of certain metaphysical and ethical knowledge once thought limited to religion and to provide the foundations for ways of life seems to me worthy of the same kind of wariness that, ironically, science first taught me to have about religion. If science warns us to be skeptical of traditionalism, of settled but unexamined views, of knowledge claims poorly based on hard evidence, on acts of faith that admit of no falsifiability, why should I not bring that same set of attitudes to science itself? That interesting magazine, The Skeptical Inquirer, dedicated to getting the hard facts to debunk superstition, quackery, and weird claims by strange groups, does not run many articles devoted to debunking science or claims made in behalf of the enlightenment it can bring us. (I believe it has yet to publish even one such article, but I may be wrong about that.)

Maybe that is not so surprising. Such rebelliousness seems utterly un- 21 acceptable to scientism, utterly at odds with its solemn pieties and liturgical practices. To question the idea of scientific progress, to suggest that there are valid forms of nonscientific knowledge, to think that societies need something more than good science and high technology to flourish is to risk charges of heresy in enlightened educated circles every bit as intimidating as anything that can be encountered in even the most conservative religious groups. The condescension exhibited toward the "religious Right" surely matches that once displayed by Christianity toward "pagans." Even a Republican-dominated, conservative Congress knows it can far better afford politically to drastically cut or eliminate funding for the National Endowments for the Humanities and the Arts than for the National Science Foundation or the National Institutes of Health.

Now I come to the heart of my problem with the ideology and faith of sci-   22
entism. Like any other human institution and set of practices, science needs to
be subject to moral, social, and intellectual judgment; it needs to be called to task
from time to time. Ideally that ought to be done by institutions that have the cultural clout to be taken seriously and by means of criteria for judgment that cannot themselves easily be called into question. Religion itself has always had this
notion as part of its own self-understanding: It believes that it -churches, theolo-
gies, creeds-stands under the higher judgment of God and recognizes that it can
itself fall into idolatry, the worship of false gods. One might well complain that
the churches have seemed, in fact, exceedingly slow in rendering negative judgment upon themselves. Even so, they have the idea of such judgment and on
occasion it has indeed been exercised.

Unfortunately—and a profound misfortune it is—science no longer has se-   23
riously competitive ways of thinking or institutions that have a comparable prestige and power. Science no longer has a counterweight with which it must contend, no institution or generally persuasive perspective that can credibly pass
judgment on scientific practices and pretensions. No secular force or outlook or
ideology exists to provide it. Religion once played that role: Popes, prelates, and
preachers could once rain some effective fire and brimstone down on science,
often enough mistakenly yet sometimes helpfully. But religion, too concerned to
protect its own turf, too unwilling to open its eyes to new possibilities and forms
of knowledge, offered mainly condemnation along with, now and then, some
lukewarm support. Moreover, the gradual secularizing of the cultures of the developed countries of the world, relegating religion to the domestic sphere, took away
religion's platform to speak authoritatively to public life. Scientific modernism
was there to fill the gap, and it has been happy to do so. It is not possible to utter
prayers in public schools, but there are no limits to the homage that can be lavished upon science and its good works.

The absence of a counterweight to the ideology of science has a number of   24
doleful effects. It helps to substantiate the impression that there is no alternative,
much less higher, perspective from which to judge science and its works. If you
are the king of the hill, all things go your way and those below you are fearful or
hesitant to speak out. It helps as well to legitimate the mistaken belief that all
other forms of knowledge are not only inferior but that they are themselves
always subject to the superior judgment of science. Accordingly, claims of religious knowledge of a credible kind were long ago dismissed by science. At its best,
science is benignly tolerant of religion, patting it on the head like a kindly but

wiser grandparent. At its worst, it can be mocking and dismissive. The kinds of knowledge generated by the humanities fare a little better, but not all that much.

From the perspective of my own field, bioethics, it is distressing to see the 25 way that claims for the value or necessity of scientific research are treated with an extraordinary deference, usually going unquestioned. A recent federal panel on embryo research, for instance, set the issue up as a struggle between the moral status of the embryo, on the one hand, and that of the "need" (not just desire on the part of researchers) for embryo research, on the other. In a fine display of nuanced, critical thinking, the panel took apart excessive claims for the rights of embryos, urging "respect" but allowing research. As for the claims of research, they were accepted without any doubts or hesitations at all; they seemed self-evident to the panel, not in need of justification. Even Henry VIII, the king of his hill, hardly got that kind of deference, even from those luckless wives he had beheaded. In a culture saturated with the ideology of science, there seems hardly any forceful voice to call it to account.

If there was a loyal opposition, it would not let the claims and triumphal- 26 ism of the scientific establishment go unchallenged. It would treat that establishment with respect, but it would fully understand that it is an *establishment*, intent on promoting its own cause and blowing its own horn, critical of its opponents and naysayers, and of course never satisfied with the funds available to it (funds that, if forthcoming in greater quantity, will someday find a cure for cancer, discover the molecular basis for disease, give us cheap energy generated by cold fusion, etc., etc.). A loyal opposition would bring to science exactly the same cool and self-critical eye that science itself urges in the testing of scientific ideas and hypotheses. One of the great intellectual contributions of science has been its methodological commitment to self-criticism and selfrevision; and that is one reason it came to triumph over religion, which has not always shown much enthusiasm for skepticism about its key doctrines.

But if self-criticism and self-revision are at the heart of the scientific 27 method, then a good place to begin employing them is at home, on the scientific ideology that culturally sustains the whole apparatus. A loyal opposition would do this not only to temper exaggerated self-congratulations on the part of science but also to keep science itself scientific.

The insuperable limitation of the scientific method is that it cannot be used 28 to criticize the ideology of science or its methods. To try to do so only begs the question of its validity. In the end, we judge that method more by its fruits and consequences than by its a priori validity. The problem here is that science cannot tell us what consequences we ought to want, what kind of knowledge we need, or what uses are best for the knowledge that science demonstrates. Science, that is, is far more helpful with our means than our ends. Good science cannot tell us how to organize good societies or develop good people (or even tell us how to define "good") or tell us what is worth knowing. There is no scientific calculus to tell us how much a society should invest in scientific research; that is a matter of prudence.

It is here that the other forms of knowledge ought and must come into play: 29 the knowledge developed by the humanities or the "soft" social sciences; the political values and structures created by democratic societies, built upon argument, some consensus, and some compromise. My own domain, that of the humanities, was long ago intimidated by science. It does not complain about the grievous disparity between research resources lavished upon it in comparison with science. Those humanists who dare enter the church of science and mutter to its high priests are given the back of the scientific hand, quickly labeled as cranks or, black mark of black marks, Luddites. The scientific establishment should help to encourage and support other forms of knowing and should be willing to learn from them; that would be to display the openness and creativity it touts as its strength. It does not, however, take the fingers of even one hand to count the number of Nobel laureates in science who have petitioned Congress for stronger support for the humanities.

What is a proper role for religion in a society captured by the ideology of   30 science? Its most important role, the one it has played from time to time with other principalities and powers, would be simply to urge some humility on science and to call it to task for pretentiousness and power grabbing. Science ought to stand under constant moral judgment, and there is an important role for religion to play in formulating some of the criteria for such judgment. It is thus proper for religion to remind science of something religion should always be reminding itself of as well: Neither science nor religion are whole and entire unto themselves. Religion stands under the judgment of God (it tells us), and science stands under the judgment of the collective conscience of humankind (which religion does not tell us). Religion can remind the world, and those in science, that the world can be viewed from different perspectives. And it can remind that world, including science, what it means to attempt, as does religion, to make sense of everything in some overall coherent way. There is no need to agree with the way in which religion comprehends reality in order to be reminded of the human thirst for some sense of coherence and meaning in the world.

There has always been an aspect of science that overlaps with supernatural 31
religion. That is the kind of natural piety and awe that many scientists feel in the
face of the mysteries and beauty of the natural world. This can be called a kind
of natural religion, and some scientists easily make the move from the natural to
the supernatural, even if many of their more skeptical colleagueswho also share
the sense of natural awe-do not follow them in taking that step. This natural awe
frequently expresses itself in a hesitation to manipulate nature for purely self-
interested ends, whether economic or medical. The concern of ecologists for the
preservation of biodiversity, the hesitations of population geneticists about germ-
line therapy, the worry of environmentalists about the protection of tropical
forests or of biologists for the preservation of even rare species, all testify to that
kind of natural piety. It is here that there is room for an alliance between science
and religion, between that science that sees the mystery and unprobed depths of
the natural world and that religion that sees nature as the creation and manifestation of a beneficent god.

It is important, for that matter, that science find allies in its desire to keep 32
its natural piety alive and well. The primary enemies of that piety are the casual
indifference of many human beings to nature and the more systematic despoiling
of nature carried out in the name of the market, human betterment, or the satisfying of private fantasies and desires. Environmentalism has long been tom by a
struggle that pits conservationists against preservationists. Conservationists
believe that the natural world can be cultivated for human use and its natural
resources protected if care is taken. Preservationists, and particularly the "deep
ecologists," are hostile to that kind of optimism, holding that nature as it is needs
to be protected, not manipulated or exploited. Conservationism has a serious and
sober history and has been by no means oriented toward a crude exploitation of
nature. But it is a movement that has often been allowed to shade off into that
kind of technological optimism that argues that whatever harm scientific progress
and technological innovation cause, it can just as readily be undone and corrected by science.

This is the ideology of science taken to extremes, but a common enough 33
viewpoint among those who see too much awe of nature, too much protec-
tionism, as a threat to economic progress. Religion could well throw its weight
behind responsible conservation, and it would not hurt a bit if some theologians
and church groups took up the cause of deep ecology. That is an unlikely cause
to gain great support in an overcrowded world, and particularly in the poverty-
stricken parts of that world. But it is a strong countercurrent worth introducing

into the larger stream of efforts to preserve and respect nature. A little roughage in the bowels helps keep things moving.

Perhaps the cultural dominance of science is nowhere so evident as in a fea-   34
ture of our society frequently overlooked: the powerful proclivity to look to numbers and data as the key to good public policy. Charts, tables, and graphs are the
standard props of the policy analyst and the legislator. This is partly understandable and justifiable. With issues of debate and contention, hard data is valuable.
It can help to determine if there is a real problem, the dimensions of that problem, and the possible consequences of different solutions. But the soft underside
of the deification of data is the too frequent failure to recognize that data never
tells its own story, that it is always subject to, and requires, interpretation.

There is no data that can carry out that work. On the contrary, at that point   35
we are thrown back upon our values, our way of looking at the world and society, and our different social hopes and commitments. The illusion of the inherent
persuasiveness of data is fostered by scientism, which likes to think that there can
be a neutral standpoint from which to assess those matters that concern us, that
scientific information plays that role, and that the answer to any moral and social
battles is simply more and better information.

The dominance of the field of economics in social policy itself tells an in-   36
teresting story: the need to find a policy discipline that has all the trapping of science in its methods and that can capture its prestige. It is a field that aspires to be
a science and that speaks the culturally correct language of modeling, hypothesis
testing, and information worship, And it has been amply rewarded for its troubles, recently gaining the blessing of a Nobel prize for its practitioners to signal its
status as a science, and for many years capturing the reins of public power and
office in a way unmatched by any other academic discipline.

There is a prestigious government Council of Economic Advisors. There is   37
not now, and probably never will be, a Council of Philosophical Advisors, or Historical Advisors, or Humanistic Advisors. But then, that is likely to be the fate of
any field that cannot attach itself to the prestige of science. It will lack social
standing, just as religion now lacks serious intellectual standing. Note that I say
"intellectual standing." There is no doubt that religion can still have a potent
political status or that religion can from time to time make trouble for science (or,
more accurately, make trouble for the agendas of some scientists, for example, for
those who would like to do embryo research). But in the larger and more enduring world of dominant ideas and ideologies, science sits with some serenity, and
much public adulation, in an enviable position. It is interesting to note what no

one seems to have noticed. In the demise of communism as a political philoso-phy and a set of political regimes, one of its features has endured nicely: its faith in science. That is the one feature it shared with the Western capitalist democ-racies that triumphed over it. It is also, let it be noted, a key feature of a market ideology, the engine of innovation, a major source of new products, and-in its purported value neutrality-a congenial companion for a market ideology that just wants to give people the morally neutral gift of freedom of economic choice, not moralisms about human nature and the good society of a kind to be found in the now-dead command economies of the world.

Allow me to end as I began. There was a time when I hoped my own field, 38 bioethics, might serve as the loyal opposition to scientific ideology, at least its bio-medical division. In its early days, in the 1960s and 1970s, many of those first drawn to it were alarmed by the apparently unthinking way in which biomedical knowledge and technologies were being taken up and disseminated. It seemed important to examine not only the ethical dilemmas generated by a considerable portion of the scientific advances but also to ask some basic questions about the moral premises of the entire enterprise of unrelenting biomedical progress. That latter aspiration has yet to be fulfilled Most of those who have come into the field have accepted scientific ideology as much as most scientists, and they have no less been the cultural children of their times, prone to look to medical progress and its expansion of choice as a perfect complement to a set of moral values that puts autonomy at the very top of the moral hierarchy. Nothing seems to so well serve the value of autonomy as the expanded range of human options that sci-ence promises to deliver, whether for the control of procreation or the improve-ment of health or the use of medical means to improve our lives. Not many peo-ple in bioethics, moreover, care to be thought of as cranks, and there is no faster way to gain that label than to raise questions about the scientific enterprise as a whole. Bioethicists have, on the whole, become good team players, useful to help out with moral puzzles now and then and trustworthy not to probe basic premis-es too deeply. Unless one is willing to persistently carry out such probes, the idea of a loyal opposition carries no weight.

Can religion, or bioethics, or some other social group or force in our socie- 39 ty call science to account when necessary? Can it do so with credibility and seri-ous credentials? Can it do so in a way that helps science to do its own work bet-ter, and not simply to throw sand in the eyes of scientists? I am not sure, but I surely hope so. I can only say, for my part, that I left one church and ended in the pews of another one, this one the Church of Science. In more ways than one-in its self-confidence, its serene faith in its own value, and its ability to intimidate dissenters it seems uncomfortably like the one I left. How can it be made to see that about itself?

No

Is Science a Religion?

Richard Dawkins

It is fashionable to wax apocalyptic about the threat to humanity posed by the   40
AIDS virus, "mad cow" disease, and many others, but I think a case can be made that *faith* is one of the world's great evils, comparable to the smallpox virus but harder to eradicate.

Faith, being belief that isn't based on evidence, is the principal vice of any   41
religion. And who, looking at Northern Ireland or the Middle East, can be confident that the brain virus of faith is not exceedingly dangerous? One of the stories told to young Muslim suicide bombers is that martyrdom is the quickest way to heaven—and not just heaven but a special part of heaven where they will receive their special reward of 72 virgin brides. It occurs to me that our best hope may be to provide a kind of "spiritual arms control": send in specially trained theologians to deescalate the going rate in virgins.

Given the dangers of faith—and considering the accomplishments of rea-   42
son and observation in the activity called science—I find it ironic that, whenever I lecture publicly, there always seems to be someone who comes forward and says, "Of course, your science is just a religion like ours. Fundamentally, science just comes down to faith, doesn't it?"

Well, science is not religion and it doesn't just come down to faith. Al-   43
though it has many of religion's virtues, it has none of its vices. Science is based upon verifiable evidence. Religious faith not only lacks evidence, its independence from evidence is Its pride and joy, shouted from the rooftops. Why else would Christians wax critical of doubting Thomas? The other apostles are held up to us as exemplars of virtue because faith was enough for them. Doubting Thomas, on the other hand, required evidence. Perhaps he should be the patron saint of scientists.

One reason I receive the comment about science being a religion is because   44
I believe in the fact of evolution. I even believe in it with passionate conviction. To some, this may superficially look like faith. But the evidence that makes me believe in evolution is not only overwhelmingly strong; it is freely available to anyone who takes the trouble to read up on it. Anyone can study the same evidence that I have and presumably come to the same conclusion. But if you have a belief that is based solely on faith, I can't examine your reasons. You can retreat behind the private wall of faith where I can't reach you.

Now in practice, of course, individual scientists do sometimes slip back into   45
the vice of faith, and a few may believe so single-mindedly in a favorite theory that they occasionally falsify evidence. However, the fact that this sometimes happens doesn't alter the principle that, when they do so, they do it with shame and not with pride. The method of science is so designed that it usually finds them out in the end.

Science is actually one of the most moral, one of the most honest disciplines   46
around—because science would completely collapse if it weren't for a scrupulous adherence to honesty in the reporting of evidence. (As [famous magician] James Randi has pointed out, this is one reason why scientists are so often fooled by paranormal tricksters and why the debunking role is better played by professional conjurors; scientists just don't anticipate deliberate dishonesty as well.) There are other professions (no need to mention lawyers specifically) in which falsifying evidence or at least twisting it is precisely what people are paid for and get brownie points for doing.

Science, then, is free of the main vice of religion, which is faith. But, as I   47
pointed out, science does have some of religion's virtues. Religion may aspire to provide its followers with various benefits-among them explanation, consolation, and uplift. Science, too, has something to offer in these areas.

Humans have a great hunger for explanation. It may be one of the main   48
reasons why humanity so universally has religion, since religions do aspire to provide explanations. We come to our individual consciousness in a mysterious universe and long to understand it. Most religions offer a cosmology and a biology, a theory of life, a theory of origins, and reasons for existence. In doing so, they demonstrate that religion is, in a sense, science; it's just bad science. Don't fall for the argument that religion and science operate on separate dimensions and are concerned with quite separate sorts of questions. Religions have historically always attempted to answer the questions that properly belong to science. Thus religions should not be allowed now to retreat from the ground upon which they

have traditionally attempted to fight. They do offer both a cosmology and a biology; however, in both cases it is false.

Consolation is harder for science to provide. Unlike Religion, science can-   49
not offer the bereaved a glorious reunion with their loved ones in the hereafter.
Those wronged on this earth cannot, on a scientific view, anticipate a sweet
comeuppance for their tormentors in a life to come. It could be argued that, if the
idea of an afterlife is an illusion (as I believe it is), the consolation it offers is hollow. But that's not necessarily so; a false belief can be just as comforting as a true
one, provided the believer never discovers its falsity. But if consolation comes
that cheap, science can weigh in with other cheap palliatives, such as pain-killing
drugs, whose comfort may or may not be illusory, but they do work.

Uplift, however, is where science really comes into its own. All the great   50
religions have a place for awe, for ecstatic transport at the wonder and beauty of
creation. And it's exactly this feeling of spine-shivering, breath-catching awe -
almost worship this flooding of the chest with ecstatic wonder, that modern science can provide. And it does so beyond the wildest dreams of saints and mys-
tics. The fact that the supernatural has no place in our explanations, in our
understanding of so much about the universe and life, doesn't diminish the awe.
Quite the contrary. The merest glance through a microscope at the brain of an
ant or through a telescope at a long-ago galaxy of a billion worlds is enough to
render poky and parochial the very psalms of praise.

Now, as I say, when it is put to me that science or some particular part of science,   51
like evolutionary theory, is just a religion like any other, I usually deny it with
indignation. But I've begun to wonder whether perhaps that's the wrong tactic.
Perhaps the right tactic is to accept the charge gratefully and demand equal time
for science in religious education classes. And the more I think about it, the more
I realize that an excellent case could be made for this. So I want to talk a little bit
about religious education and the place that science might play in it.

I do feel very strongly about the way children are brought up. I'm not entire-   52
ly familiar with the way things are in the United States, and what I say may have
more relevance to the United Kingdom, where there is state-obliged, legally
enforced religious instruction for all children. That's unconstitutional in the
United States, but I presume that children are nevertheless given religious
instruction in whatever particular religion their parents deem suitable.

Which brings me to my point about mental child abuse. In a 1995 issue of   53
the *Independent*, one of London's leading newspapers, there was a photograph of
a rather sweet and touching scene. It was Christmas time, and the picture showed

three children dressed up as the three wise men for a nativity play. The accompanying story described one child as a Muslim, one as a Hindu, and one as a Christian. The supposedly sweet and touching point of the story was that they were all taking part in this nativity play.

What is not sweet and touching is that these children were all four years 54 old. How can you possibly describe a child of four as a Muslim or a Christian or a Hindu Or a Jew? Would you talk about a four-year-old economic monetarist? Would you talk about a four-year-old neo-isolationist or a four-year-old liberal Republican? There are opinions about the cosmos and the world that children, once grown, will presumably be in a position to evaluate for themselves. Religion is the one field in our culture about which it is absolutely accepted, without question—without even noticing how bizarre it is—that parents have a total and absolute say in what their children are going to be, how their children are going to be raised, what opinions their children are going to have about the cosmos, about life, about existence. Do you see what I mean about mental child abuse?

Looking now at the various things that religious education might be ex- 55 pected to accomplish, one of its aims could be to encourage children to reflect upon the deep questions of existence, to invite them to rise above the humdrum preoccupations of ordinary life and think *sub specie alternitatis*.

Science can offer a vision of life and the universe which, as I've already 56 remarked, for humbling poetic inspiration far outclasses any of the mutually contradictory faiths and disappointingly recent traditions of the world's religions.

For example, how could any child in a religious education class fail to be 57 inspired if we could get across to them some inkling of the age of the universe? Suppose that, at the moment of Christ's death, the news of it had started traveling at the maximum possible speed around the universe outwards from the earth? How far would the terrible tidings have traveled by now? Following the theory of special relativity, the answer is that the news could not, under any circumstances whatever, have reached more than one-fiftieth of the way across one galaxy-not one-thousandth of the way to our nearest neighboring galaxy in the 100-million-galaxy-strong universe. The universe at large couldn't possibly by anything other than indifferent to Christ, his birth, his passion, and his death. Even such momentous news as the origin of life on Earth could have traveled only across our little local cluster of galaxies. Yet so ancient was that event on our earthy time-scale that, if you span its age with your open arms, the whole of human history, the whole of human culture, would fall in the dust from your fingertip at a single stroke of a nail file.

The argument from design, an important part of the history of religion,   58
wouldn't be ignored in my religious education classes, needless to say. The children would look at the spell-binding wonders of the living kingdoms and would consider Darwinism alongside the creationist alternatives and make up their own minds. I think the children would have no difficulty in making up their minds the right way if presented with the evidence. What worries me is not the question of equal time but that, as far as I can see, children in the United Kingdom and the United States are essentially given no time with evolution yet are taught creationism (whether at school, in church, or at home).

It would also be interesting to teach more than one theory of creation. The   59
dominant one in this culture happens to be the Jewish creation myth, which is taken over from the Babylonian creation myth. There are, of course, lots and lots of others, and perhaps they should all be given equal time (except that wouldn't leave much time for studying anything else). I understand that there are Hindus who believe that the world was created in a cosmic butter churn and Nigerian peoples who believe that the world was created by God from the excrement of ants. Surely these stories have as much right to equal time as the Judeo-Christian myth of Adam and Eve....

When the religious education class turns to ethics, I don't think science   60
actually has a lot to say, and I would replace it with rational moral philosophy. Do the children think there are absolute standards of right and wrong? And if so, where do they come from? Can you make up good working principles of right and wrong, like "do as you would be done by" and "the greatest good for the greatest number" (whatever that is supposed to mean)? It's a rewarding question, whatever your personal morality, to ask as an evolutionist where morals come from; by what route has the human brain gained its tendency to have ethics and morals, a feeling of right and wrong?

Should we value human life above all other life? Is there a rigid wall to be   61
built around the species *Homo sapiens*, or should we talk about whether there are other species which are entitled to our humanistic sympathies? Should we, for example, follow the right-to-life lobby, which is wholly preoccupied with *human life*, and value the life of a human fetus with the faculties of a worm over the life of a thinking and feeling chimpanzee? What is the basis of this fence we erect around *Homo sapiens*—even around a small piece of fetal tissue? (Not a very sound evolutionary idea when you think about it.) When, in our evolutionary descent from our common ancestor with chimpanzees, did the fence suddenly rear itself up?

... [S]cience could give a good account of itself in religious education. But it 62
wouldn't be enough. I believe that some familiarity with the King James version
of the Bible is important for anyone wanting to understand the allusions that
appear in English literature. Together with Book of Common Prayer, the Bible
gets 58 pages in the *Oxford Dictionary of Quotations*. Only Shakespeare has more.
I do think that not having any kind of biblical education is unfortunate if children want to read English literature and understand the provenance of phrases
like "through a glass darkly," "all flesh is as grass," "the race is not to the swift,"
"crying in the wilderness," "reaping the whirlwind," "amid the alien corn," "Eye-
less in Gaza," "Job's comforters," and "the widow's mite."

I want to return now to the charge that science is just a faith. The more 63
extreme version of this charge—and one that I often encounter as both a scientist
and a rationalist—is an accusation of zealotry and bigotry in scientists themselves
as great as that found in religious people. Sometimes there may be a little bit of
justice in this accusation; but as zealous bigots, we scientists are mere amateurs
at the game. We're content to *argue* with those who disagree with us. We don't
kill them.

But I would want to deny even the lesser charge of purely verbal zealotry. 64
There is a very, very important difference between feeling strongly, even passionately, about something because we have thought about and examined the
evidence for it on the one hand, and feeling strongly about something because it
has been internally revealed to us, or internally revealed to somebody else in history and subsequently hallowed by tradition. There's all the difference in the
world between a belief that one is prepared to defend by quoting evidence and
logic and a belief that is supported by nothing more than tradition, authority, or
revelation.

Postscript
Is Science a Faith?

The conflict between science and religion is deep and broad. The root reason 65
may be simply that science says, "Check it out—don't take anyone's word for the
truth," while religion says, "Take the word of your preacher or your scripture.
Believe—but don't even *think* about checking." Scientific skepticism is always a
threat to established authority. It challenges old truths. It revises and replaces
beliefs, traditions, and power structures.

Does this mean that science is a threat to society? Those who share the 66
beliefs under attack often think so. They may believe that the Bible or the Koran is a much better guide to the nature of the world than science is. They may

believe in crystal power and magic spells. They may tie knots in their electric cords to trim the size of their electric bills. They may even be postmodernist university professors who say that science is just a "useful myth," no different from any other fiction. Or they may, like Callahan, wish that there were some segment of society with sufficient stature to sit in judgment over science, to criticize it, and perhaps to rein it in, certainly to keep it from arrogantly quashing other views, such as those of religion. And although most Americans welcome the benefits of science and technology, they are often very leery of the unrestricted inquiry that characterizes science and challenges tradition. See, for example, Janet Raloff, "When Science and Beliefs Collide," *Science News* (June 8, 1996); Gerald Holton, *Einstein, History, and Other Passions: The Rebellion Against Science at the End of the Twentieth Century* (Addison-Wesley, 1996); and "Science Versus Antiscience?" *Scientific American* (January 1997). Even some scientists feel threatened by the conflict between their professional and private beliefs. Some have therefore spent a great deal of effort searching for ways to reconcile science and religion. For instance, Leon Lederman and Dick Teresi write about the quest for the most fundamental fragment of the atom in *The God Particle* (Dell, 1994). Stephen Hawking, in *A Brief History of Time* (Bantam Books, 1988), expresses the thought that science might lead humanity to "know the mind of God."

Can these scientists be speaking in more than metaphorical terms? Perhaps   67 not, for science deals in observable reality, which can provide at best only hints of a designer, creator, or God. Science cannot *provide* direct access to God, at least as people currently understand the nature of God. Still, it is not only creationists who see signs of design. Some scientists find the impression of design quite overwhelming, and many feel that science and religion actually have a great deal in common. Harvard University astronomer and evangelical Christian Owen Gingerich says that both are driven by human beings' "basic wonder and desire to know where we stand in the universe." It is therefore not terribly surprising to find the two realms of human thought intersecting very frequently or to find many people in both realms concerned with reconciling differences. See Gregg Easterbrook, "Science and God: A Warming Trend?" *Science* (August 15, 1997).

On the other hand, some scientists find attempts to reconcile science and   68 religion strange at best. Eugenie Scott, of the National Center for Science Education, insists that "science is just a method" and that people who see God in the complexity of biology or astronomy are "going beyond their data" and misusing science "to validate their positions." Paul Gross, former director of the Woods Hole Marine Biological Laboratory and coauthor of *Higher Superstition: The Aca-*

demic Left and Its Quarrels With Science (Johns Hopkins University Press, 1994), even fords those who see God in science frightening. More recently, Gross, Norman Levitt, and Martin W. Lewis coedited *The Flight from Science and Reason* (New York Academy of Sciences, 1997) to consider the opposition to the scientific, rational approach to the world that now finds wide expression in many nonscientific academic areas.

Are such views no more than an illustration of Callahan's claim that science—or "scientism"—has become an ideology and a faith as intolerant of others as any religion? Certainly some feel that science can provide many of the same rewards as religion. See Chet Raymo's *Skeptics and True Believers* (Walker & Company, 1998), in which he seeks a kind of spirituality without belief, finding all the awe, wonder, and mystery anyone could wish in the universe revealed by science.

Does the Theory of Evolution Explain the Origins of Humanity?

YES: Daniel C. Dennett, from *Darwin's Dangerous Idea: Evolution and the Meanings of Life* (Simon & Schuster, 1995)

NO: Edward B. Davis, from "Debating Darwin: The 'Intelligent Design' Movement," *The Christian Century* (July 15, 1998)

Issue Summary

YES: Philosopher Daniel C. Dennett argues that Charles Darwin had in his theory of evolution by means of natural selection the single best idea of all time. Far from being replaceable, he asserts, the theory has made its religious predecessors quite obsolete.

NO: Professor of the history of science Edward B. Davis reviews three books about evolution to support his assertion that the theory of evolution by means of natural selection does not adequately explain our existence. Davis maintains that religious views of evolution should be discussed in public schools.

Before science came along, the usual answer to questions such as "Why do ele-   1
phants have trunks?" or "Why is the sky blue?" was "Because God made it that
way." No one could add any more. Today children still hear such answers in Sunday School, but the rest of us generally believe that more complete and satisfying
answers have come from scientists who were not satisfied with "God's will" as an
answer. It has long been a dogma of scientific faith that "why" questions are
unreasonable to ask. They are teleological; that is, they presume that there is an
intent or design behind the phenomena we wish to explain. As an answer. "God's
will" is out of bounds largely because accepting it means accepting that it is a
waste of time to look for other answers. Outside science, on the other end, "God's
will" is very much in bounds. This leads to a continuing struggle between the
forces of faith and the forces of reason. Conservative Christians the southern
United States, Texas, and California have mounted vigorous campaigns to

require public school biology classes to give equal time to both biblical creation-ism and Darwinian evolution. For many years, this meant that evolution was hardly mentioned in high school biology textbooks.

For a time, it looked like evolution had scored a decisive victory. In 1982   2 federal judge William K. Overton struck down an Arkansas law that would have required the teaching of straight biblical creationism, with its explicit talk of God the Creator, as an unconstitutional intrusion of religion into a government activ-ity: education. But the creationists have not given up. They have returned to the fray with something they call "scientific creationism," and they have shifted their campaigns from state legislatures and school boards to local school boards, where it is harder for lawyers and biologists to mount effective counterattacks. See Gary Stix, "Postdiluvian Science," in "Science Versus Antiscience?" *Scientific American* (January 1997). "Scientific creationism" tries to show that the evolutionary approach is incapable of providing satisfactory explanations. For one thing, it says that natural selection relies on random chance to produce structures whose deli-cate intricacy really could only be the product of deliberate design. Therefore, there must have been a designer. There is no mention of God—but, of course, that is the only possible meaning of "designer" (unless one believes in ancient extraterrestrial visitors). Scientific creationists reinforce their claim that evolu-tion is inadequate by seeking weaknesses in the evidence—fossils, anatomy, embryology, DNA, and more—that more conventional biologists cite in their own discussions of evolution and natural selection. They hope to thereby weak-en the credibility of evolutionists. At the same time, scientific creationists can present the quest for weaknesses in the evolutionists' argument as perfectly appro-priate scientific skepticism—after all, they are scientific creationists.

William Johnson, associate dean of academic affairs at Ambassador Uni-   3 versity in Big Sandy, Texas, offered another argument for replacing the theory of evolution in a 1994 speech reprinted in "Evolution: The Past, Present, and Future Implications," *Vital Speeches of the Day* (February 15, 1995). He argued that the triumph of Darwin's theory "meant the end of the traditional belief in the world as a purposeful created order... and the consequent elimination of God from nature has played a decisive role in the secularization of Western society. Darwin-ian theory broke man's link with God and set him adrift in a cosmos without pur-pose or end." Johnson suggested that evolution-and perhaps the entire scientific approach to nature-should be abandoned in favor of a return to religion because of the untold damage it has done to the human values that underpin society. Matt Cartmill, in "Oppressed by Evolution," *Discover* (March 1998), is less extreme as

he argues that scientists need to exercise more humility and refrain from assertions about the presence or absence of "divine plans or purposes."

In the following selections, Daniel C. Dennett argues that Charles Darwin's   4
theory of evolution by means of natural selection is more accurate than the reli-
gion-based alternatives. Dennett asserts that in Darwin's idea lies our hope of
finding the truest meaning of life. Edward B. Davis discusses three books espous-
ing the "intelligent design" (ID) view. He is critical because he feels that ID proponents fail to recognize that "the philosophical landscape has changed" since
Darwin's day. However, he also states that religious views should not be completely rejected.

Yes
Darwin's Dangerous Idea: Evolution and the Meanings of Life

Daniel C. Dennett

We used to sing a lot when I was a child, around the campfire at summer camp,   5
at school and Sunday school, or gathered around the piano at home. One of my
favorite songs was "Tell Me Why."...

>   Tell me why the stars do shine,   6
>   Tell me why the ivy twines,
>   Tell me why the sky's so blue.
>   Then I will tell you just why I love you.
>   Because God made the stars to shine,
>   Because God made the ivy twine,
>   Because God made the sky so blue.
>   Because God made you, that's why I love you.

This straightforward, sentimental declaration still brings a lump to my   7
throat—so sweet, so innocent, so reassuring a vision of life!

And then along comes Darwin and spoils the picnic. Or does he? ... From   8
the moment of the publication of *Origin of Species* in 1859, Charles Darwin's fundamental idea has inspired intense reactions ranging from ferocious condemnation to ecstatic allegiance, sometimes tantamount to religious zeal. Dar-

win's theory has been abused and misrepresented by friend and foe alike. It has been misappropriated to lend scientific respectability to appalling political and social doctrines. It has been pilloried in caricature by opponents, some of whom would have it compete in our children's schools with "creation science," a pathetic hodgepodge of pious pseudo-science.[1]

Almost no one is indifferent to Darwin, and no one should be. The Darwinian theory is a scientific theory, and a great one, but that is not all it is. The creationists who oppose it so bitterly are right about one thing: Darwin's dangerous idea cuts much deeper into the fabric of our most fundamental beliefs than many of its sophisticated apologists have yet admitted, even to themselves.   9

The sweet, simple vision of the song, taken literally, is one that most of us have outgrown, however fondly we may recall it. The kindly God who lovingly fashioned each and every one of us (all creatures great and small) and sprinkled the sky with shining stars for our delight—*that* God is, like Santa Claus, a myth of childhood, not anything a sane, undeluded adult could literally believe in. *That* God must either be turned into a symbol for something less concrete or abandoned altogether.   10

Not all scientists and philosophers are atheists, and many who are believers declare that their idea of God can live in peaceful coexistence with, or even find support from, the Darwinian framework of ideas. Theirs is not an anthropomorphic Handicrafter God, but still a God worthy of worship in their eyes, capable of giving consolation and meaning to their lives. Others ground their highest concerns in entirely secular philosophies, views of the meaning of life that stave off despair without the aid of any concept of a Supreme Being-other than the Universe itself. Something is sacred to these thinkers, but they do not call it God; they call it, perhaps, Life, or Love, or Goodness, or Intelligence, or Beauty, or Humanity. What both groups share, in spite of the differences in their deepest creeds, is a conviction that life does have meaning, that goodness   11

But can *any* version of this attitude of wonder and purpose be sustained in the face of Darwinism? From the outset, there have been those who thought they saw Darwin letting the worst possible cat out of the bag: nihilism, They thought that if Darwin was right, the implication would be that nothing could be sacred. To put it bluntly, nothing could have any point. Is this just an overreaction? What exactly are the implications of Darwin's idea—and, in any case, has it been scientifically proven or is it still "just a theory"?   12

Perhaps, you may think, we could make a useful division: there are the parts of Darwin's idea that really are established beyond any reasonable doubt, and   13 then there are the speculative extensions of the scientifically irresistible parts. Then if we were lucky perhaps the rock-solid scientific facts would have no stunning implications about religion, or human nature, or the meaning of life, while the parts of Darwin's idea that get people all upset could be put into quarantine as highly controversial extensions of, or mere interpretations of, the scientifically irresistible parts. That would be reassuring.

But alas, that is just about backwards. There are vigorous controversies   14
swirling around in evolutionary theory, but those who feel threatened by Darwinism should not take heart from this fact. Most—if not quite all—of the controversies concern issues that are "just science"; no matter which side wins, the outcome will not undo the basic Darwinian idea. That idea, which is about as secure as any in science, really does have far-reaching implications for our vision of what the meaning of life is or could be.

In 1543, Copernicus proposed that the Earth was not the center of the uni-   15
verse but in fact revolved around the Sun. It took over a century for the idea to sink in, a gradual and actually rather painless transformation. (The religious reformer Philipp Melanchthon, a collaborator of Martin Luther, opined that "some Christian prince" should suppress this madman, but aside from a few such salvos, the world was not particularly shaken by Copernicus himself.) The Copernican Revolution did eventually have its own "shot heard round the world": Galileo's *Dialogue Concerning the Two Chief World Systems*, but it was not published until 1632, when the issue was no longer controversial among scientists. Galileo's projectile provoked an infamous response by the Roman Catholic Church, setting up a shock wave whose reverberations are only now dying out. But in spite of the drama of that epic confrontation, the idea that our planet is not the center of creation has sat rather lightly in people's minds. Every school-child today accepts this as the matter of fact it is, without tears or terror.

In due course, the Darwinian Revolution will come to occupy a similarly   16
secure and untroubled place in the minds—and hearts—of every educated person on the globe, but today, more than a century after Darwin's death, we still have not come to terms with its mind-boggling implications. Unlike the Copernican Revolution, which did not engage widespread public attention until the scientific details had been largely sorted out, the Darwinian Revolution has had anxious lay spectators and cheerleaders taking sides from the outset, tugging at the sleeves of the participants and encouraging grandstanding. The scientists themselves have been moved by the same hopes and fears, so it is not surprising that the relatively narrow conflicts among theorists have often been not just

blown up out of proportion by their adherents, but seriously distorted in the process. Everybody has seen, dimly, that a lot is at stake.

Moreover, although Darwin's own articulation of his theory was monu- 17 mental, and its powers were immediately recognized by many of the scientists and other thinkers of his day, there really were large gaps in his theory that have only recently begun to be properly filled in. The biggest gap looks almost comical in retrospect. In all his brilliant musings, Darwin never hit upon the central concept, without which the theory of evolution is hopeless: the concept of a *gene*. Darwin had no proper *unit* of heredity, and so his account of the process of natural selection was plagued with entirely reasonable doubts about whether it would work. Darwin supposed that offspring would always exhibit a sort of blend or average of their parents' features. Wouldn't such "blending inheritance" always simply average out all differences, turning everything into uniform gray? How could diversity survive such relentless averaging? Darwin recognized the seriousness of this challenge, and neither he nor his many ardent supporters succeeded in responding with a description of a convincing and well-documented mechanism of heredity that could combine traits of parents while maintaining an underlying and unchanged identity. The idea they needed was right at hand, uncovered ("formulated" would be too strong) by the monk Gregor Mendel and published in a relatively obscure Austrian journal in 1865, but, in the best-savored irony in the history of science, it lay there unnoticed until its importance was appreciated (at first dimly) around 1900. Its triumphant establishment at the heart of the "Modern Synthesis" (in effect, the synthesis of Mendel and Darwin) was eventually made secure in the 1940s, thanks to the work of Theodosius Dobzhansky, Julian Huxley, Ernst Mayr, and others. It has taken another half-century to iron out most of the wrinkles of that new fabric.

The fundamental core of contemporary Darwinism, the theory of DNA- 18 based reproduction and evolution, is now beyond dispute among scientists. It demonstrates its power every day, contributing crucially to the explanation of planet-sized facts of geology and meteorology, through middle-sized facts of ecology and agronomy, down to the latest microscopic facts of genetic engineering. It unifies all of biology and the history of our planet into a single grand story. Like Gulliver tied down in Lilliput, it is unbudgeable, not because of some one or two huge chains of argument that might—hope against hope—have weak links in them, but because it is securely tied by hundreds of thousands of threads of evidence anchoring it to virtually every other area of human knowledge. New discoveries may conceivably lead to dramatic, even "revolutionary" *shifts* in the Darwinian theory, but the hope that it will be "refuted" by some shattering break-through is about as reasonable as the hope that we will return to a geocentric vision and discard Copernicus.

Still, the theory is embroiled in remarkably hot-tempered controversy, and   19
one of the reasons for this incandescence is that these debates about scientific matters are usually distorted by fears that the "wrong" answer would have in-tolerable moral implications. So great are these fears that they are carefully left unarticulated, displaced from attention by several layers of distracting rebuttal and counter-rebuttal. The disputants are forever changing the subject slightly, conveniently keeping the bogeys in the shadows. It is this misdirection that is mainly responsible for postponing the day when we can all live as comfortably with our new biological perspective as we do with the astronomical perspective Copernicus gave us.

Whenever Darwinism is the topic, the temperature rises, because more is at   20
stake than just the empirical facts about how life on Earth evolved, or the correct logic of the theory that accounts for those facts. One of the precious things that is at stake is a vision of what it means to ask, and answer, the question "Why?" Darwin's new perspective turns several traditional assumptions upside down, undermining our standard ideas about what ought to count as satisfying answers to this ancient and inescapable question. Here science and philosophy get completely intertwined. Scientists sometimes deceive themselves into thinking that philosophical ideas are only, at best, decorations or parasitic commentaries on the hard, objective triumphs of science, and that they themselves are immune to the confusions that philosophers devote their lives to dissolving. But there is no such thing as philosophy-free science; there is only science whose philosophical baggage is taken on board without examination.

The Darwinian Revolution is both a scientific and a philosophical revolu-   21
tion, and neither revolution could have occurred without the other. As we shall see, it was the philosophical prejudices of the scientists, more than their lack of scientific evidence, that prevented them from seeing how the theory could actually work, but those philosophical prejudices that had to be overthrown were too deeply entrenched to be dislodged by mere philosophical brilliance. It took an irresistible parade of hard-won scientific facts to force thinkers to take seriously the weird new outlook that Darwin proposed. Those who are still ill-acquainted with that beautiful procession can be forgiven their continued allegiance to the pre-Darwinian ideas. And the battle is not yet over; even among the scientists, there are pockets of resistance.

Let me lay my cards on the table. If I were to give an award for the single   22
best idea anyone has ever had, I'd give it to Darwin, ahead of Newton and Einstein and everyone else. In a single stroke, the idea of evolution by natural selection unifies the realm of life, meaning, and purpose with the realm of space and
time, cause and effect, mechanism and physical law. But it is not just a wonderful scientific idea. It is a dangerous idea. My admiration for Darwin's magnificent
idea is unbounded, but I, too, cherish many of the ideas and ideals that it *seems*
to challenge, and want to protect them. For instance, I want to protect the campfire song, and what is beautiful and true in it, for my little grandson and his
friends, and for their children when they grow up. There are many more magnificent ideas that are also jeopardized, it seems, by Darwin's idea, and they, too, may
need protection. The only good way to do this-the only way that has a chance in
the long run—is to cut through the smokescreens and look at the idea as
unflinchingly, as dispassionately, as possible.

On this occasion, we are not going to settle for "There, there, it will all   23
come out all right." Our examination will take a certain amount of nerve. Feelings may get hurt. Writers on evolution usually steer clear of this apparent clash
between science and religion. Fools rush in, Alexander Pope said, where angels
fear to tread. Do you want to follow me? Don't you really want to know what
survives this confrontation? What if it turns out that the sweet vision—or a better one—survives intact, strengthened and deepened by the encounter? Would-
n't it be a shame to forgo the opportunity for a strengthened, renewed creed, settling instead for a fragile, sickbed faith that you mistakenly supposed must not
be disturbed?

There is no future in a sacred myth. Why not? Because of our curiosity.   24
Because, as the song reminds us, *we want to know why*. We may have outgrown
the song's answer, but we will never outgrow the question. Whatever we hold precious, we cannot protect it from our curiosity, because being who we are, one of
the things we deem precious is the truth. Our love of truth is surely a central element in the meaning we find in our lives. In any case, the idea that we might preserve meaning by kidding ourselves is a more pessimistic, more nihilistic idea
than I for one can stomach. If that were the best that could be done, I would conclude that nothing mattered after all....

At what "point" does a human life begin or end? The Darwinian perspective lets   25
us see with unmistakable clarity why there is no hope at all of *discovering* a tell-
tale mark, a saltation in life's processes, that "counts." We need to draw lines; we

need definitions of life and death for many important moral purposes. The layers of pearly dogma that build up in defense around these fundamentally arbitrary attempts are familiar, and in never-ending need of repair. We should abandon the fantasy that either science or religion can uncover some well-hidden fact that tells us exactly where to draw these lines. There is no "natural" way to mark the birth of a human "soul," any more than there is a "natural" way to mark the birth of a species. And, contrary to what many traditions insist, I think we all do share the intuition that there are gradations of value in the ending of human lives. Most human embryos end in spontaneous abortion—fortunately, since these are mostly *terata*, hopeless monsters whose lives are all but impossible. Is this a terrible evil? Are the mothers whose bodies abort these embryos guilty of involuntary manslaughter? Of course not. Which is worse, taking "heroic" measures to keep alive a severely deformed infant, or taking the equally "heroic" (if unsung) step of seeing to it that such an infant dies as quickly and painlessly as possible? I do not suggest that Darwinian thinking gives us answers to such questions; I do suggest that Darwinian thinking helps us see why the traditional hope of solving these problems (finding a moral algorithm) is forlorn. We must cast off the myths that make these old-fashioned solutions seem inevitable. We need to grow up, in other words.

Among the precious artifacts worth preserving are whole cultures them-   26
selves. There are still several thousand distinct languages spoken daily on our planet, but the number is dropping fast (Diamond 1992, Hale et al. 1992). When a language goes extinct, this is the same kind of loss as the extinction of a species, and when the culture that was carried by that language dies, this is an even greater loss. But here, once again, we face incommensurabilities and no easy answers.

I began... with a song which I myself cherish, and hope will survive "forever." I hope my grandson teams it and passes it on to his grandson, but at the   27
same time I do not myself believe, and do not really want my grandson to believe, the doctrines that are so movingly expressed in that song. They are too simple. They are, in a word, wrong—just as wrong as the ancient Greeks' doctrines about the gods and goddesses on Mount Olympus. Do you believe, literally, in an anthropomorphic God? If not, then you must agree with me that the song is a beautiful, comforting falsehood. Is that simple song nevertheless a valuable meme? I certainly think it is. It is a modest but beautiful part of our heritage, a treasure to be preserved. But we must face the fact that, just as there were times when tigers would not have been viable, times are coming when they will no longer be viable, except in zoos and other preserves, and the same is true of many of the treasures in our cultural heritage.

The Welsh language is kept alive by artificial means, just the way condors are.   28
We cannot preserve *all* the features of the cultural world in which these treasures
flourished. We wouldn't want to. It took oppressive political and social systems, rife .
with many evils, to create the rich soil in which many of our greatest works of art
could grow: slavery and despotism ("enlightened" though these sometimes may
have been), obscene differences in living standards between the rich and the poor
and a huge amount of ignorance. Ignorance is a necessary condition for many
excellent things. The childish joy of seeing what Santa Claus has brought for
Christmas is a species of joy that must soon be extinguished in each child by the
loss of ignorance. When that child grows up, she can transmit that joy to her own
children, but she must also recognize a time when it has outlived its value.

The view I am expressing has clear ancestors. The philosopher George   29
Santayana was a Catholic atheist, if you can imagine such a thing. According to
Bertrand Russell (1945, p. 811), William James once denounced Santayana's
ideas as "the perfection of rottenness," and one can see why some people would
be offended by his brand of aestheticism: a deep appreciation for all the formulae,
ceremonies, and trappings of his religious heritage, but lacking the faith. Santayana's position was aptly caricatured: "There is no God and Mary is His Mother." But how many of us are caught in that very dilemma, loving the heritage,
firmly convinced of its value, yet unable to sustain any conviction at all in its
truth? We are faced with a difficult choice. Because we value it, we are eager to
preserve it in a rather precarious and "denatured" state–in churches and cathedrals and synagogues, built to house huge congregations of the devout, and now
on the way to being cultural museums. There is really not that much difference
between the roles of the Beefeaters who stand picturesque guard at the Tower of
London, and the Cardinals who march in their magnificent costumes and meet
to elect the next Pope. Both are keeping alive traditions, rituals, liturgies, symbols, that otherwise would fade.

But hasn't there been a tremendous rebirth of fundamentalist faith in all   30
these creeds? Yes, unfortunately, there has been, and I think that there are no
forces on this planet more dangerous to us all than the fanaticisms of fundamentalism, of all the species: Protestantism, Catholicism, Judaism, Islam, Hinduism, and Buddhism, as well as countless smaller infections. Is there a conflict
between science and religion here? There most certainly is.

Darwin's dangerous idea helps to create a condition in the memosphere   31
that in the long run threatens to be just as toxic to these memes as civilization
in general has been toxic to the large wild mammals. Save the Elephants! Yes,
of course, but not *by all means*. Not by forcing the people of Africa to live

nineteenth-century lives, for instance. This is not an idle comparison. The creation of the great wildlife preserves in Africa has often been accompanied by the dislocation—and ultimate destruction—of human populations. (For a chilling vision of this side effect, see Colin Turnbull 1972 on the fate of the Ik.) Those who think that we should preserve the elephants' pristine environment *at all costs* should contemplate the costs of returning the United States to the pristine conditions in which the buffaloes roam and the deer and the antelope play. We must find an accommodation.

I love the King James Version of the Bible. My own spirit recoils from a God   32
Who is He or She in the same way my heart sinks when I see a lion pacing neurotically back and forth in a small zoo cage. I know, I know, the lion is beautiful but dangerous; if you let the lion roam free, it would kill me; safety demands that it be put in a cage. Safety demands that religions be put in cages, too—when absolutely necessary. We just can't have forced female circumcision, and the second-class status of women in Roman Catholicism and Mormonism, to say nothing of their status in Islam. The recent Supreme Court ruling declaring unconstitutional the Florida law prohibiting the sacrificing of animals in the rituals of the Santeria sect (an Afro-Caribbean religion incorporating elements of Yoruba traditions and Roman Catholicism) is a borderline case, at least for many of us. Such rituals are offensive to many, but the protective mantle of religious tradition secures our tolerance. We are wise to respect these traditions. It is, after all, just part of respect for the biosphere.

Save the Baptists! Yes, of course, but not *by all means*. Not if it means tol-   33
erating the deliberate misinforming of children about the natural world. According to a recent poll, 48 percent of the people in the United States today believe that the book of Genesis is literally true. And 70 percent believe that "creation science" should be taught in school alongside evolution. Some recent writers recommend a policy in which parents would be able to "opt out" of materials they didn't want their children taught. Should evolution be taught in the schools? Should arithmetic be taught? Should history? Misinforming a child is a terrible offense.

A faith, like a species, must evolve or go extinct when the environment   34
changes. It is not a gentle process in either case. We see in every Christian subspecies the battle of memes—should women be ordained? should we go back to the Latin liturgy?—and the same can also be observed in the varieties of Judaism and Islam. We must have a similar mixture of respect and self-protective caution about memes. This is already accepted practice, but we tend to avert our atten-

tion from its implications. We preach freedom of religion, but only so far. If your religion advocates slavery, or mutilation of women, or infanticide, or puts a price on Salman Rushdie's head because he has insulted it, then your religion has a feature that cannot be respected. It endangers us all.

It is nice to have grizzly bears and wolves living in the wild. They are no   35 longer a menace; we can peacefully coexist, with a little wisdom. The same policy can be discerned in our political tolerance, in religious freedom. You are free to preserve or create any religious creed you wish, so long as it does not become a public menace. We're all on the Earth together, and we have to learn some accommodation. The Hutterite memes are "clever" not to include any memes about the virtue of destroying outsiders. If they did, we would have to combat them. We tolerate the Hutterites because they harm only themselves—though we may well insist that we have the right to impose some further openness on their schooling of their own children. Other religious membes are not so benign. The message is clear: those who will not accommodate, who will not temper, who insist on keeping only the purest and wildest strain of their heritage alive, we will be obliged, reluctantly, to cage or disarm, and we will do our best to disable the memes they fight for. Slavery is beyond the pale. Child abuse is beyond the pale. Discrimination is beyond the pale. The pronouncing of death sentences on those who blaspheme against a religion (complete with bounties or rewards for those who carry them out) is beyond the pale. It is not civilized, and is owed no more respect in the name of religious freedom than any other incitement to cold-blooded murder.[2] . . .

Long before there was science, or even philosophy, there were religions.   36 They have served many purposes (it would be a mistake of greedy reductionism to look for a single purpose, a single *summum bonum* which they have all directly or indirectly served). They have inspired many people to lead lives that have added immeasurably to the wonders of our world, and they have inspired many more people to lead lives that were, given their circumstances, more meaningful, less painful, than they otherwise could have been. . . .

Religions have brought the comfort of belonging and companionship to   37 many who would otherwise have passed through this life all alone, without glory or adventure. At their best, religions have drawn attention to love, and made it real for people who could not otherwise see it, and ennobled the attitudes and refreshed the spirits of the world-beset. Another thing religions have accomplished, without this being thereby their *raison d'être*, is that they have kept *Homo sapiens* civilized enough, for long enough, for us to have learned how to reflect more systematically and accurately on our position in the universe. There is much more to learn. There is certainly a treasury of ill-appreciated truths embedded in the endangered cultures of the modern world, designs that have accumulated details over eons of idiosyncratic history, and we should take steps to record it, and study it, before it disappears, for, like dinosaur genomes, once it is gone, it will be virtually impossible to recover.

We should not expect this variety of respect to be satisfactory to those who   38
wholeheartedly embody the memes we honor with our attentive—but not worshipful—scholarship. On the contrary, many of them will view anything other than enthusiastic conversion to their own views as a threat, even an intolerable threat. We must not underestimate the suffering such confrontations cause. To watch, to have to participate in, the contraction or evaporation of beloved features of one's heritage is a pain only our species can experience, and surely few pains could be more terrible. But we have no reasonable alternative, and those whose visions dictate that they cannot peacefully coexist with the rest of us will have to quarantine as best we can, minimizing the pain and damage, trying always to leave open a path or two that may come to seem acceptable.

If you want to teach your children that they are the tools of God, you had   39
better not teach them that they are God's rifles, or we will have to stand firmly opposed to you: your doctrine has no glory, no special rights, no intrinsic and inalienable merit. If you insist on teaching your children falsehoods—that the Earth is flat, that "Man" is not a product of evolution by natural selection—then you must expect, at the very least, that those of us who have freedom of speech will feel free to describe your teachings as the spreading of falsehoods, and will attempt to demonstrate this to your children at our earliest opportunity. Our future well-being-the well-being of all of us on the planet-depends on the education of our descendants.

What, then, of all the glories of our religious traditions? They should cer-   40
tainly be preserved, as should the languages, the art, the costumes, the rituals, the monuments. Zoos are now more and more being seen as second-class havens for endangered species, but at least they are havens, and what they preserve is irreplaceable. The same is true of complex memes and their phenotypic expressions. Many a fine New England church, costly to maintain, is in danger of destruction. Shall we deconsecrate these churches and turn them into museums, or retrofit them for some other use? The latter fate is at least to be preferred to their destruction. Many congregations face a cruel choice: their house of worship costs so much to maintain in all its splendor that little of their tithing is left over for the poor. The Catholic Church has faced this problem for centuries, and has main-

tained a position that is, I think, defensible, but not obviously so: when it spends its treasure to put gold plating on the candlesticks, instead of providing more food and better shelter for the poor of the parish, it has a different vision of what makes life worth living. Our people, it says, benefit more from having a place of splendor in which to worship than from a little more food. Any atheist or agnostic who finds this cost-benefit analysis ludicrous might pause to consider whether to support diverting all charitable and governmental support for museums, symphony orchestras, libraries, and scientific laboratories to efforts to provide more food and better living conditions for the least well off. A human life worth living is not something that can be uncontroversially measured, and that is its glory.

And there's the rub. What will happen, one may well wonder, if religion is 41 preserved in cultural zoos, in libraries, in concerts and demonstrations? It is happening; the tourists flock to watch the Native American tribal dances, and for the onlookers it is folklore, a religious ceremony, certainly, to be treated with respect, but also an example of a meme complex on the verge of extinction, at least in its strong, ambulatory phase; it has become an invalid, barely kept alive by its custodians. Does Darwin's dangerous idea give us anything in exchange for the ideas it calls into question?

. . . [T]he physicist Paul Davies proclaim[ed] that the reflective power of hu- 42 man minds can be "no trivial detail, no minor by-product of mindless purposeless forces," and [i] suggested that being a by-product of mindless purposeless forces was no disqualification for importance. And I have argued that Darwin has shown us how, in fact, *everything* of importance is just such a product. Spinoza called his highest being God or Nature (*Deus sive Natura*), expressing a sort of pantheism. There have been many varieties of pantheism, but they usually lack a convincing *explanation* about just how God is distributed in the whole of nature. . . . Darwin offers us one: it is in the distribution of Design throughout nature, creating, in the Tree of Life, an utterly unique and irreplaceable creation, an actual pattern in the immeasurable reaches of Design Space that could never be exactly duplicated in its many details. What is design work? It is that wonderful wedding of chance and necessity, happening in a trillion places at once, at a trillion different levels. And what miracle caused it? None. It just happened to happen, in the fullness of time. You could even say, in a way, that the Tree of Life created itself. Not in a miraculous, instantaneous whoosh, but slowly, slowly, over billions of years.

Is this Tree of Life a God one could worship? Pray to? Fear? Probably not. 43 But it *did* make the ivy twine and the sky so blue, so perhaps the song I love tells a truth after all. The Tree of Life is neither perfect nor infinite in space or time, but it is actual, and if it is not Anselm's "Being greater than which nothing can be conceived," it is surely a being that is greater than anything any of us will ever conceive of in detail worthy of its detail. Is something sacred? Yes, say I with Nietzsche. I could not pray to it, but I can stand in affirmation of its magnificence. This world is sacred.

Notes

1. I will not devote any space [here to] cataloguing the deep flaws in creationism, or supporting my peremptory condemnation of it. I take that job to have been admirably done by others.

2. Many, many Muslims agree, and we must not only listen to them, but do what we can to protect and support them, for they are bravely trying, from the inside, to reshape the tradition they cherish into something better, something ethically defensible. That is-or, rather, ought to be-the message of multiculturalism, not the patronizing and subtly racist hypertolerance that "respects" vicious and ignorant doctrines when they are propounded by officials of non-European states and religions. One might start by spreading the word about For Rushdie (Braziller, 1994), a collection of essays by Arab and Muslim writers, many critical of Rushdie, but all denouncing the unspeakably immoral "fatwa" death sentence proclaimed by the Ayatollah. Rushdie (1994) has drawn our attention to the 162 Iranian intellectuals who, with great courage, have signed a declaration in support of freedom of expression. Let us all distribute the danger by joining hands with them.

No
Debating Darwin: The 'Intelligent Design' Movement

Edward B. Davis

"The time has come," the lawyer said,   44
"To talk of many things,
Of Gods, and gaps, and miracles,
Of lots of missing links,
And why we can't be Darwinists,
And whether matter thinks."
                                        —with apologies to Lewis Carroll

From Edward B. Davis, "Debating Darwin: The `Intelligent Design' Movement," The Christian Century (July 15-22, 1998). Copyright © 1998 by The Christian Century Foundation. Reprinted by permission of The Christian Century.

In 1874, 15 years after Charles Darwin published *On the Origin of Species,* 45
the great Princeton theologian Charles Hodge replied with his own book, *What
Is Darwinism?* Darwin had proposed that natural selection, a blind, purposeless
process operating through random variations, had produced the myriad forms of
life that inhabit our planet. Hodge contended that this denial of design in nature
"is virtually the denial of God." Hodge noted that although Darwin might personally believe in a creator who had in the distant past "called matter and a living germ into existence," Darwinism implied that God had "then abandoned the
universe to itself to be controlled by chance and necessity, without any purpose
on his part as to the result, or any intervention or guidance." Such a God was "virtually consigned, so far as we are concerned, to nonexistence." Thus Darwinism
was "virtually atheistical."

The authors of the three books reviewed here [*Darwin's Black Box: The Bio-* 46
chemical Challenge to Evolution, Michael J. Behe; *Defeating Darwinism by Opening
Minds,* Phillip E. Johnson and *The Creation Hypothesis: Scientific Evidence for an
Intelligent Designer,* Edited by J. P Moreland] understand Darwinism as Hodge did,
and like Hodge they believe that a God who is not involved in creation and with
human beings in obvious, highly visible, scientifically detectable ways is no God
at all. They seek to marshal evidence for the truth of Christian theism, based
partly on the perceived deficiencies of Darwinian evolution. Although certain
elements of their position may warrant further consideration, it is neither very
convincing nor particularly original.

In the century and a quarter since Hodge leveled his pen at the offending 47
theory, many Christians have come to terms with evolution. They have done this
in different ways, however. Some evolutionists who maintain belief in God, especially those who are theologically moderate or conservative such as Richard Buhe
and Howard Van Till, regard science and theology as separate (though ultimately
complementary) modes of knowledge. In this view, science deals with mechanism
and material reality ("how"), while theology deals with meaning and spiritual reality ("why"), which are in another domain or on another level. This approach is
best summed up in the famous phrase that Galileo borrowed from Cardinal Baro-
nio: "The Bible tells how to go to heaven, not how the heavens go."

Other thinkers, including liberal Protestants such as Ian Barbour and 48
Arthur Peacocke, employ more integrative models. They decry the intellectual
schizophrenia and theological insulation of the separation model, proclaiming
instead the need for a genuine conversation between theology and modern science that shapes both enterprises. But much of this conversation is dominated by
one side: many leading advocates of integration are process theologians or panen-

theists (believing that God includes the world as a part of God's being) who call for doctrinal reformulation in light of modern scientific knowledge but do not intend to ask scientists to reformulate their theories in light of theology.

Indeed, none of these Christian evolutionists proposes what might be called   49 a Christian *science*, one in which Christian beliefs influence the actual content of scientific theories so that the rules of science might be different for Christians than for non-Christians. Instead they represent various Christian *views of science* in which the rules of science are assumed to be the same for all scientists in a particular discipline, without regard to their religious beliefs, and with differences arising only at the level of personal worldview.

In other words, adherents of all of these views accept methodological nat-   50 uralism, which claims that scientific explanations of phenomena always ought to involve natural causes—which are usually understood as mechanistic causes operating without any intelligence or purpose *apparent within the phenomena themselves*. Whether or not any intelligence or purpose has been imposed upon natural processes from the outside is a separate question that science alone is not competent to answer, although scientific knowledge may have some influence on the kinds of answers one might offer. Science is seen as religiously neutral; evidence for or against theism has to be found elsewhere.

The books under review reject the notion that methodological naturalism   51 is religiously neutral. They also reject the idea that evolution is compatible with theism. All three books offer a highly sophisticated form of antievolutionism known as intelligent design theory (ID).

The essence of ID and the motivation behind it are clearly explained by   52 Phillip Johnson. Theistic evolution, he argues, is a "much-too-easy solution" that "rests on a misunderstanding of what contemporary scientists mean by the word evolution." Like Cornell biologist William Provine and Cambridge biologist Richard Dawkins, Johnson defines evolution as "an unguided and mindless process" that admits no possibility of being a divine work. It implies that "our existence is therefore a fluke rather than a planned outcome."

To prevent students from being indoctrinated with this type of irreligion,   53 Johnson offers them a primer on thinking critically about evolution and a brief account of ID. The latter is essentially the opposite of the strong biological reductionism associated with Dawkins, according to which (in Johnson's accurate description) "everything, including our minds, can be 'reduced' to its material base." For Johnson, matter is preceded both ontologically and chronologically by intelligence, in the form of the information necessary to organize it into living things, and this is "an entirely different kind of stuff from the physical medium [e.g., DNA] in which it may temporarily be recorded."

A principal goal of the ID movement is to convince scientists that in-   54 formation cannot and does not spring from matter, which they understand as brute and inert. This is essentially the same dualistic conception of matter that was shared by 17th-century founders of mechanistic science such as Rend Descartes, Robert Boyle and Isaac Newton. Although the mind-matter distinction remains philosophically problematic, and although some types of dualism may be possible to defend, most contemporary scientists (including most Christian scientists) no longer hold to this type of dualism, even if they retain the mechanistic science with which it was once linked. The same is true of many contemporary theologians, especially those committed to panentheism or process theology. They generally hold a more active view of matter and its capabilities, believing either that matter itself can think or that cognition arises out of it in some naturalistic manner yet to be determined. An important flaw in the program of the ID adherents is that they don't really confront the fact that the philosophical landscape has changed, and they fail to engage those Christian thinkers who recognize this.

Johnson bases his case substantially on Michael Behe's notion of "irreduc-   55 ible complexity"—the idea that because certain parts of living organisms are so complex, and are composed of many separate parts that cannot function properly on their own, we cannot account for them (in reductionistic fashion) as merely the products of blind selection. Rather, we are forced to invoke a deus ex machina who assembled the parts supernaturally according to a preconceived design. Johnson uses this strong form of the teleological argument to challenge both materialism and naturalism. He calls his strategy "the wedge" and sees himself opening up a crack in scientific materialism.

Behe attempts to widen that crack. A biochemist at Lehigh University, he   56 is not a creationist in the sense in which that word is most often used. For example, he believes that the earth is billions of years old, something self-styled scientific creationists deny, and he thinks that natural selection can account for much of life's diversity, which an old-earth creationist like Johnson probably does not accept (if so, he is awfully quiet about it). What natural selection cannot explain, in Behe's opinion, is how the original building blocks of living things were formed.

Darwin's Black Box, a detailed study of certain biochemical machines in   57 humans and other organisms, is aimed at realizing one of Darwin's worst nightmares. Darwin worried that the origin of complex organs such as the eye would be difficult to explain in terms of the gradual, stepwise evolutionary process outlined by his theory. The best he could do was to speculate that the complex eye might have developed from simple light-sensitive cells that could give a competitive advantage to an organism that possessed them. But the molecular biology of vision, as Behe notes, was a "black box" to Darwin. Darwin and his contemporaries took the simplicity of cells for granted, treating them as black boxes that needed no further explanation.

Now that we know how complex even the simplest cells are, Behe argues, we can   58
no longer ignore the question of how they originated, nor can we deny the lack of progress in answering that question within a Darwinian paradigm. Behe examined every issue of the *Journal of Molecular Evolution* (a top journal in the field) since it began in 1971. He could not find even one article that "has ever proposed a detailed model by which a complex biochemical system might have been produced in a gradual, step-by-step Darwinian fashion." This lack of an explanation, Behe says, is "a very strong indication that Darwinism is an inadequate framework for understanding the origin of complex biochemical systems."

Reviewers in scientific journals are generally highly critical of Behe. But   59
some of the critics, including biochemist James Shapiro of the University of Chicago, think that Behe has pinpointed a real problem in evolutionary theory, a problem that invites novel approaches-though not the invocation of an intelligent designer, which would mean giving up hope of a scientific (or naturalistic) solution.

Notre Dame philosopher of science Ernan McMullin argues perceptively   60
that Behe's proposed solution is itself just another "black box," for his appeal to ID slams the door on further inquiry at the level of secondary causes, denying in principle our ability to learn how irreducibly complex structures were assembled. Van Till takes this point further, arguing that we must distinguish between the claim that the world is a product of creative intelligence (a belief he shares with the ID camp) and the additional claim, implicit in the ID position, that certain products of that intelligence could not have been assembled naturalistically.

Behe realizes that it will be difficult for most scientists to give ID fair consideration, mainly for philosophical rather than purely scientific reasons. The scientific community, he notes, is committed to methodological naturalism, which rules out a priori any appeal to design. Furthermore, "many important and well-respected scientists just don't *want* there to be anything beyond nature." It's true that many scientists regard methodological naturalism as intimately linked to the   61 worldview of philosophical materialism. A challenge to one is a challenge to the other. But there is no necessary connection between the two positions. Many scientists (including most Christian scientists) accept methodological naturalism without extrapolating from it to philosophical materialism.

Since the ID proponents reject the middle-ground position of a theist who   62
practices methodological naturalism, their challenge will probably produce more heat than light. This likelihood is increased by the highly apologetic thrust Of certain essays in *The Creation Hypothesis*, edited by Biola University philosopher J. P. Moreland. Consider, for example, the title of the essay by Canadian astrophysicist Hugh Ross, head of Reasons to Believe, a Pasadena-based ministry specializing in apologetics: "Astronomical Evidences for a Personal, Transcendent God." Or consider Moreland's own essay, "Theistic Science and Methodological Naturalism," which presents the two as competing alternatives. The latter distinction is drawn even more starkly by Johnson, who refers elsewhere to methodological naturalism as "methodological atheism" and to those Christian scientists who defend it as "mushy accommodationists."

As Moreland defines it, theistic science claims that God "has through di-   63
rect, primary agent causation and indirect, secondary causation created and designed the world for a purpose and has directly intervened in the course of its development at various times," including "history prior to the arrival of human beings." Primary causes are "God's unusual way of operating; they involve his direct, discontinuous, miraculous actions," whereas "secondary causes are God's normal way of operating." Either way, Moreland stresses, "God is constantly active in the world, but his activity takes on different forms,"

In spite of this clear affirmation that God is never absent or inactive in the   64
creation (and similar statements by others), the ID program is widely viewed as being committed to a "God-of-the-gaps" theology. In such a theology (as Dietrich Bonhoeffer noted with objections) God is invoked only when natural explanations fail.

It is not accurate to say that Behe and Johnson's God is merely a God of the   65
gaps, if by that we mean a God who has nothing else to do but occasionally finetune the clock-like workings of the universe. Nevertheless, their argument does rely on a God-of-the-gaps strategy. That is, they argue from the existence of gaps in our knowledge of nature to the existence of gaps in the actual processes of nature, and on the basis of these gaps they infer that there is an agent outside of nature. What makes this a sophisticated God-of-the-gaps theory, and distinguishes their project from garden variety creationism, is that they justify their appeal to divine causation by pointing not simply to the absence of plausible

naturalistic explanations but to the presence of an irreducible complexity which suggests to them that no naturalistic explanation for the phenomenon in question *can* be found.

Pointing out the inadequacies of any received theory, including Darwinian   66
theory, is important work. But to my mind, the most important part of the ID program is not what it denies but what it affirms, namely, that some real causes might not be purely mechanistic, and that this line of inquiry might prove productive. Some interesting and fruitful science has been done by scientists who hold such a view. Newton, for example, offered no mechanical explanation for gravitation (prompting Leibniz to call it a "perpetual miracle"). Kepler based his hypothesis about the orbital radii of the planets on the assumption that God, in laying out the solar system, used the five Platonic solids as "archetypal causes."

For ID to fit into this category of fruitful science, however, its advocates will   67
have to spell out much more closely what an account of the origin of biological diversity based on ID would look like and show how this perspective would further scientific inquiry rather than hinder it. I remain skeptical that this will happen, but the movement is still in its infancy, and it has some very bright people associated with it. They may prove me wrong.

Thus far ID is only a highly sophisticated form of special creationism, usu-   68
ally accompanied by strong apologetic overtones that tend to keep the debate at the ideological level. All too frequently science becomes a weapon in culture wars, denying in practice the clean theoretical distinction between science and religion that is otherwise widely proclaimed. Provine has said that "evolution is the greatest engine of atheism ever invented." Johnson would agree, though of course he thinks the engine is faulty while Provine thinks it's true. Johnson's audience would be much smaller if scientists like Provine and Dawkins did not make it so easy for him to equate evolution and methodological naturalism with atheism, but in fact that pair does speak for a good number of scientists and other academics. Because their approach flies in the face of the beliefs of many religious Americans, antievolutionism is not likely to go away any time soon, whether or not Johnson and his associates convince many scientists to adopt their program.

We could move a long way toward correcting the excesses of both the Johnsons   69
and the Provines if public education were more genuinely pluralistic. As long as public education essentially ignores the religious values of many families and pretends to remain neutral toward religion while actually promoting secularism, many religious people will feel disenfranchised. Johnson is at his best when he

decries what he elsewhere calls "scientific fundamentalism," the tendency of scientific materialists to monopolize the conversation about science in public schools.

Johnson effectively analyzes the film version of *Inherit the Wind*, the play 70 that depicts the Scopes trial [1925 trial of Tennessee high school teacher for teaching evolution] as the triumph of academic freedom over an ignorant, intolerant fundamentalism. Henry Drummond, whose character is loosely based on Clarence Darrow, warns Matthew Harrison Brady, the character drawn from William Jennings Bryan, not to deny others freedom of thought, and asks him to consider that there could come a time when a law would be passed "that only *Darwin* should be taught in the schools!" This, Johnson tells us, is exactly what happened:

> The real story of the Scopes trial is that the stereotype it promoted helped the 71 Darwinists capture the power of the law, and they have since used the law to prevent other people from thinking independently. By labeling any fundamental dissent from Darwinism as "religion," they are able to ban criticism of the official evolution story from public education far more effectively than the teaching of evolution was banned from Tennessee schools in the 1920s.

Johnson wants Americans to think more critically about evolution and 72 about tough religious questions related to it; so do I. In my opinion, the teaching of evolution should be coupled with serious discussions both of its perceived religious implications and of the various ways religious thinkers have responded to it. Public schools seem unable to undertake such highly inclusive, controversial conversations, given the prevailing interpretation of the antiestablishment clause of the First Amendment. An accomplished legal theorist, Johnson might better direct his efforts toward persuading his colleagues to reconsider their interpretation of the Constitution rather than toward criticizing the basic tenets of what remains scientifically a well-supported theory of the origin of biological diversity.

POSTSCRIPT
Does the Theory of Evolution Explain the Origins of Humanity?

In October 1996 Pope John Paul II announced that "new knowledge leads us to 73 recognize that the theory of evolution is more than a hypothesis." This endorsement had little noticeable impact on the creationism-evolution debate because creationism is a thing of fundamentalist Protestant sects. The debate between creationists and evolutionists will thus go on for the foreseeable future. Nor do the creationists seem likely to grow more moderate in their demands; at the extreme, they crave to replace all of human knowledge with something more consistent with their scriptures. See Jack Hitt, "On Earth as It Is in Heaven: Field Trips With the Apostles of Creation Science," *Harper's* (November 1996).

The debate has at times turned abusive, as it did in May 1996, when bi-   74 ologists attempting to inform the Ohio House Education Committee of how thoroughly the evidence supports the theory of evolution were heckled, jeered, and shouted down. See Karen Schmidt, "Creationists Evolve New Strategy," *Science* (July 26, 1996). As Janet Raloff notes, in "When Science and Beliefs Collide," *Science News* (June 8, 1996), harsh reactions to scientists are not surprising, considering that nearly half the U.S. population misunderstands or rejects "many of the basic precepts and findings of science." And these reactions are not seen only in churches and before legislative committees but also at academic meetings. As Barbara Ehrenreich and Janet McIntosh note, in "The New Creationism: Biology Under Attack," *The Nation* (June 9, 1997), there is a movement among feminists, cultural anthropologists, social psychologists, and other academics, amounting to a kind of "secular creationism" that insists human beings are not shaped by their biology, unlike all other living things, and shouts down all mention of Darwin, DNA, and even science. This "new creationism. . . represents a grave misunderstanding of biology and science generally," say Ehrenreich and McIntosh, but it is not about to go away, because secular creationists do not brook contradiction of their cherished beliefs.

Stephen Jay Gould, in "The Persistently Flat Earth," *Natural History*   75 (March 1994), makes the point that irrationality and dogmatism serve the adherents of neither science nor religion well: "The myth of a war between science and religion remains all too current and continues to impede a proper bonding and conciliation between these two utterly different and powerfully important institutions of human life."

The argument from design is well critiqued by Kenneth R. Miller in "Life's   76 Grand Design," *Technology Review* (March 1994). Also invaluable is Ronald L. Numbers, *The Creationists: The Evolution of Scientific Creationism* (Alfred A. Knopf, 1992).

Jacob Bronowski (1908–1974), a Polish-born intellectual, was trained as a mathematician but eventually studied and wrote on the sciences, technology, poetry, the relation between creativity in the arts and the sciences, and man's attempts to control nature throughout history. A mathematician, a literary critic, a playwright, a scientist, and an acclaimed Renaissance man, Bronowski earned an M.A. degree at Jesus College, Cambridge, England, in 1930, and a Ph.D. in 1933. His extremely wide-ranging career includes lecturing at University College in England; serving as wartime researcher for the British Ministry of Home Security during World War II, when he studied the effects of the atomic bomb; and working at multiple posts at the Salk Institute for Biological Studies in San Diego and posts at Oxford University, Massachusetts Institute of Technology, the University of Rochester, Oregon State University, Yale University, Columbia University, and the National Gallery of Art; and serving as head of projects for the United Nations Educational, Scientific, and Cultural Organization (UNESCO).

Bronowski also worked as a British Broadcasting Corporation (BBC) commentator on atomic energy and other scientific and cultural subjects.

Bronowski came to the United States in 1964. He wrote that, after 1932, he realized it was not enough to work at a desk, was more important and what was defending human decency. It was then that Bronowski turned his attention to studying connections between art and science. Among his writings are *The Poet's Defence* (1939; retitled and reprinted, 1966); a study of William Blake (1943; retitled and reprinted, 1965); *Science and Human Values* (1965; rev. ed., 1972), his most acclaimed work; and *The Ascent of Man* (1973), essays based on a BBC television series, his most popular work. Bronowski believed that the progress of science could best be understood by recognizing the interdependence of the sciences, arts, literature, and philosophy. He emphasized the universality of human nature and the need to control violence in modern society.

The Nature of Scientific Reasoning

Jacob Bronowski

What is the insight in which the scientist tries to see into nature? Can it indeed   1
be called either imaginative or creative? To the literary man the question may
seem merely silly. He has been taught that science is a large collection of facts;
and if this is true, then the only seeing which scientists need to do is, he supposes, seeing the facts. He pictures them, the colorless professionals of science, going
off to work in the morning into the universe in a neutral, unexposed state. They
then expose themselves like a photographic plate. And then in the darkroom or

laboratory they develop the image, so that suddenly and startlingly it appears, printed in capital letters, as a new formula for atomic energy.

Men who have read Balzac and Zola are not deceived by the claims of these   2
writers that they do no more than record the facts. The readers of Christopher Isherwood do not take him literally when he writes "I am a camera." Yet the same readers solemnly carry with them from their schooldays this foolish picture of the scientist fixing by some mechanical process the facts of nature. I have had of all people a historian tell me that science is a collection of facts, and his voice had not even the ironic rasp of one filing cabinet reproving another.

It seems impossible that this historian had ever studied the beginnings of a   3
scientific discovery. The Scientific Revolution can be held to begin in the year 1543 when there was brought to Copernicus, perhaps on his deathbed, the first printed copy of the book he had finished about a dozen years earlier. The thesis of this book is that the earth moves around the sun. When did Copernicus go out and record this fact with his camera? What appearance in nature prompted his outrageous guess? And in what odd sense is this guess to be called a neutral record of fact?

Less than a hundred years after Copernicus, Kepler published (between   4
1609 and 1619) the three laws which describe the paths of the planets. The work of Newton and with it most of our mechanics spring from these laws. They have a solid, matterof-fact sound. For example, Kepler says that if one squares the year of a planet, one gets a number which is proportional to the cube of its average distance from the sun. Does anyone think that such a law is found by taking enough readings and then squaring and cubing everything in sight? If he does, then, as a scientist, he is doomed to a wasted life; he has as little prospect of making a scientific discovery as an electronic brain has.

It was not this way that Copernicus and Kepler thought, or that scientists   5
think today. Copernicus found that the orbits of the planets would look simpler if they were looked at from the sun and not from the earth. But he did not in the first place find this by routine calculation. His first step was a leap of imagination—to lift himself from the earth, and put himself wildly, speculatively into the sun. "The earth conceives from the sun," he wrote; and "the sun rules the family of stars." We catch in his mind an image, the gesture of the virile man standing in the sun, with arms outstretched, overlooking the planets. Perhaps Copernicus took the picture from the drawings of the youth with outstretched arms which the Renaissance teachers put into their books on the proportions of the body. Perhaps he had seen Leonardo's drawings of his loved pupil Salai. I do not know. To me, the gesture of Copernicus, the shining youth looking outward from the sun,

is still vivid in a drawing which William Blake in 1780 based on all these: the drawing which is usually called Glad Day.

Kepler's mind, we know, was filled with just such fanciful analogies; and we know that they were. Kepler wanted to relate the speeds of the planets to the musical intervals. He tried to fit the five regular solids into their orbits. None of these likenesses worked, and they have been forgotten; yet they have been and they remain the stepping stones of every creative mind. Kepler felt for his laws by way of metaphors, he searched mystically for likenesses with what he knew in every strange corner of nature. And when among these guesses he hit upon his laws, he did not think of their numbers as the balancing of a cosmic bank account, but as a revelation of the unity in all nature. To us, the analogies by which Kepler listened for the movement of the planets in the music of the spheres are farfetched. Yet are they more so than the wild leap by which Rutherford and Bohr in our own century found a model for the atom in, of all places, the planetary system? 6

No scientific theory is a collection of facts. It will not even do to call a theory true or false in the simple sense in which every fact is either so or not so. The Epicureans held that matter is made of atoms 2000 years ago and we are now tempted to say that their theory was true. But if we do so we confuse their notion of matter with our own. John Dalton in 1808 first saw the structure of matter as we do today, and what he took from the ancients was not their theory but something richer, their image: the atom. Much of what was in Dalton's mind was as vague as the Greek notion, and quite as mistaken. But he suddenly gave life to the new facts of chemistry and the ancient theory together, by fusing them to give what neither had: a coherent picture of how matter is linked and built up from different kinds of atoms. The act of fusion is the creative act. 7

All science is the search for unity in hidden likenesses. The search may be on a grand scale, as in the modern theories which try to link the fields of gravitation and electromagnetism. But we do not need to be browbeaten by the scale of science. There are discoveries to be made by snatching a small likeness from the air too, if it is bold enough. In 1935 the Japanese physicist Hideki Yukawa wrote a paper which can still give heart to a young scientist. He took as his starting point the known fact that waves of light can sometimes behave as if they were separate pellets. From this he reasoned that the forces which hold the nucleus of an atom together might sometimes also be observed as if they were solid pellets. A schoolboy can see how thin Yukawa's analogy is, and his teacher would be severe with it. Yet Yukawa without a blush calculated the mass of the pellet he expected to see, and waited. He was right; his meson was found, and a range of 8 other mesons, neither the existence nor the nature of which had been suspected before. The likeness had borne fruit.

The scientist looks for order in the appearances of nature by exploring such   9 likenesses. For order does not display itself of itself; if it can be said to be there at all, it is not there for the mere looking. There is no way of pointing a finger or camera at it; order must be discovered and, in a deep sense, it must be created. What we see, as we see it, is mere disorder.

This point has been put trenchantly in a fable by Karl Popper. Suppose that   10 someone wishes to give his whole life to science. Suppose that he therefore sat down, pencil in hand, and for the next twenty, thirty, forty years recorded in note-book after notebook everything that he could observe. He may be supposed to leave out nothing: today's humidity, the racing results, the level of cosmic radia-tion and the stockmarket prices and the look of Mars, all would be there. He would have compiled the most careful record of nature that has ever been made; and, dying in the calm certainty of a life well spent, he would of course leave his notebooks to the Royal Society. Would the Royal Society thank him for the treasure of a lifetime of observation? It would not. The Royal Society would treat his notebooks exactly as the English bishops have treated Joanna Southcott's box. It would refuse to open them at all, because it would know without looking that the notebooks contain only a jumble of disorderly and meaningless items.

Science finds order and meaning in our experience, and sets about this in   11 quite a different way. It sets about it as Newton did in the story which he himself told in his old age, and of which the schoolbooks give only a caricature. In the year 1665, when Newton was 22, the plague broke out in southern England, and the University of Cambridge was closed. Newton therefore spent the next 18 months at home, removed from traditional learning, at a time when he was impa-tient for knowledge and, in his own phrase, "I was in the prime of my age for invention." In this eager, boyish mood, sitting one day in the garden of his wid-owed mother, he saw an apple fall. So far the books have the story right; we think we even know the kind of apple; tradition has it that it was a Flower of Kent. But now they miss the crux of the story. For what struck the young Newton at the sight was not the thought that the apple must be drawn to the earth by gravity; that conception was older than Newton. What struck him was the conjecture that the same force of gravity, which reaches to the top of the tree, might go on reaching out beyond the earth and its air, endlessly into space. Gravity might reach the moon: this was Newton's new thought; and it might be gravity which holds the moon in her orbit. There and then he calculated what force from the earth (falling off as the square of the distance) would hold the moon, and compared it with the known force of gravity at tree height. The forces agreed; Newton says laconically, "I found them answer pretty nearly." Yet they agreed only nearly: the likeness and the approximation go together, for no likeness is exact. In Newton's science modern sciences is full grown.

It grows from a comparison. It has seized a likeness between two unlike 12 appearances; for the apple in the summer garden and the grave moon overhead are surely as unlike in their movements as two things can be. Newton traced in them two expressions of a single concept, gravitation: and the concept (and the unity) are in that sense his free creation. The progress of science is the discovery at each step of a new order which gives unity to what had long seemed unlike.

Questions for Discussion

1. What is scientific reasoning? How does it differ from other kinds of reasoning?
2. Where does the erroneous image of scientists as merely reporting facts come from?
3. If science is not "a collection of facts" (Paragraph 2), what is it? Why can science not be just a collection of facts? What is a "fact"?
4. How do new scientific theories develop? How are old ideas transformed into new ones?
5. What is the purpose of science?
6. Why can good science never be purely objective? Why will pure objectivity not work? In what way should scientists be subjective?
7. Bronowski says in Paragraph 8, "All science is the search for unity in hidden likenesses." What examples does he include to illustrate that statement? What does that statement mean?

Questions for Reflection and Writing

1. Describe the process by which scientists think. Consider Copernicus and Kepler: What were their processes? How does their way of thinking still describe how scientists think today?
2. Define a type of reasoning, besides scientific, with which you are familiar. Examples might include artistic reasoning, intuitive reasoning, and historical reasoning. Describe the thinking process, providing examples from your experience, and explain how this process works.
3. Look up Leonardo da Vinci's drawing of the proportions of the body and William Blake's *Glad Day*, mentioned in Paragraph 5. Write an essay in which you explain how these drawings illustrate scientific thought. Other artworks on scientific topics could also be used in your essay.

Primo **Levi** (1919–1987), Jewish chemist and author, was born in Turin, Italy, and stayed there for most of his life. He received a B.S. summa cum laude from the University of Turin in 1941. After becoming active in the Italian Resistance in 1943, Levi was deported to Auschwitz concentration camp in Oswiecim, Poland, and was held there from 1943 to 1945. Considered one of the most important chroniclers of conditions for Jews in World War II, Levi was one of only three Italian partisans to survive Auschwitz.

He published his first book in 1947, *Se questo è un uomo* (*If This Is a Man*), published in America as *Survival in Auschwitz: The Nazi Assault on Humanity*. Levi told the *Los Angeles Times* that he aimed "to be a witness" without overemphasizing his status as a victim. Other works include *La Tregua* (1958; 8th ed. 1965; translated as *The Reawakening*, 1965), *La chiave a stella* (*The Monkey's Wrench*, translated 1986), *Se non ora, quando?* (*If Not Now, When?*, 1982), *Other People's Trades* (essays, translated 1989), and *The Sixth Day, and Other Tales* (short fables, 1990). Levi became increasingly distressed at the dwindling attention to the Holocaust and died in an apparent suicide in 1987.

Hydrogen

Primo Levi

It was January. Enrico came to call for me right after dinner: his brother had gone   1
up into the mountains and had left him the keys to the laboratory. I dressed
in a flash and joined him on the street.

During the walk I learned that his brother had not really left him the keys: 2
this was simply a compendious formulation, a euphemism, the sort of thing you
said to someone ready to understand. His brother, contrary to his habit, had not
hidden the keys, nor had he taken them with him; what's more, he had forgotten
to repeat to Enrico the prohibition against appropriating these same keys, and the
punishment threatened should Enrico disobey. To put it bluntly, there were the
keys, after months of waiting; Enrico and I were determined not to pass up the
opportunity.

We were sixteen, and I was fascinated with Enrico. He was not very active,   3
and his scholastic output was pretty meager, but he had virtues that distinguished
him from all the other members of the class, and he did things that nobody else
did. He possessed a calm, stubborn courage, a precocious capacity to sense his
own future and to give it weight and shape. He turned his back (but without con-

tempt) on our interminable discussions, now Platonic, now Darwinian, later still Bergsonian; he was not vulgar, he did not boast of his virile attributes or his skill at sports, he never lied. He knew his limitations, but we never heard him say (as we all told each other, with the idea of currying comfort, or blowing off steam): "You know, I really think I'm an idiot."

He had a slow, foot-slogging imagination: he lived on dreams like all of us,   4
but his dreams were sensible; they were obtuse, possible, contiguous to reality, not romantic, not cosmic. He did not experience my tormented oscillation between the heaven (of a scholastic or sports success, a new friendship, a rudimentary and fleeting love) and the hell (of a failing grade, a remorse, a brutal revelation of an inferiority which each time seemed eternal, definitive). His goals were always attainable. He dreamed of promotion and studied with patience things that did not interest him. He wanted a microscope and sold his racing bike to get it. He wanted to be a pole vaulter and went to the gym every evening for a year without making a fuss about it, breaking any bones, or tearing a ligament, until he reached the mark of 3.5 meters he had set himself, and then stopped. Later he wanted a certain woman and he got her; he wanted the money to live quietly and obtained it after ten years of boring, prosaic work.

We had no doubts: we would be chemists, but our expectations and hopes   5
were quite different. Enrico asked chemistry, quite reasonably, for the tools to earn his living and have a secure life. I asked for something entirely different, for me chemistry represented an indefinite cloud of future potentialities which enveloped my life to come in black volutes torn by fiery flashes, like those which had hidden Mount Sinai. Like Moses, from that cloud I expected my law, the principle of order in me, around me, and in the world. I was fed up with books, which I still continued to gulp down with indiscreet voracity, and searched for another key to the highest truths: there must be a key, and I was certain that, owing to some monstrous conspiracy to my detriment and the world's, I would not get it in school. In school they loaded me with tons of notions which I diligently digested, but which did not warm the blood in my veins. I would watch the buds swell in spring, the mica glint in the granite, my own hands, and I would say to myself: "I will understand this, too, I will understand everything, but not the way they want me to. I will find a shortcut, I will make a lockpick, I will push open the doors."

It was enervating, nauseating, to listen to lectures on the problems of being   6
and knowing, when everything around us was a mystery pressing to be revealed: the old wood of the benches, the sun's sphere beyond the windowpanes and the roofs, the vain flight of the pappus down in the June air. Would all the philosophers and

all the armies of the world be able to construct this little fly? No, nor even understand it: this was a shame and an abomination, another road must be found.

We would be chemists, Enrico and I. We would dredge the bowels of the   7
mystery with our strength, our talent: we would grab Proteus by the throat, cut
short his inconclusive metamorphoses from Plato to Augustine, from Augustine
to Thomas, from Thomas to Hegel, from Hegel to Croce. We would force him to
speak.

This being our program, we could not afford to waste any opportunities.   8
Enrico's brother, a mysterious and choleric personage, about whom Enrico did not
like to talk, was a chemistry student, and he had installed a laboratory at the rear
of a courtyard, in a curious, narrow, twisting alleyway which branched off Piazza
della Crocetta and stood out in the obsessive Turinese geometry like a rudimentary organ trapped in the evolved structure of a mammalian. The laboratory was
also rudimentary: not in the sense of an atavistic vestige but in that of extreme
poverty. There was a tiled workbench, very few glass receptacles, about twenty
flasks with reagents, much dust and cobwebs, little light, and great cold.Onour
way we had discussed what we were going to do now that we had "gained access
to the laboratory," but our ideas were confused.

It seemed to us an *embarras de richesses*, and it was instead a different embar-   9
rassment, deeper and more essential: an embarrassment tied to an ancient atrophy of ours, of our family, of our caste. What were we able to do with our hands?
Nothing, or almost nothing. The women, yes—our mothers and grandmothers
had lively, agile hands, they knew how to sew and cook, some even played the
piano, painted with watercolors, embroidered, braided their hair. But we, and our
fathers?

Our hands were at once coarse and weak, regressive, insensitive: the least   10
trained part of our bodies. Having gone through the first fundamental experiences of play, they had learned to write, and that was all. They knew the convul-
sive grip around the branches of a tree, which we loved to climb out of a natural
desire and also (Enrico and I) out of a groping homage and return to the origins
of the species; but they were unfamiliar with the solemn, balanced weight of the
hammer, the concentrated power of a blade, too cautiously forbidden us, the wise
texture of wood, the similar and diverse pliability of iron, lead, and copper. If man
is a maker, we were not men: we knew this and suffered from it.

The glass in the laboratory enchanted and intimidated us. Glass for us was   11
that which one must not touch because it breaks, and yet, at a more intimate contact, revealed itself to be a substance different from all others, sui generis, full of
mystery and caprice. It is similar in this to water, which also has no kindred forms:

but water is bound to man, indeed to life, by a long-lasting familiarity, by a relationship of multifarious necessity, due to which its uniqueness is hidden beneath the crust of habit. Glass, however, is the work of man and has a more recent history. It was our first victim, or, better, our first adversary. In the Crocetta laboratory there was the usual lab glass, in various diameters and long and short sections, all covered with dust, we lit the Bunsen burner and set to work.

To bend the tube was easy. All you had to do was hold the section of tube   12
steady over the flame: after a certain time the flame turned yellow and simultaneously the glass became weakly luminous. At this point the tube could be bent: the curve obtained was far from perfect, but in substance something took place, you could create a new, arbitrary shape; a potentiality became act.Wasn't this what Aristotle meant?

Now, a tube of copper or lead can also be bent, but we soon found out that   13
the red-hot tube of glass possessed a unique virtue: when it had become pliable, you could, by quickly pulling on the two cold ends, pull it into very thin filaments, indeed unimaginably thin, so thin that it was drawn upwards by the current of hot air that rose from the flame. Thin and flexible, like silk. So then silk and cotton too, if obtainable in a massive form, could be as inflexible as glass? Enrico told me that in his grandfather's town the fishermen take silkworms, when they are already big and ready to form the pupa and, blind and clumsy, try to crawl up on the branches; they grab them, break them in two with their fingers, and pulling on the two stumps obtain a thread of silk, thick and coarse, which they then use as a fishing line. This fact, which I had no hesitation in believing, seemed to me both abominable and fascinating: abominable because of the cruel manner of that death, and the futile use of a natural portent; fascinating because of the straightforward and audacious act of ingenuity it presupposed on the part of its mythical inventor.

The glass tube could also be blown up; but this was much more difficult. You   14
could close one end of a small tube: then blowing hard from the other end a bubble formed, very beautiful to look at and almost perfectly spherical but with absurdly thin walls. Even the slightest puff of breath in excess and the walls took on the iridescence of a soap bubble, and this was a certain sign of death: the bubble burst with a sharp little snap and its fragments were scattered over the floor with the tenuous rustle of eggshells. In some sense it was a just punishment; glass is glass, and it should not be expected to simulate the behavior of soapy water. If one forced the terms a bit, one could even see an Aesopian lesson in the event.

After an hour's struggle with the glass, we were tired and humiliated. We   15
both had inflamed, dry eyes from looking too long at the red-hot glass, frozen feet,

and fingers covered with burns. Besides, working with glass is not chemistry: we were in the laboratory with another goal. Our goal was to see with our eyes, to provoke with our hands, at least one of the phenomena which were described so offhandedly in our chemistry textbook. One could, for example, prepare nitrous oxide, which in Sestini and Funaro was still described with the not very proper and unserious term of laughing gas. Would it really be productive of laughter?

Nitrous oxide is prepared by cautiously heating ammonium nitrate. The lat-   16
ter did not exist in the lab; instead there was ammonia and nitric acid. We mixed them, unable to make any preliminary calculations until we had a neutral litmus reaction as a result of which the mixture heated up greatly and emitted an abundance of white smoke; then we decided to bring it to a boil to eliminate the water. In a short time the lab was filled with a choking fog, which was not at all laughable; we broke off our attempt, luckily for us, because we did not know what can happen when this explosive salt is heated less than cautiously.

It was neither simple nor very amusing. I looked around and saw in a cor-   17
ner an ordinary dry battery. Here is something we could do: the electrolysis of water. It was an experiment with a guaranteed result, which I had already executed several times at home. Enrico would not be disappointed.

I put some water in a beaker, dissolved a pinch of salt in it, turned two   18
empty jam jars upside down in the beaker; then found two rubber-coated copper wires, attached them to the battery's poles, and fitted the wire ends into the jam jars. A minuscule procession of air bubbles rose from the wire ends: indeed, observing them closely you could see that from the cathode about twice as much gas was being liberated as from the anode. I wrote the well-known equation on the blackboard, and explained to Enrico that what was written there was actually taking place. Enrico didn't seem too convinced, but by now it was dark and we were half frozen; we washed our hands, bought some slices of chestnut pudding and went home, leaving the electrolysis to continue on its own.

The next day we still had access. In pliant obsequiousness to theory, the   19
cathode jar was almost full of gas; the anode jar was half full: I brought this to Enrico's attention, giving myself as much importance as I could, and trying to awaken the suspicion that, I won't say electrolysis, but its application as the confirmation of the law of definite proportions, was my invention, the fruit of patient experiments conducted secretly in my room. But Enrico was in a bad mood and doubted everything. "Who says that it's actually hydrogen and oxygen?" he said to me rudely. "And what if there's chlorine? Didn't you put in salt?"

The objection struck me as insulting: How did Enrico dare to doubt my   20
statement? I was the theoretician, only I: he, although the proprietor of the lab

(to a certain degree, and then only at second hand), indeed, precisely because he was in a position to boast of other qualities, should have abstained from criticism. "Now we shall see," I said: I carefully lifted the cathode jar and, holding it with its open end down, lit a match and brought it close. There was an explosion, small but sharp and angry, the jar burst into splinters (luckily, I was holding it level with my chest and not higher), and there remained in my hand, as a sarcastic symbol, the glass ring of the bottom.

We left, discussing what had occurred. My legs were shaking a bit; I experi- 21 enced retrospective fear and at the same time a kind of foolish pride at having confirmed a hypothesis and having unleashed a force of nature. It was indeed hydrogen, therefore; the same element that burns in the sun and stars, and from whose condensation the universes are formed in eternal silence.

Questions for Discussion

1. What is the main difference between Enrico and Levi? How does Levi explain that difference? Do you think Enrico might have had a different explanation?

2. What does Levi's memoir help you understand about the mind of a scientist? According to what is implied in the essay, what traits must a young person have to become a good scientist?

3. Why did Enrico and Levi feel constrained by their schooling? Why did they feel they must do something physical? What can they get from one method of gaining knowledge that they cannot get from the other?

4. What fascinates Levi about the heated glass? What thoughts does the one small experiment set off?

5. Why did the men of Levi's family compare poorly to the women? How does his thoughts about his family connect to what he is saying about chemistry?

6. In writing as an older man of an experience when he was sixteen, what does Levi add to the narrative that a sixteen-year-old would probably not notice?

7. How does Levi create suspense?

Questions for Reflection and Writing

1. Write about a time when you sought knowledge at the expense of propriety or safety. Tell the story of your seeking and describe what you learned (or did not learn) as a result.

2. Write about your aspirations. Compare yourself to a friend or to a sibling or other relative. Write your essay in the style of a memoir, as Levi has done.

3. Choose one element of the periodic table. Research and relate its characteristics, history, and any interesting stories connected with it.

Can Humans Go to Mars?

YES: John Tierney, from "Martian Chronicle," *Reason* (February 1999)

NO: Neil de Grasse Tyson, from "Space: You Can't Get There From Here," *Natural History* (September 1, 1998)

Issue Summary

YES: John Tierney, a columnist for *The New York Times*, argues that it is technically and economically possible to establish a human presence on Mars.

NO: Neil de Grasse Tyson, the Frederick P. Rose Director of New York City's Hayden Planetarium, counters that space travel is an impractical dream.

The dream of conquering space has a long history. The pioneers of rocketry the   1
Russian Konstantin Tsiolkovsky (1857-1935) and the American Robert H. Goddard (1882-1945)—both dreamed of exploring other worlds, although neither lived long enough to see the first artificial satellite, Sputnik, go up in 1957. That success sparked a race between America and the Soviet Union to be the first to achieve each step in the progression of space exploration. The next steps were to put dogs (the Soviet Laika was the first), monkeys, chimps, and finally humans into orbit. Communications, weather, and spy satellites were then designed and launched. And on July 20, 1969, the U.S. Apollo Program landed the first men on the Moon. See Buzz Aldrin and Malcolm McConnell, *Men from Earth* (Bantam, 1989).

There were a few more Apollo landings, but not many. The United States   2
had achieved its main political goal of beating the Soviets to the Moon and, in the minds of the government, demonstrating American superiority. Thereafter, the United States was content to send automated spacecraft (computer-operated robots) to observe Venus, Mars, and the rings of Saturn; to land on Mars and study its soil; and even to carry recordings of Earth's sights and sounds past the distant edge of the solar system, perhaps to be retrieved in the distant future by intelligent life from some other world.

Humans have not left near-Earth orbit for two decades, though space tech-   3
nology has continued to develop through communications satellites, space shuttles, space stations, and independent robotic explorers such as the Mariners and
Vikings and-landing on Mars on July 4, 1997—the Pathfinder craft (now the
Sagan Memorial Station) and its tiny robot rover, Sojourner.

Why has human space exploration gone no further? One reason is that   4
robots are now extremely capable and much cheaper; see David Callahan, "A
Fork in the Road to Space," *Technology Review* (August/September 1993). Although some robot spacecraft have failed partially or completely, there have been
many grand successes that have added enormously to humanity's knowledge of
the earth and other planets.

Another reason for the reduction in human space travel seems to be the   5
fear that astronauts will die in space. This point was emphasized by the explosion
of the space shuttle *Challenger* in January 1986, which killed seven astronauts and
froze the entire shuttle program for over two-and-a-half years. Still another is
money: Lifting robotic explorers into space is expensive, but lifting people into
space—along with all the food, water, air, and other supplies necessary to keep
them alive for the duration of a mission—is much more expensive. And there are
many people in government and elsewhere who cry that there are many better
ways to spend the money on Earth.

In the following selections, John Tierney states that it is already technically   6
possible to establish a human presence on Mars and that there are several practical
ways to raise the necessary funds. Furthermore, he adds, to go to Mars—or even to
dream of doing so—serves the cause of human liberty. Neil de Grasse Tyson argues
that space travel is an impractical dream. To go to Mars—or elsewhere in the
universe—will require enormous technical breakthroughs, he concludes.

Yes
Martin Chronicle

John Tierney

A couple of years ago, after hearing an engineer named Robert Zubrin rhap-   7
sodize about his plan for a privately financed expedition to Mars, I tried out the

From John Tierney, "Martian Chronicle," *Reason* (February 1999). Copyright © 1999 by The Reason Foundation. Reprinted by
permission of The Reason Foundation, 3415 Sepulveda Blvd., Suite 400, Los Angeles, CA 90034. www.reason.com.

idea on America's masters of marketing. I sent an outline of the scheme to Bill Gates, Ted Turner, Barry Diller, Peter Uberroth, television executives such as ABC's Roone Alredge and NBC's Don Ohlmeyer, the leaders of DreamWorks, and a long list of other people whose names tend to be accompanied by the word visionary. I wasn't asking for money, just for their thoughts on how humanity's interplanetary adventure could be packaged profitably, but most of them didn't even want to think about it. Except for a few enthusiasts, they couldn't imagine how you could make the trip interesting enough to pay the bills. How could you hold the audience for such a long trip to such a desolate place?

"Personally," Barry Diller explained, "I don't care about going to Mars."   8

Personally, I did. But I didn't presume to know as much about the mass   9
audience as Diller and his fellow moguls. They knew how short the public's attention span could be; they remembered how quickly people had gotten bored
with the Apollo program. What, really, was the point of going to Mars? If the idea
made any commercial sense, why wasn't someone working on it? I wondered if
Zubrin was hopelessly unrealistic—until this past summer, when he managed to
get 700 people from 40 countries to travel to Boulder, Colorado.

Officially, it was the founding convention of the Mars Society. Unofficial-   10
ly, it was the Woodstock of Mars, a horde of scientists, entrepreneurs, schoolteachers, lawyers, writers, engineers, college students, musicians, computer geeks,
and assorted hustlers wearing "MARS OR BUST" buttons. They ranged from
space hobbyists to the president of a company working on a privately financed
mission to survey an asteroid. They debated the cost of spaceships and whether
to power the Mars land rover with a nuclear reactor. They bought Mars trinkets
and pictures. They analyzed details ranging from the proper Martian calendar
(there are dozens of competing systems) to the mechanics of creating a breath-
able atmosphere on Mars.

And they cheered Zubrin, who is one of the more riveting engineer-orators   11
in history. A short man with intense dark eyes and a passionate speaking style—
he can bring to mind Savonarola—he railed at the stagnation that would afflict
humans without a frontier to conquer. He extolled the Europeans who crossed
the Atlantic 500 years ago to find freedom in the New World and the Africans
who left the comforts of the tropics 50,000 years ago for the cold, harsh regions
where they were forced to develop the tools that made civilization possible.
"Humans did not leave paradise because they ate of the tree of knowledge," he
proclaimed. "They ate of the tree of knowledge because they left paradise." The
audience gave him a two-minute standing ovation.

In some ways it was reminiscent of the passion for space back in the 1960s,   12
but not even the moon landings had ever aroused such a zealous corps of volunteer mission planners. These people wanted much more than another Apollo
program, whose achievements they dismissed as "flags and footprints." Their
heroes were from earlier eras of exploration: Columbus, the Pilgrims, Lewis and
Clark, the settlers of the American West. As they put it in their society's founding declaration, "The settling of the Martian New World is an opportunity for a
noble experiment in which humanity has another chance to shed old baggage
and begin the world anew."

They were dangerously close to utopianism—which at first seemed odd,   13
given that Zubrin and a good many of the others are libertarians. Ordinarily, libertarians are too busy opposing politicians' utopian schemes to be preaching their
own. But as they fantasized about casting off the chains of earthly governments,
the Mars-libertarian connection began to make sense. Mars gives libertarians a
rare chance to be *for* something, to present a grand vision of freedom instead of
merely trying to fend off the latest excesses of big government. Building the future
is a splendid alternative to the drudgery of deregulating and privatizing the present. Spaceships and extraterrestrial colonies evoke the sort of emotions inspired
by cathedrals in the Middle Ages—or, to use a more recent example, by modern
architecture in *The Fountainhead*.

Libertarians can appreciate Mars in a way that Barry Diller and his fellow   14
moguls can't. A desolate planet free of earthly institutions is more appealing to
libertarians than it is to the corporate elite, just as the New World was more
appealing to the Pilgrims and other contrarians than it was to the European aristocracy. It will take some doing to settle Mars, but libertarians have a crucial
advantage. They're not expecting government bureaucrats to do the job. They
know better than to count on NASA.

Four decades after the Lewis and Clark expedition, the American West had been   15
mapped by trappers and was being rapidly settled by farmers. It has now been
nearly four decades since the first explorers went into space, and what do we have
to show for it? Chiefly two government programs that have created lots of jobs
and produced massive cost overruns: the space shuttle and the space station. Rick
Tumlinson, the president of the Space Frontier Foundation, is grateful that
NASA did not exist in Thomas Jefferson's day.

"Suppose," Tumlinson says, "that when Lewis and Clark returned from their   16
trip, Jefferson had told them, 'Mr. Clark, you develop a Conestoga shuttle. Mr.

Lewis, I want you to build a national cabin.' And 30 years later they had three or four Conestoga shuttles, and they were just beginning to build the national cabin. That's where we are today."

Admittedly, space poses more logistical challenges than the American   17
West. But NASA has shown a genius for complicating those challenges. It is burdened not only by bureaucratic inefficiency and pork barrel politics (every superfluous job means votes in someone's congressional district) but also by the public's aversion to risk. Private explorers can afford to fail and risk lives; NASA's leaders are expected by politicians and the press to prevent any loss of life or damage to "national prestige." They're forced to avoid another *Challenger* disaster at all costs.

"The cost of space travel ought to be declining with new technology, but   18
it's not," says Edward L. Hudgins, director of regulatory studies at the Cato Institute. "About three decades after the Wright brothers' flight, the commercially viable DC-3 was flying. But today the cost of placing payloads into orbit on the shuttle is 10 times higher than it was during the Apollo program. By contrast, in the past 20 years the cost of airline tickets per passenger mile has dropped by 30 percent, and the cost of shipping oil has dropped 80 percent."

NASA's profligacy became absurdly obvious in 1989, when the agency was   19
asked by President Bush to plan a mission to Mars. It responded with a $400 billion proposal to build a 1,000-ton interplanetary spaceship the length of a football field, which would have carried all the fuel for the return voyage. It would have been assembled in orbit because it was too large to be launched from Earth—" the battlestar *Galactica*," as Zubrin dubbed it. At the time he was an engineer at Martin Marietta Astronautics and a member of an informal group called the Mars Underground that met occasionally to dream of interplanetary travel. He and a colleague at Martin Marietta, Donald Baker, came up with an alternative to NASA's battlestar *Galactica* by adopting the philosophy of Roald Amundsen, the entrepreneurial Norwegian who explored the polar regions early this century.

Besides winning the race to the South Pole, Amundsen was the first person   20
to sail the Northwest Passage, which he accomplished by avoiding the mistakes of the British Navy. As the NASA of its day, the Royal Navy in the 19th century sent one lavishly provisioned expedition after another in search of the Northwest Passage, but the large ships kept getting stuck in the Arctic ice, and when the food ran out the men had to return home (or perish, as many of them did). Amundsen, who was financing his own expedition, bought a small fishing boat and took a crew of just six. Unable to bring huge stores of food, he learned to live

off the land by hunting caribou as he maneuvered the small boat through the ice all the way from the Atlantic to the Pacific.

"Amundsen's expedition was a brilliant example of a small group of ex-   21
plorers succeeding on a shoestring budget," Zubrin says. "Lewis and Clark's was another. Before their journey, armies with big baggage trains had failed to make any significant penetration in the American West. But Lewis and Clark managed to cross the continent with just 25 men."

To reach Mars, Zubrin proposed replacing NASA's huge ship with a vessel   22
small and light enough to be launched directly from Earth. It would not need to carry fuel for the return trip because the Martian explorers, like Amundsen, would exploit local resources: the carbon dioxide in the Martian atmosphere, which when combined with hydrogen brought from Earth, could be converted to methane and liquid oxygen to fuel the return voyage. Zubrin built a machine to demonstrate how easily it could be done, and eventually NASA adopted his idea. It redesigned the Mars mission, lowering the cost estimate from $400 billion to $55 billion, and is contemplating a trip sometime after 2010.

But Zubrin, who's now the president of his own firm in Boulder, Pioneer   23
Astronautics, has pared down NASA's plans to come up with a still cheaper mission. He figures that within a decade a private entrepreneur could get to Mars and back for a mere $5 billion. He's been promoting this idea in lectures and in a book, *The Case for Mars*, that has been translated into half a dozen languages and attracted letters from thousands of Mars enthusiasts around the world. (See "Spaceship Enterprise," *Reason*, April 1997.)

Other engineers estimate the cost of a private mission might be more like   24
$10 billion, maybe up to $20 billion, but even at those prices the trip is not an absurdly extravagant dream. NASA's budget for a single year is $13 billion. For the estimated cost of building and operating the space station, $100 billion, you could send a fleet of Zubrin's ships to Mars. By NASA standards, the cost of a private Mars mission is chump change.

But by venture capital standards, it's a lot of money for a highly speculative   25
endeavor. To pay for the mission, Zubrin and members of the Mars Society have been analyzing the financing techniques of pre-NASA explorers and looking for new ideas. Some possibilities:

The Mars Prize   Zubrin tried selling this idea during a dinner with then House   26
Speaker Newt Gingrich, who got so enthusiastic that the meal lasted for four hours. But Gingrich never followed through on the proposal, which calls for

Congress to promise $20 billion to the fast explorers who reach Mars and return. In case that prize isn't enough to interest entrepreneurs in such a risky all-or-nothing venture, Zubrin also envisions offering smaller bonuses for achieving technical milestones along the way, like sending the equipment for making fuel to Mars.

Prizes have been used in the past to spur public-private ventures in ex-   27 ploration. Fifteenth-century Spanish and Portuguese rulers offered financial inducements to captains who ventured down the African coast and across the Atlantic. In the 19th century, the British Parliament offered cash awards for reaching the North Pole and for venturing westward into the Arctic ice: a prize of £5,000 for reaching 110 degrees west, double that for reaching 130 degrees, and triple that for 150 degrees.

For politicians, the most appealing aspect of the Mars Prize is that they   28 could reap the publicity of announcing it without having to pay for it immediately. They could present themselves as both patrons of exploration and opponents of make-work government programs. NASA would surely object to the proposal, and so might libertarian purists, who could argue that there's no need for the public to finance any kind of Martian adventure. But to some extent, the knowledge gained from Martian exploration would be a public good; so would the national glory, for whatever that's worth. And there's always the preservation-of-the-species argument: By supporting the exploration of a potential new home, the public is buying insurance against Earth's becoming uninhabitable.

The Mars Prize would certainly be more defensible than NASA's current monopoly on public funds for space exploration. Still, there's no reason the trip must be financed by the government. Entrepreneurial explorers have long profited from the fortunes and egos of . . .

Rich Patrons   In 1911, William Randolph Hearst offered a $50,000 prize to the   30 first person to fly across America in less than 30 days. Calbraith Perry Rodgers immediately set out to win it in a plane called the *Vin Fiz*, named after a carbonated grape drink manufactured by his sponsor, the Armour Meat Packing Company. He endured 15 accidents on the way from New York to Los Angeles, one of which landed him in the hospital for a month. lie didn't meet the deadline—it took him 84 days—but he did complete the trip. Other prizes have been offered for human-powered flight (a $200,000 award claimed in 1978, when the *Gossamer Albatross* flew a mile) and for the first manned, completely reusable spaceship (a $10 million award, announced in 1996 by the X Prize Foundation, that has yet to be claimed).

The Mars Prize would be an expensive proposition, but modern-day Hearsts   31
such as Bill Gates could afford to offer it. Or they could directly finance expeditions, the way wealthy gentlemen supported polar exploration at the start of the
century. Robert Peary, for instance, was bankrolled by the Peary Arctic Club, a
group of businessmen who paid for the privilege of basking in his company and
achieving geographic immortality. Peary and other polar explorers named mountains and glaciers after the American, British, and Norwegian plutocrats who
financed the discoveries. Mars' most prominent features, like its 18-mile-high
volcano and 2,800-mile-long version of the Grand Canyon, have already been
named, but the first explorers there-and certainly the first settlers—could exercise their prerogative to assign new names.

The patrons of Arctic expeditions also sometimes paid to tag along for part   32
of the trip. Peaty brought wealthy sponsors on his ship; Frederick C. Cook was
accompanied by a sportsman who wanted to hunt. The Mars mission—six
months traveling there, two years on the surface, and six months back—might be
too grueling a vacation for the typical billionaire. But plenty of other people
would pay for a chance to go along, and there's a clever way to get hold of their
money.

The Mars Lottery   Perhaps the most promising new idea at the conference in   33
Boulder came from someone outside the aerospace industry. Alex Duncan, a local
resident with experience in the commodities business, proposed an international
Mars Lottery, modeled on the lottery based in Lichtenstein that raises funds internationally for the Red Cross. A Mars Lottery could be headquartered anywhere
and reach a global audience through the Internet.

Besides the usual cash prizes, which could be awarded fortnightly or month-   34
ly, the Mars Lottery would have two big selling points. First, participants would
know that a portion of the proceeds was going to support a private expedition to
Mars. Second, and more important, participants would be buying a chance to go
themselves. Duncan proposed that all the winners of the regular drawings
become eligible for a grand prize: a berth on the first ship to Mars, assuming that
the winner of this grand drawing met the physical and mental requirements for
the voyage. Duncan figures that the proceeds from this lottery could pay for the
whole Mars mission within three to five years.

A variation on his scheme would be to give the winner of each regular   35
drawing the option of trying out for the mission at the explorers' training camp,
which would probably be in the Arctic (to simulate the frigid conditions on

Mars). The leader of the crew could evaluate dozens, maybe hundreds, of different winners and choose one or two for the trip. This system would produce a better crew and also increase the appeal of the lottery, because each winner would be getting an Arctic adventure in addition to the cash prize.

Media and Marketing   The Summer Olympics last just three weeks and gen-   36
erate more than $2 billion in fees from television networks and corporate sponsors. The three-year Mars mission has the potential to make much more money, possibly enough to pay for itself, solely with the revenue from media rights and corporate tie-ins.

Just as Henry Morton Stanley charged the expenses of his African journeys   37
to the *New York Herald*, just as Sir Ernest Shackleton paid for his Antarctic voyages with best-selling books and international lecture tours, the Mars explorers could tap into the global appetite for adventure stories. And just as Shackleton exploited the new media of his day—at his lectures in 1910 he showed the first movies from the Antarctic—the Mars explorers could reach a paying audience through new cable channels and Web sites. The media coverage of the mission would attract the same kind of sponsors who pay to be part of the Olympics. Outdoor gear makers and high-technology firms would have a special incentive to have their logos and products associated with the adventure.

Although some sponsors would be reluctant to get involved with a project   38
that could fail spectacularly and fatally, others (especially those selling products to young males) would be attracted by the aura of danger. But the dangers must seem worthwhile, the mission shouldn't come off as a pointless stunt. If the trip appeared to be just a longer version of *Apollo 11*, another enterprise that left nothing but flags and footprints, it would be less appealing to the audience—and therefore to potential sponsors. That's one reason that Zubrin and his disciples focus on analogies with Columbus instead of Neil Armstrong. The vision of Mars as the New World lends the first trip gravitas.

But why would anyone, especially a libertarian devoted to free markets, believe   39
that a Mars colony would be a good investment? The first humans on Mars will encounter horrific dust storms, temperatures of minus 70 degrees Fahrenheit, and an unbreathable atmosphere. If they stood on the Martian surface without a pressurized suit, their blood would expand and burst out of their veins. Why would it pay to stick around?

At first glance, Mars has none of the commercial opportunities that drew   40
the first Europeans to America. Columbus, who was financed by merchants as

well as by Queen Isabella, crossed the Atlantic with the intention of making money. Even after his first goal, a trade route to the Orient, proved unattainable, there were other attractions for investors. The Spanish conquered the natives and took home gold; the French and Dutch set up trading posts in North America to acquire furs.

Mars offers no such inducements, unless you count the souvenir value of its 41 rocks. Otherwise the minerals in its crust appear to be of little value. Science fiction writers like to imagine humans profitably mining asteroids and other planets, but there's no looming scarcity of minerals on Earth. The prices of metals and most other natural resources have been falling for millennia. Unless the prices here rise dramatically, or the cost of interplanetary shipping plummets, space miners won't be able to profitably export Mars' resources in the foreseeable future.

But Mars does have some resources of local value: water, carbon dioxide, 42 and real estate. It contains as much dry land as all the continents on Earth, and the leaders of the Mars Society have big plans for it. They want to "terraform" Mars by injecting chlorofluorocarbons into its atmosphere and setting off a runaway greenhouse effect. As the planet thawed, the atmosphere would thicken with carbon dioxide released from melting ice caps and soil. Add some trees and plants to convert the carbon dioxide into oxygen, and before long humans could be breathing comfortably as they strolled in shirt sleeves on the green planet.

This scheme sounds outlandish today, but there was a time when Europeans 43 couldn't imagine settling the American wilderness either. The Spanish and French leaders, as well as the officials of the Dutch West India Company, didn't initially emphasize permanent settlements of families. They sent mainly single men—soldiers, traders, and trappers—on temporary assignments to extract resources. America was a nice place to exploit, but you wouldn't want to live there.

"From the Spanish point of view," Zubrin says, 'the only parts of the 44 Americas that were valuable were the places with civilized Indians that could be taxed. They dismissed the rest as a howling wilderness. The British had a different notion of where wealth comes from. They created farms and towns in New England, turning the wilderness into a domain where social reproduction could occur."

The British settlers, motivated by a yearning for religious freedom, even- 45 tually outnumbered and expelled the Spanish, French, and Dutch from most of North America. Isolated from Europe, they created new kinds of communities with new kinds of liberties. 'Humanity needs room to play and experiment with ideas in human governance," Zubrin says. "In 1776 Thomas Paine wrote, 'We hold it in our power to begin the world anew.' So they did, and so do we. People will endure the risk and hardships of emigrating to Mars if, like the colonists in America, they can find a higher level of freedom." . . .

Already a few entrepreneurs are looking to launch their own missions into   46
space. Two companies, hoping to tap the adventure travel market, have announced plans to build space planes that will take customers for a brief ride just outside the atmosphere. Another firm, Space Dev, has raised $20 million as part of its plan to send scientific instruments to survey an asteroid and sell the data to scientists. But the Mars mission requires investment of another order of magnitude, and even enthusiasts like Zubrin aren't sure the private sector will take the risk anytime soon. As he hopes for a private mission, he's also lobbying for an old-fashioned NASA program.

"I'm a hard libertarian about rights on Mars, but not about getting there,"   47
he says. "With something as risky as Mars, it would be useful for the government to absorb some of the up-front costs. Spanish merchants weren't willing to back Columbus' first trip without royal involvement. Lewis and Clark were funded by the U.S. government-and then, as soon as they came back and said there's beaver there, John Jacob Astor's people did their own private exploration that ultimately was much more extensive than the government's. The American government also stimulated the private sector by setting up forts in the frontier, which attracted peddlers who established trade routes in the area. If the government set up a research base on Mars, it would stimulate private competition to lower the costs of delivering cargo."

Once the cost of transport to Mars dropped, real estate speculators might begin   48
to see the planet's potential. One member of the Mars Society, Richard Allen Brown, has proposed that a private company divide Mars into a million plots, each 25,000 acres, and sell bonds giving a 100-year option on each plot. By charging $20,000 for each bond, the company could raise $20 billion. It would invest this capital conservatively and use the income, about $1 billion a year, to finance the exploration and settlement of Mars over the course of a century. If you bought a bond and the land eventually became valuable, you (or your heir) could exercise the option to trade in the bond for a deed to the land. If after 100 years the option still hadn't been exercised, your heir could redeem the bond for the original capital investment of $20,000,

Mars bonds would not be for the timid investor. Even if the land did   49
become valuable, there's no guarantee that your deed to the land would be recognized, because for now there's no internationally recognized method of claim-

ing land in outer space. The vagaries of space property law make another great topic of discussion among Mars Society members. (See "A Little Piece of Heaven," *Reason*, November 1998). But then, the first investors in the New World did not have secure property rights either.

"People in England were buying and selling Kentucky back in the 1600s,   50 when it might as well have been Mars," Zubrin says. "No British citizen had been there, and it wasn't clear that British law would prevail-the French and Spanish had claims there too. But the king of England would sell patents to a nobleman, who would sell pieces to capitalists willing to speculate on the British. They'd hire someone to survey it, and then, if there were good prospects, they'd sell the land at a profit or start developing it by sending in settlers."

. . . [It is] the largest real estate project in history, and it illustrate[s] why   51 Mars is a no-lose proposition for libertarians. If colonizing the Red Planet ever becomes a practical possibility, we should be ready to get there before anyone else starts writing the rules. And even if colonization never becomes practical, even if Mars never becomes a free new world, just imagining it is good for the libertarian soul.

No
Space: You Can't Get There from Here

Neil de Grosse Tyson

From listening to space enthusiasts talk about space travel, or from watching   52 blockbuster science fiction movies, you might think that sending people to the stars is inevitable and will happen soon. Reality check: It's not and it won't the fantasy far outstrips the facts.

A line of reasoning among those who are unwittingly wishful might be,   53 "We invented flight when most people thought it was impossible. A mere sixty-five years later, we went to the Moon. It's high time we journeyed among the stars. The people who say it isn't possible are ignoring history."

My rebuttal is borrowed from a legal disclaimer often used by the in-   54 vestment industry: "Past performance is not an indicator of future returns." Analysis of the problem leads to a crucial question: What does it take to pry

From Neil de Grosse Tyson, "Space: You Can't Get There from Here," *Natural History* (September 1998). Copyright © 1998 by The American Museum of Natural History. Reprinted by permission of *Natural History*.

money out of a population to pay for major initiatives? A quick survey of the world's famously funded projects reveals three common motivations: praise of person or deity, economics, and war. Expensive investments in praise include the Great Pyramids, the Taj Mahal, and opulent cathedrals. Expensive projects launched in the hope of economic return include Columbus's voyage to the New World and Magellan's round-the-world voyage. Expensive projects with military or national defense incentives include the Great Wall of China, which helped keep out the Mongols; the Manhattan Project, which designed and built the first atomic bomb; and the Apollo space program.

When it comes to extracting really big money from an electorate, pure   55
science—in this case, exploration for its own sake—doesn't rate. Yet during the 1960s, a prevailing rationale for space travel was that space was the next frontier; we were going to the Moon because humans are innate explorers. In President Kennedy's address to a joint session of Congress on May 25, 1961, he waxed eloquent on the need to reach the next frontier. The speech included these oft-quoted lines:

> I believe that this nation should commit itself to achieving the goal, before   56
> the decade is out, of landing a man on the moon and returning him safely
> to the earth. No single space project in this period will be more impressive
> to mankind, or more important for the long-range exploration of space; and
> none will be so difficult or expensive to accomplish.

These words inspired the explorer in all of us and reverberated throughout the   57
decade. But nearly all of the astronauts were being drawn from the military—a
fact I could not reconcile with the rhetoric.

Only a month before Kennedy's Moon speech, Soviet cosmonaut Yuri   58
Gagarin had become the fast human to be launched into Earth orbit. In a rarely
replayed portion of the same address, Kennedy adopts a military posture:

> If we are to win the battle that is now going on around the world between   59
> freedom and tyranny, the dramatic achievements in space which occurred
> in recent weeks should have made clear to us all, as did Sputnik in 1957,
> the impact of this adventure on the minds of men everywhere who are
> attempting to make a determination of which road they should take.

Had the political landscape been different, Americans (Congress in particular)   60
would have been loath to part with the money (more than $200 billion in 1998

dollars) that accomplished the task. In spite of Kennedy's persuasive phrases, the debates that followed on the floor of Congress demonstrated that funding for Apollo was not a foregone conclusion.

A trip to the Moon through the vacuum of space had been in sight, even if   61 technologically distant, ever since 1926, when Robert Goddard perfected liquid-fuel rockets. This advance in rocketry made flight possible without the lift provided by air moving over a wing. Goddard himself realized that a trip to the Moon was finally possible but that it might be prohibitively expensive. "It might cost a million dollars," he once mused.

Calculations that were possible the day after Isaac Newton introduced his   62 law of universal gravitation show that an efficient trip to the Moon—in a craft escaping Earth's atmosphere at a speed of seven miles per second and coasting the rest of the way takes about a day and a half. Such a trip has been taken only nine times—all between 1968 and 1972. Otherwise, when NASA sends astronauts into "space," a crew is launched into Earth orbit a few hundred miles above our 8,000-mile-diameter planet. Space travel, this isn't.

What if you had told John Glenn, after his historic three orbits and suc-   63 cessful splashdown in 1962, that in thirty-seven years, NASA was going to send him into space once again? You can bet he would never have imagined that the best we could offer was to send him into Earth orbit again.

Space. Why can't we get there from here?   64

Let's start with money. If we can send somebody to Mars for less than $100   65 billion, then I say, let's go for it. But I have a friendly bet with Louis Friedman, the executive director of the Planetary Society (a membership-funded organization founded by the late Carl Sagan, and others, to promote the peaceful exploration of space), that we are not going to Mars any time soon. More specifically, I bet him that there will be no funded plan by any government before the year 2005 to send a manned mission to Mars. I hope I am wrong. But I will only be wrong if the cost of modern missions is brought down considerably, compared with those of the past. The following note on NASA's legendary spending habits was forwarded to me by a Russian colleague:

THE ASTRONAUT PEN   66
During the heat of the space race in the 1960s, the U.S. National Aeronautics and Space Administration [NASA] decided it needed a ballpoint pen to write in the zero gravity confines to its space capsules. After considerable research and development, the Astronaut Pen was developed at a cost of approximately $1 million U.S. The pen worked and also enjoyed some

modest success as a novelty item back here on earth. The Soviet Union, faced with the same problem, used a pencil.

Unless there is a reprise of the geopolitical circumstances that dislodged   67
$200 billion for space travel from taxpayers' wallets in the 1960s, I will remain unconvinced that we will ever send *Homo Sapiens* anywhere beyond Earth's orbit. I quote a Princeton University colleague, J. Richard Gott, a panelist who spoke a few years ago at a Hayden Planetarium symposium that touched upon the health of the manned space program: "in 1969, [space flight pioneer] Wernher von Braun had a plan to send astronauts to Mars by 1982. It didn't happen. In 1989, President George Bush promised that we would send astronauts to Mars by the year 2019. This is not a good sign. It looks like Mars is getting farther away."

To this I add that, as we approach the millennium, the only correct pre-   68
diction from the 1968 sci-fi classic 2001: *A Space Odyssey* is that things can go wrong.

Space is vast and empty beyond all earthly measure. When Hollywood   69
movies show a starship cruising through the galaxy, they typically show points of light (stars) drifting past like fireflies at a rate of one or two per second. But the distances between stars in the galaxy are so great that for these spaceships to move as indicated would require traveling at speeds up to 500 million times faster than the speed of light.

The Moon is far away compared with where you might go in a jet airplane,   70
but it sits at the tip of your nose compared with anything else in the universe. If Earth were the size of a basketball, the Moon would be the size of a softball some ten paces away-the farthest we have ever sent people into space. On this scale, Mars (at its closest) is a mile away. Pluto is 100 miles away. And Proxima Centauri, the star nearest to the Sun, is a half million miles away.

Let's assume money is no object. In this pretend-future, our noble quest to   71
discover new places and uncover scientific truths has become as effective as war for drumming up funds. If a spaceship sustained the speed needed to escape Earth—seven miles per second—a trip to the nearest star would last a long and boring 100,000 years. Too long, you say? Energy increases as the square of your speed, so if you want to double your speed, you must invest four times as much energy. A tripling of your speed requires nine times as much energy. No problem. Let's just assemble some clever engineers who will build us a spaceship that can magically summon as much energy as we want.

How about a spaceship that travels as fast as *Helios B*, the U.S.-German   72
solar probe that was the fastest-ever unmanned space probe? Launched in 1976,

it was clocked at nearly 42 miles per second (150,000 miles per hour) as it accelerated toward the Sun. (Note that this is only one-fiftieth of one percent of the speed of light.) This craft would cut the travel time to the nearest star down to a mere 15,000 years—three times the length of recorded human history.

What we really want is a spaceship that can travel near the speed of light.   73
How about 99 percent the speed of light? All you would need is 700 million times the energy that thrust the Apollo astronauts on their way to the Moon. Actually, that's what you would need if the universe were not described by Einstein's special theory of relativity. But as Einstein correctly predicted, while your speed increases, so too does your mass, forcing you to spend even more energy to accelerate your spaceship to near the speed of light. A back-of-the envelope calculation shows that you would need at least 10 billion times the energy used for our Moon voyages.

No problem. These are very clever engineers we've hired. But now we learn   74
that the closest star known to have planets is not Proxima Centauri but one that is about fifteen light-years away. Einstein's theory of special relativity shows that, while traveling at 99 percent of the speed of light, you will age at only 14 percent the pace of everybody back on Earth, so the round-trip for you will last not thirty years but about four. On Earth, however, thirty years actually do pass by, and everybody has forgotten about you.

The distance to the Moon is 10 million times greater than the distance   75
flown by the original *Wright Flyer*, built by the Wright brothers. But the Wright brothers were two guys with a bicycle repair shop. *Apollo 11*, the first moon landing, was two guys with $200 billion and ten thousand scientists and engineers and the mandate of a beloved, assassinated president. These are not comparable achievements. The cost and effort of space travel are a consequence of space's being supremely hostile to life.

You might think that the early explorers had it bad, too. Consider Gonzalo   76
Pizarro's 1540 expedition from Quito across Peru in search of the fabled land of oriental spices. Oppressive terrain and hostile natives ultimately led to the death of half Pizarro's expedition party of more than 4,000. In the classic account of this ill-fated adventure, *History of the Conquest of Peru*, William H. Prescott describes the state of the expedition party a year into the journey:

At every step of their way, they were obliged to hew open a passage with   77
their axes, while their garments, rotting from the effects of the drenching rains to which they had been exposed, caught in every bush and bramble, and hung about them in shreds. Their provisions spoiled by the weather,

had long since failed, and the livestock which they had taken with them had either been consumed or made their escape in the woods and mountain passes. They had set out with nearly a thousand dogs, many of them of the ferocious breed used in hunting down the unfortunate natives. These they now gladly killed, but their miserable carcasses furnished a lean banquet for the famished travelers.

On the brink of abandoning all hope, Pizarro and his men built from scratch a   78
boat large enough to take half the remaining men along the Napo River in search of food and supplies:

> The forests furnished him with timber; the shoes of the horses which had   79
> died on the road or had been slaughtered for food, were converted into
> nails; gum distilled from the trees took the place of pitch; and the tattered
> garments of the soldiers supplied a substitute for oakum. . . . At the end of
> two months, a brigantine was completed, rudely put together, but strong
> and of sufficient burden to carry half the company.

Pizarro transferred command of the makeshift boat to Francisco de Orellana, a   80
cavalier from Trujillo, and stayed behind to wait. After many weeks, Pizarro gave up on Orellana and returned to the town of Quito, taking yet another year to get there. Pizarro later learned that Orellana had successfully navigated his boat down the Napo River to the Amazon and, with no intention of returning, had continued along the Amazon until he emerged in the Atlantic. Orellana and his men then sailed to Cuba, where they subsequently found safe transport back to Spain.

Does this story have any lessons for would-be star travelers? Suppose one of   81
our spacecraft with a shipload of astronauts crash-lands on a distant, hostile planet—the astronauts survive, but the spacecraft is totaled. The crew adopts the spirit of our sixteenth-century explorers. Problem is, hostile planets tend to be considerably more dangerous than hostile natives. The planet might not have air. And what air it does have may be poisonous. And if the air is not poisonous, the atmospheric pressure may be 100 times higher than on Earth. If the pressure is okay, then the air temperature may be 200° below zero. Or 500° above zero. None of these possibilities bode well for our astronaut explorers, but perhaps they can survive for a while on their reserve life-support system. Meanwhile, all they would need to do is mine the planet for raw materials; build another spacecraft from

scratch, along with its controlling computers (using whatever spare parts are musterable from the crash site); build a rocket fuel factory; launch themselves back into space; and then fly back home.

I needn't dwell on the absurdity of this scenario.   82

Perhaps what we really need to do is to engineer life-forms that can survive   83 the stress of space and still conduct scientific experiments. Actually, such "life" forms have already been created. They are called robots. You don't have to feed them. They don't need life support. And most importantly, they won't be upset if you don't bring them back to Earth. People, however, generally want to breathe, eat, and eventually come home.

It's probably true that no city has yet held a ticker-tape parade for a robot.   84 But it's probably also true that no city has ever held a ticker-tape parade for an astronaut who was not the first (or the last) to do something or go somewhere. Can you name the two *Apollo 16* astronauts who walked on the Moon? Probably not. It was the second-to-last moon mission. But I'll bet you have a favorite picture of the cosmos taken by the orbiting robot known as the *Hubble Space Telescope*. I'll bet you remember the images from the Mars robotic lander, *Pathfinder*, and its deployed rover, *Sojourner*, which went "six-wheeling" across the Martian terrain. I'll further bet that you remember the *Voyager's* images of the Jovian planets and their zoo of moons from the early 1980s.

In the absence of a few hundred billion dollars in' travel money, and in the   85 presence of hostile cosmic conditions, what we need is not wishful thinking and science fiction rhetoric inspired by a cursory reading of the history of exploration. What we need, but may never have, is a breakthrough in our scientific understanding of the structure of the universe, so that we might exploit shortcuts through the space-time continuum-perhaps through wormholes that connect one part of the cosmos to another. Then, once again, reality will become stranger than fiction.

Postcript
Can Humans Go to Mars Now?

In 1996, a team of researchers, led by Everett Gibson of NASA's Johnson Space   86 Center, reported that in the interior crevices of meteorite ALH 84001—blasted from the surface of Mars some 14–18 million years ago, crashed on the ice of Antarctica 13,000 years ago, and found in Antarctica's Allan Hills in the mid-1980s—are structures that look much like fossils from the dawn of life here on Earth.

Current thinking is that the Martian "fossils" are simply mineral forma-   87
tions. But the possibility that there might be-or might have been life on Mars has
been enough to increase the level of interest in sending scientists to Mars to see
for themselves. And perhaps it would be possible to do so without bankrupting
the nation, as Robert Zubrin and Richard Wagner suggest in *The Case for Mars:
The Plan to Settle the Red Planet and Why We Must* (The Free Press, 1996). Another recent book on Mars is Jay Barbree and Martin Caidin with Susan Wright,
Destination Mars: In Art Myth, and Science (Penguin Studio, 1997).

Interest in Mars expeditions is hardly new. During the Bush administration,   88
the Synthesis Group of the White House Science Office, given the task of finding the best way to go to Mars, concluded that the benefits of such a mission
would include, besides simply getting to Mars, job creation, investment in science
and technology, and stimulated innovation.

The Synthesis Group's report included a call for the development of a new   89
"Heavy Lift Launch Vehicle" (HLLV) to reduce the cost and difficulty of getting
materials into orbit. Such a cargo vehicle has been discussed for years as a supplement to the Space Shuttle, with a great deal of emphasis on its value for constructing space stations as well as interplanetary spaceships. The dream continues—see Stanley Schmidt and Robert Zubrin, eds., *Islands in the Sky: Bold New
Ideas for Colonizing Space* (Wiley, 1996)—but an HLLV has never been approved,
and it seems very unlikely that NASA will be able to find funds for any major
new launch system that would make a Mars mission possible.

Do we need to send people to Mars? Won't robots do? These questions are   90
timely, for 1997 was the year when humans finally returned two decades after the
robotic Vikings—to Mars with the Pathfinder lander and its accompanying
Sojourner rover. The prospects for a renewal of manned space exploration, much
less a trip to Mars, seem dim. Much more likely may be combining robot explorers with a "virtual reality" feature that would let Earth-bound humans "ride
along"; see John Merchant, "A New Direction in Space," *IEEE Technology and
Society Magazine* (Winter 1994).

Is It Ethical to Sell Human Tissue?

YES: David B. Resnik, from "The Commodification of Human Reproductive Materials," *Journal of Medical Ethics* (December 1, 1998)

NO: Dorothy Nelkin and Lori Andrews, from "Homo Economicus: Commercialization of Body Tissue in the Age of Biotechnology," *Hastings Center Report* (September 1998)

ISSUE SUMMARY

YES: Professor David B. Resnik argues that it is morally acceptable to sell body parts that do not have the potential to become human beings.

NO: Dorothy Nelkin and Lori Andrews contend that treating body parts as salable property endangers individual and cultural values, encourages exploitation, and threatens to turn people into marketable products.

The April 1999 issue of *Scientific American* offers readers a special section on "The Promise of Tissue Engineering." David J. Mooney and Antonios G. Mikos discuss "Growing New Organs." Roger A. Pedersen writes about "Embryonic Stem Cells for Medicine." Michael J. Lysaght and Patrick Aevischer cover "Encapsulated Cells as Therapy." Nancy Parenteau discusses "Skin: The First Tissue-Engineered Products: The Organogenesis Story," and in that word *products* lies the crux of a vigorous debate.

Researchers have found a great many ways to use human genes, organs, and cells, and the substances they produce, to save lives. They have obtained patents on their discoveries and have founded businesses to meet health care needs. And—not at all coincidentally—they have made money. See Karen Wright, "The Body Bazaar," *Discover* (October 1998).

To some, such practices seem reminiscent of slavery and the sale of men, women, and children as if they were things instead of people. Others think of grave robbers who would sell corpses to medical schools for dissection by anatomy students. Reports that the Chinese use the organs of executed criminal for the organ-transplant market have not helped. Neither have proposals to use cells taken from aborted fetuses to treat patients such as the 500,000 Americans with Parkinson's disease, a progressive deterioration of the brain marked by progressively worsening tremors and other movement difficulties. Drugs are of limited value for this disorder and have serious side effects. However, researchers have theorized that if the damaged portion of the brain could somehow be replaced or if the brain's production of the chemical dopamine (one of many chemicals that carry signals from cell to cell within the brain) could be supplemented by living, growing fetal tissue, patients could at least be helped. See the Council on Scientific Affairs and Council on Ethical and Judicial Affairs, "Medical Applications of Fetal Tissue Transplantation," *Journal of the American Medical Association* (January 26, 1990).

In the mid-1970s, soon after abortion was legalized in the United States,   4
the National Institutes of Health (NIH) established a moratorium on (a suspension of) federal funding of research using human fetuses, either alive or dead. Legislation soon changed the moratorium to a ban, with the only exception being research intended to aid the fetus. In 1988, an NIH panel declared that the government should fund research on fetal tissue transplantation, and in 1992, Congress voted to end the ban. However, then-president George Bush vetoed the legislation because he felt that it might encourage abortion. The ban on federal funding for fetal tissue research remained in place until 1993, when President Bill Clinton ended it. However, in 1994, a presidential directive barred government-funded researchers from making human embryos for research purposes. The debate continued; See Jon Cohen, "New Fight over Fetal Tissue Grafts," *Science* (February 4, 1994).

Among the most recent results of fetal tissue research has been the isolation   5
of embryonic stem cells, which are capable of differentiating to become all or most of the cell types in the body. In 1998, researchers announced that they had been able to induce these cells to multiply in the lab and that there was immense potential for repairing and replacing damaged organs and tissues. See Gregg Easterbrook, "Medical Evolution," *New Republic* (March 1999).

Some ethicists insist that because the stem cells come from embryos, they   6
and their use should fall under the fetal research ban. But they promise to be much more versatile and useful than fetal tissue, and they can be obtained from "extra" embryos, left over from in vitro fertilization work, instead of from aborted fetuses.

If the work succeeds, embryonic stem cells will become a major component 7
of an industry that now sells engineered skin and other organs, blood and blood
products, sperm and eggs, antibodies, cytokines, and other components of the
human body for medical purposes. In the selection that follows, David B. Resnik
argues that it is morally acceptable to sell such things as long as they do not have
the potential to become human beings.

Dorothy Nelkin and Lori Andrews are less accepting. They studied several 8
body-as-property disputes that "reflect a conviction that turning tissue, cell lines,
and DNA into commodities violates body integrity, exploits powerless people,
intrudes on community values, distorts research agendas, and weakens public
trust in scientists and clinicians."

Yes
The Commodification of Human Reproductive Materials

David B. Resnik

The burgeoning reproductive assistance industry has created an uneasy tension 9
between individual economic interests and human dignity. On the one hand,
people who donate sperm or eggs claim to have a right to remuneration for goods
and services. If a person has a right to sell blood or hair, then that person should
have a right to sell gametes. On the other hand, the commodification of tissues
which have the potential to become adult human beings threatens human dignity and other moral values. Matters become even more complicated when we consider ownership of human genomes, since genomes are not simply pieces of tissue, but are blueprints for making and regulating organisms.

This essay develops a framework for thinking about the moral basis for a 10
market in human reproductive materials. It argues that the commodification of
gametes and genes is morally acceptable although there should not be a market
for zygotes, embryos, or genomes. This position may be at odds with current property laws of many countries, which forbid the buying and selling of bodies and
body parts, but the paper is concerned with moral, not legal issues. However, this
essay may have some bearing on the morality of current or pending statutes, regulations, or court decisions.

The Moral Basis for Commodifying Body Parts

Before turning to this paper's main topic, it will be useful to discuss the moral basis   11
for the commodification of body parts in general. Commodification is a social
practice for treating things as commodities, i.e., as properties that can be bought,
sold, or rented. Since commodities are alienable—they can be sold—it is possible to regard something as a form of property but not as a commodity. For example, we might view voting rights as a type of property but not as a type of commodity, since voting rights may be acquired, lost, or owned, but not sold.

Even if we treat a thing as a commodity, we may impose restrictions on its   12
commerce for moral, social, economic, or political reasons. For example, condo-
miniums are commodities that are bought, sold, and rented with various restrictions pertaining to redecorating, pets, sub-leasing, pricing, etc. Thus, one may distinguish between two forms of commodification: complete commodification
(commodification with no restriction) and incomplete commodification (commodification with restrictions). This distinction allows us to focus more clearly
on the paper's main question: should human reproductive materials be treated as
complete commodities, incomplete commodities, or not as commodities at all?

The moral basis for treating these body parts or products as commodities   13
stems from the body-as-property view found in libertarian political thought,
which holds that the body and its parts may be bought, sold, and rented. This philosophy traces its conceptual ancestry to the seventeenth century philosopher
John Locke, who argued that each individual's body belongs to that individual,
and that individuals can acquire other properties by appropriating them from
nature and mixing their labor with those things. This position implies that individuals also own their body parts and products. Locke's views on property still
play an important role in contemporary debates, and modern libertarians have
refined his position.

In the bioethics literature, several writers have defended the body-as-prop-   14
erty view. According to Andrews, the principle of autonomy provides a basis for
treating the body as property. Most of our autonomous choices presuppose some
control over our own bodies. If we think of ownership of an object as a collection
of rights to control the use of the object, then autonomous individuals own their
bodies, body parts, and body products. Many of the most important standards in
medical ethics also reflect this viewpoint. For example, invasive medical procedures require ethical justification. The very notion of an invasion of the body
draws on the body-as-property image, since an invasion is an intrusion into a territory. The doctrine of informed consent also draws on the body-as-property view.

Informed consent holds that competent individuals have a right to exclusive control over their bodies, and exclusive control over an object is a characteristic of ownership.

For the purposes of this essay, I will accept the body-as-property view. I real-   15
ize that this is a controversial position, but I will not defend it fully here. (I refer the reader to other authors for further discussion.) Instead of defending this view, I will consider some arguments against commodification and use them to argue for incomplete commodification of the living body (I include the word "living" here to indicate that this discussion does not apply to cadavers, unless indicated otherwise.)

Why might one regard the body as commodity but resist its complete com-   16
modification? To answer this question it will be useful to address two important moral arguments against commodification. The first argument appeals to Kant-ian concerns about human dignity and person hood; the second examines the social consequences of ownership practices, attitudes, and policies. I will discuss these arguments in different contexts throughout this essay.

Unconditional Value

According to the Kantian argument, commodification of the human body treats   17
people as things that can be bought and sold. If human beings can be bought and sold, then they have a market value and can be treated as mere objects by them-selves or other people. According to Kant, it is always wrong to treat people as mere objects, since human beings have inherent moral worth and dignity. Although objects can be treated as commodities and can be assigned a market value, human beings should not be treated as commodities and should not be assigned a market value. Human beings have an unconditional or absolute value. Thus, commodification of human beings is inherently wrong because it violates human dignity and worth.

I accept this Kantian position. However, I think it is possible to treat human   18
bodies as commodities without violating human dignity and worth. Although Kant uses the term "humanity" in describing our moral obligations, it is clear from reading his work that this term refers to the rational nature in human beings, i.e., "persons" or "rational agents". Kant recognized that the body houses many ele-ments, such as emotions, physical desires, and so on, that are distinct from the body's rational nature. If we accept this separation of person and body, then one might commodify the body without treating a person as a commodity. Thus, bodies that do not contain persons, such as anencephalic newborns, bodies in a

persistent vegetative state (PVS), or cadavers, could be commodified without violating the dignity or worth of persons.

Unrealistic Portrait

However, this argument paints an unrealistic portrait of the connection between   19
persons and bodies. The body is not like a coat that we can wear or a tool that
we can use. Although it is possible to distinguish between the person and the
body, these two entities are intimately connected in human beings. Selling a living human body is virtually the same thing as selling a person, and hiving exclusive control over someone else's body is tantamount to slavery. Only those who
maintain a rigid mind/body dualism will not concede that there is an intimate
relationship between the mind and body.

Yet this close connection only holds between the whole body and the per-   20
son; it does not hold between parts (or Products) of the body and the person.
Although we think of persons as being connected to whole bodies, we do not
think of persons as being tied to particular body parts or products. One does not
lose a part of one's self by cutting one's hair, urinating, or donating blood. Thus,
it is important to distinguish between a whole human body and its parts or products. Doing something to a part of the body does not imply doing something to
the whole body, and selling a part (or Product) of the body need not imply selling a whole body. Hence, one may commodify a part or product of the body without commodifying the whole body. (Some people view their personal identity as
being closely connected to certain parts, such as the brain or heart, but this observation does not undermine my general point.)

With this distinction in mind, one might hold that parts of the body may   21
be commodified even if the whole body should not be. Since the whole body is
intimately connected to the person, it should not be viewed as alienable property. Hence, the whole body should not be treated as a complete commodity. But
we can treat parts of the body as alienable even if the whole body should not be
treated this way. Thus, one may hold that selling a whole body is immoral but
regard commerce in human tissue as morally acceptable. However, there still may
be some good reasons for regulating the sale of body parts. For instance, one might
hold that it is immoral to sell body parts that are essential to the body's proper
functioning because this form of commerce would imply murder, suicide, or other
forms of killing. People may sell one kidney but not two kidneys, since human
bodies cannot function without two kidneys. (A person might still give away his
or her second kidney, but I will not address that question here.) some organs, such

as the heart and brain, may not be sold, given our current medical limitations and philosophical views about the connection between the person and the brain.

The second argument against treating bodies as commodities addresses slip-   22
pery slope concerns: although it is not inherently wrong to sell body parts or products, the acceptance of this practice will lead to adverse social consequences as we move toward complete commodification of the body. According to Kass, if we allow body parts or products to be sold, then we will start to view the whole body as an object or commodity. This attitude will lead to the dehumanization and objectification of people. Our downward slide might start with the selling of body parts, but will lead to trade in children, anencephalic babies, cadavers, and PVS patients. Eventually we will sell adults into slavery. To preserve our belief in the inherent worth of human life and dignity, we must not view any part of the body as having commercial value.

While I appreciate the force of this argument, I think that we can avoid   23
these adverse social consequences by regulating the market in body parts or products. We could forbid the sale of things whose commercialization would have an adverse impact on our respect for human life and dignity, such as human cadavers, PVS bodies, anencephalic newborns, and so on. Informed consent would also seem to be a wise restriction on any commerce in body parts or products. By requiring that sellers and buyers give informed consent before transaction takes place, we may be able to avoid many pitfalls. One of the biggest threats from a market in body parts comes when other people are allowed to treat a person's body as a commodity without that person's consent.

Other writers object to commodification on the grounds that it undermines   24
the gift relationship that currently exists between donors and recipients of human organs. A market in body parts and products will eventually destroy this relationship by transforming it into an economic transaction. I do not find this argument very convincing since many commodities that are routinely bought and sold are also given as gifts, such as clothing, land, cars, and labour. People will always have reasons and motives for giving gifts, even when those gifts have commercial value. The mere fact that an object can be bought or sold need not destroy our ability to transfer that object as a gift.

Some writers have pointed out that commodifying parts of the body might   25
lead to a practice where people are required to sell body parts or products to pay outstanding debts or to meet the demands of retributive justice. Thus, the phrase "it cost me an arm and a leg" would be too real to invoke laughter. However, I think we can avoid these disturbing consequences if we enact some restrictions

on the transference of body parts or products. For instance, we could make it illegal to take body parts or products to pay debts or administer punishments.

Finally, one might argue that the selling of body products could lead to the   26
exploitation of the economically worse-off members of our society. People might sell their kidneys out of economic hardship. But why would we think it is wrong to sell body parts out of economic need? After all, people take on many dangerous and degrading occupations for economic reasons. If it is wrong to sell kidneys out of economic need, then it is also wrong to work in a coal mine or deliver pizzas in dangerous neighborhoods. The problem with working under these conditions is not the economic transaction itself; it is the fairness of the transaction. We have laws that protect people from exploitation and regulate working conditions. Similar laws could also apply to a market in body parts and products.

The preceding arguments against commodification all suggest a common   27
response: body parts and products, but not the whole body, should be regarded as incomplete commodities. In order to answer Kantians' concerns about the objectification of people, we should not permit a market in while, living, human bodies; in order to address the slippery slope argument, we should regulate the market in body parts and products. I will now apply this analysis to the comodification of human reproductive materials, paying special attention to the two main arguments against commodification.

The Commodification of Reproductive Materials
Is it immoral to buy and sell sperm, eggs, zygotyes, embryos, or genomes? . . .   28

Commodification of Gametes
If it is morally acceptable to commodify body parts or products, then gametes may   29
be bought and sold, since gametes are body products. If individuals can buy and sell blood, hair, or tissue, then they should also be allowed to buy and sell gametes. However, the two arguments against commodification pertain to the sale of gametes. First, one might object to the commodification of gametes on the grounds that gametes are unlike other cells and tissues. Sperm and eggs contain half a human genome and can unite to form a zygote. A zygote can become a child if it implants in a uterus and develops normally. Thus, selling gametes is dangerously close to selling persons, since gametes can become persons. Although I agree that gametes (germ cells) are unlike other body cells (somatic cells), I do not find this argument very persuasive. Selling gametes is not the same thing as selling persons or zygotes, since gametes are not even potential persons.

A gamete is more like half of a blueprint for making a house (person) than a whole blueprint (zygote) or house that is under construction (fetus or child).

Second, one might argue that the commodification of gametes will have   30 adverse effects on other social values, such as our respect for human life and dignity. The commodification of gametes could create a market in children or adults, or it could lead to the exploitation of poor women for their eggs. For example, suppose that sperm are sold in fertility clinics and are advertised in magazines and newspapers. The market could set a price for gametes and those people with the "best" qualities could demand the highest prices for their reproductive materials. I think this type of development could threaten our notions of human dignity and worth; hence, we may need to regulate the market in gametes. Since the selling of gametes has not yet invaded our popular culture, this situation bears watching. In any case, this argument only shows that gametes should be treated as incomplete commodities.

The Commodification of Zygotes and Embryos

One might also argue that zygotes and embryos (henceforth just zygotes) can be   31 commodified on the grounds that they are simply body products. If gametes can be bought and sold, then zygotes can also be bought and sold. To make full sense of the objections to this argument, we must say something about when a human organism becomes a person, since the Kantian view forbids a market in persons but not a market in bodies, as such. If we follow the Kantian account of personhood, then a human being does not become a person until he or she can understand and follow moral imperatives. Thus, zygotes and other later stages of development are not persons. Kantian concerns about the objectification of persons therefore have little bearing on the selling of zygotes.

However, zygotes are potential persons. Zygotes, unlike gametes, have a   32 complete set of genetic instruction and normally also have their own genetic identity. Although human development depends on many different environmental factors and gene-environment interactions, zygotes are much more like adult human beings than gametes. As potential persons, zygotes merit special moral concern. Potential persons merit special moral concern because the way we treat these beings can have a profound effect on the way we treat actual persons. A society that allows babies to be bought and sold is more likely to allow adults to be bought and sold than one that does not. Likewise, a society that allows zygotes to be bought and sold is more likely to accept a market for children and adults than one that does not. Moreover, this is not a problem that can be handled simply through regulation, since a market in zygotes would imply a profound change in our understanding of human beings and could lead to the commodification and objectification of children and adults. Since even a limited market for zygotes can create this dangerous slippery slope, zygotes should not be commodified. ...

The Commodification of Genomes

The last issue I would like to consider is the ownership of human genomes. To understand issues pertaining to the commodification of genomes and their parts (i.e., genes or gene fragments), it is important to realize that there is a fundamental difference between genomes, gametes, and zygotes. Gametes and zygotes are physical entities that can be produced, destroyed, corrupted, stored, or harvested; genomes and genes, on the other hand are not mere physical entities. Gametes and zygotes have spatial-temporal boundaries; genomes and genes cannot be located in any particular time or place. Genomes and genes are essentially information for making and regulating organisms. As information, they constitute abstract objects that can be realized in biochemical structures or represented by linguistic symbols. They are more like software than hardware. In legalistic terms, genomes (and genes) are best viewed as intellectual property.   33

Viewing the genome as intellectual property has important implications for moral arguments for and against its commodification. Western intellectual property laws distinguish between items that can belong to individuals and items that cannot be owned. For example, people cannot own scientific laws or concepts. People also cannot own natural phenomena, such as benzene, but they may patent processes for making benzene. The general thrust of these laws is to distinguish between ideas (or abstract objects) and tangible expressions or applications of those ideas. Ideas are common resources and cannot be owned by individuals, although particular expressions or application of ideas can become person property. Thus, these laws assume that only tangible expressions of ideas can be commodified.   34

There are two moral arguments for distinguishing between ideas and their expressions or applications. If we think of ideas as natural resources, then Locke's views on property imply that ideas can be treated as common resources. People may own things that result from adding labor to those ideas, for example, inventions or original works, but they may not own the ideas themselves. According to the utilitarian approach to intellectual property, intellectual property laws should promote social utility through encouraging scientific and technological progress. The most effective way to promote this kind of progress is to encourage the sharing of ideas, data, and theories while allowing scientists and inventors to   35 profit from and receive credit for their works. Thus, there is a solid moral basis for laws that treat ideas as common resources but allow the ownership of particular expressions or applications of ideas.

I believe that the preceding discussion of intellectual property can provide 36 us with some insights into the commodification of human genomes. If we treat genomes as intellectual property, then genomes are natural phenomena. As such, they are common resources that may not be owned, although individuals may own particular expressions or applications of genomes. If I invent a technique for analyzing, sequencing or cloning a genome (or one of its parts), then I may patent that invention; if I create an original work describing a genome (or one of its parts), then I may have copyrights that govern the reproduction of that work. Hence, people may buy and sell invention and original works pertaining to the genome or genes, but they may not buy or sell naturally occurring genomes or genes.

Having said this much in favor of some form of ownership of the genome, 37 I would like to address the two objections to commodification discussed previously. We can imagine some objectionable forms of ownership pertaining to the genome. For example, biotechnology companies have patented genetically engineered mice. What if a company attempted to patent a genetically engineered human being? Since patents govern the buying, selling, and production of inventions, this form of ownership would entail the ownership of persons, since the patent would allow the company to control the production and marketing of whole human bodies. Copyrights on the whole genome could result in similar problems. A person who copyrighted an entire genome would be able to sell these copyrights to interested buyers. Although this form of commerce would not constitute commodification of a whole human body, it could threaten our respect for human life and human dignity: a society that allows copies of genomes to be bought and sold is more likely to allow human beings to be bought and sold than one that does not. Selling copyrights to an entire genome is very much like selling a zygote, since genomes can be used to make zygotes.

On the other hand, patents and copyright on parts of the genome would 38 not entail the commodification of whole human bodies and probably would not threaten our respect for human life and human dignity. Patents or copyrights on individual genes would be no more pernicious than patents or copyrights on artificial body parts, such as artificial skin, blood, or heart valves. Thus, copyrights and patents can be extended to parts of the genome, but they should not be applied to the whole genome. However, there may be some good reasons to regulate the market in gene patents and copyrights in order to prevent slippery slope effects. For instance, we might choose to restrict the marketing of human genes used for the sole purpose of genetic engineering; we might forbid people or companies from acquiring a whole genome; we might take steps to prevent companies from obtaining monopolies on human genes, and so on. Hence, the entire human genome should not be regarded as a commodity, although parts of the genome may be regarded as incomplete commodities.

No
Homo Economicus

Dorothy Nelkin and Lori Andrews

In recent years, biotechnology techniques have transformed a variety of human   39
body tissue into valuable and marketable research materials and clinical products.
Blood can serve as the basis for immortalized cell lines for biological studies and
the development of pharmaceutical products; the catalogue from the American
Tissue Culture Catalogue lists thousands of people's cell lines that are available
for sale. Snippets of foreskin are used for the development of artificial skin. Biopsied tissue is used to manufacture therapeutic quantities of genetic material.

Body tissue also has commercial value beyond the medical and research   40
contexts. Placenta is used to enrich shampoos, cosmetics, and skin care products.
Kary Mullis, a Nobel Prize-winning geneticist, founded a company called Star
Gene that uses gene amplification techniques to make and market jewelry, containing DNA cloned from famous rock stars and athletes. The idea, says Mullis,
is that "teenagers might pay a little money to get a piece of jewelry containing the
actual piece of amplified DNA of somebody like a rock star."

There is also a market for services to collect and store one's tissue outside   41
the body. People can pay to store blood prior to surgery or embryos in the course
of in-vitro fertilization. A Massachusetts company, BioBank, stores excess tissue removed during cosmetic or other surgical procedures for the patient's
future use. New companies such as Safe-T-Child and Child Trail have formed
to collect and store tissue samples to identify children who have been kidnapped. And a company called Identigene advertises on taxicabs and billboards

From Dorothy Nelkin and Lori Andrews, "Homo Economicus: Commercialization of Body Tissue in the Age of Biotechnology," *Hastings Center Report*, vol. 28, no. 5 (September/October 1998). Copyright © 1998 by The Hastings Center. Reprinted by permission. References omitted.

(call 1-800-DNA-TYPE) for a service to collect tissue for DNA identification that would establish paternity in child support disputes. There are about fifty private DNA testing centers in the United States, hundreds of university laboratories undertaking DNA research, and over 1,000 biotechnology companies developing commercial products from bodily materials.

These expanding markets have increased the value of human tissue, and   42
institutions with ready access to tissue find they possess a capital resource. Access to stored tissue samples is sometimes included in collaborative agreements between hospitals and biotechnology firms. In a joint venture agreement, Sequana Therapeutics, Inc., a California biotechnology firm, credited the New York City cancer hospital, Memorial-Sloan Kettering, with $5 million in order to obtain access to its bank of cancer tissue biopsies that could be useful as a source of genetic information.

Physicians who treat families with genetic disease are approaching geneti-   43
cists and offering to "sell you my families"—meaning that they will, for a fee, give the researcher their patients' blood samples. Scientists who isolate certain genes are then patenting them and profiting from their use in genetic tests. Hospitals in Great Britain and Russia sell tissue in order to augment their limited budgets. Between 1976 and 1993 Merieux UK collected 360 tons of placental tissue each year from 282 British hospitals and sent them to France for use in manufacturing drugs. Human tissue has become so valuable that it is sometimes a target for corporate espionage and theft.

In the United States the potential for commercial gain from the body grew   44
as consequence of legislative measures that were enacted in the 1980s to encourage the commercial development of government-funded research. Legislation allowed universities and nonprofit institutions to apply for patents on federally funded projects and also provided tax incentives to companies investing in academic research. At the same time, changes in patent law turned commercial attention toward research in genetics. A landmark U.S. Supreme Court case in 1980 granted a patent on a life form—a bacterium—setting the stage for the patenting of human genes. In the mid-1980s the U.S. patent Office began granting rights for human genes. It has since received over 5,000 patent applications and has granted more than 1,500, including patents for bone and brain tissue and DNA coding for human proteins.

Today, joint ventures between industry and universities are thriving, and   45
research scientists are increasingly tied to commercial goals. Industry has become a significant source of funding for genetics research. As Francis Collins observed,

companies have resources for gene hunting that the academies cannot match: "It's important not to ignore the way things have changed in the last 3 years in human genetics [because of industry]. Gene hunting used to be a purely academic exercise." Nearly every major geneticist is associated with a biotechnology firm; some as directors, others as consultants. And scientists, hospitals, and universities are patenting genes.

The body, of course, has long been exploited as a commercial and mar-   46
ketable entity, as athletes, models, prostitutes, surrogate mothers, and beauty queens are well aware. Yet there is something strange and troubling about traffic in body tissue, the banking of human cells, the patenting of genes. In the 1984 public hearings concerning anatomical gifts, Albert Gore, then a U.S. Congressman, was troubled by a growing tendency to treat the body as a commodity in a market economy: "It is against our system of values to buy and sell parts of human beings.... The notion has perhaps superficial attraction to some because we have learned that the market system will solve lots of problems if we just stand out of the way and let it work. It is very true. This ought to be an exception because you don't want to invest property rights in human beings.... It is wrong."

But what is troubling about the commodification of the body? What is the   47
problem with the growing interest in human tissue for the manufacturing of pharmaceutical or bioengineered products? Clearly the interest in the body is driven by instrumental and commercial values; but so too, as Gore suggested, are most technological endeavors. Moreover, much of the body tissue useful for biotechnology innovation—hair, blood, sperm—is replenishable. And we normally regard body materials such as umbilical cord blood, foreskin, and the tissue discarded after surgery—and, in some cases, even the excess embryos created for in-vitro fertilization—as simply refuse, like bloodied bandages and other medical wastes. Why not, then, view the body as a useful and exploitable resource if this can advance scientific research, contribute to progress, or provide lifesaving benefits to others? Why are there demonstrations against the privatization of cord-blood, lawsuits against the commercialization of cell lines, protests against the patenting of genes? Why are commercial developments in the removal, storage, and transformation of human tissue controversial?

To answer these questions, we undertook a study of several prominent dis-   48
putes over the ownership of the body, the collection of human tissue, and its distribution as a resource. These disputes reflect the collision between commercial claims for body tissue and individual interests or cultural values. They reflect a conviction that turning tissue, cell lines, and DNA into commodities violates

body integrity, exploits powerless people, intrudes on community values, distorts research agendas, and weakens public trust in scientists and clinicians.

Historical Controversies

Research and clinical uses of body parts have been controversial since the early 49 days of anatomical dissection. The process of cutting and fragmenting the body once evoked images of evil, and Dante-esque visions of Hell. As the Renaissance brought growing interest in anatomy, the use of bodies in medical schools was gradually accepted.…

Today, old tensions have taken on new dimensions as the commercial 50 potential of human tissue has caught the entrepreneurial imagination. Few laws are in place to address the proper uses of cells, tissues and genes. Instead, disputes over the ownership, collection, and distribution of human tissue have ended up in the media and in the courts.

The Ownership of Body Tissue

John Moore, a patient with hairy cell leukemia, had his spleen removed at the 51 University of California, Los Angeles, School of Medicine in 1976. His physician, Dr. David W. Golde, patented certain chemicals in Moore's blood purportedly without his knowledge or consent and set up contracts with a Boston Company, negotiating shares worth $3 million. Sandoz, the Swiss pharmaceutical company, paid a reported $15 million for the right to develop the Mo cell line.

Moore began to suspect that his tissue was being used for purposes beyond 52 his personal care when UCLA cancer specialists kept taking samples of blood, bone marrow, skin, and sperm for seven years. When Moore discovered in 1984 that he had become patent number 4,438,032, he sued the doctors for malpractice and property theft. His physicians claimed that Moore had waived his interest in his body parts when he signed a general consent form giving the UCLA pathology department the right to dispose of his removed tissue. But Moore felt that his integrity was violated, his body exploited, and his tissue turned into a product: "My doctors are claiming that my humanity, my genetic essence, is their invention and their property. They view me as a mine from which to extract biological material. I was harvested."

The court held that clinicians must inform patients in advance of surgical 53 procedures that their tissue could be used for research, but it denied Moore's claim that he owned his tissue. Who then should reap the *profits* from parts taken from an individual's body? The court decided that the doctor and biotechnology company rather than the patient should profit. The decision rested on the promise of biotechnology innovation. The court did not want to slow down research by "threaten[ing] with disabling civil liability innocent parties who are engaged in socially useful activities, such as researchers who have no reason to believe that their use of a particular cell sample is against a donor's wishes." The court was concerned that giving Moore a property right to his tissue would "destroy the economic incentive to conduct important medical research."

Justice Stanley Mosk, dissenting, objected to the notion that the body—   54
"the physical and temporal expression of the unique human persona"—could be regarded as a product for commercial exploitation. For, he argued, the spectre of direct abuse, of torture, of involuntary servitude haunts the laboratories and boardrooms of today's biotechnological research industrial complex (p. 515).

The privileging of biotechnology companies encouraged a genetics gold   55
rush. In 1992 Craig Venter, a molecular biologist, left the National Institutes of Health to form the Institute for Genomic Research (TIGR), where he compiled the world's largest human gene data bank containing at least 150,000 fragments of DNA sequences. The Institute for Genomic Research was initially funded by a $70 million grant from a firm, Human Genome Services (HGS). Two months after the agreement, HGS contracted with SmithKline Beecham, which gained an exclusive stake in the database with first rights on patentable discoveries. Geneticist David King described the situation: "you have a corporation trying to monopolize control of a large part of the whole human genome, literally the human heritage. Should this become private property?"

The concerns about commercial exploitation of the body expressed in   56
Moore have assumed more complex dimensions in disputes over the collection of human tissue in a global context. Scientists and biotechnology companies are searching the world for disease genes. But critics have viewed the collection of tissue from indigenous populations as a violation of cultural values, and associate these efforts with past forms of exploitation.

Collecting Tissue from Indigenous Populations

Because people from isolated populations may have unique body tissue, western   57
geneticists, biotechnology companies, and researchers from the human Genome Diversity Project (HGDP) are seeking blood and hair samples from indigenous groups throughout the world. Their goals are to find disease genes by identifying families with a high rate of genetically linked conditions; to develop genetic tests and therapeutic products; and to "immortalize" the DNA from "vanishing populations."

In March 1995 researchers from the National Institutes of Health [NIH]   58
obtained a virus-infected cell line from a man from the Hagahai tribe in Papua,
New Guinea. The cell line, which could be used to develop a diagnostic test,
became patent number 5,397,696. Accused of exploitation, the NIH withdrew
the patent claim in December 1996 Meanwhile, Sequana Therapeutics, collabo-
rating with the University of Toronto, collected DNA samples from the island of
Tristan de Cunha for research on asthma and then sold the rights to develop therapeutic technologies for $70 million to a German company, Boehringer Ingel-
heim. Western scientists are also negotiating contracts to collect DNA samples
from Chinese families with genetic diseases. But china's eugenics policies include
efforts to identify families with genetic abnormalities so as to prevent them from
reproducing. Thus the DNA samples may also be a valuable resource for Chinese
authorities seeking to implement oppressive eugenics laws.

The HGDP has confronted angry opposition. Indigenous groups view the   59
taking of their tissue as exploitation. They have accused the program of violating
community values, "biopiracy" or "biocolonialism," one more effort to divide
their social world. A representative of an indigenous group opined, "You've taken
our land, our language, our culture, and even our children. Are you now saying
you want to take part of our bodies as well?" Some objections reflect beliefs,
expressed in collective rituals involving blood or body parts, about the social
meaning of body tissue—its role in maintaining the integrity of the community
and the relationship of the individual to the collective. Others believe that their
future might be compromised by the collection of their DNA. Once scientists
have what they need from them, there would be no reason to help them stay
alive. This pessimistic view was fueled by researchers who promoted the project
as a way to "immortalize" the cell lines of groups that will become extinct.

Indigenous groups also question the relevance of the scientific work to their   60
own health needs, which have less to do with genetic disease than with common
disorders such as diarrhea. They argue that DNA is collected, often without adequate knowledge or consent, and then used for products relevant only in wealthy
nations. ...

In response to concerns about exploitation of indigenous resources, the   61
United Nations Convention on Biodiversity (1192) had sought to assure that
national governments receive just compensation for commercial use of both
human and agricultural resources. But the interest in genetic resources suggests
that this approach may lead to further exploitation of indigenous groups as they
become profit centers for their governments. Moreover, some groups do not want

compensation—the very idea of commercializing the body offends them and contradicts their world view. For them, the body has a social meaning tied to colonial history, traditional communal rituals, and concerns about continued exploitation. …

Theft—The Ultimate Symbol of Commodification

Products that attain commercial value are inevitably subject to theft, a not   62
uncommon form of redistribution. The traffic in body parts has persisted, spurred as in the nineteenth century, by a shortage of organs and tissue. Body parts have been bought from coroners, stolen from the site of accidents, and sold to meet the demands of industry and medicine. Today, cell lines are a target for international espionage. In a sting operation, agents of the Food and Drug Administration posed as representatives of a tissue bank and ordered tissue from a California dentist who tried to sell them body parts at a discount. In France, a government investigation exposed an embezzlement scheme in which private companies billed local hospitals for synthetic ligament tissue that, it turned out, came from human tissue, which in France cannot legally be bought and sold.

Funeral home personnel and coroners have also engaged in tissue theft. In   63
one case, a morgue employee allegedly stole body parts and sold them nationally —a situation uncovered unexpectedly when the body of a twenty-one-day-old infant was exhumed for other purposes and found to be missing his heart, lungs, eyes, pituitary gland, aorta, kidneys, spleen, and key brain parts. In Britain seventeen people who contracted Creutzfeld Jacob disease from human growth hormone accused the Medical Research Council and the Department of Health of unlawfully buying, from mortuaries, the pituitary glands form 900,000 bodies to extract the growth hormone. The tissue was taken without the consent of the individuals before death or their families, in violation of British law.

Demands for spare embryos have also led to undercover redistribution in   64
the in vitro fertilization business. At the University of California at Irvine, over 75 couples were affected by theft of eggs and embryos at the university clinic where Dr Ricardo Asch had apparently been secretly selling some of the eggs extracted from his infertility patients to other patients who were duped into thinking they were from legitimate donors. More than forty civil lawsuits were filed. In July 1997 the university agreed to pay $14 million to seventy-five couples; two dozen lawsuits still remain. Embryo theft was "predictable, almost inevitable," says Boston University health law professor George Annas. "The field [of in-vitro fertilization] is so lucrative and so unregulated that someone was just bound to do it."

Problems With the Business of Bodies

References to body parts in the medical and scientific literature increasingly   65
employ a language of commerce—of banking, investment, insurance, compensation, and patenting. Gene sequences are patented; cord blood is a "hot property,"
the body is a "medical factory.' Companies "target" appropriate markets for their
products. Pathology organizations lobby the government to allow them to use
stored tissue samples without consent, for they view such samples as "treasure
troves" or "national resources" for research. Geneticists talk of "prospecting" for
genes. The body is a "project"—a system that can be divided and dissected down
to the molecular level. In a striking statement in the *Moore* case, the defendant,
UCLA, claimed that even if Moore's cells were his property, as a state university
it had a right to take the cells under "eminent domain."

The body tissue disputes we have described—over the ownership collec-   66
tion, and distribution of body tissue—raise questions about the assumptions
underlying this language of commerce. Who will profit? Who will lose? How will
exploitation be avoided? They reflect conflicting beliefs about the body. Is body
tissue to be defined as waste, like the material in a hospital be pan? Is it refuse that
is freely available as raw material for commercial products? Or does body tissue
have inherent value as part of a person? Are genes the essence of an individual
and a sacred part of the human inheritance? Or are they, as a director of SmithK-
line Beecham purportedly claimed, "the currency of the future."

Disputes suggest that commodifying human tissue, usually without the per-   67
son's knowledge or consent, is troubling because it threatens the well-being of
individuals and violates social assumptions about the body. And they suggest that
commercialization can also have serious implications for science and medical
practice.

Individual Concerns. Commercial interests continue to evoke fears of patient   68
exploitation. John Moore's experience suggested that the commercial interests of
doctors can encourage them to take more tissue than is needed for the benefit of
their patients. Physicians or institutions with economic interests can also easily
influence the decisions of individuals in vulnerable situations. Patients who are
hospitalized may be reluctant to withhold consent. New parents, at an uncertain
time in their lives, are vulnerable to the pitch of cord blood company salesmen.

The market incentives to treat body tissue as a valuable and collectible   69
commodity may also have troubling psychological effects. Psychologists have
found that a sense of coherence and body integrity is essential to individual development and a person's sense of self, and that control over what is done to the

body or its parts is important to psychological well-being. Some people try to place limits on how their body is used. In light of past research exploitation, some African-American women refuse to allow amniotic tissue to be collected for prenatal diagnosis out of concern about the uses that could be made of this tissue. And some families with genetic diseases who provided tissue to trusted researchers for investigations related to their disease object when they learn their tissue was to be sold to commercial enterprises for unrelated research. Using individuals' tissue in ways that violate their beliefs can disturb their sense of self-agency.

The potential for commercialization creates incentives for researchers and   70 physician to ignore patients' wishes and their beliefs about the body. Jewish tradition maintains that as man was created in the image of God, in death the body should retain the unity of that image. Consequently, in the Orthodox Jewish community, the body must be buried whole. Unauthorized taking of tissue for commercial use would violate these religious beliefs about the body. . . .

Social Concerns.   The body is not just a neutral object. We have, says historian   71 Anthony Synnott, "imposed layers of ideas, images, meanings and associations on these biological systems which together operate and maintain our physical bodies. Our bodies and body parts are loaded with cultural symbolism." The norms that guide the disposition of body tissue reflect community ideals and social priorities. The history of blood donation, for example, suggests the importance of beliefs about the relationship of blood to communal values. Giving blood and body tissue is a way to affirm social connectedness by linking donors to strangers and donations to the public good. "Donations" based on economic self-interest rather than altruism tend to be devalued.

. . . [C]ritics [have] viewed commercialization as violating the social values   72 involved in free and anonymous donation. They questioned the legitimacy of treating human tissue as private property and worried about fairness and equity in its distribution. So too in the patent disputes. . . .

Commercial interests in the body also evoke more general moral and reli-   73 gious reservations. The Boston-based Council for Responsible Genetics declared that "[t]he commercialization and expropriation of these life materials is a violation of the sanctity of human animal, an plat life." If secular groups are vaguely uncomfortable about patenting the body, religious groups are more explicit: they believe that patenting turns the body into a product, violating the sovereignty of God and the "inherent sanctity of life." The issue, said a representative from the Southern Baptist Convention, "is going to dwarf the pro-life debate within a few years."

Implications for Science and Medicine

The business of bodies affects the fiduciary relationship between doctors and   74
patients. Medical research and clinical practice are ideally considered distinct
from the motives of the market. We are leery of scientists who have profit
motives in the outcomes of their research or clinicians who have economic
interests in particular procedures. Yet a 1996 study of 789 biomedical papers published by academic scientists in Massachusetts found that in 34 percent, one or
more authors stood to make money from the results they were reporting. This
was because they either held a patent or were an officer or advisor of a biotech
firm exploiting the research. In none of the articles was this financial interest
disclosed.

Patenting in biomedicine hardly enhances trust. Nor does it necessarily   75
encourage the best research. Though considered essential to protect discoveries
and provide incentives for investment in research, patenting may actually
impede research. Surveys find that patenting has led to reductions in openness
and data sharing, delays in publication, and tendencies to select research projects
of short-term commercial interest. In several cases, corporations with vested
interests have tried to suppress the publication of research findings that were not
in their interests. Strains over conflicting commitments have caused some
researchers to sever their commercial ties. . . .

. . . [C]ommercialization of body parts may prevent patients from obtaining ' 76
appropriate health care services by obstructing the distribution of research benefits. Patent rights allow the researcher who identifies a gene to earn royalties on
any test or therapy created with that gene. A British hospital that tested a patient
for cystic fibrosis was asked to pay royalties because a private company held the
patent on the gene. Some laboratories are giving up a useful hormone test to
determine whether a fetus has Down syndrome because the royalty fees exceed
Medicaid reimbursement. A patent monopoly on cord blood storage would ham-
per the development of community cord blood banks, leaving patients who do
not have the money to store their infant's blood without a remedy if their child
develops a disorder requiring a cordblood transplantation. The real costs in such
cases are borne by patients denied appropriate treatment.

There is growing concern that market principles have been improperly   77
applied. People have obtained commercial rights without making an inventive
contribution or without determining the purpose of their discovery. Dr. Mark
Bogart merely noted the correspondence between a particular hormone level and
the chance that a fetus has Down syndrome, yet he was granted a patent and is

trying to collect a fee for each diagnostic test relying on measurement of that hormone. Protesting health care providers have filed suit to challenge the patent.

Similarly, numerous patents have been issued on partial gene sequences, 78 even though the patent seekers did not know what the sequences did. In July 1991 Human Genome Sciences received a patent on the DNA sequence for the CCR5 receptor on immune system cells. Now it has been found the receptor opens cells to HIV infection, providing a basis for the development of treatments for HIV infection. But every researcher developing such a treatment will have to pay a licensing fee to Human Genome Sciences.

Incidents like these trouble even venture capitalists. Michael Heller and 79 Rebecca Eisenberg of the University of Michigan School of Law point out a paradoxical consequence of the grant of biotechnology patents: "A proliferation of intellectual property rights upstream may be stifling life-saving innovations further downstream in the course of research and development."

The Policy Response

The law has not yet settled with respect to controlling commercial interests in 80 body tissue and resolving questions of consent and compensation for the use of cells and genes. However, we are beginning to see some efforts to extend to this area the principles of consent and noncommodification that were developed to regulate organ donation. Certain professional organizations are emphasizing the need to obtain patient consent even if the tissue used has already been removed from the patient's body. When researchers sought to analyze previously collected tissue samples at the Centers for Disease Control, an advisory group pointed out that "retaining tissue samples or immortalizing cell lines may violate cultural or religious beliefs." Guidelines issued by the American College of Medical Genetics require that patients be asked for consent before research is done on their tissue samples and that patients have an option to have their samples withdrawn or destroyed at that time.

But the policy world is going further, questioning whether commercializa- 81 tion of the body should be allowed even with patient consent. Some scientists as well as activists have challenged the patenting of human genes. And at least one government ha stepped in to challenge the transformation of a research tissue bank into a private company resource: when a French foundation holding the DNA fragments of 5,000 diabetics tried to sell this database to an American biotechnology company, the French government intervened; the ownership of this resource remains in dispute.

Robert Bellah has observed that "[a]ll the primary relationships in our soci- 82
ety, those between employers and employees, between lawyers and clients,
between doctors and patients... are being stripped of any moral understanding
other than that of market exchange." In this climate, developments in biotechnology are increasingly linking the biomedical sciences with the aggressive commercialization that is invading nearly every sector of human life. But as biomedical research becomes more closely tied to commercial goals, the encroachment
of the market is triggering a growing sense of disillusionment and mistrust. For the
encroachment of commercial practices on the human body is increasingly challenging individual and cultural values, encouraging exploitation through the collection and use of tissue, and turning tissue (and potentially people) into marketable products.

Postscript
Is It Ethical to Sell Human Tissue?

As noted in the introduction to this issue, the ethics of selling human organs, tis- 83
sues, cells, and products is hardly a new issue. But it has been given a new urgency
by the recent discover of embryonic stem cells. Ethicists Karen Lebacqz, Micheal
M. Mendiola, Ted Petters, Ernie W. C. Young, and Laurie Zoloth-Dorfman
reviewed the situation at some length in "Research with Human embryonic Stem
Cells: Ethical Considerations," *Hastings Center Report* (March 1999), concluding
that such research can be performed even though there are a number of unan-
swered questions, including those of control of fetal tissue, global justice, and consensus in a pluralistic society.

American society as a whole seems to agree that it is appropriate to forge 84
ahead, albeit with some caution. For the moment, only two companies,
Advanced Cell Technology (ACT) of Worcester, Massachusetts, and Geron
Corporation of California, are progressing with plans to develop embryonic stem
cells as a medical resource, using only private funds. On April 12, 1999, the NIH
posted on its Web site a "Fact Sheet on Stem Cell Research" (http://www.
nih.gov/news/pr/apr99/od-21.htm) saying, "After a thorough analysis of the
DHHS, [Department of Health and Human Services] concluded that the congressional prohibition on the use of DHHS funds for certain types of human
embryo research does not apply to research utilizing human pluripotent stem cells
because such cells are not embryos. . . . [C]urrgent law permits federal funds to be
used for research utilizing human pluripotent stem cells. The National Institutes
of Health (NIH) plans to move forward in a careful and deliberate fashion to

develop rigorous guidelines that address the special ethical, legal, and social issues relevant to this research. The NIH will not fund research using human pluripoent stem cells until guidelines are developed and widely disseminated to the research community and an oversight process is in place." Proposed guidelines were scheduled to be published in the *Federal Register* during the summer of 1999.

Caution is necessary because the issue—particularly its link to embryos and   85 abortion—has aroused opposition from conservative legislators and pro-life activists. There is even considerable disagreement on whether or not federal law permits NIH to fund the research, despite its claims. In May 1999, senate Majority Leader Trent Lott (R-Mississippi) said that the ban on federal funding of human embryo research was not about the be lifted despite a draft recommendation of the National Bioethics Advisory Commission (NBAC). See Joyce Howard Price, "Pro-Lifers Gear up to Guard Ban on Stem Cell Research," *Washington Times* (May 30, 1999). At its 32nd meeting in June 1999, the NBAC affirmed that "federally financed scientists be allowed to derive embryonic stem cells from human embryos and conduct research on stem cells derived by others" ("Ethics Panel Recommends Stem Cell Use," *The New York Times* [June 30, 1999]).

For other views of this issue, see Emanuel D. Thorne, "Tissue Transplants: 86 The Dilemma of the Body's Growing Value," *The Public Interests* (Winter 1990); Andrew Simmons, "Brave New Harvest," *Christianity Today* (November 19, 1990); Stephen G. Post, "Fetal Tissue Transplant: The Right to Question Progress," *America* (January 12, 1991); and John Fletcher, "Human Fetal and Embryo Research: Lysenkoism in Reverse—How and Why?" in Robert H. Blank and Andrea L. Bonnicksen, eds., *Emerging Issues in Biomedical Policy, vol. 2* (Columbia University Press, 1993).

Chapter 10
NATURE AND THE ENVIRONMENT

Rachel Louise Carson (1907–1964), professor, aquatic biologist, editor, and writer, was born in Springfield, Pennsylvania, and died in Silver Spring, Maryland. She received a B.A. degree from the Pennsylvania College for Women in 1929 and an M.A. from Johns Hopkins University in 1932 before pursuing further graduate study at Marine Biological Laboratory in Massachusetts. Carson was variously affiliated with the University of Maryland, on the zoology staff; with the U.S. Bureau of Fisheries; and with Johns Hopkins University. She held memberships in the American Ornithologists' Union, the National Institute of Arts and Letters, the Royal Society of Literature, the Audubon Society, and the Society of Women Geographers. Her extensive awards and honors include the George Westinghouse Science Writing Award in 1950; the National Book Award in 1951 for *The Sea Around Us*, a Guggenheim fellowship, and numerous medals, honorary citations, and degrees. Carson's mother led her to a love of nature, which she successfully combined with her desire to write. She began publishing at the age of ten. Widely praised for her vivid descriptions of the sea in the nonfiction best-seller *The Sea Around Us* (1951; rev. ed., 1966, reprinted, 1989) and in *The Edge of the Sea* (1955; reprinted, 1980), Carson went on to write her most influential and controversial book, *Silent Spring* (1962; limited ed., 1980; 25th anniversary ed., 1987), which sold over 500,000 hardcover copies. *Silent Spring* criticizes farmers for using environmentally hazardous chemicals and illustrates the devastation these chemicals wreak upon both animals and humans. Heavily documented, *Silent Spring* precipitated such public concern that President John F. Kennedy subsequently launched a federal investigation into the problem. In May 1963, the President's Science Advisory Committee agreed with Carson and urged more stringent controls and further research.

The Obligation to Endure

Rachel Carson

The history of life on earth has been a history of interaction between living things   1
and their surroundings. To a large extent, the physical form and the habits of the
earth's vegetation and its animal life have been molded by the environment.
Considering the whole span of earthly time, the opposite effect, in which life
actually modifies its surroundings, has been relatively slight. Only within the
moment of time represented by the present century has one species—man—
acquired significant power to alter the nature of his world.

During the past quarter century this power has not only increased to one of   2
disturbing magnitude but it has changed in character. The most alarming of all
man's assaults upon the environment is the contamination of air, earth, rivers,

and sea with dangerous and even lethal materials. This pollution is for the most part irrecoverable; the chain of evil it initiates not only in the world that must support life but in living tissues is for the most part irreversible. In this now universal contamination of the environment, chemicals are the sinister and little recognized partners of radiation in changing the very nature of the world—the very nature of its life. Strontium 90, released through nuclear explosions into the air, comes to earth in rain or drifts down as fallout, lodges in soil, enters the grass or corn or wheat grown there, and in time takes up its abode in the bones of a human being, there to remain until his death. Similarly, chemicals sprayed on croplands or forests or garden lie long in soil, entering into living organisms, passing from one to another in a chain of poisoning and death. Or they pass mysteriously by underground streams until they emerge and through the alchemy of air and sunlight, combine into new forms that kill vegetation, sicken cattle, and work unknown harm on those who drink from once pure wells. As Albert Schweitzer has said, "Man can hardly even recognize the devils of his own creation."

It took hundreds of millions of years to produce the life that now inhabits   3 the earth—eons of time in which that developing and evolving and diversifying life reached a state of adjustment and balance with its surroundings. The environment, rigorously shaping and directing the life it supported, contained elements that were hostile as well as supporting. Certain rocks gave out dangerous radiation; even within the light of the sun, from which all life draws its energy, there were shortwave radiations with power to injure. Given time—time not in years but in millennia —life adjusts, and a balance has been reached. For time is the essential ingredient; but in the modern world there is no time.

The rapidity of change and the speed with which new situations are creat-   4 ed follow the impetuous and heedless pace of man rather than the deliberate pace of nature. Radiation is no longer merely the background radiation of rocks, the bombardment of cosmic rays, the ultraviolet of the sun that have existed before there was any life on earth; radiation is now the unnatural creation of man's tampering with the atom. The chemicals to which life is asked to make its adjustment are no longer merely the calcium and silica and copper and all the rest of the minerals washed out of the rocks and carried in rivers to the sea; they are the synthetic creations of man's inventive mind, brewed in his laboratories, and having no counterparts in nature.

To adjust to these chemicals would require time on the scale that is nature's;   5 it would require not merely the years of a man's life but the life of generations. And even this, were it by some miracle possible, would be futile, for the new chemicals come from our laboratories in an endless stream; almost five hundred annually find their way into actual use in the United States alone. The figure is staggering and its implications are not easily grasped—500 new chemicals to which the bodies of men and animals are required somehow to adapt each year, chemicals totally outside the limits of biologic experience.

Among them are many that are used in man's war against nature. Since the   6 mid-1940s over 200 basic chemicals have been created for use in killing insects, weeds, rodents, and other organisms described in the modern vernacular as "pests"; and they are sold under several thousand different brand names.

These sprays, dusts, and aerosols are now applied almost universally to   7 farms, gardens, forests, and homes—nonselective chemicals that have the power to kill every insect, the "good" and the "bad," to still the song of birds and the leaping of fish in the streams, to coat the leaves with a deadly film, and to linger on in soil—all this though the intended target may be only a few weeds or insects. Can anyone believe it is possible to lay down such a barrage of poisons on the surface of the earth without making it unfit for all life? They should not be called "insecticides," but "biocides."

The whole process of spraying seems caught up in an endless spiral. Since   8 DDT was released for civilian use, a process of escalation has been going on in which ever more toxic materials must be found. This has happened because insects, in a triumphant vindication of Darwin's principle of the survival of the fittest, have evolved super races immune to the particular insecticide used, hence a deadlier one has always to be developed—and then a deadlier one than that. It has happened also because destructive insects often undergo a "flareback," or resurgence, after spraying, in numbers greater than before. Thus the chemical war is never won, and all life is caught in its violent crossfire.

Along with the possibility of the extinction of mankind by nuclear war, the   9 central problem of our age has therefore become the contamination of man's total environment with such substances of incredible potential for harm—substances that accumulate in the tissues of plants and animals and even penetrate the germ cells to shatter or alter the very material of heredity upon which the shape of the future depends.

Some would-be architects of our future look toward a time when it will be   10 possible to alter the human germ plasm by design. But we may easily be doing so now by inadvertence for many chemicals, like radiation, bring about gene mutations. It is ironic to think that man might determine his own future by something   11 so seemingly trivial as the choice of an insect spray.

All this has been risked—for what? Future historians may well be amazed by our distorted sense of proportion. How could intelligent beings seek to control a few unwanted species by a method that contaminated the entire environment and brought the threat of disease and death even to their own kind? Yet this is precisely what we have done. We have done it, moreover, for reasons that collapse the moment we examine them. We are told that the enormous and expanding use of pesticides is necessary to maintain farm production. Yet is our real problem not one of *overproduction?* Our farms, despite measures to remove acreages from production and to pay farmers *not* to produce, have yielded such a staggering excess of crops that the American taxpayer in 1962 is paying out more than one billion dollars a year as the total carrying cost of the surplus-food storage program. And is the situation helped when one branch of the Agriculture Department tries to reduce production while another states, as it did in 1958, "It is believed generally that reduction of crop acreages under provisions of the Soil Bank will stimulate interest in use of chemicals to obtain maximum production on the land retained in crops."

All this is not to say there is no insect problem and no need of control. I am   12
saying, rather, that control must be geared to realities, not to mythical situations, and that the methods employed must be such that they do not destroy us along with the insects.

The problem whose attempted solution has brought such a train of disaster   13
in its wake is an accompaniment of our modern way of life. Long before the age of man, insects inhabited the earth—a group of extraordinarily varied and adaptable beings. Over the course of time since man's advent, a small percentage of the more than half a million species of insects have come into conflict with human welfare in two principal ways: as competitors for the food supply and as carriers of human disease.

Disease-carrying insects become important where human beings are crowd-   14
ed together, especially under conditions where sanitation is poor, as in time of natural disaster or war or in situations of extreme poverty and deprivation. Then control of some sort becomes necessary. It is a sobering fact, however, that the method of massive chemical control has had only limited success, and also threatens to worsen the very conditions it is intended to curb.

Under primitive agricultural conditions the farmer had few insect problems.   15
These arose with the intensification of agriculture—the devotion of immense acreages to a single crop. Such a system set the stage for explosive increases in specific insect populations. Single-crop farming does not take advantage of the principles by which nature works; it is agriculture as an engineer might conceive it to be. Nature has introduced great variety into the landscape, but man has displayed a passion for simplifying it. Thus he undoes the built-in checks and bal-

ances by which nature holds the species within bounds. One important natural check is a limit on the amount of suitable habitat for each species. Obviously then, an insect that lives on wheat can build up its population to much higher levels on a farm devoted to wheat than on one in which wheat is intermingled with other crops to which the insect is not adapted.

The same thing happens in other situations. A generation or more ago, the   16 towns of large areas of the United States lined their streets with the noble elm tree. Now the beauty they hopefully created is threatened with complete destruction as disease sweeps through the elms, carried by a beetle that would have only limited chance to build up large populations and to spread from tree to tree if the elms were only occasional trees in a richly diversified planting.

Another factor in the modern insect problem is one that must be viewed   17 against a background of geologic and human history: the spreading of thousands of different kinds of organisms from their native homes to invade new territories. This worldwide migration has been studied and graphically described by the British ecologist Charles Elton in his recent book *The Ecology of Invasions*. During the Cretaceous Period, some hundred million years ago, flooding seas cut many land bridges between continents and living things found themselves confined in what Elton calls "colossal separate nature reserves." There, isolated from others of their kind, they developed many new species. When some of the land masses were joined again, about 15 million years ago, these species began to move out into new territories —a movement that is not only still in progress but is now receiving considerable assistance from man.

The importation of plants is the primary agent in the modern spread of   18 species, for animals have almost invariably gone along with the plants, quarantine being a comparatively recent and not completely effective innovation. The United States Office of Plant Introduction alone has introduced almost 200,000 species and varieties of plants from all over the world. Nearly half of the 180 or so major insect enemies of plants in the United States are accidental imports from abroad, and most of them have come as hitchhikers on plants.

In new territory, out of reach of the restraining hand of the natural enemies   19 that kept down its numbers in its native land, an invading plant or animal is able to become enormously abundant. Thus it is no accident that our most troublesome insects are introduced species.

These invasions, both the naturally occurring and those dependent on   20 human assistance, are likely to continue indefinitely. Quarantine and massive chemical campaigns are only extremely expensive ways of buying time. We are faced, according to Dr. Elton, "with a life-and-death need not just to find new technological means of suppressing this plant or that animal"; instead we need the basic knowledge of animal populations and their relations to their surroundings that will "promote an even balance and damp down the explosive power of outbreaks and new invasions."

Much of the necessary knowledge is now available but we do not use it. We 21 train ecologists in our universities and even employ them in our government agencies but we seldom take their advice. We allow the chemical death rain to fall as though there were no alternative, whereas in fact there are many, and our ingenuity could soon discover many more if given opportunity.

Have we fallen into a mesmerized state that makes us accept as inevitable 22 that which is inferior or detrimental, as though having lost the will or the vision to demand that which is good? Such thinking, in the words of the ecologist Paul Shepard, "idealizes life with only its head out of the water, inches above the limits of toleration of the corruption of its own environment. . . . Why should we tolerate a diet of weak poisons, a home in insipid surroundings, a circle of acquaintances who are not quite our enemies, the noise of motors with just enough relief to prevent insanity? Who would want to live in a world which is just not quite fatal?"

Yet such a world is pressed upon us. The crusade to create a chemically ster- 23 ile, insect-free world seems to have engendered a fanatic zeal on the part of many specialists and most of the so-called control agencies. On every hand there is evidence that those engaged in spraying operations exercise a ruthless power. "The regulatory entomologist . . . function as prosecutor, judge and jury, tax assessor and collector and sheriff to enforce their own orders," said Connecticut entomologist Neely Turner. The most flagrant abuses go unchecked in both state and federal agencies.

It is not my contention that chemical insecticides must never be used. I do 24 contend that we have put poisonous and biologically potent chemicals indiscriminately into the hands of persons largely or wholly ignorant of their potentials for harm. We have subjected enormous numbers of people to contact with these poisons, without their consent and often without their knowledge. If the Bill of Rights contains no guarantee that a citizen shall be secure against lethal poisons distributed either by private individuals or by public officials, it is surely only because our forefathers, despite their considerable wisdom and foresight, could conceive of no such problem.

I contend, furthermore, that we have allowed these chemicals to be used 25 with little or no advance investigation of their effect on soil, water, wildlife, and man himself. Future generations are unlikely to condone our lack of prudent concern for the integrity of the natural world that supports all life.

There is still very limited awareness of the nature of the threat. This is an 26 era of specialists, each of whom sees his own problem and is unaware of or intol-

erant of the larger frame into which it fits. It is also an era dominated by industry, in which the right to make a dollar at whatever cost is seldom challenged.
When the public protests, confronted with some obvious evidence of damaging
results of pesticide applications, it is fed little tranquilizing pills of half truth. We
urgently need an end to these false assurances, to the sugar coating of unpalatable
facts. It is the public that is being asked to assume the risks that the insect con-
trollers calculate. The public must decide whether it wishes to continue on the
present road, and it can do so only when in full possession of the facts. In the
words of Jean Rostand, "The obligation to endure gives us the right to know."

Questions for Discussion

1. How did DDT come to be so depended upon in the United States and Canada? Why were alternative pesticides not used?
2. Why is time a key factor in dealing with the effects of pesticides?
3. According to Carson, what are the central problems of our age? Why are
   these problems central? Why is Carson so concerned about these problems?
4. What problems did pesticides solve? What new problems were created when
   pesticides began to be used?
5. How does Carson balance alarmist phrases such as "chain of evil" (paragraph
   2) and "impetuous and heedless pace of man" (paragraph 4) with the calm
   language of a scientist?
6. Describe Carson's tone: Is it calm? demanding? concerned? Point to words
   and phrases that exhibit this tone.
7. Is Carson an alarmist? Is this essay, first published in 1962, still relevant
   today?

Questions for Reflection and Writing

1. List Carson's main and supporting points, writing an outline if you want.
   Study how she puts together her argument, and consider how you might
   apply a similar technique to an argumentative paper.
2. What is your reaction to Carson's essay? What pesticides should be used, if
   any? Should all pesticides be banned? How should farmers ensure that their
   crops are not destroyed by insects and disease? How should environmentalists ensure that the environment is not destroyed?
3. What countries continue to use DDT? What is being done in those countries to curb the use of this and other dangerous pesticides? Or do you think
   no pesticides should be banned? Research the use and subsequent banning
   of DDT and other pesticides in the United States. Report objectively on
   your findings, or take a stand and write a documented opinion essay.

Gretel Ehrlich is a writer and rancher who lives in Wyoming. A former filmmaker, she first visited Wyoming to film a documentary on sheepherders and later married a rancher there. Her writing has been published in a number of magazines, including *Harper's* and the *Atlantic*. It has been gathered into a highly praised volumn, *The Solace of Open Spaces*. She has to her credit two other books: *Heart Mountain* (1988), and *Islands, the Universe, Home* (1991).

The Solace of Open Spaces

Gretel Ehrlich

It's May and I've just awakened from a nap, curled against sagebrush the way my 1
dog taught me to sleep—sheltered from wind. A front is pulling the huge sky over me, and from the dark a hailstone has hit me on the head. I'm trailing a band of two thousand sheep across a stretch of Wyoming badlands, a fifty-mile trip that takes five days because sheep shade up in hot sun and won't budge until it's cool. Bunched together now, and excited into a run by the storm, they drift across dry land, tumbling into draws like water and surge out again onto the rugged, choppy plateaus that are the building blocks of this state.

The name Wyoming comes from an Indian word meaning "at the great 2
plains," but the plains are really valleys, great arid valleys, sixteen hundred square miles, with the horizon bending up on all sides into mountain ranges. This gives the vastness a sheltering look.

Winter lasts six months here. Prevailing winds spill snowdrifts to the east, 3
and new storms from the northwest replenish them. This white bulk is sometimes dizzying, even nauseating, to look at. At twenty, thirty, and forty degrees below zero, not only does your car not work, but neither do your mind and body. The landscape hardens into a dungeon of space. During the winter, while I was riding to find a new calf, my jeans froze to the saddle, and in the silence that such cold creates I felt like the first person on earth, or the last.

Today the sun is out—only a few clouds billowing. In the east, where the 4
sheep have started off without me, the benchland tilts up in a series of eroded red-earthed mesas, planed flat on top by a million years of water; behind them, a bold line of muscular scarps rears up ten thousand feet to become the Big Horn Mountains. A tidal pattern is engraved into the ground, as if left by the sea that once covered this state. Canyons curve down like galaxies to meet the oncoming rush of flat land.

To live and work in this kind of open country, with its hundred-mile views,   5
is to lose the distinction between background and foreground. When I asked an
older ranch hand to describe Wyoming's openness, he said, "It's all a bunch of
nothing—wind and rattlesnakes—and so much of it you can't tell where you're
going or where you've been and it don't make much difference." John, a sheepman I know, is tall and handsome and has an explosive temperament. He has a
perfect intuition about people and sheep. They call him "Highpockets," because
he's so long-legged; his graceful stride matches the distances he has to cover. He
says, "Open space hasn't affected me at all. It's all the people moving in on it."
The huge ranch he was born on takes up much of one county and spreads into
another state; to put 100,000 miles on his pickup in three years and never leave
home is not unusual. A friend of mine has an aunt who ranched on Powder River
and didn't go off her place for eleven years. When her husband died, she quickly
moved to town, bought a car, and drove around the States to see what she'd been
missing.

Most people tell me they've simply driven through Wyoming, as if there   6
were nothing to stop for. Or else they've skied in Jackson Hole, a place Wyomin-
gites acknowledge uncomfortably because its green beauty and chic affluence are
mismatched with the rest of the state. Most of Wyoming has a "lean-to" look.
Instead of big, roomy barns and Victorian houses, there are dugouts, low sheds,
log cabins, sheep camps, and fence lines that look like driftwood blown haphaz-
ardly into place. People here still feel pride because they live in such a harsh
place, part of the glamorous cowboy past, and they are determined not to be the
victims of a mining-dominated future.

Most characteristic of the state's landscape is what a developer euphemisti-   7
cally describes as "indigenous growth right up to your front door"—a reference
to waterless stands of salt sage, snakes, jack rabbits, deerflies, red dust, a brief
respite of wildflowers, dry washes, and no trees. In the Great Plains the vistas
look like music, like Kyries of grass, but Wyoming seems to be the doing of a mad
architect—tumbled and twisted, ribboned with faded, deathbed colors, thrust up
and pulled down as if the place had been startled out of a deep sleep and thrown
into a pure light.

I came here four years ago. I had not planned to stay, but I couldn't make   8
myself leave. John, the sheepman, put me to work immediately. It was spring, and
shearing time. For fourteen days of fourteen hours each, we moved thousands of
sheep through sorting corrals to be sheared, branded, and deloused. I suspect that
my original motive for coming here was to "lose myself" in new and unpopulat-

ed territory. Instead of producing the numbness I thought I wanted, life on the sheep ranch woke me up. The vitality of the people I was working with flushed out what had become a hallucinatory rawness inside me. I threw away my clothes and bought new ones; I cut my hair. The arid country was a clean slate. Its absolute indifference steadied me.

Sagebrush covers 58,000 square miles of Wyoming. The biggest city has a   9
population of fifty thousand, and there are only five settlements that could be called cities in the whole state. The rest are towns, scattered across the expanse with as much as sixty miles between them, their populations two thousand, fifty, or ten. They are fugitive-looking, perched on a barren, windblown bench, or tagged onto a river or a railroad, or laid out straight in a farming valley with implement stores and a block-long Mormon church. In the eastern part of the state, which slides down into the Great Plains, the new mining settlements are boomtowns, trailer cities, metal knots on flat land.

Despite the desolate look, there's a coziness to living in this state. There are   10
so few people (only 470,000) that ranchers who buy and sell cattle know one another statewide; the kids who choose to go to college usually go to the state's one university, in Laramie; hired hands work their way around Wyoming in a lifetime of hirings and firings. And despite the physical separation, people stay in touch, often driving two or three hours to another ranch for dinner.

Seventy-five years ago, when travel was by buckboard or horseback, cow-   11
boys who were temporarily out of work rode the grub line—drifting from ranch to ranch, mending fences or milking cows, and receiving in exchange a bed and meals. Gossip and messages traveled this slow circuit with them, creating an intimacy between ranchers who were three and four weeks' ride apart. One old-time couple I know, whose turn-of-the-century homestead was used by an outlaw gang as a relay station for stolen horses, recall that if you were traveling, desperado or not, any lighted ranch house was a welcome sign. Even now, for someone who lives in a remote spot, arriving at a ranch or coming to town for supplies is cause for celebration. To emerge from isolation can be disorienting. Everything looks bright, new, vivid. After I had been herding sheep for only three days, the sound of the camp tender's pickup flustered me. Longing for human company, I felt a foolish grin take over my face; yet I had to resist an urgent temptation to run and hide.

Things happen suddenly in Wyoming, the change of seasons and weather;   12
for people, the violent swings in and out of isolation. But goodnaturedness is concomitant with severity. Friendliness is a tradition. Strangers passing on the road

wave hello. A common sight is two pickups stopped side by side far out on a range, on a dirt track winding through the sage. The drivers will share a cigarette, uncap their Thermos bottles, and pass a battered cup, steaming with coffee, between windows. These meetings summon up the details of several generations, because, in Wyoming, private histories are largely public knowledge.

Because ranch work is a physical and, these days, economic strain, being "at   13
home on the range" is a matter of vigor, self-reliance, and common sense. A person's life is not a series of dramatic events for which he or she is applauded or exiled but a slow accumulation of days, seasons, years, fleshed out by the generational weight of one's family and anchored by a land-bound sense of place.

In most parts of Wyoming, the human population is visibly outnumbered   14
by the animal. Not far from my town of fifty, I rode into a narrow valley and startled a herd of two hundred elk. Eagles look like small people as they eat car-killed deer by the road. Antelope, moving in small, graceful bands, travel at sixty miles an hour, their mouths open as if drinking in the space.

The solitude in which westerners live makes them quiet. They telegraph   15
thoughts and feelings by the way they tilt their heads and listen; pulling their Stetsons into a steep dive over their eyes, or pigeon-toeing one boot over the other, they lean against a fence with a fat wedge of Copenhagen beneath their lower lips and take in the whole scene. These detached looks of quiet amusement are sometimes cynical, but they can also come from a dry-eyed humility as lucid as the air is clear.

Conversation goes on in what sounds like a private code; a few phrases   16
imply a complex of meanings. Asking directions, you get a curious list of details. While trailing sheep I was told to "ride up to that kinda upturned rock, follow the pink wash, turn left at the dump, and then you'll see the water hole." One friend told his wife on roundup to "turn at the salt lick and the dead cow," which turned out to be a scattering of bones and no salt lick at all.

Sentence structure is shortened to the skin and bones of a thought. Descrip-   17
tive words are dropped, even verbs; a cowboy looking over a corral full of horses will say to a wrangler, "Which one needs rode?" People hold back their thoughts in what seems to be a dumbfounded silence, then erupt with an excoriating perceptive remark. Language, so compressed, becomes metaphorical. A rancher ended a relationship with one remark: "You're a bad check," meaning bouncing in and out was intolerable, and even coming back would be no good.

What's behind this laconic style is shyness. There is no vocabulary for the   18
subject of feelings. It's not a hangdog shyness, or anything coy— always there's a robust spirit in evidence behind the restraint, as if the earth-dredging wind that

pulls across Wyoming had carried its people's voices away but everything else in them had shouldered confidently into the breeze.

I've spent hours riding to sheep camp at dawn in a pickup when nothing 19 was said; eaten meals in the cookhouse when the only words spoken were a mumbled "Thank you, ma'am" at the end of dinner. The silence is profound. Instead of talking, we seem to share one eye. Keenly obser ved, the world is transformed. The landscape is engorged with detail, every movement on it chillingly sharp. The air between people is charged. Days unfold, bathed in their own music. Nights become hallucinatory; dreams, prescient.

Spring weather is capricious and mean. It snows, then blisters with heat. 20 There have been tornadoes. They lay their elephant trunks out in the sage until they find houses, then slurp everything up and leave. I've noticed that melting snowbanks hiss and rot, viperous, then drip into calm pools where ducklings hatch and livestock, being trailed to summer range, drink. With the ice cover gone, rivers churn a milkshake brown, taking culverts and small bridges with them. Water in such an arid place (the average annual rainfall where I live is less than eight inches) is like blood. It festoons drab land with green veins; a line of cottonwoods following a stream; a strip of alfalfa; and, on ditch banks, wild asparagus growing.

I've moved to a small cattle ranch owned by friends. It's at the foot of the 21 Big Horn Mountains. A few weeks ago, I helped them deliver a calf who was stuck halfway out of his mother's body. By the time he was freed, we could see a heartbeat, but he was straining against a swollen tongue for air. Mary and I held him upside down by his back feet, while Stan, on his hands and knees in the blood, gave the calf mouth-to-mouth resuscitation. I have a vague memory of being pneumonia-choked as a child, my mother giving me her air, which may account for my romance with this windswept state.

If anything is endemic to Wyoming, it is wind. This big room of space is 22 swept out daily, leaving a bone yard of fossils, agates, and carcasses in every stage of decay. Though it was water that initially shaped the state, wind is the meticulous gardener, raising dust and pruning the sage.

I try to imagine a world in which I could ride my horse across uncharted 23 land. There is no wilderness left; wildness, yes, but true wilderness has been gone on this continent since the time of Lewis and Clark's overland journey.

Two hundred years ago, the Crow, Shoshone, Arapaho, Cheyenne, and 24 Sioux roamed the intermountain West, orchestrating their movements according to hunger, season, and warfare. Once they acquired horses, they traversed the spines of all the big Wyoming ranges—the Absarokas, the Wind Rivers, the

Tetons, the Big Horns—and wintered on the unprotected plains that fan out from them. Space was life. The world was their home.

What was life-giving to Native Americans was often nightmarish to sod-   25 busters who had arrived encumbered with families and ethnic pasts to be transplanted in nearly uninhabitable land. The great distances, the shortage of water and trees, and the loneliness created unexpected hardships for them. In her book *O Pioneers!*, Willa Cather gives a settler's version of the bleak landscape:

> The little town behind them had vanished as if it had never been, had fall-   26 en behind the swell of the prairie, and the stern frozen country received them into its bosom. The homesteads were few and far apart; here and there a windmill gaunt against the sky, a sod house crouching in a hollow.

The emptiness of the West was for others a geography of possibility. Men   27 and women who amassed great chunks of land and struggled to preserve unfenced empires were, despite their self-serving motives, unwitting geographers. They understood the lay of the land. But by the 1850s the Oregon and Mormon trails sported bumper-to-bumper traffic. Wealthy landowners, many of them aristocratic absentee landlords, known as remittance men because they were paid to come West and get out of their families' hair, overstocked the range with more than a million head of cattle. By 1885 the feed and water were desperately short, and the winter of 1886 laid out the gaunt bodies of dead animals so closely together that when the thaw came, one rancher from Kaycee claimed to have walked on cowhide all the way to Crazy Woman Creek, twenty miles away.

Territorial Wyoming was a boy's world. The land was generous with every-   28 thing but water. At first there was room enough, food enough, for everyone. And, as with all beginnings, an expansive mood set in. The young cowboys, drifters, shopkeepers, schoolteachers, were heroic, lawless, generous, rowdy, and tenacious. The individualism and optimism generated during those times have endured.

John Tisdale rode north with the trail herds from Texas. He was a col-lege-   29 educated man with enough money to buy a small outfit near the Powder River. While driving home from the town of Buffalo with a buckboard full of Christmas toys for his family and a winter's supply of food, he was shot in the back by an agent of the cattle barons who resented the encroachment of small-time stockmen like him. The wealthy cattlemen tried to control all the public grazing land by restricting membership in the Wyoming Stock Growers Association, as if it were a country club. They ostracized from roundups and brandings cowboys and ranchers who were not members, then denounced them as rustlers. Tisdale's death, the second such cold-blooded murder, kicked off the Johnson County cattle war, which was no simple good-guy-bad-guy shoot-out but a complicated class struggle between landed gentr y and less affluent settlers—a shocking reminder that the West was not an egalitarian sanctuary after all.

Fencing ultimately enforced boundaries, but barbed wire abrogated space. It was stretched across the beautiful valleys, into the mountains, over desert badlands, through buffalo grass. The "anything is possible" fever—the lure of any new place—was constricted. The integrity of the land as a geographical body, and the freedom to ride anywhere on it, were lost. 30

I punched cows with a young man named Martin, who is the great-grandson of John Tisdale. His inheritance is not the open land that Tisdale knew and prematurely lost but a rage against restraint. 31

Wyoming tips down as you head northeast; the highest ground—the Laramie Plains—is on the Colorado border. Up where I live, the Big Horn River leaks into difficult, arid terrain. In the basin where it's dammed, sandhill cranes gather and, with delicate legwork, slice through the stilled water. I was driving by with a rancher one morning when he commented that cranes are "old-fashioned." When I asked why, he said, "Because they mate for life." Then he looked at me with a twinkle in his eyes, as if to say he really did believe in such things but also understood why we break our own rules. 32

In all this open space, values crystalize quickly. People are strong on scruples but tenderhearted about quirky behavior. A friend and I found one ranch hand, who's "not quite right in the head," sitting in front of the badly decayed carcass of a cow, shaking his finger and saying, "Now, I don't want you to do this ever again!" When I asked what was wrong with him, I was told, "He's goofier than hell, just like the rest of us." Perhaps because the West is historically new, conventional morality is still felt to be less important than rock-bottom truths. Though there's always a lot of teasing and sparring, people are blunt with one another, sometimes even cruel, believing honesty is stronger medicine than sympathy, which may console but often conceals. 33

The formality that goes hand in hand with the rowdiness is known as the Western Code. It's a list of practical do's and don'ts, faithfully observed. A friend, Cliff, who runs a trapline in the winter, cut off half his foot while chopping a hole in the ice. Alone, he dragged himself to his pickup and headed for town, stopping to open the ranch gate as he left, and getting out to close it again, thus 34

losing, in his observance of rules, precious time and blood. Later, he commented, "How would it look, them having to come to the hospital to tell me their
cows had gotten out?"

Accustomed to emergencies, my friends doctor each other from the vet's   35
bag with relish. When one old-timer suffered a heart attack in hunting camp, his
partner quickly stirred up a brew of red horse liniment and hot water and made
the half-conscious victim drink it, then tied him onto a horse and led him twenty miles to town. He regained consciousness and lived.

The roominess of the state has affected political attitudes as well. Ranchers   36
keep up with world politics and the convulsions of the economy but are basically isolationists. Being used to running their own small empires of land and livestock, they're suspicious of big government. It's a "don't fence me in" holdover
from a centur y ago. They still want the elbow room their grandfathers had, so
they're strongly conservative, but with a populist twist.

Summer is the season when we get our "cowboy tans"—on the lower parts   37
of our faces and on three fourths of our arms. Excessive heat, in the nineties and
higher, sends us outside with the mosquitoes. In winter we're tucked inside our
houses, and the white wasteland outside appears to be expanding, but in summer
all the greenery abridges space. Summer is a go-ahead season. Every living thing
is off the block and in the race: battalions of bugs in flight and biting; bats swinging around my log cabin as if the bases were loaded and someone had hit a home
run. Some of sum-mer's high-speed growth is ominous: larkspur, death camas, and
green greasewood can kill sheep—an ironic idea, dying in this desert from eating
what is too verdant. With sixteen hours of daylight, farmers and ranchers irrigate
feverishly. There are first, second, and third cuttings of hay, some crews averaging only four hours of sleep a night for weeks. And, like the cowboys who in summer ride the night rodeo circuit, nighthawks make daredevil dives at dusk with
an eerie whirring sound like a plane going down on the shimmering horizon.

In the town where I live, they've had to board up the dance-hall windows   38
because there have been so many fights. There's so little to do except work that
people wind up in a state of idle agitation that becomes fatalistic, as if there were
nothing to be done about all this untapped energy. So the dark side to the grandeur
of these spaces is the small-mind-edness that seals people in. Men become hermits;
women go mad. Cabin fever explodes into suicides, or into grudges and lifelong
family feuds. Two sisters in my area inherited a ranch but found they couldn't get
along. They fenced the place in half. When one's cows got out and mixed with the
other's, the women went at each other with shovels. They ended up in the same
hospital room but never spoke a word to each other for the rest of their lives.

After the brief lushness of summer, the sun moves south. The range grass is   39
brown. Livestock is trailed back down from the mountains. Water holes begin to
frost over at night. Last fall Martin asked me to accompany him on a pack trip.
With five horses, we followed a river into the mountains behind the tiny
Wyoming town of Meeteetse. Groves of aspen, red and orange, gave off a light
that made us look toasted. Our hunting camp was so high that clouds skidded
across our foreheads, then slowed to sail out across the warm valleys. Except for
a bull moose who wandered into our camp and mistook our black gelding for a
rival, we shot at nothing.

One of our evening entertainments was to watch the night sky. My dog, a   40
dingo bred to herd sheep, also came on the trip. He is so used to the silence and
empty skies that when an airplane flies over he always looks up and eyes the distant intruder quizzically. The sky, lately, seems to be much more crowded than it
used to be. Satellites make their silent passes in the dark with great regularity. We
counted eighteen in one hour's viewing. How odd to think that while they cir-
cumnavigated the planet, Martin and I had moved only six miles into our local
wilderness and had seen no other human for the two weeks we stayed there.

At night, by moonlight, the land is whittled to slivers—a ridge, a river, a   41
strip of grassland stretching to the mountains, then the huge sky. One morning a
full moon was setting in the west just as the sun was rising. I felt precariously balanced between the two as I loped across a meadow. For a moment, I could believe
that the stars, which were still visible, work like cooper's bands, holding together
everything above Wyoming.

Space has a spiritual equivalent and can heal what is divided and burden-   42
some in us. My grandchildren will probably use space shuttles for a honeymoon
trip or to recover from heart attacks, but closer to home we might also learn how
to carry space inside ourselves in the effortless way we carry our skins. Space represents sanity, not a life purified, dull, or "spaced out" but one that might accommodate intelligently any idea or situation.

From the clayey soil of northern Wyoming is mined bentonite, which is   43
used as a filler in candy, gum, and lipstick. We Americans are great on fillers, as
if what we have, what we are, is not enough. We have a cultural tendency toward
denial, but, being affluent, we strangle ourselves with what we can buy. We have
only to look at the houses we build to see how we build against space, the way we
drink against pain and loneliness. We fill up space as if it were a pie shell, with
things whose opacity further obstructs our ability to see what is already there.

J. Baird Callicott

J. Baird Callicott was born in 1941 in Memphis, Tennessee. He attended Rhodes College in Memphis, graduating with honors in philosophy in 1963. He earned his master's degree in philosophy at Syracuse University in 1966 and then taught at the University of Memphis for three years. After completing his doctorate in 1969, Callicott went to the University of Wisconsin-Stevens Point, where, in 1972, he taught the nation's first course in environmental ethics in 1973. He directed the Environmental Studies Program from 1980 to 1986 and was appointed Professor of Natural Resources in 1984. Callicott received the University of Wisconsin-Stevens Point's Academy of Letters and Science Distinguished Achievement Award in 1986 and its University Scholar Award in 1995. Callicott became Professor of Philosophy and Religious Studies at the University of North Texas in 1995. He has accepted visiting professorships in the United States and abroad, and is currently president of the International Society for Environmental Ethics.

Callicott's publications include *Clothed-in-Fur and Other Tales: An Introduction to an Ojibwa World View* (1982), *In Defense of the Land Ethic: Essays in Environmental Philosophy* (1989), *Earth's Insights: A Survey of Ecological Ethics from the Mediterranean Basin to the Australian Outback* (1994), and *Beyond the Land Ethic: More Essays in Environmental Philosophy* (1999).

Our reading is from the final section of Callicott's 1993 essay "The Search for an Environmental Ethic." In this section, entitled "The Ecocentric Approach to Environmental Ethics," Callicott advocates *ecocentrism*, the position that moral consideration should be given not only to individual living things (human and nonhuman), but to the interdependent "biotic community" (the community of all living organisms) as such. Building on Charles Darwin's theory of natural selection (the theory that, if an organism acquires a trait that enables it to adapt to its environment, it tends to survive and transmit this trait to its offspring) and Aldo Leopold's "land ethic," Callicott argues that ethics has a biological basis and that all living things are "equally members in good standing of one society or community." Accordingly, we have a moral obligation to other living beings and to the biotic community as such. Callicott also holds that we have a greater obligation to human beings than to nonhuman beings, and a greater obligation to some human beings than to others. He argues that we should be mindful both of the biotic community as a whole (striving to enhance its diversity, integrity, stability, and beauty) and of its individual members (treating any given plant or animal respectfully when it is necessary to use it for our needs).

The Search for an Environmental Ethic

J. Baird Callicott

IV. The Ecocentric Approach to Environmental Ethics
The Ecological Connection: Symbiosis and Wholeness *Evolution* links human   1
beings with the rest of nature *diachronically* (through time). It posits common ori-

gins, temporal continuity, and hence phylogenetic kinship and shared experience among species. . . .

Ecology unites human beings with the rest of nature synchronically (at one time). Prior to the emergence of ecology, the Western concept of living nature was characterized reductively. Nature was perceived to be very much like a roomful of furniture—that is, a collection or mere aggregate of individuals of various kinds, relating to one another in an accidental and altogether external fashion with no functional connection with one another.   2

From an ecological point of view, however, the living natural world is much more fully integrated and systemically unified than it had habitually been represented. The biotic mantle of the earth, from an ecological point of view, is one because its living components are reciprocally coevolved and mutually interdependent. Each living thing, while retaining its identity as an individual, is embedded in a matrix of vital relationships, a "web of life." A being's specific complex of characteristics, its essence, in classical terminology, is inconceivable apart from such a matrix. From the perspective of an ecologically informed evolutionary world view, organisms acquire their specific characteristics through interactive adaptation to other organisms. Hence individual living things, including human beings, are internally related to one another. That is, each is what it is because of its relationships with other kinds. Living beings thus are hardly conceivable in isolation from the matrix that has shaped them.   3

Ecologists have attempted to express the peculiar integration and systemic unity of living nature disclosed by their science with a governing metaphor, the "biotic community," and the closely associated metaphor of an "economy of nature." Environmental degradation and destruction, particularly in the form of biological impoverishment, is represented, accordingly, as similar to a severely depressed human community in which roles or professions in the human economy began to disappear. Ecologists identify three generic professions in the economy of nature: producer (green plants), consumer (animals), and decomposer (fungi and bacteria). Each of these categories is divisible into a myriad of specialties. Some specialized professions are more important than others in the economy of nature, as in human economies. And this importance has nothing to do with psychological complexity. Indeed, living things at the bottom of the psychological order are at the basis of the functional order of life on Earth—phytoplankton, fungi, rhizobial bacteria, to mention only a few.   4

The currency, the coin of the realm, in the economy of nature is not a material—like minted gold or silver or paper money—but solar energy. In Aldo   5

Leopold's characterization, the economy of nature, in the last analysis, consists of "a fountain of energy flowing through a circuit of soils, plants, and animals. Food chains are the living channels which conduct energy upward, death and decay return it to the soil."[1] Let this poetic description not disguise one fundamental fact. The currency of the economy of nature, energy, passes not (as the coin of the realm in the human economy) from hand to hand, but from stomach to stomach. What makes the world go round, literally, is one living thing eating another.

A secular environmental ethic that is as thoroughly informed by ecology as   6
by evolution would have a holistic *as well* as an individualistic dimension. That is, *both* the biotic community as such *and* (not, I emphasize, instead of) its individual members, would be morally considerable.[2] And a secular environmental ethic that is well informed by ecology would determine what is right and what is wrong for individual members to do, to one another and to the whole, not by uncritically exporting the ethics of the human community into the biotic community, but by reference to the very different structure and organization of the biotic community.

A Plea for a Holistic Approach to Environmental Ethics   . . . A holistic or eco-   7
centric environmental ethic was adumbrated in A *Sand County Almanac*, the widely read and admired "gospel" of environmental philosophy, by Aldo Leopold. For the most part, contemporary moral philosophers searching for a coherent, adequate, and practicable environmental ethic have failed to explore and develop Leopold's "land ethic" to the extent that they have, for example, Bentham's[3] even briefer remarks about the moral considerability of sentient animals. This is, in large measure, because a holistic approach to ethics is so unfamiliar and represents such a radical departure from long-established modern traditions of Western moral philosophy. One prominent moral philosopher has even called Leopold's land ethic "environmental fascism," because of its holistic char-acteristics.[4] This impression has unfortunately been invited and abetted by Leopold's few philosophical partisans who have imprudently emphasized the holistic aspects of the land ethic at the expense of its provisions for the moral consideration of individuals. I shall accordingly first explore and develop its conceptual foundations and moral precepts, and then show how it does not, in fact, lead to the untoward moral consequences its critics have thought that it must.

The Biological Basis of Ethics   In sharp contrast to traditional Western   8
humanism and its extensions, the Leopold land ethic is firmly grounded in biological concepts, as the following remark indicates: "Ethics, so far studied only by

philosophers, is actually a process in ecological evolution. Its sequences may be described in ecological as well as philosophical terms."[5] The conceptual foundations of the land ethic, at the outset, therefore, promise to be in harmony with the new organic world view.

According to Leopold, "an ethic, ecologically, is a limitation on freedom of   9
action in the struggle for existence."[6] This biological characterization of ethics suggests at once an evolutionary paradox: How could "a limitation on freedom of action" possibly have evolved—that is, have been first conserved and then spread through a population—given the unremitting "struggle for existence"? It would seem that an ethical organism, an organism that tended to limit its own freedom of action, would be severely disadvantaged in the struggle for existence and would, thus, fail to survive and reproduce. So how can evolutionary theory be squared with the manifest *existence* of moral behavior?

Darwin tackled this problem in *The Descent of Man* "exclusively from the   10
side of natural history."[7] Darwin's explanation of how natural selection could produce "a moral sense or conscience" assumes that morality or ethical behavior is based on *feelings* (love, affection, sympathy, and so on), as [Scottish philosopher] David Hume (1711–1776) had claimed. For an evolutionary account of ethics, feeling or emotion provides a sufficiently primitive and generic animal capacity with which to begin.

Darwin begins with the observation that for many species, and especially   11
mammals, prolonged parental care is necessary to ensure reproductive success. Such care, he argues, by extrapolation from our own animal experience, is motivated and facilitated by a certain strong emotion that adult mammals (in some species perhaps only the females) experience toward their offspring—parental love (or perhaps, motherly love). The capacity for such a feeling would thus be selected as part of a species' psychological profile, since such a capacity would strongly contribute to reproductive success.

Once established, Darwin argued, the "parental and filial affections" per-   12
mitted, among the primate ancestors of Homo sapiens, the formation of small family or clan social groups, perhaps originally consisting only of parents and offspring. Now these and similar "social sentiments" or "social instincts," such as "the all-important emotion of sympathy," Darwin reasoned, "will have been increased through natural selection; for those communities which included the greatest number of the most sympathetic members would flourish best, and rear the greatest number of offspring."[8]

As family group competed with family group, ironically, the same principles   13
that at first would seem to lead so directly and inevitably toward greater and

greater mutual aggression and rapacity led instead toward increased affection, kindness, and sympathy, for now the struggle for limited resources is understood to have been pursued collectively. Those groups that included "the greatest number of the most sympathetic members" may be supposed to have outcompeted those whose members were quarrelsome and disagreeable. "No tribe," Darwin tells us, "could hold together if murder, robbery, treachery, and so on, were common; consequently, such crimes within the limits of the same tribe 'are branded with everlasting infamy,' but excite no such sentiment beyond these limits."⁹

Not only did competition select for more intense sympathy and affection   14 within group limits or boundaries, but for casting social sentiments even wider, since larger social groups make possible more division of labor and hence greater economic efficiency. Indeed, in competition among the most internally peaceable and cooperative groups, the larger will win out. Thus there arose a tendency for extended family groups to merge into larger social units.

The Double Correlative of Morality and Society   This evolutionary explanation of the origin of ethics, to which Leopold alludes near the beginning of "The Land Ethic,"¹⁰ clearly issues in a fundamental principle, namely, *that ethical relations and social organization are correlative* in two ways: (1) the perceived boundaries of a society are also the perceived bound-aries of its moral community and (2) a society's structure or organization is reflected in its ethical code of conduct. Some comments on both points follow.

Original human societies consisted of extended families and clans. Subsis-   16 tence hunting and gathering determined both their size and organization or structure. Correspondingly, original human ethics were narrowly circumscribed and xenophobic, and they stressed virtues that contributed to small-group survival— for example, the virtues of sharing, courage, loyalty, deference, obedience to elders, and so on. Ethical behavior toward out-group members was not enjoined. Indeed, such persons could be exploited, or even tortured and killed, without violation of the clan code of conduct.

When clans eventually merged into tribes, there occurred a corresponding   17 growth in the boundaries of the moral community: one was required to behave morally toward members of one's tribe as well as members of one's family or clan. And as tribal social structure is more complex, involving specialized social roles as chieftain, warrior, priest, doctor, and so on, the corresponding ethical code became more elaborate and finely articulated.

As tribes eventually merged into larger social units—nations or coun-   18 tries—corresponding extensions of moral boundaries occurred along with corresponding modifications and amplifications of the older ethical rules and precepts. There also occurred radical changes in economic patterns of existence and in social organization. These changes in social organization were reflected in correlative changes in ethics. In large, heterogeneous societies, for example, there emerged the moral ideals of individual liberty, privacy, and equality. (Such modern moral principles are not only not recognized in familial and tribal ethics but are, in clan and tribal codes, regarded more as vices than virtues.)

Today we are witnessing the merger of nations into a global community. 19 This "global village" has become an emergent reality because of multinational economic interdependence and because of transportation and communications technologies. Corresponding to this emergent global phase in human social evolution is the current humanitarian or "human rights" moral ideal.

Transition from Humanistic to Environmental Ethics   According to Aldo 20 Leopold, "All ethics so far evolved rest upon a single premise: that the individual is a member of a community of interdependent parts. . . . The land ethic simply enlarges the boundaries of the community to include soils, waters, plants, and animals, or collectively: the land."[11] Since ethics have evolved and changed correlatively to the growth and development of the putative social or communal organization, and since the natural environment is represented in ecology as a *community* or society, an ecocentric environmental ethic may be clearly envisioned.

Moral precepts—for example, against murder, robbery, treachery, and so 21 on—may be regarded as the cultural specification or articulation of the limitations on freedom of action to which our social sentiments predispose us. Moral behavior has a genetic basis, but it is not "hard-wired." In the process of enculturation, we are taught both the appropriate forms of behavior and toward whom they should be directed. The people around us are socially classified. Some are mother, father, brothers, and sisters; others uncles, aunts, cousins; still others are friends and neighbors; and in former times, some were barbarians, aliens, or enemies. This representation plays on and provides substance to our "open" feelings toward others and produces subtly shaded moral responses. And should the cognitive representation of our relationships change, our moral responses would change accordingly. If one is told, for example, that a person previously thought to be a stranger is actually a long-lost relative, then one's feelings toward him or her are likely to be altered whether it is true or not. Or when religious teachers tell us we are all "brothers" and "sisters" beneath the skin, our moral sentiments are stimulated accordingly. How the social environment is cognitively represented therefore is crucial to how it is valued and to our moral response to it.

Now, the general world view of the modern life sciences represents all forms   22
of life on the planet Earth both as kin and as fellow members of a social unit—
the biotic community. The Earth may now be perceived not as it once was, as the
unique physical center of the universe, but rather as a mere planet orbiting
around an ordinary star at the edge of a galaxy containing billions of similar stars
in a universe containing billions of such galaxies. In the context of this universal
spatial-temporal frame of reference, the planet Earth is very small and very local
indeed, an island paradise in a vast desert of largely empty space containing physically hostile foreign bodies separated from Earth by immense distances. All the
denizens of this cosmic island paradise evolved into their myriad contemporary
forms from a simple, single-cell common ancestor. All contemporary forms of life
thus are represented to be *kin, relatives, members of one extended family.* And all
are equally members in good standing of one society or community, the biotic
community or global ecosystem.

This cosmic/evolutionary/ecological picture of the Earth and its biota[12] can   23
actuate the moral sentiments of affection, respect, love, and sympathy with
which we human mammals are genetically endowed. It also actuates the special
sentiment or feeling (call it patriotism), noticed by both Hume and Darwin, that
we have for the *group as a whole* to which we belong—the *family* per se,[13] the *tribe*,
and the *country* or *nation*. From the point of view of modern biology, the earth
with its living mantle is our tribe and each of its myriad species is, as it were, a
separate clan.

Thus the land ethic—in sharp contrast to traditional Western humanism   24
and extensionism—provides moral standing for both environmental individuals
and for the environment as a whole. In Leopold's words, "a land ethic changes
the role of Homo sapiens from conqueror of the land community to plain member and citizen of it. It implies respect for fellow-members *and also* respect for the
community as such."[14]

Holism   Respect for wholes, for the community as such and its various subsys-   25
tems, is a theoretical possibility for the land ethic because it is conceptually and
historically related to the Humean-Darwinian moral philosophy. Both individual
members of society and the community as such, the social whole (together with
its component divisions), are the objects of certain special, naturally selected
moral sentiments. Beauty may be in the eye of the beholder, but it does not follow from this that only the eye of the beholder is beautiful. Similarly, there may
be no value without valuers, but it does not follow from this that only valuers are
valuable. Both beauty and intrinsic value are bivalent concepts; that is, both

involve subjective and objective factors. *Intrinsic value* is, as it were, "projected" onto appropriate objects by virtue of certain naturally selected and inherited intentional feelings, some of which (patriotism, or love of country, is perhaps the most familiar example) simply have social wholes as their natural objects. We may value our community per se, for the sake of itself, just as we may value our children for the sake of themselves. Wholes may thus have intrinsic value no less problematically than individuals. . . .

As "The Land Ethic" proceeds, it becomes more and more holistic, that is, 26 more and more concerned with the biotic community per se and its subsystems and less and less individualistic—less and less concerned with the individual animals and plants that it comprises. Toward the middle, Leopold speaks of the "biotic right" of species to continuance.[15] Finally, in the summary moral maxim of the land ethic, the individual drops out of the picture altogether, leaving only the biotic community as the object of respect and moral considerability: "A thing is right when it tends to preserve the integrity, stability, and beauty of the biotic community; it is wrong when it tends otherwise."[16] . . .

The Dangers of an Untempered Holistic Environmental Ethic   . . . What are 27 the moral (to say nothing of the economic) costs of the land ethic? Most seriously, it would seem to imply a draconian policy toward the human population, since almost all ecologists and environmentalists agree that, from the perspective of the integrity, diversity, and stability of the biotic community, there are simply too many people and too few redwoods, white pines, wolves, bears, tigers, elephants, whales, and so on. Philosopher William Aiken has recoiled in horror from the land ethic, since in his view it would imply that "massive human diebacks would be good. It is our species' duty to eliminate 90 percent of our numbers."[17] It would also seem to imply a merciless attitude toward nonhuman individual members of the biotic community. Sentient members of overabundant species, like rabbits and deer, may be (as actually presently they are) routinely culled, for the sake of the ecosystems of which they are a part, by hunting or other methods of liquidation. Such considerations have led philosopher Edward Johnson to complain that "we should not let the land ethic distract us from the concrete problems about the treatment of animals which have been the constant motive behind the animal liberation movement."[18] From the perspective of both humanism and its humane extension, the land ethic appears nightmarish in its own peculiar way. It seems more properly the "ethic" of a termitarium or beehive than of anything analogous to a human community. It appears richly to deserve Tom Regan's epithet, "environmental fascism."

The Relation of the Land Ethic to Prior Accretions   Despite Leopold's narra-   28
tive drift away from attention to members of the biotic community toward the
community per se, and despite some of Leopold's more radical exponents who
have confrontationally stressed the holistic dimension of the land ethic, its theoretical foundations yield a subtler, richer, far more complex system of morals
than simple environmental holism. The land ethic is the latest step in an evolutionary sequence, according to its own theoretical foundations. Each succeeding
step in social-moral evolu-tion—from the savage clan to the family of man—does
not cancel or invalidate the earlier stages. Rather, each succeeding stage is lay-
ered over the earlier ones, which remain operative.

A graphic image of the evolution of ethics has been suggested by extension-   29
ist[19] Peter Singer. Singer suggests we imagine the evolutionary development of
ethics to be an "expanding circle."[20] According to this image, as the charmed circle of moral considerability expands to take in more and more beings, its previous boundaries disappear. Singer thus feels compelled by the logic of his own theory to give as much weight to the interests of a person (or, for that matter, a sentient animal) halfway around the world as to the similar interests of his own children! "I ought to give as much weight to the interests of people in Chad or Cambodia as I do to the interests of my family or neighbors; and this means that if people in those countries are suffering from famine and my money can help, I ought
to give and go on giving until the sacrifices that I and my family are making begin
to match the benefits the recipients obtain from my gifts."[21] When he chooses to
give preference to his own or his children's interests, he has, according to his own
account, morally failed. This is because the basic moral logic of traditional Western humanism and its extensions rests moral considerability on a criterion that is
supposed to be both morally relevant and *equally* present in the members of the
class of morally considerable beings. Hence, all who *equally* qualify are equally
considerable. The circle expands as the criterion for moral considerability is
changed in accordance with critical discussion of it.

A similar but crucially different image of the evolution of ethics has been   30
suggested by Richard Sylvan and Val Plumwood (formerly the Rout-leys).
According to them,

What emerges is a picture of types of moral obligation as associated with a   31
nest of rings or annular boundary classes. . . . In some cases there is no sharp
divisionbetween the rings. But there is no single uniform privileged class of
items [that is, rational beings, sentient beings, living beings], no one base
class, to which all and only moral principles directly apply.[22]

The evolutionary development of ethics is less well represented by means 32
of Singer's image of an expanding circle, a single ballooning circumference, within which moral principles *apply equally to all*, than by means of the image of annular tree rings in which social structures and their correlative ethics are nested in
a graded, differential system. That I am now a member of the global human community and hence have correlative moral obligations to all mankind does not
mean that I am no longer a member of my own family and citizen of my local
community and of my country, or that I am relieved of the peculiar and special
limitations on freedom of action attendant upon these relationships.

The Place of Human Beings in the Land Ethic Therefore, just as the existence 33
of a global human community with its humanitarian ethic does not submerge and
override smaller, more primitive human communities and their moral codes, neither does the newly discovered existence of a global biotic community and its
land ethic submerge and override the global human community and its humanitarian ethic. To seriously propose, then, that to preserve the integrity, beauty, and
stability of the biotic community we ought summarily to eliminate 90 percent of
the current human population is as morally skewed as Singer's apparent belief
that he ought to spend 90 percent of his income relieving the hunger of people
in Chad and Cambodia and, in consequence, to reduce himself and his own family to a meager, ragged subsistence.

However, just as it is not unreasonable for one to suppose that he or she has 34
some obligation and should make *some* sacrifice for the "wretched of the earth,"
so it is not unreasonable to suppose that the human community should assume
some obligation and make *some* sacrifice for the beleaguered and abused biotic
community. To agree that the human population should not, in gross and wanton violation of our humanitarian moral code, be immediately reduced by deliberate acts of war or by equally barbaric means does not imply that the human population should not be scaled down, as time goes on, by means and methods that
can be countenanced from a humanitarian point of view. How obligations across
the outermost rings of our nested sociomoral matrix may be weighed and compared is admittedly uncertain—just as uncertain as how one should weigh and
compare one's duty, say, to one's family against one's duty to one's country. In the
remainder of this essay, I shall go on to discuss some general considerations applying to this problem. . . .

The Place of Individual Nonhuman Beings in the Land Ethic Sylvan and 35
Plumwood have developed the view that Leopold briefly suggests, namely, that

an ecosystemic ethic primarily provides not rights but *respect* for individual non-human members of the biotic community. Although the concept of respect is singular and simple, its practical implications are varied and complex. These thinkers further suggest that American Indian environmental attitudes and values provide a well-developed rich exemplar of *respectful* participation in the economy of nature, a participation that permits human beings morally to eat and otherwise consumptively to utilize their fellow citizens of the organic society:

> The view that the land, animals, and the natural world should be treated with   36
> *respect* was a common one in many hunting-gathering societies. . . . Respect
> adds amoral dimension to relations with the natural world. . . . The conven-
> tional wis-dom of Western society tends to offer a false dichotomy of use ver-
> sus respectful nonuse . . . of using animals, for example, in the ways character-
> istic of large-scale mass-production farming . . . *or* on the other hand of not
> making use of animals at all. . . . What is left out of this choice is the alterna-
> tive the Indians . . . recognized . . . of limited and respectful use.[23]

A great deal of controversy has surrounded the hypothesis of an American   37
Indian land ethic. Recent studies, empirically based on actual cultural materials, have shown beyond reasonable doubt that at least some American Indian cultures did in fact have an ecosystemic or environmental ethic and that such an ethic maps conceptually onto the Leopold land ethic. In other words, some American Indian cultures—among them, for example, the Ojibwa of the western Great Lakes—represented the plants and animals of their environment as engaged in *social* and *economic* intercourse with one another and with human beings. And such a social picture of human-environment interaction gave rise to correlative moral attitudes and behavioral restraints. The Ojibwa cultural narratives (myths, stories, and tales), which served as the primary vehicles of enculturation or education, repeatedly stress that animals, plants, and even rocks and rivers (natural entities that Western culture regards as inanimate) are *persons* engaged in reciprocal, mutually beneficial exchange with human beings. A cardinal precept embellished again and again in these narratives is that nonhuman natural entities, both individually and as species, must be treated with respect and restraint. The Ojibwa were primarily a hunting-gathering people, which perforce involved them in killing animals as well as plants for food, clothing, and shelter. But they nevertheless represented the animals and plants of their biotic community as *voluntarily* participating in a mannerized economic exchange with people

who, for their part, gave tokens of gratitude and reimbursement and offered guest friendship.

For example, in one such Ojibwa story called "The Woman Who Married   38
a Beaver," we find a particularly succinct statement of this portrait of the human-animal relationship. Here is an excerpt from the story:

> Now and then by a person would they be visited. Then they would go to   39
> where the person lived, whereupon the person would slay the beavers, yet
> they really did not kill them; back home would they come again. . . . In the
> same way as people are when visiting one another, so were the beavers in
> their mental attitude toward people. . . . They were very fond of the tobac-
> co that was given them by the peo-ple; at times they were also given cloth-
> ing by the people.
>
> When finally the woman returned to her own (human) kin, she was   40
> wont to say, "Never speak you ill of a beaver! . . . Just the same as the feel-
> ings of one who is disliked, so is the feeling of the beaver. And he who never
> speaks ill of a beaver is very much loved by it. In the same way as people
> often love one another, so is one held in the mind of the beaver; particular-
> ly lucky then is one at killing beavers."[24]

Contemporary Life in Accordance with an Ecosystemic Environmental Ethic   41
Of course, most people today do not live by hunting and gathering. Nevertheless, the general ideal provided by American Indian cultures of respectful, restrained, mutually beneficial human use of the environment is certainly applicable in today's context. An ecosystemic environmental ethic does not prohibit human use of the environment; it requires, rather, that that use be subject to two ethical limitations. The first is holistic, the second individualistic.

The first requires that human use of the environment, as nearly as possible,   42
should enhance the diversity, integrity, stability, and beauty of the biotic commu-nity. Biologist René Dubos has argued that Western Europe was, prior to the industrial revolution, biologically richer *as a result* of human settlement and cul-tivation.[25] The creation and cultivation of small fields, hedgerows, and forest edges measurably (objectively and quantitatively) enhanced the diversity and integrity and certainly the beauty of the preindustrial European landscape. Eth-nobotanist Gary Nab-han has drawn a similar picture of the Papago inhabitation of the Sonoran desert.[26] Human occupation and use of the environment from the perspective of the quality of the environment as a whole do not *have* to be

destructive. On the contrary, they can be, as both hunter-gatherers and yeoman farmers have proved, mutually beneficial.

The second, individualistic ethical limitation on human use of the environ-   43 ment requires that trees cut for shelter or to make fields, animals slain for food or for fur, and so on should be thoughtfully selected, skillfully and humanely dispatched, and carefully used so as to neither waste nor degrade them. The *individual* plant, animal, or even rock or river consumed or transformed by human use deserves to be used respectfully.

Surely we can envision an eminently livable, postmodern, systemic, *civi-*   44 *lized* technological society well adapted to and at peace and in harmony with its organic environment. Human technological civilization can live not merely in peaceful coexistence but in benevolent symbiosis with nature. Is our current *mechanical* technological civilization the only one imaginable? Aren't there alternative technologies? Isn't it possible to envision, for example, a human civilization based on nonpolluting solar energy—for domestic use, manufacturing, and transportation—and small-scale, soil-conserving organic agriculture? There would be fewer material things and more services, information, and opportunity for aesthetic and recreational activities; fewer people and more bears; fewer parking lots and more wilderness.

In the meantime, while such an adaptive organic civilization gradually   45 evolves out of our present grotesque mechanical civilization, the most important injunction of ecosystemic ethics remains the one stressed by Leopold—subject, of course, to the humanitarian, humane, and life-respecting qualifications that, as I have just argued, are theoretically consistent with it. We should strive to preserve the diversity, stability, and integrity of the biotic community.

The most serious moral issue of our times is our responsibility to preserve   46 the biological diversity of the earth. Later, when an appropriately humble, sane, ecocentric civilization comes into being, as I believe it will, its government and citizens will set about rehabilitating this bruised and tattered planet. For their work, they must have as great a library of genetic material as it is possible for us to save. Hence, it must be our immediate goal to prevent further destruction of the biosphere, to save what species we can, and to preserve the biotic diversity and beauty that remain.

Notes

1. Aldo Leopold, A Sand County Almanac, with Essays on Conservation from Round River (New York: Ballantine Books, 1970, p. 253. [J.B.C.] Leopold (1886–1948) was an American naturalist. A Sand County Almanac, and Sketches Here and There was first published in 1949. [D.C.A., ed.]
2. morally considerable: deserving of moral consideration. [D.C.A.]
3. Jeremy Bentham (1748–1832) was an English jurist and philosopher. [D.C.A.]
4. Tom Regan, The Case for Animal Rights (Berkeley, Calif.: University of California Press, 1983), p. 362. [J.B.C.]
5. Leopold, Sand County Almanac, p. 238. [J.B.C.]
6. Ibid. [J.B.C.]
7. Charles Darwin, The Descent of Man and Selection in Relation to Sex (New York: J. A. Hill, 1904 [first published 1871]), p. 9. [J.B.C.] Darwin (1809–1882) was a British naturalist. [D.C.A.]
8. Darwin, Descent of Man, p. 107. [J.B.C.]
9. Ibid., p. 118. [J.B.C.]
10. "The Land Ethic" is a section of A Sand County Almanac, pp. 237–264. [D.C.A.]
11. Leopold, Sand County Almanac, p. 239. [J.B.C.]
12. biota: the animal and plant life of a region. [D.C.A.]
13. per se: as such (Latin). [D.C.A.]
14. Leopold, Sand County Almanac, p. 240. [J.B.C.]
15. Ibid., p. 247. [J.B.C.]
16. Ibid., p. 262. [J.B.C.]
17. William Aiken, "Ethical Issues in Agriculture," in Earthbound: New Introductory Essays in Environmental Ethics (New York: Random House, 1984), p. 269. [J.B.C.]
18. Edward Johnson, "Animal Liberation vs. the Land Ethic," Environmental Ethics 3 (1981): 271. [J.B.C.]
19. extensionist: one who advocates extensionism, the view that moral consideration should be extended beyond human beings to nonhuman beings. [D.C.A.]
20. Peter Singer, The Expanding Circle: Ethics and Sociobiology (New York: Farrar, Straus & Giroux, 1981). [J.B.C.]
21. Ibid., p. 153. [J.B.C.]

22. Richard Routley and Val Routley, "Human Chauvinism and Environmental Ethics," in *Environmental Ethics*, ed. Don Mannison, Michael McRobbie, and Richard Routley (Canberra, Australia: Department of Philosophy, Research School of the Social Sciences, Australian National University, 1980), p. 107. [J.B.C.]

23. Ibid., pp. 178–179. [J.B.C.]

24. Thomas W. Overholt and J. Baird Callicott, *Clothed-in-Fur and Other Tales: An Introduction to an Ojibwa World View* (Washington, D.C.: University Press of America, 1982), pp. 74–75. [J.B.C.]

25. See René Dubos, "Franciscan Conservation and Benedictine Stewardship," in *Ecology and Religion in History*, ed. David Spring and Eileen Spring (New York: Harper & Row, 1974), pp. 114–136. [J.B.C.]

26. Gary Paul Nabhan, *The Desert Smells Like Rain: A Naturalist in Papago Indian Country* (San Francisco: North Point Press, 1982). [J.B.C.]

Chief Seattle (ca. 1786–1866) was born near Puget Sound and became chief of both the
Duwamish and Suquamish tribes of the Northwest. He worked toward peaceful coexistence
with the white settlers of the area. What follows is an eloquent plea for both racial harmony
and ecological responsibility, but the authorship of the piece is in question. No trace of the original letter can be found among President Pierce's letters, or at the Bureau of Indian Affairs, or
at the National Archives—though at least one of these sources would likely contain some evidence of such a document. The possibility remains that what has endured here over the years
was transcribed from one of Seattle's speeches.

Letter to President Pierce, 1855

Chief Seattle

We know that the white man does not understand our ways. One portion of the   1
land is the same to him as the next, for he is a stranger who comes in the night
and takes from the land whatever he needs. The earth is not his brother, but his
enemy, and when he has conquered it, he moves on. He leaves his fathers'
graves, and his children's birthright is forgotten. The sight of your cities pains
the eyes of the red man. But perhaps it is because the red man is a savage and
does not understand.

There is no quiet place in the white man's cities. No place to hear the leaves   2
of spring or the rustle of insect's wings. But perhaps because I am a savage and do
not understand, the clatter only seems to insult the ears. The Indian prefers the
soft sound of the wind darting over the face of the pond, the smell of the wind
itself cleansed by a mid-day rain, or scented with the piñon pine. The air is precious to the red man. For all things share the same breath—the beasts, the trees,
the man. Like a man dying for many days, he is numb to the stench.

What is man without the beasts? If all the beasts were gone, men would die from   3
great loneliness of spirit, for whatever happens to the beasts also happens to man. All
things are connected. Whatever befalls the earth befalls the sons of the earth.

It matters little where we pass the rest of our days; they are not many. A few   4
more hours, a few more winters, and none of the children of the great tribes that
once lived on this earth, or that roamed in small bands in the woods, will be left
to mourn the graves of a people once as powerful and hopeful as yours.

From *Native American Testimony: An Anthology of Indian and White Relations,* edited by Peter Nabokov (1977).

The whites, too, shall pass—perhaps sooner than other tribes. Continue to   5
contaminate your bed, and you will one night suffocate in your own waste. When
the buffalo are all slaughtered, the wild horses all tamed, the secret corners of the
forest heavy with the scent of many men, and the view of the ripe hills blotted
by talking wires,° where is the thicket? Gone. Where is the eagle? Gone. And
what is it to say goodby to the swift and the hunt, the end of living and the beginning of survival? We might understand if we knew what it was that the white man
dreams, what he describes to his children on the long winter nights, what visions
he burns into their minds, so they will wish for tomorrow. But we are savages. The
white man's dreams are hidden from us.

Questions for Discussion
1.   What view of the land does Chief Seattle express in this piece?
2.   When the author uses the word "we" in the first paragraph, to whom does
     he refer?
3.   What makes the description in paragraph 2 a good description?
4.   How does the author use the notion of tribes in the letter? Does this usage
     remain consistent throughout?
5.   Do you take at face value the author's referring to Native Americans as "sav-
     ages"? Explain what the term means in context.

Questions for Reflection and Writing
1.   What, if anything, was difficult to understand due to the letter's date of com-
     position? Is it still worth reading? Why or why not?
2.   Compose a letter responding to Chief Seattle in which you attempt to
     explain how race relations and the state of the environment have changed
     since his lifetime.
3.   Would you read this piece differently if it were determined that it was not a
     letter to the President, but rather a speech given by Chief Seattle, tran-
     scribed by a white person? What if it were simply written by a white person
     and ascribed to Chief Seattle? Explain.

talking wires i.e., the telegraph

Henry David Thoreau (1817–1862) was born in Concord, Massachusetts, graduated from Harvard, and taught school briefly. He was an essayist, naturalist, editor, lecturer, and social critic. Among his works are *A Week on the Concord and Merrimac Rivers* (1849), *The Maine Woods* (1865), and *Cape Cod* (1865). On July 4, 1845 Thoreau moved into a cabin on the shores of Walden Pond, on land belonging to Ralph Waldo Emerson, and lived alone there for two years. "Economy" is taken from Thoreau's masterpiece, *Walden: Or, Life in the Woods* (1854), which recounts his solitary, reflective existence there.

Economy

Henry David Thoreau

Near the end of March, 1845, I borrowed an axe and went down to the woods by   1
Walden Pond, nearest to where I intended to build my house, and began to cut down some tall arrowy white pines, still in their youth, for timber. It is difficult to begin without borrowing, but perhaps it is the most generous course thus to permit your fellow-men to have an interest in your enterprise. The owner of the axe, as he released his hold on it, said that it was the apple of his eye; but I returned it sharper than I received it. It was a pleasant hillside where I worked, covered with pine woods, through which I looked out on the pond, and a small open field in the woods where pines and hickories were springing up. The ice in the pond was not yet dissolved, though there were some open spaces, and it was all dark colored and saturated with water. There were some slight flurries of snow during the days that I worked there; but for the most part when I came out onto the railroad, on my way home, its yellow sand heap stretched away gleaming in the hazy atmosphere, and the rails shone in the spring sun, and I heard the lark and pewee and other birds already come to commence another year with us. They were pleasant spring days, in which the winter of man's discontent was thawing as well as the earth, and the life that had lain torpid began to stretch itself. One day, when my axe had come off and I had cut a green hickory for a wedge, driving it with a stone, and had placed the whole to soak in a pond hole in order to swell the wood, I saw a striped snake run into the water, and he lay on the bottom, apparently without inconvenience, as long as I stayed there, or more than a quarter of an hour; perhaps because he had not yet fairly come out of the torpid state. It appeared to me that for a like reason men remain in their present low and primitive condition; but if they should feel the influence of the spring of springs arousing them, they would of necessity rise to a higher and more ethereal life. I had

previously seen the snakes in frosty mornings in my path with portions of their bodies still numb and inflexible, waiting for the sun to thaw them. On the 1st of April it rained and melted the ice, and in the early part of the day, which was very foggy, I heard a stray goose groping about over the pond and cackling as if lost, or like the spirit of the fog.

So I went on for some days cutting and hewing timber, and also studs and   2 rafters, all with my narrow axe, not having many communicable or scholar-like thoughts, singing to myself.

> Men say they know many things;
> But lo! they have taken wings—
> The arts and sciences,
> And a thousand appliances;
> The wind that blows
> Is all that anybody knows.

I hewed the main timber six inches square, most of the studs on two sides only, and the rafters and floor timbers on one side, leaving the rest of the bark on, so that they were just as straight and much stronger than sawed ones. Each stick was carefully mortised or tenoned by its stump, for I had borrowed other tools by this time. My days in the woods were not very long ones; yet I usually carried my dinner of bread and butter, and read the newspaper in which it was wrapped, at noon, sitting amid the green pine boughs which I had cut off, and to my bread was imparted some of their fragrance, for my hands were covered with a thick coat of pitch. Before I had done I was more the friend than the foe of the pine tree, though I had cut down some of them, having become better acquainted with it. Sometimes a rambler in the wood was attracted by the sound of my axe, and we chatted pleasantly over the chips which I had made.

By the middle of April, for I made no haste in my work, but rather made   3 the most of it, my house was framed and ready for the raising. I had already bought the shanty of James Collins, an Irishman who worked on the Fitchburg Railroad, for boards. James Collins' shanty was considered an uncommonly fine one. When I called to see it he was not at home. I walked about the outside, at first unobserved from within, the window was so deep and high. It was of small dimensions, with a peaked cottage roof, and not much else to be seen, the dirt being raised five feet all around as if it were a compost heap. The roof was the soundest part, though a good deal warped and made brittle by the sun. Doorsill there was none, but a perennial passage for the hens under the door board. Mrs. C. came to the door and asked me to view it from the inside. The hens were driven in by my approach. It was dark, and had a dirt floor for the most part, dank, clammy, and aguish, only here a board and there a board which would not bear removal. She lighted a lamp to show me the inside of the roof and the walls, and also that the board floor extended under the bed, warning me not to step into the cellar, a sort of dust hole two feet deep. In her own words, they were "good boards overhead, good boards all around, and a good window"—of two whole squares originally, only the cat had passed out that way lately. There was a stove, a bed, and a place to sit, an infant in the house where it was born, a silk parasol, gilt-framed looking-glass, and a patent new coffee-mill nailed to an oak sapling, all told. The bargain was soon concluded, for James had in the meanwhile returned. I to pay four dollars and twenty-five cents tonight, he to vacate at five tomorrow morning, selling to nobody else meanwhile: I to take possession at six. It were well, he said, to be there early, and anticipate certain indistinct but wholly unjust claims on the score of ground rent and fuel. This he assured me was the only encumbrance. At six I passed him and his family on the road. One large bundle held their all—bed, coffee-mill, looking-glass, hens—all but the cat; she took to the woods and became a wild cat and, as I learned afterward, trod in a trap set for woodchucks, and so became a dead cat at last.

I took down this dwelling the same morning, drawing the nails, and   4
removed it to the pond side by small cartloads, spreading the boards on the grass there to bleach and warp back again in the sun. One early thrush gave me a note or two as I drove along the woodland path. I was informed treacherously by a young Patrick that neighbor Seeley, an Irishman, in the intervals of the carting, transferred the still tolerable, straight, and drivable nails, staples, and spikes to his pocket, and then stood when I came back to pass the time of day, and look freshly up, unconcerned, with spring thoughts, at the devastation; there being a dearth of work, as he said. He was there to represent spectatordom, and help make this seemingly insignificant event one with the removal of the gods of Troy.

I dug my cellar in the side of a hill sloping to the south, where a woodchuck   5
had formerly dug his burrow, down through sumach and blackberry roots, and the lowest stain of vegetation, six feet square by seven deep, to a fine sand where potatoes would not freeze in any winter. The sides were left shelving, and not stoned; but the sun having never shone on them, the sand still keeps its place. It was but two hours' work. I took particular pleasure in this breaking of ground, for in almost all latitudes men dig into the earth for an equable temperature. Under the most splendid house in the city is still to be found the cellar where they store their roots as of old, and long after the superstructure had disappeared posterity remark its dent in the earth. The house is still but a sort of porch at the entrance of a burrow.

At length, in the beginning of May, with the help of some of my acquain-   6
tances, rather to improve so good an occasion for neighborliness than from any
necessity, I set up the frame of my house. No man was ever more honored in the
character of his raisers than I. They are destined, I trust, to assist at the raising of
loftier structures one day. I began to occupy my house on the 4th of July, as soon
as it was boarded and roofed, for the boards were carefully feather-edged and
lapped, so that it was perfectly impervious to rain, but before boarding I laid the
foundation of a chimney at one end, bringing two cartloads of stones up the hill
from the pond in my arms. I built the chimney after my hoeing in the fall, before
a fire became necessary for warmth, doing my cooking in the meanwhile out of
doors on the ground, early in the morning: which mode I still think is in some
respects more convenient and agreeable than the usual one. When it stormed
before my bread was baked, I fixed a few boards over the fire, and sat under them
to watch my loaf, and passed some pleasant hours in that way. In those days, when
my hands were much employed, I read but little, but the least scraps of paper
which lay on the ground, my holder, or tablecloth, afforded me as much entertainment, in fact answered the same purpose as the Iliad.

Questions for Discussion

1. What does Thoreau borrow at the beginning of this essay? How does he
   return it? What do you make of the second act?
2. What happens to the Collins's cat? Why does this matter?
3. One can view "Economy" as a process analysis. What process does Thoreau
   analyze? How else could you classify this essay?
4. How does Thoreau relate to reading in this piece? Where do you find your clues?
5. Explain the title of this essay.

Questions for Reflection and Writing

1. Do you agree with Thoreau about the value of solitary existence? Why or
   why not? Do you think being alone—at times, at least—is an essential part
   of being human, or a personality preference?
2. Self-reliance is a vital part of *Walden*. Note Thoreau's interactions with his
   neighbors throughout this essay. What attitude does he seem to have toward
   them? Is this attitude consistent throughout? Explain. What might this have
   to do with self-reliance?
3. Read up on psychologist B. F. Skinner's *Walden Two*. (Better yet, read the
   book.) How does Skinner transform Thoreau's understanding of the ideal
   human life?

Loren Eiseley (1907–1977), an anthropologist, an educator, and a poet, was one of the most highly respected and prolific scientific writers of the twentieth century. Born in Lincoln, Nebraska, Eiseley was educated at the University of Nebraska (B.A., 1933) and at the University of Pennsylvania (A.M., 1935; Ph.D., 1937). His graduate field work took him to the American West, where he did research on the remains of the earliest humans in North America. He taught anthropology at the University of Kansas, from 1937 to 1944, and at Oberlin College, from 1944 to 1947, before joining the faculty at the University of Pennsylvania, where he taught anthropology and history of science until his death in 1977. He was the curator of early man at the University of Pennsylvania museum and served briefly as the university's provost. He was also a visiting professor at several other leading universities. The recipient of numerous honors and awards for public service, Eiseley is also known for his work as a conservationist and nature lover. In 1964 and 1965 he was a member of a presidential task force on the preservation of natural beauty, advising the Department of the Interior. He was the recipient of numerous awards and over thirty-five honorary degrees. He contributed scores of scientific studies and articles to scholarly journals, but also wrote essays and books on scientific subjects for lay readers. Eiseley's major works include *The Immense Journey* (1957), *Darwin's Century: Evolution and the Men Who Discovered It* (1959), *The Firmament of Time* (1960), *The Unexpected Universe* (1969), and *The Invisible Pyramid* (1970).

How Flowers Changed the World

Loren Eiseley

If it had been possible to observe the Earth from the far side of the solar system   1
overthe long course of geological epochs, the watchers might have been able to
discerna subtle change in the light emanating from our planet. That world of long
ago would,like the red deserts of Mars, have reflected light from vast drifts of
stone and gravel,the sands of wandering wastes, the blackness of naked basalt, the
yellow dust of endlesslymoving storms. Only the ceaseless marching of the clouds
and the intermittent flashes from the restless surface of the sea would have told a
different story, but still essentially a barren one. Then, as the millennia rolled
away and age followedage, a new and greener light would, by degrees, have come
to twinkle across thoseendless miles.

This is the only difference those far watchers, by the use of subtle instru-   2
ments, might have perceived in the whole history of the planet Earth. Yet that
slowly growing green twinkle would have contained the epic march of life from

the tidal oozes upward across the raw and unclothed continents. Out of the vast chemical bath of the sea—not from the deeps, but from the element-rich, light-exposed platforms of the continental shelves—wandering fingers of green had crept upward along the meanderings of river systems and fringed the gravels of forgotten lakes.

In those first ages plants clung of necessity to swamps and watercourses.   3 Their reproductive processes demanded direct access to water. Beyond the primitive ferns and mosses that enclosed the borders of swamps and streams the rocks still lay vast and bare, the winds still swirled the dust of a naked planet. The grass cover that holds our world secure in place was still millions of years in the future. The green marchers had gained a soggy foothold upon the land but that was all. They did not reproduce by seeds but by microscopic swimming sperm that had to wriggle their way through the water to fertilize the female cell. Such plants in their higher forms had clever adaptations for the use of rain water in their sexual phases, and survived with increasing success in a wet land environment. They now seem part of man's normal environment. The truth is, however, that there is nothing very "normal" about nature. Once upon a time there were no flowers at all.

A little while ago—about one hundred million years, as the geologist esti-   4 mates time in the history of our four-billion-year-old planet—flowers were not to be found anywhere on the five continents. Wherever one might have looked, from the poles to the equator, one would have seen only the cold dark monotonous green of a world whose plant life possessed no other color.

Somewhere, just a short time before the close of the Age of Reptiles, there   5 occurred a soundless, violent explosion. It lasted millions of years, but it was an explosion, nevertheless. It marked the emergence of the angiosperms—the flowering plants. Even the great evolutionist, Charles Darwin, called them "an abominable mystery," because they appeared so suddenly and spread so fast.

Flowers changed the face of the planet. Without them, the world we   6 know—even man himself—would never have existed. Francis Thompson, the English poet, once wrote that one could not pluck a flower without troubling a star. Intuitively he had sensed like a naturalist the enormous interlinked complexity of life. Today we know that the appearance of the flowers contained also the equally mystifying emergence of man.

If we were to go back into the Age of Reptiles, its drowned swamps and   7 birdless forest would reveal to us a warmer but, on the whole, a sleepier world than that of today. Here and there, it is true, the serpent heads of bottom-feeding dinosaurs might be upreared in suspicion of their huge flesh-eating compatriots. Tyrannosaurs, enormous bipedal caricatures of men, would stalk mindlessly across the sites of future cities and go their slow way down into the dark of geologic time.

In all that world of living things nothing saw save with the intense concen- 8
tration of the hunt, nothing moved except with the grave sleepwalking intent-ness of the instinct-driven brain. Judged by modern standards, it was a world in slow motion, a cold-blooded world whose occupants were most active at noon-day but torpid on chill nights, their brains damped by a slower metabolism than any known to even the most primitive of warm-blooded animals today.

A high metabolic rate and the maintenance of a constant body tempera- 9
ture are supreme achievements in the evolution of life. They enable an animal to escape, within broad limits, from the overheating or the chilling of its immediate surroundings, and at the same time to maintain a peak mental efficiency. Crea-tures without a high metabolic rate are slaves to weather. Insects in the first frosts of autumn all run down like little clocks. Yet if you pick one up and breathe warmly upon it, it will begin to move about once more.

In a sheltered spot such creatures may sleep away the winter, but they are 10
hopelessly immobilized. Though a few warm-blooded mammals, such as the woodchuck of our day, have evolved a way of reducing their metabolic rate in order to undergo winter hibernation, it is a survival mechanism with drawbacks, for it leaves the animal helplessly exposed if enemies discover him during his peri-od of suspended animation. Thus bear or woodchuck, big animal or small, must seek, in this time of descending sleep, a safe refuge in some hidden den or burrow. Hibernation is, therefore, primarily a winter refuge of small, easily concealed ani-mals rather than of large ones.

A high metabolic rate, however, means a heavy intake of energy in order to 11
sustain body warmth and efficiency. It is for this reason that even some of these later warm-blooded mammals existing in our day have learned to descend into a slower, unconscious rate of living during the winter months when food may be difficult to obtain. On a slightly higher plane they are following the procedure of the cold-blooded frog sleeping in the mud at the bottom of a frozen pond.

The agile brain of the warm-blooded birds and mammals demands a high 12
oxygen consumption and food in concentrated forms, or the creatures cannot long sustain themselves. It was the rise of flowering plants that provided that energy and changed the nature of the living world. Their appearance parallels in a quite surprising manner the rise of the birds and mammals.

Slowly, toward the dawn of the Age of Reptiles, something over two hun- 13
dred and fifty million years ago, the little naked sperm cells wriggling their way

through dew and raindrops had given way to a kind of pollen carried by the wind. Our presentday pine forests represent plants of a pollendisseminating variety. Once fertilization was no longer dependent on exterior water, the march over drier regions could be extended. Instead of spores simple primitive seeds carrying some nourishment for the young plant had developed, but true flowers were still scores of millions of years away. After a long period of hesitant evolutionary groping, they exploded upon the world with truly revolutionary violence.

The event occurred in Cretaceous times in the close of the Age of Reptiles.   14 Before the coming of the flowering plants our own ancestral stock, the warm-blooded mammals, consisted of a few mousy little creatures hidden in trees and underbrush. A few lizard-like birds with carnivorous teeth flapped awkwardly on ill-aimed flights among archaic shrubbery. None of these insignificant creatures gave evidence of any remarkable talents. The mammals in particular had been around for some millions of years, but had remained well lost in the shadow of the mighty reptiles. Truth to tell, man was still, like the genie in the bottle, encased in the body of a creature about the size of a rat.

As for the birds, their reptilian cousins the Pterodactyls, flew farther and   15 better. There was just one thing about the birds that paralleled the physiology of the mammals. They, too, had evolved warm blood and its accompanying temperature control. Nevertheless, if one had been stripped of his feathers, he would still have seemed a slightly uncanny and unsightly lizard.

Neither the birds nor the mammals, however, were quite what they seemed.   16 They were waiting for the Age of Flowers. They were waiting for what flowers, and with them the true encased seed, would bring. Fish-eating, gigantic leather-winged reptiles, twenty-eight feet from wing tip to wing tip, hovered over the coasts that one day would be swarming with gulls.

Inland the monotonous green of the pine and spruce forests with their   17 primitive wooden cone flowers stretched everywhere. No grass hindered the fall of the naked seeds to earth. Great sequoias towered to the skies. The world of that time has a certain appeal but it is a giant's world, a world moving slowly like the reptiles who stalked magnificently among the boles of its trees.

The trees themselves are ancient, slow-growing and immense, like the red-   18 wood groves that have survived to our day on the California coast. All is stiff, formal, upright and green, monotonously green. There is no grass as yet; there are no wide plains rolling in the sun, no tiny daisies dotting the meadows underfoot. There is little versatility about this scene; it is, in truth, a giant's world.

A few nights ago it was brought home vividly to me that the world has   19 changed since that far epoch. I was awakened out of sleep by an unknown sound in my living room. Not a small sound—not a creaking timber or a mouse's scurry —but a sharp, rending explosion as though an unwary foot had been put down upon a wine glass. I had come instantly out of sleep and lay tense, unbreathing. I listened for another step. There was none.

Unable to stand the suspense any longer, I turned on the light and passed   20 from room to room glancing uneasily behind chairs and into closets. Nothing seemed disturbed, and I stood puzzled in the center of the living room floor. Then a small button-shaped object upon the rug caught my eye. It was hard and polished and glistening. Scattered over the length of the room were several more shining up at me like wary little eyes. A pine cone that had been lying in a dish had been blown the length of the coffee table. The dish itself could hardly have been the source of the explosion. Beside it I found two ribbon-like strips of a velvety-green. I tried to place the two strips together to make a pod. They twisted resolutely away from each other and would no longer fit.

I relaxed in a chair, then, for I had reached a solution of the midnight distur-   21 bance. The twisted strips were wistaria pods that I had brought in a day or two previously and placed in the dish. They had chosen midnight to explode and distribute their multiplying fund of life down the length of the room. A plant, a fixed, rooted thing, immobilized in a single pod, had devised a way of propelling its offspring across open space. Immediately there passed before my eyes the million airy troopers of the milkweed pod and the clutching hooks of the sandburs. Seeds on the coyote's tail, seeds on the hunter's coat, thistledown mounting on the winds—all were somehow triumphing over life's limitations. Yet the ability to do this had not been with them at the beginning. It was the product of endless effort and experiment.

The seeds on my carpet were not going to lie stiffly where they had dropped   22 like their antiquated cousins, the naked seeds on the pine-cone scales. They were travelers. Struck by the thought, I went out next day and collected several other varieties. I line them up now in a row on my desk—so many little capsules of life, winged, hooked or spiked. Every one is an angiosperm, a product of the true flowering plants. Contained in these little boxes is the secret of that far-off Cretaceous explosion of a hundred million years ago that changed the face of the planet. And somewhere in here, I think, as I spoke seriously at one particularly resistant seedcase of a wild grass, was once man himself.

Questions for Discussion

1. "Today we know that the appearance of the flowers contained also the equally mystifying emergence of man," Eiseley writes in Paragraph 6. How so? How *did* flowers open the way for human life?

2. How *did* flowers change the world?
3. What is important to understand about pollen and warm-blooded birds in the context of human evolution?
4. How do the exploding wistaria pods tie everything together for Eiseley? Why does he gather and line up on his table several species of angiosperms?
5. How does Eiseley present so clearly and succinctly the process of transformation between a flowerless world and a world inhabited by humans? What techniques does he use to describe the process?
6. Eiseley uses much figurative language, such as "chemical bath of the sea" (Paragraph 2), "wandering fingers of green" (Paragraph 2), and "naked planet" (Paragraph 3). Where else does he use images such as these? How do such images help to make this essay more interesting than scientific writing often can be?
7. What do you think of the strategy of condensing geological events that stretched over billions of years into a fast, smoothly flowing narrative? Does that strategy distort the facts?

Questions for Reflection and Writing

1. List the key events in the process of geological change, as Eiseley has described them. How does each key event lead to the next?
2. Find another piece of popular science writing and critique it. Compare its writing style to that of Eiseley. Point out techniques used by both writers to make the material accessible to lay readers, and evaluate the degree of success of both writers.
3. Take a difficult or poorly written piece of scientific writing and rewrite it, adding images, comparisons, examples, and so forth, to make it interesting.

Is Limiting Population Growth a Key Factor in Protecting the Global Environment?

YES: Paul Harrison, from "Sex and the Single Planet: Need, Greed, and Earthly Limits," *The Amicus Journal* (Winter 1994)

NO: Betsy Hartmann, from "Population Fictions: The Malthusians Are Back in Town," *Dollars and Sense* (September/O ctober 1994)

Issue Summary

YES: Author and Population Institute medal winner Paul Harrison argues for family planning programs that take into account women's rights and socioeconomic concerns in order to prevent world population from exceeding carrying capacity.

NO: Betsy Hartmann, director of the Hampshire College Popula tion and Development Program, counters that the "real problem is not human *numbers* but undemocratic human *systems* of labor and resource exploitation, often backed by military repression."

The debate about whether human population growth is a fundamental cause of ecological problems and whether population control should be a central strategy in protecting the environment has long historical roots.   1

Those who are seriously concerned about uncontrolled human population growth are often referred to as "Malthusians" after the English parson Thomas Malthus, whose "Essay on the Principle of Population" was first published in 1798. Malthus warned that the human race was doomed because geometric population increases would inexorably outstrip productive capacity, leading to famine and poverty. His predictions were undermined by technological improvements in agriculture and the wide spread use of birth control (rejected by Malthuson moral grounds), which brought the rate o fpopulation growth in industrialized countries under control during the twentieth century.   2

The theory of the demographic transition was developed to explain why Malthus's direpredictions had not come true. This theory proposes that the first-effect of economic development is to lower death rates. This causes a population   3 boom, but stability is again achieved as economic and social changes lead to lower birth rates. This pattern has indeed been followed in Europe, the United States, Canada, and Japan. The less-developed countries have more recently experienced rapidly falling death rates. Thus far, the economic and social changes needed to bring down birth rates have not occurred, and many countries in Asia and Latin America suffer from exponential population growth. This fact has given rise to a group of neo-Malthusian theorists who contend that it is unlikely that less-developed countries will undergo the transition to lower birth rates required to avoid catastrophe due to over population.

Biologist Paul Ehrlich's best-seller *The Population Bomb* (Ballantine Books, 1968) popularized his view that population growth in both the developed and developing world must be halted to avert world wide ecological disaster. Ecologist Garrett Hardin extended the neo-Malthusian argument by proposing that some less-developed nations have gone so far down the road of population-induced resource scarcity that they are beyond salvation and should be allowed to perish rather than possibly sink the remaining world economies.   4

Barry Commoner, a prominent early critic of the neo-Malthusian perspective, argues in *The Closing Circle* (Alfred A. Knopf, 1971) and his subsequent popular books and articles that inappropriate technology is the principal cause of local and global environmental degradation. While not denying that population growth is a contributing factor, he favors promoting ecologically sound development rather than population-control strategies that ignore socioeconomic realities.   5

Enthusiasts for population control as a sociopolitical and environmental strategy have always been opposed by religious leaders whose creeds reject any overt means of birth control. Recently, the traditional population control policy planners have also been confronted with charges of sexism and paternalism by women's groups, minority groups, and representatives of developing nations who argue that the needs and interests of their constituencies have been ignored by the primarily white, male policy planners of the developed world. At the September 1994 World Population Conference in Cairo, organizers and spokespeople for these interests succeeded in promoting policy statements that reflected sensitivity to many of their concerns.   6

In the following selections, Paul Harrison argues that " population growth combined with. . . consumption and technology damages the environment." He proposes "quality family planning and reproductive health services, mother an child health care, women's rights and women's education" as a four-point pro-   7 gram to rapidly decrease population growth. Betsy Hartmann asserts that "the threat to livelihoods, democracy and the environment posed by the fertility of poor women hardly compares to that posed by the consumption patterns of the rich or the ravages of militaries." She proposes greater democratic control over resources rather than narrow population control as an environmental strategy.

Yes
Sex and the Single Planet: Need, Greed, and Earthly Limits

Paul Harrison

Population touches on sex, gender, parenthood, religion, politics—all the deep-   8
est aspects of our humanity. Start a debate on the topic, and the temperature quickly warms up. In the preparations for next year's World Population Conference in Cairo, the link between population growth and environmental damage is one of the hottest topics.

The sheer numbers involved today make it hard to ignore the link. The last   9
forty years saw the fastest rise in human number sin all previous history, from only 2.5 billion people in 1950 to 5.6 billion today. This same period saw natural habitats shrinking and species dying at an accelerating rate. The ozone hole appeared, and the threat of global warming emerged.

Worse is in store. Each year in the 1980s saw an extra 85 million people on   10
earth. The second half of the 1990s will add an additional 94 million people per year. That is equivalent to a new United States every thirty-three months, another Britain every seven months, a Washington every six days. A whole earth of 1800 was added in just one decade, according to United Nations Population Division statistics. After 2000, annual additions will slow, but by 2050 the United Nations expects the human race to total just over 10 billion—an extra earth of 1980 on top of today's, according to U.N. projections.

If population growth does not cause or aggravate environmental prob lems,   11
as many feminists, socialists, and economists claim, then we do not need to worry about these numbers. If it does, then the problems of the last decade may be only a foretaste of what is to come.

At the local level, links between growing population densities and land   12
degradation are becoming clearer in some cases. Take the case of Madagascar.

From Paul Harrison, "Sex and the Single Planet: Need, Greed, and Earthly Limits," *The Amicus Journal* (Winter 1994). Copyright © 1994 by *The Amicus Journal*, a quarterly publication of The Natural Resources Defense Council, 40 West 20th Street, New York, NY 10011. Reprinted by permission. NRDC membership dues or nonmember subscriptions: $10 annually.

Madagascar's forests have been reduced to a narrowing strip along the eastern escarpment. Of the original forest cover of 27.6 million acres, only 18.8 million acres remained in 1950. Today this has been halved to 9.4 million acres—which means that habitat for the island's unique wildlife has been halved in just forty years. Every year some 3 percent of the remaining forest is cleared, almost all of that to provide land for populations expanding at 3.2 percent a year.

The story of one village, Ambodiaviavy, near Ranomafana, shows the   13 process at work. Fifty years ago, the whole area was dense forest. Eight families, thirty-two people in all, came here in 1947, after French colonials burned down their old village. At first they farmed only the valley bottoms, which they easily irrigated from the stream running down from the hill tops. There was no shortage of land. Each family took as much as they were capable of working. During the course of the next forty-three years, the village population swelled ten times over, to 320, and the number of families grew to thirty-six. Natural growth was supplemented by immigration from the over crowded plateaus, where all cultivable land is occupied. By the 1950s, the valley bottom lands had filled up completely. New couples started to clear forest on the sloping valley sides. They moved gradually uphill; today, they are two-thirds of the way to the hilltops.

Villager Zafindraibe's small paddy field feeds his family of five for only four   14 months of the year. In 1990 he felled and burned five acres of steep forest land to plant hill rice. The next year cassava would take over. After that the plot should be left fallow for at least six or seven years.

Now population growth is forcing farmers to cut back the fallow cycle. As   15 land shortage increases, a growing number of families can no longer afford to leave the hillsides fallow long enough to restore their fertility. They return more and more often. Each year it is cultivated, the hillside plot loses more top soil, organic matter, nutrients.

The debate over this link between population growth and the environment has   16 raged back and forth since 1798. In that year Thomas Malthus, in his notorious *Essay on Population*, suggested that population tended to grow faster than the food supply. Human numbers would always be checked by famine and mortality.

Socialists from William Cobbett to Karl Marx attacked Malthus's argu-   17 ments. U.S. land reformer Henry George, in *Progress and Poverty* (1879), argued that the huge U.S. population growth had surged side by side with huge increases in wealth. Poverty, said George, was caused not by over population, but by warfare and unjust laws. Poverty caused population growth not the other way around.

In modern times, U.S. ecologist Paul Ehrlich has played the Malthus role. 18 "No geological event in a billion years has posed a threat to terrestrial life comparable to that of human over population," he argued back in 1970, urging compulsion if voluntary methods failed. His early extremism (such as suggesting cutting off aid to certain Third World countries) has mellowed into a more balanced analysis (for example, he acknowledges the need for more than just contraceptives to attack the problem). But doomsday rhetoric remains in his 1990 book, *The Population Explosion*, which predicts" many hundreds of millions" of famine deaths if we do not halt human population growth.

Today's anti-Malthusians come in all shades, from far left to far right. For 19 radical writers Susan George and Frances Moore Lappé, poverty and in equality are the root causes of environmental degradation, not population. For Barry Commoner the chief threat is misguided technology. Economist Julian Simon sees moderate population growth as no problem at all, but as a tonic for economic growth. More people mean more brains to think up more solutions. "There is no meaningful limit to our capacity to keep growing forever," he wrote in 1981 in *The Ultimate Resource*.

Other voices in the debate focus on ethics and human rights. Orthodox 20 Catholics and fundamentalist Muslims oppose artificial contraception or abortion. A wide range of feminists stress women's rights to choose or refuse and downplay the impactof population growth. "Blaming global environmental degradationon population growth," argued the Global Committee on Women, Population and the Environment before Rio, "stimulates anatmosphere of crisis. It helps lay the ground work for an intensification of top-down population control programs that are deeply disrespectful of women."

There is no debate quite like this one for sound and fury. As the forgoing 21 examples show, positions are emotional and polarized. Factions pick on one or two elements as the basic problem, and ignore all the others. Thinking proceeds in black-and-white slogans.

Often debaters seem to be locked in to the single question: Is population 22 growth a crucial fact or inenvironmental degradation—or not? However, if we frame our inquiry in this simplistic way, only two answers are possible—yes or no—and only two conclusions—obsession with family planning, or opposition to family planning. Both of these positions lead to abuse or neglect of women's rights.

There has to be away out of this blind alley. Perhaps we can make a start by 23 accepting that all the factors mentioned by the rival schools are important. All interact to create the damage. Sometimes one factor is dominant, sometimes another. Population is always there. In some fields it plays the lead role, in others no more than a bit part.

Most observers agree that it is not just population growth that damages the environment. The amount each person consumes matters too, and so does the technology used in production and waste disposal. These three factors work inseparably in every type of damage. Each of them is affected by many other factors, from the status of women to the ownership of land, from the level of democracy to the efficiency of the market. If we adopt this complex, nuanced view, much of the crazy controversy evaporates, and the hard work of measuring impact and designing policy begins.   24

A number of success stories have emerged. One hallmark of these successes is the recognition that population should bean integral part of long-range resource management.   25

Take a snapshot at one particular moment, and there is no way of saying which of the three factors carries the main blame for damage. It would be like asking whether brain, bone, or muscle plays the main role in walking. But if we compare changes over time, we can get an idea of the irrelative strengths. Results vary a lot, depending on which country or which type of damage we are looking at.   26

In Madagascar, population growth bears the main blame for deforestation and loss of biodiversity. As described before, the island's rainforests have shrunk to a narrow strip. Increased consumption—a rise in living standards—and technology tend to play less and less of a role in this devastation. Incomes and food intake today are lower than thirty years ago. Farming methods have not changed in centuries.   27

Population growth is running at 3 percent a year. When technology is stagnant, every extra human means less forest and wildlife.   28

By contrast, population growth played only a minor role in creating the ozone hole. The main blame lay with rising consumption and technology change. Between 1940 and 1980, world chlorofluorocarbon (CFC) emissions grew at more than 15 percent a year. Almost all of this was in developed countries, where population grew at less than 1 percent a year. So population growth accounted for less than 7 percent (one-fifteenth) of increased CFC emissions.   29

A central issue in the controversy is whether we are on course to pass the earth's carrying capacity—the maximum population that the environment can support indefinitely. Malthusians like Dennis and Donnella Meadows suggest in   30 their book *Beyond the Limits* that we have already passed the limits in some areas such as alteration of the atmosphere. Anti-Malthusians like Julian Simon insist that we can go on raising the limits through technology.

Here, too, acompromise comes closer to reality. Humans have raised the   31
ceiling on growth many times in the past. When hunter-gatherers ran short of wild foods, they turned to farming. When western Europeans started to run out of wood in the seventeenth century, they turned to coal. The process continues today. When one resource runs down, its price changes, and we increase produc-tivity or exploration, bring in substitutes, or reduceuse. In other words, we do not just stand by and watch helplessly while the world collapses.We respond and adapt. We change our technology, our consumption patterns, even the number of children we have. It is because we can adapt so fast that we are the dominant species on earth.

So far adaptation has kept us well stocked with minerals despite rising use.   32
It has proved Malthus wrong by raising food production roughly in line with the five-and-a-half-fold growth in population since his time. But it has not worked at all well in maintaining stocks of natural resourcesl ike forests, water, sea fish, or biodiversity, nor with preserving the health of sinks for liquid and gaseous wastes such as lakes, oceans, and atmosphere. These are common property resources—no one owns them—so what Garrett Hardin called the "tragedy of the commons" applies. Everyone overuses or abuses the source or sink, fearing that if they hold back others will reap the gains.

Problems like erosion, acid rain, or global warming are not easy to diagnose   33
or cure. Sometimes we do not even know they are happening until they are far advanced, as in the case of the ozone hole. Like cancer, they build up slowly and often pass unseen till things come to ahead. Farmers in Burkina Faso did not believe their land was eroding away until someone left a ruler stuck into the soil; then they saw that the level had gone down an inch in a year.

Environmental quality follows a U-shaped curve. Things get worse before   34
they get better, on everything from biodiversity and soil erosion to air and water quality. But everything hinges on how long the down swing lasts—and how seri-ous or irreversible are the problems it gives rise to. Given time we will develop institutions to control over fishing or ocean pollution, stop acid rain or halt glob-al warming. But time is the crux of the matter. Adaptable though we are, we rarely act in time to prevent severe damage. In one area after another, from whales to ozone holes, we have let crises happen before taking action.

Over the next few decades we face the risk of irreversible damage on sever-   35
al fronts. If we lose 10 or 20 percent of species, we may never restore that diversity. If the global climate flips, then all our ability to adapt will not stave off disaster. Rather than wait for global crisis, prudence dictates that we should take
action now.

However, the way we look at causes deeply affects the search for solutions.   36
That is why the debate on population and environment matters. If we say that
damage results only from technology, only from over consumption, only from
injustice, or only from population, we will act on only one element of the equation. But damage results from population, consumption, and technology multi-
plied together, so we must act on all three. And we can not neglect the many factors from in equality to women's rights and free markets that influence all others.

Consumption will be the hardest nut to crack. Reducing over consumption may   37
be good for the soul, but the world's poorest billion must increase their consumption to escape poverty. The middle 3 billion will not willingly rein in their ambitions. The middle classes in India and China are already launched on the consumer road that Europe took in the 1950s. They are moving faster down that
road, and their consumer class probably out numbers North America's already.
Even in the rich countries, consumption goes on growing at roughly 2 percent a
year, with hiccups during recession. Consumption can be cut if consumers and
producers have to pay for the damage they do through higher prices or taxes—
but, politically, it is not easy. Politicians who threaten to raise taxes risk electoral
defeat.

So technological change must reduce the *impact* of consumption. But it will   38
be a Herculean task for technology to do the job alone. The massive oil price rises
of 1973 and 1979–80 stimulated big advances in energy efficiency. Between 1973
and 1988 gasoline consumption per mile in western countries fell by 29 percent.
But this technology gain was wiped out by arise in car numbers of 58 percent, due
to the combined growth of population and consumption. The result was a rise in
gasoline consumption of 17 percent.

Population and consumption will go on raising the hurdles that technology   39
must leap. By 2050, world population will have grown by 80 percent, on the U.N.
medium projection. Even at the low 1980s growth rate of 1.2 percent a year, consumption per person will have doubled. Technology would have to cut the damage done by each unit of consumption by 72 percent, just to keep total damage
rising at today's destructive rate.

Yet the International Panel on Climate Change says we ought to *cut* car-   40
bon dioxide output by 60 percent from today's levels. If incomes and population
grow as above, technology would have to cut the emissions for each unit of consumption by a massive 89 percent by 2050. This would require a 3.8 percent
reduction every year for fifty-seven years.

Such a cut is not utterly impossible, but it would demand massive commit-   41
ment on all sides. Introducing the 85 miles-per-gallon car could deliver a cut of
almost exactly this size in the transport sector, if it took ten years to go into mass
production, and another fifteen years to saturate the market. But the combined
growth of population and car ownership could easily halve the gain.

Technology change will have a far easier job if it is backed by action on the   42
population front. Population efforts ares low-acting at first: for the first fifteen
years the difference is slight. The U.N.'s low population projection points to what
might be achieved if all countries did their best in bringing birth rates down. Yet
for 2010, the low projection for world population is only 1.2 percent less than the
medium projection. Over the longer term, though, there are big benefits. By 2025
the low projection is 7.3 percent less than the medium—621 million fewer people, or a whole Europe plus Japan. By 2050 the low figure is 22 percent or 2.206
billion people less—equal to the whole world's population around 1930.

With a concerted effort in all countries (including the United States),   43
world population could peak at 8.5 billion or less in 2050 and, after that, come
down. And it is clear that this would reduce environmental impact and lower the
hurdles that improved technology will have to leap.

What do we need to do to bring it about? Here, too, the debate rages.   44
Diehard Malthusians talk of the need for crash programs of" population control."
Horrified feminists answer that a woman's fertility is her own business, not a target for male policy measures. The objective should be reproductive health and
choice, not simply bringing numbers down, they argue.

Yet this conflict, too, is an artificial one. The best way to bring numbers   45
down fast is to pump resources not into crash or compulsory programs narrowly
focused on family planning, but into broad women's development programs that
most feminists would welcome. How do we get enough resources out of male governments to do this properly? Only by using the arguments about environment
and economy that feminists do not allow.

Coercion and crash programs defeat their own aims." Population control"   46
is impossible without killing people: the term implies coercion and should be
dropped forthwith. Coercion rouses protests that sooner or later bring it to an

end. India's brief and brutal experiment with forced sterilization in1975–76 led within a year to the fall of Indira Gandhi's government. The progress of family planning in India was set back a decade.

Mass saturation with just one or two family planning methods is equally   47 doomed to failure. With female contraceptives, side-effects are common: women need good advice and medical backup to deal with them or avoid them. Left to handle them alone, they will stop using contraceptives and go on having five children each. Once mistrust has been aroused, it will make the job harder even when better programs are finally brought in.

If we want to bring population growth rates down rapidly, we must learn   48 from the real success stories like Thailand. In the early 1960s, the average Thai woman was having 6.4 children. Today she is having only 2.2. This represents a drop of 3.5 percent per year—as speedy as the fastest change in technology.

Such success was achieved, without a whiff of coercion, by universal access   49 to a wide and free choice of family planning methods, with good-quality advice and medical backup. Mother and child health was improved, women's rights were advanced, and female education leveled up with male.

All these measures are worth while in their own right. They improve the   50 quality of life for women and men alike. And there are economic spin-offs. Thai incomes grew at 6 percent a year in the 1980s. A healthy and educated work force attracts foreign investment and can compete in the modern high-tech world.

Quality family planning and reproductive health services, mother and child   51 health, women's rights, and women's education—this four-point program is the best way to achieve a rapid slow down in population growth. It can improve the quality of life directly, through health and education benefits, and it improves the status of women. It creates a healthy and educated work force. It gives people the knowledge with which they can fight for their own rights. It might also help to raise incomes, and it will certainly help to slow environmental damage.

With its human, economic, and environmental benefits, there are few pro-   52 grams that will offer better value for money over the coming decades.

NO

Population Fictions: The Malthusians Are Back in Town

Betsy Hartmann

In the corridors of power, the tailors are back at work, stitching yet another invis-   53
ible robe to fool the emperor and the people. After 12 years in which the Reagan
and Bush administrations downplayed population controlas a major aim of U.S.
foreign policy, the Clinton administration is playing catch-up. World attention
will focus on the issue this month in Cairo, when leaders from the United States
and abroad gather at the United Nations' third International Conference on
Population and Development. Cloaked in the rhetoric of environmentalism
and—ironically—women's rights, population control is back in vogue.

At the U N's second International Conference on Population in Mexico   54
City in 1984, the Reagan administration asserted that rapid population growth is
a "neutral phenomenon" that becomes a problem only when the free market is
subverted by "too much governmental control of economies." Under the Republicans, the U.S. withdrew funding from any international family planning agencies that perform abortions or even counsel women about them. Aid was cut off
to the International Planned Parenthood Foundation as well as the UN Fund for
Population Activities (UNFPA).

The Clinton administration, by contrast, is requesting $585 million for   55
population programs in fiscal year 1995, up from $502 million the year before.
This aid is channelled through the U.S. Agency for International Development
(USAID), which has made population control a central element of its new "Sustainable Development" mission for the post Cold War era. The USAID's draft
strategy paper of October 1993 identifies rapid population growth as a key "strate-
gic threat" which "consumes all other economic gains, drives environmental
damage, exacerbates poverty, and impedes" democratic governance."

Clinton's more liberal stand on abortion is certainly welcome, but even   56
that has yet to translate into effective Congressional action or foreign policy.
Announced in April, USAID's new policy on abortion funding overseas is still
very restrictive: It will finance abortion only in cases of rape, incest, and life
endangerment, the same conditions the Hyde amendment puts on federal

From Betsy Hartmann, "Population Fictions: The Malthusians Are Back in Town," *Dollars and Sense* (September/October 1994). Copyright
© 1994 by Economic Affairs Bureau, Inc. Reprinted by per-mission. *Dollars and Sense* is a progressive economics magazine published six
times a year. First-year subscriptions cost $18.95 and may be ordered by writing to *Dollars and Sense*, 1 Summer Street, Somerville, MA
02143.

Medicaid funds. Along with the mainstream environmental movement, the administration pays lip service to women's rights but continues to back practices—such as promoting long-acting contraceptive methods like Norplant without follow-up medical care—that are actually harmful to women's health.

Population Myths

It is true that population growth (which is actually slowing in most areas of the   57
world) can put additional pressure on resources in specific regions. But the threat
to livelihoods, democracy and the global environment posed by the fertility of
poor women is hardly comparable to that posed by the consumption patterns of
the rich or the ravages of militaries.

The industrialized nations, home to 22% of the world's population, consume   58
60% of the world's food, 70% of its energy, 75% of its metals, and 85% of its wood.
They generate almost three-quarters of all carbon dioxide emissions, which in turn
comprise nearly half of the man made greenhouse gases in the atmosphere, and are
responsible for most of the ozone depletion. Militaries are the other big offenders.
The German Research Institute for Peace Policy estimates that one-fifth of all
global environmental degradation is due to military activities. The U.S. military
is the largest domestic oil consumer and generates more toxic waste than the five
largest multinational chemical companies combined.

What about the environmental degradation that occurs within developing   59
countries? The UNFPA's *State of World Population* 1992 boldly claims that population growth" is responsible for around 79% of deforestation, 72% of arable land
expansion, and 69% of growth in livestock numbers." Elsewhere it maintains that
the" bottom billion," the very poorest people in developing countries," often
impose greater environmental injury than the other 3 billion of their citizens put
together."

Blaming such a large proportion of environmental degradation on the   60
world's poorest people is untenable, scientifically and ethically. It is no secret that
in Latin America the extension of cattle ranching—mainly for export, not
domestic consumption—has been the primary impetus behind deforestation.
And it is rich people who own the ranches, not the poor, as most countries in
Latin America have a highly inequitable distribution of land. In Southeast Asia
the main culprit is commercial logging, again mainly for export.

In developing countries, according to USAID, rapid population growth   61
also" renders inadequate or obsolete any investment in schools, housing, food
production capacity and infrastructure." But are increasing numbers of poor peo-

ple really the main drain on national budgets? The UN's 1993 *Human Development Report* estimates that developing countries spend only one-tenth of their national budgets on human development priorities. Their military expenditures meanwhile soared from 91% of combined health and education expenditures in 1977 to 169% in 1990. And in any case, the social spending that there is often flows to the rich. A disproportionate share of health budgets frequently goes to expensive hospital services in urban areas rather than to primary care for the poor, and educational resources are often devoted to schools for the sons and daughters of the wealthy.

The "structural adjustment" programs imposed by the WorlBank have not   62
helped matters, forcing Third World countries to slash social spending in order to service external debts. The burden of growing in equality has fallen disproportionately on women, children, and minorities who have borne the brunt of structural adjustment policies in reduced access to food, health care and education. But in USAID's view, population growth is at the root of their misery: "As expanding populations demand an even greater number of jobs, a climate is created where workers, especially women and minorities, are oppressed."

A Costly Consensus

In the collective psyche of the national security establishment, population   63
growth is now becoming a great scapegoat and enemy, a substitute for the Evil Empire. A 1992 study by the Carnegie Endowment for International Peace warned that population growth threatens" international stability" and called for" a multilateral effort to drastically expand family planning services." A widely cited February 1993 *Scientific American* article by Thomas Homer-Dixon, Jeffrey Boutwell and George Rathjens identifies rapidly expanding populations as a major factor in growing resource scarcities that are" contributing to violent conflicts in many parts of the developing world."

In the pages of respectable journals, racist metaphors are acceptable again,   64
as the concept of noble savage gives way to post-modern barbarian. In an *Atlantic Monthly* article on the" coming anarchy" caused by population growth and resource depletion, Robert Kaplan likens poor West African children to ants. Their older brothers and fathers (and poor, nonwhite males ingeneral) are "re-primitivized" men who find liberation in violence, since their natural aggression has not been "tranquilized" by the civilizing influences of the Western Enlightenment and middle-class existence.

The scaremongering of security analystsis complemented by the population   65
propaganda of mainstream environmental organizations. U.S. environmentalism
has long had a strong neo-Malthusian wing which views Man as the inevitable
enemy of Nature. The Sierra Club backed Stanford biologist Paul Ehrlich's 1968
tract *The Population Bomb*, which featured lurid predictions of impending famine
and supported compulsory sterilization in India as "coercion in a good cause."

By the late 1980s, population growth had transformed from just one of sev-   66
eral preoccupations of the mainstream environmental movement into an
intense passion. Groups such as the National Wildlife Federation and the
National Audubon Society beefed up their population programs, hoping to
attract new membership. Mean while, population lobbyists such as the influential Population Crisis Committee (renamed Population Action International)
seized on environmental concerns as a new rationale for their existence.

The marriage of convenience between the population and environment   67
establishments led to many joint efforts in advance of the 1992 UN Conference
on Environment and Development (UNCED) in Riode Janeiro. In 1990,
Audubon, National Wildlife, Sierra Club, Planned Parenthood Federation of
America, and the Population Crisis Committee began ajoint Campaign on Population and the Environment. Its major objective was "to expand public awareness of the link between population growth, environmental degradation and ther
esulting human suffering."

Despite their efforts, the U.S. population/environment lobby had a rude   68
awakening at Rio. In the formal intergovernmental negotiations, many developing nations refused to put population on the UNCED agenda, claiming it would
divert attention from the North's responsibility for the environmental crisis. At
the same time the nongovernmental Women's Action Agenda 21, endorsed by
1500 women activists from around the world, condemned suggestions that
women's fertility rates were to blame for environmental degradation.

In the aftermath of Rio, "the woman question" has forced the population/   69
environment lobby to amend its strategy. Many organizations are emphasizing
women's rights in their preparations for the Cairo conference. Women's empowerment—through literacy programs, job opportunities, and access to health care
and family planning—is now seen as a prerequisite for the reduction of population growth.

While this is a step forward, the population/environment lobby largely   70
treats the protection of women's rights as ameans to population reduction, rather
than as a worthy pursuit in itself. Its inclusion—and co-optation—of feminist

concerns is part of a larger strategy to create a broad population control "consensus" among the American public. Behind this effort is a small group of pow erful actors: the Pew Charitable Trusts Global Stewardship Initiative; the U.S. State D epartment through the office of Timothy Wirth, Undersecretary for Global Affairs; the UNFPA; and Ted Turner of the powerful Turner Broadcasting System, producer of CNN.

Although the Pew Initiative's "White Paper" lists "population growth and   71 unsustainable patterns of consumption" as its two targets, population growth is by far its main concern. Among Pew's explicit goals are to "forge consensus and to increase public understanding of, and commitment to acton, population and consumption challenges." Its targeted constituencies in the United States are environmental organizations, religious communities, and international affairs and foreign policy specialists.

Pew and the Turner Foundation have sponsored "high visibility" town   72 meetings on population around the country, featuring Ted Turner's wife Jane Fonda, who is also UNFPA's "Goodwill Ambassador." At the Atlanta meeting, covered on Turner's CNN, Fonda attributed the collapse of two ancient Native American communities to over population.

To prepare for the Cairo conference, the Pew Initiative hired three opinion   73 research firms to gauge public understanding of the connections between population, environment and consumption so as to "mobilize Americans" on these issues. The researchers found that the public generally did not feel strongly about population growth or see it as a "personal threat." Their conclusion: An "emotional component" is needed to kindle population fears.Those interviewed complained that they had already been over exposed to "images of stark misery, such as starving children." Although the study notes that these images may infact "work," it recommends finding "more current, targeted visual devices." Ones trategy is to build on people's pessimism about the future: "For women, particularly, relating the problems of excess population growth to children's future offers possibilities."

Sacrificed Rights

Whatever nods the new "consensus" makes towards women's broader rights and   74 needs, family planning is its highest priority. USAID views family planning as "the single most effective means" of reducing population growth; it intends to provide "birth control to every woman in the developing world who wants it by the end of the decade."

The promotion of female contraception as the technical fix for the "pop-   75
ulation problem" ignores male responsibility for birth-control and undermines
the quality of health and family planning services. The overriding objective is to
drive down the birth rate as quickly and cheaply as possible, rather than to
address people's broader health needs.

In Bangladesh, for example, at least one-third of the health budget is devot-   76
ed to population control. The principal means is poor-quality female sterilization
with incentives for those who undergo the procedure, including cash payments
for "wages lost" and transportation costs, as well as a piece of clothing (justified
as "surgical apparel"). The World Bank and population specialists are now herald-
ing Bangladesh as a great family planning success story. But at what human cost?
Because of the health system's nearly exclusive emphas is on population control,
most Bangladeshis have little or no access to primary health care, and infant and
maternal death rates remain at tragically high levels.

Lowering the birth rate by itself hashardly solved the country's problems.   77
Poverty in Bangladesh has much more to do with inequitable land ownership and
the urban elite's strangle hold over external resources, including foreign aid, than
it does with numbers of people. The great irony is that many people in
Bangladesh wanted birth control well before the aggressive and often coercive
sterilization campaign launched by the government with the help of the World
Bank and AID. A truly voluntary family planning program, as part of more comprehensive health services, would have yielded similar demographic results, without deepening human suffering.

The prejudice against basic health care is also reflected in the UN's first draft   78
of the "Program of Action" for the Cairo conference. It asks the international
community to spend $10.2 billion on population and family planning by the year
2000, and only $1.2 billion on broader reproductive health services such as mater-
nity care. After pressure from women's groups and more progressive governments,
the UN raised this figure to $5 billion, but family planning still has a two-to-one
advantage. Meanwhile, the Vatican is attacking women's rights by bracketing for
further negotiation any language in the Cairo document which refers to abortion,
contraception or sexuality. Women are caught between a rock and a hard place,
bracketed by the Vatican, and targeted by the population establishment.

The current focus of population programs is on the introduction of long-   79
acting, provider-dependent contraceptive technologies. The hormonal implant
Norplant, for example, which is inserted in a woman's arm, is effective for five
years and can only be removed by trained medical personnel. But often, these

methods are administered in health systems that are ill-equipped to distribute them safely or ethically; In population programs in Indonesia, Bangladesh and Egypt, researchers have documented many instances of women being denied access to Norplant removal, as well as receiving inadequate counselling, screening, and follow-up care.

A number of new contraceptives in the pipeline pose even more serious problems, interms of both health risks and the potential for abuse at the hands of zealous population control officials. The non-surgical quinacrine sterilization pellet, which drug specialists suspect may be linked to cancer, can be administered surreptitiously (it was given to Vietnamese women during IUD checks without their knowledge in 1993). Also potentially dangerous are vaccines which immunize women against reproductive hormones. Their long-term reversibility has not yet been tested, and the World Health Organization has expressed some concern about the drugs' interaction with the immune system, especially in people infected with the AIDS virus. Simpler barrier methods, such as condoms and diaphragms, which also protect against sexually transmitted diseases, continue to receive considerably less attention and resources in population programs since they are viewed as less effective in preventing births.

Recently, a network of women formed a caucus on gender issues in order to pressure USAID to live up to its rhetoric about meeting women's broader reproductive health needs. The caucus emerged in the wake of a controversial USAID decision to award a $9 million contract for studying the impact of family planning on women's lives to Family Health International, a N orth-Carolina-based population agency, rather than to women's organizations with more diverse and critical perspectives.

Progressive environmentalists also intend to monitor USAID's planned initiative to involve Third World environmental groups in building "grassroots awareness around the issue of population and family planning." They fear that USAID funds will be used to steer these groups away from addressing the politically sensitive root causes of environmental degradation—such as land concentration, and corporate logging and ranching—toward a narrow population control agenda.

Trouble at Home

Within the United States, the toughest battle will be challenging the multi-million dollar public opinion "consensus" manufactured by Pew, the State Department, and CNN. Not only does this consensus promote heightened U.S.

involvement in population control overseas, but by targeting women's fertility, it helps lay the ground, intentionally or not, for similar domestic efforts.

The Clinton administration is considering whether to endorse state policies   84
that deny additional cash benefits to women who have babies while on welfare. (This despite the fact that women on welfare have only two children on aver-age.) A number of population and environment groups are also fomenting dan-gerous resentment against immigrant women. The Washington-based Carrying Capacity Network, for example, states that the United States has every right to impose stricter immigration controls "as increasing numbers of women from Mexico, China and other areas of the world come to the United States for the purpose of giving birth on U.S. soil." And in many circles, Norplant is touted as the wonder drug which will cure the epidemic of crime and poverty allegedly caused by illegitimacy.

Such simple solutions to complex social problems not only don't work, they   85
often breed misogyny and racism, and they prevent positive public action on finding real solutions. Curbing industrial and military pollution, for exam ple, will do far more to solve the environmental crisis than controlling the wombs of poor women who, after all, exert the least pressure on global resources.

The real problem is not human *numbers* but undemocratic human systems   86
of labor and resource exploitation, often backed by military repression. We need to rethink the whole notion of "carrying capacity"—are we really pressing up against the earth's limits because there are too many of us? It would make more sense to talk about "political carrying capacity," defined as the limited capacity of the environment and economy to sustain inequality and injustice. Viewed this way, the solution to environmental degradation and economic decline lies in greater democratic control over resources, not in a narrow population control agenda.

Postscript
Is Limiting Population Growth a Key Factor in Protecting the Global Environment?

Harrison extols the virtues of Thailand's population-control program, which he   87
claims has achieved success in significantly reducing birth rates without coercion while promoting women's health care and female education. He implies that this policy has contributed to a growth in average income and the ability to "compete in the modern high-tech world." He does not, however, respond to Hartmann's argument that such policies alone do not ensure a reduction in environmental degradation.

Anyone with a serious interest in environment. 831
read Paul Ehrlich's *The Population Bomb* (Ballantine B
Commoner's *The Closing Circle* (Alfred A. Knopf, 1971). 88
tressed by the arguments contained in Commoner's popular
thored a detailed critique with environmental scientist John F.
Commoner answered with a lengthy response. These two no-holds
were published as a "Dialogue" in the May 1972 issue of the *Bulletin*
ic Scientists. They are nteresting reading not only for their technical co
also as a rare example of respected scientists airing their professional and
al antagonisms in public.

Another frequently cited, controversial essay in support of the n
Malthusian analysis is "The Tragedy of the Commons," by Garrett Hardin, which
first appeared in the December 13, 1968, issue of *Science*. For a thorough attempt
to justify his authoritarian response to the world population problem, see
Hardin's book *Exploring New Ethics for Survival* (Viking Press, 1972).

An economic and political analyst who is concerned about the connections 90
among population growth, resource depletion, and pollution—but who rejects
Hardin's proposed solutions—is Lester Brown, director of the World watch Insti-
tute. His world view is detailed in *The Twenty-Ninth Day* (W. W. Norton, 1978).
Anthropologist J. Kenneth Smail argues that we have already exceeded the car-
rying capacity of the planet and need to reduce the world's population in "Beyond
Population Stabilization: The Case for Dramatically Reducing Global Human
Numbers," *Politics and the Life Sciences* (September 1997).

Anyone willing to entertain the propositions that pollution has not been 91
increasing, natural resources are not becoming scarce, the world food situation is
improving, and population growth is actually beneficial might find the late econ-
omist Julian Simon's *The Ultimate Resource* (Princeton University Press, 1982)
amusing, if not convincing.

For an assessment of needs and strategies to control population growth by 92
several international authorities, including Commoner, see "A Forum: How Big
Is the Population Factor?" in the July/August 1990 issue of *EPA Journal*. Ehrlich's
present views, which have been somewhat modified in response to criticism by
feminists and people from less-developed countries, are presented in an article
that he coauthored with Anne Ehrlich and Gretchen Daily in the
September/October 1995 issue of *Mother Jones*. A series of articles on the connections among population, development, and environmental degradation are
included in the February 1992 issue of *Ambio*.

say is part of a special section entitled "Population, Consump- 93
ament" in the Winter 1994 issue of *The Amicus Journal*, which
articles focusing on the needs and concerns of people of less-devel-
.s, along with brief statements representing the views of people from
world about the issues that were to be debated at the 1994 Cairo pop-
nference. TheSpring 1994 issue of that journal includes an essay by Jodi
.on that addresses some of the same concerns raised by Hartmann. Dis-
.ied environmentalist Michael Brower addresses the population debate in
all 1994 issue of *Nucleus*, the magazine of the Union of Concerned Scien-
.. A provocative response to the Cairo meeting is the article by Norway's
ame minister and sustainable development advocate Gro Harlem Brundtland
.n the December 1994 issue of *Environment*. Gita Sen, in "The World Programme
of Action: A New Paradigm for Population Policy," *Environment* (January/Febru-
ary 1995), describes and analyzes the World Programme of Action, which is the
main working document emanating from the Cairo conference. Robin Morgan,
in" Dispatch from Beijing," *Ms.* (January/February 1996), reports on the follow-
up UN Fourth World Conference on Women, which was held in Beijing in 1995.

In her book *Reproductive Rights and Wrongs: The Global Politics of Population* 94
Control, rev. ed. (South End Press, 1995), Hartmann offers a radical critique of
the extent to which the women's rights movement has accepted the politics and
rhetoric of what she refers to as the "population establishment."

Joanne Stichweh, *Paradigms Lost*

834

Artist's Statement

Paradigms Lost

Joanne Stichweh

The imagery in my painting is a natural outgrowth of my interest in art history. As an art historian and a contemporary painter, I am interested in producing paintings that combine allusions to works from throughout the history of art with popular icons and images, juxtaposing motifs derived from art historical sources both ancient and modern. The following passage from Nathan Knobler's *The Visual Dialogue* illustrates the link between art-making and human nature:

> "Image making is an essential human characteristic. Since Paleolithic time the unique ability to transform physical material into icons and illusions, signs and symbols, has affirmed the deeply rooted need of our species to arrange combinations of marks and colors, solids and voids for the satisfaction of individuals and their social groups.
>
> . . .
>
> This combination of symbols . . . illuminates the past and provides instruction on the nature of our present condition."

Nicholas Hill, *Sanctuary*

Artist's Statement

Sanctuary

Nicholas Hill

The compositional elements in *Sanctuary* are juxtaposed and combined so that the viewer can find a variety of visual access points to the piece. In a parallel fashion, the narrative content of the imagery is intentionally open-ended. The viewer's interpretations and associations are essential elements in viewing the work.